D1022282

The Sounds of Silence

THE SOUNDS
OF SILENCE

The National Library of Poetry

Laura Fiorini, Editor

Jennifer Duncan, Assistant Editor

Angela Hughes, Assistant Editor

The Sounds of Silence

Library of Congress
Cataloging in Publication Data
ISBN 1-57553-426-6

Proudly manufactured in The United States of America by
Watermark Press
One Poetry Plaza
Owings Mills, MD 21117

Foreword

Throughout life, we store information collected from experiences and try in some way to make sense of it. When we are not able to fully understand the things which occur in our lives, we often externalize the information. By doing this, we are afforded a different perspective, thus allowing us to think more clearly about difficult or perplexing events and emotions. Art is one of the ways in which people choose to externalize their thoughts.

Within the arts, modes of expression differ, but poetry is a very powerful tool by which people can share sometimes confusing, sometimes perfectly clear concepts and feelings with others. Intentions can run the gamut as well: the artists may simply want to share something that has touched their lives in some way, or they may want to get help to allay anxiety or uncertainty. The poetry within *The Sounds of Silence* is from every point on the spectrum: every topic, every intention, every event or emotion imaginable. Some poems will speak to certain readers more than others, but it is always important to keep in mind that each verse is the voice of a poet, of a mind which needs to make sense of this world, of a heart which feels the effects of every moment in this life, and perhaps of a memory which is striving to surface. Nonetheless, recalling our yesterdays gives birth to our many forms of expression.

Melisa S. Mitchell
Editor

Editor's Note

Maguire learns
As the horses turn slowly round the which is which
Of love and fear and things half born to mind.
He stands between the plough-handles and he sees
At the end of a long furrow his name signed
Among the poets, prostitut[es]. . . .
Here with the unfortunate
Who for half-moments of paradise
Pay out good days and wait and wait
For sunlight-woven cloaks.

–Patrick Kavanagh, "The Great Hunger"

Irish poet Patrick Kavanagh's poem "The Great Hunger" is a portrait of the fictional peasant farmer Patrick Maguire, whose life is replete with half-consciousness. Throughout the poem, Maguire has brief flashes of insight into his condition—one of continuous, cyclic repetition—but has neither the means nor the motivation to act in order to change it. Kavanagh presents Maguire as Everyman: He muddles through life with little passion or happiness, barely recognizing the world's and his own indifference to the desperate inalterability of his situation. Maguire communicates superficially at best with the land he works and with the people in his town, rendering him indifferent to his own fate as well as to that of others. The passion of life and of the land escape him: His inability to fully comprehend his life and the life around him leaves his own existence desolate and devoid of meaning.

Like "The Great Hunger," Brian Shields' poem, "Chorus from 'The Wind'" (1), explores man's indifference to nature and to his own fate. The poem's persona observes a wind storm from a window; however, he and the other observers at this gathering somewhat willfully refuse to garner any message or meaning from the intensity and the "rage" of the wind:

> . . . we stand together, aloof, removed, looking out
> contentedly, surveying nature's rage. The sun, warm on our faces—
> dull, listless, sleepy—is the only thing to penetrate here.

The persona and the other party members are unable to notice things on a deeper level—nothing "penetrate[s] here." They "witness" only superficially the anger, failing to recognize its significance as an "angry parent wake-up call" spurring them to action; instead, they remain immersed in the tedium of trying to engage in meaningful conversation with the other participants.

Shields depicts their indifference to their surroundings as mirrored in their inability to connect on a more vital plane with the people around them. The persona and the guests are all

> *picking idly through the remains*
> *of the afternoon's conversations, already fully gorged,*
> *seeking some glimmer of wit or succulent phrase*
> *to formulate existence into that tidy, understandable, sedative package.*

The series of adjectives Shields employs to describe that which the party-goers attempt to comprehend through their communication—the "package" of existence—illustrates their need for a simple, comforting conclusion. They want an explanation of existence that will ease their minds, which will, in effect, sedate them without bringing any form of blinding, brilliant revelation, causing them to fall even farther into their stupor of security. Comparably, they seem to yearn desperately for meaning, yet they communicate cursorily, pushing aside the meaningful in lieu of the banal, "slam[ming] and grappl[ing] in the air; / rattle-clatter nervous fingers seek[ing] introspective diversion." If closely examined, perhaps their lives would prove insignificant—a realization that might be too difficult for these individuals to endure. However, at the same time that they sincerely want meaning, they shy away from it. They choose the truths others present to them instead of discovering their own:

> *"Well, that is it then," they would say,*
> *amid the clatter of coffee spoons, "Yes, that is it—I'm sure...."*

The participants' need for security and stability only allows them to maintain this idle chatter, symbolizing their refusal and inability to delve more deeply into their collective conditions.

Much as the tree branches must have "wakefulness" screamed into them by the wind's rage, Shields suggests that the indifferent party partici-pants must be similarly shaken before they will recognize any faint hint, "some glimmer of wit or succulent phrase," of greater meaning in their lives. Nature, the "angry parent," does its best, but it appears as though humanity's capacity for reason nullifies nature's efforts. The people stolidly remain "looking out / contentedly surveying nature's rage"—their lives are rife with half-conscious-ness. Even the brilliant power of nature cannot move them into awareness and out of their indifference. The poem's last two stanzas explicate the disability conferred by the condition of being human: Although the "Worms and seeds buried deep" do not directly witness or "see the rage," they "feel the quivering root"—they know their roles and importance without question in the grand scheme of life. Mankind, on the other hand, is also "buried deep" and "secure" but it will not risk that security to come into a greater consciousness that may be unpleasant; humanity "will not wake."

Humankind's disconnection from the land and inability to acknowledge meaning in human life is a modern theme to which Shields gives an original twist and a deft dissection. Therefore, it is for the profoundly thought-provoking illustration of humanity's indifference to its own condition that the judges have awarded Brian Shields the Grand Prize in the contest associated with *The Sounds of Silence*.

Similarly to Brian Shields' party-goers, the persona in Rolf Uher's poem, "Meeting L. C." (276), takes no action to combat his own indifference. The persona reads the work of the relatively anonymous "L. C." every night after an initial, obviously enrapturing introduction to this person's writings. In order to have "fulfilled [his] debt of lines every night," the persona exerts arduous and diligent effort in his pursuit of reading "the seven-thousand words" L. C. wrote. This author, through his written descriptions, teaches the persona "about chances of the unbridled nights," the risks involved, and, one may assume, the gratification gained from embracing those chances. However, the persona's inability to take action due to fear of the risks involved surfaces when Uher writes that the persona "took to [his] heart the most courageous" of L. C.'s words: The persona reads and absorbs only the most heroic and inspiring words, still failing to assimilate those words and to translate them into action. His remaining static even after being so inspired by L. C.'s works is a disclosure of the fact that the persona is more comfortable with living vicariously through L. C.'s words than with doing the living himself.

In another vein, while the persona devours all of L. C.'s words and allows them to inspire him, he still does not take action either by writing himself or by attempting to live the scenarios presented by L. C. The persona sits and reads

> *between milk and bread*
> *between un-payable French cognac*
> *and the glance from immortal brown eyes*
> *which could fill pages between soft music*
> *and the air from dusty tubes. . . .*

No creativity emerges in the persona, who may only be able to recognize half-consciously the potential for literary creation. He is wholly unable to create anything in actuality; "the glance from immortal brown eyes" only "*could* fill pages" [italics mine]—it has the potential to inspire the persona to write but it remains as merely a possible inspiration since the persona cannot shrug off his resignation to his inert life in order to write or to engage in life as an active participant. The persona waits for things to happen to him instead of actively pursuing their fruition. Sitting in

> *rooms in which darkness shines*
> *and in which we wait*
> *for the courageous fulfilling of these words,*

the persona expects that life will simply befall him while he takes no action to make life fulfilling for himself. His inspired interior does nothing to manifest itself in his outer life, leaving him static and unchanged, waiting for life to happen.

Stolidity toward one's own life becomes man's disregard for his fellow man's plight in Laura Meester's poem, "The Last Hand" (225). Meester's exploration of man's extreme incapacity to sympathize with human disaster suggests that this dearth of emotion stems from the modern apathy caused by inurement to mishap through the proliferation of violence and catastrophe constantly viewed in the media. The poem's speaker describes a sinking passenger ferry, "Its rusty, naked hull absurdly exposed," as it slips beneath the water into "an underworld of chaos." The poem opens with a masterful setting of the scene: "Mist fades into un-mist." Initially, a gull is the witness of this calm, natural sea as it disperses the last effects of night. However, the scene shifts and a vulture enters; its "shrill shrieks . . . pierce the atmosphere" and it is the solitary witness that "views a passenger ferry tipping eerily slowly." The plight of the people on the ship is entirely absent from the poem; although they must be experiencing great fear and turmoil, Meester echoes modern indifference by not describing it.

The sea is similarly unconcerned with those whom it devours. Meester creates this compelling metaphor of the boat's passengers as consumed by a sea of indifference while also asserting that the modern world is over-saturated with images of disaster, much as the passengers are drowned in the waters of the ocean:

> *The sea, seasoned saltier with blood, broods and wails,*
> *A wanton child whose eye was larger than his stomach.*

After describing the sea's unconcern, debunking the theory of "pathetic fallacy" that asserts nature's sympathy with mankind's struggles, Meester presents humanity's inability to feel any inkling of commiseration with its fellow man:

> *Beyond an eternity,*
> *The last hand succumbs and dissolves below the water,*
> *While the world, unaffected, sips cappuccino,*
> *Its disjointed awareness duly gained from tomorrow's daily:*

> *Missed faded into un-missed.*

iv

The people who read about the deaths in "tomorrow's daily" paper are unconcerned and go about their lives as if nothing has changed. The deaths of the ferry's passengers mean nothing to humanity as a whole, and Meester subtly suggests that this incapacity of mankind to feel sorrow at another's death is infinitely tragic and detrimental to the human condition: Our failure to react to real-life tragedy and sorrow denigrates humanity as a whole.

An inability to act in order to countervail an overabundance of feeling as opposed to detachment emerges in Anita Danch's poem, "Pentimento" (57). The word "pentimento" in visual art is "the reappearance in an oil painting of original elements of drawing or painting that the artist tried to obliterate by overpainting. If the covering pigment becomes transparent, as may happen over the years, the ghostly remains of earlier marks may show through," (Encyclopedia Britannica Online). "Pentimento" comes from the Italian word *pentirsi* which means "to repent"; the artist "repented," or changed his mind, about the original work and painted over it.

In Danch's poem, the original, underlying painting depicts a seascape. The over-painting is one of an individual sleeping on a "yellow bed." In a traditional pentimento, the under-painting emerges by itself, which the original painting in this poem seems to be doing, but in Danch's poem the speaker also helps the under-painting resurface by using horse-hair paintbrushes to remove the current painting. She "repents" her second, more recent painting: "Each morning / you are tickled by bristles." The sleeping person may be a lover that the speaker painted over the seascape, a tribute to the place of importance this lover once held in the speaker's heart. However, time's effects override the speaker's inability to forget this person: The world erodes the painting much as time erodes the memory of this past love.

The imagery Danch employs in depicting the slow fading of the foreground painting making way for the ocean is that of violent upheaval:

> On your sill,
> white water is trapped
> in glass bubbles.
> You can see through them sea gulls crash up in the air,
> shattering their orange feet
> and falling lightly
> down into the brown mud.

Using words like "trapped," "crash," "shattering," and "falling," Danch shows the reader that the speaker must have devoted much of her life to the over-painting's human subject, the lover, and that the separation was painful and perhaps brutal. The lover cannot alter his fate: The speaker's memory of him will further erode as time and the artist both conspire to annihilate the painting. The poem's speaker halfheartedly assists time in eroding the second painting, but her seemingly indifferent unwillingness to take action either to completely destroy the painting or to recreate it indicates a paralysis, an acceptance of the fate that time and nature deal to the death of this relationship:

> *In the corner,*
> *salty sea waves lick your wall.*

This conclusion of devastation and silent, unavoidable destruction closes Danch's poem with an intriguing assertion: Although time may alter and decay our memories, we must play an involved role in actively maintaining our art forms, our lives, and our memories—and, in some cases, both those memories that we wish to hold and those that we wish to release.

Several other poets captivated the judges with their unique perspective on maintaining their passion for life and spurring others on to that passion through their works. Pay close attention to the following poets and their individual approaches to poetry: Carolyn Robinson's "Ode to BHB" (274), Martyn Iannece's "Control" (73), Sasha Semienchuk's "The Murmur of the Rolling Sands Keeps Me Awake" (192), Elzy Taramangalam's "The Byzantine Scribe" (91), Brooke Prior's "All Has Lessened..." (134), Collin Douglas' "Powerless" (227), and Sarah Brown's "To a Clandestine Lover" (36).

Laura Fiorini
Editor

Acknowledgments

The publication of *The Sounds of Silence* is a culmination of the efforts of many individuals. Judges, editors, associate editors, customer service representatives, data entry personnel, office administrators, and administrative services staff have all made invaluable contributions to this effort. A special thanks goes to Mary Catherine Saporito, Anne Jacobs, Rick Ivy, Todd Thompson, and Melisa Mitchell. I am grateful for the assistance of these fine people.

Cover Art: Steve Kimball

vi

Grand Prize

Brian Shields / Beaverlodge, AB

Second Prize

Sarah Brown / Toronto, ON
Anita Danch / Toronto, ON
Colin Douglas / Fewick, ON
Martyn Iannece / Toronto, ON
Laura Meester / Mount Hope, ON

Brooke Prior / Ottawa, ON
Carolyn Robinson / Mississauga, ON
Sasha Semienchuk / Wesmount Montreal, QC
Elzy Taramangalam / Halifax, NS
Rolf Uher / Koeln, Germany

Third Prize

Alexander Ary / Montreal, PQ
Joanne Barrass / Washington, UK
Pauline Blendick / Etobicoke, ON
Morton Bodanis / Saint-Laurent, QC
Alison Bodurtha / Mississauaga, ON
Geneinne Bondy / Windsor, ON
A. Bruce / Salt Spring Island, BC
Bhaswat Chakraborty / Scarborough, ON
Lesia Charko / LaSalle, QC
Kary Cook / Manning, AB
Sr. Michaela Davis / Oxon, UK
Evadne D'Oliveira / Don Mills, ON
Judith Ennamorato / Schomberg, ON
Severino Enopena / Manila, Philippines
Sarah Fenn / North Bay, ON
Janet Gallagher / Rothesay, NB
Mariana Gardner / Norfolk, UK
Iidija Gasperlin / Toronto, ON
K. Gordon / Nepean, ON
Jamie Gregor / Halifax, NS
Jeremy Grootenboer / Brampton, ON
Ryan Harrison / Courtenay, BC
Jim Head / East York, ON
Siobhan Hicks / Whitby, ON
William Hunter / Vancouver, BC
Yuko Ishii / Saitama, Japan
Kurt Jackson / Kelowna, BC
Tiffany Jones / Toronto, ON
Jeffrey Jutai / Toronto, ON
Wayne Jutila / Thunder Bay, ON

Rosie Livingstone / Johannesburg, South Africa
Fini Lokke / Froerup, Denmark
Ingrid MacIsaac / Lower Sackville, NS
Lawrie Manson / Markham, ON
Julie Maurice / Windsor, ON
Kim McKay / Eastern Passage, NS
Jeremy Mcleod / London, ON
Teresa Mead / Courtenay, BC
Peter Ohler / Vancouver, BC
James Olcese / Hamburg, Germany
Annie Polushin / Rimbey, AB
John Potter / Bandung, Indonesia
Derek Robinette / Voima Uy, Finland
Jayne Russell / Mississauga, ON
Scott Satterfield / Chiang Mai, Thailand
Adam Segal / London, ON
M. Simms / Aylmer, QC
Sheri South / Westmount, QC
Robert Sproule / Scarborough, ON
Tanya Thomas / Furdale, SK
Ioana Timariu / North York, ON
Kathy Treybig / Calgary, AB
Shashank Tripathi / Hong Kong, China
Milena Urbanajc / Oakville, ON
Neil Verma / Montreal, QC
Tyler Volsky / Edmonton, AB
William Walton / North Bay, ON
Megan Watson / Newmarket, ON
Shannon Watts / Saint John, NB

Chorus from "The Wind"

The enraged wind in my picture window
screams wakefulness into listless branches.
Still brittle with the sleep of winter, they slam and grapple in the air;
rattle-clatter nervous fingers seek introspective diversion,
hoping this rage will pass them by;
sun-parched, barren, yellow-gray, desolate eyes squint a reluctant greeting,
mute response to this angry parent wake-up call.

Yet, we stand together, aloof, removed, looking out
contentedly, surveying nature's rage. The sun, warm on our faces—
dull, listless, sleepy—is the only thing to penetrate here.

Having arrived late, I witness guests picking idly through the remains
of the afternoon's conversations, already fully gorged,
seeking some glimmer of wit or succulent phrase
to formulate existence into that tidy, understandable, sedative package,

"Well, that is it then," they would say,
amid the clatter of coffee spoons, "Yes, that is it—I'm sure. . . ."

Worms and seeds buried deep
don't see the rage but feel the quivering root;

buried deep we are secure,
we will not wake.
        Brian Shields

Life's Corridor

One very ordinary day,
I lost my way.
The how, the why—
No one can say.
Each day, I travel
Further back in my mind
To places and friends
From another time.
I'm now society's shame.
I slipped through the cracks.
Yet try, try as I do,
I can't find my way back.
So I walk life's corridor
Opening door after door,
Becoming smaller and smaller,
Until I am no more.

Peter D. Babington

Fall

Fall is so fun
When I get to run.
One way, other way,
Out of the leaves I come.

Raking up the leaves,
Then I go and jump,
Popping out my head.
Piew! I smell a skunk.

Oh, all the pretty colors
Falling from the trees.
Eating all the apples,
Watch out for the seeds.

Look at all the geese
Flying where they'll stay.
They'll love it there down south,
Where it's hot out every day.

Oliver Blumenfeld

My Place

This place
shines like
a coin
catching the sun
on the bottom of a deep
fountain.

The rocks are polished
by the water's fingers,
and the deep, soft moss
hangs on the cliff like
a foliate beard.

No longer
able to resist,
I run down the dirt path
and dive through
the surface of the pond
as if entering
lucidity
from
a dream.

Sue Fogarty

Dreamland

I remember the days of yore,
The songs I heard came from the core.
Birds seemed to twitter all day long
Each time your footsteps neared my zone.

But then I was only eighteen,
The world seemed full of roses then.
Time stood still when e'er our eyes would meet,
Awkward moments, but life made sweet.

What else is there to ponder on?
The years we shared, lit by the moon,
'Neath stars and trees, swayed by the breeze,
Sheltered and cuddled and caressed.

Visions of you in fantasy
Whispers love in ecstasy.
You looked eighteen, forty, sixty;
I love it most, you at seventy.

A thousand thanks, Oh Lord, to thee
For hours, lively in rhapsody.
As visions of a loved one float,
Our souls dance in dreamland showboat.

Pacita Labayen Aliermo

Wee Laddie

The wee laddie marched on as he played.
Stalwart did he seem; to watch I stayed.
His bagpipes were piping loud and clear;
Crowds began to gather close to hear.

His kilt swayed to gently in the breeze.
Every song he played, the crowd did please.
I thought as I saw him standing tall,
Surely, love inspired him, was his call.

The wee laddie played and marched along,
'Round and 'round his stage with every song.
Now and then someone would wipe a tear,
As his music roused a mem'ry dear.

The melodies, yes, one that I heard,
Resounded as sweetly as a bird,
Showed me the wee laddie in each man,
Softly playing bagpipes in God's plan.

W. Diane Van Zwol

Greatest Gift

It's not the love songs you dedicate to me,
It's not the ring I wear on my finger,
It's the tender kisses you give me
And the soft touch of your hands.

You can offer me the moon,
You can offer me the stars,
You can offer me the impossible,
But nothing matters . . . just your loving heart.

My love for you is true,
My heart belongs to you,
And my greatest gift of all
Would be your true, undying love.

Tania Valdes

Post-Adoption

Amidst a colourful array of fading petals
Emerge the flowers closest to my song,
Strung along the pathway of my dwelling place.
In my garden, stems standing so strong:
Reaching up to overtake the others,
Scattered amidst a fenced-in field of wild,
Dispersed amongst the pastels, they take over,
Flowers of black—now I can't hold my child.

Beyond the fence, I see the petals,
And through the cracks protrude the leaves of gold.
Before my grave, I'll see my fruit of labour,
My lot re-multiplied except for weeping.
For though my eyes are clamped,
And though my heart is now in disarray,
When I see her next we'll all be laughing,
As love escapes the boundaries of today.

Jill Campbell

Mystery Lies

Deep beneath the darkest sea,
There's many a secret,
For you and for me
For those who dare
The mystery lies
Deep beneath the darkest sea.

At dawn "The Conqueror" leaves the dock
With sails set high
He finds his spot
Amongst the others, wide open and free
In search of the mystery, beneath the sea.

His courage and strength, engraved underneath the bow,
The eagerness awaits, to be fulfilled somehow
Deep beneath, the darkest sea.

Joanie Mooney

The Things I Carry

It's 7:30 a.m.
I'm half awake
And my foot's out the door.
Onward I go
In withered old shoes,
Bearing treads no more.
I carry on.

With school books in backpack
Strapped over my shoulder,
Another cold day, moving on I feel older.
These are the things that I carry.

School's in session, but I'm not there.
Sorry couldn't make it, are my woes of despair
Inside myself.
These are the burdens I carry.

Everybody has problems
I find everyday.
So now I must think
In a positive way.
These are the thoughts that I carry.

Thomas Webber

Being

Trying to make decisions,
Trying to look serene,
Hoping the right direction,
Hoping to hold my scream.

Expecting something not seen,
Expecting to find my place,
Thinking, I haven't been.
Thinking, something to erase.

Working, my own projections.
Working, what I am going to be.
Holding, my reservations.
Holding, what lives in me.

Trying, Hoping, and Expecting,
the things I want to be.
Thinking, Working, and Holding,
my God is helping me.

Rafael Lopez

Where Do We Stand

The moment I saw you
I wanted to be more than friends
My feelings for you are true
From the first time I saw you
    until the end

Just when we are getting closer
I feel you push me farther away
This is quite a poser
Because now I feel like a castaway

I need you to understand
That I am trying to be bolder
For you are the only man
That has always given me
    the cold shoulder

I really need to know
How you feel inside
For I want to know if you are
    friend or foe
Because my feelings will not be denied

My feelings for you grow strong
Each time you came around
Even if we are destined to be wrong
Sometimes a love can be found

Shannon Robbins

Lost in Your Eyes

My heart pounds and flutters.
I feel my blood pressure rise.
My cheeks flush with colour
When I look into your eyes.
Can you see the way I feel?
I'm lost in your piercing gaze.
I just can't help loving you.
Love has put me in a daze.
When my eyes meet with yours
I can't help but look away.
Still, my eyes are wandering.
I want to look at you all day.

Ralph Adrian Xavier

Shadows

Embodied and warmed by radiance,
rays burst through containers
to sunshine's golden,
there is no end to this light
the source casts no shadows
seen by those in shadow's light
until it falls on rusted might,
right or left it may go
over or under to and fro
eventual destiny will
rest no more passing around
obstructed vision
wanting to find that source of light
in the very own shadow's sight

Samuel Y. Lee

Seaing

Driving, catching glimpses of sea
makes me twelve years old
when only ever seen on holiday
Durban and Cape Town
seeing it virgin
once a year
perhaps ten times
in life

Now sea
every
single
day

Driving the sun is strobe light
through infantry of trees
lancing into my head without shades
scrambling the lobes
I want to cry
But I'm driving

Gareth Campbell Flood

To the Love of My Life

The day you asked me out
May have caused a tiny doubt
Then a kiss you gave to me
And I knew it was meant to be
Your eyes a deep, dark brown
Never once caused me to frown
You had a quality I never knew
Your faithfulness is my only clue
You always listen and always care
Hurting me in any way you'd never dare
All my love I will give to you
For you, there's anything I'd do
We've had our share of things go wrong
But fixed it with the words of our song
We'll always have our love to share
In my heart I'll always care
People like you are hard to find
Always, you are on my mind
I hope forever our love will last
And remember things
   we've done in the past

Stacey Dale

From a White Pine Tree

In memories, my boyhood days I still see
As in the shade of a big White Pine Tree,
Sitting on top of a split-rail fence, like a squirrel,
Watching the clouds above unfurl.
Much of the country farmland I could see—
The country life that was meant for me.
The barns and stables and corrals,
The cows, being milked, tied in their stalls.
I remember the swine, sheep, and goats,
The big fields of corn, barley, and oats.
I almost hear the babbling spring-fed stream.
I see working in the fields, the Old Grey Team.
The barnyard fowl of different breeds,
The pigeons, flying about with ease,
I remember the birds singing, as they ate the cherries
And the long rows of strawberries.
The gooseberry bushes near the grape vines.
Memories of my boyhood life are so Divine.
I have many memories that make my heart swell,
Like Mother a'ringing the old dinner bell.

William J. Lambert

A Cry for Help

Oh, young generation, we're crying out to thee.
We have failed the land and deep,
We are wandering as lost sheep.
Help cleanse the world from sin and set it free.

Oh, young generation, we have sinned before the Lord,
With your help that error we can swing.
Help us, God's mercy it may bring,
If we together take to heart God's holy word.

Oh, young generation, God knows the thoughts of man.
Sadly, injustice and hate prevail,
Peace in the world still seems to fail.
Let's strive so God saves the world if He still can.

Oh, young generation, exalt in the Lord with dignity.
Help clear away the great unrest.
With our wisdom we can try our best,
So with repentance let's face the Lord in unity.

Oh, young generation, with enthusiasm great,
The world is yours to dominate.
Let not that it should deteriorate,
But strive to give to God a worldwide peace and faith.

Rosie Duch

Midnight Sonnet

Look how the sky's pale eye in quiet sight
Night's hidden secrets soft and black unveils,
Transforming wispy clouds with surreal light
And waking shadows whose vague, confusing trails
And forms eclipse the stars with inky stillness.
Such waiting bound within eternal motion
Reflects the state of my own soul, tremulous;
Minding the present moment in the ocean
Of memory (as if thought could time freeze),
And pausing in a sigh of borrowed breath
That now, like living mist curled 'round the trees
Of woods deep-rooted in the earthy death,
Escapes, by eastern winds drawn far away
To live again and greet the cautious day.

Bryn Williams

Lonely

I feel all alone in this big world that I live in,
Nobody there to care for me.

People are everywhere:
Laughing and crying,
Singing and dancing.

Through good times and bad,
In sickness and in health . . .
Friends are there for you when it really counts.

People think that they have it bad;
They think that they are not as rich as others,
But they are not the ones living on the street.

All I wanna be is a normal teenager,
With someone to laugh with,
Someone to cheer me up with when I am blue.

True friends are awesome,
Considering they are hard to find!

     Melissa Daniel

The Village on the Lake

From above, the lake is placid, mirror still,
and through the mist is heard the late loon's call.
The trees cast their flambeau to fulfill
the ever-changing, never-changing beauty of the fall.

The heron makes its way on languid wings,
the sea gull dives in search of prey,
and from his nest the blackbird sings.
Below, the otter slips and slides in gleeful play.

The changing times have stilled the water mill,
the haunting whistle of the train is heard no more,
straining horses no longer breast the hill,
and steamers no longer ply the shore.

But nature does not heed man's whims,
and keeps for us through all eternity
the beauty and the grace of living things
in one closely bound fraternity.

     Harry Hargreaves

Untitled

Maybe it meant nothing to you
And you were lying the whole time
Even though you told me your heart was true
You have just committed an un-forgiven crime

You led me on day and night
To make me think you were Mr. Right
You didn't really care how I felt
You chewed me up, then spit me out

You can't imagine the pain I feel
Nobody can see me drowning
Into my thoughts of the good times we had
Only few, but never frowning

Now I have to pay the cost
And I suffer when I see you or when you call
But "it's better to have loved and lost
Than never to have loved at all"

     Krystal Newman

Friendship

It's time to mend the fences
With those friends that we've annoyed.
Hopefully we'll discover that
They haven't been destroyed.

For, Friendship is the most important
Of any treasures we may possess.
Material things we can use each day,
But old friends we can caress.

Each morning as I greet the day,
I think of each Old Chum.
I review those happy times we shared,
Those days of Carefree Fun.

As I grow older, so grows their worth,
And as I survey the scene,
Friendship's Value has outgrown by far
Any Material advances I've seen.

     Bill Ott

Big Mac

I wandered into town this day
To earn a couple of bucks,
Then be on my way.
I sat down on a roadside bench;
There's a Big Mac.
Just across the way.

So I thought, what the heck,
A fella's got to eat.
I'll buy a hamburger
With my last two bucks;
It will be my treat.

Just as I was about to eat,
A stranger came along;
He looked at me, but did not speak,
So I said, let's share.
He gulped his down and turned around
And slowly walked away.
Then he stopped;
He barked and wagged his tail.
It just made my day.

     Ray Morley

Melanie Tessier

Midnight's moon glows brightly
Enhancing a castle as the roses are
Left in the garden sleeping,
And a princess dreams as a unicorn stands
Next to her castle,
Intertwining with angels, as they
Enchant the surrounding beauty.

The sun rises and morning arrives with
Every rose leaving a
Sparkle of beauty to be
Seen by all, and
In the distance, a unicorn
Enchants the sparkle
Resting in the eyes of the princess.

     Steve Gillespie

For the Sake of Freedom

Staying to find what's new to life
makes me begin right where I stand.

There I see birds coming to the sea
as if exchanging views
on where they went,

Letting the wind carry them on its back
in sympathy with the way things are.

Then altogether came to my attention,
not for my sake, but for their own.

Fini Lokke

For M

I long to rise one morning
And finally find I'm free
To spread my wings far beyond
This cage of destiny.

I long to live the hour
When my feet touch the ground
And find I'm the man again
Who feels safe and sound.

I long to seize the second
When my agony subsides
And my constant ailing
Far from me hides.

I long to grasp the moment
When my heart grieves no more,
And life is breathed in fully,
Free from pain evermore.

Pheadra Farah

She-Wolf

Once the silvery huntress of the wild,
Keen to scent the wind
Before her savage kill,
Still in death she lives.
Shadowed she-wolf, bullet gray,
Howling from a granite rock,
Blind to the hunter's pointed gun,
Dreams of running free
In the midnight sun.

Kathryne B. Roberts

Confused

My mind has been shadowed
with things people say,
but sometimes things
just happen that way.

You don't know who is
right or wrong.
Your life just seems like
an endless song.

Then when your mind's journey
comes to an end,
you make it seem like
it was all just pretend.

Britt Anakaer

Trials

Sometimes, I just can't see it, Lord.
I don't seem to understand,
But I know that You are in control.
All things are in Your hand.

I can't see the reasons why, oh, Lord,
All these trials I receive.
That all things work together for good, dear Lord,
Please help me to believe.

Some of the reasons now, oh, Lord,
I'm beginning to see.
The trials and tests of different sorts
Help me be what You want me to be.

You're doing more, more . . . much more, oh, Lord,
Than I at first could see.
The trials are bringing answers to prayer.
You know what is best for me.

Roberta Hildebrand

Tender Thoughts

If the thoughts of my heart
Were to be released from the restraints that hold them
If the vault of tenderness thoughts opened
The true and only true words
Would spill out in a tidal wave of feelings
That would spread throughout
And come tumbling through my weak pencil
Filling the blank lines
With so much emotion
You would be taken back
If the lock were broken
And the thoughts let out
You would be taken back
By the fears and emotions, sadness and happiness
That cowered onto the bleak and lonely page
If the truest form of words
Were released from the locks and chains
That keep them bound inside my small, little body
Thoughts destined to be kept away from human touch
You would be taken aback

Renee David

Petal Bed

In this petal bed, fingers spread
To sprinkle the dust of life,
Weaving the tapestry of kaleidoscope worlds
Like something conjured from a dream.

Ivy upon the lattice entwine,
Silent colours scream the mixed columbine.
Pink sun drops drip like dew,
Sweet as balm, savoury and new.
Crystalline rainbows that the sunlight captures
Send the bees into dizzy raptures.
The rhinestones buds of jaundiced grace
Bow to the pretty maids of satin and lace.
Back the stargazer lily bronze and brass,
Chilean jasmine sparkles like glass.

As the click, clack, creeping myrtle glows,
Throughout this garden everything grows.

Megan Evans

Illusions

At least my body will be touched,
giving the illusion of what everyone says is true:
the illusion that I have the capacity to be loved,
that I am smart enough and average enough to be loved;
the illusion of sheer lust transforming
into pure desire for the real me,
the transformation of my soul into a righteous being,
not just a lonely, desperate creature.
Any place of my being is willing to change for love,
and the transition stage of my life has always been sex.
Learned, ingrained behaviors are immortal,
ergo will never cease, only metamorphose.
How pathetic my illusions are.

    Kary L. Cook

Beaming Sunshine over the Treetops

Graciously the setting sun,
Beams such beauty and brightness,
Yellow and Gold!
Glistening through my window pane,
The time of day to be home, the sparkle is momentary.
When the clouds come and go some days,
Sunshine is blanketed by the fluff
Of the strata as it floats by in its heavenly path.
My eyes light up to the Glory of it all.
"Oh! How we are Blessed!"
Each day is surprisingly different!
The dream of tomorrow in my thoughts,
The evergreens sway with the wind,
While the sun peeks past her bows,
Surely to goodness! What will tomorrow bring?
A day to behold!
Why, I can see the sunset still,
Leaving my heart with the color of Glory
As the treetops straighten and grow taller,
Waiting in a peaceful night for the morrow.

    Patricia E. Thompson Davidson

The Woman Called Me

The troubled child I once was
has grown just like the wings of a dove.

The scared child I use to be
has grown stronger mentally.

The frightened child of yesteryear
doesn't hide in a corner;
she has no tears.

The woman that has taken her place
stands before you, poised with grace,

To welcome you home with loving hands,
To tell you her secrets and know you understand,

To walk with her and say not a word,
To touch her soul and set it free like a bird.

The woman that I have become,
The woman that has struggled and won,

The woman that you have set free
is the woman they call
ME.

    Gail Ferguson

Words

Words, words, beautiful words
How grand to see them play
You can make them dance and jingle
Or even make minds sway

You can make words kind and gentle
Or cutting as a knife
They can make a lover happy
Or make someone take a life

Words, words, beautiful words
Flowing swiftly on a page
They touch the young and tender
They reach the wise, old sage

But the words we find in the Bible
Are the best loved words of all
For, they tell us of a Saviour
Who gave His life for all

    Audrey Morrow

I Stopped Loving You Today

I stopped loving you today
Your treatment of me doesn't go away
If you don't change, I pray
I'll leave you flat

In times of war and peace
I sat and waited for your release
You were number one in my life
Till I became your wife

What makes you think
You can hurt me like you do?
If you don't smarten up
These shoes won't come walking
Back to you

You can find another to fill your bed
I don't belong in it
My love for you is dead

I feel weak when you come my way
A kiss you don't deserve
I will turn my head the other way
'Cause I stopped loving you today

    Grace Del Bel

Why?

Brothers and sisters
of mankind,
why stand still
in the frame
of two minds?
Why resist
the sacred kind,
pictured and framed
in the realm
of one mind?
Why?

    Sylvia Brewster

Melody

There is no music.
The violin notes polished by the wind
are running away though my fingers,
sinking in the dark corners of winter.
I recreate in my mind
the unique ecstasy of melody
and dance along with the stars.
This is an unknown world for most,
sinfully delirious for me.
Oh! Let me continue in this trance,
where my untangled thoughts
flow to gentle
meadows surrounded by sunflower beds.
Oh! Let me continue in this trance.
Let me be the commander
of my tired heart.
Just this one time,
let me eternize my soul
in the transparency of my melody.

Martha C. Iturralde

C.K.

With a step that is soft.
I climb, see stairs,
And when at the top
I hope to see you there,

But the chair is empty,
The room is the same,
And in my heart I know
I shall never see you again.

My loss is great,
Not in possessions, you know,
But in the love
That I lost so long ago.

I try to capture all of our dreams,
But so out of sight they all seem.
So, I close my eyes and you are there.
I hold you fast. Gone is my despair.

Jean M. MacKenzie

The Final Battle

A sword through the army
As a hawk
Through a flock of geese.
Terror
Killed every man.
Closed in combat—such a combat.
Calves racing about in dread and
Terror,
Wrestling to the bottom.
"Off with the heads!"
The call was heard out fifty-two miles.
Flesh to blood,
Blood to bone,
Bone to marrow,
Destroyed.

Kristina Austin

Jolly Ole Moon

Over the hilltops I see the moon
Like a jolly face on a gay balloon
It seems to say as it soars up high
Have fun with me ere the dawn is nigh

It rises as bright as a ball of fire
With its laughing face that I admire
It sends its glow over all the Earth
That warms our feelings and stirs our mirth

Come laugh with the moon and lighthearted be
Don't despair of the world and thee
Forget your troubles and cares of the day
Let the moon with its moonbeams chase them away
That laughing face away up high
In the starlit heavens in a darkening sky
Spreads its cheer over all the land and sea
Make the most of life be as gay as he

Ruth Johnson

Questions

My children have asked me many things:
Why do snakes crawl, but birds have wings?
Where do butterflies live through the winter's cold?
Why is a moonbeam so hard to hold?

Is it true that elephants never forget?
And why is water always wet?
When the wind takes a kite for a ride in the sky,
how far can they see when they're up so high?

A plane is so heavy and makes such a sound,
how can it possibly take off from the ground?
Why are there rainbows after the rain
when the sun begins to shine again?

The mind of a child is a magical place
that grows when he's learning as if in a race
to find every answer to all he may see.
I wonder what the answers will be?

Science explains the dynamics of flight
for birds and butterflies, for planes and a kite.
Science gives answers, that's true without doubt,
But, oh! It leaves the magic out!

Jessie M. Burr

The Seasons

In the summer, the warm breeze blows,
leaving a tickle in my nose.
The sun shining through my window makes
it easier to get out of bed.
When I go outside, birds fly above my head.

In the autumn, the leaves start to fall;
the geese begin to fly south, making a goose call.

In the winter, the pond freezes over;
now there is no more green clover.

In the spring, which is the best,
all the birds make new nests.
The flowers start to bloom, and the grass turns green.
The snow goes away, hoping not to be seen.

Rachelle E. Gylander

On the Death of Diana—Princess of Wales

I sit at my window overlooking the Bay as I share in the sorrow of
those so far away. The Queen speaking from the palace window—
mourners and flowers beyond belief—the walk-about of the Royals
shaking hands and sharing the mourning and grief. Emotions of each
of us handled in our own private ways; memories will linger
the rest of our days.

The world is lonely, the world needs love; this love Diana craved,
of which she gave the world so much. The tabloids' ravishing photos
and stories of the lonely princess filled our needs.
We devoured them—now the whole nation bleeds.

Diana's unique funeral on worldwide TV was beamed to everyone
across the sea. The casket draped with the Royal banner and roses,
with one single card, "Mummy," slid out of the hearse. The Welsh
guard, sidestepping together, placed it atop the gun carrier; young
and old could feel no worse. The Royals slowly walking behind—with
every step a bit of solace they find. The steady clip-clop of the
horses' feet as they wended their way down the flower-strewn street.
Every minute the toll of the bell,
letting London know that all was not well.

A service so touching, "The stars spell out your name,"
sang Elton John as we watched the candle's flame.
Tears fall from the eyes of both young and old;
for years and years Diana's story will be told.

    Lenore Layton

State of Denial

Is your death enough to freeze my lust?
Will it purify my brain?

Will you dance about in my waking dreams
until I go insane?

The phantom of my dying heart can never release its hold.
You are my lifeline to the waking world, braided, psychic gold

When your quivering heart beats its final drum,
I will be alone,

without lust, without love, without pain or fear,
empty, just flesh and bone.

    Kenneth J. Paulson

What Is a Friend?

A friend is a very special person in your life;
Next to your parents, brothers, sisters, husband, or wife.
She's a person who's always there to give you an ear;
She's someone to turn to when you are in despair.

A friend is a person you can lean to when you have a problem,
Someone who is much concerned when you are in pain;
A person who helps you out when you are in trouble
Is someone who uplifts your heart and gives strength to your soul.

A true friend does not envy whatever goods you get
Nor rejoice at any misfortunes or adversities you've met;
She's there to cheer you up when you are in distress,
She's always there to share with you both failures and success.

A friend is a person who can be relied upon;
Your lives are open books, your secrets shared as one.
A person who safeguards your interest and protects it from harm,
No matter what happens, she's always there to lend you a hand.

A friend is a person loyal and true;
She never pretends but is always frank and honest with you;
And when things go wrong, she's there to defend,
For she is a true and a real friend.

    Anuasily Rivera Deveza

My Real Life "Teddy Bear"

In memory of my Pepere, 1934–1995. May he rest in peace.
Everyone knew this man as "The Big Guy,"
The one with the loud voice who wouldn't be shy.
He was always loved like a child's teddy bear
'Cause everything he did showed how much he cared,
Like the touch of his hand when you'd cross the street,
Or the treats you'd get when you tickled his back and feet.
He was always there throughout good and bad.
The smile on his face would never make you sad.
You thought he'd always be there through your life,
To see you get married with that wonderful husband or wife.
But sometimes, when you don't even know,
That magical person must go.
But when he left, I first wondered: Did his love go too, or will I find
That when he left, it stayed behind?"
The last time I saw him, his happiness was away,
To think an hour would turn into an endless day.
But although he is gone, and his smile is away,
It was replaced with an inner light that is here to stay.
I can but say he is something rare,
A sensitive person who isn't afraid
To care and he was also and will always be my Pepere!

Stephanie Lavergne

The Will to Survive

Life always amazes us when we are not aware
of other people and their problems, of what they may hold dear.

Some may suffer in silence—no one can possibly know
in hearts they have nothing their pain they won't show.

They smile and act normal—a surprise to many
may have nothing of benefits of life not even a penny.

But then—money isn't everything people at places like the
Hope Cottage teach us, we can all have loss and fall
to be fragile and weak gives us inside strength after
we've often lost it all.

The will to survive—the strongest of wills outshines great
losses and certainly, in us, instills—
The mere fact, it always will.

Sheila Valentine

A Dream of Dolphins

Gleaming, smooth, wet, silky skin,
dolphins, porpoises, and sea lions
dive happily in and out of the dark,
expansive, unruffled ocean-space.

I stood and watched, drawn by their friendly fun.

Giant, round bodies splashing gracefully
hardly make a sound.

A mysterious force called me to play by their side.

A bottomless, cloudless, womb that has no beginning or end.

Putting aside my spectacles to jump,
a sea-cow playfully chewed the frame.

Like a dolphin, I wove in and out of the
blissful, mystical, wet waves.

Knowing earth was my home,
quietly I crept away to the house
at the top of the hill.

Without my spectacles, I could see
the dolphins dreaming me.

Eva Lewarne

If I Could Play the Viola

If I could play the viola,
I would sit on a rotten log
On a warm summer afternoon,
With grass thick and tired,
A dog panting in the shade.
A dog that has no collar.

I would play "Elegy" by Benjamin Britten,
Wearing a cheap cotton dress
With two buttons missing
And with an uneven hem,
With sandals on my feet
That flap noisily as I walk.

I would place my viola close to my cheek,
Forgetting the world around me,
My soul trembling with the pluck of the strings.

If I could play the viola,
I would play the "Elegy" . . . on a warm summer day.

Miriam Batts

Life after Death

If there's life after death, is it pleasure or pain?
It must come to us all someday.
And then perhaps we'll know if we lived life in vain
And just how much we've got to pay.

Do you think that we really must pay for our sins?
After all, we didn't ask to be born.
Do you think that the rich man's the one that wins
Or the man who planted the corn?

Do you think that it matters? Does God really care
If on Earth we're successful or not,
Or is it a fact that as long as we share,
God's kingdom in Heaven we've got?

There's no way of knowing until our time's up
Just what is in store for us all.
So, till that time, come, fill the cup!
Perhaps there's just nothing at all!

Barry E. Nortion

To See Another Day

Gazing out around at a restless night,
Seeing the wounded, hearing their pain,
Knowing their heartache.

Listening to faraway blasts like thunder
Threatening to break apart the ground
On which we fight.

Seeing the explosions lighting up the sky,
Blindingly bright, the only sign of life
In an otherwise-dead night.

Hearing the whistle as the dawn breaks,
Charging at fire, no hope for me now.

No more will I hear those deafening sounds.
No longer will I breathe the scent of death,
Not to see another day like this one,
Never again to see another day.

Jillian Maloney

At Sunset

The clouds all billow soft and free
With colors like a Christmas tree.
The edges marked with color bright
Tells us it will soon be night.
At sunset

We can all find patterns there.
Animals far beyond compare,
Fluffy puppies floating by
Disappear at blink of eye.
At sunset

Sun hits water—casts a glow;
It's very sad to see it go.
The birds all rush on silent wings
As, far away, one bravely sings.
At sunset

Silence not . . . last rays of light
Usher in the peaceful night.
One last glance and home we trod.
Tomorrow's in the hands of God.
At sunset

Dorothy Mazurik

Going out to Play

Three bonny boys one sunny day
decided to go outside and play.
"What will we do?" Kerry said,
and then upended onto his head.

"I know, let's play hide and seek
down by that old stony creek,"
said Blair, as he pushed Kerry down
with a laugh and then a frown.

For, Kerry had shown Blair his fist
and then his arm did quickly twist.
"Stop your silly fighting, you two,"
said Jason, kicking with his shoe.

"Stop it! What's going on here?"
shouted Mum, and sounding severe,
"If you really want something to do,
there's plenty of work for you."

"We are all right!" yelled Jason.
"We're just having plenty of fun."
And as work was what they feared,
three bonny boys quickly disappeared.

Noline A.V. Johnson

The Symbols

From their cozy, sandy tombs,
They came struggling out
To seek the salty water
That beckons them to come.

And with short little pauses,
They struggled with all their might
To avoid any danger
Lurking behind the night.

Though some will be victorious,
And they are the lucky ones,
Some will stumble and fall
And be a part of none.

And those who are victorious
Will never look behind
As they glide into the water
To fill their souls with freedom.

Yet, never could they know
That each of them will bear
The symbols of these deaths
Atop their shiny shells.

Ahmad Faisal Aljunied

Normal and Abnormal

It is normal
to be abnormal
in an institution of abnormal
It is abnormal
to be normal
in an institution of abnormal
What is normal
in our world
of abnormality
What is abnormal
in our world
of normality
If the psychiatrists
knew the answers
to these questions
abnormalities
would not persist
and institutions of abnormalities
would not exist
on this side of Jordan

Vivian Paulette Aston

Kitten

Chasing sunbeams, lavender, and mier,
In the clover, through the grass,
Feel of dewdrops on my fur.
New to this world, being born in May,
Scampering to fro, a bonny wee lass.
Swaying her tail, "That's enough," as if to say,
Antics galore, Mom "Sam" hopes a cure.

Fluffy and soft, any child's delight,
Cuddly, pointy ears, two white feet,
Green eyes, defense against mice and might.

Upside down, around and round,
Topsy-turvy, flipsy-flopsy,
Feelin' ten feet tall,
I weigh one pound.

Evelyn Hunter Clark

Coming Home

As I sit in silence, the tears rolling down
my cheeks meet in a single river.
Years have passed by; I still miss you so.
I won't ever understand why he called you home.

I lie awake in the midnight hour; as the
moon casts a shadow across the room, I close
my eyes in hopes that you will be there.
Waiting in silence for sleep, I find myself
alone, hoping, praying,
no one to talk to about my mere existence.
There is no escape from the rushing thoughts
that are running like a whirlwind in my mind
as I wait for him to call me home to be with you again.

Till then, I will wait in vain and talk to
my angels, my guardian angels.
Although you are not here beside me, I feel
your presence, watching, sharing my every battle,
my every heartbeat.
Never am I alone, just lonely.
I will be coming home one day, and we shall be
together once again.

Cindy Lussier

The Last Crossing Station

Where are the eyes of thee
To bring me a sight of passionate love?
Where are the lips of thee
From which to quench me with wine?
Where are the hands of thee
Whose touches bring me peace?

Where are you my dearest pearl, my joy?
Come closer to me to make a good join.
Two we are, one we have to turn.
And the love we make is of no sin.
It's love. It's just a magic game.

I and you, he and she, and all of us are there,
Crossing the dark cloud in a treacherous life
Whose infidelity her nature is.
Over her surface, evenly we float
And suddenly she throws us away.
Then nothing we become, even something before we were.
We die, lying in between the dusty bed,
Which is the musk of the finality down there.

Dirar A. Aldaim

I Was a Stranger

I heard the streets were paved with gold,
I only found them wet and cold.
Hurrying people with no time to spare;
my hope quickly turned to despair.
I was lonely and lost without a home,
without a friend; I was completely alone.
I was a stranger in a strange land
with no one around to take my hand.
The stars came out, I needed to rest.
Time to seek shelter, I went up west.
People slept in cardboard boxes,
they lived their lives like cunning foxes.
Empty bottles lay at their feet,
their clothes were anything but neat.
Old newspapers were their blankets,
their breakfast, leftovers from street markets.
I found a box and lay down to rest;
my courage then was put to the test.
My new-found friends held out a hand:
I was a stranger in a strange land.

Brenda Hammersley

A Special Date

Outside it's softly snowing,
And all the streets get white.
Deep in the snow our house is.
The chimney smoke is like a soft grey kite.

The sky gets dark, the forest black.
It's getting late, it will be night.
Today a silent darkness
Is covering the world of light.

Just one light—a star—still on the sky
Sends soundless shine so silver bright,
Gives winter earth a secret light.
It warms the house that special night.

So different is the world today.
I guess, I dream so soon to seem.
It will be time: A day for all
To think of wonderful Christmas balls!

Slowly days get short, nights get long,
Children singing holy songs.
They are counting days and counting lights
And they can hardly wait for the merry Christmas date!

Trudi E. Graf

Untitled

Dedicated to Abner on his eighty-seventh birthday
Dearest Abner, light of my life,
Lucky the day I became your wife.
We have had our ups and downs,
But we managed, despite our frowns,
To have a good life with lots of love,
And it's you I am always thinking of.
So stay healthy and happy, and live many years,
And for you I stand up and shout, "Three cheers!"
For your good nature, generosity, and handsome looks
We could never find your equal even in books.
So happy birthday for your four score and seven.
To be with you is better than Heaven.

Gertrude Kushner

Heaven-Sent

In loving memory of Doctor Irving Levy
You left a legacy of love,
A name that bears great pride.
Your devotion went beyond the call;
You put your needs aside.

You gave us all you had to give;
You shared our joy and grief.
The time you took to call your own
Was truly far too brief.

You gave your heart to many;
You were a friend to all.
Great comfort came from knowing that
We needed just to call.

A more devoted doctor
This world will never know.
You were a gift from Heaven that
God sent to us below.

Your presence made a difference;
Your passing brings great pain.
May all our love surround you
Until we meet again.

Tina Cooper

Fiery Arrogance

Little fiery flame
Dancing on a candle's wick,
You may be surprisingly hot to the touch,
But your arrogance is short-lived.
For, at my own will,
I can choose when to
Extinguish your existence.

Tanya Thomas

Basking in the Sun

Quivering
I watched
as the lizard
mistook my
midriff for
the twig of
a sponge
see-sawing
his bloated
green coat
with the rhythm
of my breath
and when
at last
he finished
basking in
the sun
he departed
leaving me
unnerved

Gea Grace Littler

Revolver

Last night I stepped out in the chill
Through time's elusive door
Into a place where I had been
A life of years before

I pulled my fine coat tightly round
Shivering through old bones
Embarrassed by a childhood thought
Of being all alone

I bit my lip and shook a bit
And struggled to be brave
In awe of the short journey
From the cradle to the grave

   Tim Akins

Snow Bird of Youth

The autumn whirls and whorls and whines
And changes into winter.
I sing to you, a black thing on a bough.
From my pedestal of ebony,
I disgorge my blurred
   and melancholy notes
On the world's white manuscript.

I flutter and flit and fly to spring.
In the lean twilight of an April day,
I bob and throb on a swaying grey twig
And in the solitude I sing
Of Earth's essence, crackly in my throat,
Transmuting God to note.

Lonely over fastness of snow,
I swerve and sweep and soar
   along the wind;
I flitter among the shadowy lights of night
And cry a crazy song of night and snow
And the sweet, soft air; oh, hear me!

I tremble and tumble and fall to Earth.
I heard the pellets
   before I was twenty-one.

   Robert Weekes

Solitude

A drizzling rain
hides like a veil
pale, blue-green, distant hills.

The only sound
you hear around:
smooth dropping on the lawn.

The grass is wet,
so are my feet—
my heart feels wide and free!

It's like a dream—
where has time gone?
I feel I am on Earth alone. . . .

   Doris Kyburz

My Guardian Angel

I must have a guardian angel, for how else can
I explain that when all seems lost, and I feel abandoned,
My angel shows me the way.

He sits on my shoulders and urges me on, every day
From dusk 'til dawn.
I cannot doubt the existence, for without my belief
I'm sure to stray.

My angel sent from above encourages me onward,
With hope and excitement to succeed:
With my angel ever present, a bond I know will endure,
To keep me safe, out of harm's way.

Whatever obstacle I incur, my angel is ever present
I'm sure. How else can I explain the sunshine all
Around me, even on a rainy day?

   Margaret Dignard

England's Rose

Where have all the flowers gone? Long time passing. . . .
Diana, a magnificent flower, a budding rose
Riding life's problems created by those nearest you,
Who never tried to understand or even lend a hand.
Winter fell that dark night in Paris by the Seine;
The world lost a saviour, Heaven's gain.

So many of us had never met you, Diana,
Yet you put meaning into our lives.
You gave your heart to the poor, the sick, those in need.
You were no candle in the wind.
Your flame within our hearts will continue to burn,
To inspire and help us to understand and learn,
Ensuring that the babies of the world,
The ones we adore, grow up in peace,
To love, be kind, to not make war.

You know, dear, sweet queen of hearts,
It's hard to realize how or why
You could have been taken from us.
We are heavy with sadness,
But if there be such a person as Christ,
We pray: please look after our Di . . . she was so nice.

   Norman St. Paul

Resurrection

Reaching for the stars undaunted,
Tasting the moon, metallic and insubstantial,
Ocean waves touch tender, salty tears.
Pitching me ashore, sensuous as the sun,
Kissing the sandy beach, unfurled into an

Unsuspecting universe; holding hands with
Its disciples, but I am woman, sunlight,
An unchained voice in a tight circle.
Is there room for singing and rocking
A cradle of shattered dreams?

Like a ship's sails facing the wind . . .
Howl as it may, I still travel
Into the night, even beyond darkness,
And shine with my own inner light,
Un-eclipsed by a darkening sky.

   Mary Helen Mitchell

For Gordon

I stood, an interloper in the final chapter of your life,
Silently watched you struggle and try to hold on.
As with laboured breath you watched the seasons pass,
Weighted down by indecision when earthly hope was gone.

That broken, weary room while family held your hands,
Whether to go or stay you had to decide,
Became a celestial cocoon suspended in time
Where angels beckoned you home . . . and I cried.

Like the sweet, pungent whisper of autumn's wind,
You shed your prison of tired, earthly sod.
And I envied, as for one brief, spectacular moment I saw
You loosen here your hold and grasp the hand of God.

A cord deep within reverberated with the crescendo
Of heavenly shouts and never-dreamed-of charms
That pierced far across the great divide
As God welcomed you home and picked you up in His arms.

I suppose I could have imagined your footsteps firm,
Your stride sure and quick as in days before.
I probably dreamed I felt the first, sweet breath you breathed
As my ears were teased with the echoes of wonders in store.

    Geneinne Bondy

Tale of the XXth Century Cerpent

Sadistically crucified my soul by your ignorance
Six feet demise trapped in your mind
Haunting nightmare shakes your scream
Forever glance at my pain, in water rings in a clear lake

Stubborn images reflect in mirrors
Your solution a pull of the trigger, a slash of a blade
My scars stain my skin
My insides have no vacancy to new scars

I've fallen to rage, you will need me
I am the deceased, dirty king
I'll reflect my hate and pain to your virgin sins
Snake bite with the crushing effect of payback

Suffocate by guilt, you deserve it, for your misjudgment on thee
Suffer my wrath

XXth Century Cerpent
    Jim Kouri

I Have Seen Death

I have seen the face of death:
He was not a hollow skull
With grim and empty eyes;
He was not cloaked in darkness, nor did he ride a pale horse;
He did not carry a sickle,
And the foul smell of rotting flesh did not surround him like perfume.

He was a young man
With smiling blue eyes
Who laughed and cried, just like me;
He wore clothes from the Gap and smelled like Old Spice;
He flew planes for a living;
He carried chewing gum; he quit smoking, you see.

He was a hero and the boy next door,
A patriot and a husband,
A father, a brother, and a son;
Yet when he went forth into the sky,
He caused the fires of hell to burn,
And the stench of rotting flesh was left in his wake.

    Althea Monteiro

Angel

Dedicated to Catherine Arlett and Jane Houang

She was not a movie star, but she was beautiful.
She had never invented a cure for a disease or fought in a war,
But she was a hero.

She was not famous, yet hundreds knew her.
She touched the lives of so many,
Yet she was not a saint.

She was a person full of love, and now that love is gone.
She will never be forgotten—
We won't allow it.

Her smile would warm your heart, and her laughter spread like wild fire.
She was a friend.

She gave all of us the strength, confidence, and courage
To face what lay ahead.
Although she is gone,
Her light still shines.

She is remembered in all of our hearts,
As one more precious angel
Who was taken too soon.

> *Kim Arlett*

Nature

Nature is the beauty, created not by man but by the earth.
You can plant a tree or a flower but only the earth can make it grow.
Nature is not only plants it is animals and you, too.
You are part of nature, you are beautiful.
Just because you see a person or a plant you don't like
Doesn't mean it's not beautiful.
If you smell or hear something you dislike doesn't mean it
Should be erased from existence, it could be treasured by someone else.
Love nature, for it makes a great sacrifice in your honor.
It lives through all the animals you kill and all the trees you cut down.
Don't take it for granted, it may not be around forever.
Allow the future to enjoy it as you did. Love nature always.

> *Elicia Gavey*

A Sea of Faces

A sea of faces waving as the ship set out to sea,
The billowing smoke flowed from the stacks; the air flowed through it as we dined.
Yet in the air a cool breeze flew, if only we knew.
Surrounded by the ocean blue, the cool breeze blew right through,
A sea of faces waving that we were never again to see.

A sea of faces waving as the ship was in the sea,
Our fate was sealed as we sailed out, by the Titans some would shout.
Others would say we sealed our own,
Oh! How could we have known?
A sea of faces waving that we were never again to see.

A sea of faces waving with the ship far to sea,
The sun sunk low off the bow; whatever can become of us now?
A crash of ice, the screeching steel,
A jagged edge ran from the keel,
A sea of faces waving that we were never again to see.

A sea of faces waving with the ship beneath the sea,
Down we sank to the water below; lives were lost to the darkness low.
Of the few that survived the daze,
Their eyes would forever hold a glaze,
The sea of faces waving that I again would never see.

> *Tanis Thorlakson*

A Thief

A tear is a thief, for it steals a smile;
with powerful effusion it cascades no style.
Your life is content, then enters a blow,
grasping the core within your soul.

Bitter, salty tears slither their taste,
bathing your sorrow, embracing your face.
A flutter of butterflies visit at night,
cramming for comfort, searching for flight.

The veil of darkness soon pales into dawn;
a new day is born a new smile inches on.
The thief is a rendezvous of somber grey,
a metamorphic release, paving your way.

Barbara Moyer

The Rocking Chair

I remember Mom's old rocking chair,
solid wood and painted white.
It held a spot out on the porch,
where she viewed the world both day and night.

When a summer day was sultry and still,
and the house was stifling hot,
we kids would sit on the glider swing
and rock away the time with our thoughts.

My mom would spend the afternoon
watching the birds and bees flit by;
seated in her old rocking chair,
all kinds of sights she would spy.

I can hear the chair softly rocking,
and see my Mother's pensive gaze,
and know the hours of silent repose
that chair brought, and I cease to amaze.

It simplified my young life
to see business put to rest.
I learned to take time to reflect,
and my imagination was put to the test.

Deidre Simpson

Then Come with Me

Have you ever . . . run in the woods,
Feeling as fleet and free as a deer
Bursting forth, elegance exposed, for a time?
Then come with me! Hurry.

Have you ever . . . walked in the woods,
Seeing the lush, green growth of the seed
Bursting forth, at spring's first sign?
Then come with me! Explore.

Have you ever . . . stood in the woods,
Smelling the warm and pungent air
Bursting forth, full of cedar, fir, and pine?
Then come with me! Inhale.

Have you ever . . . sat in the woods,
Listening to the chatter of the birds and squirrels
Bursting forth, the air full of excited rhyme?
Then come with me! Enjoy.

Rowena J. Ramsden

Keeping Us Apart

How many days of the
    week go by,
How many hours of the
    day do I cry?
How many rivers are on
    this Earth?
That's how much I think
    you are worth.
When I awake each morning
    at dawn,
My thoughts for you are
    very strong.
Will I ever stop this
    longing for you
Or just keep feeling
    the way I do?
Maybe if I told you, just
    how I feel,
Things might come together
    And would be real.
Feelings of you fill my heart.
What, then, is keeping us apart?

Gloria Johnson

Mom's Secret

I like to get along with folk
And run away when some evoke
An argument, so voices rise
And anger flashes in the eyes.

While others moan the ice and snow,
I dare not speak, for this would show
An oddity, to rankle them,
For others rarely feel the same.

But when a snowstorm starts to pitch
Its frosted mountains in each ditch,
A warmth, like springtime,
    wraps my soul.
Gloom's gone! With joy my heart is full.

For, secretly, it's just the sound
Of hearing family homeward bound:
In summertime they're scattered wide
But snowstorm time, they come inside.

Esther Fitch Crandall

Treasure Land

'Tis no blarney from Killarney,
Nor indeed from county Cork,
That your ship without a rudder,
Safely harboured in New York,
Is a blessin'; since your messin'
All about on waves o' chance
On a trip in winds a'howlin',
Banshee wails, gale's bold advance
Assailed the silk, but failed 'cause milk
O' due kindness and the wand
O' Lady Luck did guide your ship
Into slip o' dreams that bond!

John L. Newey

Illusions of Love

First love, first impatience,
First infatuation, first obsession,
First dream, first hope,
First wish, first desire,
First touch, first kiss,
First warmth, first chill,
First doubt, first fight,
First tear, first regret,
First spring, first flowers,
First present, first gift,
First compromise, first apology,
First truce, first promise . . .

Summiya Nizamuddin

Of This Time

This tree-half lies
cut up,
still, not as if
you were quiet
before today,
but—still!

You knew pages
before they were born,

proud works in bud
when each night becomes a dawn;

You opened
daily unlearned secrets;
you hosted
countless feathered parties,

toughly weak
putting hands together,

bookmarks to a future year
when birds and trees and works were rare.

John Cooper

I Love You, Mom

Strong, fearless
Selfless, brave
Carry with you
These traits to your grave

Giving, caring
Of feminine gender
Glow on high
In your elegant splendour

Toil, sweat
Laugh, weep
You overcome with bare limbs
High mountains steep
I try to see through your eyes
You are not old, yet so wise

Then descend from great heights
With humble appearance
As though an award
Would not be in accordance
I love you, Mom, for all you've done
Thank you, Mom; you shine like the sun

Ayinka-Asahkee Brown

To Feel Once More

To feel once more the childlike touch of rain,
Throw off these weights and chains that bind us old
And see through eyes not yet so full of pain.

When all that was so cherished filled our wain,
A summers breeze not soothing now, but cold;
To feel once more the childlike touch of rain.

A well to dip their cups so much to gain,
To pierce beyond the arrogance and bold
And see through eyes not yet so full of pain.

The collected years echo back in vain,
Deaf ears not listen to the lessons told,
To feel once more the childlike touch of rain.

Within ourselves the secret to us plain,
To sit in peace and comfort with the fold,
And see through eyes not yet so full of pain.

Our meadowed past pressed flat where we have lain,
With memories so dear as life we hold.
To feel once more the childlike touch of rain
And see through eyes not yet so full of pain.

Rodney Legault

North Country

The geese have started flying south
across a gloomy grey sky.
We look up at them with envy
and think of winter as they pass by.

Sometimes winter seems dark and so long
when one sees only ice and snow,
but the hope for spring can be so strong,
and we dream of flowers that bloom and grow.

Many people are just like the birds,
they go south to a warmer land
where they lie on a beach and enjoy the sun,
where the view of the ocean is grand.

But every winter does go by
and another spring comes forth,
when across a bright blue sky
the geese come flying north.

Anna M. Ward

Remember

Condescending truth,
Transcending time to find you,
The heavens have shut the door,
That I might not enter therein.
All the lore of waves pounding a fallen man,
Driven by a fallen land,
Lacking purpose and reason
To discern fact from fiction,
Now all is still within.
On the sands, we desperately trudge on
To be forgotten
Or washed away in the wake.
A long-forgotten memory that plays in my soul
Day and night, night and day,
I want to be remembered
Or forgotten:
I lose either way.

Donald Armoogam

A One-Way Ticket

A one-way ticket can take you to fortune and fame,
Can take you to pleasure, or take you to pain.

A one-way ticket can start out slow,
But at the end of the line, you're out of control.

A one-way ticket is a lonely ride,
With nowhere to run and nowhere to hide.

A one-way ticket's a dead end trip;
Along its tracks lie ruins that drip . . .

Ruins that drip with the blood and the waste
Of a life led by greed, lust, and haste.

A one-way ticket doesn't have to be fatal,
If we're willing to change before the final battle . . .

A battle that's waged for our lives and our souls,
With Good versus Evil, each wanting control.

A one-way ticket's the ride of your life,
But you can change tracks and stop the fall of the knife.

Get help if you need it and do not despair,
Because a one way ticket can be exchanged for return fare.

George P. Giles

Hidden Meanings

I scream, and no one hears.
I growl, and no one fears.
I cry myself to sleep at night,
Yet everyone thinks that I'm all right.

I think it's because I hold it all inside.
My feelings are something I try to hide.
Sometimes I feel like no one understands me.
I often wonder how that can be.

I smile and say that I'm okay,
So the people just nod and move on their way.
The days blow by like the ones before,
And they will be followed by many more.

To express my feelings, I'll write poetry.
Each has a hidden meaning that no one can see.
I guess I express myself more than I know.
That's probably why I blossom, bloom and grow.

Sometimes my feelings get out of control.
They leap through my chest and break through my soul.
When I'm done crying, the frustrations are gone.
I'll pull myself together, and then I'll move on.

Heidi Allison

Tears

Tears, what a strange part of emotion.
Tears shed in a day can almost fill an ocean.
Tears will appear when I am happy and glad;
Tears will appear when I am angry or sad.
Tears will appear at the most inopportune times.
For each tear shed, I wish I had a dime.
Tears are not discreet as to time and place,
And they always do such wonders for my face.
The tears, face, and nose always win the fight;
When emotions are out of control, it's a pitiful sight.
Tears should not be allowed to act as an "emotions thief."
After all, tears can be controlled with a handkerchief.

Mary Freeman

My Soul

Wish me a wish,
and I'll wish you more.
Give me a kiss,
and I'll give you more.
Tell me truth,
and I'll show you more.
Whisper me a dream,
and I'll tell you more.
Send me an angel,
and I'll find you more.
Buy me nothing,
and I'll still love you more.
Catch me when I fall,
and I'll never let you go.
Cry for me,
and I'll cry more.

Evelyn Theoharis

Nothingness

I asked for love
And I knew not
What I asked.

I searched for God.
I knew not Whom
I sought.

I longed to pray,
Yet all I could
Do was be!

And in that vast
Nothingness,
I learned
That God
Was loving me.

Sister Patricia Kelly

Yearning

Be still, my heart, before you bust.
Is this true love or just pure lust?

I met a man the other night,
He sent shivers down my spine.
Oh, what I'd give to hold him tight
And have the right to call him mine.

His hair is blond and curly,
And a cleft deep in his chin.
I'd give up my wealth forever,
If I could be with him.

His voice was gentle when he spoke,
Not a tremor nor a slur;
It made me want to cuddle
On a bare rug made of fur.

A fire in the fireplace,
Champagne sparkling in a glass,
If I could hitch my star to his,
That's all I'd ever ask.

Penny Buchanan

Untitled

And I left you
all alone
days of love
those days are gone

And you hate me
your eyes show
full of darkness
now I know

And I'll love you
remembering May
forever, and until
our dying day

Marijana Govorcin

Aspire to Succeed

From our own resistance
limitations come;
while obstacles hinder,
dreams are left behind.

There is little room
when discouragement hits.
For, to fight against yourself,
a lonely battle occurs.

With negative anguish,
truth is ignored,
goals are abandoned,
life stands still.

To have been defeated
before the attempt
yields a quitter
with certainty lost.

Try to prevail,
regain all strength
that's been too long hidden
and allow the challenge to be—
experienced.

Donna F. Grimsley

R.I.P.

Today they laid Mom to rest.
They laid her body into the ground.
A few of us from our family
Were there, all gathered around.

For those of us who could not go,
Our prayers are with you, Mom.
You'll never be forgotten,
Not by anyone.

Now we know you've been laid to rest.
We will rest then too,
Knowing that you're in God's hand,
For we know He loves you.

Terrance Keith Nichol

Falling Rainy Stars

Quietly, softly—like in dream—
on that rainy day
the tiny golden leaves,
autumnal but still dreaming about the spring,
were falling down with rain. . . .
I listened to the rhythm of Heaven,
music of flying stars on the roof of my car.
I watched the gold from the sky in various sparks—
How they are flying down to choose their own place
on wet and colorful natural space. . . .

Oh, yes!
Even the forest feels sad and crying after summer's gone;
it pours the rainy tears for summers of many years.
My feelings and dreams were also within
in all their beauty and richness.
The sky and forest were in tears,
like me with many unfulfilled dreams,
with many from Heaven falling stars. . . .

Marinko Grk Croata

The End

Down the path of innocence we travel,
the children of dew and sunfire.
Baptized in spring rains,
we explore the enchanted castles of life.
Wallowing in gardens of peace and contented flesh,
we refuse to stop and ponder the move of our future,
never watching the sunset of our youth,
of our dreams, of our happiness, or of our faith.
Slipping beneath the icy waters of life,
to the courts of the damned and the rule of silence,
down the deserted highways of the dead,
soon, without realization,
we shall tread in their footsteps,
walk the shattered walls of time for oblivion
in the blackness of death, the soft bee sting of sadness.
We will not miss our former lives,
nor the company of others,
we shall only miss ourselves.

Emma Bowers

Reflections on Finding a Soul Sister

A soul wanders lost,
Pondering its worth and existence.
It peers into doorways and windows,
Ever searching for something like it,
And sometimes there's a glimmer of hope.
The soul finds one not unlike itself;
Perhaps more beautiful than she,
Perhaps more pure,
Perhaps even more tortured,
But that glimmer fades with time.
Until someday
When the soul happens upon another, so perfect
And so like her
She could never see herself without the other.
That glimmer of hope brightens each day that their
Friendship grows,
Strong and pure,
Beautiful and tortured.

Nicole Pastuch

Our Revolution

WHERE IS OUR SELF-ESTEEM?
Your revolution will give it to you.

Internalize that you are a beautiful person . . .
that we are all equally beautiful.
It's hard work . . . we are here to learn.

Integrity, compassion, the "we generation," the age of peace . . .
our evolution.
Tolerance is not enough.
To love strangers, sacrifice is not required . . .
it is a feeling; a new happiness is the result . . .
when we realize we're all in this together.

Awareness of feelings and why we do what we do . . .
is the revolution. Reflect!

End of us: them. Now . . . We! (I)

Hitler rose because he made us feel good about ourselves.
We needed hate to unite us . . . before the revolution.

The end of acting . . . a waste of energy.

Prozac, war, divorce, crisis morale, Woodstock,
I've been to the land of no colour . . . everything is connected.

We will understand ourselves, we will save the world:
We will save our worlds.

START YOUR REVOLUTION.
Robin Campbell

Wild Weather

Nymphs of lightning begin their wild dancing throughout the skies.
Thor followed into the black and grey clouds, grumbling
loud and mumbling with sighs.
Crystal raindrops fall and sink into the Earth's walls.
Swiftly the wild winds begin and wipe out all.
The smiling sun comes out to wrap the planet in a golden shawl,
Colors of all different hues that soon faded away,
Leaving all in a happy and glorious day.
L. Evans

Peace

Mist entwined in treetops obscures the world
to the water's edge, reluctantly leaving
torn shreds like shades clinging to tree and sand.
As it vanishes in the warmth of the rising sun,
my lake is revealed: blue-black stillness,
remote and unmoved, remembering in its
worn rock shores, eons Precambrian before man.

Now on the rim of distant hills, the sun's bright fury
lights leaves, trees, until a hill brooding,
buried in darkness, is roused in sudden glory.
Small birds begin their morning song, tentatively
testing the new day, while close by one
improvises for me, as the sun, spectacular
spendthrift, pours over the sand at my feet.

Patterns widen on the still-quiet surface of the lake
where a mother duck, all care and petulant
concern, gruffly scurries her brood.
And over the trees, a proud flash of black and white
flies to join his mate, leaving his long loon-call vibrating in my skull,
answering echoes rising from distant hills.
Ellen I. Fry

Songs of the Soul

The music speaks from the heart
and gazes out on the window of my world.
All the colours and sounds are heightened to their full crescendo,
awash with memories, un-faded by the passage of time.
Experience the rise and fall of the notes as they transcend your essence
to the horizons of the worlds.
The full scope of emotions are orchestrated in their turn,
dictated by the melody arranged by the minstrel of the universe.
The body is wrapped in a sonorous caress
likened to the touch of a longtime lover.
The symphony of reverberations serenade the spirit with a
resonance in tune with the ever turning Circle of Life.
The anthem of the spirit intensifies the harmony
and manifests the measure of my soul.
The lyrics chant the brilliant spectrum of sensations
encompassed in the life experiences—bittersweet and heartfelt.
The essence of the composition
is reflected in the gathering of power of the mirror within.

My soul will sing its songs,
The notes spinning through time on the wheel of existence.
Come, sing with me.
    Cathy Robinson

Watching the Birds

Lurking upon the window ledges
hand gathering bread crumbs to feed these migrant creatures
so willing to find a sanctuary
you're losing their heads
in the electric wires overhead.
Or being knocked from those high perches when as they enter their habitat
that's being intruded by those idiots
with no comprehension of a bird's lot.
Leaving these perches they twitter and sing
of their own meanderings
How free and unfettered they appear to be
I wish I could share in such carefree revelry
and somehow be just as free as they appear to me.
    S. Olympia Heber Adams

My Brother Brian

Oh! How I despised my brother
for all the torment that his own inactions had put me through.
I did not care for a long time who my brother was until . . .

What I knew of my brother then
was that he was useless, he was not a fighter nor an athlete.
He was brown, curly-haired, taller, uncoordinated; I don't want him
on my team because I hate him, brother.

I remember I was being pushed around by one kid at school, and my brother found out and
pushed him down repeatedly in my defense.
I remember I was on the monkey bars and I hung trapped, choking on one of the straps from
my book bag with no one else being able to help me until my brother came.
I remember I was being chased with only my brother to protect me.
I remember the piggybacks and the shoelace tying he would do for me.

What I remember most now is that he loved me,
that brown, curly-haired, taller, uncoordinated,
I don't want him on my team because I hate him brother.
I say this as tears stroll down my face,
"I hate you, I really love you."
    Stephen Halden

Equality Not Dominancy

Never give up; time is on my side.
Be wise, be strong,
Send love and energy his way,
And it won't be long,
And long can be today.
It can also be many moons away.

Equality, not dominancy, is what I strive for,
So I'll pull back the curtain and open my door.

My dream will be reality.
He'll flow as one with me.
We'll know everything is right
And we'll hold on to each other tight.

We'll always be free
And committed to each other for an eternity,
And when we are not physically sharing the same space,
We'll still be with each other in whatever place.

My love will be only for you,
As I don't know who else I want to give it to.
No one else will have the privilege
Of sharing my heart and soul from deep within.
Equality, not dominancy, is where it will all begin.

Jaye Low

Shillelagh

I had an old shillelagh that came from Ireland
I had it hanging on the wall and it sure looked so grand

Last night when I came down the stairs to have a wee nightcap
I spied a little leprechaun taking a wee nap

And I noticed that my little stick was lying on his lap
Then suddenly he woke up when heard the running tap
So I asked him if he would join me in a little, wee nightcap

He got up from my rocking chair
He danced and jumped with glee
But still he held my little stick
And tapped it on his knee

He said he travelled far and wide
And "I have finally come to you
For, this is my old father's stick
I tell the truth to you"

He said his father's getting old and now he can't go out
Without this little walking stick, he cannot get about
He said if he could have it that he'd bring good luck to me
That I would ever want for naught that he would care for me
I told him he could have it, if he'd promise that he'd see
That one day he would help me to cross the Irish sea

Dennis Joseph Kelly

Reflections of Love

As I sit thinking today of a love perfect
That was figured, signed to the right,
Then with the knot tied would gently reflect
To hold and carry through thick and blight
Then came a call, as if directed
From the great one, so right
Thus with the blink of an eye, or so affected
My love was vanished to a world ever bright

Harold Hewson

Beauty of the Ocean

The sound of the waves carries
My cries across the shore;
The sand beneath my feet
Cools my aching soul.
The sun in my face warms
My cold heart;
The breeze through my hair
Mellows my drastic mind.
To wash away into the sunset,
Is an oasis.

Cindy Tansky

The Canoe

In a sheltered bay,
In a rocky inlet,
There lay
A small canoe.

A sea gull calling,
The moan of the wind,
The rising and falling
Of the canoe.

Lonely and wild,
The shoreline was harsh.
The canoe looked mild,
Yet it belonged.

Her master was late,
Yet patiently
She would wait
Till he came.

Sheltered in the bay,
Floating among the rocks,
She quietly lay—
The small canoe.

Valerie Friesen

Crane Shoot

Wake up, Russel, let's go hunt cranes.
The sky is clear, no sign of rain.
Coffee's on, so grab your gun.
Let's head for the hills and have some fun.

You hide there, behind that tree.
I'll hide in the bush down on my knees
And wait for the cranes to fly overhead.
With any luck, we'll shoot them dead.

Here they come, all neck and wings:
Gangling, awkward, ugly things.
They're fun to shoot and tasty too,
Slow cooked in jerky, or in stew.

Now the season is at the end.
You're heading home.
Good-bye, old friend,
Until next fall when the cranes will fly.
We'll blast some more holes in the sky.

David Leapard

There's No Doubt

I've never seen green eyes
filled with so much love;
I never thought I'd find
what I found in your touch.
Heaven sent you
to make my life complete.
Every moment that we share
will live forever in my mind;
every memory that we make
is sure to out-last time.
I know when I hold you close
I'm holding love that's true—
there's no doubt about it.
He moves Heaven and Earth;
it started something that's still going strong.
All the time I've been waiting . . .
I don't have to wait anymore.
I don't have to look very far now
for someone who understands;
he sees through to the heart of me.

Valerie Lynn Marie Zimmel

To My Son in Heaven

My son, why did you have to die?
My heart is aching and I cry.
Why did you leave your daughter small
you loved so much protecting all?
It was your birthday 34,
you could have had so much more.
I came to visit you that night,
to see you, and we hugged so tight.
Our last hug in our life, my son,
I said "Good-bye" and then went home.
Then came the call to work from you:
you don't feel good, you're worried too.
We found you lying on your bed,
with clothes on and so cold and death.
My son, you're gone; I loved you, dear.
Your child is sad and needs you here.
And then, I saw you one last time,
it looked to me you only sleep.
All pain was gone out of your face.
I didn't cry, to not disturb this
beautiful peace.

Helga Eschrich

Emptiness

I searched deep within my soul
to find the cause of this empty hole.
Searching through my broken mind,
what I've lost I cannot find.
My pain is so intense, so deep,
these tortured memories are all I keep.
Tears have fallen for the past.
I must go, I must leave at last.

Holly Prophet

My Lost Love

It's heartrending to know
I've lost my second beau.
I never meant to do what I did!

My crying all the whole night long
Didn't help me right the wrong,
And here it's morning and I'm feeling spent.

He was everything I'd wished for all these years.
To think of him just brings on all the wasted tears.

I can see him when we first met
And feel the passion that we both felt.
So, I'm wondering if I'll ever love again.

Now the time has slowly passed,
And I know someone will ask,
Wherever did your old flame go?

Then I'll turn my head and sigh
And explain the reason why.
Then my heart will suffer once more.

Had I not been foolish when
We were young and only friends,
My love now would only soar.

Jean S. Brown

First Love

Your first love is like you're in a dream state.
It seems so unreal and far away
That you'll hope it will never fade or die away.
It only occurs once in your lifetime
But it will be treasured forever.
Although it may come and go
Like a cool summer breeze,
The memories will never become vague,
And that is why your first love is such a special
Occasion that you should never leave in vain . . .
Because it will leave your head hanging down in shame.
Since love is like a fun, new game . . .
So many things to learn and play,
So many wonderful things to share
With that special someone who cares.

Christina Thompson

Island Kingdom

There is an Island Kingdom of Ix
With the neighbouring vales and fjords
Each considered the Center of Earth.
Each a wealthy one or some two thousand souls,
With great Capitals, Institutions and Kings
—Beware, be wise and conform.

In youth we are taught to be not OK
—Though others less so
Keeping distance, introvert proud
Extrovert modest—and quite self effacing

As missionaries preaching our way of life,
We flag tolerance, science, compassion
As emigrants, advisors to rest of the world
Lone Valemen yearn lifelong for Center of Earth
Where the immigrants are lifelong rejected.

Henning Jensen

The Sky at Night

Oh, the wonder of the sky at night
The stars they shine so very bright
There are planets, meteors, and comets, too
And twinkling stars with a tinge of blue

The planets revolve around the stars
Their names are Saturn, Jupiter, and Mars
There's Pluto, Neptune, and Uranus, too
The brightest is Venus, that really is true

Seven chief stars make up the "Plough"
Why only seven, I know not how
The Milky Way forms a nebulous band
With a myriad of stars, I understand

The moon in the sky is very bright
It illuminates the sky at night
It has craters, "mountains" and "valleys," too
I'd like to go there—wouldn't you?

Neil Armstrong was first to walk on the moon
The astronaut arrived the month after June
To astronomers, the stars are a wonderful sight
Oh, how they love the sky at night

    Janet McBride

My Path

My path is full of pebbles and stones of misfortune,
and I have no time to dream about fortune;
each step of mine should be as fast as it can
so that I can reach the highest that I can.

Lightning may strike east and west all its bright
or it can strike before my feet with all its might.
I must keep going no matter day or night,
for I know I will soon reach the height.
Oh, God, guide me in this darkest night
'cause you are the light that can guide me right.

    Jaywant Patil

Been It Is

I see fire as I stare at those cold, misty eyes
A frown hiding every fancy smile
The warmth of her laughter brings a bitter chill
Those sweet gentle caresses are gone forever

What has become of the once majestic flower?
Glittering rust consumes its royal petals
Venomous bees corrupting its precious nectar
The fragile bloom, once proud, slowly withers

Immortal lies of sweet-perfumed tongues
Blind the innocence of this woman
The bait's eaten, the sinker and the hook are swallowed
Too late to realize she had been poisoned

Pale, shallow laughters fills the stillness
Echoing into the dark abyss
Should have laughed with her, but I'm afraid
That the truth in the lie will be revealed

Arrogant eyes—why not stare at the ground?
Hear and see with your heart her whispering moans
The fire in her eyes now dying down
She is too weak to stand alone on her own

    Alfred R. Cadavos Jr.

My Love

I hope you know how much I care
My heart and soul I now can share
I'll hold you in my arms at night
Our love for each I know is right
Every moment that I'm away
You'll be safe, I hope and pray
For, when you're safe within my arms
You know I shall keep you from harm
Our lives began to intertwine
Once you pledged to be mine
I love you more than you may know
My love for you I now can show

    C. Edward Cochran

Old Tree

Spreading its branches in beauty
To those who would rest 'neath its shade,
It has sheltered many a traveller
And the carefree children that played.

A tree house perches high in its branches,
Where secrets were shared every day,
And thoughts flood over my memory
That time cannot take away.

To one of the more trusty branches,
Was tied a strong, sturdy swing
That took us high in the heavens
As if borne on a magical wing.

The children no longer play here,
But the tree has not lost its power;
For, a couple, old and weary,
Sit 'neath its shade by the hour.

Old tree, you shall not see the axe man.
We will guard you from any such fate;
For, a thing of such beauty and stature,
Mere man could never create.

    June E. Willis

In Salome's Garden

Insulated to protect my feet
from getting wet,
and these are strange woods
of clever craft and intent.
There are leaks
when something sneaks
or crawls in,
and slithers smoothly
under your skin.
In Salome's garden,
from the first taste
of medicine—
bitter on my tongue,
poisoned from her dancing.
Under the sky,
left on the plate
to bleed to death,
in Salome's garden
of clever craft and intent.

    Anastasia Papageorgiou

The Poem

I sit writing
On a clean sheet of paper
A poem of true love—
Even though my love was gone—
The words flowing
Like a rhythmic dance,
Foreboding,
Yet inviting.
I press harder,
Getting more into the mood of the poem,
An art,
A story from deep within.
Then it all falls apart.
I scream in horror!
My lead breaks,
As does my heart once again.
I cry.
My tears blot out the words,
Blurring them,
Erasing them.
I'm left again with a clean sheet of paper.

Michael Bitaxi

My Life

Into this world, I came with a scream
A slap on the butt started this dream
I went from 0 to 16 in a blast
Today, tomorrow is now my past
Oh, the joyous time of being a teen
Sticky girls and hot summer dreams
Not a care or concern in my mind
Everything for me was going fine
It seemed in a blink and a second of time
I was all of twenty-nine
Now quite ready for life, this child
Took a wife and all is running wild
Now I look back on tomorrow
My dreams and plans are yesterday's sorrow
Now it is time for all of you to see
That this life or dream is at its end for me
For I am now just ninety-three

Len Sawatzky

Untitled

Little kids play marbles
in the rain,
they smile
beyond the pain
they carry inside.

Andrea Druhar

Stranger

I see you,
the total stranger
in front of me.
But you don't seem so unknown:
I've seen you before
in my dreams.

Emma Hansson

ONE PERFECT ARCH

At the filmy dawn infused with blazed light
Or gentle evenings of moonlit nights,
By my window there curved a graceful arch,
Frilly tendrils dangled from exotic vines,
Enshrouded with scented flowers of sorts.

A wondrous rainbow, this arch reminds me
Of a fragment of nature in hues and shades
Resplendent—it seems as it bends over Earth
A mighty covenant between God and men.

Beneath the bridges along the bustling roads.
Where silvery beams nightly shimmer
On the wanton ripples upon the greenish sea,
A concrete arch sustains the load of cruising mortals
Uniting man and man, all races and creeds.

And as I journey through the paths of life,
Above and below these arches prevail.
One heavenly day behind me curved a living arch,
Warm, touching, has skin and pores.
It pats my back, lifts my soul,
This arm of a friend, my one perfect arch.

Ma. Bonita Valdez-Cruzada

The Knells

Euphonious, and lightly falleth,
a melody to awaken the angels,
my troubled sleep hath she stolen,
as sadly did sing the knells.
Joyous and childishly splendid,
whispereth her nightly hymns
that shatter time's lifeless frown
with childhood's laughter and dreams.
When sharpest scythe shall harvest the crops,
and clouds still bear the bitter seeds
from which shall bud the fruits, most sweet?
Beauteous and solemnly walketh,
into garlands she weaveth her tears.
In her last procession she marcheth
under a rain of lonesome leaves;
as painful as life that doth wither,
she shall welcome the anguish of birth.

Yisrael S. Levin

Despair

The women before showed the way,
Their emotions in check, no tears to betray,
Wounded souls robbed of dreams,
Oceans of tears slowed to streams.
Stoic shoulders bear the same cross,
Empty of hope, and all share some loss.
The look in a starving orphan girl's eyes,
The same in a runaway street teen's disguise,
In a young mother's face deserted for drink,
Babes in arms left alone to think,
In the mirror's image of a middle-aged wife
Forgotten for a husband's mid-life strife,
At last in a dying grandmother's face,
Cancer approaching, patiently waiting with grace.
Life's quest called them to struggle and endure,
Sisterhood shared privately, knowing pain has no cure.
The exact same look by all to share,
Locked in the eyes with a lonely, empty stare.

Michele Keenan

Growing Old

Who are these men and women, existing in this home,
Staring up and down the halls, not sure where to roam?
Some walk, some shuffle slowly and carefully along,
Others are in wheelchairs humming long-forgotten songs.

Their old and tired faces, sometimes happy, sometimes sad,
Show no remembrance of loved ones who call them Mom or Dad.
Are they still there somewhere, deep inside their hearts?
Where is that part of them that somehow just departs?

There is a lady rocking, a child that's long since gone;
The doll that she is holding takes the place of flesh and bone.
Another has a shopping bag she carries all the time;
Perhaps she thinks she's going out; who knows what's in her mind?

There is no place they are going, but many they have been.
Forgotten in their memory are the places they have seen.
Now they are lost in hallways and don't know where they eat.
They sit the same place every meal but still can't find their seat.

It's sad to watch these people, the youth of days gone by,
Now so frail and feeble and waiting just to die.
They, like us, were young once, filled with life and zest,
Living in the moment and trying to do their best.

> *Margaret Barrington*

Eternal Desiring

In the innermost chamber of your being, there lies a magical place
Where you find yourself with the Beloved, face to face.

Here, a love has existed before you knew,
Awaiting your discovery as you grew.

You sleep while your heart is wide awake;
Only the flame of union will heal its ache.

Lovers are not destined to meet somewhere.
They lie in each other, completely unaware.

To reach the Beloved, follow the road from your soul;
You're sure to arrive with a visible goal.

You are bound to tire of everything,
Except eternal desiring . . . the hearts all sing.

> *Mona Moosavian*

Golden-Haired Angel

I pick up the paper and what do I see?
A Golden-Haired Angel staring back at me.
My eyes tear up just to see her image,
lovely in feature and in her deeds.
This lovely creature has touched the world.
From those with debilitating illnesses to the removal of land mines,
she strived to make a difference.
A tragic accident has torn her from us,
her children to be denied their greatest archangel.
Britain's brightest rose has flourished and been crushed by our endless
thirst for knowledge of this fair and rare beauty.
Many a life was touched by this most treasured shining star.
A most gracious and rare beauty has glistened in the sun,
brightening the days with her smile and her sweetly serene charm.
The world's blackest hour eclipsed in her death,
deeply mourned is our Golden-Haired Angel.

> *Dawn Goodwin Holroyd*

Dearest Diana

A sudden cloud of sadness blocked out the sunny skies
because of human madness—Princess Diana dies!

The world and countless millions are struck by unbelief,
by shock and woeful sorrow and paralyzing grief!

We lost a gracious princess, a warm and caring friend
to those of dreadful burdens—we mourn her brutal end—

The world is crushed with anguish—a world Di knew so well,
a ground swell of emotions—truer than words can tell!

We're in the grip of grieving for someone we applaud,
affectionate in service to mankind and to God!

Diana, in your lifetime you have accomplished much
by simply deeply caring and by your gentle touch.

Your magic made us love you, your bright and flickering flame,
your fascinating candle of beauty and of fame!

Our tears of loss and mourning fall on Canadian soil,
bereft of your compassion, encouragement, and toil.

We're left to face the challenge—Lord, strengthen us, we pray!
Diana, thanks for leading and for showing us the way!

Schelte Brandsma

Dying Customs

I sit here looking back upon the time of my grandfather,
    who has told me of the time before the white man came.
He told me of the life of the Indians, of the times long ago,
    his grandfather told him of, when we were truly free.
When we had land to thrive upon,
    now we live on Reserves.
When we had game to thrive upon,
    now we have scarcely few.
When we had freedom to thrive upon,
    now we have none.
When we used to live in long houses,
    now we live in shacks and such.
When our dancers were heard for miles,
    now they stand still due to the dying of the drum.
When our songs were praised upon,
    now are drowned out by some rock-n-roll tape.
When our children learned from the elders,
    now learn from computers and such.
I have lived in this world a long time
    without an Indian life.
We, the Indians, are dying;
    thus, I am no more.

Wilfred Oliver Jamieson III

Parents

There's a time in life
That we all look back,
Remembering our childhood,
The good and the bad.
Did they bring us up right?
Did they do their best?
Was it God that guided them for the rest?
You made them angry,
You made them cry,
You made them disappointed,
And sometimes you even lied.
But the tears that you both shared
And the hugs and kisses that were there
Always made it hard to tell them that you care.

Love and parents are like waters on a shore,
Further the tide, the heart that breaks,
Closer the wave, the heart that shakes.
Life is funny in its ways; we want to tell them we love them so,
Return the hugs and kisses, but instead our lives continue on.
When the day comes to tell them, it's all to late, for they have gone.

Charlotte Nardelli

A DREAM

When I was twelve, my dream was bold.
I travelled far to find my goal,
To catch the dream the way I hold.
Chances are there to clear my road,
Struggling first as I was told.
At last . . . I've reached the other
          side of the world.

I waited that long to reach this place,
Bestowed upon the Earth, the hardships arose,
Bared, the cold and lonely roamed.
Breathlessly sigh the days gone by,
Pouring tears across my eyes,
Confusing days beyond good-bye.

The voice floating in the air with a rhyme,
The singing heart was formerly divine.
The trees so greenly flowing beneath the sky,
Now, it turns into a silhouette.
The burden of the soul stuck in the depths,
Release me, Oh Lord, so I can be safe.

Temistocles-Amiceta Magtibay deMesa

Green Survival

Such wonders of Earth ancient
Old growth with natural wilderness
Where Pacific breakers pound and roar
Along the wet, west coast, old-growth forest
Where giant cedar silent stand in wild valleys.
'Tis here that you may seek and find
The true landmarks of this land.
In the ancient, wild valleys of this land,
Clendenning Valley, Upper Elaho Valley, Upper Lillooet
Valley, and Mehatl Valley, rivers, lakes, and streams,
The true heritage old-growth forest,
The true heritage old-growth habitat,
The true heritage of this land
Prove beyond shadow of a doubt
That this is their land as we are all
Only immigrants to the new province-land.
Let it stay ancient, old-growth forest only.
History tells you as a rare, open-window woodland
Is ancient forest land and only as a heritage park,
Otherwise open-window woodlands in the future.

Victor Gallagher

The Horizon

The sky supreme hailed the euphoric Earth,
For, from the seclusion, unity would take birth,
And into verses of sweet union,
Drown the melancholy strain of diversity,
And would sound distant the sermon of adversity.

The sky, the majestic groom,
The Earth, the bride in elegant bloom,

Leading on the symphony, the mighty zephyr,
The resplendent Earth, now blooming in green attire,
The glowing radiance of a sapphire-studded heaven
And a garland across the sky, with shades of seven.

The rites performed, two became one,
And together they carved the horizon.

Kapildev Jagtiani

Will You Be There?

Will you be there when I'm down
     to pick me up from off the ground?

To laugh with me when times are great
     and hold me close when I'm afraid?

To wipe my tears and sympathize
     when you see pain deep in my eyes?

I need to know how much you care,
     so I ask you . . . will you be there?

Teresa Oliver

Another Tale

The passing dove with song so fair,
Whose white wings seem to fill the air.
The bold, the able, time that it seems,
Near silent sky and waiting dreams.

Just past Tall Timber Road,
Eld gray castle from clouds have told.
One wolf snarls, another does play,
Lies Queen Field with much to say.

All of it, its natural charm,
Oh, fragrance from each flower's arms,
Where fields of bloom are really gold,
And clover sleep with heart a'fold.

Through a field,
To and fro.
Friends all
Where the free winds blow.

Every bridge is built so high—
Enough to float a lullaby.
The stream sings together with me;
All of this for you to see.

Lynda Barkhouse

No Sorrow for Autumn

As summer ends, the fall begins:
A flower's bittersweet fate,
From flourishing beauty unparalleled
To victim of Autumn's abate.

Each blossom lowers its head
To undress, in resignation bows over,
As Autumn's cool air removes
The garments of a springtime clothier.

Their bare heads are laid to rest
In a cold, white, winter bed,
Leaving all to crave their colours:
Golden yellow, pink, and red.

Then stretching after winter's sleep,
When springtime rolls around,
They stand proud, arrayed again
In the warm and watered ground.

Life's beauties are like flowers;
Take comfort if they go away,
Although out of view for a season,
Sure to return a warmer day.

Patsy Payne

Hilton's Philosophy

Hale and hearty at seventy-sight
Inching through life by His fate . . .
Living and loving the whole day long
Thoughts of beauty—a perpetual song
Others may think it's finished and through
Nor I! How about another twenty-two?
Here in Guyana, it's hard and rough
Each day bringing me just enough
Not undaunted, I'll see it with you
Rough or tough, the skies are blue
Yet it often makes me wonder
Life's so complicated that I ponder
Each morn dawns, clear skies and birds
Whistling tunefully—suggesting words
Indicative of Him who planned it all
Soulful, satisfying . . . a perfect mall.

Hilton Henry Lewis

For Mother's Day

Life is planted in arid soil,
Nothing will grow unless you toil
To see gentle blossoms near,
It has grown from a mother's tear.

Giuseppe Favaro

Dad Died

When Dad died,
I felt, for the first time,
The uncertainty of the Earth,
The harshness of the wind,
And the bitter sting of falling rain.

Martha Mallon

Read

Read, read, say ye to me
Use your eyes, for you shall see
A guiding light that shines so bright
To help you see on through the night

Read, read, say ye to me
Unlock the door with calmest key
You will find a gold-filled mine
Of riches that empower the mind

Read, read, say ye to me
Tell me what it is you see
All the words' vivacious verve
Your thoughts' enlightenment
   they do serve

Read, read, say ye to me
I accept, so shall it be
To me remind a tie that binds
All the treasures I can find

David Grosfield

Feeling Heaven's Bliss on Earth

Oh, what a beautiful day!
The birds sing so sweetly and gay.
The sparrows too chirp and hop about,
Just right for the month of May!

The tiny ladybird curiously crawling
Through the blade of green grass,
And the trees that rustle with the wind
All make me sigh with great pleasure . . .

And what should I see above my head but
White fluffy clouds all blended
With the light passionate blue of the sky—
Which of course makes me cry.

The wind not only blows through the trees,
But also onto my face and through my hair.
And as I raise my head and
Take a deep breath, I caught sight of the sun's glare.

Oh, what a beautiful day,
Not only to enjoy
But also to live through
And drink and savour the beauty of it all!

Farzana Aboobakar

The Majestic

My frog had died and gone to Heaven,
He liked the numbers six and seven.
My sadness, following his death,
Has left me very short of breath.
"'Tis only for the best," i muttered—
'Twas no use, my world was shattered.
A bustle squabbled in my head,
My eyes were mesmerized, and gazed.
The raunchy being i'd been left to be
Was that of no tranquillity.
And so the Satan, having seen my gloom,
Could easily lure me into doom.
I took one stride—but then i winced
'Cause i saw something on TV:
A man, no higher than an elf,
Taught "how to decorate your inner self."
Oh, then at once i realized,
The Satan had me paralyzed.
But i sat down, and with a grin quote i to my raven:
"As long as he left me channels six and seven."

Michal Weiss

Alba

if at the moment of death
                my corpse hangs—upside down
I will burn my bones at the tips of ilalang grass
so that my mysterious muteness will the better learn
the art of taming death

Oh, eastern dawn of my soul,
teach me the breath of poetry
that you have hidden at the promontory of silence
for I have cast my lot in a struggle
with death and with my self

        but who is has spread wide the seed
        in the hearts of the children of poetry
        "if life has succeeded in separating us
        let then death in its farthest reaches
        make us one"

Poet Hartanto

Sweet Spring

The wild emanates from within a nest,
So gently cradling life.
Its frailty and splendor, so early in sweet spring,
Entwines our very hearts and souls,
Nurturing, and lessons learned revel in the joy.
In spite of all life's miseries,
First learn how to sing.
In spite of all life's mysteries
Still learn how to fly.
Winter arrives. The nest is empty, cold:
Loneliness, sorrow, and tears.
Harsh bitterness soon turns to warmth.
Sweet spring has thus returned.
Elated hearts, reunion comes;
Nest is built anew.
Oh, sweet spring, wondrous sweet spring,
Embrace the gentle wind!

Deborah Maidment

Let Us Be . . . Lest We Be

Let us be frank
And never try a prank,
Lest we be beaten with a plank.
Let us be ever telling the truth
That all will hear and believe,
Lest we be known as liars.
Lest us be careful about rumors
And never take them as gospel truth,
Lest we be breakers of social mores.
Let us be no supporters of bloody wars
Nor our consent to any kind of evil give,
Lest, out of the blue,
We be baffled by Frankenstein's monsters.
Let us be good and kind
And welcome the poor we find,
Lest we be those that never mind.
Let us be filled with fear of God and
Keep His laws and our nation's, too,
Lest we be known as lawbreakers
And be given the punishment by law prescribed.

Frank Reubis

Memories

Memories diffuse, grieve me no more.
Like the wave that leaves remote the shore
and onto a fresh horizon, let my beliefs retire,
for they are wearied, disdained, and set afire.

Memories diffuse, grieve me no more.
Like the cloud that spares the desert a pour,
retread your trail, save me a tear,
fly over and beyond, distant from here.

Memories diffuse, grieve me no more.
Like winter, the tyrant of seasons four,
cold, indifferent, lifeless, you leave me so pale,
defenseless, so bitterly frosted in hail.

Memories diffuse, grieve me no more.
Like death, passive, stinging till the very core,
seek not my soul, yet vanish far into the far-gone . . .
and let loose my spirit from here on!

Kapildev Jagtiani

Harbors on My Soul

A deep, emotional vessel
on a sea of turmoil,
being tossed from port to starboard
with a sullen spray of speech.

An ocean full of phrases
that prey upon my mind,
that linger in the quiet mist
and harbors on my soul.

Janette Mcnamara-Comeau

St. Valentine's Day

Hearts and flowers and candy
Are appearing everywhere.
With fancy cards, with bows and lace,
That day is drawing near.

St. Valentine's, the day of love,
And Cupid with his bow,
And little arrows filled with love
Will soon be letting go.

He shoots them here and everywhere
With hardly any thought,
And you can't hear or feel them
Until they hit your heart.

So on the fourteenth of the month,
Be careful not to tarry,
Or you'll be next to fall in love
On the fourteenth of February.

Adam Lewis

See Things Grow

They say we call the sky a window
of everlasting shades of blue.
They call the eyes the windows to your soul
to see if you are true.

Windows that reflect time and pain,
of drought and no harvest rain,
crops are withering within its grief,
the greenness is gone from every leaf.

Your eyes reflect the un-shed tears
of the hardships you have suffered many years.
Community spirit is at an all-time low;
you wonder if it is time to go.

The grass is gone and the land is bare;
there is no one else left to care.
Money is low and bills are high;
your last cow is ready to die.

There are no answers to this mess;
we are praying for the rain—more than less.
We're not a third world country,
so let's help each other and see things grow.

M. J. Wright

If I Were a Cloud

If I were a cloud,
Soft and feathery,
High up in the day light sky,
I would let you up on me
For a soft trampoline ride,
For your happiness means much to me,
You brighten up my day,
Your smile and laugh are special
Because you are my friend.

Raman Srivastava

the edge of waiting

cutting the bend
in the river
the edge of waiting

rolls on
and long-necked stillness
stands on one leg

at deep night rest curves
around the smouldering breaths
of fire and cedar lovers

sometimes my paddle
doubles where the blade
meets the shaft

a long-necked shadow
wings self-ward
spilling stars in its wake

from this perspective
the speckled trout
dreams the great blue heron

Kim Mallett

Lost Souls

I knew you were out there
I felt you wanting, waiting
Wandering in despair
Reaching out for me, anticipating
How I've yearned beyond compare
This feeling is quite sedating
I've searched everywhere
For one worth relating

Anna Teixeira

A Love Lost

He holds on to something
That he no longer has—
A love lost.
He holds on to the hope
That he may have her back—
A love lost.
She no longer loves him,
Not he way she did once before—
A love lost,
A love no longer found.

Tanya Brencic

The Farewell

Sit down by the side of my chair, my boy.
You have only a moment, I know,
But wait until I give you some parting advice.
It is all that I have to bestow.

God gave you to me in your cradle, my child.
I have taught you the best that I knew,
And if God in his mercy permits me to live,
I'll never stop praying for you.

In your satchel you'll find a book, my child.
It's the book of all books, the best.
It will teach you to live and help you to die
And lead you to the home of the blest.

Christina Brown

Untitled

Somehow, I don't want to know
how well your thoughts cohere.
I've concocted something sticky, too:
a crumbling mound of apple pie.
I can still wish for a cure
as I watch it discolor your teeth.
Until this moment, I've never felt
so alone—lost like that forbidden
crumb skinny-dipping in your carton of milk.
Even it turns sour as I struggle
to regain the consciousness
I lost blaming you.
Actually, the only time I blame you is when
I rediscover sleep—and I am sorry.
I'm sorry that the horrible mask I chose
to obscure me frightened you,
so you see how linearity rejected me
and I ran away and hid my head in
a crumpled paper bag.

Sari Sotamaa

Nullification (Tilintetgjorelse)

Like acid
the words dripped from your tongue
and burned themselves
into me.

Your eyes
stretched their
hands out and
strangled my soul.

I am no more.

Translated by Peter Stewart Richards

Original text: (This is the same poem, but in Norwegian)
Som syre
dryppet ordene fra din tunge
og etset seg
fast i meg.

Dine oeyne
strakte sine
hender ut og
kvalte min sjel.

Jeg er ikke mer.

Elin Gyda Sjoelie

A Saviour Within

All your thoughts linger upon the one you believe in.
You search in your heart and visualize the future that lies beyond,
An infinite life of love and completion.

You build a home with a foundation that is pure,
Fulfilling dreams together, allowing happiness to prevail,
Concluding a chapter in the lonesome life that was held in low regard.

Yet, you must be aware of binding hearts and sweet pleasures,
For it all can be wiped away forever by the humble creature before you,
One that has turned into a rabid beast gone wild,
   devouring all that you held close.

A wounded heart is left hanging and a soul left dying,
Blackened marks shown for morning kisses,
   and hateful words served at random,
A pleading hand is all that will be seen, begging for the love in disguise.

A saviour is there to watch this feeding of betrayal,
One who was there to strengthen, to love,
   and should be seen in high regard.
The friend is you, a saviour within,
   the only one who can pull you through and save your life.

> **Sharlene Ready**

In the Blink of an Eye

I can hear the sadness in his little voice; he hates to say good-bye.
Quietly he asks, "How many more sleeps, Mommy,
Till you come home?"
The wasted years I've missed watching him grow,
The love of a child can't be bought with silver and gold.
As I choke on my tears, I can't find the words to say,
"Soon, my little man, soon. You be a good little boy now. I love you."
He slowly hangs up the phone.
Each time he drifts a little farther away.
Each time my heart breaks a little more.
Farther down the road, great pain will be the price I'll have to pay.
The setting sun fills the sky with bright colors of purple, blue—
A warm yellow glow—another day is now gone, the future unknown.
I hope one day this child of mine
Will not feel unloved or cheated in any way.
The only wish I have, oh, Lord: Please give us more time.

> **Beth Mason**

Reality

I wonder where you are now, the sky begins to snow,
drifting ever aimlessly to the ground below.

The street's a sea of black, wet and very sleek;
you come across a man who's cold and his body's weak.

Your eyes are empty vessels, yet you stop to help the man,
take him for a walk through nature's wonderland.

Ahead you see a mountain, like none other seen before,
and you search for the key to its mystical door.

But the mountain's a sheet of ice, and there are no footholds;
A solid mound of frozen tears, of stories gone untold.

Recognition flickers in your eyes, you now know what to do
as the poor, cold man you gave a hand was always really you.

The feelings once denied, the ones that were replaced,
have now become a mountain that you will have to face.

> **Laurie Carr**

Cowboy

There's a man out on the trail, the sun of a different breed
Who follows the path of ancient ways and lives by an unspoken creed.
Touched by the hand of Satan, that makes his life seem grim,
His pure heart and honesty are why the angels watch over him.

Everyone's always wondered what's in this man's head,
The mind behind what makes him do what'd kill another man dead.
Freedom from the city space is what draws him to the plains,
Where hardly any time is spent worryin' about capital gains.

He's drifter, a loner, an all-around friend.
He's been around and back that mythical, so-called bend.
Always a smile on his face and quick to lend a hand,
Loyal, proud, and committed to ride for his chosen brand.

Seldom ever starting his day after the morning sun,
Never laid his head to rest until all the work was done.
Not one to ever back down in the face of uncertainties,
Just too cocky or confident to ever be brought to his knees.

A small part of him is a show off for the benefit of womankind.
Another part is purely luck, forever savin' his scrawny behind.
A ladies' man by nature, no woman could hope to tame,
A soul worthy of recognition, and Cowboy is his name.

> *Mike L. Long*

A Young Man's Plea for Cancer

Must death be our answer
For my poor mother who lay with cancer?
She has taken the hardships and the rugged road
And everything else that life could hold.
She's never asked for very much, just for a little happiness,
And that's not much.
She has fought the battle,
She has fought it brave.
She has taken all that her life gave.
She did the best that she ever could.
To have faith is something she always would.
And now the time has come to pass.
Life for her no more will last.
And so I say to the world out there,
Don't let death be our answer.
Help us, please, to find the cure for cancer.
So please give.
Research is the only answer.

> *Richard Barkley*

Wisdom

I realize now life must go on.
Having Dreams I used to ponder about
I now feel compelled to do something about
No longer in control of things I used to take for granted
I now thank God my perspectives have changed of what I wanted
I have instilled in my children, they have the power to do whatever they desire
Even with life's unforeseen tragedies for unknown reasons
They ignite the flames of your fire
My life on this Earth will not be in vain
As God gave me strength to live with this pain
To go through life without pain and sorrow
Would rob you today of learning for tomorrow
Appreciate life's moments Day after Day
Never knowing the faith coming you way
Wounds can be healed, Frustrations forgotten
Hearts will be broken
Your dignity and soul
You will always control

> *Lise Peisley*

The Bleeding Heart

The first time I saw you, I knew:
Knew you were special, unique,
And I liked that.

I grew to love you, deep within my heart,
A secret longing to be with you.
But I was scared, unsure about what you would say.

I hid my feelings, telling only a few,
And when you found out, you rejected me,
Saying, "Now get lost."

My heart fell to pieces,
Like a precious crystal goblet, broken,
Shattered, an empty void.

Tears, like rain, poured down my cheeks,
For I still loved you.
Now, I will never love again.

My heart still bleeds from the wound;
It will never heal because I know,
Know it will never be,
Because you rejected me.

Jodine Droux

To a Clandestine Lover

On some black night or sunny summer day,
A knock, a ring, a shout will make me know
You will not come again—that you are gone.
I know about these things—don't ask me how.
I'm really not on speaking terms with God,
But once I let a Gypsy read my palm.

I shall not beat my fist against my breast
Or throw myself in tears upon a bed;
I'll listen, but not quite, to eulogies,
Converse with mourners, swallow sips of tea,
Above your dust place roses with great care,
Then toss my black-veiled hat upon a chair.

Upon a sullen cliff above the bay,
I'll watch the stubborn tide cleave to the sea;
Bereft, undone, I'll turn and walk away,
Crushing Devil's Paintbrush with my feet,
Tear a bough from some decrepit tree
And smash it on my knee.

Sarrah Brown

Remembrance Day

The sun is shining past a cloud,
Beneath the sun, a very large crowd.
The people in the crowd were crying,
Because of all the people dying.
They bowed their heads in a moment of prayer
For all the men and women who died there,
All the people who fought for their country
To make us all feel safe and free.
The people in the crowd ask, "Why?"
To why the people had to die.
Poppies grow around Flanders Field
To symbolize how we all feel.
So, remember the people who died in the war
And what Remembrance Day is for.

Trish Lawson

Wishing and Waiting

The wish to be,
Not the will to do;
The freedom of choice,
But to choose not to;

The sense of sight,
But afraid to see;
To express "I am,"
Then hasten "to be";

The chance to fly,
But then wait too long;
The chance to sing,
Then forget the song;

When the fact is so plain,
That it's hard to believe;
When the trees are so green,
That you can't see their leaves;

When it seems so right,
That it has to be wrong,
Then you're waiting for life,
And you've waited too long.

K. Jill McMurray

The Pain of Love

I gave you love, and
you gave me pain
that flowed through my
eyes like rain.
Your love and care
seemed to vanish into the air.
I was kind, but you
played with my mind, and
when you said good-bye,
I felt so alone
I had to cry.
I tried with all my heart, but
our love fell apart.
Will the pain . . . ever go away?

Ronald Lapointe

Imprisoned

Trust the Emptiness
That Beauty that you thought was lost
shall suddenly appear to you
and Time, an alchemy
destined to babies, deviates
when by some longing's magnet
is mislead
Silence-proof
Resists
the obvious violation
of the accepted way to measure
those kisses you've been hiding
inside your sight's
open prison
The hand over-adroitly approaches
caresses that no one
has had the chance
to grab.

Konstantinos Bouras

In Pace Requiescat

I give in, I must not
The pull of death is too strong
Afraid in life I'll do something wrong
See all the mistakes I've made
Can't wait for the day I'll be in a grave
And the world will be rid of me
While I'll be sleeping peacefully
Always been an annoying bother
Always been a problem to others
There's no other way
Lead me to my grave
It's all for the best
Just let me rest

Joy Devera Guintivano

Fluttering Wings

From the core, beyond,
Fluttering of wings I heard.
The soul is flying,
Flying beyond the mortals.
Beyond, and above Heaven,
The soul is fluttering,
Fast to cross the boundary
Of this translucent life.
Wasted for long, long years,
The agony and the sins
All perished in moments,
And the soul has vanished
Like the sweet kisses
He poured on our cheeks
That tasted saline?
Who'll tell us? He is silent!

P. K. Mohanan

Dice

When the loaded dice thrown
unchecked
By some queer circumstance
Fall to disrupt my life,
A jagged tear appears.
Then, each night is agony,
As my mind seethes
In unchartered seas.
Each day dawns
With a promise of new hope,
But the hours pass by
In mock sympathy.
I sit like a beggar
And wait for them
To take pity
And drop a wish fulfilled
Into my empty bowl.
But then, fate does not discriminate,
Nor judge the good or bad
Accordingly; it simply loads the dice
To throw where it will.

S. Nandini Shinde

Forgotten Past

Long ago when the skies were bright,
Long ago when there was no night,
Long ago when the heavens were near,
Long ago when there was no fear,

Long ago when we all learned to fight,
We all were so bold that we lost all our sight.
The skies widened up and shed us some light
And told us that life would last all the night.

We still didn't learn and we still didn't care,
And in all the fighting we lost someone dear.
We realized then the meaning of life
But we all had the wounds that were cut by the knife.

The knife we learned was the symbol of war.
The spirits that died were the ones that would soar.
The pain that we felt deep down inside
Was the shame and the guilt we were trying to hide.

Tara Thame

My Best Friend

Among the tombstones I wander along,
Listening to the birds as they sing my sad song.
How my heart's full of sadness, full of despair
Of a world I think's cruel, not often very fair.
They sing of the loneliness and emptiness within
Where I once felt happiness. Will I ever feel it again?
They sing of my fight to survive till the end,
When death overcomes me and I'm free once again.
The graveyard becomes quiet. I hear a voice sadly say,
"Child, you didn't ask for help along the way.
I've been by your side as the years have passed.
I love you, my child, why do you not ask?"
Tears stream down my face as I kneel and pray,
"Lord, I've been such a fool! Please show me the way!
To know that I have such a friend like you near,
With your love and guidance, I have nothing to fear."
The air fills with the music of a thousand birds singing.
In the distance, the chimes of Heaven's bells are ringing.
The angels are rejoicing from far and from wide
As I start a new life with my best friend at my side.

Kathy Thomas

Mind vs. Heart

Sometimes the hate inside our minds
Can be too much to bear,
And the love we have inside our hearts
Will show its true colors there.

Sometimes the sorrow in our minds
Tells us to give it up,
But with the joy we have inside our hearts
We shall overcome!

Sometimes the wars within this world
Take innocent little children.
The thoughts inside our minds and hearts
Must be peaceful and forgiving.

Your heart knows the right way to go,
And your mind will let it win,
But if of love, peace, and joy you are lacking,
Your heart will surely give in.

Maria Purves

Our Cottage

On a river bank stands our cottage of white and green,
So thankful from any highway cannot be seen.

Very peaceful, quiet, and so still,
Our visits linger until we have our fill.

While resting from life's toils and stress,
Animals can be seen from the great wilderness.

Ducks, rabbits, foxes, and birds of gray and blue,
Bears, caribou, and squirrels to name a few.

Sometimes crossing the river with such splendor and pride,
All gazing eyes follow a moose to the other side.

In the stillness of night rippling water is heard,
And the morning dawn blends with love-singing birds.

Winter, Spring, Summer, and Fall,
At our cottage we gratefully enjoy them all.

Each season bringing its own special treat,
Such as meat, fish, and berries we can eat.

No matter what season of the year it may be,
We're off to our cottage with that special key.

   Alfreda Snow

Paradise Found

Whenever you have crossed your personal hell
and are ready to make peace with the world and yourself,
and have come to think that only friendship is really worthwhile . . .

among all kinds of relationships,
you'll find me there, waiting for you,
out on the brim of hell, at the edge of happiness . . .

as one who stood there once before
and has known the experience and has survived the pains,
sensing the victory and measuring the price of knowledge,

as one who has finally become a true friend of himself. . . .

   Lena Calomiris

Chorus from "The Wind"

The enraged wind in my picture window
screams wakefulness into listless branches.
Still brittle with the sleep of winter, they slam and grapple in the air;
rattle-clatter nervous fingers seek introspective diversion,
hoping this rage will pass them by;
sun-parched, barren, yellow-gray, desolate eyes squint a reluctant greeting,
mute response to this angry parent wake-up call.

Yet, we stand together, aloof, removed, looking out
contentedly, surveying nature's rage. The sun, warm on our faces—
dull, listless, sleepy—is the only thing to penetrate here.

Having arrived late, I witness guests picking idly through the remains
of the afternoon's conversations, already fully gorged,
seeking some glimmer of wit or succulent phrase
to formulate existence into that tidy, understandable, sedative package,

"Well, that is it then," they would say,
amid the clatter of coffee spoons, "Yes that is it—I'm sure. . . ."

Worms and seeds buried deep
don't see the rage but feel the quivering root;

buried deep we are secure,
we will not wake.

   Brian Shields

Conversation with a Friend

As I head toward my destination after calling it a night,
my ears ring with fragmentary echoes of our recent conversation.

A smile readily appears at remembered jests.
I sharpen my syntax for further trysts
and relish the sharp bite of your stiletto wit.

The cinema of recollection brings images to life,
as if peering through a frosted window pane,
watching the characters of a play, their faces shadowed by firelight.

I see arms raised in expressive gestures.
Voices ominously punctuate the points made and hum in earnest
anticipation to interject an impatient thought.

Time becomes irrelevant and cannot break the trance.
Compelled by tired bodies, obligations, and tomorrow,
cronies frown parentally and force an agreeable descent.

We lay aside our intellect, though the subject is never concluded.
Inspiration, kind moments, and enjoyment form an aura about me.

The history is thoughtfully noted and delightfully captured in memory
To be retrieved at some future hour in private contemplation.
> ### *Kathy Lynn Treybig*

The Truth

Do you think there are more people in Heaven or hell?
I don't think there is anyone who has lived to tell.
There has and always will be good and bad,
and I think one of the worst people I know is my dad.
But it is not all his fault; it is the drugs, I say.
Either way it is his price to pay.
When I was younger I used to say,
Don't worry, my dad will be nice today.
But as the days, weeks, months and even years rolled by,
I began to believe the only thing that mattered to him was being high.
Whether it be true or not,
One single birthday card was the last thing I ever got.
> ### *Rachael Morrison*

A Christmas Reflection

Snow begins to fall from the endless skies
As trees with crystal branches glisten before my eyes.

This winter landscape of timeless beauty,
A true gift from nature, never failing its duty.

Lit Christmas trees in windows everywhere,
The feeling of this wondrous season is in the air.

Though this season may often be very cold,
There is a warmth in my heart that will never grow old.

On Christmas Eve, as I sleep and I dream of what will be,
Visions of gifts of love and of joy dance inside of me.

Rays of a winter sunrise wake me on Christmas morn'.
Feelings of love for my family and friends will never, ever be torn.

As I reflect upon the year that has gone by,
There are things that will make me smile
And some that will make me sigh.

But I am thankful for all that was, now that it is done,
And I look forward to the new age to come:

So cold and yet so warm, so fast and yet so timeless,
So white and yet so green, so busy and yet so serene.
> ### *Shawn C. E. Berry*

She Walks in Silence

She walks in silence like the night,
    Of ghastly things and sickly moon,
    And all that's ugly and a'fright
    Shall pounce upon her very soon:
    Her fearful, lonely, wretched blight
    That is the cannon of her doom.

One roar the more, one scream the less,
    Had half impaled the pretty day
    That reaps the horror of Unrest
    And quickly ushers joy away;
    The mirror of her face distressed
    When keeping 'marish dreams at bay.

And so these winds and o'er the land,
    So harsh, so cold yet aggravate
    The sickly sounds of sinking sands,
    But tell her gloom: The Outcast State—
    A mind whose clock turns awful hands,
    A heart that loves too long, too late.

Philip Raglione

Coping?

You plan for expectations,
Tomorrow's slumber deep,
But what's the point in staying up
When it hurts to sleep?
Working hard in preparation for things to become grand,
Complete faith in your deliverance to the Promised Land,
Imagine the pain, the disbelief
If it proves untrue.
When at last the time runs out,
Then what shall you do?
Will you impose on others
Come the rainy day
Or are you proud enough to chance
The independent way?
Perhaps your planted feet shall stand
In victorious display.
Perhaps the rain will come too fast,
And you'll be swept away.
It all depends on your belief of what will come to be.
Can you control your fate, or is it destiny?

Alexander van der Wijst

Coming Home

In the night, emotions need not be revealed
Darkness in its blessed sweetness
Is a golden haven to battered souls
Who are too weak to fight a losing battle

Mending a war-torn soul
Is to stitch a seam through a blanket of air
I have not the strength to raise myself
From the fire that turned my heart to ashes

Time is the sword
Sharpened by the wheel of despair
Future is the hand that runs me through
That sends me to the darkness
In its blessed sweetness
I have finally come home

Siobhan Hicks

Expanding Consciousness

The deep reality comes home
To my restless mind's surprise.
There are Spiritual Beings helping us
As from cosmic sleep we rise.

The more we dare to open up
To the powerful energy flow
Of the Spiritual love that heals us,
The clearer our hearts will grow.

No longer can doubts and fears
Hold us in confusion.
When inner Spiritual light comes on,
We see they were illusions.

Every single thought we have,
Everything we may feel,
Gives energy to the elusive dark
Or to the Radiant Light that's Real.

How great the opportunity
In this time of rapid change
To create a vital, waking world
And extend our conscious range.

Sara C. Marriott

Friends

Many people have entered my life
To quickly disappear,
So I never dreamed that when we met,
Your friendship I'd hold dear.

Now it doesn't seem to matter
How far we are apart,
For no matter where you are,
You'll be always in my heart.

Donna Lainchbury

When He Looks at Me

My breath quickens
As my man I see
I feel a warm glow all over
When he looks at me

His playing eyes
Sparkle with glee
At the blush on my face
When he looks at me

I feel so special
I feel so free
As I bask in his love
When he looks at me

We gaze at the stars
While I'm in his arms
I feel happy as can be
When he looks at me

We roam around
Then he takes me home
I give him a kiss
When he looks at me

Crystal Shesterniak

Glacier

Have you ever seen the mighty machine
Of nature's best coming to rest
Between mountains tall,
Cutting a swath, devouring all
That lies in its path?
Cold and hard, yet a glorious hue
Of pink and blues,
Sparkling awesome,
Crawling forward, ever onward,
Until at the edge of a beautiful sea
Breaks up with a thunderous roar
For all to behold. A glacier, it's nature.

Brenda Hodgson

Cycles

Fading light
The sound of the cold whispered
Heard by ears deaf
And answered mutely

Phantom shroud
To cloak, to shield
The eternally immobile
Sway in the darkness

The life-giver
Encases the dying
Embers torch a thousand hands
Then fall to the ground

Reborn somehow
The death brings life to another
Grasping at the sky
Always grasping

Melissa Bernert

Going through the Fire

Tests are to improve life.
Don't get scared, we all have to share
this sparkling tear of failure
like the Blacksmith's knife

cutting us into pieces,
banging us to start releasing
oxygen and lose molecules
the Blacksmith has in mind for my use.

After all that banging and testing,
it's really tiring.

Look at his finished product:
I'm as strong as iron.

Ricardo Guzman

Kamploops Sage Brush

Where the trees end, the sage blooms
Grey-blue above the snaking river

In the wilderness of the dry soil
Swaying pure and uncontaminated

Timidity of the small, yellow flowers
Emits a wild fragrance of the harsh world

Mariko Kubo Holland

Heartache

To my grandfather, deceased June 14, 1997—I love you, Pappa
My heart still aches with sadness,
and silent tears still flow.
What it meant for me to lose you,
no one will ever know.
It hurt me on the inside even though
it didn't show.
I wish that everything could just be the same
and all of this was just a little game,
that you would be back with me,
laughing and having fun like we used to always do.
But just to let you know,
I'll be missing you.

Seann Kirkby

Family Tree

A jungle creature by Darwin's theory is my ancestry,
whilst the man on the box avows to disagree,
irreverently decrying, "Deny this family tree!"

Generations ago, my hair was abundant,
which time by design selects to wear away;
today, I weave onto my crown—onto vanity.
Nakedness I had, once adorned by ivy leaves,
now my shame hidden in animal skins.
There is no trace of my tail,
for to Earth I am bound,
thusly burdened upon my two feet,
bending my spine into life's arches.
Is my life a gift from the primate
or Paley's argument for a God?
As time lifts my descendants to a higher order,
decried by the pious upon sandaled feet,
shall life deny my family tree?

Iidija Gasperlin

Right on Time

Right on time, opening, allowing a small light.
Through this space a new face,
Squirming and moving like in space,
Time moving, making a place,
A little light,
A little darkness,
A little fright,
A little guy,
On a precious night,
Right on time.

Marie Newman

Counting Lizards

One two bad form
Three to tell
I'm going home
Showdown match together rain
Four to keep the beast's disdain
Five eruptions primal green
Six has evil keen and seen
Seven shores where are you God
Where eight the boys keep sniffing my corpse
Number nine my resurrection from pool of blood
Let them all know in Aldus and in Morse
In ten I'll be back to take my revenge
Bring the sugar

Lance Windom

September Pain

For my Alaskan Malamute and cancer research

My puppy, my friend . . .
This was our last walk together, but it goes on to eternity.
You sensed my sadness when we left the yard . . .
And I cried to see your pain . . . when you whined in the car.
You sniffed my hair for the last time and weren't able to curl your tail.
You whimpered when I went inside to see the vet . . .
To write away your life. . . .
I cried and cried as you licked my hand, afraid to see me go.
The howl of loss cut through my heart as I turned and walked away.
Why, my friend, did it come to this?
I want to remember all our happy times from puppyhood to now,
But all I see are your sad brown eyes.
As I leave you in that cage . . .
As you lie down low, not wanting me to leave,
The pain just grows and grows and grows . . .
I love you, dog, you silly thing,
And now . . . it is too late.
Good-bye, my friend.
I'll try to stand the pain. . . .

> ### Robert Wiebe

A Run with Time

The newborn opens his eyes and asks, "What is time?"
The answer is unheard. To an infant there seems no time.
Yet Father Time takes that child within his long embrace.

The teenager asks without interest, "What is time?"
The answer is mute. To an adolescent there seems no time.
They shrug off the arms of time yet grasp for immortality.

The young adult asks with frustration, "What is time?"
The answer is a dare. Time has become their competitor.
Will they have reached success by 30? Can they beat time?

The middle-aged adult asks with fear, "What is time?"
The answer is harsh. The corners of his eyes wrinkle, and
gray hairs mask his scalp. Time is no more friend but foe.

The senior shuts his weary eyes and asks, "What is time?"
The answer is a heavenly knowledge—Time is but life!
An ethereal glow beckons him . . . time has finally run away.

> ### Leslie Broddy

Untitled

Shuddering spasms of God's softened tears are thirstily inhaled
by the parched, dry earth.
The wind and the trees wildly dance together,
as if both their spirits and souls celebrate the plenty
that has unfolded in our own lives.

Although unmoving, the solid mass of rocks seems to sing vibrant melodies,
Innocently portraying the contagious laughter of newborn children.
Fallen autumn leaves rhythmically step around my carefree thoughts;
The brilliance of their colors acts as glass prisms.
I am surrounded by the dancing reflection of life's own creator.
For the first time in my long life, I feel as if I am at one
with the greatest father of all,
To whom I will eternally aspire to heed.
For, in my forgiving heart, I have learned to appreciate details and
to thoroughly love.
And for this, I will continuously roam within the fallen boundaries of his
unselfishly given life.

> ### Tara Wheeler

Syrinx

As beautiful as the Dawning day,
As lithe as Rowan tree limbs,
I yearned for you, I loved you, I wanted you.
Am I that horrific, that death was more appealing?
Such a senseless waste of life, such a senseless waste of love,
Love that could have lasted, love that should have lasted,
Love so rich and passionate,
Why did you shun me?
I would have shown you the world; I would have given you the moon.
The grove is my home, and sacred. The grove could've been our home.
Love burns for you still
In these bestial veins.
The reeds you became, the reeds I picked,
Fashioned into flutes, fashioned by passion, fashioned by hurt.
Haunting melodies I play on them,
Keeping your memory alive.
The sound they make comforts me; the sound they make taunts me,
Reminding me of you, reminding me of my love, reminding me of you.
Close to my heart you will always be,
Your name always on the edge of my lips.

Pan Forester

Colony 3

We who have loved the day
are not given to idle fears and misplaced emotion.
The World is not ending, nor is this time any worse than those
that have preceded it:
A long time ago,
Yesterday.
We dreamt that nothing would change,
but change it did, and we the dreamers were changed also.
But,
we are still here—wiser perhaps, older certainly.
More battered by life than we thought possible,
we remember days we have loved.
God willing,
they may come again
with sunshine in the morning and the long, sundowner evenings,
the talk of friends, and the laughter of children.
Remember this always:
God is not malicious.

A. Bruce

The Picture

Softly, she said she would not draw the picture, for
Angels would not fly in Heaven abroad. And the
Clouds that she smoked would forever be melting, as
Long as she could have a wish in her well. And the

People then stared at her, blank as the paper, un-
Knowing of wishes and clouds in her mind. And they
Said that she had to make use of her fingers or
Else in return they would steal her loft picture at

Night in her sleep, and she'd never awake. And she
Laughed at the people obsessed with the truth. And she
Told them her truth was as real as the sky that she
Danced on, and danced as she broke yellow pencils and

Drew what she dreamt when she felt what she meant. But they
Stood, their demand high above as the ceiling, so
High up above she could not even find. And so
She shook her head as they sent her to bed where she

Drew her own picture of the unconscious mind.

Yvette Marie Ivanic

High Expectations

Everybody said they shall be the one—
the one to lead in every sphere.
Everybody had such high expectations;
it would be a crime to let
society down.

But, alas, the sands of time
have passed
swiftly through the hourglass of life.
But what has happened
is a crime,
creating wounds that could take an eternity
to heal.

They have now become the ridicule of society.

Adrian Dastur

Looking Glass

I watch you through my looking glass,
and as you act out your part
I reflect on what was,
and what might have been.
And when I see her in your arms,
my stomach tightens,
my heart slows.
My eyes see only her,
her perfection, her beauty.
And staring back at me through the looking glass
are my faults, my imperfections.
Watching her with you,
seeing her smile,
hearing her laugh,
I hear only you and what you said to me.
The words still echo in my mind.
The memories are still vivid.
She acts only as a painful reminder,
of what I had,
and what I lost.

Ileana Brito

Enlightenment

Each man is an island . . . marooned on lonely seas,
Absorbed in his search for joy
Wallowing in his personal tragedies.
The more he earns, the more he yearns.
He knows not what he is searching for,
Yet he keeps knocking on every door. . . .
He seeks success and finds insomnia and stress.
He tries for love but gets control and pain instead.
He goes for religion but dogma spoils the holiness.
Television temporarily allays his fears,
Sex temporarily suspends his tears,
But all the time Judgement Day nears!
And then, on some quiet and uneventful day,
Enlightenment dawns in a sunburst of ecstasy!
It was always within, that which he searched for outside,
Glowing like a jewel, blushing like a bride!
Unbelievable sweetness, nestling inside!
Universal love floods his heart and being!
The Spirit awakens full of Light and All-Seeing
He sees in its glow, all souls as One!

Indra Hathiramani

Unknown

There's noises all around.
They come from every room.
I can't stop thinking about life;
everyone's so different.
Life is always changing.
Why do I feel like dirt?
I don't know why I am here.
I'll never know my purpose.
I'll never know who we are.
I know I'll never know!
We will only know who we want to be.
I love it when it pours outside.
I love it when it thunders and lightnings;
It makes me feel so alive.
I wonder if there is a Heaven and hell.
I catch myself wondering:
Do I want to die?

Andrea Wienecke

The Other

The smile that adorns his face
does little to convince me.
The eyes, glacial, uncompromising,
are all that I can see,
and whilst his lips are firm,
straight, and wrinkle-free,
the orbs grow and cannot conceal
his mockery of me.
Those tacit times when not one sound
is uttered betwixt lip and breath
to those it overawes,
unleashing gravity in death
of union once so certain;
but I, the knowing, concerned when he
speaks and lips move incessantly,
not I in his thoughts, in his reverie.
She stole his love from me.

Joanne Barrass

whisper

alone
in solitude
i stand in the corner

leaves rustle
the wind howls . . . threateningly

i flew off
onto the wings of the night

and drifted away
i would disappear
  from this uncaring world

a pity i can't scream my feelings out
because the ears in this world are biased
i have to whisper to myself
this world is dying

Tan Tze-Ming

Lady Di

You're dead—Lady Di,
And the die is cast.
Nothing will last.
The Present, The Future are Past.
At a standstill is Time.
Frozen Time,
Frozen Love,
Do Di, Lady Die.
An Icon of LOVE
—Loving us from above—
MOTHER DI.

Joseph Bonnici

Where?

in a place
all alone
your friends are gone

your soul is dark
empty is your heart

there is only you
and nothing you could do

your biggest fear:
it will never disappear

you can't express
your heart's a mess

and no one
to lean on

in a place
all alone
and all your friends are gone

Patrick Stoepper

Two

Deep within a human's mind,
the physical characteristics
and mental changes a person
goes through are understandable.
All in all, the person's perspective
toward life changes as he/she matures;
therefore, a woman enters a man's life
and changes this poem into reality.
Mystical features that come
   to a man's mind
lift his soul and personality that brings
a gleaming, white sparkle to his eyes
as a reflection from the supernatural world.

Ryan Brown

Forest

A man walked into a forest.
He looked around and fell to the ground.
He got up and looked around,
and a tree fell to the ground.
The tree got up and looked around,
and the man fell to the ground.

Tomi Alanen

Natasha

My daughter's face shines in my eyes.
Like a dream I watch its beauty change,
Reshape, and glow with my aching pride.

Could I die now, or dare I ask for more?
Like her birth, her confidence consumes my breath.
My heart pumps iron, and my lips bleed.

This woman, this actor drives herself.
Like my passions, she will not stop
Until life has captured her moment,
And her life, my life, watches the justification
Of New York and its demanding stages,
The costumes of our lives cast aside for dramas
Yet to close, kisses yet to be kissed,
And, this moment, I am with her and content.

Jim Head

My Love for You

The moon was full when first we met
I knew it'd be one night I'd never forget
For when you held me close
I shivered from my head to my toes
And when you softy whispered my name
I knew I would never be the same

That night I knew I had fallen in love
And, as we kissed, I thanked my lucky stars above
Like flowers that bloom in the spring
My love for you made me want to sing
To awaken each morn' with you by my side
My love for you I knew I could no longer hide

Your dreams became mine
Everything seemed just fine
If only I could've loved you less
Then my life wouldn't be in such a mess
You knew you had your way right from the start
You took all you could, then broken my heart
Sure, maybe you loved me in your own way
But, it just wasn't enough to make you want to stay

Sarah Jane King

Luxury

I bought flowers instead of bread.
I passed by mountains of shiny apples . . .
I just looked at juicy oranges.
I sat in the sun, not rushing to work.
I listened to music played by four Guatemalans,
making time with my feet,
my body vibrating with the pluck of strings.
I wandered over by the keyboard player,
smiled at him, moved by his melodies,
I felt love for the musician.

There was not a cloud in my heart,
as clear as the sky I looked upon.
Wind came stealthily
and visited with the waves in secret rendezvous.
Flowers of colours spilled out of their containers,

And I did not have to buy the bread.

Miriam Batts

You Used To

You used to call me "Darling," but now it's simply "Sal."
Your loving smile that once was mine is now that of a pal.
Our early morning cuddle, now a coffee in a huddle,
And your tender touch is gone—there's trouble.

Should I worry? Should I fret? It can't be true. And, yet . . .
That feeling's gone, that look is gone, that touch is gone. I try to not forget
The loving times, the happy times. We used to romp and frolic,
And now it's chores instead of play; I've acquired a work-aholic.

But, just for now, amuse myself. He tells me it's not over.
A few more years, some long, hard work, and we'll be high in clover.

I feared to love so many years; it makes me hurt, you see.
My weakness shows, my mind is fogged. I love too much, I know.
But maybe if we take the time and reacquaint each other,
This, too, will pass; we'll realize love's there, just undercover.

You used to call me "Darling," but now it's simply "Sal,"
And yet today you said, "Sweetheart," and I was filled with joy.
Could it be I feign your love? No, no. It's just a ploy
To test my faith, to try my mind. For now, I must consider,
This pair is new at ties that bind. We'll make it work. I know it.

Sally Rylance

The Flight of Icarus

In Darwin's prison, imagination and necessity,
an invention of escape conceived
upon arched, waxed wing of science,
dreamed by man loved and reviled,
for desired master over all that he could see.

Exponential curves of math assailed the heights of finite wrath.
For escape from a sun-less island cage
in a maelstrom sea of information,
technology was the key to the sage,
so Icarus soared to the light borne upon a melting plight.

William Hunter

Giant Sunflower

Winding down these shallow stairs
the air is murky with the smell of gloom
faces peering, eyes so wide, glazed from horror nationwide

The tide is turning as hearts once frozen (in glacial tombs)
begin to beat once more, once more

I fear that beauty loves a flower
brief in flowering radiance
ageless, dying in ignorance

I dreamt I was a giant sunflower and someone plucked my seeds
ate me, spit me out, and left me doomed to face the sun
half-naked (sunflower face, petals for hair, human body exposed
breasts heaving, legs straight, and throbbing feet rooted into Mother Earth)
and in my dream where all is possible
I grew more seeds and found more sap
fluttering my leaves in the summer breeze
and for a moment in time, I lived forever. . . .

My sunflower face was touched by God
My forgotten grace was founded by strength

I looked all around me in the field of my friends
their petals were fragrant, and we were alive—once more, once more

Phyllis Dermatas

I Mourn

I mourn, I mourn; not for death . . .
But for that every breath
That passes without taking His name,
Leaving my conscience to burn in dreadful shame.

I mourn, I mourn; not for a dead body . . .
But for the poor, naked body
That lies on the street without any clothes.
Shame! We never take pity, but that sight we loathe.

I mourn, I mourn; have you heard . . . ?
For the poverty in the world,
For the baby of the poor woman whose breasts have dried
The milk that the child did not get—cried and died.

I mourn, I mourn; not for some accident . . .
But for the reason why God in this world me He sent
To witness the miseries
Where humanity is seldom seen.

I mourn, I mourn; my mourning keeps going in circles. . . .
I hope day and night for Miracles!
I wish this were a better place to live
Where everybody had ample love to give.

Parminder Kaur Kalsi

Saying Good-Bye

As we look at the pictures with all the lines and creases,
Listening to you tell stories of your nephews and nieces,
One thought continues to creep into my mind:
Why someone so young, gentle, and kind?
So many questions, so few answers I have to give.
I pray every night, with all my heart, you will live.
You've asked me in so many ways, why?
It takes everything I have not to break down and cry.
Now the days are growing near;
When I look in your eyes I see emptiness and fear.
It's like the illness rips out your insides and tears you apart.
I don't give you a beginning or a head start.
They ask me to help you, but not to get close.
I'm only human: That's what bothers me most.
As we sit, I see a calmness come over you.
I feel happy, also sad and blue.
The fight has come to the end.
There's a place in my heart for you, dear friend.

Vickie Brown Embury

The Universe Beside

Standing beneath the night sky, staring into the vastness of space,
I watch as a molten rock of ice seems suspended in time.
In reality, however, the gods look on as this intruder tears
through the peaceful sanctuary of the heavens,
disturbing the frail place they call home.
As this force hurtles toward Earth, I sense an anticipation of uncertainty,
not millions of miles away, however, but of just a few feet.
I can feel a presence in myself that I never believed possible—
one that seemed to grow out of the frosted breath
that the two of us exhaled.
As the warmed air gently floated through our chilled lips,
I came to an understanding as to how one is to survive within our universe.
Looking far out into the darkened sky, I tried to find the one spot
that could capture my imagination and dazzle me with brilliant fascination.
But the harder I looked, the more I came to realize that the greatest
star in my universe was not a gaseous mixture of fire burning out of
control in a place I could never be, but instead she was
where I could touch, hold, and even kiss. She was there, beside,
in a place I hope she would want to stay. Our universe.

Michael Parsons

Wishes for You

These, my special friend,
Are the wishes I have for you.
You are very special to me;
May all these wishes come true:
I wish you good fortune, my friend,
For without it life can be rough.
Even though, in this world today,
It is hard to be fortunate enough,
I wish you great luck my friend
In accomplishing whatever your life goals may be,
For I know you will some day,
And right beside you to help you reach them will be me.
Last and most importantly,
My friend, I wish you love,
For without it life can be blue,
And when you do find love, my friend,
Then all these wishes I have for you, my friend,
Will have finally all come true.

Tamatha Guthrie

Revelations of an Exiled Heart

Disembarking in a sterile desert
my head was spinning with plans of greatness
enmeshing my feelings
my thoughts
the very epiphany of my soul
my deepest core
thereby testing the waters of my dreams
the stability of the ground my feet lay upon
leaving my heart to choke in the sand
abating ever so slowly
that it sets me to tears
watching my dreams
wafting through like a breeze
erupting memories of the girl I once was
once upon a time
amidst a long-lost dream

Ghia Osseiran

Happy Marriage Poem

Gangrene of boredom floating up in the room

He is eating patiently at the table
End with the rusty knife cutting a pus cuticle
And from his gullet coming out
Breath smelling of alcohol and undigested food

She is whiningly giving a birth
On the bed of web

From the huge stomach of pitch
A cross-eyed baby is coming out
Made from mechanical movements
Of galvanized limbs

On the wall
Near the Villar's picture of the sleeping boy in the field
A picture of a happy couple
With their rickets heads

From the poisoned air
Death flays
Are falling all over the place

Slobodan Djurasovic

Don't Tell Me a Lie

With anger, I reach for the door
and walk into your room.
A vodka bottle lies on the floor,
the lingering smell of her cheap perfume.

I glance outside the window,
watching the falling rain.
I can't believe I trusted you, so
I close my eyes to shut out the pain.

The silence is broken with a sigh.
I feel myself falling apart.
With my head in my hands, I cry.
A knife has been stabbed
    through my heart.

I'm losing control of my will.
Tears run down from my eyes.
It's you I want to kill,
but it's a part of me that dies.

Sandy Elia

it's time to stop it's time to start

pain for pain and cry for cry
consistency of preparation
endless end and start-less start
delinquency of animation

hits of destiny bits of ignorance
sporadic satisfaction
sips of poison whips of hormone
erotic interaction

or was it
erotic consistency
sporadic delinquency
interaction preparation
satisfaction animation

and let it be
erotic preparation
sporadic animation
consistency interaction
delinquency satisfaction

anyone lost in tiME

Dragan Mirkov

Solace

Of all the dreams and aspirations
I've held inside my heart,
To find that one to share my life
Has been there from the start.

And yet although it is the one
That holds fast above the rest,
It is the least in my control;
I clutch at it at best.

But the tide will bring my ship to me
Whether I wander from the shore.
So then I find dreaming not so hard,
Waiting, not such a bore.

Joanna Groves

It Is Love

It resists analysis in words,
It does not yield to the theorist.
It is personal,
It must be felt directly.

It has pleasures, epiphanies,
Ecstasies, and disillusionment.
It has burdens and duties.
It takes time.

It has a variety of emotions,
Fierce satisfactions, swooning delights.
It shares in the horrors of jealousy,
Desperation, and obsession.

It is confidence, honesty,
Tenderness, generosity, and sweetness.
If it's real, it's forever.
It is love.

Kimberly Dawn Raycroft

Need

My insides burn
As I wait for you.
I don't know who you are,
But still I wait for you.
I will let you whisk me away
And lead me far from here.
I will let you hold my heart
To keep me safe and warm.
I see you so vaguely in my dreams
(A shadowed one so soft and light),
But you are always in my heart
(I feel you live within me).
For you and only you, I will wait forever
(Which is no time at all for you).
But until Forever,
My insides burn
As I sit here and wait for you.

Shannon McIlveen

SOPHISTICATED LONGING

From the seashore, deep in the sea,
Sophisticated longings,
To throw away and never be
The part of my belongings.
The sunset's calling every night
At the horizon's glory—
Is telling me, "That's not all right!"
How could I say such a story?
If to thy order disobey,
A distant desperation
To another vault of Heaven, pray
To find angelic station
Of music and orchestral drum,
And what could I discover?
From other galaxy to come
That hopeless still my lover!
Thy sphere again is teaching high,
The art to purport feeling.
A longing lives and I shall die,
How deep could be thy meaning?

Neli Fatu de Valahia

Life, Living, Loving

My love for thee is unexplainable
As the fear of losing you is untameable

Life goes on with hopes and desires
As dreams are a wait that often tires

Ceasing the moment is truly profound
As is keeping two feet on stable ground

Living a fairy tale is a puzzling concept
As being alive is an astonishing prospect

Freezing the spirit captures beautiful treasures
As freeing one's thoughts of extreme measures

Loving your companion is infrequently a task
As is keeping each other happy without having to ask

Candice Ostrowski

Life Change

Was mistreated and abused,
My reason for being so confused
Not knowing where to go or where to turn,
Feeling trapped, as my heart burns

Suffering slowly deep down within,
Wishing for happiness to shine in.
As the days, weeks and years go by,
Anticipation of a better life, cross my mind

Sitting there reflecting, the way life is,
Will it continue just like this?
Agonizingly these questions plague my fears,
Why go through this, why am still here?

Swiftly as the eagle, flies away,
Life changed to a brand new day
Like a bed of roses, only few thorns inside,
Life could only get better, at last I found my pride.

And if you listen, closely to my heart,
You'll hear the beat of these wonderful words at last
I'm free, as free as the world turns.
Free, as freely, as my heart burns.

Nedra Johnson-Aswad

My Son! My Life!

It was great joy I felt the day you were born.
It was deep pride I felt when to school you were shown.
A young boy to me on loan,
To mold and guide
Into a good man someday full grown.

And over the years you grew to be
Everything I wanted and expected to see:
An outstanding athlete with academic prowess,
Handsome! Proud! Destined for success!!

Although at times great sadness I feel,
The baby, the boy, this man, now so real!
This wonderfully exciting job to me given
At which over the years so hard I have striven
Will end as sure as my life has been driven.

My fine handsome son will soon take a wife,
And so will end the most important part of my life.

Peggy A. Tucker

Golf

Golf, that game I dared to play instead of farming and making hay,
was what my friends said I should try
and play with them as time goes by.
At first I dubbed them off the tee, now in the pond and shooting three.
I'm in the bush, I'm in the rough, this bloody game, it sure is tough.
I'm on the green in three or four, and in the hole in nine or more.
One day while playing with Bill Munro,
he said, "Those clubs have got to go.
What you need, Norm, are clubs like Ping,
and stop your playing like a ding-a-ling."
So, now with new clubs in my bag,
my thoughts of par make me feel glad.
I'll be on in three and down in five. It sure feels good to be alive.
The nineties are a score of the past. I sure do hope my luck will last.
I'm in the eighties and getting lower,
and joined the ranks of the club house "blowers."
I'm breaking eighty and doing fine,
this sure has been a real tough nine.
A few more games and I'll arrive at that magic number of seventy five.
Happy Birthday, Norm, you Ding-a-ling.
>   *William Munro*

Giving

One's life to service, while feeling honestly inclined,
may distinguish between necessity or control not easily defined!
A smile often touches lives with warmth, as love can impart,
or experience a cold glare that pierces one's heart!
Each morning to waken making choices within,
whether positive or negative, from whence to begin?
To initiate each day with an extra mile,
or left unfinished—was it really worthwhile?
Revel needlessly when guarding each ungrateful thought
instead of reciprocating goodness from the bottom of your heart!
Do I applaud or justify each deed I've fulfilled,
or accepted a gift in a pretense still chilled?
When a giver levied pay-backs, running interest that's high,
Oft given with a purpose in mind, how do you decide?
To Give and Receive with sincerity enrolls
a growth that's enriched to nourish the soul!
Charity feels good, as it functions both ways
and dissolves the greed that most often preys!
Love's commitment involves trust with another each day,
A True Disciple of God in every way!
>   *Patricia Palmer*

Atalasa Pine Forest

We frolicked where sweet violets with fragrant roses grew,
at the edge of Atalasa Pine Forest.
Our father took us, as children, there,
and all through spring and summer we picnicked and feasted under the pines,
and as brazen-sweet pine strung our nostrils,
we gathered sweeter violets for Mother.
And we played hide and seek and musical chairs,
using pine trunks for chairs.
Then something transcendental and rare touched our inspired hearts.
For, the remote but friendly forest became an enchanted
and divine paradise for all of us children.
We still have vivid memories of those magical days.
We also picked asparagus and shy mushrooms for our mother
to cook asparagus soup.
And as the vermilion day grew cooler, and we had our fill of chasing angel
butterflies, we all trekked back, all in a file,
like Boy Scouts by the side of Snake Brook,
Father being the leader of the pack,
before dusky night fell on the "Magnificent-Excellence" of all-mothering,
all-caring, and "Divine" Mother Nature!
>   *Eftalon Harman*

Deliverance

You stood there in your triumph,
your fist strangling my heart.
I could hear your wicked laugh burning silent through my soul.
Each painful tear that fell dry from my eyes tried to drown you,
but you knew how to swim.
Rampant in your power,
consumed by the rush of your sexual prowess,
you were blind while I braved your silent, selfish ritual.
You never saw me, I was invisible,
and then I became more nothing to you
than I was in the beginning—
now just the shadow of a whore.
Somehow you remained the same,
untouched, unchanged, and smiling.
As I looked at you, I saw your cruel heart
and it startled me into remembering mine.
As you stood there, I knew you never thought of me.
As you looked at me, I wasn't wearing anything,
not a thread of human dignity or honour,
and my soul screamed as I turned and slowly walked away.

> ### *Kathleen Kennedy*

Please Stop the Blame

Rich against poor, "majority" against "minority,"
Black against white, brother against brother,
Parents against children, please stop the blame!

Nation against nation, blood against blood,
Why does this happen, why does this go on,
Teaching our children these shameful deeds?
Please stop the blame!

Politics, religion, race, culture, status,
Each blaming the other, not accepting their own responsibilities.
Please, please stop the blame!

Bloodshed and tears, heartache and pain,
Why must this go on? Who are we to judge
Those we stand beside, those who share our space?
Please, please stop the blame!

Why must innocence die to have hatred take its place?
War over love, hatred over unity?
Death over life?
Someone please, please, stop the blame,
Before it's too late to turn back!

> ### *Cory Whitecap*

Springtime Resurrection

Springtime green returns each year,
Renewing resurrection
With newborn life of every kind,
Some of which to mention . . .
Sunshine rising with the dawn,
Doe gives life to newborn fawn,
Springtime snows refresh the land,
Restore anew the life at hand,
Winter's treasures ever so long,
And then the peeper's chorus of song;
Hepatica, trilliums, marsh marigolds too,
Lily of the valley and crocus of blue.
Mr. Fox, Mrs. Fox, and baby foxes too,
Live wild and free within our midst, preferable to a zoo.
These young foxes like puppies play, amusing one another,
which I have witnessed with my eyes, just as their tamed brother.
Spring time comes but once a year,
Renewing resurrection
For the betterment of our natural world.

> ### *Elizabeth W. Fraser*

The Unibird

Two birds above the mountain,
gliding high toward the sky
in opposite directions,
then approaching each other
at top speed.

In their love dance,
tips of wings are touching,
bodies merging into one body:
circling . . . waltzing . . . moving slowly . . .
separating into dazzling dives.
Uniting, separating, uniting, separating
immeasurable times.

In final union,
one bird flies off into the universe,
on its way to the stars. . . .

Vanishing forever
while the sun is disappearing behind the horizon,
coming back the next morning
to enlighten a new day and another two birds
above the mountain
gliding high . . . toward the sky.

Guido Hoogenboom

Look Around

What a brisk, clear night tonight.
Fall is on its way, and the stars are shining bright—
The leaves red, orange, and gold,
A light breeze, a little chilly, a little cold.
Cars rush by the road ahead,
Not a soul in sight: The night is dead.
Nature's so beautiful and so dear,
But somewhere tonight someone sheds a tear.
As the leaves blow and pass me by,
I sit here and think, one needs an open eye.
Because with all the bad comes the good,
And I believe that each person should
Take a look around—there's much to be grateful for.
Pick up that broken heart that's lying on the floor.
Love hurts and to all death does come,
But after awhile the pain goes numb.
Fate decides which way we will go.
Our part is to breathe and take things slow.

Michelle Ertel

6 p.m. News

The eye of Medusa,
inevitable TV screen,
turns us into stone,
heart and all.

Orchestrated by Jerry Springer,
New York amoeba slowly expands
with its shrink-wrapped justice,
with cops and robbers,
with adultery and talk-to-the-hand
immunizing, dehumanizing
conditioning us for the 6 p.m. news:
A billion eyes swallow blood, our daily venom.

On desolate streets,
hooligan ghosts ruffle garbage.

Ioana Timariu

Life and Death

Life and Death: The two are one—
The crying babe, the setting sun.

Life brings Death. Death brings Life.
'Tis the cause of all strife.

The body decayed down to soil,
Drags us down into turmoil.

Yet, with that soil, can Life regain—
The newborn baby yet free from pain.

Each passing moment, the baby cries.
Each passing moment, the baby dies.

Life and Death: The two are one—
The crying babe, the setting sun.

Jason Tremoyne

Another Day

The sun sets,
The sun rises.
Someone is born,
Another dies.
One hand reaches in healing.
A second strikes in anger.
Beauty fades,
And a flower blooms.
Where the sun rises,
It will set again.
And where there is dusk
Somewhere there is dawn.

Carolyn Nonkes

What Is It Worth?

What is it worth to fight?
What is it worth to die?
What is it worth to beat?
What is it worth to bleed?
What is it worth to steel?
What is it worth to kill?
What is it worth to a sword?
What is it worth to a lord?
What is it worth to a country?
What is it worth to the world?

Josh Grottick

The Storm

Once again as I sit,
I must endure the thunder:
the thunder of his anger,
the thunder of his rage.
The lightning flashes from his eyes
and strikes me in my heart.
I must never show the fear or hurt
I feel deep inside.
For, I know this storm will pass,
and there will be time
for tears to quietly heal
the many scars that will never show.
They say thunder cannot hurt you—
then why does it break my heart?

Darlene Brush

Home

Home is small, Home is big,
Home is a wonderful place for you to live.
There you'll find safety and love,
parents, brothers, sisters
making you laugh.

Georgia Christoforou

Drosophila Melanogaster

Splayed for review,
They look for what's new
Inside my core.
I am no more.

Is there something to gain
By visiting pain
On a body so small?
Am I no good at all?

Do they derive
Some reasons why
We are what we are,
And have we come far?

Perhaps with some luck
In future I'll cut
And split them in two
To see just what's true!

David Pember

S T O N E S

Homeless stones close your eyes
in oblivion with wild wind
embrace hot blood of rivers
when volcano burns the Earth
with lava of words
to be again
the bright temple of Silence

Mihail Petkov

The Unveiling (Of the Mind)

It always remains a
    mystery
waiting to be
    unveiled

Like an intricate
    Puzzle Box
all it needs is a
    Nimble Hand
to pry it open to
reveal its internal
    workings

Its true identity
finally shows itself
the onlookers await
in silence

A picture show
runs across the ceiling
the show is black
and silent

Roger Rousseau

Night Shift Murmurs

Anthony was no show, Jeremy moves too slow
I feel tired also, but the clock said let's go
We worked all week, as a horse
Hated it like kids their chores
Finish the job as good sports
To earn the pay cheque, of course

Now that the week is over
Got our bills somewhat covered
The weekend let us get recovered
Monday it's time to start things all over

L. K. Matyus

Paper Tiger Army

We're living now in the void
The void left by two great paper tigers
Paper tigers that threatened to spit fire at each other
Paper tigers that would both burn if they did
How strange it is to live here
Here in the vacuum that was left behind
Vacuum that sucks in every scavenger with an appetite
Sucking them into combat with each other
Fighting for the scraps of civilization
Fighting to create a kingdom for themselves
Hoping to control a remnant of the paper tiger
Wishing to be a paper tiger also

David J. Doles

The Human Fate

Oh! What a humankind
With no qualities to find
You move West
You move East
All's the same, everywhere

Humans turn against each other
For the greed of mankind, killing one another
Laws broken every time
Making way for the corrupt
To lead a short life span
For man's selfish comfort

Poverty has its tentacles spread across the globe
Injustice looms around the world
What a misery in the midst of agony
In this tiny spot of the universe

Oh! Homo sapiens
What will be thy fate?
For in the days to come
Generation are bound to suffer

Dr. Suresh Alex

Raindrops and Tears

Silence in the night, raindrops on my window,
It sounds like music in my ears.
I pull aside the curtain, watch rivulets flow,
Windows, water, faces wet with tears.
Although there's no way to know
As I confront all the years,
Is it tears of joy, or tears of sorrow?
I do not know; I cover myself, close my ears.
Maybe I'll try to find out tomorrow.

A. P. Segers

Cries of a Soul

Sadness lies in one darkened soul
One life torn up with so many holes
Reflections of an image filled with emptiness and tired, vacant eyes
The soul hurts to live, but looks forward to die
Fighting its demons, the soul starts to weaken—for, winning is rare
So to God the losing soul cries out in prayer
Give me guidance or rid me from this world of judgement and despair!
A soul pleads to its maker at its greatest time of need
No signs are given, no images come to mind, no messages received
The soul then asks itself, "Will the pain of hurting ever stop?"
It answers to its own image, "It could be all over, way up high, as quick as a drop!"
"It's freedom I want!", the soul rants and raves
Hoping its cries are heard and the awaited golden road soon paved
The restless soul wants to cry no more, no more wiping away of tears
No more burdens with worries and the struggles of unwanted fears
One lost soul of a shattered mind and a broken heart
Waits out its time on the world until its turn to part

Maria G. Slogar

The Fortress

The sentinels appear sullen as they stand guard
Protecting what once was such sacred ground,
Lighthearted melodies played by an unknown bard
Seem to envelop the valley with such sweet sounds,
The likes of which had not yet been found.

The Bastions of our gardens still stand,
For they alone bear witness to our mere history.
They have somehow become strangers in a strange land,
Since we inflicted upon them the poisons of hate and misery
And all despicable facets of our self-proclaimed infamy!

We silently watch as they weaken and fall,
Each one different despite looking the same,
These minions of nature that once stood so tall
Have been poisoned and scarred by ignorance's bright flame,
And yet, Man still wears a guise to hide his guilt and shame.

David Maynard

1997

I walk out my door
I am greeted by fine, crisp weather.
Walk further down, people piled into their cars
Scurry past to a destination where beeper's ring,
Black slim line telephones shrill,
The incessant clickety-clack of keyboards,
And the mediocre buzz of people's voices.
Am I destined to face this too?
The endless frustrations,
The dependency on technology,
Deadlines to face!
I doubt Mother Nature had this on her agenda.
She created nature for a reason.
A reason that has been forgotten,
All thanks to man's inability to appreciate her services.
Now generations follow, and will, in the same life of constant rushing.
Is nature dead? Did we kill ourselves in the process too?
Why?
Because we wish to die rich—
In the material world.

Gia Pereira

My Love

To my husband, the one I love, it has been one year today!
Love just cannot stay away.

Love takes a long time to mold and it is just growing bold.

Love reflects the love we have for ourselves and for each other.
I want to keep continuing to grow and never leave the show.

All my love and pride run ridged and high.
For, all my family and you are the center of my eye!

Debbie Baer Gilbert

A Warrior's Prayer: Remember Me

Come, stay with me between the many miles of memory.
How oft I yearned a whispered glance
Of youth and grace and endless chance.
No mortal I, nor mortal be;
A soul in agony no more, come live with me.
Come stay with me, in memory of I,
A wanton will to clasp your life to mine
In walks through dreams of suns.
To will the light into my heart of pain,
Come kiss these lips I give to thee in prayer.
I found your hand in mine, again.
How many times we gazed into the eyes of life!
How many times my suns arose in thee!
How many times mine eyes will search again, till you come to me. . . .
Come walk with me and ask of me my constancy
To fare thee grace, and fare thee absent ill, for return I will.
Come rise, this night will be the longest bliss.
Come sweet lips, kiss the longest kiss,
For come again, I will; be still, be still.
For, come again, I will.

Anne Bauer

Spouse's First Quarrel

I look at him: My Darling . . . My Darling?
Not today—but once he was!
He kisses the top of my head, before bed—why the pause?
Is it because
He sees the flaws that Newly-Wedded Love perforce denies?
Are love's sweet lies
Erased—replaced by Ruthless Truths and Disillusion's Sighs?!
There was a time, His Darling was I; 'twas written on his face.
I fell from Grace! What Intimate Misdeed can work this woe?
I'm as innocent as on the day we wed!
Who can retrace
The heedless steps that led to this nothingness
From Marriage Bed? I love him still!
But, still—can I forgive his lack of faith,
his callousness—his chill?

Elmay Crow

Ennui

Serenity in thy agitated life is what thy heart hath
Been searching for. . . .
Tranquility amidst adversity, thy mind hath to explore.
In the seventeen abrupt years of thy entity,
Noble life hath been filled with animosity.

Grudge in thy heart, fear in thy soul . . .
Yearning for help to lift thee from thy fall,
Hath seen thy life totally in vain. . . .
Release thee from world's deceitful chain—

And seeing thy life in such predicament . . .
Never hath happiness nor contentment.
Now thy conscience pondered thee to seek the divine providence.
Ennui in thy life, thy heart hath despised, and now thy
soul cherishes thy humble existence.

Kimi Lou P. Baluyut

The Ghetto

In the ghetto where chances
Of life are slim and the light of hope begins to dim
The cave of death caves in and people leave
Their little beds to end their lives in the grasp of God's hand
But even though they're dead they remember
The ruins in which their lives came to an end

Zachary Schwartz

On the Acropolis

What are we doing here, ten thousand of us daily?
Worshipping has-been gods, unreal as
The Bold and the Beautiful and twice as nasty—
everything we wannabe in our darkest fantasies:
selfish, moody, partisan, immortal?
(One half of our moon is always in shadow.)

A professor from a little-known American college
and his wife, a Japanese tour group, young
men with geometric haircuts and been-there-done-that
T-shirts, my family from South Africa: Few of us
student architects, fixated on perfect
caps and columns, all of us with our reasons.

Posing self-consciously for camera or video,
we carve ourselves into this frieze of history.
No one much minds the scaffolding on the Parthenon—
how else shall we shore up our century's ruins?
Propitiation is the name of the game: lest-we-forget
those who preceded us, so we in turn will be remembered.

Rosie Livingstone

Time Change

It seems like only yesterday—
I drank at the fountain in our playground,
I danced in the concert at school,
I sang as a lover in our college play,
I was a young bride, dressed in tulle.

It seems like only yesterday—
My infant sons were born, and motherhood surfaced;
My inborn maternal instincts were on display.
My life challenged—wiped out in a flash—
Thoughts, hopes, dreams in disarray.

It seems like only yesterday—
Sadness enfolded me.
I was plunged into depths of despair.
All around me were darkness and devastating fear—
Then inside me—I heard it—a prayer.

But then today—yes, only today—
I caught the breath of spring air,
Young hearts touched me, young voices I hear,
Fresh, fragrant blossoms beckoned, called.
Then, without warning—new horizons were clear.

Bernadette Le Roux

Mother Teresa

Toll the bell solemnly, weep to its tone,
For Mother Teresa has left us alone.
The poor of the poorest she loved with her heart,
True angel of mercy, fulfilling her part.
To combat the squalor, to clean up the dirt,
To feed the unfortunates, quenching their thirst.
Surrounded by pestilence, famine, and death,
She was risking her life to the very last breath.
Her love universal was known round the Earth.
She was loved and adored from the day of her birth.

She was born of rich parents, her life could have been
One of infinite leisure and comfort serene,
But she chose to forego it, let luxury pass,
To live like a nun of the gaunt lower class.
She was full of good works till she reached eighty-seven.
May the trumpets all sound as she rises to Heaven.

P. Roy Wilson

Angel by My Side

I have met an Angel
Standing on a Cloud,
His eyes so warm and loving,
His smile a ray of sunshine.

Each morning as I wake,
He greats me with a smile.
His words are like a melody
That touches me like the wind.

He's there watching over me,
Wherever I may be.
He finds me when I'm lost
And carries me when I'm weak.

He guides me through the day,
Protects me through the night.
His arms are there to comfort me
When no one else can see.

I have met an Angel
Standing on a cloud. . . .

Marie Savoie

Unseen Voices

Voices reaching out of darkness,
Talking to those who cannot hear.
They shout of victories.
They whisper of sorrows.
But no one takes time to listen.
Shadows moving amongst the crowds,
Yet, in the crowds, they move unseen.
They walk tall with pride.
They hunch over in fear.
But no one takes time to watch.
Who are these unheard, unseen people?
They hear all that goes on.
They see all that happens.
They want someone to notice,
But no one takes time to care.

Lawrence Mcclafferty

Summer Afternoon

The day was like a dandelion
The sun slid through his hair
Apple blossoms fell like snow
The dream was everywhere

The black-eyed birds described the sun
His face was fresh and bright
The deep blue sky and lilac scent
The quiet summer light

The wind asked every tree to dance
The air flamed up to gold
I took his sunburned hand and knew
We never would grow old

Kate Lunau

Untitled

Lying awake at night, thinking,
Where is here?
Not knowing where here is
is scary.
It mortifies and immobilizes
even the strongest.
Being lost
is frustrating, tiring:
burned out
like a rusted car
in a back alley,
an empty shell
left on the beach
because it's ugly.
Where is here?
Not knowing causes wandering
and indecision.
Sleep does not exist.
Where is here?
To know means here can be there.

Cody Todd

The Hug from the Heart

The hug from the heart
Holds on to love
Embracing its power
To bring peace to the soul.

The hug from the heart
Holds on to freedom
Embracing its spirit
To bring peace to the mind.

The hug from the heart
Holds on to emotion
Embracing its comfort
To bring peace to the body.

Scott Young

Out of Lips

Tell me secrets out of lips
long-since kissed
tell me of the time
cut stockings
of the time
in my grandmother's kitchen
when flour became war paint
and tarts became the body of Christ
tell me secrets out of lips
burned with liquor
burned with time
burned with mine
burned with lies
tell me secrets out of lips
parched with cold
with ice and wind
the wind that carries your name to my ears
from three hundred miles
parched with loneliness
pass me secrets from your lips to mine

Sarah Fenn

Marana

In a mysterious world we walk,
In the "O" of the goddess eye.
Behind the firs she peeps, shy.
Along the snow banks, she drapes her laces.
Down by the river, you may see her traces.
She blows across the lake, icily caressing faces.
No one knows what she knows
About the birds and the beasts,
The trees and the streams.
When night falls in deep blue hue,
The moon sails overhead—ivory, new.
Perhaps you may see her sitting in the dark,
Under the rustling leaves where crickets hum.
Linger there despite your fear
And as you wait, look.
She comes near,
Soft like a breath of mountain air.

Jennifer Sutton

I Love

I love my England, the white cliffs rising steeply
from the sea, a placid English channel that gives us
peace and security.

Henley, the Thames, oars flashing in the sunlight,
Oxford eight striving for supremacy to express and
show a sportsman's view, a happy world, love and
fun for me and you.

A ceremonial parade, gay kilts, bagpipes and drums,
Edinburgh castle. Pageantry and colour, great joy for
dads and mums, as well as boys and girls, which to
me is joy enough. An old romantic, no doubt, but it's
what I like to shout about.

'Tis fyne that I wouldst sit wi ye in a tavern drinking,
meadows bright wi' country green, auld Edinburgh
towne not yet for sleeping. That's my England, the
pulse of a country well worth the keeping.

Now perchance were I to gain my dream,
no smoky vehicles or factories would e'er be seen.
The horse and cart, a country lane, a sultry day.
Ah! That's if only I could have my way.

Norman St. Paul

Pentimento

You sleep in your yellow bed,
washed up by horse-sweat.
Each morning
you are tickled by bristles.

On your sill,
white water is trapped
in glass bubbles.
You can see through them sea gulls crash up in the air,
shattering their orange feet
and falling lightly
down into the brown mud.

Your curtain is skin-coloured, torn, and dripping
sticky, thick drops like tar.

In the corner,
salty sea waves lick your wall.

Anita Danch

But a Lifetime

I have but a lifetime to repay my mother
for the pangs she felt giving birth.
Is that enough?
She was always at my side, rearing me,
molding me into someone special.
How can I shatter her hopes and dreams?
For, I am but a channel
of all the hopes she's ever had for herself,
and she has walked the path much farther than I.
Dream, fly, explore, ask, wonder, love,
even if it means falling, for she is there reminding me
to take notes along the way should I fall again,
never judging my mistakes, just carefully sharing her own,
and in the process healing me with tender accolades.
Can I even think the day will come when she's not here . . .
my friend, my mentor?
But she will live on through me, and my choices
will reflect the truths she so well taught,
for how I live each day is thanks enough
when I have a lifetime of my mother's love.

> ### *Donna Hines*

Playing Soccer in Suits

Soccer is never played in suits.
President Clinton and the Brazilian soccer legend Pele did this on
Wednesday, 15th October 1997.

We all know uniforms of different categories,
but never will a suit be a soccer uniform.
Clinton stressed, "Every child enters this world with a great gift from God,
the power to dream." How can this be digested?

"Every child enters this world with a great gift from God"—
babies never choose whom to be their parents; "the power to dream"—
neither do parents know who their babies will be.

They will have played the soccer in uniforms, but they wanted to give
meanings to Clinton's words . . . with a great gift from God.
The word "gift" alone is denoted by the suit, of which even Jack and Jill
wish to have worn, as nobody wishes to be poor.

> ### *Justin James Mlomba*

Untitled

If I could put to music all the words that I have written
People would whistle the melodies
Carrying forever that special note
But seeing as I can't play guitar, or even beat a drum
You can read it as poetry, or you can start to hum
For, the verses that I write, they all seem to rhyme
So you can put a beat to it, if you take the time
It may not be Top Forty; it may never make the charts
To some it is a curse, to others, it is art
I write it down as it comes to mind
'Cause if I don't, it's gone, lost for all time
I have written verses of love and verses of despair
It's the way I show my feelings and my willingness to care
To open oneself is never an easy task
So take the time to read these words—it's all I'll ever ask
To know the poet behind the pen, whom you may never see
For, Shakespeare I am not, and will never pretend to be
I'm just a man, gifted with many things
Oftentimes I wonder and wish that I could sing
So I could put to music all the words that I have written

> ### *Jim English*

Footprints on the Moon

Translated by Sylvia Mittler

Even within the ice of my soul,
I still feel the sound of your breathing
undoing the world, fiery smoke of burnt-out fireflies.

This evening with the full moon,
the torrents of thoughts contracted, dry, empty,
to bar the escapeway to the past,
for barefoot dreams turn bloody
upon the footprint of your searing decision.

And when midnight comes,
new canyons will fill with blood
and ashes from the burnt-out fireflies
to erase the moon's smile
in your ironic shadow, condemned,
wandered within the skin of the white birch.

Tomorrow, as dawn breaks, you will be forgotten,
sucked into the suffering rattle of the blistered city,
outside memory, outside loss,
insubstantial, shabby exorcism, burnt vestment of no value.

A fine dust from your ashes
will dry up the rivers of transparent blood.

　　　　Avra Tsambis Michailidis

Baby

Hi, Mommy . . . I know you're there.
The way you rub our tummy shows you really care.
Yes . . . I know we're growing and getting really round,
But before you know it, I'll be there in a leap and a bound,

It's really comfy and natural in this warm place,
Yet I just can't wait to meet you face to face.
You know, I hear you talking all the while.
I wish you could see how those words make me smile.

I know in a short time you'll be so proud of me,
You and me on walks for everyone to see.
I promise to love you and grow up strong,
'Cause with a mommy like you, how can I go wrong?

　　　　D. J. Goodman

The Season

The weather, it comes in four kinds of seasons
From the Mater above for more than one reason.
The spring, it unfolds to the beautiful Earth
As the buds come alive like a newborn birth.
The blades of grass push their way through the ground
As the sun reaches down to strengthen their crown.
Summer is welcomed in lands near and far,
Where parks come alive with children from afar.
The lakes are busy with swimming and skiing
Where people are traveling for many a reason.
The beauty of nature has changed now to fall.
The leaves have now changed to yellow, orange, gold, and brown.
The grass has now faded, and flowers have passed,
And the wind makes a rustling noise in the back.
As we turn now to winter, so bleak and so cold,
The Master above showers us with snow,
But the beauty beneath it lies here to rest,
And you ask this question—which season is best?
There's four kinds of seasons—which one could you miss?
Because in each kind of season, we know God exists.

　　　　Fay Beart

The Dreamer

I am a dreamer of dreams,
And through my visions,
My dreams become realities.

I am a student of life,
And through my adventures,
My experiences become lessons.

I am a weaver of words,
And through my skills,
My words become stories.

I am a singer of songs,
And through my voice,
My songs become music.

I am a pursuer of happiness,
And through my quests,
My happiness becomes joy.

I am a maker of love,
And through my creations,
My love becomes spirit.

I am a piece of the universe, and through my truth,
My soul becomes divine . . . and It becomes me well!

Melanie Howe

A Melody of Love

A subtle look is all it takes
to warm my soul, to hold my heart,
and keep it captive from all other's wanting.

Consumed with emotion, an aching need
to have you close, to feel your warmth,
a soft, fresh kiss is all it takes to melt me.

You give me pleasure, give me pain.
I feel a passion that unfolds
each time you lay your eyes and hands upon me.

Thinking of all I want to share,
experience, with only you,
to bond in body, mind, and spirit, colliding.

So, lover, beware, for if you dare
I am yours in all the ways you want and need.
Please say you'll share life's melody with only me.

Sandra Romanelli

The Trap

The trap has been set, but will it work?
I have laid the scent and baited the area,
All there is left to do is to patiently wait.
Yet, with baited breath, I sense her approach.

She enters the scene, oblivious to my schemes.
A shout of glee erupts within me
But does not escape.
Soon my prey will be snared in my gentle embrace.

At the very end,
At the pinnacle of suspense,
She senses her plight and turns away,
Away from my gentle but now empty embrace.

Without her essence to fill my veins,
My vessel begins to crumble from within,
And yet she walks away, now oblivious to my pain.
My trap has failed, and so I shed my humble skin.

Normand Bergeron

Water Lily

O' water lily,
You are so dainty.
They're glad you're not tiny,
And so am I.
Your color shines
Brighter than the stars in the sky.

O' water lily,
You're such a cutie.
You float on your bed
And never have said,
"The world is boring
When the water is pouring."

O' water lily,
You are so fascinating.
You've more admirers
Than the prosperous king.

Wendy Wang

The Final Fight

The twilight in my head
Portends impending night.
Oh, Honey! In the bed,
I'll start the final fight.
I have the master keys;
I'll open your heart.
You brought me to my knees.
You forced me to start.
No need to resist—
The fortress will fall.
Un-clenching my fist,
I'll break up the wall.
Love twinkles on my palm;
This arm is my deep.
You whispered so calm,
"I wanna go to sleep!"
The half light of dawn
Is tickling my neck.
My shackles are torn.
I'll never be back. . . .

Victor Kotelnikov

Ode to Diana

I didn't follow close
Till you came along
You were the glue
That kept the family strong

You showed the world
That you had grace
While you put a smile
On everyone's face

Oh, Diana,
As we now part
You will always be remembered
Straight from the heart

Don Boulding

Death of a Potential Masterpiece

She is a boulder.
The tear of the years scales the stone,
effectively corroding her.
We chisel the surface, molding dead art
like hardened clay
deprived the warm, sculptor hands.

We trouble the material,
no longer malleable,
pondering its possible usage.
It really holds no purpose,
this bleak, impoverished earth,
once the potential of velvet rope barriers
conjuring thoughts of rich antiquity.

The cracks of dehydration,
now veins of dust devoid of liquid life force,
pervade the pale parchment.
The surrounding air is particulate:
dust cells and oxygen,
the frame of stasis.

Megan Watson

The Fear of Death?

Foreboding death,
oh, Foreboding DEATH,
why do I fear thee?
In darkness you embrace me,
in brightness you engulf me.

In the silence of the night,
whence the candle flame burns bright,
you stand before me bare
with anguish and fervent stare.

The hour has come,
my end is near and calm.
Foreboding death,
oh, Foreboding DEATH,
why don't I fear thee?
Maybe it is not thee that I fear,
maybe it is life that I fear.

Unforgiving Life,
oh, Unforgiving LIFE,
why do I fear thee . . . ?
Is death the ultimate of LIFE or
is life the ultimate of DEATH?

Joyce Lim

I Will Always Love You

I will always love you,
No matter what your faults
    may be.
I will always love you
As long as I can see.
With your qualities so fine,
I will always love you,
And you always will be mine.

Lila Hutt

Autumn's Own Heart

As magnificent shades of nature's gold fell,
the earth sighed
with its newly covered ground.

For a moment now, with a longer distance to gaze,
the trees looked barren
and almost seemed de-crowned.

How wonderful are the dreams autumn hides,
preparing for winter
and its cold to subside.
Pause for a reason and notice this gift
of one of Mother Nature's
sensational shifts.

As the fall that surround us
contemplates with itself for what's in store,
the time that keeps on turning
will bless us with more.

So pause for a moment
until nature's new start,
be consumed and be comforted
straight from Autumn's own heart.

Chuck Beamish

Flowering Attraction

A bud slowly sprouting up into
The all-consuming, lustrous light
Delicate in its entirety—
Care and attention must be given
To ensure healthy growth—
A transformation into a gleaming jewel.
A spark gradually developing between
Two people, the dawning of a new day;
Sensitive throughout time—
Consideration and reflection must be shared
For development to occur,
Continuing on its passionate journey.
Blooming unexpectedly with a medley of shades
Amidst an air of fragrance, cherished by all,
The sensuous effect overwhelming,
A sign so strong all-encompassing,
Yet the thorns can be unforgiving.
A symbol of hurt, broken hearts: misunderstanding.
Whereas the essence of the rose will eventually wither,
that of true love shall prevail;
Tranquil and pure, it grows toward eternity.

Nicholas Ma

On the Laundry Day

Laundry shouldn't have been so long
And you don't have to do it once either.
Now there is nothing to put on in drawers,
On hangers, on couches, or on chairs.
So don't accuse me of being obscure or naughty,
'Cause I am so naked.
If you mind, either buy
Something extra for me tomorrow or
Advise me a day
Before laundry.

Mustafa Mencütekin

Untitled

Redeemed by His blood from sin and fear.
Entirely enshrouded by His love, even right here.
Defended from deceptions by relying on His word.
Empowered by Prince Emmanuel in our lowly abode.
Eternal life is granted exclusively in His name.
Merits of His sacrifice all may humbly claim.
Experience the joy of redemption and eagerly share.
Remain forever with Jesus as a royal heir.

Michael N. A. Pedrin

The Flower

I would not have chosen this ground
so barren and hard, devoid of life,
until I came.
But by chance a seed was dropped by bird,
by wind, perhaps a squirrel, I know not which.

My path is to accept what's given,
make the best of it, use the power
of being alive
to grow a flower, nectar for the bees,
scent for all, a thing of beauty ever so fleeting.

Then die but in death, swelling with
the birth of new seeds, ready to scatter.
And start new lives; I know not where,
whether barren or fertile, beauty in a new spot,
life beyond my death.

Norman Ayers

Carrying On

I'm standing here in the night,
My love for my friends the only light.
Alone against my darkest fear,
But I sense all my friends are near.
Only together we face the fight,
Nothing can stop our hearts' might.
With our hearts' strength, the battle's won,
With all our love, we can't go wrong.
And at the crack of dawn,
I know I will always carry on.

Victoria Alfred

Living Room Couch

I fell asleep on the couch in my living room
and dreamed of dreary days.
With a yell and a knife, I woke up from the molasses
that held my soul together.
On subliminal thoughts and high-strung notes,
I took the pen on the desk and ripped the casket open.
With white powdered doves and blue tainted flesh,
I left the corpse of my memories rotten.
Like Heaven and hell, I saw tapestries of pain
and dead baby dolls crumble into innocence.
In murderer's hands, the blood in the sky
covered black birds in the sea.
My eyes became heavy like feathers of hate,
and the acid of love tempted me with lustful language.
And throughout all this pain, no point came to mind,
except that never again will I sleep on the couch . . .

. . . in my living room.

Cherri Low Horn

The Preacher

With the skill of a prize fighter,
He gives his message,
Quietly jabbing away,
Waiting for the right moment
To throw the big punches.

The truth of his words
Rings in your head,
As if hit by a punch,
The conviction in your belly,
Like a set of body blows.

His comic relief,
Like the bell for the end of the round,
A little pep talk
To start you up again,
Ready to receive the next punch.

But this is one fight
You will always win,
As long as you have listened and received.
For, every punch and jab
Brings you closer to the Lord.

Hamish Muir

Outside and Inside

i've broken the walls
between memory and reality

i'm hurt
and thrown away
covered in dirt
wishing myself away

shadows of trees
over closed windows
your heart

i dream outside and inside
of losing you
our sky is empty
close our eyes
while the world cries
for us
outside and inside

Viktor Blanke

Tribute to Diana

Trees, maples, oaks, or whatever,
Are beautiful, as everyone knows,
But no flower is as lovely
As the English rose.

She was so beautiful,
As everyone knows;
She was Princess Diana,
The English Rose.

Everyone loved her,
From everywhere.
We will all miss her deeply,
And we will always care.

Lois V. Welch

Retired

It seems like I've waited ever so long
For this time to come along,
And now it's here, I can see
All patience and hard work had to be.

With so much to do along the way,
There weren't enough hours in my day,
Especially quality time for myself.
Many projects were put on the shelf.

But now that I have time for me,
I still do much but now leisurely.
What once was a chore, now is fun,
And hopefully it has just begun.

A timepiece I no longer wear.
There are no limits, so who's to care
When I come and where I go,
Except my mate who keeps me in tow?

I appreciate the trip along the way
Now that I have made it here today.
Each day I become more inspired
And truly grateful to finally be retired.

Sandy Eldridge

Realia

Neither happy nor unhappy,
the real stands between us.

What can we do then, to explain
that what is palpable is not enough,

that the impression our steps have left
on the green grass means more to us?

What were the streets without them,
and what would things be without hands?

They would be real, but to us
they would be obsolete, and die.

Fini Lokke

The Storm

Quite the storm was she . . .
the winds blew one way,
the waves crashed the other way.
But I, the captain who is me,
kept ship from drowning,
drowning to the bottom of the sea.
The waves were fierce,
the rain was wet,
and the winds were mighty strong.
After awhile, I grew tired
and I couldn't fight anymore.
The ship was about to capsize;
it swayed toward
the vast ocean floor.
But then, Mummy pulled the plug . . .
dried me off and sent me to shore,
where, in my bed,
I was scared no more.

Rachelle Lamour

Lost Dreams

Of decaying buildings on the side of a hill,
Once someone's dream place, now silent and still.
Left alone in disrepair,
A legacy of grim despair.
Dreams abandoned, hopes released,
Established, built; suddenly ceased.
A homestead started, a new life begun,
Reduced to a fragment of dreams undone.

Albert Kildaw

Fate

For one to know is for one to see
No matter how much you try to be
Like a person who knows not when
The person who can always bend
The truth in such a little way
That some not know what to say
But the day will come when they will find
That they can't lie in their own mind
That their destinies are written in a stone slate
That you will never be able to deny your own fate

Nick Robson

Snowflakes

Shimmering snowflakes floating though the air,
Dancing through the vast, open space,
Exploring golden treasures not yet seen by humankind.

A snowflake's desire to clothe open space,
To bring a freshness and harmony to humankind,
To blanket and soothe every emotional crevice,
A temporary solution masking unresolved emotions.

Snowflakes melt, removing the masks,
Revealing emotional pain and scars,
Continuing to explore with the head and the heart.

It is only when we listen to our heart, and
Act with our head,
That all mental anguish will vanish,
Bringing peace to humankind.

Ann Nelson

In My Own Shadow

Yellow leaves, dry and rough, hanging on the branch,
Chilled with breezing winds, waiting to break,
A prime of my youth recklessly beyond reach
Let my past haunted in grief silently speak,
Waiting for the stem withered away in the meadow,
Utmost, I wish to stay in my own shadow.

Doubt of future sincerity in my present joy,
Day by day counsel of truth will testify,
Irritating to my insanity with great annoy,
Nothing but to hope my innocent will justify
That I may no longer suffer in sorrow,
Utmost, I wish to rest in my own shadow.

Those days were gone, sweeping rapidly into darkness,
Still lying to myself those things will be better,
Storming every reverie, leaving hope strangled in madness,
All of my life taste nothing more than bitter,
Fear losing the battle I wish to be a sparrow,
That I may fly and vanish in my own shadow.

Cheng Lam

Musings from a Hospital Bed

Oft' in the silence of the night, I stir from a gentle sleep;
I seem to feel the fleeting touch of a childish kiss on my cheek.
Then memory will bring to me a glimpse of my children fair;
It seems I can hear them whisper,
"Dear Mother, we wait for you here.

"The house seems strangely quiet, the sun not quite so bright.
We miss your smile and bedtime song when you'd tuck us in at night.
When we fall and skin our knees, the pain doesn't go away
As it did when you kissed it better, and we would go back and play.

"Daddy seems so lonely, the smile has left his eyes.
When he thinks there is no one near, we often hear him cry."

It's good to know my dear ones miss me while I'm away,
And every night when lights are out,
I too close my eyes and pray:

"Dear Lord, tho' my days are lonely, help me to be of good cheer.
Help me to merit those wonderful words,
"'Dear Mother, we wait for you here.'"

> *Eve Headley*

Queen Elizabeth II

O', my queen, will you listen to my plea?
Will you dare send your greetings to a poor soul?
How afflicted and sorrowful, my heart is pounding!
At your arrival in St. John, Newfoundland
For the Canada Day of July 1st, Nineteen Ninety-Seven,
Did you see what I saw?
Surely you must know that life is not a piece of cake.
Surely you are well aware that love has no "C".
The throne must be lonesome at time of crumbling.
But you are my queen and you did answer when the phone rang.
Remember, I have always been your loyal subject out of seven.
There was a time when at home we dearly shared your picture.
Oh! What a queen you were to us.
You always seemed to know what to do.
Does God still save the queen in time of need and rest?
Surely the monarchy regime is still the best.
Nostradamus in his book of prophecies mentioned your courage
And exhorted you to show compassion to all of us.
If there was a way I could get in touch with Your Majesty,
Many blessings of God will accompany your pilgrimage.

> *Bernard Beland*

Thoughts from a Canoe

In early morning peacefulness, we paddle in the quietness
With scarce a ripple on the lake.
How great our God who did this make to be enjoyed by us!

We see His hand in everything, the changing leaves; the jay's blue wing,
Pleated pecker in his flight—oh, what a majestic sight
With crimson crown to cap his head!

I think of one He wore instead. It too was red,
Made thus by thorns that pierced His head
When on Golgotha's hill He shed His blood for me.

I am unworthy of such love that brought You from Your throne above
To lay aside Your kingly crown
And to this sinful world come down for me.

Oh, let me live my life for You in everything I say and do
That others, by my life, may see the One who wore that crown for me.

And when this life of toil is past, and I shall live with You at last,
Then I will have a crown to cast to You.

> *Sylvia Weaver*

Attaining Success

Urged on by my ambition, I struggle every day,
In spite of all conditions, to keep my sorrow away,
And all the time I'm trying, with my body and my brain
To labour, never sighing, and some success attain.

Success is not only skill and deeds, it's in the things you do and say.
It's in the person you are each day.
It is laughter and the struggle for a goal,
And everything you need in the shaping of your soul.

I haven't come to glory yet, but there's the hope I will.
I keep going still, because I know that true happiness is only found inside,
And I'd rather be a failure than the one who never tried.

So I tell myself, as I start to smile, that life is good and its chores worthwhile.
So keep your dreams and follow where they lead you
With faith that someday you will reach your quest
Because we work for something better than that which is now our best.

And all the time you're trying, fighting pressures, pain, and stress,
Just remember, before sighing, that you will attain success.

Stephanie Fiorini

Waterlily

Rolling with the ripples but firmly held,
swaying without self-consciousness, without self-doubt,
a face echoed across the water,
brilliant and inviting in the noon sun,
simple beauty rising out from the murky bottom.

When I stare into your core, your dazzling heart,
I am wading through fields sun-deep to my knees.

Pinching the stem, I contemplate, reading truth in the depths,
to pluck you from your roots would make you wither,
turn your scent into stench, force rot.

A miscreant, I return in malevolence:

I'll strangle the chord and expose you to the world,
I'll let you breathe the exhaled air,
I'll sing the songs myself,

and when the dew is licked off your lips in the relentless sun,
and when, withdrawn into yourself, a curling, tightening frown,
I'll float you upon the river,
Entwined, we'll sink together.
I'll drink the waters with you, in vain.
I'll remember the times, sun-deep.

Jeremy Grootenboer

Devotion

Into that silver maelstrom
Women touched divine love at last.
Cling to the sweet breast like a clingstone.
We're born without symbol—
All illogical stories and sick memories,
Day by day getting thick hide.

They came to preach to me: "Everything has another face."
Ready for salvation, put my muse out from this obstruction!
Above the revolt, into the thirst,
I wish to live like a link as a reward for your wound.
If you forgive me, I want to have some reason that's true.
Where's the feast? Why are you so innocent?

We saw the fashion wreckages lie around.
And he burnt out the wings to fly like Vincent van Gogh.
Yes, there's a mistake on our life,
Sometimes it makes us cruel.
But your fearless love will save us—
Love's a joy even while a despair.

Yuko Ishii

Beach

The waves are crashing upon the shore,
I slowly walk the beach once more.
The long-gone sunset over the sea still glows,
The quiet summer breeze softly blows.
The night is young, the tide soon to rise,
The sun has now long left the skies.
The moon and stars glow on the water,
The feeling of presence couldn't be odder.
The prints of footsteps follow me
And forever disappear into the sea.
I start home again, snug in my coat,
Watching the sea gulls on the water afloat.
Good-bye, moon, stars, waves and sand,
Good-bye, cold ground where I stand.
Good-bye to the sea and its beautiful sight
Until I return tomorrow night.

Nicole Van Ostaeyen

Images

With their hands, sculptors awaken
sleeping images in the stone,
and substance is no more a dream.

Poets yearn to feel the pulse,
to glimpse the quintessential core of what is real.
Who else sees the phoenix in the ashes,
the sign beneath the seal?
They shape and sharpen this discernment
on the wheel of words, moulding an image.

I cannot possess the solidarity
of every chiselled stone;
these are not given to all to own
or even constantly to see.

Yet, insubstantial words are always mine,
and for each poet's voice I am an aeolian harp;
when the winds of their thoughts
pluck my soulstrings, my spirit sings.

Sr. Michaela Davis

Everyone Is Special

Everyone is special in their own little way.
Everyone is different, but we all live day to day.
Some like the sunshine, others like the rain.
Some like thunderstorms, others like pain.
Some people are skinny some people are small.
Some people are chunky, and others are tall.
Some people are quiet, some might talk a lot.
Some people are sneaky and some can be bought.
Some people are cute with little curls in their hair.
Some people play dirty while others play fair.
We all may be different, we might know what to say,
But we all know we are special in our own little way.
Some may be rich and always have some cash.
Some may be stingy and always keep a stash.
Some may be grumpy and keep things in deep.
Some have bad days and some might not sleep.
Some may write letters to everyone they know.
Some always smile and never let their thoughts show,
But everyone has feelings, so watch what you say.
Remember: Everyone is special in their own little way.

Sandra R. Coens

Heavenly Father

Father, you've lifted me high.
Your touch removes the sadness
that once had filled my soul.
Your wisdom comes to me,
now once again I'm whole.

Father, the silent tears did fall,
the droplets onto your palm.
You wiped the fear within me.
All fright turned into calm.

Father, strength from you I've needed
to see me through the storm.
Your love like wind-to-sail
brought chaos to a norm.

Father, deep inside my soul
I feel your love.
Side by side we walk now
this garden path called Life.
My love for you is eternal!

Nancy J. Hazel

A Very Perfect Day

I do not need a fancy heart
With kisses and a bow
To tell me in a flowery verse
What I should already know.

I do not need a costly gift
Presented as a sign
That although the days
  have come and gone,
I'm still yours and you are mine.

I only need your loving smile
Each time I look your way
For this to be from start to end
A very perfect day!

Kathy Marleen Harris

My Friends

My friends can be seen
bathing in the dawn,
their clothes torn,
their faces smiling.
They're bleeding.
My friends are fighting in the corner;
they're hugging each other,
passionately avoiding
the affection they feel.
My friends are unusual.
Their eyes are flowering in the night
while they can't sleep.
They talk about fairies
and the beauty one can find
in a man's scar.
And it is an irony,
like those symbols of a wasted youth
suffocating in my hand,
that their dreams are made of feathers,
but their wings are made of sand.

Spyros Hadziantoniou

I Watched the Morning Come

I opened up my eyes ere dawn
And saw a doe and fawn,
They walked along the garden fence,
Soon, into mists were gone

I opened up my eyes again,
And saw the early sun
Start sliding down the mountain side,
Like firelight on the run.

I opened up these eyes once more,
My world was filled with light,
I heard the birds sing morning songs
In absolute delight.

Now I sit here and look upon
This new day that's begun
With wonder beating in my heart
That I've another one
To live with love, to make the most
Of moments that are mine,
Contentment sits upon my knees
While on delight I dine.

Frances Bryan Radford

Loss of a "Lifetime"

I feel so terribly lost
As I no longer can recall the past.
All the memories I cherished so
Have slowly faded away.

I must have loved and lost,
For I have an aching in my heart
And I feel deep down within me
That there is someone
   missing from my side.

Will I ever know again
The "who" and the "where"
   and the "when"
Of those lovely, smiling faces
In the pictures by my bed?

Time passes for me slowly
As I lie here in my bed.
The only joy that I have now
Is that I still know how to pray.

People come to see me
And some of them call me "Mom,"
So why should I despair
When I'm surrounded
   by people who care?

Gemma Leyne

Taiwan the Green

By Pacific's western shore,
Beauteous isle, our green Taiwan.
Once suffered under alien rule,
Free at last to be its own.
Here's the basis of our nation:
Four diverse groups in unity,
Come to offer all their varied skills,
For the good of all and a world at peace.

John Jyigiokk Tin

Daze

Weather away into sweet nothingness,
Dry my soul until it shrivels.
Blow the hot winds this way
And bug me no end with drivel.

Tell me stories about your mischief.
Tell me why you ever left the nonsensical world,
Closest people to my heart,
Little fairies on the grass

Little swords from a seed
Rising up through the weed,
Rising up to the sun,
Stained: red and green and brown.

Lift me up into your arms.
Place me high up in a tree.
Try and fear away my calms.
Then laugh heartily at me!

Take me to a wooded park.
Tell me why the sky is dark.
Tell me why my life is screwed.
Tell me I'm your favourite mood.

Noellé Desouza

Convolutions of the Mind

My brain pounds and swirls as if filled
with the creative thoughts of all men
since the birth of eternity.
As a boiler reaches critical point—
with no safety valve—
so the confines of my mind
totter over the abyss
between genius and insanity.
Do I alone experience this turmoil
or does all humanity by its limitations
become enmeshed in this relentless cauldron;
that will not let them go?
Is this what sets man apart,
leading him to the stars
or eternal perdition?

Phyllis M. C. MacKinlay

Tonight Hunter

May my words comfort you.
May they hold you close tonight.
May they keep you warm and safe from harm.
May they protect you from loneliness.
Who will tap upon your door tonight?
Who will whisper, "Let me in!"
May these words silence that voice,
For these words are made of love:
Love that is eternal and strong,
A love who mourns in your absence,
Who shivers for the warmth of your arms,
A love with ears that ache to hear your soft voice
With its powerful and comforting tone.
May my vow of love that I placed upon your finger
Reach out into the night and take hold of dreams,
Dreams your weary head may rest upon
While you lay so far from home.
May my prayers for dawn
Wake you softly.
May my calling voice lead you home to my awaiting arms.

Mindy Le Blanc

Brotherhood

The airfield is still and quiet tonight,
So until dawn, when aircraft spread their wings,
I shall rest, sleep sound, and also be
Quite happy to live in a country of things
That are essential to complete man's dreams.

For tomorrow our dreams may be shattered,
And taken on the wings of war,
All broken, lost and scattered o'er the sea,
There goes our peace, and when the battle's o'er
The sun rises, the start of a new day is here.

We look out over the frozen land
And realize that the work of God's hand
Has been destroyed by the hand of man.
God told us it would not be good
To fight amongst our brotherhood.

For God has set the time and place
For His return to Earth, our home.
Then all mankind shall see His face.
What shall we do when that time comes.
Shall we be worthy to be called His sons?

David Noseworthy

Blessings

Today I walked within the wood;, it was a glorious sight.
The maples, oaks, and beech glittered in the light.
The forest floor was covered with a tapestry so grand,
Of gold, orange, brown, red, and green covering the land.

The geese flew overhead in a sky so hazy blue,
Honking to their loved ones to follow where they flew.
Silently I stood listening to the sound of geese,
Enjoying all the beauty, revelling in the peace.

Deeper still I wandered.
A crack I heard so clear.
Turning about, I thrust my eyes
To see what might be near.

A sudden wind, a brush so close,
It brought a sudden fear.
A deer leaped round in front of me,
Turning back to peer.

Let's give thanks to God above
For such a wondrous day
And for the blessed life He gives to us,
In each and every way.

Joyce Dunn

First Love

My heart feels a void and a pain it's never had.
It once was filled with love and happiness,
Now it's only sad.
I would have given you the stars in the sky
And made your dreams come true,
But your love for me just wasn't there,
But I guess I kinda knew.
You will always have a place in my heart,
And you will be there 'til the end,
For you will always be my first true love,
And now you will always be my friend.

Michael Desmarais

Love Is in the Air

*Dedicated to my wonderful boyfriend,
Pat Irvine*

The sun is shining,
The flowers are in bloom.
My love for you
Is just starting to break through.

There's love in the air.
It comes with spring.
It's the time of the year
We hear wedding bells ring.

Your words so sweet,
Your touch so soft,
I know it's love
'Cause I'm already lost.

You see the first robin
And make a wish.
I still remember mine—
It was our first kiss.

Pam McLellan

Dreams

When restlessness causes night's despair,
And fiendish creatures do appear
To battle sense and create fear,
Subconsciously I struggle there.
Peacefully, she sleeps on.

So real, I battle fierce and long,
Determined to out-last the throng
Of demons with their eerie song.
I will protect, for I am strong.
Safely, she sleeps on.

I wake with beaded brow and moan.
Exhausted, worn, I stretch and groan,
For I had vanquished all alone
While she lay resting, quiet, prone.
Contented, she sleeps on.

Then daylight comes and morning breaks.
She stirs and murmurs, then awakes.
Her smile dispels the awful fakes
Of devils that had made me quake
While she slept on.

C. Cornelius Harnett

True

Only when we see the world
As it was, is, and shall ever be,
Can we hope to find
True death

And only when we see ourselves
As we were, are, and shall never be
Can we hope to find
True life

Richard Evans

Untitled

Across the county
and by the sea,
around the river bend
and beneath a tree,
you'll always be there for me.

In my dreams,
in my sleep,
in my imagination,
I see you there with me.

But then I see reality,
and it finally hits me:
You're not there for me,
you're not there with me.

So now I see the county,
the sea, and the rivers,
finding myself beneath a tree,
but there's just a slight, tiny difference:
You're not there with me.

Claudia Salcedo

The Sea

For some, it is to take the helm
So gallantly and set the sails
Across a shimmering sea,
To call the cries, command
The cannon fire, and grasp the railings
Looking on beyond the forging prow.

For some, to fire guns down there,
To glory in the roaring dark
Across a shimmering sea,
To bleed in blood and scream
In pain, perhaps, and wrench the cables,
Confronting tar-wood and each other.

For some, to hoist the ensign,
It spreads and sparkles true and clear
Above a shimmering sea,
To pipe the tunes so proud
Amidst the day and look from mast that
Nearing from afar the foe they see.

For some, at last the home shore's sight,
Loved coves then cliffs drift nearer by.

Alastair Matthews

A Bird Flying through the Air

I look around, and away up high
I see a bird flying by.
Now it's gone and time to time,
I think as if I were just flying by.
It'd be magical,
It'd be fun,
I would just take off and be on the run.
Then I'd land I know not where,
Then I'd be human and all aware,
But a bird flying through the air.

Charlotte Mckenzie

Scared

As he runs across the enemy lines,
his heart sinks to his stomach.
The sand he runs upon sticks to his sweat.
He doesn't know if he's there yet.
He falls to the ground, his chest in pain;
he sees his life flash back again.
He wasn't ready yet to die,
he said to himself in the black coloured sky,
and as his spirit drifts away,
another soldier dies today.

Amanda Di Maggio

Untitled

Arriving through misty eyes of resilience,
short, crystalline memories
like silk, honey upon our fingertips
protrude from impaled emotions and shattered dreams.
Distances have changed our views.
Enigmatic ambitions bind us to the clock
with brief laughter, unfolding for insecure pretences.
But anything can be made to look sinister,
like your naked moonlight reflection
or the sweetness of your breath.

Jase Botting

Rage Within

Rage,
An all consuming control,
One that binds fragile threads of insanity,
One that unravels the mystery of the human condition!

Black out,
Rationale no longer is an option,
Let alone even a thought.
Come with me down this road of childhood torment!

Easy to blame others,
Less easy to take a hold of strings of self-control.
Combine fear with stupidity,
One may dance in the shadows of my beings!

Most of your life, you walk as the missing link,
Blocking out your past, struggling with your present,
Uncertain of your future,
Knowing only too well the dynamics of your success.
Grow the hell up, you weak, little man!

Frank Arthur Gode

His Shadow Joins Us as One

As the sun rose, dusk arrived to end his days.
We now feel empty, with many voids.
How dare the sun shine on such a sad day!
But . . . life goes on;
One must pick up the pain and continue.
Although the move is slow, it's forward.
Whether together or alone, we all share his shadow;
We are strength and comfort for each other.
Stand tall when you can,
Falter when you need,
For now Martin is a shadow of memories.
Just remember I'm in that shadow, right beside you,

Patti Steenhuisen

Spook

A white cat with big yellow eyes
Who was not old, but very wise
Running up to you, then racing away
Wanting you to come and play
Making you laugh after a hectic day

Disliking a new kitten entering his space
Hissing and growling he would give chase
Thinking he was a human, not a cat
Swatting at me for pointing a finger and talking to him like that
Turning away, leaving me to look at his back

Behaving as though he were a child
Pouting while the kitten ran around the house wild
Putting his paws up on my leg and reaching up to me
Wanting to me to pick him up and hold him, you see
Showing the new kitten this is where he wants to be

Giving me nothing but joy and love
Living now in a cat Heaven above
Easing the pain with which my heart sears
Having to put him to sleep after seven years
Loving him so much, put me in tears

Darlene Billett

Mother and Daughter

In a joyous way, at heart, it is sad for a daughter and a mother,
Their lives on Earth were far apart, but each one knew the other.
They shared the same ideas, holding out their arms with love,
And now they are together in the realm that is above.
The daughter of the world had strength to overcome her fear,
The mother of the world was wise, her heart was pure and clear.
The both of them together, always helping out the poor,
A mother and a daughter, with much suffering to endure.

Theresa and Diana felt the suffering and the pain;
Still, they always had a smile and a love that will remain.
They have shown the female side of God with dignity and pride;
They will never be forgotten, they have left a mark inside.
The mother and the daughter opened windows that were locked.
They were humans, just like us, that's why the world is shocked.
They have shown their good example, their devotion, and their love.
Now they can help us twice as much from the realm that is above.

Noel Harpur

Burning Light

All that I reckon, right or wrong
and all the feelings, weak or strong,
can make a heart survive or lost, for I believe there's time for all.

The hour has come to wake and cry
for righteous days and hopeful sights,
and everything a man deserves in our
small world, lost paradise or else we call,
deprived of ornaments that soul needs most.

Life is too short to be ignored for wealth
and power, pleasure or fame, as vanity is the source of death
that lures one's senses sink in depth—
instead of vivid mood for love and care—
strength of human soul's nourishment, I'd say.

No words of comfort I dare offer; only a knife
I plunge into the earth, becoming light, becoming
sense against the deadly kingdoms that rule the Earth.
Hear the voice of thousand years, brought by the winds
to what I write. Hear mankind's mourning, but overall,
hear its echoed cries beyond the mighty crystal walls—
"Peace, freedom, no more lies."

Virginia Protopappa

Humans Communicate Best

Scientists say that humans communicate best.
Philosophers think we know all the answers,
But we don't.

Doctors conclude we're smart because of the size of our brains.
Priests say it's all a gift of God,
But it isn't.

Humans don't communicate well at all.
We're always fouling up our sentences,
Breaking hearts, and messing minds.

It's only because we have thumbs that we have technology.
Dolphins could build computers if they didn't have flippers.

Sometimes it would be best if we had no words at all,
Just communicating with thoughts and feelings.

Because then we wouldn't always mess things up,
Hurting people because of our mistakes.

> *Betty R. Macrae*

A Page of History

His hands red with blood, and sweat upon his brow,
He was the first to breathe, rest, and weep
On the land we now call our own.
He built a home and a barn and nurtured the land.
Nearly a century has passed since he has rested his weary hands.

Due to his blood, sweat, and tears,
We now live on his land, in his home, and our cattle in his barn.
His barn battered with age, leaning with the wind's every gust,
His land overgrown with shrubs, no longer fertile as it once was.
Tears stream down our cheeks as we think of the history our land keeps.

He will survive in photographs and memories,
But the blood, the sweat, and the tears he shed have dried.
As the wind blows, the barn will fall,
The land will wither and die, the home will rot with age,
And we will turn to the next page of our history.

> *Kerrie-Lynn Kossatz*

Orchid

I cannot have the sun and an Orchid
In the same picture.
The stem and plumage creature will bend away,
While the other will slide into the wavering horizon, dragging the day.

I cannot hope to experience the night
When a fog of fatigue rolls over me like the sound of wars,
When I rest like a hole in the sky, dulled to its surrounding light.
But a black hole is simply a part of the universe choked on its own stars.

The tree is powerless to retain its most blazing garments,
Born in the fall, when things are waning.
For, at their most explosive, they are thin like spiders' silk
And fall to the rapture of a windy squall.

On the ascent of sun
Or assert of moon,
I wish to observe every fruitful hour.
I hope to emerge with the blossoming flower.

Oh, Orchid, you bend to the sun, not to me.
I enter the sky by watching my reflection in the sea.
I see the larks with a softened eye.
I meet the ground by resting my face against the sky.

> *Jamie Gregor*

Two Little Girls

Those two girls were a gift, in fact,
Tossed over our wall in a gunny sack.
That's blonde "Grace," slimmer of the two . . .
And next to her, "Sister," the one that is black.
Grace landed on her nose;
We could hear her wailing her woes.
Sister had bruised one small, soft ear.
Our mother cat came running in fear.
Felina, our cat, had also arrived
with a crush of kittens . . . in a bag!
Felina became to the pups both nanny and mother.
She washed and soothed them and allayed their fears.
And here they have lived for these four years . . .
Happily, with their mother, the cat.
The dogs were perfectly reared and trained.
Climbing low tree branches is their game,
Locally earning a good bit of fame,
A unique mixture of dog and cat.
We love them truly, just for that.

Laura Bateman

Listen to Your Heart

Are you used to listening to your heart?
Aren't you? My honey, hurry up!
Did you do enough to keep it working good?
Ask yourself; don't spare any food.

Can you tell the beating of your heart?
Can't you? I'm sorry you are tied.
But force and order you to pull yourself together.
For God's sake, be confident of this forever.

How are you doing? How do you feel?
Pardon me, indeed, it's not my deal.
No problem, I'll say I started just to live.
Hopefully, I love, but heartily believe.

Christina Babadjanian

Far from Nowhere

Far from nowhere,
Where the blue bird sings,
Joy bird tweets,
And in the distance bells ring,
There is a little boy
Lost among the trees.

The boy hasn't got a care,
Not a care in the world.
Blue bird comforts him,
Puts him to sleep.
She'll always be there,
Have a shoulder on which he may weep.

The animals are his friends,
Trees provides him with food,
Birds provide him with nests,
And roosters awake him from his slumber.
This is his home, a land of magic:

A world that neither you nor I could understand,
A world of love and laughter, joy and cheer,
And it can only be understood by magic.

Bara Mann

Sonnet to Diana

Standing with the common people
awaiting our final good-byes.
Tenor bell tolls in the steeple
as I join the millions who cry.
Procession of Cortege is long.
Air frozen silent and still
except for the horse hoofs' sad song,
as they carry her up the hill.
The mourning crowds will regress,
but the legend must remain.
A girl, became our Princess,
and Diana was her name.
Do good deeds—do your part.
Keep her alive in your heart.

Kathleen Boyd

Shadows

My weary eyes that are sore,
stare upon the open door.
And there I see a figure black,
I sense, I feel is staring back.

My body numb, full of fear,
listening for what I may hear.
And in the shadows, a movement falls
back into my old cracked walls.

Are my eyes playing tricks on me,
or is that what I really see?
Crawling slowly, closer now,
beads of sweat drip from my brow.

Shaking, I peak around the frame;
to my relief, everything's the same.
Turning to jump back into bed,
a jagged knife cuts me dead.

April Hughes

Tribute to Georgia O'Keefe

Man and woman,
we become each other.
I harden—you soften.
I grow rational,
you, sentimental.
We are one,
both male and female.
We compromise in tolerance,
amenable to influence,
willing to change.
The red and yellow
that become orange.
We age,
rugged like mountains
full of ocean
surrounded by desert.
Our character grows with struggle
in extreme climates,
creating new dimensions
of humanity.

Judith Kent Fawkes

Old Things

Old things I sell.
From the cellar I take them,
From the loft,
From the secret places
Only to me known.
Old books I sell,
With underlined sentences inside;
With them I achieved nothing.
Old, petty things I sell.
As for me, they make me sad,
Because they wake memories in me.
As for you, they will be
Just as new.

Vladimir Gavrovski

I Found Someone

I needed a shoulder
To lean on today
Someone to listen
And know what to say

A shoulder so strong
Yet gentle and kind
With no limitations
Reading my mind

Somehow that shoulder
Is always there
At times when most needed
My times of despair

Someone is walking by my side
Watching over me
Putting a smile back on my face
Helping to see things differently

I think I found a special friend
Who's never far away
I think I found an angel
And I'm glad he's here to stay

Shirley Anne

Control

lying together weary,
halfhearted conversation
flapping lazily
around us,
shrugging off desire,
I think I've mended myself, but
you reach out,
trace the bones of my back,
broken clay and shells
half-buried under flesh,
fingers over
palm pushing muscle,
your nail catches
and describes an arc in pale fruit,
blood through milk to the surface,
and when you stop,
I bend
like a flower in your shade.

Martyn Iannece

A Life without Love . . . Is a World without Love

The want to be with
someone with a warm soul,

To touch a special
heart with one's mind,

Feeling near as a breath
but being miles apart,

Speaking but one word,
and the night so restful,

Touched with one and
their potential for being,

Feeling of knowing
someone wants to listen,

To know a mutuality
of spirit, based on acceptance,

Let us not postpone the
time when we can love
another completely for
himself, as he is.

A life without love . . . is a world without love.

Lynn Ann Gloade

A Mother's Love

For all those nights you lay awake,
Forgave me for all my mistakes,
You always knew just what to do,
Your prayers were there to guide me through.
The hugs meant so very much
When a young boy needed his mother's touch.
As my life changed, you stood by me
Through the sorrow and heartache that were meant to be.
Your strength always there, just a call away,
To say, "Thanks, Mom," now I'll have a good day.
Some things changed; I see pain in your eyes,
But I will never leave your side.
I will care for you, and my prayers are strong
From a giver who taught me right from wrong.
You were there for me; now the time has come
To say, "I love you, Mom" . . . this is your son.

Sandy Meloche

My Only True Love

Little by little, it's hard to say
What love has in store for me today.
It is somewhat different for me to believe
When it is time for him to leave,
For when my true love is here to stay,
I'll thank the Lord for that special day.

Before my love had come along, it took
Some time for him to belong,
For he belonged to someone, not me.
I'll have him forever if I can make it be.

I'll love him forever, for I know it takes time.
But I know in a while I will make him mine.
I'll love and keep him forever in my heart.
Together and forever we will never be apart.

Karen Turpin

The Thoughts of Man

The thoughts of man
are blended into today's society,
contrasted like the sun and snow.

To compare them is only the beginning
and to know them,
a different meaning.

For, an appearance is only an image
so misleading.
Loneliness and bitterness can be hidden by hatred,
beauty by vanity,
and sadness by mistaken love.

To compare our thoughts
is an experience of life in itself,
a part of living and loving,
but most of all
a feeling of being.

Karen Proehl

You Came

I walked the sky empty-handed
Without the affection my heart demanded.
I slept at night in scenes of black;
I was a train that had fallen off the track.

But then you came and opened my eyes.
There you were with no disguise.
Now my thoughts are no longer blue,
Because all I think about is you.

I thought I was blind but I was just in the dark;
All I needed to see was a little spark.
I thought I was deaf but I just wasn't listening
To the voices in my head that were screaming.

But then you came with the key to my heart
To help me on the journey I was about to start.
You brought the colour into my dreams,
And now I know what love truly means.

Martine Legault

In Memoriam

A rosebud that early bloomed,
So carefully for the throne groomed.
A beacon of hope, the morning light,
The helping hand, the loving heart,
Never receiving what's her due,
Gave unselfishly, made the old new.
Child of a broken home,
Consort of a cracked crown,
In her lifetime a legacy:
Angels now mourned one of their own,
For she was an angel of mercy.
It rains . . . it pours . . . and never clears.
Heaven cannot hold back its tears.
The senior amongst her peers,
Tutor in courage, dispeller of fears,
The humblest amidst the meek,
The strength and comfort of the weak,
The ever windblown golden mane,
The sideways glances, the blue eyes
By tragedies clouded, which reflected her inner pain.

Samuel Ferenji

Tomorrow, What Will Be?

Last year his newborn feet didn't stand
And in his crib he cried,
Until his mother held his hand
And showed to him life's stride.

Last month he climbed the school bus stairs
But felt not that he fit
Until his brother exchanged glares
And found him where to sit.

Last week he cried, he wasn't paid
Through his fault he was fired,
His tears were shameful and afraid
Until by his dad, hired.

And yesterday his bed was bare
No wife caressed his heart,
Till his sister taught him, how to care
And showed him where to start.

Today he fell on merciless land,
Perhaps tripped by a stone?
But, no one helped him up, to stand
Now, he was all alone.

Ghila Ashtor

Survivors

Look at this evergreen . . .
With hardly any roots,
Perching in a deep crevice
On the slope of a rocky mountain.
Year after year, it points to the sky,
Majestically standing straight and tall.
By all odds, it ought not to be there.
Look at it—it is a point of inspiration.
The perfect Christmas tree,
It should be spared.

Look at this lonely Shasta daisy . . .
Growing in the crack of the cement parking lot.
Tall and slender and reaching for the sun,
It ought not to be there.
Yet there it is, exquisite in full bloom.
It brings forth much character.

Are we not more than flowers?
Are we not more than trees?
We, too, must reach for God:
Contemplate, concentrate, and be a survivor.

Marguerita Pilon

To Be Seasoned4775

Spring of my virgin wish,
Romanticized versions put to the test.

Summer of my virtuous lust,
Fulfillment a never ending quest.

Fall of my unerring trust,
Laughable to think me blessed.

Winter of my constant regret,
Join me in my cynical fest.

Jolie-lynn Trenholm

Cry of Nature

I am a songbird.
Rejoice in the mirth of my melodies.
Journeys I have taken,
Tears of joy and sadness,
Propel me on my way.

I am a stone never moved from position,
Revelling in my social history.
I am whole where I stand.
If you move me, I may crumble
Into nothingness.

I am tall and majestic
Speaking through my beauty.
I appeal to your sense of nature.
Woodcutter,
Do not cut me down!

Assumpta Padden

Clouds

Fluff in the sky
Incomprehensible
They're something sensible
Clouds beaming by

Atmospheric anomaly
Up there so high
Bizarre in their shape
I wish I could fly

Dark and they're ominous
And they will live
For me there is death
Suck in the clouds
With one massive breath
Still streaming by

Jason Belanger

Dreams

Advocates of unpredictable dreams,
Drifting like clouds over the hills,
Let us merge with the life stream
That cares for our every whim.

Dust of memories
Stretches as far as one can see,
Keeps still-unexpected mystery
Waiting for the unattainable to be.

Lost inside soothing frontiers,
Primary thoughts nonetheless,
Knit together secret desires,
Left with nothing but emptiness.

New bounds to reality
Through uncertainty lead the way;
No more fear, doubt, or scrutiny
In awe of resisting destiny.

As young birds fluttering their wings
Endlessly repeat attempts to fly away,
Thus remain dreams, seemingly senseless,
Yearning for the search of happiness.

Dominique Aguessy

Second Born

A thunder roll, a lightning strike,
Dark brown eyes pierce a stormy night.
I tuck you in, sweet dreams I pray—
Little motorcycle sounds ride the Milky Way.

You toss and turn; it's three a.m.
Wisps of blonde hair, like a shooting star,
Headlight the journey across the hall—
Little motorcycle sounds ride the Milky Way.

Like Neil Armstrong, I step upon the moon;
A heavenly smile shoots across the room.
Sleepy-eyed, I pick you up.
With tiny arms, you hold on tight—
Little motorcycle sounds ride the Milky Way.

A picturesque sunrise overhead,
Long, silk eyelashes eclipse our bed—
Little motorcycle sounds
Bridge Heaven and Earth.
Good morning, son!
How did you sleep last night?

Darryl Patterson

Jumbled Celebration

Strange voices whisper through the night,
Curious eyes stare in the dark
As the light drowns out the feeling of loneliness
And transforms it into something of happiness.
Prayers unheard,
Still voices proceed to exclaim the disfunction of truth,
Disfunction of life and love,
Lonely as the day closes and turns into night.
Forgetful the Mind,
Full of absently remarked confusions and thoughts,
Passing through a valley of sin:
Travelling the road of danger, death refuses to let go.
Life is caged in nothingness, as we are in our bodies.
Memories forgotten as the mind deteriorates,
The fading of the sun reminds the mind of yesterday,
Torturing, enlightening,
Never again to be filled with passions, alone, scared,
Afraid of the unknown as it awaits our arrival.
Forgive all sins, we are impaired;
We are . . . Human.

Holly Mills

Butterflies . . . Wings of Flight

With my gaze, I see a sight
Of color and movement in the light
Floating, playing with such delight
Winged flowers are in flight

Scattering in directions without course
No reason for shame or to show remorse
Their purpose must be served both day and night
Winged flowers are in flight

Changing seasons come, their time to end
Now my heart aches to see them again
To feel spring sun with warming light
Winged flowers are in flight

Brian Hornyak

Variations

The swan is weeping a glazed lute on the icy waters.
The Emperor's ceremonial boat is the absurd time keeper
That is counting the disappearance of the quick sands.
The hunter's melting eyes are sinking deeper and deeper
While wolves are biting the indifferent celestial lights.

The virginal doe is lost on the Eve of the feast day.
The moon is showering the Earth with wounded light.
Weeds are laughing in the terrestrial progress.
The burdened doe is silenced by the returning storm
When mirrors are crying at the unwanted vigil moving past.

The clouds are touching the sky above the fading doe.
The flowers of the fungi are drinking from the celestial mist.
The hunters have broken the glass of the starched silence.
The Moon is sifting the absence of noise in the distance.
Hurry . . . hurry . . . the paths are melting . . . the paths are moving . . .

The paths are chasing the ill-fated . . . the hunters . . . the doe. . . .

     Mariana Zavati Gardner

You Are My Heaven

At times I refer to You as Mother Nature.
When the going gets tough, I blame You for my troubles.
If I want to masquerade as a sophisticate,
I refer to You as Master Time
although I realize that every creature
in Your sun-veiled valleys is unique.

If I but challenge one of Your humblest stars,
countless others adorn Your dark space with lights
from here to the end of time, too distant for a man to reach,
and You remain unknown for what You are.

Things are developing and growing on Your authority.
There isn't anything that's nothing, only what's meant to be.
We look for our beginnings far and wide,
yet our own brains can call us blind,
for Your world is without limits like Your greatness
that we can't grasp with all known the unknown in it.

Yet in moments when my time seems at a standstill,
I somehow sense Your presence in every inch and atom
of this mysterious Universe.
Indeed, I sense You are my Heaven, You are my Earth.

     Veneranda Ciemins

I Lit a Small Candle

I lit a small candle late last night.
It flickered so slowly but burned so bright.
The spirits told me someone was to pass away
And that I should sit quietly and pray.

I lit another candle this morning at early dawn.
It only flickered brightly a minute or two—things were beyond.
A soul had departed to Heaven above.
The spirit had been there with God's pure love.

I lit the third candle to say my prayers
To also talk to God, he's the one who cares,
A short trip through time when your mind is in need,
It's time well spent, time to receive God's precious seed.

I'll light another tonight, just at the last of daylight.
It'll be for my Aunt; she left with God on a morning flight.
The great eagle spirit came in silently and took her soul away.
Now an eternity with God is where she's going to stay.

I'll light another candle tomorrow morning at sunrise.
It should flicker slowly and burn mighty brightly.
God's help is always there, we just need to pray,
And life is but a whisper of time, on Earth where we stay.

     James B. Souter

She Sits Majestic

Nestled in the Owings Mills of Maryland,
Amid the wonders of a literary State,
The National Library of Poetry sits, majestic in suite fifteen thirty-nine,
Inspiring young writers to explore their somnolent thoughts,
Ordering poetic verses to come to the fore, from topics of
Nature to romance, even futuristic, any style or subject will do.
Anthologies are born from this cultural mix.
Largest poetry organization in the world, we laud you!

Libraries everywhere should overflow with your works.
Immense knowledge in them is found, from poems written in iambic
Pentameter, to those with
Blank verses, penned with brilliance of the writers,
Rhythms and
Rhymes,
Yuletide themes and

Off-rhymes clothed in
Figurative language, personified like actors on a stage!

Priceless organization, the persona of an
Optimistic man emanates everywhere and
Affects us into poetic gear: enthusiastic Howard Ely, excellent try!

Norma Williams Seymour

I Need Your Love

I can't leave you alone, I am so in love with you.
No words can express, make me feel wanted and loved,
As I am feeling for you.

I feel for you, oh, loved one,
I really do.
I am so much in love with you every day, make me feel
Wanted and cherished. Make me yours tonight.

Girl, I try to make you understand that I want this love
To be real. What about us—I'm in need of your love—what
About us? On and on we go.

Oh, love me, baby, because I know just what I need,
I'm in need of your love.
And what about us making love
Till the breaking of dawn?

Oh, cherish my love, I want to love you, now and always,
Till the break of dawn. I want to love you. I'm in need of

You, in need of your love, as much I need your love.

Angela Wilkinson

Memories

Memories are in our hearts,
And in our minds as well.
But the way they mean the most to us,
Is through the sharing that we tell.

Memories are happy times,
Of special scenes untold.
The loved ones within our lives,
Are remembered and unfold.

Memories are sometimes sad,
As life is meant to be.
The way we've treated others,
Accepting experiences that we see.

Memories are sometimes hard,
When to forget the times being rough.
But if we lived those days with courage,
We can say they were good but tough.

Memories are not just thoughts, of family and friends.
It's our own individual ways of life, that God for us intends.

Memories have come, and others; they will go.
But most important to leave for others are the actions that we show.

Sally Saunders

A Thought in the Dark

We often ill-use and even abuse
The things that we're given for free.
A keen sense of touch, we don't think about much,
Or the fact that we're able to see.

The music we hear with a sensitive ear
Is taken for granted as well,
And how do we choose our food if we lose
The power to taste and to smell?

Have you ever thought, some people can't talk,
And then there are those that can't eat,
And before you complain of your bunions,
Just think of the ones without feet.

So, if you think fate and misfortune
Have kept you from making your mark,
Consider if you lost your senses.
You'd be just a thought in the dark.

Malcolm Benjamin

Death Wish

She embraced winter cold, was chilled by summer sun.
She was different, different from anyone I had met before;
She found death alluring and life, at best, a bore.
A weary sojourner on planet Earth,
Longing for death ever since her birth,
Blest with health and beauty, intelligence to match,
Potential swan unwilling to hatch,
She grew up, married, and went to work,
Yet joy she seemed to shirk.
She sought professional help and the experts all agreed:
"Nothing's seriously wrong," labelling her "bad seed."
She prayed to God, but her heart wasn't in it,
When, finally, she reached her limit.
She slit her wrist and welcomed death,
Whispering, "Peace at last," with final breath.
I wonder why we couldn't reach our friend?
Is this the way it had to end?
How can we help others dealing with such strife?
Such a sad little tale of a sad, young life,
Such a sad little tale of a sad, young life.

Jean Clayton

A Leap of Faith

Swirls of lavender, smoke, and grey,
Like a cloak engulf the day.

Heartfelt sobs, breath-filled gasps,
A mother's pain—how long it lasts.

This world hath many paths and turns
Yet the "straight and narrow" for her son she yearns.

"I am the light; to thine self be true."
Just words? Just psalms?—Who are you?

Then tear-filled eyes begin to see
The calm, the quiet, the serenity.

The clouds disperse, the sky is bright.
The burden upon her soul takes flight.

Peaceful sighs now contemplate
The comfort from her "leap of faith."

Karen Corney

Why?

WHY IS OUR LOVE FORBIDDEN
LOCKED AWAY, FOREVER HIDDEN
A RAFT ADRIFT ON STORMY SEAS
A TREASURE CHEST, WHO
HOLDS THE KEY
A LONE DOVE SOARS THROUGH
CLOUDY SKIES
NOT KNOWING WHERE HER
FUTURE LIES
DON'T SHED THOSE TEARS
THE LOCK'S UNDONE
THE DOOR IS OPEN
WE ARE ONE

Belinda Egan

Cliché

there is a man
behind the eyes
of a working-class woman,
and she will scratch out a song
for him
to give him something to move to,
but he,
with his selective step,
passes through her mind like a fly
through a fly-wire screen
in summer,
and this man,
beating against her eyes,
tries to explain his love for her
with bunches
of discounted flowers,
and he knows that he'll be victorious
if he ever
runs
away from her

Mathew Hamilton

A Blinded Army

For one reason they had come.
For one reason they will remain.
For years it has been this way;
Why not then can we hope to sway?
The mother, the daughter, and the son,
Must they always have to come?
Look and see, toward each other,
So mean they are to one another.
Can they see what ought not to be,
Or must they be whom they can see?

Standing on a stage so high,
I see that naught and other make nigh.
Though many, many people who could,
They never, ever understood.
The thought that hit them in the face
Came in our open, empty space:
The workings of the common slob,
Shown here as a faceless blob,
Often moves away, does bob,
Thus in the manner of the Mob.

Mark Knezevic

Easter Day

Families unite,
Sweet delight
In memoriam of
Nature's Emporium.

Daffodils and tulips bloom,
Summer warmth is coming soon.
Bunnies will go hopping
Through farmers' new cropping.

Morning dew glisten,
Freedom song listen;
Finches, robins, and jays,
Warm and brighter days.

Special regard prayers,
Christ Lord bares
Reminders of sacrifice,
Spirituality heals nice.

Pastel colours are bright,
Sneak baskets at night;
Eggs in decoration
For the young generation.

Laura Jane Culhane

Eden

Cut apples, cut apples.
Poison and seeds.
Cut apples. Cut apples.
Hot, twisted trees.

Root-weary orchard.
Strangled neglect.

Rough. Juiceless. Ragtime.
Pollen suspect.

Savage nests.
Skeletons appeased.

Leaning like
Van Gogh,
thick hands on
thick knees.

Worm bites.
Aphids.
Amber-broached bees.

Cut apples. Cut apples.
Poison and seeds.

Peter Ohler

Time

Flashing before our very eyes
Slipping out of our grasp
We reach out to catch it
But it slides through our fingers
Eluding us once again
Dreams are not impossible
Prove your point
Because no one lives forever

Ellie Nguyen

Enchantment

The water ripples onto the dam
as I lie on the bridge watching the clouds.
My soul is embraced with calm and harmony
as I lie there watching the Earth follow its course.
A frog passes by, hopping with the joy of freedom,
turns to me and it seems that he winks at me!
I smile, for today is a special day,
A day on which the world takes a new form.

Then a droplet lands in the water,
then another and another.
I realized that it was raining.
I stood up and turned to the field.
It shone like a million jewels
and it smelled like the most beautiful perfume.
I stood there looking at my surroundings,
my hair wet from the rain,
the field smelling, and the creek glistening.
Now I leave this place of wonders.
As this special day passes by,
I say good-bye.

Andrea Lothrop

My Home on the Street

Worthless and useless and all alone,
Deep in despair, life's expressed in a groan.
Oh, why can't I be someone special to me?
An existence that's wasted, no relevance I see.

It hurts to be nothing, a truth deep within.
Even death can't release my torment of sin.
Plagued by the odds that are stacked against me,
Irrelevant and useless is all I can be.

I'm trapped in a prison with nowhere to go,
A belief that's embedded so far down below.
A mistake from beginning, I started out wrong.
My will wouldn't die, so life's fiber grew strong.

Silent cries in the darkness are heard from afar.
Only warmth filled with love can heal every scar.
This love I'll not know in my cold concrete space,
For the streets of the city don't offer much grace.

For, life's core has been damaged, rejected, and bruised,
My foundation for growth so weak and abused.
So if this is the start of who I'm to be,
My question to God is . . . why did you make me?

Jan Ricci

Heavenly Dreams

Last night I went to Heaven
But only for a while
Once again to see your sweet face
Once again to see your smile
You said, "Come walk with me, child"
As you took me by the hand
Together we strolled, through God's promised land
As you turned to face me, as you gently kissed my brow
I awoke with the morning light to the reality of now
An angel you have become watching over me
And every now and then I visit Heaven
I see you in my dreams

Darlene S. Morgan

Life

No matter our wealth, we all need good health,
And friends, many or few by what we do.
If on our way we wish for a good day—
Give each person respect as we also expect,
When we toil with might, yet things not right,
But find real stress, with all in a mess,
We must just sit down, not fret and frown.
Think to turn effects around, so we'll have found
We can conquer the strife; that's life!

Annie L. McLennan

Emulsive Hand

The hand is on the table,
clouded over in black mist.

Scraggled flowers
(pick your favorite variety)
are falling limp over the brass urn;
their image inscribed on its fat belly,

And soon to become . . . black!

Paws of the family manx, flex,
and twist into view; pouncing

On walled shadows; becoming Halloween.
Your floral tribute blends

Into ghostly midnight,
shedding petals to pile like snowflakes

On winter's photographic negative
and yielding to its illusive,

Emulsive hand

That marks out is territory
with a toothy grin,

Glowing white heat inside the forbidden orange
of Jack-O-Lanterns (rotting into black).

Ronda L. Wicks

In the Garden

Come walk with me, my dearie,
In the garden, oh, so cheery,
Where the roses and the lilies are in bloom.
Together we will wander
Among the flowers over yonder,
Where the sweet-smelling fragrance fills the room.

I will pick a pretty flower
For my lady of the hour,
And place it gently in her auburn hair.
I will tip a glass to toast
The one I love the most,
And may we continue to be a loving pair.

As the raindrops gently fall
Among the flowers short and tall,
And as they gently bow their heads from falling rain,
May we return again some day
To this land so far away,
And maybe in the garden stroll again.

Velma Peters

Believe Me

In me liquid pain pours
Freely without tears—
Deep, profound wells of sorrow
Disbelief, disappointment.
Where? With whom? When?
Can I open the flood gates?
Dark, long nights, cowering
Doubts bridge the edge of me.
Reality is, pain is, worry is.
Churling waves wash
The pain without freshening water.

Did I not give you faith?
Profound . . . hope, trust me.
I know liquid sorrow, dulled not
By time but increased until the cup
Overflows. But I am here, carrying you,
Carrying your grief. Trust me. Have faith.
Faith is strong. All is right as I want it.
Now, believe, trust.
I am with you all days.

Marilyn Stoppleworth

The Wedding Pledge

It is with my best friend,
I herewith pledge;
To share this life together
—Till death parts one from us.
Share we will
Not our laughs, our joys,
But also our pains and tears;
Not only our ups and highs,
But our downs and lows as well:
Our successes and our failures,
Our trials and our tribulations.
It is with my best friend,
I herewith pledge;
Through all the hard and stony paths of life
You will never again, my love
Take that path alone:
For I will always be there at your side
—Till death parts one from us.

Lal Kumar

The Ride . . .

Her hair blows in the wind
like the mane
of the wild beast she's astride

And his blows, streaked with grey
from the wild life
of the machine he rides

both horses, flesh and steel,
bring rumbles to the Earth
like thunder from a distant storm,

both so different
yet so much the same
as freedom rides from life's daily chains

Kurt Jackson

Elephants

Large and gentle
great bodies
saunter through
the hot horizon
Vivid pinks, reds
frame
their faded gray skin
Trunks sway
to and fro
to and fro
to the beat
of their
heavy
heavy
feet
Massive
ears flap
to the music
of the
savannah

Zoe Simpson

Word Things

Words are flat things,
Walk-upon-a-mat things,
Throw-them-in-a-hat things,
Use them back-to-back things.
Words are scary things,
Very, very, wary things,
Sweet-tasting berry things,
Fingers-through-your-hair things.
Words are cutting things,
Time-to-go-a-nutting things,
Smelly, old, fish-gutting things,
Sharp-edged, jutting things.
The words I say,
The words you hear,
Are never quite the same.
They're only words,
They're Memory's birds,
And experience is to blame.

Cheryl-Ann Lloyd

The Search

There has to be more
What is it I am searching for??
My world is so confusing
Always myself I am abusing
Looking for a way out
I scream and shout
Alone at night I cry
My body aches to die
But I continue the fight
Forever choosing between wrong and right
I must be strong
Must search for where I belong
I search for you my friend
But always come to a dead end

Daniel Hogan

A Journey of Time

Through oceans of time, on a ship of immortality,
I keep my watch.
Past whirlpools of despair, to an island of hope,
I set my course.
After a lifetime to the power of eternity,
I arrive.
I arrive at a world that no longer resembles
The one in what is left of my dreams.
In a form of nothing, I wander.
Through a labyrinth of faces, I seek only one.
Give me opportunity,
And if withheld from it long enough,
I'll break free,
Twice as strong,
Twice as wise,
More eager to cheat death,
Embrace life,
And find that which allows me to do so.

Robyn Hemington

The Forgotten Fisherman

Alone he sits, tired and forgotten by friends
that passed and family uncaring.
The fisherman of long ago whose youthful hair,
old man's white and bright blues eyes now clouded,
his smile that used to light the world has grown dim.

With misty eyes he searches the horizon for ghost ships
and faces past, for laughing eyes and lips that kissed.
And through the mist of his old man's eyes, he sees
the face with sparkling eyes and smiling lips—
the smile that frees his tired and lonely heart.

With outstretched arms he slowly rises
and walks toward the ocean's edge.
The water seeps into his shoes,
but he does not feel cold or damp, only the blinding
tenderness for his mistress and love: the sea.

As she gently surrounds his now-frail body,
He smiles again and whispers,
"I have come home to rest, my love."

Michelle O. Russinow

From a Kids with Cancer Nurse

The children arrive at our door,
Not feeling well and looking poor.
We give them chemotherapy and pray
That they may live to run and play.
Some go on to grow and thrive,
While others do not have the drive.
We use everything in our power,
But some will only have an hour.
We give them unto the supreme being's care,
For he will know to judge them fair.
In the end we hope to be
A sound support for the family.
We too have feeling and feel lost,
For tears, sorrow, and sadness are our cost.
But as we grieve and hope for no more,
Another sick child arrives at our door.

Diane Arndt

The Big Day

As we put on our dresses for the big day,
We still cannot believe it's only hours away.
Later, when we are at the aisle and the piano starts to play,
I still cannot believe it's the big day.
Everybody looks so happy, yes, including me,
I almost have the best seat in the house,
Though everyone can see.
I look at my mom; there's a tear in her eye.
I look at my grandma; she begins to cry.
I feel an urge to burst into tears;
I haven't felt this way in years.
As a tear rolls down my face, I wipe it just in case.
I look at my sister; she's crying too.
I tell my mom through my mind, she's just as bad as you.
When Pastor says, you may kiss the bride,
I feel a burst of happiness inside.
I had a lot of good times in a lot of different ways,
But this is the best out of all of my big days.

    Sarah Stewart

The Woman Child

A child reluctant to forsake the world of fantasy,
A budding woman, hands outstretched, to grasp fate avidly,
Consistent in inconstancy, bestriding both her worlds:
While surging on, she's looking back! Dear, wistful little girls!

She's so confused, her mind, her deeds! Emotion rules her life.
"I will," "I won't," such turbulence brings anguish, fear, and strife.
But, child of mine, take heart and cheer, this format's all too true:
The paradox of little girls was old when Earth was new.

Soon, fledgling dear, you'll bridge the gap, at first uncertainly;
Your faltering initial step will come painstakingly,
Then eagerly you'll stand erect, adventure beckons, draws
An ardent, joyous, new recruit, impatient for a Cause.

    Margaret Power

You're a Sad Child

You say you're sad because you're sad.
Others say it's psychic. It's age. It's chemical.
Go see a shrink or take a pill,
Or you can just hold in your sadness like a faceless doll.
You need some sleep.

But you can't forget your sadness.
It's still there, and you must tell them about it.
Your sadness. Your confession.
Whatever was done to you the day of the party,
When you came inside flushed with the sun,
And you said to yourself in the bathroom,
I am not one of the popular girls.

My darling, when it comes right down to it,
And the lights go out as the storm rolls in,
And you're trapped in your little body
Under a warm blanket in your own bed,

And the lightning strikes but it does not hit you.
It ignites the doll beside your head, or else the floor, or else the pillow.
And you realize none of us is,
Or else we all are.

    Nicole Axworthy

A Day of Love

Come, take my hand and play.
The misty morning's still unplanned.
An oak-rope swing and a step-stone brook await
The childish laughter of two full-grown.
Come, play along with me on dewy, flaxen fields this morn'.

Come, take my hand and run.
The sky's autumn murky-rained.
Laughing, dripping, wet-wool sweet, we'll share
Memories in the summerhouse retreat.
Come, run again with me and watch afternoon autumn rain.

Come, take my hand and walk
Upon the cool, rain-soft sand.
Indigo gentles copper's light, as sunset
Sleeps, soothed by the night.
Come, walk awhile with me and hushed-whisper smile.

Come, take my hand, then go.
Make no promises, I'll not demand.
The midnight sky's a starry blaze and there will be
More perfect Indian summer days.
Please go, my friend, for now;
Perhaps soon we'll spend the day again.
Lois Elaine Wright

Prayer for My Boyfriend

Holy Father full of grace, bless my boyfriend's hands and face.
Bless his hair that never curls and keep him safe from all the girls.
Bless his hands so big and strong
    and help him keep them where they belong.
Bless his eyes that shine like stars
    and make him love me more than his cars.
Bless his lips that are divine and always keep them close to mine.
Bless us later, oh, Lord, so we may marry.
Bless his kids that I may carry.
But if he's not there on judgement day,
    I'll know he went the other way.
Then I'll give the angels back their wings,
    golden chains, and everything.
Just to show what love can do, I'll go to hell . . . 'cause I love you.
Pat Archibald

A Precious Gift

As I gaze into my son's eyes,
I see a forgotten youth and innocence.
I see an unquestionable trust.
I see an everlasting love. . . .
He is my beautiful son.

I remember the growing pains.
I remember the vulnerability.
I remember the sensitivity. . . .
He is my beautiful son.

He is there with a comforting arm when I am saddened.
He buckles over with laughter when I tell a joke.
He shares his ideas when he thinks I need help.
He shares the joy when I am celebrating. . . .
He is my beautiful son.

As I sit in my kitchen looking out at the river,
I wonder—what did I ever do to deserve such a precious gift?
He is my beautiful son.
Diane Heans

Yesterday's Tomorrow

When I first looked in your eyes,
I felt something I couldn't deny.

I felt something down so deep,
I felt it even in my sleep.

I've never felt a love so strong,
I kept it buried for so long.

But then I realized that it was time
To show the way I felt inside.

Every time I'd see you, I'd say, "There's no way,"
And I regret it to this very day.

I love absolutely everything about you.
I love every little thing you do.

When I'm in your arms, I wish to stay there forever.
Every second we're apart I think about us together.

When you hold me in your arms, I breathe you in so deep.
I wish that forever your heart I can keep.

Sometimes we're so close, other times we're so far apart,
But no matter how far, you'll always have my heart.

April Eldridge

The Struggle for True Love

My heart cries out in the dead of night
For one chance at a love and a hope there might
Be an angel watching from the heavens above
That might grant me the wish for a love
To last my whole life through.

But, alas, once again my heart has called out in vain,
And so shall that deep loneliness always remain.
For, a love to me shall always be the untouched wine,
And alone my heart and I shall dine
On the thoughts of a love so rare and forgotten
That my God has now and again forsaken.

But dare I continue the fight that rages within?
For, to do such, where shall my heart begin?
For, the feelings of love grow unbridled and untamed.
This is a love that is not to be shamed,

Or how shall it end, or dare I even try?
But as for my heart, it will always cry
For the two it loves and shall always hold dear.
For, if untried or forgotten, there shall always be a fear
Of what might have happened if I would have dared
And pursued that love, and not have been scared.

John Heinrichs

Being Lonesome

Here I am just sitting here,
So sad and lonely and not full of cheer.
As I am watching people go by,
I am sitting here all alone with a tear in my eye.
Just waiting and watching the sunny sky,
I hear many cars and trucks as they go by.
As time goes by, will this day ever end?
I am so happy now; I hear at the door, Jesus,
My Master, my Saviour, and my Friend.

Inez V. Fitzpatrick

Children

The record is playing
The clock is ticking
I hear the laughter
Outside my window

Little boys and girls playing
Singing nursery rhymes
With no care in the world

Children are so innocent
So beautiful inside

Children are protected for the present
But protection won't keep them
forever

All children grow up
They face their future
No longer as children

Tara Singh

Forgotten

The music is peacefully playing
While my head rests after the day.
A single carnation smiles at me
The bloom of stillness, but cheer.
Day start, day finish,
Back to my room I lie,
Look around,
Outside the clouds make creatures
Only seen by children,
Seen by me long before.
I see an eagle soar
Through my far cloud castle.
I realize I haven't been there for so long.
I close my sight of my problems
To see there stands my domain.
There stands me, a little princess.
Inside I play, dance with the enchanted,
Then little pixie friends prance around me,
Laughing, leaping:
The world without worry,
The land of dreams,
The heaven of a child.

Elizabeth Buri

For Sara

Beyond the leaf
at the edge of the tree,
in the surrounding air,
it is there. . . .

I am touched by its majesty,
the rhythm, and the hum. . . .

Somewhere inside of me
it takes a hold and

I feel the water behind my eyes
begin to well. . . .

Bernard Hart

Waves of Darkness

Night has come at last
the end of another day.
As waves of darkness envelop me,
in endless hope I pray.

Please let tomorrow bring happiness,
to this lonely heart afraid.
Please let tomorrow bring love,
an end to my long wait.

This is the tomorrow of my yesterday.
My prayers unanswered, still I pray.

As waves of darkness envelop me,
I dream of tomorrows that yet might be.
But I know these tomorrows
    will never be,
As waves of darkness envelop me.
        Bernadette Scollo

Untitled

You move in my mind
like a half-remembered
fairy tale
a dream
that was never quite caught
on waking
You slip in and out
of my thoughts
weaving your essence
through the strands
of my mind
Never leaving
never staying
always there
forever gone
My heart moves
eternally with you
        Margaret Stokes

Your Dream

Along the path of life,
We've dreamed a lot of dreams
Of happiness and hopes on high.
How wonderful, it seems.

It would be nice to see them happen,
One by one anew.
How exciting it would be,
To have your dream come true.

A dream, we know, is the wish
Your heart has stored away,
Though for now, it isn't real,
May come along one day.

Uncertain as all this may be,
Have faith in what you do,
And keep right on a'wishin'.
Your dream just might come true!
        Jimmy Embro

Silent Angel

The winds have changed, the year's gone past;
the autumn night has come at last.
I feel the chill. You keep me warm.
I close my eyes . . . your soul, I form.

My silent angel, come set me free;
you've got your wings—please fly for me.
My loving friend whose heart's so strong,
I need you now—it's been too long.

I miss you more than words can say;
I feel your presence, but you've gone away.
My gift from you, I hold so tight;
It guards my doorway through the night.

My silent angel, spread your wings;
please guide my path to what life brings.
My loving friend, don't watch in fear,
for you're my shelter from what's down here.

I don't understand; I'm still confused
why God chose you, your life refused.
An empty heart in the past four years,
I'm growing strong, but still shed tears.
        Allison Setterfield

Connections

Burning images smouldering in chaotic minds,
Whispers spoken in hushed tones echo away.
Unknown secrets held deep in many souls,
Troubles forgotten by the ones who lament.

There lies a desire to need and to belong,
A crazy search for fulfillment and destiny.
Clarity disappears as soon as it is grasped,
Leaving only confusion and despair to comfort.

Love flows like the blood in your veins;
It both empowers and sustains your existence.
To be in love adds definition and purpose;
It is a part of discovering a mystery of nature.

To be apart from your caring partner
Makes one struggle and feel incomplete.
You know something is truly missing
Even on your best days as a loner.

However, the cycle of life continues to spin,
Finally connecting the loves for good this time.
It was only a brief respite of pain in a lost reason,
Soon forgotten with that passionate kiss.
        Curtis Hettinger

Hurt

Out in the cold rain or a warm summer day,
Lady, I think about you in a very special way.

Here in the darkness, I'm lying all alone,
Always thinking to myself, when is my baby coming home?

I wrote you letters, but they never made the mail,
Took my possessions, and I put them up for sale.

Here in this coldness, I'm crying alone,
Always thinking to myself, won't you call me on the phone.
        Troy Adam Killam

Who Is

Their plight was simply to survive
And not to perish where they lie
With no food or shelter, on they strive
The anguish growing in their eyes

These are the starving, for them the world is cold
A world filled with an abundance of riches untold
Who is responsible that they may grow old
It is for all of mankind to know and behold

Henry Overholt

Me

Sitting by the fire,
Mind in a rage,
Trying to get out of this god-forsaken cage.

Fits in my mind,
Getting all confused,
Can't tell if I've been taken or used.

I want to win this fight,
I want to go far,
But I can't do it sitting at the end of a bar.

Living my life,
Going day to day,
It just doesn't match up; it just doesn't pay.

Sick of all the lies,
Sick of all the battles,
I face all my problems through the bottom of a bottle.

It's not what I want
But what I'm going to do.
Can't you see me now? It's what I'm going through.

I think I see the light.
I think it's the end.

Toby Young

Ireland—Scotland

Sometimes when I'm talking, I'm asked if I came
From Scotland the Brave, for my tongue sounds the same
As that from Ben Lomond or Bonny Dundee,
And folks tell me often, "You sound Scotch to me."
I tell these fine folks it would fill me with pride
To hail from Sweet Afton or banks of the Clyde:
But I'm really from Ireland, the country next door,
Och! Dinna ye ken? Och! Macree 'us ma stor.

From Ireland to Scotland is not very far,
Especially by ferry, from Larne to Stranraer:
From Scotland to Ireland is but a wee trip,
Indeed you can sail on the same little ship.

The Scoti from Antrim went over the sea,
They loved Scotia's scenery and settled for aye:
But we stayed behind with the shamrock's wet dew,
And we drove out the Danes by our king, Brian Boru.
We seem so alike that some can't tell between
The Tartan and Thistle, the Orange and Green.
So, if you are wondering, be puzzled no more,
To Ireland, sweet Scotland is the neighbor next door.

Robert W. Sproule

My Nephew, Benjamin

God called his guardian angels
To search upon the Earth,
For just the right parents
To welcome Benjamin's birth.

"He will not live," the doctors said.
This caused us all to grieve,
But his angel knew God's plan,
Benjamin would have a short reprieve.

Despite his weak heart and lungs
He grew and smiled with all our love
His sister sang "You Are My Sunshine"
While God prepared for his place above.

His mom and dad took lots of pictures
And taped special memories too.
Five months just went far too fast
To say "Benjamin,
   we'll always love you."

It broke our hearts to hear the news
That Benjamin left us all.
Cradled in the arms of his angel
He is now God's little doll.

Linda Payne

Husband

A husband who is loved
But sees that he's bugged,
How can you tell him
That all is not dim?
For, husband, open your eyes and ears
That we are near.
Come closer and don't fumble,
Because we all stumble.
So, husband, you're loved
But not bugged!

Simone Smith

The Passing of Time

A small class we were then;
And smaller now we are.

Some managed here to stay;
And others moved so far.

We've lost a few; they've gone ahead.
The good die young they say.

But look around; what do you see?
We've managed here to stay.

Time has a way of creeping up
On all of us you see.

It's not just him or her, you know;
It's you, and you, and me.

Use every moment that you have,
And make the most of it.

For we don't know how much time
Each of us will get.

Eric R. G. Oickle

The Lonely Tear

My life is torn apart by one;
My love for her is equalled by none.
Such beauty is yet undisclosed
For many a year: Has she dozed?

I know not how.
I know not why.
I must tell the truth—I cannot lie.
I love her true, though does she I?

My life is torn apart by one;
Her love for me, I hoped I'd won.
I love her true, but she, not I.
A lonely tear I think I'll cry!

Benjamin Brooker

Child

The kid after wedding
The kid for be wetting
The kid for night troubling
The kid is produced after night kissing
The kid for happiness
The kid is learning good and
Bad things from the world
Are you a God?
No
You are learning how to act
In the world

S. Gopala Krishnan

Let Me

I could walk,
I could run,
If you wouldn't keep me back.
I could move,
I could grow,
If you wouldn't hold me down.
I could soar,
I could fly,
If you wouldn't push me behind.
I could live,
I could love,
If you would let me.

Jodi Ingram

The Season

Winds are blowing,
Leaves are rustling,
Animals scurry to find cover.

Days get shorter,
Clouds become thicker,
The smell of snow is near.

The birds are hungry,
Chimneys bellow with smoke,
Frost carpets the fields.

The Season . . . Autumn.

Manuela Boutilier

The Christian's Calling

Because of our freely given salvation
We must go and teach to our nation
Christians detest abortion
Because it's man's distortion
Take it to prayer all you who care
Love in action
Brings the Lord's satisfaction
We are all on His team
To bring God-given self-esteem
In the comfortable pew
We Christians win very few
God does not limit us
Yet we worry and fuss
We have the answer for the junkie, thief, and prostitute
As well as for the lame, the blind, and the destitute
As Christians we must more than just exist
For we have the calling of the evangelist
If we are lukewarm the devil will swarm
I pray that those who do listen
Will be sold as a Christian

Douglas Robinson

Feline Friend

Cat to man as man to God
I cannot be as God to God,
But as man I understand
To do his will rests in his hand. . . .

Fuzz ball to caress, near hugging her to death,
In this she does protest, feeling innards pressed.
Furry feline beast, ferocious to the mouse
Or territory breached, her domain our house.

To other furry stranger, meowing she does glare.
Fur arched foreboding danger, chance alien beware.
Can I forgive our cat when chasing this or that
Knocks over flower vase so focused on her cause?

Bad luck if it did break her guilt, I feel the ache,
Knowing from the clatter something is the matter.
Runs to hide from blame, dreading angry glower,
Adam felt the same as with Eve did cower.

If I forgive our cat, this lowly, little critter,
Can God forgive his man or remain forever bitter?
He sent His only Son in mercy to forgive us.
He holds us to His breast, his tender love to give us.

Vince Pallier

The Dog's Soul

How can you say that a dog has no soul?
If you own one, you know it's not true,
For when he looks with those lovely brown eyes,
His very soul is looking at you.

No heart in this world is as loyal as his,
No human has his patience.
He lives just for you, you are his all:
To obey, stand guard, and come at your call.

In Heaven, there must be a place for a dog.
He has earned it, God bless him . . .
To be there beside God.

Blanche Powell

Peaceful is the Little One

Peaceful is the little one who lies there fast asleep.
Peace is what you make with a friend when an argument causes you not to speak.
Peace is what you feel in your heart when you show kindness to all you meet.
Peace is what you should be able to feel, day or night, walking our city streets.

Peace is looking upon each person you see with a smile that radiates love
from your face, looking past gender, race, sexual orientation, and religion,
understanding we are all part of the human race.
When peace does not exist in countries where cruelty and terror take
thousands of lives, how can our conscience ever find peace when our world
leaders determine who will survive?

When illness overcomes the body, peace is waiting beyond death.
For, eternal peace is what we pray for when we lay our loved ones to rest.
Our souls cry out for peace as we mourn their passing.
We feel anguish and heartache knowing our memories of them will be everlasting.

Inner peace does not come naturally when emotionally bound by those who have hurt you.

Replace torment and anger with forgiveness and love.

Peace will fill your heart; your life will begin anew.

Lin Dressler

Treasuring a Well-Spent Life

Years long ago, I laid my head on cold, dry sand
Close to where the seashore gave way to the ocean,
Stretching out my frail form, facing the star-filled skies;
The sound of waves gently breaking on pebbled shore,
The pale moonlight glistened over the restive sea,
And the balmy breeze caressing softly my face:
At age nine, I thought then, life must be so precious
To possess jewels like these.

Now I, past forty, stare at my weathered hands:
Tasks that they've done etched the marks of demanding dues,
And wearied strength, sapped by promises left undone,
Still prodding the heart to desire for one more blow.
And rising to heave this aging body, I dreamed
Of that moment when in my youth, I thought of this hour,
Far from the gently breaking waves on pebbled shores,
Treasuring a well-spent life.

Severino Enopena

Freedom Is a Word

They told me I was lucky when I was young,
You live in a free country unlike some.
I wondered for many a year just what these words did mean,
Not drinking water from a stream nor having skies clean,
Not gathering foods from forest, for those doors are closed,
Nor walking alone at night or to march for opinions opposed.
Don't step on the toes, for the violence did silence those
Who strapped themselves to trees
When the delays they caused were increasing the fees.
The contested view winds up being the arrested
To appease the few who own the world,
Making freedom just a word, sad to believe the lies you're told,
That politics should be about economics
So that it provides lush lining of pockets.
Wealth before Health is the call of the day,
So another sick dollar we spend for this way.
Know better than I, the rulers say, I speak for us another day,
One where people look at the sky and cry,
Where the need for clean air leads many to despair.
Leaders are trusted in employ, with our lives 'tis not yours to toy.

Anita Carter

My Angel and I

When we're living, we're giving.
When we're daring, we're sharing.
When we're bold, we're cold.
When we're not, we're hot.

My Angel and I are trying so hard not to be aggressive from the start,
But it is hard when we have to protect ourselves
Because there is only us and nobody else.

When we open up and let our guard down,
We have to make sure there is no negativity around.
As far as we are concerned, negativity can stay on the shelf,
And positivity will reign over everything else.

If you are positive in everything you do,
We'll open the door and let you through.
Don't feel you can always share our space
Because we need time to relax, unwind, and escape.

My Angel and I will always be together as one.
We'll play life away and have plenty of fun
So if you care to join us along the way,
Remember it can only be for today.

And if you look closely you will see my Angel
    that guides and travels with me.

> *Jaye Low*

Portrait of a Predeceased Poet

A vagabond wrapped in velour,
Velvet under touch,
Without any sense of smell,
Making my arm hair stand on end:
Do I have to die to have my poetry become genius?

Filthy hands applaud to haste,
Which stain their now-empty plates,
Constantly looking over to see you nod a sign of approval,
While exploring the female aspect of placing nail polish
On chewed finger nails.
And from time to time I'll take an interest in current events.

> *Jerry Grymek*

A Daughter's Prayer

Parents are a blessing, for there will never be two
more important people in my life than my parents.

God gave you to me, and me to you, with only one purpose:
That we would love each other, and I couldn't love you more.

My mother is my best friend and more.
She has never judged me, hurt me, or criticized me.
She always has an ear to listen and a shoulder to cry on.
She has a never ending love and a bond that can never be broken.

My father is the strongest person I know, and I admire him for it.
There is no other man that can compare to my father.
His wisdom, his smile, and his heart of gold
Are qualities that I've only seen in him.
My father would do anything for me and expect nothing in return.
The thing I love most about my father is the way he loves my mother.
Because with a love like that, I know I'll always be in his heart.
I am "Daddy's Little Girl."
Dear God, bless my parents.
Keep them safe, healthy, and happy,
But most of all, God, don't ever change them.
I love them just the way they are. Amen.

> *Dana Montgomery*

Imagination

In a meadow of soft, repelling memories,
A spring of water trickles down a wall of rocks.
Peaceful whisperings linger in the trees,
While doves fly gracefully in a flock.

Laughter dances among the willow's leaves,
Yet crickets chatter to break the silence.
Grass and dandelions sway in the breeze.
Echoing waters scream in defiance.

A whippoorwill's melody pierces the air.
A light envelopes the forest.
Last peek of a sun with flare,
An owl beats his wings with zest.

Inspiring scents of wildflowers waft in the meadow.
Faint lights blink in the clearing.
Lush green lands stretch miles with an iridescent glow,
Daisies, buttercups, and violets tremble while jeering.

Refreshing and peaceful all around,
Inside is where it is found.

Kelsi Serena Mehrer

A Mother's Gift

There is this place I know of
Go to it
When you feel beaten
For it is a comforting place
Where nothing can hurt you

Go to it
When you have failed, for it
Is a believing place where
You are everything you've ever dreamt of being

Go to it
When you are weak, for it is a strong place
Where nothing can make
You seem less than what you are

Go to it
When forsaken, for it is a devoted place
Where you are the only thing that matters

A place that is your sanctuary
A place where you are an entity
A place of worship
A place in my soul

Nona Irvine

Smack

The force of the blow separates the lip;
blood flows freely down his chin,
marking the clothes like teardrops.
The fury escalates—counting won't help now.
But it wasn't the hit that hurt,
only the fact that it ever happened.
He tearfully pulls away,
never letting her see him succumb.
She can no longer do any more damage.
They are lost from each other forever.

Robert Beach

Lights

Throughout my life there's always been
a guiding light along the way
to keep me on the proper path
so I will prosper, as I go.

I've lived in cities for sometime
and watched the flashings with no face;
expressionless—so cold and dead—
a big computer, underground.

Too long—I've tried to find a source
to give them meaning, then I swept,
and started greeting strangers, yes:
experimenting, in my cause.

I soon discovered hungry eyes
responding to a lot of friendly touches:
and so let the sound waves mix,
to see what happens, who believes.

I get responses just like that,
and people everywhere are nice.
They come from all around the world—
to share the light within their souls.

Todd Goyetche

The Image

Today I looked in the mirror
and saw, with some surprise,
a stranger's features in the glass
staring at me with my own eyes.

"Can this be me?" I wondered,
I look so different to me.
The wrinkles, the worried brow, the grey,
is this what my children see?

Or do they only know their mom
by how they feel, not see,
not noticing the changing flesh,
just knowing the inner me?

Alice Church

Depths

I had a witch read my palm.
She smiled, "You won't last long."
She laughed away
Into a lucid fog: my skull, my genius.

You rely on pathetic piety,
Grasping your straws. . . .
Did you ask to be here?
Did you not?
Do you doubt your own existence?
Do you hate everyone else's?

Her line is sleek;
Her form is mean.
Die with me then . . .
In a bed of opium,
A bed of fellated corpses.

Kevin Charman

The Sentinels

Silent sentinels standing,
Two stone gate posts
Bearing witness
To the passage of time.
The silence is deafening
Where once people laughed,
Cried, worked, and played.
Fields where crops once grew,
Abandoned now—
Tangled with weeds.
The only reminder of where a
Farm house proudly stood,
A pile of stone—
Once a strong foundation.
And two stone gate posts,
Silent sentinels standing.

Betty F. Goodwin

The Byzantine Scribe

Shearing my shiny hair
Into short steps,
I tried to plunge
Into the new world.
Severing my ties with the old magic
Turned me to a crone
Bled of will, bright plumes, and angles.
I wish to turn back—
To a rock, to be a step,
Emotionless with durable strength.
Can I risk being mutated into pillars
Of salt with fragments of vision
Of redemptive homelands,
Or an eternal witness of wheels
Cruising the conscience of the future
In a world of virtual reality
Seeking images
    to comprehend the present?

Elzy Taramangalam

Maturity

I'm coated in candy—
sweet, urgent.
I think of nothing else.
I'm happy for a moment.
I'm green, longing and lost.
Thoughts of indiscretions and betrayals
all wrong, head spins.
I'm giving candy,
trying to soothe,
if only for a moment.
I want to be coated in candy again—
simple, sugary, fast—
but candy has turned to earth—
green and moist,
happy and content.
Candy taste has turned sour
until the Earth revolves again.

Marla Herritt

Autumn

Autumn has come—I have watched for her lately—
She who has eyes
Like to the faces of little blue asters,
Quiet and wise.

I saw her hair that the goldenrod watches
Wave all day long.
I heard her voice in that burning red maple,
singing a song,

"I must be happy," is what she was singing.
"Swift the days roll—
Vain were those days, but to fill them with color
Bright from my soul.

"Brave must I be to face winter's destruction,
Hiding all fear—
Let me with merriment strengthen my courage
While I am here."

Margaret McCurdy

No Sympathy

I don't want any sympathy.
I just want respect for being me.
This is too hard to seek, you see,
Some respect just for being me.

Life is one long, never-ending road.
Most people treat you like a dog.
Life slaps you in the face at every turn.
What can I do to make it change? Learn.

You must be pretty or bright, that's right.
Yes, you may have to sleep alone at night.
No, that just doesn't seen right, so fight.
Life sure can bite; it isn't right.

I sit inside myself all the time.
I'm like a prisoner on a shelf; what a crime.
God, help me get out of this rut in time.
If I can't escape, I'll freak out at any time.

In ten lifetimes, most people can't live.
I say they still can't experience love.
Love comes and goes and comes and goes.
Some of them treat it like changing clothes.

Lou Ann A. Phillips

Serenity

Early morning, dew kissing my feet
An orange glow on the horizon
Mist rising from a mirrored lake
The call of loons, permeating the silence
Serenity

A row boat cascading through still waters
A quiet cove to contemplate life
The stirring of animals, awakening to greet a new day
Untouched wilderness surrounding me
Serenity

Tranquility of the heart, to be one with nature
Enjoying the riches of this great Earth
Experiencing a sense of oneness with the universe
A place to nourish my soul
Serenity

Linda Forrest-Castonguay

Ode to the River Nile

Swept away by the breath of God
We sail past fertile valleys kissed
By your soft, flowing waters of life

Veiled women wash pots in your changing currents
While children frolic in your cool, alluring form

Against your soulful shadow
Soothing sounds ring from distant minarets
Calling our crew to unfurl colorful carpets for prayer
While water buffalo and Nubian goats graze
Over green fields in gratitude for your abundant grace

Daily life softened, put to sleep by the sweet
Spell of your beguiling charm

On wings of exalted air we witness
Deserts, mountains, fields on fire
For centuries nourished by your ebb and flow
Forever singing your same sweet song

Through our Captain's eyes, we enter your enchanted
Feminine form and see in your ancient
Innocence an infinite wisdom
Deeper than the eye in the pyramid's chest

Teressa Asencia

The Carnal Man

As a child, free from guilt and innocent,
I read God's word; it was His intent
To keep me in the spiritual realm,
With me in mind, God at the helm.

He kept me free from the Carnal Man
Till worldly things, they had a hand
In keeping me here to learn and live,
And so to practice to forgive.

It's O.K. to be angry for what's right and just
To neighbour, friend, or foe, forgiveness is a must.
When sun goes down, the anger is gone.
Serenity sets in, and in my heart is a song.

No wrath is left go fester and kill;
To be healthy and happy, it is God's will.
For me to be so happy and free,
A child of God He wants me to be.

Like the strong oak tree I am to bend,
To give freely to others until the end.
The Natural Man, the Carnal man, waiting to see
The Spiritual Man living in me.

Norma B. Mackie

K

Long, dark hair flowing gently down her back.
Deep, dark, mysterious eyes holding secrets untold.
Her perfect, pouty lip turned up in a smile.
Every curve of her face pleasing to the eye.
Fingers delicate yet strong.
Her legs, long and graceful, as a final, perfect touch.
Every movement, every mannerism, alluring, sensuous.
Her spirit, unbreakable, her will, undeniable.
My soul is hers, if she but desires it.
Putty in her hands I am.

Adam Lenders

Love Is Like

Love is like a little dove,
descending from the sky above.

It's like the morning dew in spring,
sings like a bluebird on the wing,

places a smile upon your face,
soft as delicately woven lace,

shy like a doe with newborn fawns,
soars so high with the graceful swans,

sparkles like stars in the sky above,
faithful as a little dove.

Riley Fehr

My Favorite Flower

Baby faced
With soft, velvety petals of
Deep, rich hues,
Dark wines, purples, golds, and blues.

Peeking shyly
From its north side bed,
Welcoming sun, shade, and shower,
It does not know it's my favorite flower.

I care for it.
It cares not for me,
This pensive looking bloom,
The pansy.

Louise M. Kavulok

Paper Doll

As she closes her eyes
She sees herself
Consumed with emptiness
Walking through the halls
So full of laughing people
As she walks by
She blows them a kiss
And these people become paper dolls
And float away
As she comes to realize
The loneliness she's denied
She feels more and more empty
And as she comes to a door
And steps outside
She too becomes a paper doll
And floats away

Adrienne Bellamy

Avian Brush

As one,
A hundred little birds
   Whirling
   Twirling
   Swirling
Painting the air
With an avian brush

Ruth I. Kellogg

Man's Best Friend

My little dog is Pumpkin,
A daughter in my heart.
I never thought the day would come
That we would ever part.
To wake up every morning
And see her little face,
In the kitchen, in the hall,
She just was every place.
I'd take her for a walk
And always come back beat.
She'd run into the kitchen
And wait there for a treat.
And then the night would come.
As I lay down my head,
There would be my Pumpkin
Lying right beside my bed.
And now that she has passed away,
My heart will never mend.
I'll always know one thing,
And that's that we were friends.

Chris Morrow

The Busy Sunbeam

The sunbeam wandered through the room.
It seemed to be seeking out
The many things it could find
As it wandered all about.

It lit up that fine tea set,
The one with the silver rim,
Leaving there a special glow,
To be seen as the room grew dim.

The sunbeam played with silver drapes,
Caressed the fine rug on the floor.
Still, it seemed not satisfied.
Surely there must be more.

In a corner there she is,
A lady with fine grey hair.
The sunbeam, it could not leave the room.
It lingered on her rocking there.

As the sunbeam took its leave,
On the lady it left its blessing.
Surely, I cannot be wrong—
Its leave-taking most caressing.

W. Warman

Remember

I remember the day I met you,
The day God made you mine.
I remember the day he took you;
I will until the end of time.
But through all my tears and sadness,
There is one thing that makes me glad:
You chose me to share with you
All the years we had.

I wrote this down for all the world to see
How much I loved you
And you loved me.

B. A. Jackson

Crocodile in the Mountain

There is a crocodile in the mountain,
The one I am going to climb.

Crocodiles are dangerous
So I have been told.
It is best to stay away,
But I have to climb this mountain
And I know there is a crocodile in this mountain.
So, what am I to do . . . ?
No one has seen the crocodile.
It is true that crocodile tracks have been spotted,
But since crocodiles do not live in mountains
No one believes the rumours or the tales or the tracks
Or me.
And they say what do I know
About mountain climbing anyway,
Or crocodiles, for that matter.
I only know what I know:

There is a crocodile in the mountain,
The one I am going to climb.

Gina Tzav Wulkan

The Quest

You seek the fount of youth and happiness,
Elysian fields where noble deeds are done,
The Eldorado mine of prizes won,
Alladin's Lamp, the Singing Tree no less!

First follow Phoebus' chariot; that success
Behind you, give Atlanta's apples sun
To ripen, melt their glossy skins for none
But Sesame, of forty thieves the guest.

Then look out; on you doorstep, nature's gifts
To you lie there: strong arms the weak to lift,
Intelligence to see, and a heart to feel
The plight of those who bear hard fortune's weal.

Here is youth's powerhouse: a legacy
Of golden opportunity.

Gloria G. Gadoury

Come with Me on a Dream

Come with me on a dream
To a faraway land
Have you ever rode on a dove
Or walked on pink sand
Have you ever eaten apples, rainbowed and bright
Bathed with dry water
Or danced with white mice
Have you ever heard blue bells
Ring upside down
To the sounds of whatever grow under the ground
Have you ever picked flowers
And have them all say
My, what a beautiful, sunshiny day
Have you ever jumped higher than ever before
Have tree tops catch you
And open a door
To a world far beyond, but it's only a dream
Come with me and pretend
And see what's to be seen.

Veronica Nadasdi

The Voice Machine

We are told that communication is at its best these days.
With all this new, high-tech stuff out now.

It is also said that we should be able to talk to one another,
And that our voices will sound clear.

But why is it, when you dial up a store or business to ask a simple question
That you always get a voice recording that you can barely hear?

This voice recording that you are now hearing in the backdrop of
Some static tells you to stay on the line for further assistance.

But after pressing the buttons that it tells you to on your telephone keypad,
You only find yourself to be right back where you started.

So, frustrated and upset, you hang up the receiver on your telephone
Thinking to yourself, "Did I do something wrong?"

But it isn't you who made the mistake of inventing this voice machine,
So you are not the one to blame for the agony of this device.

For, sitting somewhere in a room is the inventor of this crazed gadget,
And he is the one to blame for all the torment that he has caused us.

So, I beg to differ that we really are more high-tech than we were before
The invention of this rather stupid voice machine.

> *Nicole St-Onge*

My Child

I've been retching during breakfast, lunch, and dinner, yet I smile.
Made heavy and stretched, but I am glowing.
I have been nearly split in half, yet in the next minutes forgotten all.
As I look into a part of myself, and it looks back curiously,
Angelic and sweet, wrinkled and small—will it break?
Delicate and tiny, nature's gift, my own creation,
Beauty in a miracle, my child,
Dreams have flashed and passed,
Fleeting thoughts of what this moment would be like.
Yet, nothing compares to this feeling.
May the image be forever locked in memory so that in growing old
I may look back and reflect on the person I've raised.

> *Katherine Fader*

The Unheard Voice

My hair is brown, my eyes are blue.
Who was my mother? I never knew.
Who was my father? I will never see.
Why has the world done this to me?
How did you know I wanted to die—
Not even given the chance to live, laugh, or sigh?
I won't be able to talk or look, play in the grass, or bathe in the brook.
I won't be able to run down the street
Or go to school where there are all kinds of children to meet.
I don't know about happiness, love, or fear.
I won't know this because I am not here.
My life was cut short before I was born.
From a comfortable womb I was literally torn.
No pain for my mother or father, no hospital contortion.
I never arrived here because I was an abortion.
Instead I lie above the sky, with the angels by my side.
My parents are below with a secret they truly must hide.
Although I'm in Heaven above, I will always wonder if my life
Had been granted, would somebody else
Have taken me into their arms to love?

> *Sandra McLaughlin*

Rearranging

Old Bacchus limped across the road, and dropped exhausted on the curb.
He didn't know his left from right, and couldn't tell his right from wrong.
His eyes, unfocused, tried to find a glimpse of some reality,
But there was nothing on the street related to his inner need.
Once Bacchus used to dance all night and lead his followers through fields
Of golden grain, and daffodils, and pretty girls who laughed and sang
From dusk to dawn and back again.
No end to all the revelry exploding from his finger tips.
He sent the hills and valleys wild with rollicking debauchery.

Now, Bacchus lives downgraded by a plethora of ecstasy,
Enhanced with the heroin and crack, and marijuana, speed, and all
The newest pharmaceuticals available in drug stores,
Prescribed by doctors in the know.
No wonder Bacchus sits bemused and smokes a cigarette or two.
He knows that he's outmoded, and he also knows the upstart drugs
Have opened up a can of worms far worse than one small hangover.
Poor Bacchus, once the centre of imagined dreams impossible,
Now sits bedraggled, all alone,
Dethroned.

    M. L. Dunn

My Guardian Angel

Upon my birth, you were given to be
My protector from above to watch over me.
How privileged I am to have you by my side,
God's perfect creation, my spiritual guide.
I am God's child, you are in between,
God's holy messenger, for me you intervene.
The soft-spoken whisper to choose right from wrong
Came from your very being, in truth's tune, as a song.
You insure God's will; God's will you must serve.
You assist me back on track, should my tracks take a curve.
It is God that I thank that for the good of my soul.
He'd lend me your help so that I'd be made whole.

    Tara Oakley

What Paulos Said

Said He: "Rejoice Always."
So we have a joy-joy vision:
Nothing is real but joy.
Said He: "Pray Constantly."
But we have made a science of prayer
and study it constantly.
We say: "If it's sad or mad and not glad, then it's bad."
Yet, "Give thanks in Everything" does not mean,
"Don't worry, be happy!"
Said He: "Do not despise prophesying,"
Yet we have made prophesying into story-telling and folk-taling.
We distort prophecy, we destroy prophets, we despise truth!
Said He: "But test everything,"
But we test nothing. (We deceive. We despair.)
Nothing can be tested because nothing can be judged.
Nothing can be judged because nothing can be known.
This is the wisdom that is not wisdom.
This is the trial that is naught but denial.
Said He: "Hold fast to the good,"
But we have banished the bad.
We've dispensed with Sin. We've disposed of Evil.
We wash away the good.
We have made all things corrupt but call them good.
Evil is Good. Lies are truth. Death is Life. Horror is Beauty.

    Ted Mallar

Gentle Temper

Placing your hands around my wrists,
you have become the night.
Through all my tumultuous, tumbling dreams,
my thoughts existed in flight.
But the night restrains me—in all its density,
roots me to the Earth.
And now the sun has finally slept,
while in you, I capture mirth.

Leaping across stepping-stones of light,
the stars and I raged against time.
Then you, who proposes a vehement eclipse,
you burst my world of mime.
And without an altered state of mind,
so sweetly gestured my name.
Now, in each tendered moment, I move closer to you,
and farther away from pain.

Annemarie Luck

Prologue

Once upon a time there was a man.
It was early morning.
The man felt the cold breeze chill his chin.
He looked at the green horizon and thought.
Then he looked down and said:
"I am who I am, not who you are.
Try to understand that, my friend."
The man began to walk away.
His green figure was soon lost in the haze.

Then I looked down and I thought.
I thought about the universe, the ants,
    and my niece Terry.
I was glad and happy so I sat down.
The ground was damp, but that did not bother me.
It just made me feel alive.

Then the ants came and ate me.
I never saw the old man again.

Ulfar Eliasson

Friends for Life

This life is a challenging game we play,
a game of vows and words we say.
Each one had to throw a pointed dart . . .
and you shot yours deep in my heart.
Your gentleness, your tenderness,
your everlasting love . . .
all were like a blessing from Heaven above.
You taught me meanings words cannot tell.
You broke my silence, pulled me out of my shell.
You killed my fears, you broke the spell.
When I speak of our friendship, I speak of trust.
It's as warm as sunshine, as fine as dust.
So, even if we are oceans apart,
remember: You're always in my heart.
You'll always be my truest friend,
and I mean forever, till life shall end.
"Together we will live . . .
forever we shall strive
to keep up this friendship . . .
for we are friends for life."

Heidi Tantawi

Reality

A baby is born,
The pain, the suffering,
The anguish, the blood.
Bones of my bones, flesh of my flesh.

"What have you done?"
"The serpent beguiled me."
"Cursed are you above all animals!
Crawl in the dust, and eat it, too."

"What have you done?"
"The woman you gave me . . ."
"Cursed is the ground for your sake!
In sorrow you shall eat of it

Till you return to the ground
From which you were taken.
Dust you are,
And unto dust you will return."

Linza MacDonald

Good Night

I am weak and powerless,
No matter how hard I try.
I cannot pretend to be fearless;
All I can do is cry.

So many times I have persisted
When I wanted to give up.
So many nights I have resisted
The urge to drink from Romeo's cup.

No longer can I think of why
I force myself to continue.
After tonight I shall forever lie,
Peacefully, beneath the morning dew.

Kathleen Campbell

The Hardship

A hard time waiting,
hunger and pain.
Impossibility baiting
my temper again.

A shard of glass cracking,
Soon it will splinter.
A brittle stick breaking
In a cold, glacial winter.

Spring may not mend it,
Wounded and frail.
Though a new twig may grow
Where the other one failed.

Yet again the summer nurtures
With its balmy care,
And the branch may grow
Strong and gracefully there.

There will be other winters,
But my branch is now strong,
Bracing against the wind
And whistling its song.

Misha Louise Blakely

Unique

Alone in the sand,
Shines brightly toward the evening light,
A single shell.
Rolling in of the tide
To acquaint oneself,
To stay or drift away,
Seeking to be
Unique,
Reaching out to the sunrise,
Alone in the sand.

Debbie Brown

Celebration

Far as the eyes can see
Only waves of clouds
In symmetry
Parade swiftly
Over the Castle of Peace

Clapping tree waving tree
We salute with momentous joy

Dance of the ballerinas
Leaping and swirling autumn leaves
Shimmering grass
Such excitement
Prelude to a rainbow with Sensei

Rainbows span the sky
Six celestial curtain calls
Fullness of harvest moon
And setting sun
All celebrating the Humanity of Life

Reg Kimura

If

If God hadn't made the mountains
So majestic and so tall
If he hadn't placed the creatures here,
The biggest and the small

If he hadn't made the rivers
Swiftly flowing to the sea
What would there be around us
For you and me to see?

There would be no fragrance
Of sweet blossoms in the air
Or chirping of those little birds
So colorful and rare

No fields of grain or rolling hills
No honey from the bees
No luscious fruit upon the vines
No blossoms on the trees

If God had not given us
This beauty that we share
How could we ever even know
His handiwork, his care?

Lorraine Fladager

Old Ways and New Days

When I was small, it was good times for all.
Everyone then had employment,
Students were hired at the jobs they desired,
But I was too young to enjoy it.

Long gone are the times when your chrome bumpers shined,
And in the car your seven friends sat.
Your car was full-grown, AIDS was unknown,
And a car-jack was the cure for a flat.

We're spending billions on Mars and watching the stars
While people here die of diseases.
We're hacking down trees and polluting the seas
While the ozone is floating in pieces.

So I remember the days when the cattle would graze,
And that subdivision once was a farm.
In the pond there were frogs, and bytes were from dogs,
And web-sites were found in the barn.

In the days of old, you could die from a cold,
And wars claimed men from the 'hood,
But in changing those days, with our technical ways
Why didn't we keep what was good?

Jeff Stover

Untitled

I am still after, after a great war in my soul.
I am at peace, though all around me are rough waters.
My gift is me; I am my own present,
I have learned I have the answers,
The kingdom of Heaven is within me.
It's okay to listen to my inner voice.
Deep inside there's health, a self-preserving God
who will never lead me astray.
I bid you other soldiers of Mania
find the inner Christ and follow Him to peace.

Susan Rundle

Birthdays

As future years go rolling by
No need for tears; that makes us cry.
For bodies, age doesn't matter: I promise you.
So, don't let the physical make you blue.
When two hearts love, as yours and mine,
In my eyes, you will forever shine.

Let's live the love held in our hearts.
When love is freely given, hearts never part.
Let's live the joy we both truly share,
When we each show the other we care.
Let's live the laughter our love to us brings.
These things are more important than physical things.

This birthday promise, I do here, with love vow
Each year, I will love you more than now.
For, each year's wear our bodies do show,
Our inner strength will continue to grow.
Our souls do touch, then join and blend,
So I know our love will never weaken and end.

Happy Birthday, most wonderful, kind man.
Please be mine alone, for as long as you can.

Vera Benusic

Sunny Rays on Your Birthday

Half a century you have walked through life
While doing this you have conquered many a strife
Now, we all have a special day
As we go along in life
We tend to forget that day
But today don't be coy
Celebrate your birthday, "enjoy"
For, only once in this lifetime
Fifty rays of sun
For, you will shine
Have a Happy Birthday
Enjoy, and have lots of fun

Irene Philips

Alloycracy

That precious exotica has come here.
Anywhere, to the moral and right allotted,
Unevenly on the complete opposite bestowed,
Confided to the old clowns and their tricks.
This *coterie des parvenus* for the sake of mission-ism,
They're honest for the sake of their dishonesty.
Things seem a political cafeteria.
They have you the way they wish:
Fried or grilled, mashed and garnished, or chopped,
With your values prostituted and mixed,
While your bones are frog-marched outside—
Pro publico bono, cast onto the masses
As if a dead envelope for your immortal soul.
In vain do you long to stand up to them?
It's you to serve, them to be served.
Only then can you feel yourself,
Or anarchy becomes your name.
But do not be a deal at every table;
Do not be a deal at every handshake.
Oh, Democracy, you happen to be alloyed.

Pawel Osuch

T.B.I.

It would be nice to say, to this list we don't belong,
That everything they say about us, it's all wrong.
The night this all happened we were one minute late.
That step we took then will have to wait.

If we could back off just one more day,
From what we learned, we would want it that way.
The pain we take, the headaches too,
I know for sure we would not want for you.

Do you see the scars inside my skull?
For me, it's made my life quite dull.
The things I did I have to learn again.
Will this life for me never end?

There are places to go, people to see,
There are things in life that just can't be.
I will never be completely alone,
The people on the list keep me close to home.

If you get tired and no place to go,
Watch the people on T.B.I., you know.
They have stories and can lend you an ear.
There is nothing in this world you should fear.

Keith Sherrard

The Poppy

Every year around this time
When poppies can be seen
Remember what they symbolize
Remember what they mean

This pretty little flower
That we wear upon our chest
Is not to make us happy
And is not worn in jest

It's a symbol of remembrance
Of suffering and the cost
We wear it so we won't forget
The loved ones who were lost

It reminds us of the soldiers
Who fought in two world wars
Especially those who didn't return
From distant, foreign shores

Be proud to wear your poppy
On your sweater or your vest
For it helps us to remember
Lest we forget

Aaron MacKenzie

Free to Be Free

The Earth is a circle,
No beginning nor end,
Continually revolving,
No broken edges to mend.

So why is the world
So broken inside?
Why do love and compassion
Continue to hide?

Nations and countries
Continue to divide.
That is why love and compassion
Continue to hide.

It's everyone's problem,
It's yours and it's mine.
We have to start loving,
And now is the time.

Love your neighbor,
Your ally, your friend,
Your country, your enemy.
It's now time to mend.

Donna Jamieson

In the Garden

In the garden bed
Are the flowers pink and red.
Roses, tulips, and daffodils,
To grow they don't need any pills.
They need sun and rain to grow,
And you will see it coming slow:
A blooming bud, a pretty flower,
Just with sun and a shower.

Jessica Crowe

Earth and in Between

Cloak of darkness, illusive charm
His purpose was to do me harm
I cried out with due alarm
Anxiety

White fire arc across the sky
Warrior's sword, thy blade doth fly
From thus a booming battle cry
Passion

Unseen bodies fighting brave
Send adversary to thy grave
All they had was me to save
Solace

Thy enemy had paid his fare
And slunk back to his loathsome lair
With nothing more than word of prayer
Faith

Cloak of darkness passed away
Soon morning sun will light the day
And on this rock I'll surely stay
Serenity

Curtis Stankevich

Wait a Moment, Please

Wait a moment, please . . .
Did you not understand me?
I'm the one that offered you equality.
So, wait a moment, please . . .
Before you strip me of my dignity.

Wait a moment, please . . .
Before you cast your doubt on me.
To be so cruel is to be
The devil's advocate tease.

So, wait a moment, please . . .
Before you bring down
    those who do good,
Trying to help you in life,
And take heed like you should.
So, think a moment, please.

Be still, be human, please!
You can't treat those in life like a tease,
So wait a moment, please . . .
Before you destroy what good
there is left of me. . . .
Wait a moment, please.

Eileen Sheridan

The Uncarved Block

Sits beneath the rays of the sun
Waiting to be moulded into its new form
The completed shape almost
distinguishable
But always hidden from view,
    never carved
By the process of energy or time
To what it really could have been

Pamela Stoehr

My Family

My family does not want anything to do with me.
I think they want to lose me.
Sometimes I wonder, where did I blunder?
What happened—was I kidnapped and thrown under?
I was not inventive, just very sensitive.
I have no feelings, was I full of apple feelings?
If it were not for uncles three, where would I be?
They were like brothers, like no others.
As it turns out, there is only one thing to shout:
My only family is me, my husband,
and baby make three, and I guess that is all
there will ever be.

Dianna Holigroski

Friendliness

Some people say
"To heck with friendliness;
friendliness is only for
wimps and suck-ups,"

But I say friendliness is what
I wake up and look
forward to every morning.

Friendliness is loving thy neighbor
and what makes thy neighbor friendly
and loving in return.

Friendliness makes the world
turn 'round and makes us all feel good.

Friendliness is something each and every one of us
should give and take every day.
Be friendly to others,
For, without friendliness, we would have no friends.

Emmy Wilson

Becoming

I look back upon myself,
the glimmer of youth and innocence
nothing but mere phantoms
amidst my adult soul.

As I look upon the changed world,
yearning for answers

Answers to private aspirations and
eternal lifelong failures.

I ache for understanding, I seek my
soul existence for becoming a
mother, a woman, a being.

Fears of declining our dreams and
discovering our failures—
Rejoicing in the ways of
existing accomplishments.

As I raise my eyes to the darkening sky, realization.

My most cherished creation. The beauty of a child.

To succeed where I have failed.
So innocent and pure, so loving.
He embellishes my soul with a new-found pride.
He is my success I have become.

Lisa Dobos

An Instant

Where the sun shines, now nothing grows. Where there were raging
rivers, now nothing flows. How the golden moon hung brightly—now
all is dark. The brilliant stars were all just holes in a paper mirage
of a night. Playgrounds of children playing happily,
now all is placid. Streets once filled with the sounds of
life are now silent and deserted. The bird that once flew
and would sing all day now just roosts and won't sing at all.
Oceans full of life now are toxic and unable to produce life.
Bright, sunshiny days good for walking are now overcast and
there's just thunder and lightning. The sweet, warm summer air
has now turned cold and stale. The little ant who knew his job now
walks around in the fog. All the jungles rich with life, now are
just stumps with no life in sight. The monks and the priests once
full of faith, now have lost their way. This world was once beautiful
and peaceful. All now is just a fading memory. All was
created with a name—a name that means fragrance. Once so
sweet in smell, now so putrid and vile it destroys everything.
This same name—the creator of all—now has left and
destroyed all. All that is left just a shell of dreams and
hopes. That name . . . KAORI.

> *Timothy Abriola*

Inside and Out

My arms thrown wild in the air
My head falling back catches the sun
I turn round and round
Moving and opening
A glorious dance of birth and life as colors explode and shimmer
A warming laugh fills my throat and enters the depths of my body
My arms come down
They hug my body
I welcome everyone, I give everything
I take comfort in the warm breeze and fall
Into its gentle sway of my cradle
And a tear slides down my cheek
Soft and warm, it dries in the sun
My dance—it ends
And I walk to my mirror
Such a graceful, tender complexion
My hand reaches to touch my face
And raising it, I securely fasten it in an awkward bow behind my head
I walk out the door and a tear slides down my cheek
No one can see it now

> *Brenda Erickson*

The Sun Shall Weep for Me

My eyelids feel so heavy . . . i start to drift off . . .
floating up to space, away from you, away from all this aphotic pain.
sooner or later i know i must fall, i must come back,
but i slip through the hands of time and fly.
i feel the wind scrape past my face and i hear the desperate cries of others.
i pay no attention to where or who i am; up here i feel so alive and free,
feelings i've never felt before.
my eyes darkly gaze up, and i breathe in all this joy before i collapse into the fingers of hell. . . .
i can feel myself falling, faster, and faster,
my thoughts quickly rush through my mind,
and i can see the humble stars slowly fading in the distance,
muffled by my silent cries.
the heartless sea becomes clearer, and i notice my fear-ridden face upon the crystal floor.
they warned me not to go, they said i would regret trying to escape my shame,
but as i feel the cold overpower my body and the water wrap around my weak lungs,
i realize that they were wrong.

> *danielle marie lesperance*

Wings of the Morning

This melodious morning shone luminously and bright,
Gloriously guiding me to the world of light.
Blinding me with its vast brilliance unique,
The light told me what every human alone must seek.
"You my friend, choose your own destiny,
From here to the future, be patient and see,
What gleam or what dream,
Will be done unto thee."
At that moment, I awoke from my abyssal slumber,
Pondering the words, as the obscure skies shot lightning and thunder.
I observed up to the sky and my mouth dropped in awe,
Unable to explain in my mind what my eyes just saw.
Two cupids approached the world from the heavens above,
To fill my mind with the essence of happiness and love.
Then the doves appeared from the clouds and soared,
To escort the cupids back to our Lord.
Put on the wings of the morning and fly,
There is no reason for us to weep and cry.
The shadows have been lifted for us to see,
What futures and what destinies hold for thee.

   Justin Moy

One Kind

The feeling of loneliness floats in your mind.
It tells you that you are worthless, not one of a kind.
Screams of hate tell you you're no good.
You are not loved, just misunderstood.
It takes away all confidence and fills you with fear.
Evil in sight, Satan is near!

Crying softly to yourself, you wish you could change,
Change all those mistakes that were so strange.
You want to be someone else, because your old self is so hard to find.
You need help; you are going out of your mind!

Sitting alone, listening to your heart,
Fighting off demons that might just be near.
Maybe the pureness of a tear would renew your mind,
But that tear is just so hard to find!

   Elizabeth Brink

Take the Time Today

Take the time, dear "Mom and Dad," to give them love they've never had.
Listen when they speak to you, for they have their problems, too!
Take the time to show you care—tomorrow comes, they've gone somewhere.

Take the time when you are young to look ahead before you run.
Respecting those who know what's best will help you in the final test.
Take the time to count the cost—tomorrow comes, will all be lost?

Take the time to all together pray, you will find it's best that way.
Lightens burdens, gives strength, too, for it's true—God still loves you.
Take the time now to agree—tomorrow comes, together you'll be.

Take the time to visit or write the sick, the blind, the folks tonight.
They need your hand, you will find, for stronger faith and peace of mind.
Take the time, don't procrastinate—tomorrow comes, 'twill be too late.

Take the time, think before you speak; will it strengthen or make weak?
Love that's taken years to grow can be quenched by a thoughtless blow.
Take the time, start the day right—tomorrow comes with some foresight.

Take the time at work or play to do your best in every way.
Be patient, kind, and also true to those who love and trust in you.
Take the time, control your pace—tomorrow comes, you've won the race!

Take the time the birds to hear, see the flowers grown for cheer.
Music on the roof from rain, frost designs on the window pane.

   C. W. Peddle

Ida

Weeks came;
Days passed.
You're still in my head
And I'm still wanting to know you.
I can't see you anymore
'Cause my fate took you away,
But I'm still hoping
And full of hope that we could be close
to one another someday.
I left 'cause I had to.
I know that's a stupid thing to do,
'Cause I'm not going to be able to see you every day;
I'm not going to be able to see
The precious light that makes me
A very cheerful man.
I don't think I belong to this
New place I'm attending.
I think where I belong
Is in your heart.

Friedrich Victor O. Zabala

Untitled

In a hospital room we sit tonight,
You and I by the soft night light.
As your dear, sweet mother rests beside us in bed,
Thoughts so mixed go through our heads.
I see a woman who raised a wonderful boy,
You see a mother who filled your life with joy.
I may not have known her very long,
But my love for her is very strong.
Because, you see, we share one thing for sure,
Our love for you is, oh, so pure.
I see in you a man so fine,
I'm sure she sees a son divine.
As we sit and wait for the hours to go by,
Now and then she gives a soft sigh.
We go to the chapel and kneel and pray.
We need not speak, he know what our hearts say.
Knowing the Lord will hear our prayers,
And keep us strong as we hold back tears,
I pray for strength to handle what may come,
Because I know "He will be done."

Susan Ann Myers

Untitled

Quiet as she may be, she still listens to
the loudness of the mother's voice shooting
behind her. It sings the songs we played as we
sat in our muddy outfits in the old sandbox
beneath the second story house of monsters.
The playing stopped, the cries began. We were
told to do within ourselves. We pray for the
little man with all the keys of the secrets
to be told to do as we were.
I sit now in shading trees on top of my head,
nothing but a white ceiling with a kitchen, bathroom,
and a room where more goes on than any other
place in this thoughtful place-making world.
I destroy my own face with the brushes.
He gave me the sandbox-muddy stories I still
tell to make sure I'm happy.

Candice Matthews

This Child

See this child before you,
do you know his name,
where he is going,
or direction that he came?
His clothes are peculiar,
his hair may be a mess.
There's something in his eyes,
that's different from the rest.
He's sitting at the bus stop
or knocking at your door.
If you can't see past the surface,
don't look anymore.
This child's not what he's wearing,
he isn't what you see.
It's all just window dressing,
a show for you and me.
Look at the children,
tell me what you see.
Then look again, deeper still,
at the beauty that lies within.

Linda Grenier

Dying

As we lay dying
No one knows
As we look up into the sky
No one knows
The dark clouds are forming
　and moving by
And no one knows
An angel waits from up above
And no one knows
The devil watches, dressed in a shroud
And no one knows
As we lay dying
No one knows
And life goes on
And no one knows

Audrey Fenton Roode

Echoes of Silence

A barren landscape
lies white and still.

No sounds intrude,
no animals to hear.
The birds are sleeping
or are they gone?
Where are the people
who skated the pond?

Deep in the city,
amongst raucous calls,
gulls weave and dip
before they fall.
Children's voices in the air
fade and disappear.

People crowd city walks,
oblivious to others,
not hearing the doves.
All around—above, below—
Echoes of silence seem to grow.

Joyce Evans

Let It Be Me

When I was down and out
When I was blue and about
When I was in sorrow and cold
You were there for me to hold

I have a lot of friends, yes
But not when I'm a mess
I have lots of fun with them, too
But not the kind I spent with you

Never in my life will I find
Another good friend of your kind
Never will ever find again
A friend in joy and in pain

You've been so nice and good to me
And I want to do the same, let it be
If times and things are heavy to carry
That's when you need a friend, let it be me

But if by chance we'll grow apart
By distance or by heart
Let our memories together
Warm our friendship forever

Immacion Chona Galace

Open Your Eyes

Too many words, too much to say,
I wish I could explain why I feel this way.
Impossible dreams never to come true,
I wish I weren't so in love with you.
Composed in a song that I can sing,
To you, my love is all I can bring.
If I had wings and I could fly,
I'd take you up into the sky.
I'd take you up to the heavens above
And drown you in the depth of my love.
In my dreams, I can see
That truly you were meant for me.
Open your heart, open your eyes.
I am where your future lies.

Sheila Cruz

Savior

She reached deep down
Inside his lonely soul
And found that fragment
Of his love
That he had cast away.

He gave that fragment to her
To nurture, to cherish,
To keep vital
For him, for her,
For an eternity.

She brought it forward
With magic and charm
Until it blossomed
Into ecstasy
And tenderness.

His soul is vital now, alive
From the love
Within her
That pours back into him
By pure enchantment.

Colleen Hanson

Near Summer

Paperback books tucked under the arm,
Old house blue shutters in a city with charm,
Blind man, white cane, happy expression,
Mother and child, all leave an impression.
Street musician on sax, soft, sultry tune,
Near summer day this early in June.
Smiles on the faces, children at play,
There is peace in the world, if just for today.
Old men in the park, shoe polish and spit,
Blue haired women on porches rock as they sit.
Trees coming alive, the flowers in bloom,
Honking of horns for the bride and the groom,
Boys playing ball, little girls they are skipping,
Some covered in ice cream from cones that are dripping.
Lovers hand in hand, they touch and embrace,
Artists and poets, their times that they trace.
Birds mating and nesting, everything seems to be alive,
The bees carrying pollen from flower to hive.
Life seems quite in order, so abundant, so pleasant,
Near summer day in June, perhaps this is Heaven.

J. James Gardiner

When You Look at Me

When you look at me do you whisper to others?
When you look at me do you sneer?
When you look at me do you insult me?
When you look at me do you stare?
Why?
I am human being!
How would you like it if I gasped at your approach?
So listen,
I'm a person, too.

Sierra Methot

Dreams

They steal softly into our night
With fanciful thoughts that then take flight.
Loved ones long gone hold us and smile,
And we cry and say, "Stay, stay, for a while."
Our guilt now all put behind the veil
As the child within us awakens to feel
That silver thread once more still there.
What joy we feel until the pale dawn.
To sleep, "Perchance to dream," we mourn.

Pauline Richardson

In Memory of My Mother

My mother left me for another world,
Leaving memories to unfurl.
How I miss her sweetness and grace.
No one can really take her place.
Laughter she said was good for the soul,
A sense of humor worth more than gold.
How wise she was, that mother of mine,
With love and patience all the time.
She never said, "I told you so,"
But gave me courage so I would grow
Knowing love and laughter would heal the pain.
I miss you, Mother, just the same.

Viola A. Rennie

To Be a Child

With lots of love and a house that's warm,
And doctors to inoculate me against harm,
And hospitals to go to when I'm sick,
And a school to teach what makes me tick,

But what about being a child today
Where I should work instead of play?
To carry water from a truck
Or from a river, through the muck . . .
And not know how to read a book,
Or be able to find for myself a nook
To be by myself and think about things,
Where my mind could soar, imagination take wings.
To dream of a table loaded with food . . .
Or a spot to play on the street would be good.

And who could tell mamma, out there on the "edge,"
To stop having children, with not enough beds . . . ?
And what if a flood took my home all away,
And gardens of vegetables, great fields of hay?
Would I go without, or would somebody care?
A child of the world . . . what if I were born there?

Dorothy Christie

Untitled

If there is honesty in the heart,
there is goodness in the character.

If there is goodness in the character,
there will be tranquility in the home.

If there is tranquility in the home,
there will be a sense of purpose in the nation.

When there is a sense of purpose in the nation,
there will be happiness in the world.

Think about it!

Tanyann Hamilton Belaney

Youth Gone By

An old woman stands at the chain link fence
Watching the children play
Remembering back to the time of her youth
And thinking of happier days

Her fingers are now gnarled and her hair has turned grey
And her eyes have lost most of their gleam
She yearns to take part—and run, skip, and jump
But that is now only a dream

A little girl stops and smiles up at her face
And asks would you like to join in
But the old woman says not today, I'm afraid
As my legs are too wobbly and thin

With a tear in her eye, she turns back from the fence
And wearily walks down the road
And she thinks to herself, as she shuffles along
Growing old can be such a load

Then she stops to thank God for the years she has seen
And the joy that He adds to her day
And the voices of children at play in the field
Make her smile as she goes on her way

Bob McKinnon

Ended Love

Maybe loved,
Maybe not,
Maybe missed,
Maybe forgot—

The one you thought loved
Has now disappeared.
Now dying alone
Is the one thing that's feared.

The relationship was hard,
And you both fought it out.
Now this round's at an end,
And you both lost the bout.

Now each goes on,
Finding his way.
You're still in my heart,
And for you I will pray.

Sven Amo

Hope

When times are tough
And we're down and out
Seems nothing turns out right
We only see the darkness
But then—a ray of light!
God's ways are hard to understand
We cannot see the fairness
For some, it seems, are richly blessed
And at times he forgets the rest
Of us who are sad and forlorn
And on our shoulders the cross is borne
To be carried to greater heights
Where once again we see the light
And happiness and love prevail
To wipe out all the tear-stained trails
We must be brave and carry on
Though lips are parched and bodies worn
Head held high and a smile on our face
We'll still be the "winners" in life's race!

Margaret A. Thiessen

Illusion of Man

Man, oh, man,
How wise that we are.
We have more intelligence
Than animals by far.

Mankind, oh, mankind,
What builders we are:
The cities, the ghettos,
The spaceships so far.

Man, oh, man,
What leaders we are,
Fighting all wars
No matter how far.

Mankind, oh, mankind,
How great that we are,
But I look and I swear
Better destroyers by far.

Jurrien Hoekstra

Heaven

I think I know where Heaven is.
It's deep within our souls.
It's the place we've filled with memories
of the blessings we have known.

For, Heaven is eternal peace,
a place free from hurt and pain.
I feel it when I hold God close
or when I just speak his name.

When God's light fills my heart with love,
I can drift away
to a place of quiet blissfulness,
all I have to do is pray.

Then I can feel Heaven in my heart,
when I just close my eyes.
I think of all God's given me,
and Heaven is realized.

Yes, I think I know where Heaven is:
It's deep within our souls.
Can we find a way to live there now?
Heaven only knows.
Jodi Reitberger

Lone Wolf

In the peace of night
A lone wolf howls
Shattering restful sleep
With a piece of night
It's known well
That sounds inside it deep
With cries of pain
And emptiness
In journey's climb uphill
Through skies that rain
The tearful kiss
Of washing away its will
To stand and fight
In keeping proud
And not lie down to die
In the still of night
Of moon and cloud
A lone wolf cries
Ken D. Meheden

Untitled

How lonely are the nights,
Empty are my thoughts.
To believe can destroy
What sanity you have left.

Virgin are your feelings,
Innocent are your thoughts.
What you believe will destroy
This insanity they call love.

To sleep the sleepless dreams,
Dreams of reality, so real,
They exist for all to see,
Witness to my dreams.
Mike Gregoire

Ode to Poets

Once poets spoke of love,
Of birds and bees, lawns and trees.
Once poets spoke of sadness,
Of storms and hail and harvests failed,

Once poets spoke of loss,
The son who in the war was felled,
The joyous heart where he was held,
Forever damaged, so the doctor said.

They spoke of family,
Of mothers, fathers, brothers, and sisters.
They spoke of scandal, in gentle whispers.
They spoke of kin throughout the town,
But the town is no more, the walls are down.

The metropolis embraces strangers;
There is no warning of the dangers.
Oh, kindly poet, come once more
And tell us stories of days of yore.
Ellen Smyth

No Destiny

Without dreams, we have no destiny.
Without a destiny, we become an existence.
Being an existence, we lose hope.
Having no hope, we fail to look for love.
Without love, there is an emptiness.
The emptiness becomes a hollow chamber.
Our tears gather in that chamber
Where they echo like raindrops,
Echoes of despair, for we have destroyed our dreams.
Without dreams, we have no destiny.
Deborah Lhea Turner

The Price of War

On November the 11th we remember the wars
That men have fought to keep our country safe, for

It was tragic to lose all those brave souls,
But we will always respect their goals.

For freedom they fought for everyone.
Many families were left without their sons.

Ships were sunk, men were lost,
The war would be won at any cost.

Medals were given for bravery and success
To be worn proudly on the soldiers' chests.

Some did not make it, so candles were lit.
Families received their medals in their kit.

So many bodies littered the fields,
Never claimed, so the graveyard was filled.

For our fathers and sons the war took away,
We hold our memories and wish they were here today.

Too many deaths, too many lies,
We need to learn and be more wise.

So let us think love and sign a lease
That the world will come together and cherish peace.
Amanda Shave

She Said She Loved Me

She said she loved me, but what does love mean?
Will she always be with me or will she come clean?

If she loved me, then why did she go?
Did I move too fast or was I too slow?

She said she couldn't live without me, but that was just a lie.
Someone tell me why, when she left she didn't cry.

If she couldn't live without me, then where is she now?
I've got to find her; I just don't know how.

I'm saying I still love her; without her I'm missing something.
I feel so incomplete,
Because with her no one can compete.

She said she loved me, and I love her too,
But now she's gone, and I don't know what to do.

Eugene Pruski

Rolling Hills and Piercing Daggers

Rolling hills, quiet breeze,
The words you are saying hit me like thousands of piercing daggers.
Tall trees, orange sun,
The touch of your hand against my skin, sends a multitude of shocks
through my body.

Ribbons of colour floating on air,
The feel of the cold steel bullet rips through my insides
like a meat grinder.
A rabbit hops through the grass.
The last breath I take in this world feels like suffocation.

A deer nuzzles her fawn.
The moment my eyes eternally close gives me a sense of peace.
The petals of the flower close.
The flight of my soul to Heaven leads me to freedom's door.

Pelin Oguz

The End

The deep, dark crevasse, offers solitude,
Giant mountains all around,
Miles upon miles, snow with a great magnitude
With not a whisper, not a sound.

Great, unmatched, desolate plains with nothing to show,
The cold, the wind, will get vicious.
It seems you haven't been moving, the time went so slow.

You cry for echoes again and again,
The sky blue never to change.
Suddenly from nowhere, here comes the pain.

You're close to the end when you look to the sky.
You wonder, your whole life flashes in your mind.
You suddenly think, is this it? Am I going to die?

As you doze off, you try to stay awake.
It's hard, you know you've been out for a while.
You pray to God: Please, God, give me a break!

Time has elapsed, your eyes start to water, you begin to cry.
You mutter to yourself, why? Why here? Why now?
And as you lie there, you realize you're about to die.

You think once again of your kids and your wife.
Wow, what a life!

Jarrett Belanger

She Dances

She's like a soft breeze passing through the air
Or a flurry of sea gulls springing from the sea water.
The sun's rays pass through the window glass
To fall upon her shoulders, enhancing her slight frame,
Lighting the silken threads of her shimmering dress,
And surrounding her body in a magnificent aura of golden light.

Her hands move in all directions.
Emotions flow from her fingertips,
As she gracefully takes her body
Through the motions of her breathtaking art,
Painstakingly telling us a story in vivid detail.

She floats, yet her feet touch the floor.
Finally, she sinks to its smooth surface
Like snow sweeping down from the sky.

Tanya Odile Letts

Destiny

I break through to feel the rush of the wind
upon my face and see the sun shining down to warm me.
I stand strong and free, gathering the energy
from the forces that abound from within.
Eternity stretches out her arm to me.
Calling my name ever so softly, I follow the
steps that lead to the deepest, darkest regions of my mind,
staying in this fortress until I find the truth to who and what I am.
One day I will break free for good.
One day I will stand alone and know why I am here
and what my destiny has laid out for me.

Patti-ann Jensen

Drive in the Rain

Have you ever driven in the rain when water hits the
window pane and jumps and dances on the roads like
merrymaking, happy toads?

The mist just ahead, a soft blanket on the bed,
The trees and bushes by the road bow low with their load.
The constant drumming in my ear whisks away any fears.
As we travel from here to there, I offer up a small prayer.
Thank you, Lord, for the rain; it washes and cleans the window
pane while we slither home again in the pouring rain.

Ruth Hamilton

New Song

The wind blows strongly with rippled shades of blues
And white caps upon the water as it rolls.

The poplars, willows, and maples bend their branches, too;
The cedars merely flutter tips.

I cannot hear the song of the birds in the wind,
Only that of the trees.
I've never distinguished the songs of the trees as have I the birds.

T. K. Cooke

The Soothsayer Cried

Do you know what we need more of in this country?
—The soothsayer cried.
Much more modern, medieval, Mormon, memorial, moral movies!
Some jerk!
This country isn't going to the dogs.
The dogs wouldn't touch it!
And I was having a headache, how gay and bonny!

Peter Stiernström

Golgatha

Foul wind sweeping across the rocky heath,
Bitter darkness that fills the night,
Stark, upraised mound of death,
Eyes gazing upward, eyes without sight.

Lonely sentinels, keeping eternal vigil,
Arms outspread, embracing the darkened sky;
And one, head raised, hands clenched,
Scarred and battered, supreme in a world passed by.

Naked and frozen, nailed to a cross,
Stained skin, torn and beaten in life,
And in death, untouchable, a sacred body,
Bearing no mark of an existence of strife.

Transformed being, mystic, full of hope,
In a new life, in a world without pain,
Freed from men's hands, men he had saved,
His brooding eyes stare upward again.

The yellow dawn soaks up the pithy night;
A small group silently approaches the hill;
They take his body gently off the cross,
And bear it away, shrouded and still.

Peter Grey

Untitled

Through the hustle and bustle of each day,
I take a moment to pray,
For the Lord would want it this way.
I can feel Him knocking at the door of my heart,
He whispers, "Fret not my dear child.
From you I will never depart.
My love is deep, my love is great—
Deeper than the seas or any bottomless lake.
When I called you by name,
It was so that you would never be the same.
No longer will you hang your head in shame.
I set you apart for my very own
And I have numbered the seeds that you have sown."
Heavenly Father, in all your glory and splendor,
Man never dreamed they needed a Saviour.

Sonya M. Terry

The Loss

I never knew it could hurt so much
To lose something I couldn't even touch.
We worked until we got it right,
But everything fell apart in a couple of nights.

I loved it as it grew and grew.
I was so happy to have something new.
It never worked out in the end;
I always lost my new, little friend.

I cried and cried . . . how could God be so unfair?
I didn't deserve this. I wanted my share.
My heart shattered like a window pane;
My many tears fell like summer rain.

I hope I never have to go through this again.
It hurts so much . . . I can't handle the pain.
I never knew it could hurt so much
To lose something I couldn't even touch.

Dolly Meise

Canadian Autumn

This interlude is nature's own,
When seed is set and fledgling flown.
Her ageless hands, from labour free,
Beguile the hours with artistry.
We watch the masterpiece unfold,
Retreating green, advancing gold,
And see her sorcery revealed
In russet swamp and amber field,
In purple tint and carmine blaze,
Now drenched with sun, now veiled in haze.
Entranced, we watch the landscape's guise,
Toward perfection's zenith rise,
Until, one restless, frost-tinged day
An errant wind sweeps it away.
Leaving, in wake of his retreat,
The splendor ravaged at our feet,
And autumn's gone. The vision past,
We turn to await the winter's blast.

Annie Polushin

My Life, My Love, My Happiness

My life, my love, my happiness
Some things are all the same
I live, I feel, I smile
But maybe inside has gone insane
I fight, I scream, I cry
Can't you feel my pain
My insides are being torn apart
I feel nothing but shame

My mind is going in circles
Tears are streaming down my face
My heart is pounding rapidly
Blood is burning through my veins
My hands are shaking
My knees have gone weak
I've fallen to my death
Nothing is important anymore
You took my life when you left
My life, my love, my happiness
Some things have changed
All that's here is me inside my pain

Stephanie Mavroudis

The Cult of the Cathode

The modern mind is dimly lit
By the dull, fluorescent glow
Of a television set in its deep recesses,
Churning out show after show.
We are too busy staring
To find time to be amazed,
And the message is completely lost
In our blank and mindless gaze.
We are too busy hearing
The plethora of sound
To find time to listen to the words
Great men through time expound.
If TV and computers
Are the path to civilization,
Take me to the dark ages
Where they had imagination.

Nick Kellaway

Hope Is

A state of being
A silent wish
A cry from the heart
A need of the spirit
A song for the soul
A dying man's folly
A hopeless man's desire
A blind man's vision
Life's encouragement
Fear's opponent
The freedom of feelings
The creator of dreams
A solution for uncertainty
A quest for ecstasy
The courage to carry on
The strength to confront
The reason to face reality
Something to hold onto
During hardship and triumphs
Power of the mind

Caroline Proot

Lifelessness

What once had life is dead,
Too soon the spark of hope was shed.
What once had beauty is torn,
The look of pain its face has worn.

What once saw light is cold,
Waiting for a life untold.
What once was strong is weak,
A hollow corpse that cannot speak.

What once did smile now cries,
An empty look across its eyes.
What once had colour turned grey,
And no more stars come out to play.

What once held hope up high is gone,
Now hides its grief beneath the dawn.

Carlie Kilduff

Masks

We wear elaborate masks to hide
the truth of what we feel,
of who we are or what we want,
or what we might reveal.

We play so many roles in life,
at being what's expected;
we act the parts another's written,
afraid of being rejected.

But if the part is played too long,
and life's an acted role,
then all that's looked at is the mask
and not the inner soul.

What starts as just a game, turns real,
then we begin to fear
that if the mask should slip or fall,
we'd find there's no one here.

E. F. Hughes

On Love

To judge a man but at a glance,
To see his dream and take a chance,
To hope that life's treasure I've found,
In him, where wisdom and love abound.

A man whose heart still craves and yearns,
In depths of soul his passion burns,
Whose mind engages and reveals,
Whose hands caress, uphold, and heal.

For, when I look into his eyes,
I see clear above the skies,
Over the hills, and beyond the horizon,
To capture the ecstasy of one rose and a dozen.

A man whose word is pure and kind,
A man whose sentiment can equal mine,
Who'll lead me in a lifelong dance,
All this to judge, but at a glance.

Irit Gertzbein Kowarsky

What More Do You Want?

I loved you and gave you everything,
I cared about you more than anything.
I fought for you and tried my best,
I gave you everything that I had left.

I thought of you as my special someone,
The one true friend I could always count on.
I wanted something, not too much,
Just a little loving touch.

Was I so wrong to think you cared,
To expect you to always be there?
I tried so hard, I just can't understand
Why you said "No" when I asked, "Be my man?"

Crystal Anne Chioini

Diamonds

Tiny little gems run down cheeks,
Crystal tears, precious tears,
Triggered by uncontrollable emotions—
Sadness, fear.
Priceless jewels from the mines of the soul
And the deep caves of the heart
Escape from the sockets of sight and free themselves.
Pure emotion.
Like a river.
Diamonds, precious tears.

Shara Goldsmith

Fly

You have always been there to hold and protect me.
Take me under your wing.
Kiss it and make it better.
Always knowing when to ask questions and when not to,
You never let me down.
My wings are now stronger.
They grew with love . . . your love.
Be proud of your baby bird.
She can fly.

Michelle Geroux

The Crowded Room

There was no space in the crowded room
Embracing one another with love
It wasn't just they that filled it
The strong smell of incense
Familiar songs of the sixties
Debated issues filled their night
Planning protests that would give them power
Power needed to express themselves
Flowers filled the crowded room
Exchanging them with each other
An expression of love
Smiles filled their faces
An inner peace filled their hearts
They were content to be in the crowded room

Sandra Horton

Spirit of Salmon

Fish egg, fish egg, it's time to break free,
To swim in the stream and meet your destiny.

Fish fry, fish fry, grow as fast as you can,
Swim down to the ocean, to the salt, and to the sea.
Swim under the sky and the clouds in motion,
Soon you will be free!

Big fish, big fish, jump in the air,
See this wonderful world of sky, stars, and sea.
Swim, big fish, swim free, free, free
In the endless currents of time and tide.

Look!
The sun is setting; it's time to go,
To swim back to the stream of your birth.
Time to lay eggs in the clear, cool water,
Time to sink your earthly body in the sparkling brook.

Spirit of Salmon, spirit of fish,
Leave your flesh behind you
For the majestic eagle and the big black bear.
Now you are free, free forever,
In the endless universe.

Barbara Ann Lambert

Free!

You're free as an eagle, but watch where you fly
For the dangers are many up there in the sky

There are those who soar with you who'll take you so high
To places forbidden for eagles to fly

And some who fly with you will take you so low
To dangerous places where no eagle should go

And then there are those who will make it their quest
That eagles fly free and don't need a nest

As you fly in your freedom, be sure to look down
For eagles go nowhere that lose sight of the ground

An eagle has power, but even power can fall
Make sure there is someone to hear when you call

And eagles get lonesome, hear their cry from above
For not even an eagle . . . can survive without love

Pat O'Connor

Falling

Leaves that fall from branch to ground,
Floating downward without sound,
So do leaves their place forsake
When comes storm their grace to shake.

Starts with spring buds do peek out;
Points reach skyward, pushing taut.
Fresh and green they fan their web,
Waving from anchor of branch in ebb.

Turn of weather shocks them all;
Colours break on landscape full,
Beauty as a last cry fleeting,
Display of their grandeur beaming.

Unkind is fall to leaves so vibrant;
Part of cycle plays the tyrant.
Rain assaults in drops on them,
Each taking leave of leaf's stem.

One leaf rests atop a tree;
Wind comes up and blows it free.
Where to land now must be found
Leaves that fall from branch to ground.

Helene St. Laurent

Missing You

The loneliness I feel today
Is because you are far away.

The love I feel in my heart
Grows even stronger while we're apart.

And as I gaze across the sea,
I think of the day you'll come back to me.

Tim Landry

Teardrops of Dead Love

As I rage against the dying light
That once grew so bright,
As the candle slowly burns,
The table turns.
Tears of wax fall from the sky,
Sending nothing but a lie.
Candlelight flickered past,
Candlelight dead at last.

Carolyn Whittaker

Gardener's Lament

Join us, the guild of gardeners
The uniform, if you please
Your favourite hat, a pair of gloves
And pants with dirty knees
Our homes aren't always tidy
We have no time, you see
For yonder garden beckons
That's where we love to be
So, please excuse our clothing
The un-tidiness of our place
But stop and smell our flowers
And let the sun shine on your face

Lori Dutot

Neglect

Did you know
That after I talk to you I cry?
The way you ignore me
makes me want to die.

You're always talking
to everyone but me.
It's like you don't know
or you can't see.

I am who I am
and I won't change for you.
I'll be who I want,
and there's nothing you can do.

The way you ignore me
is a loss on your behalf.
Because, no matter what you do,
you'll never hear me laugh.

Carolyn Barber

Health Hazard

This morning as I did wake
such hurried thoughts inside my head,
my tired eyes tumbled to their arising,
cold water splashed upon my face.
My hair a mess, my clothes were sagging.
My heart was screaming, to bed, to bed.
Reluctantly I crept into the race,
my body numb, my mind lagging,
my parents bent on my demise.
I promised tomorrow with feverish lies,
to sleep in is a chance I'll take.

To school I crept in my stealth,
the milky halls tinged with blue,
my morning glory slightly faded
into a tired world of shadows.
But I—I daydream of the night:
fast cars, cheap drugs, flashing light,
my thoughts of rebellion heavily weighted,
the awkward teenager somewhat jaded,
apparently hazardous to my health.

Alison Bodurtha

Gato Negro

With eyes of glowing amber glass,
tail twitching at its end,
and muscles tense with fearsome poise,
He watches for his prey.

—a mercury flicker in the dark—

The Kill.

Then . . . still.

And back again the hunter pads,
footfalls concealed by grace and the
breath of coming winter,
teasing leaves from solemn boughs and
whispering a feather to the sky,
for one last tour

of Heaven.

Rory Makosz

I Love You

I love you for you.
I love you for me.

I love you 'cause you're you
And not someone else.

There's no specific reason why I love you.
I just love everything about you
—your hands
—your face
—your strength
—and who could forget your voice!
I love you for your sense of humor
And how you make me smile when I'm feeling down.

All these things put you together.
All these things are what make you up.

And that is why I love you!

Sharon Rendle

Angel Call

A blast as the great golden trumpet sounds
From the heavens over this vast planet of ours
Where some lost and lonely souls rove 'round
The Creator summons us from beyond the stars

Diana He's called for her regal nobility
A guardian angel to stand by the AIDS victim
For caring for children and for her generosity
We'll miss you, nurturing matriarch and woman

Teresa He's called for her mildness and humility
To teach all His angels the triumph of prayer
To prudently attend to those who live in poverty
We'll miss you, transcendent nurse and care giver

John He's called for his love of wilderness
To speak to the animal kingdom with angel choirs
To aide our planet's salvation from wastefulness
We'll miss you, great voice and nature's squire

Liz Deslippe

Escape

There is this place that I know
It dreams in the heat of the sun
Yet there is a tranquil air about it
As if it breathes and lives on its own
I think
It may be a world created by us both . . .
An embrace in the warmth of the day
The passion shared on a wondrous night
Yet there is the semblance of a house
In this place, so haunting, so true
The whisper of a ghost of a dream
So slight, just sitting on the edge of a thought
Still, it must be a world we created simultaneously
The flutter of hearts beneath palms
The sweetness of a kiss pledging life after life
Yes, there is such a place in the mirage of my mind
Our haven of escape to live and to love
Where we are alone to be who we are
Together where no one can touch us
While our hearts beat as one . . .

Diane Forest

My Life

Always turmoil, always pain, knowing sadness, missing Joy
My Life, always hectic, never boring, filled with problems, lessons learned

A heavy rainfall seeming forever endless, dark clouds filling the sky
The sun lingering from behind, struggling to break through
A crack in the clouds, light breaks through, weak at first then shining stronger than ever

A beautiful sight it is, bringing with it a surprise so lovely
A rainbow so big, so bright, so strong
Symbolizing an end to what was and a beginning to what is

My life, filled with much happiness
Always much laughter, frowns long gone
A birth of new memories filed away and treasured

Blessed with great friends, always loyal and forever true
One especially, very special and rare
Pure and honest, I'm so lucky

Treats me like a precious flower, with lots of care and a gentle touch
Showers me with sweet words, lots of warmth and kindness to spare
Arms open wide, forever protected

Living for now, Past no more
Friendship so strong, Love still blooming
Forever lasting 'til the sun, moon and stars keep shining

Naurra Baroud

If I Could Tell You Anything

If I could tell you anything, this is what I want it to be:
Please don't cry, not for too long, I'm happy—a soul set free.
I want you to know I've only passed through life's next door.
I am okay, I'm still here, but now my soul can soar.
You need to remember that I also didn't want to part,
But just as I am in yours, you, too, are forever in my heart.
Every emotion that grief can bring, please know that I feel it, too.
I love you, I miss you, but we have to see this through.
This separation is temporary and the sun has set me free.
We will be reunited and only then can I promise eternity.
You need to take time to heal, and I'm sorry for your pain.
Please be strong, trust in God, he will bring us together again.
This is a journey we all must make and we have to be alone.
It is all a part of the Master's plan, a step forward on the road home.
So if I could tell you anything I'd thank you for your love,
For it is all I could take with me to Heaven and above.

Jodi Kalbhen

Eternal Bliss?

Death knocks on your door:
Do you answer or let it be?
It stares you in the face, the trembles of the floor,
the dark, cold air as you look at thee.
The passage to the gates of paradise lies beyond this door,
the blinding light of Heaven seeps through the cracks.
Not terrified, but everlasting love and bliss,
you open the door, full of death, full of eternal happiness.
Our forever Father, His hand of love,
you are carried to the Kingdom of Heaven.
No more disease, hatred, fear,
nor emptiness, pain, or tears.
Uniting with family, living in peace and harmony,
listening to music of the angel's great symphony:
Your life hasn't ended, but has just begun,
waiting for the day
the Lord's name is always praised and sung.
But would you have feared if you knew that dark door of death
meant a life with the one you love most in eternal happiness?

Stacy McGoldrick

Glorious Past and Precarious Future

On her shore, invited were the poor and the oppressed
They came from all parts of the world
From Europe, religious persecution fleeing
In America, liberty and freedom seeking
To them was offered a new vision
They could feel the good effects of that plenty of provisions
On the new land, any immigrant could experience a sort of resurrection
Something he had never lived before
His former servitude and dependence was soon forgotten
His heart became glowing and swollen
Instead of being a vagrant, he had a place of residence
From nothing to start into being
What an epoch in his life
Today, Miss Liberty has closed the door
America has her own destitutes
What has happened to America's proclaimed worthy goals
To defend the rights and the dignity of man
To live in both freedom and equality
To act in accord with reason—reason being a divine attribute?
O' America, could you return to the first seeds you sowed?

    Dan Chellumben

Roots

    I gaze up to the twinkling stars searching for truth,
    but tonight they hide, draped under a blanket of thickly fluffed clouds.
    Shamelessly, they only offer more misery. I come back to my roots.
    I hide from my present and hope to rekindle the long-forgotten past.
    Memories of running barefoot through the freshly dewed,
    prickly grass come flooding back to me like a premonition, a hazy dream.
    I look up to a glorious, sun-kissed sky, feeling the strong presence
    of the domineering mountains that enclose upon me and
    smelling the amber, pure-fresh running brook.
    As I taste the cool liquid, I feel it pouring into me,
    replenishing me, giving me strength. I turn to the encumbering trees
    for guidance and understanding, but they are deathly silent.
    They now turn away from me; I am no longer a part of nature.
    The animals, waters, and even humans have cast me out;
    that is why I returned to my birthplace.
    The cool, crisp night air sends shivers up and down my spine.
    I feel naked. The warmth of the quality down blanket
    offers no protection from the damp, relentless wind.
    Hot, salty tears trickle down my cheeks
    as the blinding crescent moon illuminates the sky.

    Cristina Barbu

Pain of Love

As the candle started to melt away in the heat of agony,
As the sun started to hide from the weight of cold,
As the leaves started to fall from the harshness of winter,
I started leaking tears just for you, the one I loved so passionately.

You had left me in awe the first time I saw,
Like a person suffering from infatuation.
I'm no expatriate to your skies
That you always stay away from me.

Neither am I a tapestry,
That you should buy me to sit on a corner for decoration.
Don't be so insinuating to ostracize me from your eyes.
Be a little generous, love for the sake of love.

The feelings I have for you,
The pain of love that I keep inside my soul,
Will always be hard to explain,
But can't you see, my love, that you are building a iron curtain between us.

    Indu Aishwarya

Give Us an Evening

give us an evening of rest,
when we can sit beside a cool stream
and rest our souls,
put our burdens down

give us an evening of gentle joy,
of quiet, melodious warmth,
of reflective rue

give us an evening away from the daggers
and despair,
away from always trying to touch the sun

give us an evening where warm winds of comfort,
black laughter and love
and nature's sweet songs
remind us of our real selves

and we will come to find full drops of joy
and rich new rhythms and more strength to fight
the new day.

give us an evening
Paul Kwasi Kafele

Eyes of Gold

She sees him with eyes of gold,
the way he walks,
the way he talks,
his every move watched by pure gold.
The golden eyes of a young girl
. . . a young girl with determination and hope
that one day he will realize
that pure gold is hard to find and will
take his chance to look at the beauty
and warmth of pure gold.
Pure gold eyes,
Pure gold heart,
Pure gold soul,
all of these in one,
in one young girl, with eyes of gold.
Janine Nowlan

Panic and Confusion

Inside my brain I hear them call—
"You should do this!" . . . "Why did you that?"
I wish to silence up them all—
Rebuking hiss! . . . Berating gnat!

First panic comes,
Confusion after.
Then their drums
Erase all laughter.

They come upon me often, oh,
Dreaded panic and confusion.
I try to push them down, but no!
Peace is but an illusion.

They reign supreme inside
Until all else is gone.
They enjoy their ride,
Till banishment at dawn.
Kathleen Seibel

The Park

There is a park where I have been,
Now only a memory left in my head.

Once you go through the gate,
You'll see that the beauty within
Brings pleasure to everyone.

The trees stand tall;
Their leaves are different shades of green,
Colourful flowers put in the right place
That smell so sweet you can almost taste.

Freshly cut grass, everything kept in trim,
Swans in the water, protected but free,
Soft ground in the park,
Safe place were children can play,

No broken seats—nice place to sit;
No graffiti—nice place to be.

Maybe one day I'll come back
To see this beautiful park,

Now only a memory
Left in my head. . . .
Martha Bowes

Drought

The Lord above, in his colour scheme
Must have forgotten the colour green
As the land turns to a darker brown
While we wait for the rain to fall

The kangaroo hops down his track
He knows it's no use turning back
There's only Death at the dam now
The kookaburra still laughs in his tree
For he can fly where the waters be
The cockatoos screech and the curlews call
The brolgas dance at their unique ball
But there's a sense of suspension in the bush
As they wait for the rain to fall

In times of plenty, with grass so green
Little thought was given to times so lean
The land was covered in cattle and sheep
Now the haze of the day sinks into the west
Now the working men have gone to rest
Everyone over this brown land kneels
And prays for the rains to fall
Teresa-Ruth Maynard

Here Am I . . .

Here am I,
standing tall,
standing against this nearby wall.

Here I stand ashamed,
Yet I find no one to blame.
Have I made the right decision
As I thought,
Or is it all for naught?

And so I move on every day,
Just so I can earn my daily pay.
Kristan MacCarthy

Best Friends

My spaniel dog will play with me.
Rebuffed, his eyes may plead,
"Don't leave me all alone today.
To cuddle is my need."

And when the world and friends betray,
My pet will understand.
He'll gaze at me with shining eyes
And come and lick my hand.

His faithfulness is endless,
And to me seems not so odd,
For if I turn dog backwards, then,
I find his name spells God!

Caryl Bowman

Peace Is Found

You are lost amid
the waves of confusion.

What can you do to find
your way back to how you were?

Don't you know that the old
cannot be recaptured?

Embrace the new, which is slightly
scuffed and more weathered . . .

Not so neat and shiny,
but tougher.

Once you realize how strong
the current is against you,
will you realize your inner strength?

Swimming was so very hard.
But now, you can float to the surface.

It is waiting.
The pain, like a large rock,
has sunk below the surface,
out of sight. . . .

Anna Kim

Death Row

Here I sit, counting away
The minutes one by one,
All because of one ill-spoken word
And speaking with a gun.

Midnight's my final hour;
Redemption will not be.
The priest declined to hear my words.
Said he, "Satan marked thee . . ."

Reminiscing brings back pain
Of times not long ago
When children believed my every word,
Then redness in the snow.

The man in the hood is here;
Time on this world is done.
The gas smells; I'm going to hell
Because I used a gun.

Henry Veltkamp

You

I see you standing over there,
With your brown eyes and blowing hair.
I pretend not to see you,
And you do the same.
We're trying to forget the grief and the pain.
We belonged together,
But you couldn't see
Just how much you meant to me.
Your heart now belongs to someone new.
I thought I meant a lot to you.
Now you're gone, and I know
Just how much I loved you so.

Robin Ferguson

Brother

So far and never near
You're here so fast, only to disappear
I wonder if you realize
How much you mean to me
Love must be a difficult thing for you to see
Your friends will come and go, Brother
But I am here to stay
So if you ever need me, Brother
I won't be far away

Stephanie Tonge

The Single Flower

From the nutrient earth emerged a flower
basking in the fresh spring sun,
wistfully dancing in the air,
awaiting tender care,
awaiting someone.

And someone came and watched it for a while.
He then came often—would look on it and smile.

Clouds formed and the sky grew dim.
The budding flower awaited for him.

There came the sun and then there came the rain,
but the smiling man did not come there again.

And before the bloom one cold, dark night there tread
footsteps on the flower in the single flower bed.

Shirley Cluney Sheppard

Release

My mask I cast aside,
All my pain exposed to your sight.
With a tear drop resting at the corner of my eye
I searched for you in the wide and endless sky.

I sensed your glow resting on my tear stained cheek.
I felt stronger, no longer alone and weak.
Your warmth encompassed me as I danced in ecstasy
The hurt and sorrow your scintillation took away from me

A sense of peace overwhelmed my entire being
So pure and mystical; an indefinable feeling
I felt a strength I never had before,
As your glow lifted me from reality's claw.

Seah Siew Hua

Behind My Fan, I Cry

Opulent city, gold upon shimmering lights
Let me go.

Gondolas will caress your skin
The softness of your gardens shall wipe your tears
Do not touch me!

I have risen early—to catch my train.
Why must you watch?

Invitingly reclined upon velvet bed
Hypnotic eyes that breathe
No, I cannot stay.

Gather the pretty Venetians into your arms
For they are more beautiful than I.

My train is leaving. I grab my fan.
Venetian lovers never say good-bye.

Lia Zuliani

Remembrance Day: Poppies to Remember

P—Poppies are grown in Flanders fields
O—On November 11th, they are worn
P—Poppies are grown in Flanders fields
P—Poppies are worn on your clothes
I—In memory of the soldiers who died
E—Enemies were defeated
S—Soldiers died for us, for democracy

T—Today is the day we wear our poppies
O—One day a year is enough to

R—Remember:
E—Every soldier who died
M—Many families torn apart
E—Every dead soul
M—Many said that there would never be another world war
B—But they were wrong
E—Even in years to come we will remember
R—Remember!

Elyte Barzilay

Winds of Fate

I stand at your grave but I do not weep,
although you are now in eternal sleep.
It was months ago that my tears were shed,
long before we chose your satin-lined bed.
I cried as I watched your health slowly fail,
your mind grow dull, your grow body frail.
A young man's walk turned to hobbled gait.
I watched you suffer an old man's fate
of eyesight dim and raspy breath.
You fought your battle and challenged death.
But as you weakened, death grew stronger.
You would not be with us for much longer.
So with breaking hearts and tear streaked eyes,
we gathered 'round, said our good-byes.
You took one last breath and gently sighed;
I was there beside you when you died.
Today a headstone will mark your place,
and although you are now in God's embrace
I will bide my time 'til the winds of fate
reunite us at Heaven's Gate.

Cindy Rona Gasoi

Souls

When your hand
took my hand,
words were not for us,
excuses for me.

As a reed in the wind
since then,
you vibrate and suffer.

As leaves of the same twig,
we palpitate
under the same light.

Our souls
are magic pearls
in a secret sea.

Alfredo Tutino

Wolf

Soundless down its path
Travelling in search of a fray
This creature of beauty
Strikes fear in its prey

Lustrous eyes, so captivating
As if peering through to the soul
Immobilizing through its stare
Mysteriously in control

As his howling resounds
Through the frigid night air
In the darkness all is silenced
Making his presence aware

Posed on the highest cliff
Un-intimidated by height
A wolf's silhouette
In the full moon's light

Marcia Rodrigues

Father Beast

Daddy? Are you there?
Daddy? Do you care?
Daddy? Are you mad today?
Daddy? What can I say?
Daddy? Why the strap?
Daddy? On my back you've
whipped a map.
Daddy? Do you hate me?
Daddy? Can't you see?
Daddy? What have I done?
Daddy? Don't yell, I'll come.
Daddy? Why down here?
Daddy? Stifle my fear!
Daddy? Who are you?
Daddy? Obey? I always do.
Daddy? It's dark in there.
Daddy? Rebel? I don't dare.
Daddy? Must I do this?
Daddy? Can I have a kiss?

Daddy? Never tell, you forbid.
Daddy? I just did.

Carmen Eva Duhaime

Alone and Sad

The shining tears
Stream down her face
She feels quite lost
And out of place

Her love has died
He's gone away
Her last respect
She'll pay

And through the cold
And misty flower
She places down
A love red flower

A symbol of the love
They had
And now she feels
Alone and sad

Pam Steiniger

Madame Butterfly

After my lustrous demimonde
ransacked the house
in search of her dead lover,
she became a monarch butterfly,
and fell upon the gravel shoulder
where she clamoured and flailed.

At the side of the road
she slowly fell asleep;
her tiny breaths and sobs
succumbed to the pain
of her crushed womb
that had borne future kings.

I cupped her in my hand
as she gave a last stroke
against the summer air,
then folded her wing;
and for her lost children
final thoughts she gave.

Jay Stephenson

The Robber Bride

She lurks
In the
Dark.
She steals
Without a
Thought.
She never looks
Back.
She can't
Afford to.
She knows.
She knows
It won't last forever.
She knows
She will be
Caught.
She knows
She has the
Upper hand.

Jaime Smith

Laurels at Your Feet

I do not know how you came my way,
But once I found you, I'll never let you go.
I came to understand by time
That you know my very feelings,
And whether you care or not,
I made of you my hero.
You can ignore me for months, for years,
Yet when you turn up, there you find me,
Ready to put laurels at your feet.

Imelda Serracino Inglott

Resigned

My root lies dying,
Pieces wither, pieces fall;
Keep me grounded, fruitless cries,
Life seeps slowly, breaths are stalled,
Eyes see backward, muttering meaningless;
Now just this place, the faces by your bedside,
And, holes, holes, wherever will I go?
In mournful cries by your bedside,
To bring your face around again—
To say "hello" and "remember when we"
But shriveling, my root lies dying;
And the memories in layered rings,
Reshape the wood in its decay.
You're going away.
I know.
No sense hoping you'll stay,
I know.

Susan J. Russell

Lady of Night

I hear the Lady sing in my ears,
I feel her presence through all my tears.
Times of laughter, times of pain,
Times of infinity as the insane.
Oh, the lady with glistening silver hair
And warm topaz eyes, more than one can bear.
She is everyone and herself all the same,
That I relate to and admire her, the Silver dame.
Life and Death she holds in her hands,
Strings of colorful patterns, wrapped in bands.
In the dark beauty of twilight's gloom,
I see her as the guardian of doom.
Her silvery words can delight and despair,
She on the back of a white unicorn mare.
At the pool on Avalon's sacred earth,
Her visions show secrets of our death and birth.

Lindsay McGee

Why Not?

Why not love me for who I am,
Instead of hating me for who I'm not?

Why not love me for what I have,
Instead of hating me for what I lack?

Why not love me for the love I feel for you,
Instead of hating me for the love you feel not?

Sherine El Difrawi

Something I Cannot Have

A thing of beauty, staring at you,
Perfection at its best, leaving nothing for the rest.
I can only dream of being with her,
For when I wake, things are as they were.

All she wants is a friend.
For, all I want is for it not to end.
For, she is kind, for she is sweet,
For she keeps my heart at a steady beat.

The love I'm willing
To share with her,
Is warming but chilling
But will always be there.
For all I write, and all I say,
I hope that she, will be mine one day.

A lot of wishes on my behalf,
Because now I realize
This is something I cannot have.

Kenneth Leduc

An Hourglass Is . . .

I sift the sands as the day goes by;
My particles slowly drift and die.
I cannot be turned back in time,
Because I control the string of lives on line.

Each heartbeat that I pour through,
A soul is made to be overly renewed.
Now, I stand, only to be overturned
As I hold on to the time that I have earned.

Time is passing us by;
We always need to allow nature to answer why,
To make us live within the fullest hourglass.
Only the souls do last . . . while our time has passed.

Tina Scarpitti

Thunder Boy

The morning is so peaceful and bright
So bright from the morning sunlight
Traffic is thinned out so light
And the birds, from tree to tree, take on short flights

The toughest little man around was thunder boy
Knives and guns were his toys
And the louder the bang, the more he'd enjoy the noise
A cool little guy with a lot of poise

Thunder boy stood three feet tall
He dressed in black overalls
And when danger was near, he'd have a ball
He'd always the right weapon for every call

One day, thunder boy was challenged by a man named Jack
A big man, all dressed in black
A man that carried his worldly possessions in a big sack
And weapons were one thing Jack did not lack

Jack pulled out a hand gun
And thought that he'd have a little fun
With spear in hand, thunder boy made a little run
Caught Jack at the end of the spear, and the fight was done

Lourie D. Passmore

Thinking of You

As I sit here all alone,
I think of you,
All that you do and say.
I feel safe in your arms.
Every time you touch me,
A chill runs down my spine.
When sweet words flow from your lips,
My whole body begins to tingle.
When your lips touch mine,
A peaceful sensation fills my soul.
Every minute of every day,
I think of you.
When I hear your voice on the phone,
I wish you were here beside me.
When you are near me,
I see but only you.
When you whisper to me,
Your voice is all I hear.
As I sit here all alone,
I think of you.

Melissa Storey

Untitled

All along the beach
I see footprints that never reach
the crowded shore or hot dog stand,
'cause they are only the
traces of a lonely dog and a
lonely man.

Marisa Cameron

Life Is a Bouquet

Beautiful to have and enjoy,
Satisfaction for the soul, the eye,
Thorns that can catch you unaware,
Sadness when it dies, but leaving
Behind the seeds for future
Bouquets forever and ever.

Dorothy Bisphop

Mother Nature? Or My Wife?

Oft' I'll watch Her, fumbling through
small bundles of forest gatherings, few
could place . . . just so.

A withering rose placed in a branch,
on window frame with lace by chance?
I think no.

The Artist has touched Her, I believe.
Her wisdom in change will not deceive
an admirer.

Her inner peace is held strong
with a passionate love that only belongs
to a lover.

I adore Her.
She is a priceless extension,
of God's creation.

Eugene F. Crawley

Living Life

To live is to be alive.
To be alive is to care.
To care is to be cared about.
To be cared about
Is to be living life.

To live is to think.
To think is to have thought.
To have thought is to be alive.
To be alive
Is to be living life.

To live is to see.
To see is to be seen.
To be seen is to have insight.
To have insight
Is to be living life.

To live is to hear.
To hear is to be heard.
To be heard is to be understood.
To be understood
Is to be living life.

Melanie Bodendorfer

The Old Man

A very bent old man
walking with a cane
slowly makes his way
down a country lane.

Now he stops to rest
beneath a shady tree.
He likes to sit and dream
of things that used to be.

In his heart, he's young again,
instead of old and frail.
Then he could run and skip
on legs that did not fail.

But now he is back again,
his reverie is gone.
Slowly he picks up his cane
and sadly shuffles on.

Clare Moyer

Love Is

Love is not a feeling,
it's a choice and a way.
Love is more than words,
not just the things we say.

Love is an opportunity
to be more than we are.
Love shines brightest in darkness
and draws those who were far.

Love is not temporary
like hardship and strife.
Love is eternal by nature
and brings with it life.

Love need not be distant
but comes when you call.
For, Love is a person,
the Lord God of all.

James David Haycock

Kings and Queens

I remember
when we were kings and queens.
We were young and immortal
We changed the world ten times
in the same night.
At the esoteric tavern,
we drank red wine among intellectuals and artists.
I loved the smoky atmosphere and words wafting in the air.
Around the wooden table,
my friends and I thought we were the chosen ones.
John Lennon was still alive—
humans had never given peace a chance.
We wanted "Hair" to be forever;
everything was so mystical!
The world was much smaller than Vietnam.
The hippies thought they were heroes.
There was so much mystery and danger
when we were kings and queens.

Avi Neto

Where Have You Gone?

There was a while of happiness
Once upon a time so long ago
When you danced and shone and sparkled
With your eyes and features all aglow

Now your face is clouded over
You hide behind a gauzy veil
I try to lift the curtain
And time and time again I fail

You look at me but do not see
I might as well be empty space
A silver mirror where you gaze inside yourself
Or a window to some distant other place

It didn't happen suddenly
You didn't vanish in a fairy cloud
Over months and years you slowly disappeared
Retreating further in your introverted shroud

I don't know why you're leaving me
I don't know where you're going to
I don't know what I could have done
To save our love and rescue you

Bruce Goodchild

A Ray of Light

Sometimes we will stand still.
Sometimes we see.
Sometimes a tiny ray of light, that far
surpasses Earthly lights of dimmer strength,
may startle us.
Its wisdom, clarity, and truth unchangeable
may show the fleetingness of our life's routine,
may also show a glorious world elsewhere,
untouchable, and yet so surely known.
We turn from such a light but slowly
to go on our path, still wonder in our eyes,
but in our hearts in one still place
remains the memory of that one glimpse,
of that one tiny ray of light,
and will become a smile that lingers,
and does become a star that guides.

Kaethe von Mandel Davis

Someday

Someday, my one true love will come along.
Someday, a dove will perch on my finger and coo in my ear.

Someday, they'll let me play on their team.
Someday, maybe I won't feel in the way.

Someday, the pain will stop.
Someday, the blood stains will be washed away by tears.

Someday, it will be safe to walk at night.
Someday, the good might fight and prevail.

Someday, the meaning of life will be known.
Someday, people might not live in strife.

Someday, we will treat each other as equals.
Someday, there will be no need for sequels.

Someday, tears will flow.
Someday, our fears will subside.

Someday, the killing will cease.
Someday, there will be peace.

Someday, someday—scenes so far away—
Someday soon our fate will be made.

It's up to you and to me to make a decision
Before someday is too late.

Denise Fuller

Untitled

Oh, my child, how can I comfort you
Or try to ease your pain?
That waterfall of tears streaming down your face
Will slowly start to stain

I didn't make the decision to leave you
I heard Him call my name
The softest, sweetest voice
It was then in my dreams that He came

The touch of His hand as He led me away
Filled me with such peace and love
It was a feeling of great freedom
Feeling as free to fly as a dove

A part of me will always be with you
My love that's in your heart will stay
Be strong with the comfort of knowing
I will again get to hold you—one day.

Jodi Howell

Sonnet

What becomes of a flower when it wilts
Or beauty when it is withered and old?
What happens to a soul, weighed down with guilt,
Or a magical tale that goes untold?
When lungs breathe their last, to where goes the air?
When minds work no more, what will think for them?
When flowing blood stops, how can the heart care?
A punishment so sad, one can't condemn;
Waiting is hard, unexpected is worse.
Not knowing, it's torture, what will happen?
Nothing goes fearless to Nature's worst curse;
Some learn to accept it, most never can.
What happens in death; who shall your soul keep?
Neither Heaven nor hell, but dreamless sleep.

Veerle L. Huygens

Far Away

Take this tear and hold it
Feel it with your heart
Take my cry and hear it
You shall play your part

Take my dreams and feel them
Scared with bitter love
Take my hand and hold it
Peace is like a dove

Take my eyes and blind me
Lead me through the way
Take my voice and speak for me
On the grass I'll lay

Take my dreams away from me
Let me see the dark
Take my thoughts away from me
I ask for no remark

Hold the darkness still for me
Let me rest in peace
Take the voices far from me
I shall be released

Victoria Wyman

Walls

Where were you when Kennedy died?—
I'm sure "We the people" know,
And when Armstrong stepped down
With Nixon soon to follow.

Mandela walked free
Only to see
His people prisoner
In their own country,

Or the wall to fall.
It's Berlin for all,
Yet, China still won't recall,
For Tiananmen still within their wall.

Is it something we helped to be
With one-sided viewing and
Centuries of complacency
Content with its part
In our wondrous history?

Gary Hindley

Fear

I am a mere shell
Of my former self,
My youth and strength
Sucked from my being
By a force laced with evil.

Fear, frustration,
Sadness, and uncertainty:
Lost and scared,
A prisoner of ill health.

Patience will tell;
Destiny will prevail.
Will hope and prayer
Save?

Laura Cooper

Sunrise

Beautiful colours
Mixed together,
Up against a shrub of heather.

The sun comes up;
The moon goes down,
As pretty as an evening gown.

Shades of purple, orange, and blue,
Red and pink and turquoise, too.
Except for sight—what does it do?

It brings us all another day,
Makes people happy, and they say,
"I see the light through golden ray."

The eye of God, it shines so bright.
It brings us all eternal light,
And mesmerizes until night.

When the dark of night is done,
And the day has just begun,
The light comes with the rising sun.

Jacqui Holiff

Loveless, She Stumbled

Loveless, she stumbled
Into the night
Upon her two feet
Snowy white
No one to hold her
Keep her upright
Abandoned
Unable to see the light

Stumbled
Into the darkness
Falling, far from Grace
A lone figure
Leaving no trace
A whisper, in silence
A cry
No one heard

Loveless, she stumbled
And now she is gone
Only our guilt
Our pain
To live on

Hope McIntyre

My Dad

Dad
Jim
Exercise
Built
House
Life
Death
Gone
My
Dad

Mike Mcmillan

Help

Where are you, where are you,
Where are you, my friend?

I need you, how I need you;
I need you to take my hand.
I want your help and guidance
Through this life, a life in great distress.

Please, dear Lord,
Please take command,
Help make me that person I know you know I am.
With your help and guidance
I know that we can.

Jeannette Barnes

I Will Love Again

I wish to forget one who I loved.
I wish to dry all the tears that I shed.
I wish to heal the pain in my heart.
In my dreams I feel you a lot—
Your lies and false promises of all sorts.
I remember your words that you will catch me when I fall;
You showered me with hollow hopes.
Your desire to see me stand happy and tall,
When it came to really loving me,
You had no skill how to cope.
But I still glorify love,
My most intent feeling,
And I still desire to love again.
How wonderful it is to still feel that in my heart.

Nicole Mann

Love's Promise

I am in a great state of bliss
All I want is the taste of your kiss
This you give with plenty of care
Deep in my heart, you know that you're there
I've never been so happy as I am at this time
I thank the Lord for making you mine
I share my possessions and my life
Maybe, someday, you will be my wife
You worry about the future, one you don't know
Don't think of the bad—together, old we will grow
By your side is where I will always be
Comforting you, just being me
Nothing in this world can split us in two
Because I've never loved anything as much as you

Rick Leaver

Civilized

We are civilized barbarians,
Living in a world we did not create.
Guilty of crimes we do not commit.
Victims of some circumstance that does not exist.
Screwed quite royally,
because we forgot to open our eyes,
when we woke up this morning.

We are civilized barbarians
and all the world is our stage.

Vivian Bigler

The Stream of Love

Upon the bank I sit placidly, watching the flowing stream, stream of passion;
I look up, gazing at the skies.
The dwelling within the bounds of that first moment arise.

I smile to the memory of your voice, your eyes;
my heart pounds to the tenderness of your love.

I shift back my eyes to the running water,
the watercourse of love,
I search for the endpoint, trying to look into the future,
but all that my heart could settle for
Is the present flow of love,
the endless love we share.

Looking up, gazing at the stars,
I feel a shivering warmth run through my blood.
After deep illusion,
I meet your magic eyes, your soft smiles, your sweet kiss,
and your affectionate heart
to be the roots that cling to the ground of my state.

Moving back to my state of mind,
I sigh with greatest ardour, close my eyes, and cry:
"I love you."

Nazli Eltahry

Good-Bye, My Little Friend

Good-bye, my little friend, I sat with you until the very end.
It saddens me to see you go, oh, how I loved you so.
I didn't have you for very long,
    never again will I hear your beautiful song.
Here you were not able to fly, but now you're free to soar the sky.
I'll never have another bird like you, the perfect shade of blue.
You looked at me in the cutest way and talked to me every day.
Benji was your name and tossing your ball was your favorite game.
You would get angry when I'd touch your orange ball,
For it was your favorite one of them all.
You laid your head on your ball and went to sleep, never to wake.
I buried it with you today as a little keepsake.
Good-bye my little friend, for now we must be apart.
I hope you know, Benji, you'll always be in my heart.

Darlene Krieger

Peace Haven

This place to where we have moved
Is truly the epitome of peace.
It's so wonderful to leave the groove
Of life in a city's streets.

Surely Paradise is trees, grass, water, and flowers,
And God put them here on Earth
For us to appreciate but not feel power
Over those unfortunate enough to have a dearth.

Surely He did not intend that wars be fought
Nor wish all the strife and poverty existing in the world today,
But then again many people forget they ought
To remember to whom they owe so much and pray.

God does not ask for our gratitude.
Rather He leaves it up to us to live our lives
With integrity and toward others a caring attitude.
Happiness within He then provides.

Peace and tranquility we now have in abundance.
The quietness so quiet you can almost hear it,
The only sounds those of nature's nuances,
Into this environment we happily fit.

Gina Perrin

Joe's River

Down in the Ottawa valley where our father was born
The echo of the music is still there and hanging around
In the morning, the sound of the river, you can hear the drop of a fin
The flowing sound of the river and the sound of the violin

The man, he was a poet, would sing a song or two
Play a tune and tell a tale and give a joke for you
The stories of the loggers are freshly on my mind
The legends of courageous men who lived there in that time

The fiddle was the center for a man who plays a tune
He never had to buy a beer in the town saloon
My mother never found a fault for this caring man
He kept her toes a tapping with love, I understand

The trees along the river, they stand so strong, you see
Like the people at the valley who made it history
When I visit the river, it surely makes me proud
It makes me want to come along and sing this poem out loud

Enjoy your life the best you can, the words he said to us
Play a tune or tell a joke or sing a song you must
The river keeps on flowing and stories always there
The music keeps on playing, you can hear it everywhere

> *Jerry Lepage*

The Ocean

The bright sun glistens on the water
as the waves gently roll across the ocean.
The boats rock on the waves as they sail with the wind.
The sea gulls squeal in the sky while
the dolphins dance freely in the water.
The sharks lurk across the ocean floor
waiting for their next prey to swim by.
On the shore, the waves walk up to meet the sand.
The children laugh, run, and play
and build sand castles on the beach.
They have smiles on their faces as
they find seashells on the edge of the water.
As the day ends, the sun leaves a mixture of colors
painted across the sky as it slowly disappears in the horizon.
No more laughter, only the sound of the waves and the sea gulls.

> *Ashley Wilson*

The Joy of Living

The joy of Living,
the vigour of "being" is revenge of a wretched life,
by a soul everlasting . . .

where the Gamble of life
is played by impregnable fate,
where the bones are kept waiting
for one who is late . . .

where the divine fragment of "God"
is trapped under a mortal net . . .
where man is just a puppet
while the world is a huge set . . .

where gold is found
in the dreary desert sand,
where the highest mountains end in a vale
but find no land . . . !

It is fun to live in such a strange world, which is beautiful and ugly as well.
Nothing resembles my varied world,
neither Heaven nor Hell . . . !

> *Pradnya Joshi*

Political Correctness

Is it good or is it bad?
To me, it seems it's very sad.
We've lost the art of enjoying laughter
At ourselves, but rejoice in the slaughter
Of anything and everything we do not agree with.

In my youth, we made fun of
Politicians, authors, countries, and sort of
Anybody and anything, and the best of it was,
The target of our fun would laugh the loudest, because
He (she?) seemed to have then what we have since lost.

A sense of humour is so precious.
What can one have more delicious?
It is unfortunate that we no longer can call
A spade a spade or, affectionately, a lady a doll
Without raising umbrage of one and all.

Short people are not short, but "vertically challenged."
The deaf are not deaf, but "hearing impaired."
Even weeds are now called "voluntary plants!"
Pray, what's the correct term for insects such as ants?
Politically correct. What a pitiful state of affairs!

K. P. Wickremasinghe

Ode to Classical Music

In times of joy or when I feel dismay,
I turn to music of the classical giants
Whose names comprise a great array—
In them I place my trust and my reliance.

Beethoven's symphonies and J.S. Bach's
Cantatas uplift the human spiritual beat.
To Mozart's Magic Flute, childlike, one harks,
While to the Strausses we waltz with our feet.

Mahler's lieders plumb the psyche's depths.
Chopin's piano notes caress in intimate steps.

Palestrina and Victoria bring us closer to God;
Smetana brings all peoples closer to their land.
With motets that guide like divine staff and rod,
Bruckner puts us in touch with the Creator's hand.

Their timeless music brings Faith, Hope, and Love
To grow in our minds and to soothe our souls!
Listen with open ear, become at peace like the Dove—
Then you will find it easier to reach Life's goals.

Michael F. Chui

Times

There are times in life
We want to remember,
Times we wish to forget,
Times we knew great happiness,
Times we knew regret,
Times we look at the world and wonder
Why thousands of children are dying of hunger,
Times we wonder why tyrants did live
Who only had death and destruction to give
To many who live in riches and grace
Who never had hardships in life they must face.
Will there ever be times when life will be
A world of love and equality?
I fear I'm a dreamer with visions afar;
Will time just be gone and we are as we are.

Edna E. Mavity

The Cracks

The cracks in the road
Have a story to tell
About where we are going
And where we have been

Some seem so destined
To just run away
The path in the pavement
The price that I've paid

As you move through this life
When your heart leads the way
Past romances like cracks
Become part of the way
That we determine what's right
And which way to go
The cracks in your heart
With old memories mend slow

Terry Lynn Howard

For Someone Special

Is love hatred?
Is hatred love?
Is it a night hawk
Or a mourning dove?

Does it cry,
Or does it weep?
Does it wash,
Or does it sweep?

Does it give,
Or does it take?
It is two,
That love will make.

It is neither hatred nor a night hawk.
Love never cries or is washed away.
For love is something warm and truthful
That is won by two, every day.

So you see, it's in all of honest hearts,
And loving souls, too,
To be wanted by someone special,
Most of all that someone that is You.

Corrie Edward

Compassion

There lies a tortured soul
after stumbling through a dark web
blinded by the pain
when something took it away
like the beating of wings
lifting the spirit beyond the weight
arms engulfed the sufferer
emphatic to the crisis
creating a new melody
their souls orchestrated together
in the power of give and take
making the one
their blended battle dismantled obstacles
destiny hovered beyond the dust
revealing the path of their journey
enlightening existence

Trevor Starratt

Untitled

A breeze caresses
The lover's nest.
Sun shines
Warmth and comfort.

Clouds are forming
Under the darkening skies.
You can hear the thunder
And feel the rage.

Lovers should never seek
Nor stray from those they keep.
Like two birds in flight,
They glide toward the morning light.

I now have found my dove
To give him my sacred love,
Holding him and giving cover
When the weather gets stronger.

Patricia Chisholm

Romancing Today

They call it lust; I felt love.
They saw deception,
I sensed trust. . . .
"Sink in his arms,
And land your arms
In the sink." They lamented . . .
They predicted . . .
They waited . . .
I couldn't wait.
I had to dry the diapers and rompers,
And scrubbed the jeans and jumpers.
"Didn't I tell you so?" said the righteous.
"Serves you right," asserted the smartest.
I slaved a lot, saved a bit,
I sink in his arms, loving his charms.
And pretty soon I turn to my girl . . .
'Don't marry in haste. . . .'
Bemused, she steps away
Leaving me to wonder about rings
And things and beautiful happenings. . . .

Lilian Loke

Loon

Loon tremolo
ripples through the lake,
dallies on the lily pad,
filters through the feathered
holy of holies,
lingers in the backwater
of my wilderness,
but does not enter.

Voice quivering
with indifference
floats aloft on caryatid winds,
pierces through the heart
of sixty million summer nights,
then tucks its songs
inside its bill,
aloof from me,
the infidel.

Bernadette Griffin

The Calm before the Storm

The sea is calm.
The air is still.
There is a silent demand
For something devastating to happen.

A small craft sails into this tranquil surrounding.
It is overcome by the peacefulness it has found
And pauses to take in the beauty and silence.

In the distance a faint rumble is heard,
Suddenly louder and louder.
There on the horizon it is spotted,
A great white tower of turbulent water.

The small craft attempts to retreat
As the wave grows in intensity and speed,
But to no avail.

The wave is here.
The craft and all who sailed it disappear.
Once again the water calms,
And the air stills.

Frank Sheldon

War Cycle

Do you hear the banished cry,
the tearless rain upon the face of time?

The war of worlds will battle on,
the years of torment among the silent strong.

Beneath the tarnished skin of faith
a light appears to hold the gate
of truth and love, a witness to all,
as the wounded begin their fall.

So weak from fight, the scars too many,
the healing time diminishes with shots
as the sun leaves the sky's peace.

A darkness shall excuse the shadowed face
as his mind loses its grace.

Evil shows no faith—a mere candle to
extinguish in the hands of hate.

As the last fool draws his card of death,
a peaceful entry will become his forgotten passage.

Bruce Loughery

Grandpa

He went to the hospital late one day,
I think it was a day in May,
The clouds went dark,
The birds didn't sing,
I felt like I was caught in the middle of a ring,
He went into critical care,
And I couldn't go in and see him there,
Gramma says that he looked scary,
But he was not quite as hairy,
He went in because he couldn't breathe,
But for me there was no breeze,
And now the house is so quiet,
He promises that he will be home soon,
But I think that he is lying.

Kristen Petherick

Friends

Some friends are truly a Special Kind,
And sometimes harder than easier to find.

Where relatives are chosen by fate alone,
Friends we choose, to each our own.

It doesn't matter if we're near or far,
A friend to me you truly are.

They say the best mirror is an old friend,
Someone on whom you can count and always depend.

When I make a fool of myself, and you feel it won't last,
We can laugh about it and put it in the past.

Though at times we may disagree,
Friends forever I hope we'll be.

I guess the feelings just weren't there,
But I have to admit I still care.

The future is not ours to see.
I guess best friends we'll have to be.

There's really only a very small few
Of Special Friends just like you.

Donna Evans

Wanted: Companionship

He says he lives in an apartment,
That he travels, and is an engineer,
How some of his children no longer speak to him.

Of course, they do not believe him.
They do not believe themselves.
They see his bedspread and silken sheets in a want ad.
Printed words on a page
Stirred their thighs so they telephoned;
Neglected, lovely thighs, announcing their names,
Dating a bedspread that has a box number.

And when they lie with him,
He relates a story of his wife to them.
They seldom answer him.
It is important to dignify their role on the bedspread.

They know their parts
Between those silken sheets.
They make-believe talk,
Speaking of roses rather than thorns.
As they part, names are written in their engagement books,
Lending a timid sort of identity to it all.

Ann Farrell

Nicole

In the spring, you gave me happiness as though
I were a child in the park.
Through summer, you were like the brilliant
sun on my waking morn'.
Like fall approaches, I become a leaf,
changing color, losing life.
There is no winter for me.
My time is done; I float softly down to die!
Please put me in a book between lost pages.
Find me there, for thus is my dead existence.

Evin Bergeron

Too Many Shades of Blue

His broken heart will never mend
His love has gone, he knows not where
But the blue of her eyes, he'll remember
Like the blue of the ribbon in her hair

He sits and wonders—is it all a dream?
She left so quickly, with no good-bye
But the blue of her eyes, he'll remember
Like the blue of a cloudless sky

Wings of birds and ocean waves
Cornflowers sprinkled with dew
Everywhere he looks, he sees
Too many shades of blue

Never again will he see her
Memories will fade with the years
But one thing he'll always remember
Is the blue of her eyes, filled with tears

He's tried to forget but he cannot
All of his thoughts seem to view
Those eyes that broke his tender heart
There's just too many shades of blue

Kathleen Heys Tushingham

Awakened

Recalling life, I awake from the dead
Ancient as sin, I lift my head
Brushing away death, I consume the sky
As sons of man stare with dry eyes
Alive as today, I shake off the rot
Slowly my mind again thinks thoughts
Inhaling the darkness, I'm so alive
I've waited centuries to arrive

Wounded Bear

Falling Star of Hope

When you want to wish
upon a falling star,
it won't be far when it falls,
for the hope within you is so deep
that nothing can affect it.
So you look into the sky each night,
waiting and hoping that
the moment will be just right.
But then unexpectedly,
the nights turn into days and the
days into weeks,
and soon enough the hope that
was deemed unchangeable
begins to wear ever so thin.
So you decide to walk
away from it all and put your
hope in something else.
But what you didn't realize was
that the day you gave up
your hope was the day that the
shooting star did fall.

Vivian E. Lee

Untitled

Friday morning,
I'm hating being awake.
A dead cat on the street:
a reminder of mortality.
At the subway,
a man with a saxophone
plays a mournful tune—
how does he know my mood?
On the train,
with no one I recognize,
feeling crowded and lonely.
Now, a pair of eyes I know
but don't feel like meeting.
Out on the street,
a lonely beggar is selling pens.
He calls to me.
"You'll be twenty-one forever," he says.
"Your lips are cherry blossoms."
I didn't buy a pen from him.

Roberta Rambaldini

Souvenir

Little grain of sand
From that inland sea,
Did you touch His foot
At Galilee?

Janet C. James

Reaching Out

Rattle the bars,
Of an ivory cage,
Escape across unknown terrain,
Abandon the rope,
That is tied to a hope
That you will evade all the pain.

Direction is constant,
Conditions are not,
Lost in the valleys and peaks,
Trapped in a car,
That is strapped to a star
Always remains out of reach.

We walked in the desert,
Baked under the sun,
Followed your parallel tracks,
The dust and the heat,
Has blistered the feet,
Of the monkeys we tie to our backs:

Graham J. Bowden

Hands

Hands tell a journey.
Creativity sifts through fingertips.

Her hands show self-mutilation:
Yesterday's burns, cuts, broken bones.

Her hands remind her.
They are her voice,
Saving her from muteness.

Debbie Wiper

Dragons

Dedicated to Bubby Reva

Dragons are extremely cool.
They like to breathe fire, eat, and drool.
They fly so high that you can't see.
They are a big part of history.
They come and attack and fight in war.
They eat you up and then they roar!
When people see dragons coming their way,
They run, run, run, so far away.
Dragons are a hideous sight,
And they usually come at night.
Dragons are sometimes very cruel,
Others are as precious as a jewel.
The nice ones come and grant you wishes;
They might be kind and do your dishes!
Dragons live way up in your mind,
And when you are lost, they are a great find.
Dragons come when you're lonely or sad.
They like to help out, and make you glad.
I hope you liked my dragon poem,
When you see your first dragon, give it a home.

Joanna Krongold Kennedy

Shilmista

Along the windswept tundra he stood,
Alone and destitute,
Forgotten and forlorn.
Passing decades and crawling time,
Cease to exist in his freeze-frame of reality.
Hoping for a break in the monotony,
He looks toward the barren lands.
All the plants and animals have withered and died,
Save only He,
The scavenger of dreams.

Kim Crosby

Sea Change

All day,
Sullen steel rods of rain
Whipped ancient cedars
And pewter-grey seas alike
Into furious chaos.

The waves, white manes streaming,
Crashed over the rocky headland
In endless sequences of spume-laced surf—
A fearsome image
Of our distracted world.

Suddenly,
A pathway of beaten silver, blindingly beautiful,
Spread over the ocean's vastness,
As the sun broke through mist and cloud,
Making a glory of the world's vital, unforgiving waters.

Slowly these waters calmed,
Turning from pewter to living indigo
Under a sky of delirious blue,
And from the depths of timeless green forests
A robin sang for territorial peace.

Sylvia King-Brown

This Is Dedicated to the One I Love

I love you, I love you, I love you,
A thousand times, I love you.

We've shared a lot through the years,
Maybe even comforted each other as one sheds tears.

We've been through so much, and
The Lord's been there to give us a special touch.

I love you so dearly and I say it so cheery.
I love you, deary!

We've been watched night and day,
That's something I know I can say.

We can't even hold each other's hand,
Just because they wouldn't and don't understand.

Yes, it is true,
They were young once too!

I wish they would let us go on.
It's not their lives it depends upon.

Maybe we'll have to take a stand
To make them understand.

I love you, I love you, I love you,
A thousand times, I love you!

Vicki Spurrell

The River

The River that runs through my veins
Is like the one that flows through plains.
She carries life, sometimes gold,
No doubt . . . she is a sight to behold.
She carves a wide or narrow path,
With mighty ease or blinding wrath.
Her waters keep secrets of yore
That people buried along her shores.

The river is etched, like someone's life,
Blessed with harmony or filled with strife.
To go on or cease . . . she knows not when.
To sail her with pride is the challenge of men.
With different rivers the world is lined,
Solemnly leading . . . to wonders new,
He who threads her waters leaves behind
The many splendid things, tender and true.

Regine Grenon

Shadows

Shadows—drifting over the misty morn',
Creeping stealthily from their curtained shore,
Seeping softly past the gossamer fence,
Blending quietly with the creviced floor.

The memory of your life slips silently
From hidden corners of forgotten time;
Your presence shakes me often from a pause
To capture mood songs from a distant chime.

A melody—your voice upon the wind;
A smile—your cheerful mask returns to me;
A breeze—your kisses calming every storm;
A fresh baked pie—your gastronomic fee.

These gentle chains envelop thoughts and dreams,
Reflecting gauzy links, invisible seams.

Janet M. Klimek

Pattern of Thought

We must awaken
We must free ourselves
From this ignorant
Pattern of thought

We need to be able
To look up at the stars and know
Who we are

We must open our minds
We must unlock the mystery behind ourselves

And think solely of the
Universe in unity

We need to be able to bloom
Into the ever-changing
World of thought
With our thoughts

We must inhale our past
And thrive on it

We must exhale our future
And learn from it

We must, we need, let us evolve

Regina Riffel

When You've Found Love

When you've found love, don't let it go.
When you've found love, let it show.
It's never right to keep it inside,
it serves no purpose for it to hide.
You are lucky if you do find love,
falling like manna from above.
Love so amazing, love so divine,
love that saves you when you toe the line.

Love that gives you peace so serene,
love that washes you and makes you clean.
Love that's free, never bought,
love that's hard to find when it's sought.

It's times like these when one can sigh,
'cause they are riding on wings so high.
The wings of that feel so light,
the wings of love that sigh in flight.

But don't be fooled, for love is like a rose,
soft to the touch and sweet to the nose
with thorns that prick your very soul,
and often shatters what was once whole.

Carla Francisco

Abortion

I have learned how, unwittingly
Seductive, the invitation of sin
Can cause a sacred blood-flood,
Drops oozing from the womb of a witch.
I have heard the tragic resistance
Of the crying climax of a child's voice
Over empty playgrounds . . . but sorry is
An impregnated word and the debris
Is presented to me like a hard-earned merit.

Nikki Botha

All Was Awake

The great moon shone its brightest
The stars seemed to go on forever
The clouds gently went along
All this wonder was awake

Clara Acton

Signs of Spring

I hear the call of wild geese,
Northbound for Labrador.
I see a cloud of eider ducks
Wing past the eastern shore.
The icy wall by the seaside
Decays in a southern wind.
I hear the red fox barking
In the lore of the western glen.
The rabbits are turning brown again,
To match the forest floor.
The tulip and the crocuses
Burst forth by the kitchen door.
I see the bulging brooks
Rush rapid to the sea
And watch the sweeping sea gull
Drift above the lea.
Days begin to lengthen
As spring blossoms bloom.
Soon comes the warm and summer sun
And passes winter gloom.

Parker Langley

He Flies with the Eagles

In memory of Jim Bond (1978–1997)
He flies with the soaring eagles now,
He walks amongst silver-lined clouds,
He drinks from the sparkling waterfalls
Of Heaven's endless bounds.

He shines with every sunrise,
He smiles on every day.
His words echo into the night, that
For him this was the way.

He feels no pain nor sorrow,
Only happiness abound.
His soul is free from worry,
He is an angel now.

Julie Wray

Only Time Will Tell

From the rose bush's bloom
To the rose petal's fall,
The regrowth of one's love
Will come for a return.

Love will make a path
Along the trails of gloom.
As the rose dies and blooms,
Only trueness will prevail.

Time is the essence of all love to be,
And love is in all time to tell.

Liane Shulak

Mighty and Wild

The trees will grow high and mighty
And the grass will rise as well.
The land of the Earth with flourish, nurtured by the sun.

Life will form in the ocean
And soon will crawl to land.
Life will thrive all over; it will meet no end.

And the reptiles stomp about, hard and strong,
And the insects fly about fast and curious.
Life lives on, mighty and wild.

And in a fraction of Earth's life to date,
Through life's ever changing way,
Humans walk the Earth so boldly.

And some of those plants are gone
And most of the animals too,
And humans' caves are buildings now.

And lives can be left to live,
And mistakes can be undone,
And life can live on, mighty and wild.

Rick Rowe

Can't Come Out

Once it's been written, once it's been said,
Some of my thoughts are best left in my head.

No one to share these thoughts in my mind;
Can't write them down for someone to find.

No one to trust, to share silent pain.
Nowhere to turn if I tried to explain.

I can't tell my family, I won't tell a friend.
To say it out loud would lead to the end.

Keep me locked up, I might go away.
Don't open the door; I have nothing to say.

Once it's been written, once it's been said,
Some of my thoughts are best left in my head.

Elaine Connah

Love

Love, many tried this word to define,
Sometimes possessive—"You've got to be mine."
Sometimes obsessive, with lust from afar,
Adoring, imaginative, and a little bizarre.
Then there's abusive, strange yet forgiving,
Begging the question, "Is this really living?"
Such definitions for most are quite scary,
Causing some to turn off and others to be wary.
The real definition is considerate and kind,
Allowing freedom for the soul and peace for the mind,
A bond that is there when presence is not,
A passion so great that it's never forgotten,
Understanding that needs no utterance at all,
Just a glance, a nod, something quite small,
Something that's firm all through the years,
Plenty of trust, no lies, and just a few tears.
Of all human feelings, it's the greatest of all,
For without it you'll never be forty feet tall.

Madeleine H. Cargeege

Love and Learn

Love is something you have to earn and is
Something to help you grow and learn.
Love is understanding and respect and
Caring so much; love is something you can feel in a touch.
Love is something you feel in your soul
And in your heart; true love is God's creation of art.
Love is patience and it's about being
Kind, and for some, it's often hard to find.
Love does conquer all; people, I'm sure,
would disagree, otherwise God wouldn't
Have made us, you see.
Love is something that all people need;
I guess you'd say it's like planting a seed.
Love grows stronger every day and
Eventually blossoms like a flower in May.
Love is not jealous or possessive; it is
A lifelong lesson, learning new things every day.
We're learning and loving in every way.
To love someone else, you have to love yourself first,
And to not love yourself is sadly the worst.

Andrea March

Spirit Love

Our love predates the dawn of time.
Such a love had to come longer
Than time itself to embrace
The chambers of this mind, this heart.
We are old souls, old memories, old stories,
Born again in different times and centuries.
Different places and lives.
Our bodies cannot contain our love,
For our love is more beautiful and pure
Then the fading sunsets of summer;
More magical and mysterious than the full moons of night.
My eyes see the visions of us in the clouds.
My ears hear the sounds of us in nature.
My heart remembers a love more precious than life.
My spirits slips
Through the atmosphere of this Earthly plane,
To lie with you as night approaches.
Our spirit love, like a circle, like a ring.
No beginning—no end—
Infinite.

T. A. Glaremin

To a Friend upon Her Father's Death

I wish could reach deep into my
small pocket of experience
and somehow dig out the
right thing to say,
yet never in my short, confused,
and generally happy life
have I ever had to deal with
a termination such as this.
And I'm not quite sure what
to think or make of this situation,
because as much as I would like
to shoulder some piece of your burden,
I am all too thankful that
I did not borrow your shoes that day.
And the farthest I can reach out to you
is not far enough to grasp these ill-timed emotions
that you now have to saddle by yourself.

Emily Rowe

The Voice

Loneliness, Isolation,
Where do I go?
Where do I run?
Everyone is gone—Emptiness.

I hear a voice.
I run the other way.
Where is everyone?
Why am I all alone?

The voice calls.
I cover my ears.
Search, search
for someone else, anybody else.

Alone in my sorrow—Darkness,
tears rolling down my cheeks.
My tears are dried
By the breath of the voice.

"I am here."
I look up—Jesus.
His voice is soft and gentle.
My darkness is shattered.

Megan Fast

Dreams

Before I dozed off to sleep,
I went to a place,
A place of beauty,
A place of love,
A place words cannot describe.
Yet, soon enough,
I had awoken . . .
How can this be?
A dream?
A thought my mind came up with?
Mere thoughts cannot be so powerful
Or can they?
Such questions cannot be answered,
Not as soon as I may think.
Yet, these questions seem to fade,
To vanish,
And my mind fills up with . . .
Dreams.

Wojciech Gryc

Crimson Kisses

Crimson kisses
In passion-filled dreams,
Tango in daisies,
Just you and me.

Eternity in paradise,
Souls intertwined,
No escape from happiness,
Bliss to the end of time.

Don't pinch me now
Afraid I shall wake
Only with memories
And your name on my lips.

Jane C. Rendall

The Foreign Beggar

Coming from a storm,
There she is to warm
Her poor body ill,
That is hungry still.
The girl at the gate
Without a fate,
What's she looking for?
Why's she in the door?
"If you understand,
I'm not from your land.
To thy God I pray,
If you let me stay!
My braids are undone.
What I had is gone.
How I feel is cold
And completely old.
Looking to thy sky,
Please don't let me die!"
God whispers above,
"I heard you, my love."

Neli Fatu de Valahia

Letting Go

We took two lives
And wove a fabric of love.
Bonded and together,
We faced the world.
Somewhere, somehow,
One thin strand unraveled,
Until all that were left
Were memories.

Janice B. Young

Walking through the Shadows

Walking through the Shadows,
Under the Dark'ned Sky,
Discovering that Love is lost,
And Life is just a lie.

Walking through the Shadows,
Leaving the dead to lie,
Knowing that your time has come,
And that you shall soon die.

Walking through the Shadows,
Feeling the end is nigh,
But then, Love, calls you back,
From under the dark'nd sky.

No longer Walking through the Shadows,
Under the Dark'nd sky,
Realizing that Love, is not lost,
And life, is anything but a lie.

Shae Hagarty

Wildlife on the Plantation

These shivering lemon tigers
in this green night—
only old palm fronds,
stripes skinny-pale
in the cool rain

Sheri South

Entity

The somber woods reach out,
Touching, communicating,
Life and death moving in the layers
Of decayed, compressed residue.

My innermost consciousness is aware
Of advancing growth,
Sighing of fallen leaves,
Shifting of spreading bark,
Unfolding of mushroom caps,
Peeping of baby birds in warm nests,
Cold, pitted, alabaster bones nearby—
Life and death bonded together,
Holding each to the beginning.

Time is a distance not thought of,
Light the shimmering cadence that nurtures,
The flowering essence that perfumes the depths,
Spreads the circling events of time
Up the destined void toward the heights.

My awareness returns to the beginning,
Where life and death are bonded together,
Each the nucleus of the whole.

Pearl M. Hall

Rift

Resentment, anger, retribution—
The acrimonious fruits of separation.
Each party an injured innocent
Ready to avenge the hateful source and cause
Of its present grief and pain.

It matters not if these indeed be real . . .
The fact of separation makes them so,
And every ounce of paranoia is added burden
To the uncertainties heaped on head and heart
To make them bow or break.

The heretofore mighty union of pride and hope
Resents the shattered image enshrined by jealous mirrors,
And every instinct in its wounded frame cries out aloud:
"Vengeance must be mine, for I will not share with you
The oblivion you seek."

Rift recognizes neither victory nor defeat,
For the skewed lines and rules of its division
Do not discriminate between warring parties.
It prefers, purposely, to inflame the constant bicker
That eternizes strife.

K. Gordon

Verdun

Through the failing mists of Verdun,
Came the most notorious of the Hun;
Their suns on fire, their sabres on hold,
The French were very brave, and yes, very bold.
But at the end of the battle,
No military colours were to fly;
For, the only honours went to the ravens,
Maggots, and flies.
For, of the 600,000 at Verdun who harried;
300,000 were never buried.

Taft Machesney

Mother

Nine months of labour, nine months of pain
Nine months of an unpredictable road, nine months of rain
Nine months of swelling, nausea, and you name it
Nine months of rapid eating, nine months of spit

Then night after night of coughing, breast feeding, and baby weeping
Night after night of Mom's being stopped from sleeping
Followed by wetness, and you don't need to guess
It's mingled of course with terrible smelling watery or hard mess

Then it is time for school: need money, need books
Home from school for dinner; he has to be home to cook
Take care of the house, have all the clothes clean
Day after day, until I am in my teens

She never murmurs, for she knows they are her chores
Her work never finishes, there is always more and more
Washing, cooking, cleaning, trimming the flowers
Baking, dusting, chopping, and so many others

Like dish washing, baking, ironing; she never quits
Bread making, shopping, sweep the yard; oh, I couldn't do it
Sometimes I wonder if mothers are machines
Well, I do hope you understand what I mean

    Maxine Fletcher

Oundre

Silent tears wash me down
as my fairy tale Prince turns back into a Frog
but hops along beside me as
my Super special Friend.
Yet, in my sleeplessly alone nights
He dons His dimpled crown
and teases me into the past, convincing me of the
beauty the future will carry into my story-book life.
Eventually . . .
But now I want to fold myself into His magical arms
as they giveaglimpse of all my desires.
But my soul screams a whisper that a glimpse is not enough,
and I need to wait for my story's happy ending.
So, for now, I battle the evil Witch loneliness,
wondering exactly which side my
kick is on.
Knowing that He is the one who will lead me out of the depths
that we created together.

    Jennifer Taylor

Flowers for Her Man

She pauses at each of the headstones as she makes her way down every row.
She murmurs a little, "How are you?"; you can tell that she's been there before.
But today, she seems a bit flustered, and she shakes as she leans on her cane.
It's a struggle holding the flowers that she's brought for the grave of her man.

She knows that he's lying there somewhere, after all, she's been every day.
She believes he's asleep down there in the deep, just waiting till she comes his way.
She cries, for today she can't find him, no matter how many graves pass.
She calls out to him to come get her, as her tears slowly fall to the grass.

For so many years she's been all alone, she's grown tired and her memory's fading.
A smile starts to grow as she thinks of her beau; she knows even now he'll be waiting.
All at once, she remembers and heads to his spot, as if she'd never been lost.
She places the flowers on the grave of her man, there beneath the little stone cross.

The light starts to dim, she's left there alone, to make peace with her God up above.
She knows that today is the last that she'll pray to be back in the arms of her love.
She swallows her deadly, dark mixture, it's the last part of her life's plan,
Then she lays her head down in the flowers that she's brought for the grave of her man.

    Dave Duncan

The Letter

I know sometimes I don't treat you as I should
And I'm sorry; it must hurt you so much.
Even so, when I'm hurt my Heavenly daddy
Is always there with healing in His loving touch.

I was just a dirty sinner, but through Christ you've made me a winner.

Being the righteous, holy God that you are,
My life on its own had fallen short by faith,
But Jesus loved me so much, He paid the price at Calvary.
And now, through Your mercy, I have been set free.
My heart cued Abba Father; You had compassion and rescued me.

You loved me before the dawn of time.
This love is one I can't comprehend—that the God of the universe
Would want to be my friend!

When there seems to be no one I can trust
And my friends all desert me, I can lean on You, Lord,
And in prayer cast all my burdens on thee.
When I'm falsely accused and the rumors won't stop,
It's awesome to know You understand and care;
You, Jesus, Son of God have also been there.

Words can't express your deserved appreciation and praise.

Holly Switzer

Never Watch the News Alone

The news on the radio depresses me.
The world through the glowing eye of television is worse.
A bulletin breaks,
    and it sickens me.
Another sex-crazed man prowls the streets,
    looking for fresh, young, and innocent prey, and I turn it off,
        feeling anger at the world and those in the media that control it.

The door opens.
I turn and she is there, and I feel relief.
The anger subsides, and I take comfort in the knowledge that
    even in this crazy world,
        I am loved.

David Bishop

Life's Windows

When I look out the window, I value what I see.
It does my spirit wonders to see a budding tree.
A flower sprouting from the earth, the grass is turning green.
It gives me a sense of life, all of the things I've seen.

A mother with her young child, an old man shuffles by.
The birds are singing in the trees, the big, blue, wondrous sky.
The stars that twinkle in the night, the moon that lights the way,
I think to myself as I stare to the sky, what a perfect ending to a day.

It wasn't always so pretty, so calm and, oh, so still.
I used to see such sadness from my last window sill.
Violence and uncertainty were a common sight.
A mother angry at her small child, on the corner there is a fight.

A drunken man staggers by; he holds his bottle to his lips.
A woman screams at passersby, her hands upon her hips.
I never noticed budding trees or flowers growing tall.
I never noticed real life down there; I never noticed it at all.

I never knew what I was missing, how great one's life could be.
If the window you're at was clearer, much clearer so you could see.
Life has been viewed so differently from each window that I've sat.
And I enjoy life's pictures that I see from the window that I'm at!

Victoria Lynne Pentney

Just My Gram and Me

She sat looking out the window, thinking of yesteryear,
thanking God for the wonderful family
He has given her through the years.
She gazed up into the sky, knowing her time was near,
making sure she said her good-byes
to the ones she knew so dear.
That night as she drifted off into her peaceful sleep,
she saw God open Heaven's gate, and ask her,
Please come home.
Her body felt so heavy and all so full of pain.
She lifted up her arms and took God's hand and sang.
For, she knew with God's great love,
we would someday meet,
and when I walked through Heaven's doors,
it's Gram that I would see.
Our hearts would ache no longer,
no sorrow or sadness be,
the circle would not be broken,
just my Gram and me.

Brenda Farbycuk

"I Love You"

when i look into your deep blue eyes,
oh! my darling, i cannot lie.
i just have to say to you, "i love you."

the blueness of the sky and deepness of the sea
are together the expression of true love i can see.
the wilderness of romance that i feel within thine eyes
gives me a feeling that i can't deny.
it just steals my heart and brings me close to you.
oh! my darling, "i love you."

the warm caress that i feel when you hold me,
the love that i feel for you when you're close to me,
the kiss that speaks a thousand words
when everything's silent and just you are here,
just steals my heart and brings me close to you.
oh! my darling, "i love you."

Tina Gangolli

All Has Lessened . . .

The phone is silent in the night.
The trees outside have lost their song.
The moon reflects and glistens pallid light.
All has lessened now you're gone.

There is no one knocking at my door,
no one left to hold me close.
Your shirt's still on the floor
where last you held me and kissed my nose.

I remember the times we've shared,
moments together, close like spoons,
things we loved, the things we dared
once together underneath the moon.

An old-fashioned fourth of July:
fireworks, holding hands, and Ferris wheels—
freedom together and we wondered why
life seemed so full, so complete, and so real.

All has lessened now you're gone.

Brooke Prior

For Him

He gives me a sense of trust,
A sense of hope and peace.
He always lifts my spirits
When his voice and words are sweet.
He has offered me a warm place,
Somewhere deep in his heart.
He has given me the chance to prove
That this is what I want.
He showed me he is honest
While my heart was on my sleeve.
He helped me understand
Why it is he really believes.

Alison McCaffrey

Millennium

The second millennium is almost dead.
It's lying rotting on its bed.
It was born in blood and pain.
It will die in grief and shame.

Progress marches on and on
Turning its victims into stone,
And man's inventions poisons spew.
I'll drink some; here's some for you.

We've plundered all the Earth, it seems,
And we've ruined wise men's dreams.
Children starve and women cry
While tyrants march men off to die.

Still we can escape if for a time,
Pay a few bucks and stand in line,
Turn a switch or press a knob,
Join the senseless, mindless mob.

Music blares out fear and rage,
And actors act it out on stage.
Love's been cheapened, hate is free.
Compassion's what I'd like to see.

Nancy Block

Forever . . .

To cry would bring such pleasure
of which you may not approve.
To see you every morning
would make my heart move.
To you I'd give such sacrifice
as other stories tell.
I'd hold you as a treasure
that evil repels.
To taste the sweetness on your lips
that taste of morning dew,
I'd kiss you with a passion so great,
I only wish you knew.
To be who we are and still love
is how I want to be.
If you only knew with what strength
I care for and love thee
to the silent oath made
when our hearts touch,
and because we have forever,
we are not rushed.

Aimee Mihalus

Godspeed

Alone she carried
The burnished golden urn
Atop the windy bluff

Lifted off the shiny lid
The powdered ashes in her hand
She gently blew so that the wind

Would bear his Earthly soul away
Waft it swiftly to the heavens
Be in God's arms without delay

Teresa Mead

Friends

I HAVE SOME FRIENDS.
THERE ARE NEW ONES NOW,
BUT THEY'RE LIKE MY OLD ONES
WHO ARE SPECIAL SOMEHOW.

SOME ARE GIGGLY,
TALKATIVE, OR BOLD.
SOME ARE SHY AND QUIET,
SOME ARE COLD.

SOME ARE BLONDE
JUST LIKE ME.
SOME ARE SMILEY
LIKE EMILY.

SOME ARE LIKE GRACE,
AND SOME ARE SMART.
SOME HAVE A NICE FACE,
AND SOME HAVE A GOOD HEART.

Lorraine K. L. Fernicola

Prayer

A day you gave me a soul
pure, cool, clear
like the water of a source
You told: "Have care of it,
protect it, don't do it any evil.
Now you go and live."
I'll give you back a dirty soul
frightened, wounded, dying
lacerated from a world
that I don't succeed in loving.
Do what you want with it.

Federico Marsili

Need for You

Dedicated to my beloved
Ever from now
To you this oath is sworn
The best I had yet unsaid
And truly mean I do spread
From a devoted heart on thee
For giving all, just you to me
Like music, well-pledged to love
That inspires as night above
To you my being till dawn
Fore'er I vow

Lisa Umoh Ndia

Second Wind

Leaves turned to color. They have fallen to the ground.
Disappearing in the wind, nowhere to be found.

Coldness surrounds me, winds up in a state.
Gray skies above me, freezing grounds are late.

Won't be long
Till memories come back,
Feelings of loneliness.
Scared I am, don't want these feelings back.

Letting thoughts loose,
Letting them run free,
Running into a fenced arena,
This time they will not capture me.

Holding me down,
Blindfold my blue eyes,
Closing my mouth shut,
But I'm still yelling, no lies, no lies, let me out.
Scared I am, weak I am not.
Last time I will be left alone
In these hellish memory walls.

Glenna D'Orazio

Mother Teresa

It will be written in black letters
In the history of the world
That cursed Saturday dawn
That cracked down with the news,
"Mother Teresa is gone."
The whole world cried with numbing pains
And burst into moan-full tears
For the demise of "the saint of the gutter."
Nature was engulfed with the pall of sorrow and gloom,
The sky expressed its far-flung sorrow
With thunder and incessant rain,
The motherless orphans cried again
With broken hearts and endless pains!

Oh, angel of love and legend of Earth,
As an incarnation you came down from Heaven
To rekindle the light of mercy and love
And to glorify your beloved Earth
With divine message and to show eternal path.
You're the burning lamp of love and inspiration,
The endless, holy sea of self-abnegation.

Amal Kumar Dutta

Untitled

The grains of sands pass through my fingers
Like lost moments in time
Each moment in time that is lost
Is a memory that cannot be cherished
Memories that cannot be cherished
Are chances not taken
Chances that are not taken
Are regrets in your past
The past cannot be changed
So, live each moment to the fullest
Close your fingers around each grain of sand
To create the moment and cherish every memory

Alison Hutfelter

Evening Song

She sings and does not cry,
though her voice, like old grass, trembles
in the last evening winds.
She tastes the ripest sorrow,
understanding now the unspoken tales of aged eyes.
Her words are not bitter; they are heavy and sweet
and speak of love—weep of love.
Like a stone her gaze falls; these eye are virgin dry,
for she hopes and waits for the fate she names love
one day to greet her again.
She sings and does not cry
when night falls and shadows like near memories haunt,
but, still, stares unmoved into that darkness
while a greater darkness still stares back.
Her heart invokes an ancient chant remembered
as hope runs wild into that fierce black night,
and still she sings, softly and sadly,
for now she sings not to cry.

Elizabeth Shepherd

Football in the Rain

Let's go play football in the pelting rain
And drown our cares in grassy pools again.

Shout our shrill voices, hoarse for sheer joy,
And belabour our beleaguered toy,

Which dead, stuck yet again in muddy pool,
Becomes a stubborn, an unyielding bull.

Let's kick the ball high with the morning's Math,
The treacherous school bell, and the teacher's wrath.

Let's all forget the rules of normal play
And play the way we know will make our day.

Forget our wings and charging at the ball,
Collide above it, lose our balance, fall.

Let the goalkeeper lead the next attack
And having scored his own goal, scamper back.

Let's shriek at lightning, but defy the thunder
That lacks the force to split and put asunder

What God had put together. Boys and Rain
Shall always play the game of joy again.

Emmanuel A. Frank-Opigo

Marionette

I'm sick of pretending that I'm just like you
Pastel, porcelain, doll-like machines
Empty witches of your own denial.
Proven evil floating in a pond of emotionless facade.

Pastel puppets,
Porcelain witches,
I will pretend no more.
I'll break the plastic, interchange molds,
I don't care.

Perfectness causes pain,
The dolls all go insane.
I'll cut the strings of your marionette.
You can't think, what would you do?
I won't be like you!

Meagan Graves

Untitled

At thanksgiving, giving time,
I eat the food, which is mine.
The gravy running the stuffing stuffed.
All the silver polished and buffed.
Mashed potatoes piling high,
turkey, casseroles, pumpkin pie.
Candles, carrots, china plates,
two glasses together with their mates.
Buns and napkins, greasy hands,
tarts and cookies, musical bands.
Cornucopias, gourds, traditions and bay,
the candles giving an eerie ray.
A prayer before the dinner meal,
family and food is a wonderful deal.

Jessie Skinner

Jesus' Shoulders

When you feel sad
and want to burst out in tears
come, cry on these shoulders

When you feel tired
from the trials of life
come, rest on these shoulders

When you feel sick
and there is no cure
come, find healing on these shoulders

When you feel thirsty
from the desert of life
come, find water on these shoulders

When you feel lonely
and seem to have no friend
come, find friendship on these shoulders

Jonathan Johnston

Dilemma

I thought I was dead,
Buried in the pale of day;
Rust spread over me.

I relished the slimy advance,
Sought shelter under its damp;
The taste in my mouth was bitter.

This music now I hear,
It touches some string
Deep inside, and I shake.

As an autumn leaf
From dry North wind;
And rust crumbles.

The melody rises,
Pieces of me sway,
Falling, hither and thither.

Stripped of flesh,
Rinsed in light
Where do I go?

Hafeez Jamali

Rotation

The bus is a microcosm:
people,
crazy people on the bus,
strangers
sitting side by side.
The frail elderly,
the restless children,
the arrogant teens,
the frustrated mothers, the crying
infants,
the prim secretaries:
All of them, on the bus

—and me.
I am on this bus,
in it,
not part of it:
a stranger on the bus,
a stranger who observes
the FUTILITY of this bus,
wheels churning, turning, going
nowhere
on this bus.

Julie Maurice

Lost

Sometimes I look around
and I'm lost.
Don't know where I am
Or what I'm here for.
Everybody has a purpose but
what is mine?
Is there a reason for my existence?
Will I leave a mark "I was here"
or will I simply pass through?
Will my dreams become reality
or remain just that—dreams?
I look and I wonder
Wondering but never knowing.
Hoping but never certain.
I know that I must believe in myself.
For there is no way without belief.
Believe that I can fulfill my dreams, that
I have a purpose.
And then, only then,
will I find it.

Mandy Tannenbaum

Wind Child

The air breathes your name
as it rushes across the waters.
It whispers it at the break of day
in a pale blue light,
and sighs it in the evening
as the horizon burns out.
Your name is whistled on the
mountain tops
and rolled along the plains,
thundered in the waterfalls
and chimed in the rain.
I hear you across the water,
wind child of my heart.

Kirinani Kankhwende

Life

What is life?
I believe it is a continual search
for the meaning of our existence,
to be found by you and me.

Life is the look of a happy child
opening his presents at Christmas.
Life is your first puppy.
Life is love.

Life is meant to be enjoyed
with those you love.
If not, you feel unfulfilled,
You feel alone with the world.

Be at peace with yourself,
Be gentle with yourself.
If you don't, who will?
Love yourself, and you will love others.

Life is pain, life is evil to be surpassed.
Life is happiness to be shared with everyone.
One must triumph over life's cruelties
and learn to be strong.

Life is an unending search
to understand yourself and those you care about.
Life is simply meant to enjoy yourself.
So enjoy, please enjoy!

Eric Le Chasseur

Love Yearning

On the farther bank of the Pearl River,
Water and sky linking together,
Cold wind interweaves with Winter drizzle.
At dust gray, long, stripped cloud layers pass by.
Floating black clouds traverse the sky.
Thick fog spreading o'er Canton me does puzzle.

Long yearning for my darling for nine years
Has left me nothing but bloody tears
As red as maple leaves in the autumn.
Look at the roses in exuberant blossom.
Look at the roses turning withered.
A coastal swallow very high hovers
And now in a circle, then low does flee,
As though to be a companion to me.
But, oh, my faraway, sweet paramour!
When shalt thou set off on your return tour?
Only the house poplar in the breeze sways
Leisurely, carefree, and in the stylish grace.
Reluctant, it stays with me always.

As usual, the neighborhood silence cloaks.

Hor-Ming Lee

It's Hard to Say (Those Words)

My heart's bleeding, and I'm tired
of convincing myself that
everything is going to be all right.
I don't think you understand how I feel . . .
to be stepped on constantly
and needles to be thrust into my heart,
and my every effort to make things better fails.
All I can do is pray that you still love me.

Mari Omori

Fraudster

With plenty to gain and nothing to fear
That was the plan or so they all said
But look at me now fear filling my head
Will she hate will she scold will she roll up and crawl
If she hates if she scolds I'll never stand tall
I tell her my name and I tell her my game
Will I expose my real aim
Her smile had froze and started to thaw
When I told her I tried she saw the flaw

Everybody's aware at the start of the day
Time goes by change fades away
Beginning with charm and all things good
Surprise her I did and leave me she did
Then a crescendo of lies, deceit and tears
Now I'm alone, alone with my fears
Of dark grey walls with a long way to fall
To a thorny brigade learning to crawl
It's simple to say and simple see
Why it's as plain as the day and as true can be
Fraudsters We are and always Will be

Pearse Fahy

Foda

Hell to think thine shire links,
How fiction fancies master.
Will canst I come, this well be done,
If not then for another.
If be it she, whose hold in me,
Then ruin comes to those who don't.
If you hate this, this loves you . . .
This love is not to you, but to feed.
You took off your clothes and stood in my way,
How do you expect me?
You always rape me with your little girl thoughts,
Gigantic teardrops.
You sop up my blood with your skirt.
Your lips brush my foul soul
And endear my worthlessness.
Lustfully waste away your time line.
I'll feel your reward: shivered flesh.
I branded you
To feed.

Judah

Experiences of Life

The lonely walk on a wet, cobbled street,
The soft whispering wind blowing my hair,
The hot, burning sand touching my naked feet
Are the knowledge of the Lord being near.

The aching limbs when a long day is through,
The departing of a dear, dear friend,
The hope that comes with a fresh day anew
Make more joyous this life with no end.

The wet, smudged tear on a lost child's face,
The old man whose dog has died,
The non-Christian friend who has found his grace
With a master now at his side,

Enjoying and experiencing these things
Give life and living a reason,
The tears, the good-byes, the compassion it brings
Are our trials for each coming season.

Fay Taylor

Dune Clouds

The dune clouds, they whistle by,
white mounds of islands in the sky.
Light twinkled from shore to shore,
as I stood contemplating at my door.

Of thick white ribbons that float up high
with movements that only dance on by,
such steps that teach one to fly,
this fluent flow that makes one cry.

The wind is cold; it opens eyes
to look upon the white-blue skies,
to broaden minds, yes, weaken hearts,
to give us all a loving start.

It shows slight movement to the eye,
a veiled dance through the blackening skies,
a lofty breeze that holds heads high
to watch the dune clouds as they fly.

To make us wish we had no fears,
to help us free all maddening tears,
it's time for all to know and see:
These shores belong to you and me.

Beth Bryer

Life and Love

Let's take this kite we call our lives
and teach it how to fly.
Let's run with it through open fields
and show it to the sky.

It will start to soar and sure enough
it will tumble to the ground.
But if we try and don't give up, it will
soon be flying 'round.

I'll be the flyer in the field, if you'll
be the kite above.
The string that goes from me to you—
let's call it our love.

The string that keeps us joined as
one may sometime almost break;
The kite comes down, the string repaired,
that's all that it will take.

A kite without a flyer just idly stands by.
They need each other so that they
can together learn to fly.

Betty Yerkie

1984

You and I
ran
as naked as childhood innocence
through rows
of indelible sprinklers
that year
oblivious
to our lingering fates
propelling us
into
adolescence.

Shirley Camia

My Home

Canada, land of my dreams,
Where fields of golden wheat grow
And long, lazy rivers flow.
Lovely lakes lie still,
Surrounded by forest and hills,
Where the beautiful sun sets,
Caresses the valleys and mountains.
This land of beautiful places is
Where people still greet you
With smiling faces.
This land where freedom flows,
Our children don't know the terrors.
Oh, how lucky we are to live
In this wonderful land: Canada.

Janina Campbell

to regain no pain

facing the sun each morning
with sincerest of regret
no more i want to greet it
with pain . . . with pain

all smiles my kin come to see me
masking their smouldering tears
hoping that i won't see them
sustain . . . sustain

like-patients wheel by to see me
sharing our ultimate truth
misery misting their moulding eyes
again . . . again

care-givers come prancing by
their frozen lips up-tilted
sated with their pointless chore
they feign . . . they feign

no more shall i endure this
for me the charades will end
for my escape i've stowed it away
to regain . . . no pain

j. e. carter

The Child of a King

A tear trickled down the cheek
Of my very best friend today,
He held, and loved and forgave me
said He'll hold me until I see,
For you are the child of a king.
For the path may be long and narrow
And the crosses seem quite a load,
Yet leaning on my Master and Savior
There is nothing He won't give for reward.
For as days pass by fast and slow
Like the grains of sand in time,
His word will teach and show
How to shed, overcome, leave behind.
He carried and nurtured and taught
Tenderly what a child aught naught,
To be ever so humble and low
Yet hold your head up high and know
You are the child of a king.

Dorothy Van Bree

The Last Hope

With every ray of sunlight and every blooming flower,
With every rippling wave and every passing hour,
I wonder . . .
"How is it that nature is so bountiful?"

With every chirping bird and every drop of rain,
With every call of love and every cry in vain,
I wonder . . .
"How come nature never fails?"

When I cry, "Give unto me all that I want!",
When I lose all but one of the numerous hopes,
I turn my eyes to that one hope, to that one saviour
To whom I owe my life!

Surprised I am—she does not turn her face away,
Even after man's endless exploitation!
She does not ask, "Why?",
Even after witnessing man's attitude of destruction!

But I fear the end is near.
It's time—she will look at us
With cold eyes,
And without any fuss, say, "No more."

Anusuya Das

Guess: Who Am I?

Named after a precious metal, I stand.
I'm the largest span of my kind.
The service I render, no one complains
As my 4,200-feet-long makes your day.

From my 746-feet towers high,
And 200 feet above the water gateway,
I enjoy the picturesque and splendid view
Of that "city of all nations" that looks so great.

Time came when I needed a touch-up look,
And where was that person for that special job?—
A courageous citizen was able to perform
And, with an unique crew, executed the work.

When enthusiasm and determination to win,
Enduring radiant sun, cold and dangerous winds,
Was the first step toward a fruitful work
Enabling them to travel around the world.

As a laudable homage to Mr. J. B. Strauss,
Whose remarkable idea materialized as the
San Francisco Golden Gate bridge,
Solid and majestically, for posterity, I stand.

Milagros F. Ramirez

Fortress of My Heart

Walls of stone, build yourselves
up around the tender chambers of
my heart, and do not crumble under
any army. Do not succumb to those
that desire to plunder your treasures,
but could never appreciate your worth.
Bar the doors and shut out the light.
Nothing can reside in the new halls of night.
Love comes softly like a thief prowling after dark,
wishing to steal that last little spark.
Guard it well, oh, Heart of mine,
if ever again the light of love in my eyes shall shine.

Taryl Guenter

On the Way to Egypt

I went through the desert
in the arms of My Mother.
Joseph was trying to shield me
from the scorching sun with his body.
My Mother!
I'll never forget Her hands.
She became one with Me.
We shared one breath.
A tamed animal, on which We were cozily settled,
was evenly striding.
I was babbling.
The lips of My Mother were copying My baby-talk.
My self-denying Mother!
Her life belonged to Me:
She bestowed it upon Me with love and tenderness.
She had always loved God,
Who granted Her life to this world,
And God went with Her through the desert
in Her arms.

Vladimir Moskovchenko

Heroin

Your heart, black as midnight,
your soul, blacker still,
with warm embrace you fooled me,
and with every bitter pill.

My friends, you killed them one by one,
you almost killed me too.
No man could ever understand,
the hate I have for you,

Not on written paper was our marriage made in hell,
but married to our needle sharp, my soul I had to sell.
Evil is too kind a word for one so dark as you.
I was weak and you were strong, that I know is true.

But now the tables, they are turned.
I yearn for you no more.
I cleansed your venom from my veins.
I've evened up the score,

All the years of pain I gave,
you stole them one by one.
All the many scars I bear,
I've turned my back, I've won.

Colin Layton

The Beach

At times when I feel down
I often think of a place where I long to be
This beautiful place is that which only I have found
It is one that only I can see

I sit on the sand
And watch the birds go by
The troubles of the world are no longer mine
I have stopped for one moment in time

If only the bad could disappear
Then everyone would be happy
The world would be such a wonderful place
If only the light could be seen

Michelle Tajudeen

Wasted Silliness

It seems
I can only write serious poems,
Grave and resolute—really.
I can't do justice
To my article poem:
Pink Flamingo with False Leg Dies.
Absurd—it deserves silliness.
But then I think—he died.
That's not funny at all.
Great science couldn't put
A simple joint in the leg.
A flamingo wasted
On their ignorance.
Why is that funny?
I think it's really sad.

Ingrid MacIsaac

Little Girl Lost

I am just a little girl lost.
My childhood was taken at any cost.
I looked for love over the years
But found instead only sorrow and tears.
My body grew up big and strong,
But somehow I never went along.
I stayed inside a girl of three
And thought that I would never be free.
But, slowly I am growing inside,
For the big me has taken me to her side.
She had to learn how to be my mom,
And now our work is getting done.
I long for the day when I'll be free,
No longer just a child of three,
No longer to be bullied and bossed,
No longer to be a little girl lost.

Beverly Lachance

Broken Fences

I've noticed people put up fences
To protect themselves
While walls work both ways—
Keep feelings inside.

I sleep under my grandmother's quilt
Although I do not rest.
Strain has torn the delicate fabric
Of the patchwork of my family.

One square is tattered,
Spotted, and uncomfortable,
Soiled by urine and indifference,
Judgement and finger-pointing.

I could cry foul and demand restitution,
Being injured by one of my own;
Except when I look at myself,
I have no stone to throw.

Broken fences can be mended,
Not so easily relations.
I cannot sew with a thread of blame
Or play with the ghosts of the past.

Irene R. Guilbaut

My Symphony

In this age of vast destruction,
With beauty all but lost—
I will write myself a symphony,
No matter what the cost.

I will use all birds of freedom
As notes of quiet might—
Like eagle's soaring melody
And hawk in silent flight.

Each piercing sound of wilderness
Will float on giant wing—
Until it reaches all the world
And teaches it to sing.

And then to play this rhapsody—
A monumental feat,
Each man will make, as instrument,
My symphony complete.

Pamela Anne MacDonald

To Breathe Again

Take a moment of every day
To take the time to look away
To think of emptiness
A void, a blank, just nothingness

To feel your fingers
Your mind, your soul
And clear the path
That leads from young to old

Place the fears and worries aside
Take in the air and wind
And teach yourself to breathe again

Patrick Bender

Losing a Friend

She was a wonderful person.
She made people laugh,
But we lost her,
Lost her to the jaws of death.

That night when she died,
The life was squeezed from her.
I wish that I was there
To save my friend.

When the news got back home,
We were all shocked.
We had to bury one,
One of our Graduates.

We grads cried.
We tried to understand
Why something like this could happen,
But we were more confused.

That day in the cemetery,
We cried as we held hands.
We put roses on her coffin
And said our last good-bye.

Jennifer Abel

Spanish Banks at 11:30 p.m.

A city sleeps.
Raindrops like bullets litter the darkened road;
One slippery corner and five miles too fast
Thrust mortality in my face,
I am inches from a long explanation.

Even the moon hides on this perilous night.
Even he can only peer from behind the hallowed clouds.
As an eavesdropper meticulously
Stoops and listens to privateness,
So the moon does to this tiny corner of existence.

There are no city lights on this trip,
Just me,
My father's car,
And the darkness.

A city wakes to find itself unchanged,
But not me, not I on this dreary night;
I never sleep.

Adam Segal

Only to Part With

She stood at the window,
Clinging to the casement,
Her eyes wide open,
Waiting in amazement.

Now it was dark.
She still stood waiting,
Only to part with
Him she was meeting.

Suddenly, like the lightning,
He appeared from nowhere,
Standing at the doorway
Like The Highwayman of yore.

Clasping her hands in his, said he,
"I can't sustain this separation, my dear."
She clung to him with flowing tears
Whispering, "Good luck. . . . Good-bye, my dear."

With the chirping of birds, she awoke.
Outside the window, the Red Ball shone.
Did he really come, or was it a dream?
Perhaps a reverie . . . that will remain ever green.

Manjari Pandey

Perceptions of Life

White is right as rain,
falling quietly on a tranquil ocean,
disturbing solitude, bringing it to chaos.

Black is as beautiful
as a starlit sky on a dreary winter's night,
bouncing off the treetops, contrasting in the snow.

Pictures worth their weight in words,
spoken a million times but never heard,
are the importance of the soul.

See the point—
of a blind, pointless existence,
breathing time, exhaling space,
understand
life is waste. It withers away.

Charlene Kelly

The Lost Sale

One by one they filed through the door hoping to snatch the best from the floor
They'd taken onerous and intricate measures
to ensure they'd procure at least some of the treasures
A low bid for one, outrageous for another "I'll buy this for Christine and that for my mother!"
"They're antiques!" they said "a gift from the past,
in the aura of our caring they're certain to last"
"Going! Going!" no more from the speaker his pallor increased as his knees grew weaker
He stared straight ahead, as if in a trance, at a crumpled old figure that began to dance
She held in her arms the effigy of a god and moved with the grace that Sultans applaud
She smiled reminiscent, the bust in her grasp, the well-to-do bidders mewed a sickening gasp
They'd seen her before, her plight was well known,
all were certain it was from Hell she had flown
"Get her out!" they cried "She'll tarnish the wares!
Go!" they ordered "Take your filth down the stairs!"
She was young at one time, many years ago, she lived upper class but who'd ever know?
A wicked parent, virtue deposed by a brother, it wasn't her fault she could not trust another
She sought comfort in alleys, safety in solitude, her collection of trinkets was a refreshing interlude
The world was her own she belonged to herself, unbounded by norms, not placed on a shelf
They witnessed her leaving and then seemed relieved
they all had concurred it was scum they'd perceived
Back at the auction all held their breath, oblivious to life and doubtful of death
She mused as she ambled but just shook her head, it wasn't she but themselves they should dread
"Older is better?" she thought with a tear "they too will be old and that much I fear!"
One by one they left through the door clutching the loot they'd snatched from the floor
Their task was complete, they left with great pleasure,
they'd blindly renounced the greatest of treasure.

  David Vass

Poem

For, here I sit, an empty room, an open mind,
trying to create a poem, a poem about writing a poem.
It has to be amazing, so spectacular that others will
gaze when they read the words on the intriguing page.
Words will roll off their tongues as they swallow an
excellence that an amateur poet has presented to them.
This poem will be strong yet gentle, must be prompt
yet dear, having all the trimmings of a wonderful piece of work.
For, here I sit, an empty room, an open mind,
capturing a unique poem, writing not just
a poem, but a poem about a poem.

  Natalie Tribe

Keep On, Keep On!

When work is slow and time is short to meet the schedules we have set,
We may at times be so distressed, that we would just as well give up.
But giving up will just abort the joy of having our goal met.
It's good to live not being pressed, but not with loss of victor's cup!

A pioneer must take the risk that his convictions may be wrong;
But even so in fearless way, making his way in unknown ground,
His work pursues silent and brisk. No man can win, fearing the gong
For errors made. No one can say what's good or bad until it's found.

Persist all times! A challenge is a test to those that care to fight;
To see their dream turned to a face, it gratifies the heart and soul.
Just bitter folk say you're a quiz when in pursuit of things that might
Bring better life. By humble act just prove your worth, reaching the goal.

Keep on! Keep on your course, all folk that merit much for brave pursuit
To make the wishful dream today become the pride of times to come!
For, your hard work will soon un-cloak new things that only the astute
Could dared have dreamed. Those that dismay will see no joy.
Their minds are numb.

  Jack Thomas Sydenstricker

Lost Daughter

Hello, I said as I stepped into their uninviting stare.
I barely noticed as they looked me over in pure disgust.
I was there to beg their forgiveness, I was to ask for help. I could read their thoughts and was
ready to spill the words that spread my lips, for I was their long-lost daughter.
A long silence ended my violent cry, please greet me warmly.
I begged with my eyes,
Look into my future not to my past, I was away long enough not to get a greeting.
Are they sorry? I could not read the plain expression.
Then her lips quivered, the dark lightened for what were seconds,
and I was able to understand her emotions that she tried not to show.
My own mother, was she worried she would not be able to support herself and I?
She kept her troubled gaze frozen ahead.
My thoughts could not have been read through the drenching storms that raced down my face,
pleading for these new strangers not to be my own parents who were cold and solid with no heart.
Who am I, I asked myself over and over—
not a word from my so-called father who was part of the shadows.
Were they so heartless not even to welcome a poor girl, daughter or not, into their caring?
No, of course not, why would they notice?
I smiled when I saw my mother was suffering as much as I.
The sky to the day was over; I was settled in a small village far away from where my other family
lay in peace. I will remember this day only as a dream but forevermore.

Samantha Miller

Name

I have been branded a letter
sometimes followed by a minus or a plus;
I have seen myself in the mirror,
my face similar to the dark features of a short, stocky man,
my body the image of a woman
who's accused me of gracing every back seat of fast cars;

I was the temperamental bully, using force with every demand,
a vivacious figure with shocking things to say and do—
all clapped their mouths with proper hands;

I have been called a foulmouthed ***** by back-stabbing traitors,
been told to go home to my barbecued dogs
and leave the fish and chips behind
to the true-blue Skips;

I have seen myself as a man and horse,
shooting stars across the sky with my bow and arrow,
basing my identity on books, cards, palms. . . .

I have been many things, but I've never been my name.

Aimee Acosta

Daniel

Soft, gentle brown eyes that comforted me
for so many years
were closed as he lay there so still.
Memories of a thousand laughs rang in my ears
and haunted my mind.
I stood frozen in pain and fear.
Why? Was all I could think of.
All the words I never said to him,
the only person in my life that understood me, he made me whole.
I didn't want to be all by myself, but now I was.
I hated the world for this,
everyone that was happy and had all their loved ones near,
I hated them.
I knew I had to let him go,
so I cried and cried.
I knew what I had to do
and so I said good-bye.
I said good-bye to a seventeen-year-old boy
who deserved to be alive
. . . but I guess he didn't think so.

Amanda Gerrior

Rainbow

A rainbow in the sky, so beautiful to the eye,
Full of signs and wonders and a promise from on high.

Some of our days are cloud and rain
and in the midst of the storm you feel the pain.

Yes, filled with tears, you feel like giving up.
On bended knees you decide to look up.

Yes, you behold with your eye
The rainbow so beautiful to the eye
Full of signs and wonders and a promise from on high—

Inspired by God.

Allan A. Radmore

Life Is a Tale

"Life is a tale," said the Bard;
And so it remains in all regards,
But not at all by an "idiot."
The rest of the line was a facade
To conceal the truth that he discovered,
The truth that every man uncovers.
But once in a lifetime, ever it occurs
To us, the living, what the life utters.
It asks us to be brave in troubles deep,
Take time out and just peep
Over the months and years, where you keep
The youngster in you who wanted a leap.
But now you know it doesn't come cheap.
The world is like a shopping mart,
And if you want to shop smart,
Never leave behind your cart.
To see the items displayed with art . . .
It will be a blunder on your part;
To reach out for the high-shelved dream . . .
Soon it would melt like a dollop of cream.

Tazeen Zahida

Burgundy

No grains in the time jar,
Her body's curves confirming,
The gnarled figure, in high element of beauty,
Her shadows leap as flames,
Within them she shifts eternally,
Caged by blown walls.

PhebeAnn Wolframe

A Couple in Love

A couple in love
C an live in harmony,
O pinions set aside,
U ntil life's little things become a never-ending ride.
P eople enjoy the shared company that
L overs of life express,
E ver ready to lend a hand when the other is in distress.
I inviting truth of love for happiness,
N eeding understanding from the one that means most,
L iving with open arms, ready to be the host,
O ffering a shoulder when the other needs to hide,
V ery loving to one another
E ven on the roughest ride.

Melissa Mcgee

Remembering

Today my mother died.
Today I lost a friend.
Today my world turned upside down
Today my world would end.

I did not lose my grip
On life's reality,
But then, my comfort zone
Just vanished suddenly.

It grieved me when you died,
But not because you died,
But on the day you died,
That day, I lost a friend.

Brunhilde N. Chin

A Slim Selection

Light creeps under eyelids.
He awakes.
One leg dangles over the edge;
Thoughts stretch forward
    and cover his day,
Wondering what to wear.

The "Mr. Right" mask
Is in the hamper
From last night,
Speckled with wine.
It will not do.

The selection is slim.
He chooses the "Innocent Face."
It is the cleanest.

A business lunch with "Miss Right,"
He reminds himself to order the quiche
No matter how good the spaghetti looks.

Janet Gallagher

Children

They are our prodigy
Our sunshine, our ray of hope
Children don't see colors or hate
Laughter and play fills their days
Look through their eyes and see
No destruction, no greed
Only peace and love
Do not smother or mistreat
Let them flourish and grow
Let us not teach them our imperfections
Instead open your heart and eyes
And just maybe you will learn
Something you did not know

Corinna Claeys

crumbs of shadows

i remember when
i thought the world
consisted of only 64
beautiful crayons

shawn prince

Indian Summer

Every year in autumn,
When Indian Summer comes
With blazing trees as war paints
And the wings off birds as drums,
The snowy clouds are his headdress
Thrown against the sky,
As blue as turquoise wampum
Where the golden grass grows high.
With his warming campfire
And his pipe smoke strays,
He fills the folds of valleys
With a delightful summer haze.
But just as you've forgotten
That none of this can stay,
As quickly as the nightfall,
He has run away,
Stealing with him his colours,
And during the chilly dawn
Frost has grown on our autumn hills,
And our Indian Summer has gone.

Tera Rowlandson

Words of Wisdom

Live each day to the fullest
As if it were your last
Don't give up or hesitate
Stop living in the past

The past has long been lived
There is nothing you can change
So look upon the future
As something to arrange

Don't depend on others
To help and see you through
Remember the only friend in life
Is the friend you have in you

Jane White

Your Puppet

You pull
all the strings
so perfectly
to make your puppets dance.
They laugh.
They sing
and bow their heads,
to an audience
of all who do not know.
But I, yes I
know . . . they only come to be
through the many moods of you.

For, just like your puppets,
you control the strings of me.
You lead me
carefully . . . completely
to the centre stage with you,
so that I can dance,
and I can sing . . .
the song you want me to.

Lena M. McPeak

The Wind

Throughout the night, by wild winds
Spirits fly, their cries so high.
No one shall see, no one shall wake,
As trees from the bitter winds will quake.
Within their roots, within their trunks,
Through their branches, through their leaves
The cold, bitter winds shall whistle,
Pitched high as the spirits cry.
Shall creep through windows, under doors,
Spirits as its riders soar
To taunt children in their dreams,
So to awake with frightened screams.

Emily Bain

Sleep

i have an appointment to keep—
my *rendezvous* with sleep.
a friend that i once knew so well,
in whose realm i've ceased to dwell.
how can i say you mean less to me now?
it's something politeness will not allow,
and yet i repeatedly postpone our date.
does it perturb you that i'm constantly late?
my once-companion, rest—
do i put you to the test?

Courtney Montgomery

Forever Diana

Tonight a new star is shining in the sky,
A sign to remind us—Diana never said good-bye.
She has never left us—look up and you will see
In this world of darkness a shining ray of light
She sends to you and me.

Tonight, a new star is shining in the sky.
God placed it there to teach us
To live in hearts we leave behind
Is not to die.

Lourena Vandersluys

In Spirit

As this Christmas comes near,
I'm more aware you're not here.
You always made my Christmases so fun,
but now I feel like they're gone and done.
I know I'll miss your funny Christmas shirts.
They would make me laugh so hard it hurt.
And I'll miss seeing that big smile on your face
When every outside light was put in its place.
Although this year those same lights still shine,
and on the outside everything looks like it's fine,
it's really not going to be nearly the same.
What makes it hard is that there's no one to blame.
I feel like there will be no Christmas without you.
But I also realize that every Christmas should be new.
You definitely won't be forgot,
a Poinsettia will be put in the usual spot.
Happy thoughts of you will be with me all day,
thoughts of the things you would do and say.
And all of the things that you did for us in the past
are now great memories that will last and last and last.

Emma C. Darby

The Death Chamber (On a Factory Pig)

On the cold and hard concrete
Solitary with none to greet
Chained sore, deformed and saddened
None their hearts gladdened
The heavy chains their heads leashed
Bowed as if a sinner each
And in the dark scarce a cry
Only the step known that they must die
Row 'pon row in anguish sure
And each good soul without a flaw
A prisoner held and bound in prisons
Vile to cruel demise few look upon
Hung and quartered and much more
The questioning infants cannot know more
And now these sorry creatures bound from living
Never know but imagine only wing
A solitude of hope against hope to know
That this is so.

John Amsden

The Farmer's Song

Womb—moist from a sanctuary replete
  With unfledged tribute, the minions of rain
    Haiya ho haiya, they rescind
      The scythe of its brazen diphthong

The warm sweat that these fields secrete
  The hoe that slakes the wrinkled terrain
    Mud stories in their fingernails pinned
      The sinner, the sinned merrily throng

In Earth's pocks of teething wheat
  Where shrivels a moist legacy of pain
    On heart's sedges, the ergot thinned
      Gently ho, gently, they sing along

Of eternal wretch of human surfeit
  (as laughter mosses on lips of grain)
    And between spliced phrases of the wind
      Glean a healthy crop of song

Shashank Tripathi

Gratitude

Dear God of Heaven and God of Earth,
Thank You for the miracle of my Rebirth.
Thank You for the life You've given to me,
And for a heart to serve, I'm grateful to Thee!
I thank You for Your mercies that are new every day,
And I'm grateful that You never tire of hearing me pray!
I thank You for my sight and I thank You for Your touch,
And I love to tell You daily that I love You very much!
I'm grateful for Your Everlasting Arms of Love
And for the Holy Spirit who descends like a Dove!
Thank You for the talents You so freely gave to me
And for my friends who are a great help
And encouragement to me!
Thank You, because You are my friend
On whom I really can depend!
I'm grateful now, but I'll be more grateful when
I'm welcomed Home to praise You,
Forevermore in Heaven!

Marie Falck

Fading Petals

A rose is but a flower
That seems to fade away
The memory of its fragrance
Will always seem to stay
A life is like the flower
It keeps blooming day by day
Grows old as time goes by
Eventually fading away
Life is never ending
As the memory always remains
Never forgetting the love that's past
To each of us day by day
Your memory will be in our hearts
As long as we remain.

Janice Pitter

Perception and Prayer

To Diana, Princess of Wales
People, people everywhere!
Expression of heartfelt sadness.
Flowers, flowers everywhere!
Symbol of love and deep devotion.
Family following the ensign-draped casket
In silent reverence.
White lilies symbolizing purity
Only Christ can give.
White lily-wreath with the envelope
To "Mummy"
Will always rend our hearts.
Tears of empathy
For two motherless boys.
May God be merciful,
Drawing them to Himself,
Who to know is
Life Eternal!

Helen Reimer Bergmann

Reality

To sharpen the saw
Is what one has to do
To get ahead today
In the world in which we live.

One must seek first
To understand,
Then to be understood
By others.

Work backwards,
Begin with the end in mind.
Then you can worry
About where to start.

Let your mind wander.
Don't stick to a plan.
You will get lost
And very frustrated.

Work at your own pace.
You have your whole life
To accomplish
What you are supposed to do.

Terra Stewart

The Meadowlark

I dreamt I heard a meadowlark,
I was transported back.

Running across a field of crocus,
Mallards nesting
In the reeds beside the pond,
Wild turkey in the grass:
I heard the thrilling, trilling song.
As sunrise lit the prairie sky.

He sang for me through all my years,
This joyous harbinger of spring.

And now I've come to rest
Where heron stalk the shore.
The lonely sound of loons
And song birds fill the winter day.
Spring came, I thought I dreamed.

I leapt from bed, and there he sat
Upon my garden gate.

Dorothy Childs

Untitled

Life is but a mystery to me:
Wild as the rapids,
Calm as the sea,
Hard as a rock,
Soft as a child's smile.

Life is but a mystery to me.
What is my purpose?
To await death,
And let my body rot within the soil?
Is my soul to be left alone
To face the unknown?

Life is but a mystery to me.
What is my duty?
Am I to help my fellow man?
Help him destroy our world?
What am I to do?

Life is but a mystery to me,
But I will teach a child to smile,
And help a man to love.
That is what I will do.

Isabella Mottillo

Remember

Good-bye, my friends,
My little ones,
You'll always be remembered
In all our hearts and in our thoughts.
You're in His Hands forever.
In God's Land we know you're free
To seek the mild and wisdom.
You're in His Hands and are carefree,
That's why they call it so heavenly.
Take care, my friends.
I hope you see,
You'll always be remembered by me.

Alice Panter

The Book of Life

The keeper of the ages is the keeper of the heart,
Eternity entwined in forgotten pages.

The ebb and flow of full moon's tide,
washed ashore, ever reaching
distant horizons, calls to beckon the sun,
its arms ever reaching, is rising, rising, rising
as time elapses into itself
un-forgotten, ever remembered.

The keeper of the heart reveals its hidden thoughts
of time beginning, to time of ended pages.

The keeper of the ages unfolds its fragile pages
of distant times and long-forgotten ages.
And therein lies the heart of hearts
upon the printed pages of the book
declared throughout all the ages!

Lesley Ann Frederick

No Title Needed

She caught the eyes of millions;
God gifted her with two sons;
She gave to so many her heart;
She had no life outside royalty and fame,
For the papparazzi always came.

The flags lowered, the tears fell,
For no one could believe;
Family cried for hours on hours
While millions came to mourn and give flowers.

Her brother is furious,
Her sons confused with sorrow;
Her heart to us all was a brand new tomorrow.

She will never die; she will never let us weep;
She is inside us all;
With so much love and concern for others,
She needs no royal title; for, she has ours she was.
The People's Princess.

My heart is with all of you in your hard times of sorrow;
If we keep thinking of our Diana, she will
Bring us a better tomorrow.

Anthony Levere

Agonizing

My soul and body ache for thee to hold,
My love; with mingled joy and longing weep,
As of thee I dream, dearest, with wishes bold
And cry, "Ah, Love! Thy dart hath struck me deep!"

One night, when normal souls were 'sleep abed,
On mine I lie awake, yet dreamt of thee,
And gazed perchance upon the moon o'erhead
Where—likeness unto thine—a face I did see.

Her lips smiled down on me from Heaven high;
Her eyes beheld me in my yearning plight;
But woe—misfortune's clouds there drifted by,
And for a while they took thee from my sight!

But so they're gone—I now would e'er have thee
To love and hold—if thou wilt but have me!

Morton Bodanis

Coming Home

Beneath the rock and clay lies a wounded soul
In search of the Earth, its strength to bring home,
To hear the birds sing, and feel the sun's warmth—
A pleasure yet to have come.
Judge not the choice or the place you came to see
While searching for the memory that brought you to me.
The sky will protect it, you know,
While settling a world yet so unknown.
Blessings are far from here now;
Protect the soul that you have found.
The Earth settles around the rock that holds it still,
While yearning for the force that can bring home the will.
Leaves will fall and snow will grace
Memories of that grounded place.
Remember the song of love, come to the place
Where memories are sweet-enduring,
From this forever embrace.

Michelle Connolly

Beauty of Life

In this modern world in which we live,
we often forget the way it was for our ancestors.
It was a time of change, a time of tradition,
a time of values different from our own.
It was a time when religion played a much
greater role in everyday life.
In this hectic world in which we live,
few ever notice the beauty or the changes.
So concerned with pressures and deadlines,
we often lose sight of the beauty of life.
If only we could see it through the eyes of a child.
If only we could slow down for a moment
and look around as if we were seeing everything
for the first time, the world would be a better place.

Susan Herns

Life

Life is like a shining flower,
As bright as a spring morning,
Filled with warm, happy laughter,
And a heart that breaks forth in singing.
Life is full of sunlight
That God sends down from above,
Giving us His blessing with a never-ending love.

Margaret E. Drake

The Eventuality of Man

As we look into the eyes of the past,
we see faint, flickering memories of what we once were.
Shadowy images dance in our minds,
as the light shines down upon the stage of life. . . .

Then death, to those who lie in their graves,
is but a final moment of true peace,
a peace that they can neither feel nor share.
In a somnolent trance, they descend into darkness.

Solitude is what envelopes their souls.
And there they are left
to continue in nonexistence,
relying only on a memory of what was once their lives.

Finnian Cole

Alone

In a corner unknown to me,
I see and hear all the fears
Hidden away—afraid to see
All the pain of all the years.

Feeling too scared to even try,
Through the tears I fear the known.
Wanting to share before I cry,
In a corner I sit alone.

J. Craig Fraser

The Tamarack Bird

There it sat quietly
on the shelf in the store,
made by an unknown Indian
from the sticks of a tamarack tree,
waiting to be moved
to where, placed in water,
it would fill the air
with the smell of tamaracks.

Gloudina Bouwer

Untitled

I may be blind
but I can see.
For, when I sleep,
I dream of thee.

I have no heart
but I feel whole.
For, love is born
within the soul.

I may be deaf
but I can hear.
My heart beats loudly
when you're near.

Although my life
may be surreal,
I know that it is
love I feel.

Melissa Kaniuk

Untitled

I hesitate, then stop to listen
Memories of this gruesome mission
Are here and there
Dead flowers lay
Never changing night by day

I hear them shriek their battle cry
Frenzied running as they die
On murdered ground
The white flag waves
Ever draining blood-filled graves

I weep for those who suffered here
Forever now must dwell in fear
And guilt for this Satanic crime
Yes all are dead
The fault is Mine

Trish Van Buren

Thoughts of All Your Loved Ones

To my dad
Grieve not
Rather let memories linger on
We will cross more rivers and bridges
Climb more mountains together

Send no flowers
For they wilt and die
But send your love and pleasant thoughts

Let the heather be your bed
Wild flowers give you freedom
God's creatures to watch overhead

We shall not separate
For, when I leave the Earth
In God's Heaven we meet again
At this union we shall
Never depart
Diane Bradbury

Death of an Ant

I killed an ant! God-given ant!
Through grassy sprigs to bed she aimed;
On little back, thread-joined back,
She dragged a corpse of her dead friend.

I blew the "Raid's" poisoned whiff
On tiny ant's desperate parts . . .
She twitched and coughed in deadly grip,
Holding her friend, kicking her limbs.

Her eyes I saw glossy and stunned,
Looking at huge, horrendous Bug!
A dragon's head she must have seen,
Spewing a gush of deadly juice.

If she could think, if she could see,
She would have asked Almighty Lord:
"Why do you let this horrid beast
Kill, when I must bring home my friend?"

Or did she think of me as God,
Avenging God for goods she stole?
Did she confess? Her pardon beg?
So that she may to Heaven go?
Aniela Ania Radek

Hear Her Here

Her velvet arm touch,
Racing the pace,
Facing the taste,
In a sunrise at four a.m.

Silent at the edge of dawn,
Among the roadside flowers of summer,
My tired eyes turn west . . .
Home, where night still lingers.

Her splendor sleep there
Unknowing,
Ever-growing,
While I can only dream.
Michael Johnston

Remembering

Quite often memories of past life come back to mind:
While growing up in my remote village,
Where there was no running water or electricity,
Life was full of basic things of all kinds.
One could sit outside at night and stare at clear sky.
Children were the happiest ones playing hide and seek.
Songs rose behind shrubs chanting,
Smart one, smart one, keep whistling
So that we can locate you where you're hiding.
Older people sat around the fire,
Busied themselves telling legends full of wisdom.
Excited and interested faces listened without boredom.
Behind houses made of straw, on branches of trees,
Owls hooted, letting people know they too were alive.
Superstitious people listened to them with fright;
They believed owls were wicked witches.
What a difference there was on a full moon night,
When young people decided to organize a dancing evening.
The sounds of tam-tam invited surrounding villages
To join in the celebration of life's simple pleasures.
Beatrice Luvwefwa

Tears Falling

Will you walk with me once in a while?
Will you share with me your smile?
Will you follow me down into my darkness?
Will you light a candle during my great despair?
Will you whisper in my ear when I am alone?
Will you take my hand and lead me back home?

Can I hold you for one long last time?
Can I pretend for a little while that you are mine?
Can we whisper each others names and pretend?
Can I wish for this never to end?
Can I stop my heart from calling your name?
Can you hold me, now everything has changed?

Will you forget me now with the passing of time?
Can I forget that for a little while you were mine?
Will you hear what my soul to you is calling?
Can I hide the tracks of my tears falling?
Katherine Wolfheart

Title of Wonder

They dance across the screen
From hour to hour,
Those transient messages of instant wealth.
"Genuine Offer!!!"
One you can't resist? Try hard.
And if you waver, think instead
Of that cold beer your dollar bill could buy,
A burger, or a streetcar ride
To somewhere more exciting.
If any of those email offers worked
And made repliers rich beyond their dreams,
Would not the advertiser keep
Those profits for himself?
I would, and so would you,
And he's not daft!
So I just hit "Delete" each time they come—
But wonder if I've turned a fortune down.
Lionel Fanthorpe

Judgement Heard

The clouds had gathered, the winds howling, he gushed; remembering her beauty
Thrilled his mind as thought rolled in.
Her physique a boutique, her stature a brochure, her character a feature.

He saw her at the ball of the teens and tods; in the moonlight vision
She shone like a sight for the gods. He grid up the coins and took up a gauntlet;
Be I a man of spirit, not a man of straw?
And without a leap in the dark, he tried to draw his love, hidden in his heart.

He approached her, touching her hips, he turned her round.
He drew her close.
Gripping her hands with one behind the other, he smoothed over her head.
With a tilt of slight, he pressed his lips on hers.
She tried to wiggle out but he chained her more, too bold to be cold.
Time ticked. Loosing herself to him, she ran her hands on his chest.
Slowly moving to a chair, she sat on him, lap to lap, lip to lip, they were.
Startled mouths widened, applause and claps filled the air.

They pondered the audacity of both, the deed similar to the past,
That of a Capulet girl and a Tybalt boy, but to disprove their tragic end
These swore: die to live, not live to die.
Thunder may roar, lightning around,
But our love they blinded shall earn in light, not beg in dark.

Krithika Kumar

True Emotions

I'm not an ordinary, everyday person, but here I am.
I keep hoping someday I'll be there for you, like you were for me,
but time can only tell.
Sometimes, I need to be alone, but they say there's no time
to think or be afraid of what's ahead of us.
I never knew it could be like this,
that you could make everything all right.
But if I'm wrong, then tell me I'm wrong.
I guess that what you'd call "you and I" is a game of chance.
Maybe I've been a fool not learning how to face things on my own.
But then again, I'll soon find out.

Candy Mabbitt

Our Undercover World of Thoughts and Feelings

Each and everyone of us is a witness
Witnesses to what this world's become
Enemies with happiness and freedom
Subtracting smiles that reflect what's to come
Inside, we see cloudy cast shadows
With signs of sunshine outlining our picture's frame
It's cold, and growing colder as we let it
Passing each other in the streets with faces of shame
Realization is the lock we need a key for
A door that's hinges rusted shut as we bypassed
Now, to open up our world and revive the setting
We'll be letting out what's been hidden for so long
Hidden is the will to share our feelings
To those who keep them inside, they will waste
Hidden is the smirk that sparked the smile
That shook this earth and started things to quake
Hidden is the overall intention to start as we once had, now again
The need to put our hand out through connection
And reach beyond to let this never end

Matthew T. McDaniel

Innocence Lost

Your stare is filled with poison, and your green words drip with envy.
Your embrace is cold and uncaring.
My glance is innocent, and I croon soft words in your ear.
I embrace you tightly, and hold onto you as if you alone were my salvation, my savior.
I am like a fallen angel.
The smacks, bruises, bumps, and cracks I take like I deserve,
And maybe I do. . . .
You raped me of myself.
I am left to drown in my own miserable existence.
You engulf me in your venomous glare,
And I melt to you.
Foolishly I believe your lies,
Thinking your kisses will make up for the pain.
I cry silken tears, you laugh mockingly
Smiling like a snake about to devour his prey.
While I am blind to your hatred,
You're the knife that cuts my wrists.
The blood is on your hands.
I am drawn to you like a vampire is drawn to blood.
I drink you, I need you. . . .

   Kristy Willson

Words . . . (The Story of On-Line Love)

I need you, I want you, I love you:
words written in light,
words set on paper with ink,
words whispered on shafts of moonlight,
words thought every day,
words dreamed every night.
Secrets of our souls, promises of rapture, dreams of together,
withered and died in the realities of distance and time.
Two hearts, introduced by chance and
cruelly stabbed by the daggers of fate,
trust was won through words to be built upon.
The challenge was made and the duel begun.
Heaven and Earth proved too strong to move,
even by words of truest love, purest love,
of hearts who had never met,
who now will never touch, and who will never know
what might have been.
Because in the end, the truth was found . . .
the words just weren't enough!

   Christine Leitgeb

Unspoken

One day you were here and the next day you were gone.
How could I have been so foolish?
How could I have been so wrong?
I didn't even say good-bye to you,
Didn't even kiss you on your cheek.
Now I sit here and I wait and wonder:
I wonder of the day when we can finally re-meet.
You didn't realize how much I loved you;
You didn't realize how much I cared.
I sat there on that hospital bed and all I did was stare.
I couldn't believe you were actually gone;
I couldn't stand the pain.
I kept telling myself that God shouldn't have taken you;
He should have taken someone else.
Now I realize that I was wrong,
For now you are in a much better place.
Earth was just holding you back from being in the most joyous state.
So even though you are dead and I will never see you again,
I want you to know you were the best father,
And you will always have a special place in my heart . . . till my very end.

   Ernalyn Puno

Dreams of Delight

I look at the stars in their heavenly height
And wonder the ocean blue
And the marvelous glow
Of the crystal snow
Wherever the paths divide.
'Tis a beautiful thing
That only the spring
Is ever prepared to hide.
I gaze in your eyes
And wonder your sighs,
And wonder what fortunate fate
Invited me here
To the atmosphere
Of the roses around your gate.
And always I dream,
In the gleam of the stars,
Of the day when my dream will come true,
And my heart may abide
In the joy and the pride
Of being together with you.

Elsie Clarey

untitled

my days were always full from the first finger
of sunlight that caressed me each morning
until the sheet of darkness that tucked me
in at the end of every day.
and never did that which filled every conceivable
space in my heart ever cross the threshold
of my lips, and fall upon your ears to find
its way to occupy your heart of hearts.
while my hands may have been upon you,
they were never really within you
as your hands touched every deepest part of me.
and when i look to my side, to your shadow remains
and i can only wish that you preceded it.
i am now awash in this flickering light, alternating
between lightness and darkness, memories and reality
and it compels me to wonder if you could ever return
to shine on me again, but i can always retreat to
those days when you and i walked hand in hand,
and i lived in your eyes and your heart of hearts.

Lawrence M. Robertson

YOU

Pieces of you, pieces of me. Fallen.
Our pain exploding, pulsing through my veins.
Helplessness. I scream into the darkness, the echo
     dulls within the black space. Alone.
I am alone. The thickening quietness.
I touch the spot where I felt your
     breath graze my moist skin. Stopping.
Holding my finger to the pulse, waiting,
     inhaling slowly. Pausing, pausing . . .
Lingering on remembrance of the moment
     when your breath was within mine.
Salivating as I swallow the richness of it.
Now, my eyes watering, stinging with loneliness
     held in the reality of alone. Emptiness.
I am losing you now. Fading. The tide is rising.
Swelling higher as it takes me inside. Protected.
Hiding in the darkness. Waiting for your breath
     to be close again.
You. Only you . . .

sharon

By the Cruel Blue Sea

Come to me, my lady,
Across the ocean blue.
Come to me, my lady,
Like the morning dew.

I have a picture of us together,
Under the willow tree.
Come to me, my lady,
Across the great blue sea.

I heard your ship was lost
And I'm crying for you, my lady,
As I stand here above the great cliff.
My nostrils take in a deathly whiff,
As I jump off the rocks into the cruel sea.

Come to me, my lady, in the deep blue sea.
Come to me, my lady; our souls are free.

As the seabirds gave their cry,
From the ocean came you and I,
Standing beneath the willow tree
Beside the cruel blue sea.
Now, our love will last an eternity.

Gerald Meyer

Copenhagen

Fifty-six degrees past memory,
beyond the veil of night,
the lamp of argon glows.
A thick, wet mist imbibes the air
like whiskey in the brain.

The cool wind,
as salted as herring
from Norwegian shores,
comes in strong from the North Sea.

This Viking land of Cnut and sons,
whose powerful oars
propelled men to dreadful clashes
for silver and bloody adventure,
this place is now for dreaming.

As the days succumb to triumphant nights,
the halogen luminescence rules
over tavern and church
like the star of Bethlehem gone supernova
in a sky devoid of stars.

James Olcese

A Wish

Oh, to walk amongst
azure fields
of the sky,

To let the wind play
upon this envelope
of mortal flesh,

To be weightless and free
from the confines of
Earthly wonders,

To Fly!

David Timpa

Gone, The Velvet of the Rose

I don't want to be
an old woman with thin lips,
that absent, gaping mouth—
gone, the velvet of the rose:

dried husk walking in the world,
seeing only inward,
lush memories,
the oasis of her desert years,
visiting them one by one
until they, too, dry up,
their spring source gone.
Do we live long after the last is gone?

If I were an old woman
with thin, dry lips,
I wouldn't want to live after
the memories.
But I wouldn't know it then, would I?
Who would I be, anyway?

Heike Schroeder

Memories of 1990

Shut out the light;
Pull the curtains;
Protect yourself from the barren night.
The key,
the bolt,
closed against the world outside,
sometimes drowned in an evening tide
of despair and desperation.
What's it for?
What's the reason?
Just to live,
to provide?

A. V. Hill

Mindful Thoughts

Trees stand as testaments to time,
Keys to lost days, and
Dreams of the future.
Sunlight shines. Creeping
Only to the edge of the woods,
Reaching for the darkness,
But eternally reaching.
Night and Dreams
Frolic with the Trees of Remembrance.
Soft music is heard as Dreams dance
Through the fingers of Light.
Mist hums a wordless tune and
Blows kisses of forgetfulness.
Night lives secluded from the Light,
And longs only for a brief affair.
Fright swims in a pond of darkness,
Surfacing when Dreams dance too close.
Piercing eyes cannot read the darkness,
And lips are the only door to its secrets.

Paula Shaver

Where Do You Go?

Tell me, where do you go when you close your eyes?
Do you seek the darkness? Do you hide inside?
Are you out in the fields that once made you smile
Or do you climb up a tree and touch the sky?

When you look in my eyes, can you read my mind?
Are the thoughts that you seek the same as mine?
As you look in the distance, eyes like sparkling wine,
Are the dreams that you have of reality kind?

Who do you turn to when everything looks dim?
Do you pray to a god or go out on a limb?
The lights have shone upon you, as bright as day.
Don't let yourself drift or be taken away.

No limits, no boundaries, no secrets to find,
Lifeless, inanimate, and spiritless inside,
Are your voyages as gifted or wonderful as mine
Or of destruction and of deception of mankind?

Tell me, where do you go, do you really go away?
Sometimes I wonder and I too wish to go away.

Michèlle Dionne

Untitled

Allegorists catch the fish where calm waters flow
Mindfully restless, a stone to throw,
Indifferent and sad as complex, as one
Turmoil envelopes from father to son.
Richly adorned with eloquent treasures,
Unaware of life's worldly pleasures,
Less of the tears that pour from the soul,
Empty the heart that has taken its toll.
Yet, try to uncover the blanket so neat,
Unrest of failure, contempt of defeat,
Never to follow the prints in the sand,
Hurt and afraid to reach for your hand,
Projecting from height a mystical air,
Young hearts in awe wistfully stare.

Old and grey are the eyes of the wise,
Rigid and tight, held within their disguise.
Call from the water the trickle and gulp,
Allowing the juice to flow from the pulp,
Hoping for, wanting an end to our screams—
Interminable they are, both memories and dreams.

Olive Brennan

Please Don't Drink and Drive

So you've had a couple of drinks
But sure you can still clearly think
And I know you've got to get somewhere
Putting everyone at risk, is that really fair?
What would you do if you killed someone?
You cannot take it back, it's already done
It might be someone you didn't know
So a little despair is all you'd show
But what if it was someone for whom you cared?
Someone with whom all the good times you shared?
Your life would never be the same
And you are the only one to blame
So please help spread the word
Even if they've already heard
A life can never be replaced
And that is something you need to face

Janette Erskine

A Friend

When did it start? It seems so hard to remember.
It's hard thinking of the exact time that it began to matter.
It seems so long ago, and yet still so short.
Who knew it would change us—too late to abort?
It was so innocent, no time to prepare.
It started so quietly—who knew it would be there?
We've come such a long way, that it's hard to understand
That we could have lost the innocent years in the end.
Time has gotten better, each year like a page;
It's better than wine that gets better with age.
At first we didn't say, no one would dare;
We had to be sure that it was really there.
It's hard to believe time passes so fast,
That we've become so comfortable, from the future to the past.
It's true! It's all true! No use to pretend.
It finally comes out—too late—we're friends!
In this day and age, it could be much worse;
Destiny could have missed us, and left us empty like a curse.
But our time line is stronger—again and again—
Looks like we're friends, from beginning to end.

    Eliane Hachey

The Happy Hunting Ground

We came across the sea by boat; we trekked across the land
For, we had to get the message to the swarthy, heathen band
The message of the great, white God who dwells in Heaven above
In a city paved with streets of gold, where angels sing of love

We didn't know that Heaven was an Indian summer eve
We hadn't walked on golden paths, strewn with autumn leaves
We hadn't heard the angels that sang among the trees
Nor did we know the smallest were the little chickadees

We hadn't seen the Northern lights or heard the wild goose call
Or felt the heaven of warm Chinooks—we didn't know at all
That before we'd come to teach them of his love that was profound
He'd been leading all the natives to the happy hunting ground

    Karen Poulsen

The Second Coming

The three came riding on their Harley's, shining brightly like a
full moon! His hair was long and flowed in the wind. His eyes
were glistening, dark pools of love. His outriders were Michael
and Gabriel, sitting taller than any man, in their black leathers
and dark sunglasses. They rode majestically behind their leader
but ever on guard! They rode down the middle of the road, their
engines idling cool and low. Toward Central Park they travelled,
neither looking left nor right. As they came in sight of the park,
the massive crowd began to cheer, Hosanna! He is here! They
waved palm leaves as they ran, creating a sea of green. On the
roadside they stood, some in tears at the sight of Jesus, others
on their knees in awe. Many saintly people were seen in the
crowd, Martin Luther, Mother Theresa, Mother Mary, Lady Di,
Mahatma Gandhi, to name a few, Francis Xavier, Martin Luther King,
John Kennedy, and Peter came into view. Jesus said, "I have
returned as My Father always foretold! Now, come and follow me;
for, peace, health, and love are now eternally yours!" Then from
all directions a rumble could be heard. It grew tumultuously
into an ear-splitting roar, as millions of leather clad angels
came riding into view, gathering the many who believed. Hosanna!

    Dale Congdon

Peace on Earth

When a child is born, he brings a lot of happiness, which no one wants to see
turned to sadness. But, as the child gets older and starts to develop,
he starts to wonder who he should trust, and that's the trouble
with mankind today. We have lost trust in one another; instead of blaming
each other for our trouble, we should learn to pray. Praying is a gift from the
good Lord above. It's a gift about singing with each other and sharing our love.

There are a lot of fears in the world today and a lot of sadness and suffering,
but I say that in everyone's heart, there is a flame that is burning, burning
for the love and understanding that we owe to one another. This cannot come
from hatred and violence or from fighting our own neighbors. We were put
on this Earth for just so many hours, maybe if we took one at a time,
our fears . . . we would conquer.

It's like a four-year-old building a castle in the sand. I'm sure he would
be very happy if his little friend offered him a hand. It doesn't matter
what age you are; we are all kids at heart. Why not make from this day
on . . . a brand new start. I think that by trusting each other more, we will be
much farther ahead; wouldn't that be someday when everyone had bread?
It would take away a lot of suffering, fighting, and killing, and I bet that
the church bells in the world would start ringing. "May God bless."

> *Gilles Chenier*

Dreams

I once dreamed of a house with no fighting,
full of love, a family of my own.
I once dreamed of a place I could call home.

I once dreamed of a relationship with no lies,
no cheating, or arguments.
I once dreamed of a perfect love.

I once dreamed of a world with no guns, bombs or war.
I dreamed of a world that was fighting no more.

However, these are all dreams, and dreams they will only be.
The perfect life, the perfect world,
but only in my imagination, never reality.

> *Barry Szaefer*

The Beauty of Summer

While strolling all around my yard on a bright and sunny day,
The beauty that surrounds me fairly takes my breath away.
Pansy faces look at me, and I'm sure I see them smile.
White daisy heads nod in the breeze, their petals so fragile.

The orange and golden marigolds are like the sunshine's rays
Reflecting off the grass so green and sidewalks 'long the way.
Petunias, snaps, and zinnias, lilies, columbines are there,
While fragrance from the roses wafts softly in the air.

Peony buds are bursting into brilliant colored blooms.
A bouquet of scented sweet peas will enhance my living room.
By the fence delphiniums send their spikes shooting to the sky.
Their purples, blues, and creamy white attract big butterflies.

Geranium pots beside the house have blooms the eye to please.
At the corner, the clematis climbs away up to the eaves.
The fifty-year-old leafy trees, with branches spreading wide,
Are support for hanging baskets of begonias side by side.

Tiny hummingbirds at feeders beat their wings and drink their fill,
While orioles and robins, from the treetops, songs they trill.
I've a Garden of Eden here on Earth to enjoy all summer's days,
And the welcome mat is always out to all who pass this way.

> *Pearl McDermand*

Honorable Janet Reno

Gloria Landau did die on the fourth of July.
The U.S. Treasury has directed!
I now respectfully request an "Official Inquest"
And have myself resurrected!

This whole thing is absurd, how did they get the word
That I no longer existed?
They want back my Social Security checks
That I "forged" they insisted!

My Bank account's frozen, I'm in a bind.
Have you ever heard of such a thing as this kind?
My passport is stamped July 28th '94
I entered the U.S. like always before.

I'm not a ghost, I can proudly boast
I live like all humans do.
I eat and sleep, read books
And go shopping too.

Way after the Treasury claimed me "dead"
I paid my quarterly tax instead!

Gloria Landau

I Dread the Night

Rolling over once again, glancing at the clock—
   Time passes with agonizing languor—
Again a silent vigil relentlessly repeated.

Memories cascading upon near consciousness—
   Gazing at the bottle—
Standing as a sentinel against reality—
   Thinking back—

How long has it been this time?
   My being cries out for peace—
Yet my cries fall upon deaf ears—

To whom shall I cry out now?
   To the Gods who have forsaken me
   to this abyss of despair?
My friends who hear not my voice crying out
   in supplication?

How I long to hold you near—feel the warmth
   and tenderness of your presence—
Yet I am alone again, condemned to repeat
   this agonizing ritual—

Seeking only and end—now my only recourse—
   picking up the bottle—
I dread the night.

Andrzej Zawalinski

A Teacher's Description

Twenty-eight children with a thousand dreams;
Fifty-six bright eyes watching life's extremes;
Twenty-eight small tongues never cease wagging;
Fifty-six fine feet dancing, dragging;
Twenty-eight noses, curious ever;
Fifty-six smart hands, clumsy and clever;
Twenty-eight bodies never sitting still;
Fifty-six wide ears listening with a will;
Twenty-eight brave hearts beating and alive;
With a million hopes—my class in Room Five!

Patricia Lewis

A Plea to the Alcoholic

Oh, rise, You Alcoholic,
Rise up and stand up straight,
You've grovelled in your plate too long,
The hour is getting late.
Your youth is quickly fading,
Redemption time is here.
You've wronged your friends and neighbours,
Make haste and have no fear.
Your wife once stood beside you,
But her love you did erase,
By sleepless nights and verbal abuse,
In your alcoholic state.
Your children once admired you,
No one could take your place,
But you've destroyed their love for you,
So many times you've turned your face.
So rise up you Alcoholic,
Rise up and stand up straight,
But "Take it Easy," "One Day at a Time"
And the future you can face.

Lois Quinn

Below Reproach

Tour de monde vilification
of copulate sobriety,
heresy abysmalized
in a hysteria of wretched contempt.
Choke back the vomit, oh, censored society,
idolize the quo-laced,
refute the ill-gotten martyrdom
of the unkempt.

Sabotage the un-marionetted pragmatists.
Saddle reproach on every blasphemous steed.
Burn all the dissidents 'cause they exist.
Let the whores read the verse,
while the outsiders bleed.

Geordie Tait

Why?

Have you ever watched the sunrise
Light the early morning dew,
Or gazed in awe and wonder
At the deep majestic blue,
Or tried to track a planet's
Endless voyage across the sky,
And from somewhere deep inside you
Heard the frightening question: WHY
Does man—in his supposed great wisdom—
Keep on tempting God and fate
With his weapons of destruction
And his multitudes of waste,
And expect this tiny planet alone to repair
All the scars and all the cancers
He has knowingly put there,
Or will he stop this slaughter
Of our land, our sea, our sky?
I think not. Alas, too late he'll pause
And ask in anguish—WHY?

Clyde Heffern

God's Ways

Very often we think God is not there,
For our plans progress nowhere.
We think that He doesn't care,
And what He does isn't fair.

In His time, He will let us know
That our plans wouldn't grow,
For we'll know what we prayed then
Was a disaster we didn't comprehend.

He knows our tomorrow and today,
So let Him have His own way.
Finally, when we put it to test,
God's plans would work the best.

Sajani Mathew

Untitled

Big brown eyes of innocence
Sparkle in naivete
Rose-coloured glasses provide a shield
From the sun's ray
Inevitably the blossoming begins
They shed tears of lost virtue
Glistening even more
Because of what they've seen

Laura Cea

Love's First Kiss

The sun has set.
The world's gone cold.
As winter's moon grows paler still,
A gentle breeze begins to stir.

It sweeps her maiden's golden hair
Across her ruby lips.
The gentleman to whom she clings
Enfolds her in his kiss.

With this kiss he does profess
His love and tenderness,
And forever they shall be filled
With the warmth of love's first kiss.

Ursula Roesch

Blood Is Thicker Than Water

I have not thought out,
I have not grown, yet I am proud,
With no feathers to show that I'm a man.
I still roam free about my land.
Wild horses I have tamed.
To me it is a serious game.
My horse and I, together we'll die.
On the war path, sounding the war cry,
Bow and arrow go hand in hand.
My brothers and I, together we stand.
The colour of our skin is not the same.
To use that excuse is very lame.
We are not the colour of night,
Nor are we the colour of a cloud,
But we are Indian and we are proud.

Keith Madeley

My Beautiful Palace

My beautiful palace,
Where once I ruled with malice,
Stood high in the darkest of all valleys
And was feared by the passing galleys.

Should a traveller pass near,
He'd feel the paralyzing fear
After hearing the macabre melodies
Played in my legendary parties.

A chalice was raised as I was praised
By the immortals who (yes, even they) were amazed
By the glamour and grandeur
Of my beautiful palace and its parlour.

But, alas, now it's gone, and life has won
Over the one whose only fear was sun.
Now the palace is naught but ashes.
I'm old and have just my memories
Of my beautiful palace,
Where once I ruled with malice.

Roope Talasmaa

A Sunray

A faint sunray at this moment of sunset
Is entering my cell and warming up my heart.
O' precious gift of God that comes down to this Earth!
I hear in your presence a heavenly choir's voices.

An Chau Nguyen

Sorrow

Give me the potion to take away all my sorrow,
All this weight of painful loneliness
That crushes and tortures me.
That one awful thing I truly fear
When I hear that dread footfall come near
And I know there is no escape.

Give me that potion to take away my fear of
Longing for you, never to be with you.
If I took such a potion of forgetfulness
And went away and then we met on some other day
And I knew you not?
How terrible that I should not remember.
Not to remember your sweet embrace,
Your kiss, your loving words, your touch,
Your breath on my face.
Your cries of love as we make our love.
To forget you?

Give me the potion to take away all my sorrow,
And I shall not drink.

Scott Farrell Strichen

Limericks

My birthday is an exciting affair.
I would like to get a teddy bear.
After all the presents comes some ice cream.
I have never seen this kind of ice cream.
What a great birthday I had.
I hope it's this great next year when my birthday comes.

Alex Newman

The Land of Everlasting Peace

For many years we'd been sailing through th' cold night,
Two super warships with the crewmen nuclear blind.
We had indoctrinated every whore and nun
With image of the evil en'my number one.

"Thou shalt not murder"—this commandment of the Lord
Was done away with; lo, it was cast overboard,
And every stray son who ignored the false alarm
Was running risk of being strung up from the yardarm.

But dawn has broken and the crewmen, we have seen,
That there is only one ship cruisin' in the sea.
We couldn't perceive in chauvinistic outer dark
That we are sailing, verily, in Noah's ark.

Should we stay bellicose or should we reach the accord,
The starboard brethren and the brethren on the port?
Can't we dispose of our weapons piece by piece
And find the promised land of everlasting peace?

We are not enemies! We have foiled Satan's plot,
The starboard brethren and the brethren on the port!
We'll do our best, behold, amid tempestuous seas—
We'll find the Holy land of everlasting peace. . . .

Boris Gryn'

Untitled

My life has been one long journey,
I have travelled many roads.
I have navigated big broad thoroughfares
teeming with the importance of life,
as well as quieter routes that use a kindlier pace,
and little tributary paths have I also frequented.

In all my wanderings to and fro,
I have stopped at many dwellings,
some great, towering palaces, and some
of the busiest of inns.

And yet in all of these places
that I had searched room by room,
I did not find that which I sought,
and so my search continued.

But now my search is over,
no more musty old buildings,
no more sorties for me,

for now my heart is content
to sit awhile at rest

in the garden of your soul.

John Campbell

Crying

I cry day and night with no one knowing;
Sometimes I feel fright to know it's showing.
I cry not tears but blood;
I cry not by eyes but by heart.
Sometimes I want to flee
Like the birds that are free,
To lift my heart from anguish,
For the pain to finish,
To gain what I want and what I need,
To flee from this world of greed.

Erin

Flying Free

Sometimes when I'm alone at night
I wish for wings I could use to take flight
Sitting, staring out the window
I wish for no limits to where I could go
When I see the birds out flying free
I wonder why it couldn't be me
It's a pain I cannot bare
Locked up here where the world's not fair
Sometimes when I dream at night
I dream I have wings, and I take flight
Shifting, soaring out the window
There is no limit to where I can go
I see the birds out flying free
And I take joy that they're flying with me
There is no pain that I have to bear
Finally now the world feels fair.

Leanne Dawson

Waited

I've waited so long for this
Waited to feel your kiss
Waited to hold you tight
Waited to be there all night
I've waited to be your man
To love you as much as I can
To be the one that makes you sing
To be your all, your everything
To be the one you run to
To be the closest man to you
I've waited months for you
But the time flew
Now it flies faster every hour
I guess it just proves love's power
I've waited to be your all
I've waited for him to fall
Finally the wait is gone
I'm on the same level you're on
No longer two, we are one
All that waiting is finally done

Derek Young

As I Sit in the Dark

As I sit here in the dark,
I think about the world
And what kind of place
I have grown to live in.

A place of happiness
And love one minute,
Then a place so cold
And full of hate the next.

This world is such a funny place,
Full of hopes and dreams
Of the young and innocent,
Destroyed by those of age and wisdom.

The silence of the night,
The recklessness of the day,
What has happened to our hopes,
Our dreams, our love, our homes?

Kari Lynn Chevalier

The Rose

As I watch all the petals
Fall to the ground,
The one left holding on is you,
And I can feel you close to my heart.
Whenever I see your smile,
My face becomes a glow.
Every time I hold you in my arms,
I know that you are safe from harm.
For, if anything were to happen to you,
The petal would leave my heart,
And I will die with you.
The thorn from the rose bush
Pricking my finger and bleeding my love
Is only one of the pains
Of sacrifice to be with you,
My sweet, sweet rose.

Trevor Forbes

Emily

I know a little girl,
She's very pretty,
As I watch her from my kitchen,
I see her sitting smiling,
She's learning about life
Sometimes funny—or in a big hurry,
Always this beautiful child
Growing, learning she
helps with her little hands
She even makes her own cheese
scrambled eggs
She sings, she dances
Emily never complains,
Her little hands play her keyboard,
"Love you always forever"
She sings.
Then it's off to home—her visit is over,
I sit and wait—till the phone rings.
Granny—it's Emily.

Doreen Polier

Post Man

Dedicated to Vince

To the postman
From your dear friends,
We're so glad to see you again.
Through the days we watch you work,
Delivering mail from here to there,
It seems like you go everywhere.
It must be hard on your poor feet,
Walking along the busy street.
You stop and talk to all your friends
But soon have to start your route again.
The day must seem so long and slow,
For you are always on the go.
Now stop and think
Before I go:
What it would be like
If you didn't know
That you're a special person
To everyone you know?

Ronda Gullickson

The 50th Wedding Anniversary

The most enjoyable day in my life will be
My Mom and Dad's 50th wedding anniversary.
April 3rd, 1982, a remarkable day for all,
Never to be forgotten, winter, spring, summer, or fall.

Two hundred seasons they shared together
With very few going to waste,
Hard times, good times, strong times, weak times,
Whatever the case.

Food in our stomachs, shoes on our feet,
Sent to school every day, was the usual beat.
Praying each morning with great anticipation,
Always providing regardless of the situation.

In sickness and health together stayed,
Giving moral support to the family they made.
Trading coupons for sugar and flour,
Trying to keep the family together every hour.

50 years, 200 seasons, 18,250 days, 4,380,000 hours,
26,280,000 minutes, any way you want it read,
Any way you want it said, the end result remains the same:
We are celebrating a 50th wedding anniversary.

Gloria Borden

Missing You

We'll miss you so much,
For you were a part
Of a life shared with us,
Sometime in the happy past.

How soon this has happened,
As you have reached the summit of your life's dream,
Leaving us filled with memories
Of the goodness you left behind.

Oh! Fate is cruel
To decide harshly on this matter,
Thus filling us all in dark dismay,
To ponder how fast life fades away.

And now that you're on your journey
To be with the Lord, God Almighty,
We shall always remember you.
In our hearts, your name is engraved, too.

We'll miss you so much,
And so with simple faith in our hearts
We pray, "Lord Jesus, please guide our friend on his way."

Julia B. Lunizo

Bless This Child

God, bless this babe You've sent to my knee
Watch over her as You watched over me
Keep her safe from all of life's harm
Safe at Your bosom, safe in Your arms

God, bless this child You've given to me
Help her to be the best she can be
Give her the comfort she'll seek when she cries
Show her the love that shines in your eyes

God, bless this woman, the one that will be
The one that was once a babe on my knee
Lead her and guide her day after day
Shine Your light on her path, show her the way

Yvonne Ellis

The Anchor

Jesus, the anchor, the anchor of my soul,
The winds can blow, the waves may roar,
But still my faith will hold.

He reaches out to me His hand; take hold and you will live.
I've given all my love for you, my life to you I give.
Though life can be like mire and clay, your foot can find no hold.
So keep your eye upon the rock; he came to make you whole.

The things in life, your sins and strife, Christ Jesus paid it all.
He held not back a drop of blood; he freely gave the call.
Even though the thieves each side were crucified with him,
Jesus came and gave his blood; he even died for them.

And even though the passersby would spit and rail "Come down,"
From the cross we put you on, and save us, this whole town.
Jesus knew they did not know he came to free their soul,
And if upon this rock they cast, their anchor it will hold.

Jesus the anchor, the anchor of my soul,
Jesus the anchor, he came to make us whole.

John A. Gee

Cold, Cold-Hearted

She's got come hither eyes and a sexy smile,
Dangerous curves and legs for miles.
Everybody wants to get a piece of what she's got.
She drives the boys crazy 'cause she's so damn hot.
Like Eve tempted Adam with an apple from a tree,
She tempts the boys like honey tempts a bee.
Like a spider weaves a web to trap its prey,
She weaves a spell from which you'll never break away.
But she's cold, cold-hearted.
If you don't know what you're doing, then don't even get it started,
'Cause she's cold, cold-hearted.
She'll play you for a fool and leave your heart broken in two.

She was an innocent girl along time ago.
She gave me her love and said she needed me so.
I left her broken and crying in the morning light.
Now she's got fire in her eyes and a heart of ice.
Now she's cold, cold-hearted.
If you don't know what you're doing, then don't even get it started,
'Cause she's cold, cold-hearted.
I played her for a fool and left her heart broken in two.

K. Geurtjens

Don't Forget Me

I'm sitting on your knee.
We're together, you and me.
We're kissing each other for the first time,
and on my skin, I feel the sunshine.
It's a beautiful day,
and you say: Together we will always stay.

That's what I dreamed one night
as a candle still was burning so bright.
I really thought it would come true,
but it didn't, 'cause now I'm here without you.
And for making memories, it's too late,
'cause too long did we wait.
So we'll just have to say good-bye,
but please don't let our friendship die,
'cause someday something will come and tear us all apart.
Then all you will have from me are these words and a place in my heart.

Michelle Peltokangas

Forever

The days of our love are gone.
The time we shared together burns on and on.
When you looked at me, I grew soft and weak.
I want to hold you near, but you're nowhere to be seen.

One time you whispered sweet words in my ear,
The lovely words and fairy tales I longed to hear.
You will always be the only one for me.
Now you're with someone new and not with me.

If you should ever need me, I'll be here with open arms.
I'm sorry I never had the chance to say the things you wanted to hear.
In fairy tales they live happily, but the pain of you is still here.
I'll remember the beauty of you smiling at me.

Once upon a time, I believed that would be you and me.
I wish you would tell me I'm the one you need.
I never imagined living without you,
And all the lovely things you said to me.
I sit here and dream that once again we'll be together,
"Forever" in eternity.

Tammy Smith

A Battle Worth Fighting

When I first got cancer, I was really sad.
There were even times when I was really mad.
The thoughts really hurt, and the needles do too,
But, you know, to get all better, this is what you have to do.
The chemo makes you tired, and you'll probably get sick,
So you just lie in bed like a big, old brick.
Your hair will fall out, that is guaranteed,
And as for the doctors, they give you what you need.
There are lots of other people there, so you will not feel alone,
'Cause they are just like you, they too want to go home.
It's okay to worry, and it's okay to cry,
But to get through this big mess, you've got to really try.
So, when you're done your treatments,
Whether it be a year, two, or three,
You'll know that for the rest of your life,
You can be cancer-free!

Brenda Pleskacz

Love's Sacrifice

Who is this Man of Adam's kind, Seed of Abraham and Sarah?
Melchizedek and Israel point the Way to this Messiah.

Could I be of His Royal Line or unworthy of His Table?
Exalted place or fate unknown, I would serve this King if able.

Might He scorn my ordained gender, even spurn my appointed race?
If that were so, humbled I'd go, reverently seeking His Grace.

The hope and promise of Heaven reserved for others, not my gain?
Death alone to end my service, yet I would praise His Holy Name.

Finally, my life forsaken, willing sacrifice discarded?
A shrouded end would I condemn, but for awe of God's Anointed.

What matters it who Christ will choose,
    for to reign and rule His Kingdom?
His Blood was spent to conquer Death,
    now His Own would die to serve Him.

Who is this Man whom I treasure, esteem above all I hold dear?
Though He slay me I will trust Him,
    and accept through my heart His Spear.

Jean Catherine Bengey

Christmas Time

The icicles, the angels, the whitest snow,
Vibrant coloured balls and mistletoe,
Candy canes, fresh smell of pine,
Popcorn strings, and holly'd vine,
Snow men, lanterns, brilliant lights,
How enchanting this is with all the sights.
Our family together, our little ones,
The wrapping of gifts, it's so much fun.
A wonderful dinner we all will share;
The carols we'll sing, will fill the air;
Santa and reindeer are busy at night,
Preparing and making gifts for tikes.
Striped, coloured stockings hung everywhere,
Filled with toy surprises, dolls, teddy bears.
What a wonderful season this can be,
As long as we all love each other and see
The closeness of Christmas, the bells and sleds
Are meant for everyone—for, this I've said,
So fill your hearts and joyous times
With glee and joy, for it's "Christmas time."

Lorraine Ruznisky

Seasons of Change

A rosebud appears
Couples sing and dance
The birds sing out
It is the season of romance

The rose has bloomed
The waters beat their drums
The children are free and playing
This is the season of fun

The winds are rising
Many hearts are chilled
Our rose has drifted away
This is the season of remembering yesterdays

The white cloak has fallen
The air is crisp and clean
Trees are naked and swaying
Under this seasons frozen dream

Krista Learmonth

That's Where

Where lilies blow after winter's snow,
Where birds fly after strong winds die,
Where deer wander and bears saunter,
That's where, that's where.

Where wild fern grows and hides the toads,
Where the wild cats roam and the spring skies storm,
Where the wildflowers bloom, their scent like perfume,
That's where, that's where.

Where butterflies gently float along,
Where the wild canaries sing their song,
Where the fish go swish in a cool mountain pool,
That's where, that's where.

Where the sun filters through before storm clouds brew,
Where the trees grow so tall, high up the mountain wall,
Where the moon shines so bright in the chill of the night,
That's where, that's where.

Margaret R. Ikola

My Dream

Last night I had a dream,
a nice sweet dream.

My dream was
us beneath a sunset

Our eyes were glassed with
the reflection of the sky's light.

The colours covered our faces
as we watched them dance.

I hope my dream comes true:
you and me in the sky light.

Teena Coon

Hesitating Your Happiness

Hesitation is just
A matter of time
To make decisions
Up in your mind.
But once they are made,
And you delay,
That's just fear
About what one will say.
Happiness is just one word
For "seize the day";
If you know what makes you happy,
Why do you hesitate and delay?

Richard Crossman

Second Chance

Yesterday he was given a second chance.
As he lay there helplessly,
Looking up at me with tears in his eyes,
He promised it would never happen again.
He had learned his lesson,
And, with time, he would pay for it.
His life was just beginning
With a bright future ahead of him.

Today he died.
What happened to his second chance?

Ushani Dookhy

Love

Love is strong and love is blind,
won't be long and then I find
all the withered way back to,
at the end I will find you
to teach you how to love and give,
only then can you truly live,
may not be for me to say
surely you shall find a way,
a way into my bleeding heart,
if only we're not far apart,
then I'll say that I love you,
see my eyes and know it's true,
maybe say you love me, too,
then my heart belongs to you!

Alexandra Krucien

Unrequited Love

Waiting, hoping, anticipating.
Smiling, laughing, nothing.
Walking by tension.
No conversation, no mention.

Hope rises, doubt remains.
Complete heart or depressing stains?
A rose, a look, a consultation.
Waiting, hoping, anticipation.

Time flies, adrenaline's rise.
Heart broken, heart lies.
Rose offered, not denied.
Given away, but not to I.

   Dudzai Pswarayi

The Mother I Want to Be

I want to be a mother kind and true,
Pure and beautiful in all that I do.
I want to be noble and loyal
And steadfast, wherever I may be.

I want to be a mother, prayerful
That my children may follow my steps.
I want to be a mother, loving
And do my very best.

I want to be a faithful mother
And put all my trust in God,
And I always want to follow
The path that the Master trod.

And when my kids are all grown up,
And I have done my very best
To lead them to life everlasting
With the Savior, forever we will rest.

   Janet Smith

Feelings

Feelings buried like seeds,
Starved of moisture and light,
Decaying in the womb of night,
Produce naught but weeds.

Feelings expressed, a tender look,
The touch of a loving hand,
Act like instant magic and
Bond two hearts as in a picture-book.

Thoughts left unspoken
Are stillborn children,
Fruit dead in blossom,
Buds withered, unopened.

A loved voice is a melody
That never, never dies;
A smile is the sunrise
That sweetens our agony.

Like the melody of a song,
Memories linger
Long after the singer
Is dead and gone!

   Pauline Finella J.D. Martin

shades of fire

amidst the changing fire
shades of shadows blend and then conspire
to fool the mind's eye

the fire dances its own song
contradicts within its own wrong
but still it is whole and why?

each shade of crimson reaching high
a cyclical rebirth of passion's cry
reach and embrace passion's birth

blue's a mood that most ignore
without, one could never understand white's door
to know blue is to live on earth

the pale white holds transcendence
for those accepting colour's descendants
it is then when one has come alive

all shades then complete
fire, life's inevitable deceit
it is whole and this is why

   Kraig X. Wenman

Destiny of Man

Implicate, explicate . . . synchronicity spawned
Order or Chaos, what be the evolutionary end?

History's lesson is clear
Eternity's spent denying the truth
Head in the sand; wrong end up
Keeping vigil of humanity's haste
Its greed, its hunger, its immorality
Riding the work ethic t'ward material gain
Masking real issues
The cost to nations, Mother Earth, to health
Is severed from conscience
Our "selves" disconnected

The threshold of evolution or entropy
Do we stand upon in the aftermath
Of our blindness and denial
Are we morally spent; skipping the rent
Will we look for the next big bang
To finally reach GOD

   John Kalyn

Diana

Diana was a lady whom we all loved;
We know she was blessed by Heaven above.
She brightened the lives of all she knew,
Although there were times she must have been blue.
She left us two princes to remember her by;
We know they'll remain an honour to Di.
We also love Charles, and love and honour our queen.
What a blow to them this must have been!
Our queen's getting older, more regal each day;
Although we loved Di, don't make our queen pay,
But tell her we love her before it's too late.
Don't wait until she reaches the "Pearly Gate."
Just hold Di's memory with those of our own;
Someday she'll return and make herself known.
God gave us his promise and that's what he'll do.
Just read your Bible and trust in him, too.

   Mildred Irwin

Never Alone Again

Someday, I will fly away,
And be with the birds where they play.
Who knows how far they go?
I'll know, when I fly away.
My hands and my legs will not take me away,
Not to the place I want to go and stay.
All of my loved ones will be there,
Except for the one for whom I love and care.
I hope someday she will fly away,
But that will be for her to say.
After I fly away, I will no longer be afraid,
The greatest one being left alone.
So lastly, when you look up in the sky
And see a flight of birds go by,
One may stop to sky hello.
Then you will know for sure: I can fly away.

Virginia E. Hodges

The Reality of Death

Death—what is it?
A cold, stiff feeling
Of being unable to move,
Not being able to see your loved ones anymore.

You cannot really explain death
Unless you have faced it.
Death comes in many forms,
Especially when you least expect it.

There is no way of escaping death.
Everyone dies sometimes in their life.
It is best to meet death face to face,
Then meet death unexpectedly and suffer from it.
Death is as cold as a meat freezer.
So there's no use of running from death;
When it's your time, it's the right time.

Death is like
A deserted road,
You do not know
Were the unknown will lead you!

Jeff Fries

Escape

Escape in the shallow twilight, dream,
Drift in silvered reflections of daylight fancies
Wrapped in a smothering shawl of peace.
Turn from the cruel white light of day.
Return to dream, see new truth
Poured from the heavy mist of doubt.
Time to smile at wild rhetoric,
A phlegmatic mood
As far removed from Earth as Elysium.
Return to dream, relax in shadow.
Countless thoughts as shoals of rough pebbles
Flood past, awakening no response in the tired mind
But flickering recollection or a momentary frown.
Only bright remnants remain to gild
This quiet time.
Return to dream.
Relax in shadow,
Calm thought.

Pauline Blendick

MY SHADOW

Tell me—and if they are lies—gentle words
To calm my heart and bless my day;
I will listen to what you say.

It has been a year that passed us by,
Leaving behind too many wounds;
For them, our hearts cry.

The story of love made you nervous . . .
I heard your pounding heart so clear. . . .
Your soul was not too far away;
In my throat, I choked the tear.

Your shadow walking by my side—
You cannot hide
Nor can you try to trace its rays;
It lay with me on a golden tray.

I am the one who cares the most,
For you know my heart you own;
All I need is a little cheer
To take away my pain and fear.
For, you know I love you, and I appear.

T. B.

Pockets Full of Dreams

Pockets full of sins
You carry silently
Their voices louder
Than yours could ever be

Sin of despondency
Sin of omission
False breath of relief
When at first you destroy the dream

To appease the dangerous myth of liability

Infirmities of the mind
Our sometimes
Insinuating whispers
That you say were
Never meant to be

Glimpses of accolades from
Aenas

If only
You had dreamed
A little harder
A little longer

M. C. Simms

Homelessness

Homelessness—
It is a problem
in this world.

It's not good.
For some, it's their life
and sad, too.

Cruel but true.
It's hard to accept,
tough to live.

Cosme R. Colon

Perspective

The sun shines bright
A nice warm light
But from planet Pluto
It's only a star

Valerie Francis

My Parents

You are my warmth
When the winter is cold
You are my light
When it's dark and bold

You are my shelter
On those stormy days
You have that shoulder
When I cry for joy or moan in pain

You have that ear
That listens always
You have that heart
That loves me without shame

Jacqueline Zena

Maybe

Maybe I should go to England,
The country I dream about,
Stand on the white cliffs of Dover
Drinking a pint of stout.

Golden sunshine will colour my day
On a Surrey hill in spring.
I'll walk through pastel fields
In search of what life can bring.

Catch a train to swinging London,
Stroll up and down famous streets,
Squat in a doorway out of the rain,
A spirit of endless beats.

Then fly up the north country
On a scooter shining bright.
Smoky rows of cottages
Rush by me in the night.

Visit a tiny graveyard
Where a doomed poet sleeps
As the river man watches silently;
Your words and music he keeps.

Brett Crowther

Words

Angry echo-voices bouncing
Off the walls
Of battered brains
A trail of bloody syllables
Lurching drunkenly
Where even "Angels fear to tread"
Fools! Close the door
Let this chapter end
Turn the last red-splattered page
And, please, forget
The tombstone

Sheene Gericke

Mysterious Fairy

The autumn's golden days have faded,
Welcomed by a white fairy
Whose garments of glistening silk await.

Patiently she weaves her gown of sugar-glossed thread
Awaiting the tunes of rivers rippling and trees a'swaying,
Singing her sonnet to the ends of her dream-filled bed

As the world sheds its silken sheet, left decaying,
The sunshine-drenched hills, no longer yellow or red,
And the fields now covered with a new colour of icing,
Her gown of glistening white ever so enticing

As the wild geese over our heads once more pass,
Rotating the point of their arrow;
Change, opening her arms, will once more trespass.

The battle will strike of thunder,
Weeping willows releasing their cries,
And the world once again will be covered with wonder,
Filling the ends of her den
From shore to shore.

Milena Urbanajc

Social Butterfly

I couldn't feel lonely forever.
I am not that kind of person.
Floating to the people
Introducing me attempting to
Find an acquaintance type of friendship.
I am known yet still a stranger,
But I still spread my wings and
Greet all even if I get confused with names
I still remember you
Even if I have trouble putting the name with a face.
I have the trill of finding a friend
In my heart
And respect for all people
I can't wait to see if she is alike
And different from me
And I always have room for those around me.
But there would come a day,
In my life as the Social butterfly
I would hear one say, "Somebody clip her wings."
Such a sad day as that and I ignore it.

Letitia Jones

Sonnet: Shall We Survive

The night that looms ahead, should it be dark,
Would we survive, my country, you and I,
Or, caught between the races' violent spark,
Be consumed in our innocence without a cry?
Bad deeds ahead their shadows throw behind,
Serving as guides to ready an escape;
And when stark terror stalks your kind,
To acquiesce to murder, theft, and rape
Would mean one's conscience is corrupt as well.
Though struggle 'gainst the blackest tyranny
Is to remove oneself within the spell
Of hopelessness, despair, and self-pity,
And should this coming night appear not bright,
Perhaps, somehow, we two would seek a light.

Evadne D'Oliveira

The Haunting of Hilltop Hall

Gaunt old house atop a hill (closely come and feel the chill),
Dark, forbidding, roof awry with toothed chimneys probing sky—

Broken windows (pulse beat rise) provide it with its sightless eyes.
On broken hinges hangs the door, whilst rotting timbers form the floor.

Furnished dark and aged with sin, dares brave souls to venture in—
Who makes to enter footsteps bold to feel fear's grip on that threshold.

(Pause awhile your time to bide.
A ghostly spirit dwells inside.)

Gliding softly (vision dread), within her arms she holds her head.
With rattling chains her presence sounds as she goes upon her rounds.

All in all, she has a ball, melting backward through a wall.
O'er her domain dwells her persona—in the likeness of Madonna.

Men—should this house you stumble by, take this heed and from it fly.
For, on all males this ghost doth thrive—
You'll never leave the place alive!

Roy Mason

Beloved Eternity?

Feeling the cold and bitter wind, yet I see only grey.
The difficult hike over the rocky road has brought me to this peak.
I find myself on a slope overlooking the bay
Where cuts and bruises are the only visual marks to the eternity I seek.

The past and the possible future merge together into the "Now."
As the seconds slowly tick by, my breath escapes into the air,
coiling wispily by my ears.
A vaporous, nebulous figure takes shape and form.
My mind can only scream, "How?"
I see a shape that was close and dear to me
and now can only draw tears.

The signal from the other side has sent me from the slope.
The shape seems to shake its head and imply,
"You must begin your life anew."
I step away from the precipice and avoid the fatal fall.
I can now live my life with hope.
For, I now know, one day we will be together forever, happy and true.

Vincent Joe

Untitled

Building up time.
Counting the moments
until the dam breaks,
and the truth comes flooding through
like the bloody afterbirth of a stillborn babe.

And, like the child,
being dead inside
and unable to repair the damage
That another has caused.

And, like the truth,
being so destructive and all consuming
washing over the innocent
in waves of anguish
and keeping those who might help,
at bay, cowering behind their intentions.

So that when the flood has ended
nothing will be left
but the salt from un-shed tears,
and the lamentations of crushed souls
who will never resurrect from beneath the truth's insufferable girth.

Danielle Moulder

Mortality Rejuvenated

You ask me about love, but I cannot answer; emotions and reality now long-forgotten,
I am inexperienced in matters of the heart and mind again, as a child.
There is a brief recall of advanced intellect and deep feelings, yet when?
A gentle caress and pure, unbridled joy at dawn's first light.
Still, emotions lie dormant in a place un-fed—malnutritioned—
memories stifled by prescribed synthetic fabrications, craving the liberation
of my unrestrained emotions. . . . So many days, months, and years have passed,
spent freedom, vitality, and expression hindered—well-hidden,
striving now to overcome this dark, insidious cloud,
the one that impairs my emotional responses and reactions;
serotonin levels gently increase—oh, so slowly.
Living day by day, finally in lieu of moment by moment,
the cloud gently dissipates, revealing a new and rare moment, metamorphosis—
sweet butterfly, unencumbered by my ineffectual, synthetic cocoon,
I turn to you and reply, "What is love?" You asked.
I vocalize my reply, a symphony carrying a melody of unrelinquished happiness,
my state of nonexistence has departed at long last.
I weep with happiness—"This is me!" I cry out! "I am real!"
Renewed vigor in mortality—my own life—having learned to love myself at last. . . .

> *Victoria E. Cowden*

Inspiration

An hour with you passes by as a moment.
I am lost in a wave of your presence.
I drown in the depths of your eyes,
So deeply, I never want to be rescued.
My breath quickens . . . my heart races at the sound of your voice,
A voice from perfect lips, with a smile that steals my soul.
Your hands, so soft and gentle . . .
The slightest touch feels like silk upon my fingers.
The smell of your hair would fill a rose with envy;
Dark and luxurious, it caresses your face like a soft blanket.
I find myself staring uncontrollably at the most beautiful of creations;
I could look forever upon the radiance I see.

> **Robert Adams**

What Price, Freedom?

A flurry of hugs and hurried kisses. Huge eyes peer from small hooded
faces; tiny mittened hands wave good-bye. The ache begins.

Children and heart are gone, lost to me again. Away with their father
to chart untested waters, pleasures, and dangers unknown.

No choice, no choice, the alternative inconceivable.
A loveless marriage escaped, but, what price, freedom?

Children scattered. The passage of time marked in giggles lost,
bedtime stories missed. No tears to dry except my own.

Phones bring small voices across the miles.
Sounds so young, so vulnerable and trusting, so incredibly far away.
They are in safe hands, but they are not my hands.

The mind charges through the days, filled with the busyness of life.
My soul is consumed in the night,
    awash in anxiety and angst and apprehension.

Relief rushes through the front door with the cold winter air. Rejoice!
No more time for "what-if's." Fears unfounded; sprites tumble in,
bright eyes shining, bursting with stories to tell.

I rush to the embrace, scooping my heart into my arms with them.
My life is reclaimed . . . until next time.

> **Heather Cressman**

Antiquity (The Past as Perceived in the Present)

In the pyramids of the sunken past
Lie buried the treasured memories of bygone days,
And lost in antiquity
While tears continue to trickle,
Forming the muttering torrent of time,
Fathomless, sun-less, bottomless.

Fay-Yaz Shah

Intimate Thoughts

To stand without you, I surely could not bare.
It warms my heart to realize that you'll always be there.

When times are hard, you know just what to say.
What surprises me the most is that you never turn away.

When good feelings come to a screeching yield,
Your arms wrap around me like a loving shield.

For more than this deed, I shall love you true,
And my heart shall forever belong to you.

You fill my life with so much fun.
I feel the best has just begun.

Tender kisses as we play,
My love for you shall never stray.

Each and every day is a special day
That leaves me with one thing left to say . . .
I love you!

Jeff Robinson

Haunted . . .

Every day I hold a hope,
A flicker, a dream of sin-less life with you.
But I pay the price, strangled by my own rope,
Hung for the thought of your wanting a future too.

The past is dead, the future is lost.
They say I'm moving on,
But I can't see the changes, only the cost.
For, the memories linger, even though you are gone.

Your voice, your touch, your scent, and your words
Are always on my mind.
The last I love you will forever be heard,
But you, my love, I have yet to find.

Kim McKay

My Special Gift

It's time once again that day of the year
When special gifts are give to those we call dear
To light up the faces, to see the pleasure
From one small token, a lifetime treasure!
I searched all over, one store, then another,
For my most precious task, a gift for your mother,
And then it came to me one night while alone,
I'll write my gift down, "Love words in a poem."
There are tears in your eyes now of joy and bliss.
Much the same were in my eyes whilst writing this!
So if ever in the future you feel you need a lift,
Read these words of love, Mother; they're "my special gift."

Carole D'arcey

A Flame to Fuel

The candlelight wavered acquaintance,
and snapped at the stillness air,
illuminating spastically
amid surroundings tender.
The life that sparkled it glowing,
a match that struck it light,
so rays to reach across two souls
bring to each self a knowing.
It cried its tears and hardened
on temperatures found to differ,
which made it feel the voices strong
and dimmed on crossing breaths.
It carried subtle words on rage
when feared its flame erupt,
so soothed its surge, not part astray,
two silent silhouettes.
On softly spoken sympathies,
en-stoked a brightness, calm
above the shadows, sorrows mend
a warmth into their hearts.

Paul H. Duguay

Ode to Snails

With Blurring Speed and Numbing Haste,
Our lives proceed at record Pace.
Days so full of work and care,
Robots blind and unaware.
Each hectic day we rise and run,
Compete to get our duties done.
The air, a soup of electronic waves,
Bombard the mind until it raves.
Like greyhounds after rabbits run,
We have no time for setting sun.
Computers, videos, TV screens,
Replace the sane and natural scenes.
Trapped in cars in unending line,
We race around a slave to time.
Like hamsters on the spinning wheel,
No time to stop and think and feel.
Look to the snails! No race to run.
Take our time. Enjoy the sun.
For, life we live and do not see
As we race to get from "A" to "B."

Peter Morry

Sand

So tiny, in the universe
Of happiness and strife,
A grain of sand is what I am
Upon the beach of life.

Eternally, the stars will shine.
The sun inflames the day,
The sea of time caresses me
On the beach where I stay.

Of all the many grains of sand
That tumble in sea-swirl,
A special one, the oyster picks
And exalts it to a pearl.

Adorn my castle, on this beach,
Made from the sands of time,
Forever will I relish love
On you, this pearl of mine.

Dennis Hill

Swing in a Backyard

Under the silent, blue moon,
By a bloody river,
No sound, no air,
Wonder who you are.

Sit on the old swing in a backyard
With the no-named you,
See your loneliness with my eyes.

You and I,
Surrounded by ghosts of loneliness,
Without any faces,
They swallowed our broken heart,
Cut our spirits into pieces.

Now only you and I,
Sitting on the old swing in a backyard,
Under the silent, blue moon,
Staring at the dark old sky,
Waiting for the day we die . . .

Kate Liu

Strength and Courage

It takes strength to be firm
It takes courage to be gentle
It takes strength to stand guard
It takes courage to let down your guard
It takes strength to conquer
It takes courage to surrender
It takes strength to be certain
It takes courage to have doubt
It takes strength to fit in
It takes courage to stand out
It takes strength to feel a friend's pain
It takes courage to feel your own pain
It takes strength to hide feelings
It takes courage to show them
It takes strength to endure abuse
It takes courage to stop it
It takes strength to stand alone
It takes courage to lean on another
It takes strength to survive
It takes courage to live

John Young

Intertwine

the branches of my heart
swirl away
blankets of crimson leaves
blankets of crimson leaves
do not break
not even a twig
every branch
the staunchness of my life

roots struggle
surviving
different arched paths

suddenly
the fragile dryness
breaks into a million pieces
proudly embracing
solitary.

Irma Banales

Alone

I think, and you are there
A conversation to myself within my mind
I look alone, but you are with me
Just as sure as were you standing by my side

A connection's made between us
On a level not apparent to the senses
The unity of every man exampled in our oneness
And that, displayed about me, an illusion

Like a movie on the screen, we sit and watch
I need not look nor hold your hand to feel your presence
The scene unfolds and takes us someplace else
We laugh, we cry, yet haven't left
And all that's just been witnessed is a lie

So too "real life" is watched from out beyond us
Observing through these eyes
That which time and distance have no hold
Both in separate spheres I catch a nuance and say, "look,"
And know your smile

Brent Winstone

Reflections in a Looking Glass

Hypnotists probe the mind for previous lives.
A format of manipulative patchwork awaits.
Transforming fact to fiction, feeding on lies,
The victims' revelations are criminal debates.

Freud fixated on sexual correlations.
Piaget guides a child in trial and error.
Darwin's evolution shakes all nations.
Engel's theory is a communist terror.

The journey to individual's identity,
Confused by scientific study method,
Spirituality and patience are reality
As evil phantoms prey on anxiety.

Whimsical actions become youthful traits.
Circumstances replace those futile games.
God has a hand in forming everyone's fate.
Heaven or hell, a road difficult not to tame.

Angeliki Nendos

Insight

Oh, dashed vitality!
The news, the dreadful, suffocating truth—
Honed razor of horror inside a stricken heart,
Peeling it within, layering in hurt,
Ah-h-h, constrictive band about the chest,
Eyes, dulled lenses through stark reality,
Aw-w-w, spiral of confusion!
Blinding, wrenching pain, draining every fiber—
Leaving behind a skeleton
To face each heavy day, holding IT in!
Outwardly un-viewed, un-shared except for one,
Down through life's lesson of years,
Knowledge gained, allowing at long last
That Divine lover of us all
To touch, completely, that gnawing, quivering place.
Then, grasping unto renewed trust,
Press on with hope and footsteps dancing
To once again seize life!

Elaine L. Osmond

The Wind

I feel the light wind blow over my innocent face,
It kisses my tiny ear,
It caresses my smooth skin,
It enriches my deep soul, like morning laughter.

The cool breeze takes away my lingering pains,
It takes me away,
Away from my life,
Away from my reality.

The calming sense of the soft air
Carries the harsh sounds
Of life and of death.

Like a good friend watching me,
It cares for my life,
It is with me at my death.

As the wind blows by, I feel it,
Love it,
Live it.

We are the wind.

Stacey Lynne Campbell

Untitled

Remember me not on that old wooden cross;
Think not of my crown that was so cruelly tossed,
But with hearts all rejoicing, think on my new birth,
Remember me gladly, all souls of my Earth.

Let not your thoughts to that Calvary scene
Remember me dying or what might have been,
But deep in your hearts attest to my life
By casting away the sword and the knife.

The sword that cuts ties of family and friend,
The knife wound of words so hastily penned,
Move now that stone of Calvary pride
Where the man of great sorrows suffered and died.

Wipe away that sad vision and picture me near.
I take form in all life you touch, see, and hear.
Believe only this: There can be no loss.
Remember me not on that old wooden cross.

My life abounds 'round you; I care for you still.
Think of me not on that faraway hill.
My spirit departed, I left man to his fate,
Then met him in love as he came to my gate.

P. Spells Palmer

Song of Love

Let us swing the cradle of prosperity.
Let us light the candle of love and unity.
Let it go away from the sufferings and the poverty.
Everyone has the right of equality.
Let us prevail everywhere in peace and in tranquility.
Let the people lead life with dignity.
Love and generosity are the pillars of humanity.
Let us adore the world with real beauty.
Noble deeds are the stairs of spirituality.
Let us sing a song of love and nobility.

Rabbani Siddiqui

Apple for Taste

Awakened by the fragrance,
You enter the kitchen.
Placed on the table,
Bursting with color and flavor,
Is a treat
Shimmering with perfection,
Tempting one who dares.
You try to look away,
But
The temptation is too great.
You envision
Plunging your teeth into her sinuous shape,
Allowing her sensuous juice to dazzle you.
Go ahead,
Take a bite of the apple.
I won't tell.

Lesia Charko

Footprints of God

May the Christ Child brighten your season
For you this Christmas day
And may these seeds grow into flowers
When you scatter them along the way
I can still see Robert's delight
As he knelt and cupped his little hands
Around a little flower
By the roadside of the BC sands

Someone like you could have planted it
For someone else to share
The beauty of God's footprint
And a boy like him aware
It gave him the greatest happiness
And he wanted us to see
That God made this little plant
To be shared by you and me

These seeds, I give you this Christmas
So you can be the one
To seed God's love forever
To be shared by everyone

Elvira Stang

Wish for 1998

So it will be ninety-eight—
Hope my wish is not too late.

All wishes seem to be the same
For years that are, that went, and that came.
They all express our dreams, desires,
That vanish as the time expires.

Yet another year is on its way:
To live it well, now let us pray,
To use its time to do some good
In peace and love, as we should,
So that when its end will come,
We can be proud of what was done!

Dr. Hana Gerzanic Hons

The Rose

If the world is washed away,
Will it grow back?
Ravaged and left to die,
Can it make it alone
And continue on its way?

The uncertainty of regrowth:
Will the flower bloom again?
Future to present, present to past,
Time will travel by.

The dark, the evil, has done its work.
Barren and empty,
The spirit waits to take root once again;
The life, the love,
All wait for the proper time.

But could they wait too long?
Can I wait that long?
Can I grow that flower back?

Brian Tucker

Longing

Time passes me by.
The future becomes present,
and the present becomes past.
Like bubbles in ocean, nothing lasts.
I long to hear your voice
and feel your presence.
My days and nights
are spent in idle thoughts,
and I don't see you.
You are not there
where thoughts are.
Thoughts of future and past
crowd my mind.
The present is the eternity,
and you, the soul of my soul,
can only be touched in
the stillness of the mind.
I can't find you in the clamour
of my thoughts that matter not.

Jadu Saha

Hidden

I withdraw into the silence of my mind
A blank mask hides the feelings
that I've placed
behind a high wall of white stone
My empty eyes reveal nothing
I remain expressionless
You speak, but I don't hear the words
They mean nothing to me
Mere sounds offer no solace
They pass over me and cannot
penetrate my unfocused thoughts
I appear to be unaffected
In truth, I've placed an iron clamp
over my heart and trapped my soul
into a tiny steel box
where it can remain untouched
and pure
for a moment longer

JK Johnson

Saint Dominick

The river Tamar eternally flows toward the sea,
winding through areas of outstanding beauty,
pursuing its course with commitment and ease
un-harnessed by men over many centuries.

History recalls at Halton Quay
an Irish prince landed from a voyage of discovery;
his safekeeping was not without design
in the year A.D. eight hundred and sixty-nine.

A fair lady joined him on the river bank,
the sister of Prince Intract of noble rank,
Saint Dominica knelt in silent meditation,
safe from her arduous indignities of exploration.

A chapel now commemorates this historic event
of people of adventure, of courage, and of good intent,
inevitably linked with the village of Saint Dominick,
founded near the neighbouring Hamlet of Bohetherick.

Charles Tribe

A Day on the Earth

The petal of a rose, a soft, sweet scent
Kissed by the dew of the morning;
Gently, as a whisper in the wind.

Plants and animals delighting
In this glorious new day,
Breathing in life's goodness.

And thus begins Earth's young life,
Perfect, glorious, and new,
Golden, refreshing.

Ages-old sun shining brightly above
Is blinding and hot,
Blistering in touch.

The land is now thirsty, as water is polluted.
This change in climate no longer is suited.

Animals are dying, rain forest destroyed.
This planet grows weary, this planet grows old.

What have we done to this marvelous Earth?
Are we too late . . .
To learn from our mistakes

And let the Earth heal?

Yvonne Redner

Artist's Point of View

A blank page, it stared hard to me,
For a long time nothing,
Nothing. Just blankness.
A dot, a great dot, yet so insignificant,
It swirls around and around.
It turns to me yet still a dot.
I feel as if it has stolen me from the natural world,
As if never to return.
I realize that it is no longer just a dot,
But a great form of dots.
Color splashed as if a beam of light
On a great kaleidoscope of gems,
The great sea of color joins together as if one,
And I see a masterpiece, yet only a picture,
A clear yet fuzzy picture,
But still a great masterpiece.

Tanya Kennedy

Untitled

The light outside slowly diminishes.
The click of the lamp disturbs the settled house.
It creaks as if ghosts walk, trying not to be heard
Like voices of children who should not be awake.
Wind whistles through the cracks of the window, almost inaudible,
Like a robber creeping in slowly,
    ready to rape you of your material possessions.
Rain seeps in through the weak and stained walls,
Unwanted and yet un-preventable,
Like someone who is different, someone who no one understands,
Who will lie with many people and yet still live alone,
Isolated, and yet in many ways set free.
Alone is no place to live but is the only way she knows.
The creaks and wind and rain are her family.
They comfort her and keep her warm at night.
The creaks keep her from believing she's alone.
The wind whispers to her delightful words,
And the rain puts her to sleep with its sweet caress.
Maybe it's not so hard being alone.
I've known no other way.

      Laura Ippolito

Good-Bye, Annick

You felt her grow inside of you for what seemed eternity;
You wanted to meet this fluttering wonder so desperately.
When she was born, she came to you and loved you right away.
You had many dreams for her—why couldn't she stay?

A frolicking child, she loved to play outdoors surrounded by the trees.
A loving girl who, like her mother, cared for many others,
She expressed herself quite clearly, so you knew the truth today.
You had many dreams for her—why couldn't she stay?

She grew into a young woman, made a family of her own.
The life she knew, the love, the dreams that you and she had sewn
Would always be a part of her. Joyce, you showed her the way.
You still had many dreams for her—why couldn't she stay?

One day, your precious girl was overtaken by disease.
Why did this evil happen? Answer me, God, please!
Annick had Jesus in her heart. He needed her today.
You had many dreams for her, but she just couldn't stay.

      Dawnallyn Kennedy

Time Spent

We have a friend who is locked away.
He is so close as we touch the stones of the wall,
His heart and soul are shielded from our touch.
Does he know in his solitude that we care, oh, so very much?

And here we wait for our friend, until he has his final day
So that again, on a special day,
Be it again, or gloom, or come what may,
All stand together, with touch and hand
To dream and be once more together.
Against the hours that mean loneliness no more,
Freedom and friendship, how sweet the sound,
To have, to hold, to love unbound.

Alas . . . here we are . . . you are there.
The time shall pass and then we'll see
That in the end, the outcome be
As sweet to you as any should be.

We long to hold and tell you true
That all is well and none are blue.
Be strong in faith, keep in heart
The love of life and friend you are.

      Marie Korpela

Ocean View

Finding myself standing by the shore,
Scanning the soft melding of perfect sky with turquoise waters,
Staring hypnotically into the cyclic, churning rolls,
Becoming transfixed, yet ethereally removed.

This time, a tortuous enemy,
The breaking wave's crushing force, knocks the flesh down,
Washing it back with choking eyes, salty nostrils, and gaping mouth,
Leaving behind a drenched, whipped semblance of sticky, encrusted granules.

Next time, a beckoning friend, the wave-master,
Crooking its finger, entices surrender, promising to enfold and comfort,
Whispering softly, calling the self of flow into perpetuity,
Effortlessly loosening the desire for human shallowness.

The brilliant sunlight gradually fades;
Cool slaps of breeze awaken, break the appeal.
Slowly, heavily, clammy legs move leaden feet backwards,
Drawing away reluctantly from the seductiveness, as light darkens.

An urgency to withdraw overcomes:
Running, tripping, dragging, making it back breathlessly to the coral balcony,
Safely now, searching the panorama through the dusky shadows,
Seeing more clearly, or perhaps more desperately, the ocean view.

> *Sharon Major*

Tidal

Like heaving waves that crash along the shore,
My love for you, uncontrolled, following the tide.
I cannot stop it, make it die, even as you slam the door.
I must remember all that's happened, all the tears I've cried.

I'd harden my heart but I'd find you again in my soul.
Outside, inside, my relentless love finds a way,
Possessing me, enticing me, I'm relinquishing control.
I have to love you, there is no other way.

A Lordly mountain might move if my love were to cease,
And any contempt for you would be as frozen fire.
With this unwanted love can I ever again be at peace—
This unrequited love so deep and so dire?

This smoldering, burning love can find no vent.
Extinguished and dead it won't be until the life in me is spent.

> *Nicole Vinette*

The Prime Minister's Car

Sleek and bold and just like new cars like this, I've only seen a few.
I couldn't help myself, I had to take a peek.
Security was called, I was locked up for a week.
None can compare by far . . . the Prime Minister's car—
Washed and polished every day, always first on the raceway.
I tried to pass myself off as the cook.
The judge said, "Throw it at him, the whole bloody book."
None can compare by far . . . the Prime Minister's car—
Tinted windows and shiny chrome, everyone wants to take her home.
I've swept the floors and washed the walls,
The guards have told me, next are the halls.
None can compare by far . . . the Prime Minister's car—
240 in a quarter mile, I gotta have her, she cranks my style.
I've been here for ages, I still have six years to go.
It feels like forever, it feels like death row.
The Prime Minister's car, wasn't it a beauty?
The Prime Minister's car, wasn't it a cutie?
I stole her and rolled her, and now I'm crushing boulders—
The Prime Minister's car . . . the Prime Minister's car . . .

> *Kathryn Regier*

I Am

I am a seeker of the past.
I wonder what will happen in the future.
I hear gay birds singing in the air.
I see Heaven in my dreams.
I want the courage to conquer all my fears.
I am a seeker of the present.

I pretend I have powers out of the impossible.
I feel a strength, a strength of unimaginable power.
I touch that power, that strength.
I worry; I fear that power, that strength.
I cry for help from that power, that strength.
I am a seeker of what is to be.

I understand the light breeze of a September afternoon.
I say, be strong in thought, in trust, and in hope.
I dream of serving the world as a U.N. Peacekeeper.
I try to be strong, I try to be brave.
I hope that my future, my destiny, will be fantastic.
I am a seeker of fate, of destiny.

Ben Wong

Forever Spring

The flowers of love are starting to bloom within my heart!
I have seen them today like on some other fine days,
Beautiful and fresh and bright.
How precious they are to me, then,
When I can enjoy their beauty!

Only too soon they wilt and die,
But others are already in bud,
Just waiting for some rays of light to shine upon them
And to be bathed in the sound of a gentle rain.

Then, happily and eagerly they bloom again
Even more beautiful, brighter, and fresher than before.
The whole world seems to shine with joy and beauty.
Oh . . . the wonder of spring within!

Nora Gignac

The Bells Toll

From the ancient steeple, come
Knocks on the echoing bronze.
Doves take off on their flights.
On the table tapers tremble
As if ready to die too.
Beneath the gentle look
Of the sweet lamb,
Black shrouds surround the box.
Litanies repeated in deep voices
Link themselves to sobs.
They weep for the dead
As they remember
Their own sure death on the morrow.
Knocks on the echoing bronze . . .

Enrique R. Fernandez-Anderson

Night Dweller

As the sunset appears the sun people go into hiding
while the night dwellers come out to sing and play
and do their thing the night dwellers
are like the moon and stars they are always there
but not always seen

Don J. McLaws

Tears

Tender
Emotion
Always
Running
Silent.

Susan Watson

No More Tears

Today the clouds are gone away
And the sun shone brighter than ever
With more time to play

The insight seems more sightly
Everyone should be on cloud nine
No one should be below

I am singing in the rain
Singing a bright and merry tune
The sun is finally here to stay

And I am ready to play

Pamela Chapaman

Last Breath

As he lies there, dying
He looks into her eyes
So soaked with tears
Her black hair
So soaked with rain
He manages a slight smile
He hopes she'll do the same
She makes the effort, but it crumbles
Her face begins to tremble more
His life is leaving fast
He lifts his arm to bring her closer
Wanting to taste her lips once more
She lowers her head down
To fulfill his dying wish
Wishing herself to be dying
Lovers lips meeting in love
And then he whispers:
"When you think of me, please smile.
You know I'd rather you forget me,
Than leave knowing I'll make you cry."

Jeff Marlow

To Be in Your Arms

To Swim of Iced Water
In the Arctic
To Crawl the Sun's Dunes
Of Sahara
To Climb a Mighty Sequoia
Only to Fall and Pick
Myself up, Surpassing the
Mount that Ever-lasts to
Walk Amongst Clouds
To Run a Marathon from
Boston through New York
I would Do all of These
To Simply be with You

Robert Park

My Vow to You

I miss you when you're not here.
You've calmed my worries and my fears.

I was lost till I found you.
Now I can start my life anew.

With you, my love, by my side,
I'll be with you until I die.

I love you with all my heart.
We will never be apart.

This, my written word, is true.
This is my solemn vow to you.
Davina J. Giesbrecht

The Labyrinth Called Love

Remember when we lived
in that burnt-out London flat:
pacing its endless corridors
in unknown states,
discovering new rhythms
or reciting old rhymes,
dying—time after time after time.

And then your music became
a cool escape, compelling
us to fresh scenes,
indulging in dreams and
opportunities.
We stood poised and ready—
hungry to exist.
Jeremy Mcleod

Me

Looking in the mirror,
I see to my surprise
a completely different person
staring deeply into my eyes.

The carefree young girl
I saw when I was five
has now become a young woman
fighting to survive.

In a world filled with madness
that surrounds me every day,
it's frightening to think
I could be killed for what I say.

Remembering the times long ago,
parties, Barbies, dances, and parks,
a time when I didn't worry about
others' remarks.

It's scary that time flies by so fast,
and what I used to call the present
has now become my past.

And when I look into the mirror,
what I see looking back at me
is the face of a young woman
where the young girl used to be.
Jenasis Mahaffy

Mystical Goddess

Come forth if you care, come forth if you dare,
Into the perspective of her mind,
Unknown to man, untouched by insanity.
Herself, her being, is ecstasy, a catastrophic happening,
A title wave leaping forth upon the rocks,
Who would tread anywhere to reach her destiny.
Her physical beauty is beyond compare
As she moves with sound tranquility,
And her pensive mood appearance combined
Causes heat to envelope me,
Her hair wind-whipped by nature's own eccentric recipe.
One feels elusive, repressive, and as they become intrigued,
Are subdued into her imagination without contempt.
She's a mystical Goddess
Who must feed upon the dewy night air to survive.
Oh, God, let this spell that has risen over me last infinitely.
'Tis like a sound fantasy that should never be shattered
But becomes stronger each time I'm in her presence.
Let my soul become entangled in hers.
Daniel Earl Devine

The Sun Is Burning Gases
(But I Still Have Good Friends)

A response to
"The Sun is Burning Gases
(Loss of a Good Friend)"

If as we grow older
We become less imaginative
And lose our innocence,
Then why:

Do people become dreamers and poets?
Do people bring children into this world?
Do people want better lives for others?

Because we have not lost our innocence,
Nor our imagination.
They have only grown and matured,
As we have done.
And why not?   They are a part of us.
Now I ask you:
What is hope?
Stuart Harsevoort

Everyone Has a Fan

Every day at a quarter to four, I was his purpose.
I occupied a few hours of each day.
To me, he was my inspiration.
I kept on 'cause he did.
I never gave up on me, 'cause he didn't.

That night, and every night after,
I saw him there, where he always was in the stands,
to the back right at the top, with the heavens set behind him,
cheering, never letting me give up.
I don't know who needed whom more,
but I know each time I felt down,
I looked up,
and I saw the old man who came each day,
right at a quarter to four.
Laurel Gadd

Aurora Borealis

I caught a glimpse of the first red glow, high in the northern sky,
and thought at first 'twas reflected light of the city we'd just passed by.
Then to the left another glow; a twin with outstretched rays
formed an arc across the sky, a span of red-gold haze.
The rays then turned to rainbow hues, sped down the Milky Way,
enfolding us within its arms, imploring us to stay.
And as I watched, my heart beat fast, such beauty to behold.
God's hand had wrought this wonderment—made not by men or gold.
My thoughts soared upward, full and free beyond my Earthbound duty,
beyond this world of sin and strife to God and all this beauty.
And then I felt within my soul the need to stop and pray.
Within his realm of hallowed light, could I but live each day
to raise my eyes up toward the light still radiant high above,
and thank him for this beauty rare, his gracious gift of love.
But on we sped—into the night, no time to stop and pray.
We had to hurry, get to sleep, tomorrow's another day.
And soon—too soon it seemed to fade; the colors washed away
and soft, sad glow still lingered on, my heart begged it to stay.
But when we reached our home at last, and I was free to stare
and gaze upon the heavens above, I found no colors there.

   Eva L. Turman

Words Condemned

I hear myself speak and know the words were spoken.
Although they are intelligible to my ears,
They resound back into my head
As scrambled, fragmented words, unclear in their interpretation.

Conceived with a desire for meaningful expression,
Pure and virgin-like, honest and open,
They return and echo in the recesses of my head,
Shattered, misunderstood, and hurting.

Receding to those dark, quiet places
Where words, thoughts, ideas, and dreams,
Will never again be expressed,
And communication will consist of a simple nod or smile.

   Karen Scott

A Time to Remember

Rays of dawn pierced the dormant forest
where persistent autumn leaves still held on.

Peacefully, alone, I walked a winding pathway
that occasionally crossed a clear, quiet stream.

In the distance, muffled waters rumbled
as feathered spirits whispered out from treetops high.

At the centre of a long wooden bridge,
I stopped above the canyon's churning waters.

I began peeling colored leaves from the iced railing
and released them to spin down, down to the river below.

With each one I thought of family and friends, now
but fond memories, held deep inside of me.

One landed upon the rocks: the unknown soldier.

Slowly, the floating leaves cascaded over the falls
to the river—and its pull—that took them all away. . . .

I grieved sadly till no more joyful faces came to mind. . . .

To my surprise, many leaves and drops of water began descending
as a breeze and as the sunlight touched the high canopy.

Turning, I parted with soft steps sounding at my side.

Again, dewdrops and tears dropped on another Remembrance Day.

   Stephen Mancinelli

Death for a Season

As the air grows colder, leaves flutter as They rain from above.
Exposed to impending death, a stream pants for breath in vain
Until one cold, dismal day the shallow gasps for air cease,
Suffocated by the strangle of Winter's bitter hand,
Its youth frozen forever.
Reflections of lilies trembling in His embrace
  as they danced together over pebbles in the springtime,
Remembered giggles of younger, fuller days
Echoing from the depths of His soul,
Lilacs, wet with Summer's rain, weep above Him,
Almost as if They knew what was to come.
Long, warm summer days float by.
Lilacs admire and adore Their image in His eyes,
Flirtatiously waving Their enticing fragrance above Him, just barely out of reach.
Sometimes Wind blows, and for a fleeting moment
A gentle kiss is His and then stolen just as quickly.
Delicate and as brief as a lover's whisper,
How quickly youth vanishes and dreams drift away.

> *Lauren Yeomans*

Dead End

Shattered dreams, broken promises, a future that will never be,
A nightmare that all too soon became reality for me.
A downhill ride on a dead-end track,
A feeling worse than being stabbed in the back,
The look in your eyes just says there is no hope for me and you.
A love that is slowly dying and taking me down, too.
A love for life that is just not there,
A feeling that I just cannot bear.
But it is time to say good-bye,
For I have lived, I have loved, now it is time for me to die.

> *Angie McArthur*

Love

Through war and peace, through boom and bust, we'll be together,
Regardless of Colour, age and of creed,
Together is the world, together is the planet.

On the cold winter's nights, and in the light lover's breeze,
The fire in our hearts will warm us,
No need for blankets, each other's all we need.

Again in the springtime, amid the new grown birds and bees,
Together in the garden,
The new virgin grasses will be our honeymoon bed.

Beneath the warmth of summer sun, we'll reflect
On the life we've been given by the single, lonely arrow
Shot from Cupid's bow.

Scattered with the russet of crisp, autumnal leaves, the path of love we walk,
Hand in hand we travel,
Forward to our destiny.

All around the planet, this world, we've had the pleasure to have graced,
All of nature stops and rises in togetherness
To bid the lovers good wishes and a hearty farewell.

> *Chris McKenna*

Wind

Wherever the wind takes me, that is where I'll go;
I may get there quickly, or I may go slow.

The wind blows me places, to lands I've never been;
No other person has laid eyes on the sights that I've seen.

The wind tosses me away to different lands, far and wide;
In most places I am open, but in some I must hide.

When the wind picks me up and carries me at night,
At the new place, I land, often shivering with fright.

When blown to a spot that fills me with fear,
I try to be brave for all who are near.

When the wind sets me down in an area that I know,
The expectations set upon me never are low.

I love being up high, but it's often down low
Where I encounter things that often help me to grow.

It doesn't matter if its blown in a gust or in a slight flow,
Wherever the wind takes me, that is where I will go.

Ryan Coltura

Darchangel

Dark Arch Angel, please allow me to ask
What did you thieve in your last sinful task?
Another soul, another life?
But this task caused you so much strife
Let me explain, Dark Arch Angel, why you fell
Evil shall only reign in Hell
Internal explosion burst his heart.
His mangled body could not handle, he fell apart
A choice to be mere mortal or something divine
His heart fought so hard to beat the flat-line
Too much blood this mortal had bled
From his body his frightened soul had fled
Life lapsing in blue, shut eyes, seeing faces he recognized
Faith in life sadly dies as his body begins to paralyze
Heavenly Kingdom God shall reign
Obediently he followed, he did not refrain
God replaced your high-rank seat
Now only hell will accept your defeat
Rise now, newborn Arch Angel, deny the blazing inferno
Once you kiss the sky, you shall then become eternal

Vicky Chan

Remember?

Mother and Father wait by the door,
Hoping that messengers will be seen no more.
Seems like only yesterday their young ones left to fight.
As I lay my head on my bed, I will not sleep tonight.

Have curfews, lights go out,
Light your candles and pray in doubt.
Wives sit still, their hearts in pain,
For their husbands are not there, they are out in the rain.

Children sit in poverty, they cannot play.
Imagine if that were you, what would you say?
Poor little boys and girls, not like you or I,
For they have no choice but to say good-bye.

Marilyn Poirer

They

Lifting their gaze to higher purpose
They didn't see the buzzards circling
To wrest control of all dimensions
They seized the right with full intention
Primitive world of blood and greed
They didn't see where it would lead
To forge their dream at any cost
Such was the nature of their thoughts
Red sand blowing on the surface
The blackened stars, the rivers purple
Sintered chains of gold and glory
Bedazzled, blind, they didn't worry
Strange dynamics so slowly unlearned
The sky grew cold as forests burned
In the shadows of their minds
Instinct crushed the reasons why
Now cinders swirl about the sun
Twisted dust of schemes undone
An epitaph to mark their race
Scars the spangled void of space.

Ron Mcforth

Forgiveness (A Sonnet)

Alone and in the dark,
shadows everywhere.
Fear leaves its solemn mark,
as into the black I stare.
Noises are made louder,
and silence screams
at the pale face of a hopeless doubter,
tortured by my dreams.
As loneliness creeps slowly in,
I close my eyes to the night
and the sin
that keeps me from Eternal Light.
. . . A smiling, tear-stained face
that was touched by God's grace.

Michelle Noordhof

Dreamscape

Last night I awoke from a dream,
Choking on a silent scream.
Outside the broken window pane
Was lightning, thunder, darkness, rain.
The Demon that hovered above my bed
Had lips of blue, eyes of red.
Grinning in victory,
It called my name as it reached for me
With hands cut by broken glass.
Should my heart be beating this fast?
The love of my life was by my side.
Her eyes were open, alert, wide.
As the Demon reached, so did she;
To her belongs the victory.
When her love touched me first,
The Demon exploded in a fiery burst.
No more nightmares—no bad dreams.
Love conquers all. So it seems.

Carl Heffern

Grandfather

Who knows what happened
When I lost that one
Outside. Outside, inside,
He died. The music
Rose in some cancerous
Crescendo. Rising up, up
Consuming me in the
Tears of joys past.
The days of my youth . . .
Ring silently over the
Cold prairie. Thoughts
Of weekends past, of
Sunshine, turn to Snow.
Slowly the Reaper's tune
Rolls; across the prairie
Rolls. Pianowire fingers
Strumming on a hollow guitar.

Christopher Bourassa

Untitled

All alone, I am an island.

Living separately, denied.

Intuition made to be isolated.

Extreme, known to be desolated.

Never near to anyone.

Affirmed one day, gone.

Thoughts of myself, shunned.

I say suffering is so grand.

Oh, life is what is now.

Numb to all my senses.

Alienation is my only living sensation.

Eleonor Sagadraca

Far Away

Sister, you mean so much to me
more than words can say.
We shared so many special times
that cannot fade away.

As you leave to journey on
I'll give my best regards.
Remember all the times we shared
those memories in our hearts.

Our children grew all hand in hand
as the years went by.
Who knows when they will meet again
once we've said good-bye.

Never let their hearts forget
All the love they shared.
Remind them of the memories
And all the ones who cared

Although you're many miles away
Our love will never end.
You're not only my sister
but you're also my best friend.

Chris Evans

Mother—Daughter

The day I was first born, your love was fresh and powerful.
Your pride made me shine.
Mother—Daughter

During my infant years, your devotion was vast and true.
Your own priorities put aside.
Mother—Daughter

Through my childish times, your sincerity was solid and pure.
Your confidence grew with me.
Mother—Daughter

During my teenage years, your patience was lasting and strong.
Your support never failed me.
Mother—Daughter

Now as a growing adult, your friendship is fortunate and divine.
Your affection always there.
Mother—Daughter

With all memories laid in my heart,
No vision or words mean more than your love.
Mother—Daughter.

Linda Cicuta

For My Sons

He's a bundle of joy when you first bring him home,
And before you know it, he is all grown.
He's the song that will live within Mommy's heart.
He's Daddy's Little Leaguer, right from the start.

Then he becomes quite the smart little scholar,
And though you can't believe it, yes, he has gotten taller.
He rushes from school with report card in hand,
And gives it to you and says, "Mom, ain't it grand?"

In the blink of an eye, in a day so it seems,
He has grown into the fine young man of your dreams.
He's not round the house, well, not much anymore,
Except to have meals, but it's not like before.

He's met this new girl—a friend, so he says,
Then it's finally happened, they're off to be wed.
The visits are few and too far between,
But you now have grandchildren to complete the scene.

So if you're as lucky and have a fine son,
Hold each precious moment just as they come.
I know that's exactly what I plan to do,
Because I have been blessed with not one son, but two.

Deborah Kilimnik

Halloween

October has a pumpkin day;
We pick pumpkins in a merry way.
I'll carve the pumpkin if I may,
Then we'll sit on the bay
And watch children play.

Witches and ghosts hunt for their prey,
While people and animals run away.
Children say "Trick-or-treat! Trick-or-treat!" all the way.
Halloween, Halloween is coming today!

Ka-Chun Yuen

Mother

I owe my merriment to your saintly devotion
That no mother could have evinced as a token
Of her endless love and tender affection.
With no motherly touch, my heart could have been broken,
And then we wouldn't be two hearts in ecstasy of emotion.
Un-forgotten, my infantile memories threaten my quietude with agonizing guilt.
For, your customary reaction to my naughtiness was forgiveness not fight.
I should have been limited to what you permitted
When my perversity was mildly indulged that way, not merited.
For me you always cared, you cried and you sacrificed,
And satiated all my desires, my wants, and all I needed.
So, I owe you warmth and reciprocal understanding.
But how can one price interminable maternal sacrifice and liking?
Because you deserve more of a liking,
Perhaps a prize for qualifying.
You, the most wonderful mother the whole world over, the praiseworthy being that never asked
having and never ceased bestowing.

Laila Bouinidane

Promises Shared

The loneliness, the emptiness creeps back into my heart.
Words once spoken, cherished memories shared, find their way back,
I look for him, long to reach out for him through empty space.
"I won't let go." I spoke these words to him.
His tomorrows would come. In my heart, I believed
If I only held him closer, tighter, he would always be here with me.
From the moment I allowed him to venture into my heart—connection.
"I won't let go." I spoke these words to him.
I would, for the first time, see inside my soul,
Because he took me there and rested inside.
I would, for the first time, experience infinite compassion for another,
Because that is what he required of me.
In him, through him, because of him I felt his never-ending strength,
His unwavering passion for life, and his total commitment to live.
"Don't let me go." He spoke these words to me.
With love, faith, and trust, I held on.
"I won't let go." I spoke these words to him.
Now, alone in his space, I stand.
Words spoken, promises shared echo in my heart.
"I will remember you." Connection broken.

Starr Swayze

Canadian Winters, Hurry Spring

Canadian winter can be so beautiful at times.
The glistening snow shimmering on the tree branches in the sunrise,
just beckoning you to stare at all this beauty
surrounded in the white blanket called snow.
Today the sky is no longer sprinkling,
showing us the star-shaped snowflakes.
In place is the gusty winds blowing the snow
from the tree branches to the ground below.
The sun is shinning, with a smile on its face,
not a cloud to be seen, what a pretty sight.
Everything sparkling in the strange crackling
and creaking as if it were night.
I'm such a fool trying to convince myself of the beauty in surroundings.
Outside of Canada much of this can't be found.
I have to dress in boots, coat, hat, and mittens on my fists.
Now shovel in hand, from surrounding my car, I have to shovel all this.
Days like this make us think of the new beginnings
with the glorious spring at least for myself,
winter clothes not for me, I'm for Spring, the best Canada can bring.

Karen Chapman

Loneliness, Happiness

There are two kinds of loneliness,
There are two kinds of happiness:

A missing you kind of loneliness, when someone you love is not around,
A having no one kind of loneliness, true love has not been found.

Happiness for a moment when a gift has been given to you,
Happiness, enduring forever, when you find a love so true.

I have the missing you kind of loneliness when you are far away,
I have the enduring forever happiness when we fell in love that day.

Whenever the two of us sometimes have to part,
The missing, you kind of loneliness tugs at my longing heart.

I am happy to have this loneliness; I save it especially for you
While you are far away; you feel the same way, too.

We found enduring forever happiness in all the things we share,
When we are far apart, both of us know in our hearts we care.

The love we share together is a special and lasting one,
It will never fade away, like the sun when the day is done.

When we are together, we make the sunshine through,
Darkness never comes when I am there with you.

So when we are apart, missing you kind of loneliness comes our way,
Enduring forever kind of happiness will help us through the day.

Debbie R. Jerome

So Sweet

For, the sand touched thy hand
Sparkles reflected light in your eyes
So sweet, petals of daisy love flew in the born air of spring
Delicate and mystic scent of miracle enveloped firm shapes of masculinity
Deep caressing breath embraced tender soft femininity
Firm strong-shaped forms captivated the nude waves that raged
The shore of the new rebirth tide

Nathalie Wilson Borges

My World

Oh, world, oh, my world, you are a lure
Your love is kind and pure

How vast and deep you are in soul
So many treasures in your body stroll

You have bestowed everything to mankind
In you they live, love, and decline

Seasons, oceans, mountains, forests, and valleys
Are the lovely symbols of your qualities

Scattered in races, religions, casts, and languages
Fighting for their own objects for ages

And they who scratch your beautiful face
Are themselves holding the way of peace

Some who with the ill feelings of lust
Fill you with ammunition, politics, pollution, poverty, and thrust

Oh, my world, my gracious world, hold their ill soul
Do your best to uphold the prestige of your goal

You—whether it is North, South, East, or West
Are kind with all from the core of your heart

You are the mother, great and kind for all of us
Save and love, we belong to you, you belong to us

Mahammad Ilyas

Butterfly Diana

From a moth to a butterfly,
She flitted place to place—
From a child to a lady, a lady of Grace.
Everyone's fantasy, she lived to the full,
Our fairy Princess we all recall.
Smiling, laughing till she was spent.
Times "Oh, so Weary," she still raised a smile.
Shaking hands of the people, the poor she smiled on.
They weep for her now, "Their Butterfly Gone."
She gave sons Harry and William. They'll remind us of her.
The day of the funeral, to them hearts will stir.
Gone is their mother and friend to the end.
How will two hearts be able to mend?
Time is a healer, we all know 'tis so.
Bad memories live longer, they never go.
Why did she die such a terrible death?
Unknown is the reason, we will never forget.
All we know now is our "Butterfly" is gone.
History will recall that she will live on.
"God bless you, Diana," our butterfly, our moth.
We will all meet one day; there will be no more wrath.

Elizabeth Facette

Touched by God's Closeness in Nature

The beautiful splendor of the leaves
Was sent from God for us to please.

The colors are more vivid this year,
Especially with sunshine when the sky is clear.
The gleaming sun on gold, orange, red, and green;
It sure is a wonderful sight to be seen.

Impressive rocks at the road's edge
Take your eyes to their top ledge,
Where sumac, evergreens, and silver birch make home,
And sometimes raccoons and deer will roam.

Each time you round a curve, it has a special look,
So much better than reading about it in a book.
A rainbow rose from across the lake,
Which prompted me a wish to make.

A real nice place to stay with waves on the shore,
From the balcony, catch the sunset, who could ask for more!
The sound of the waves is soothing to me.
It brings peaceful contentment for all to see.

The twinkling stars fill the darkened sky,
Telling God's promise to you and I.

Frances Milburn

No Dessert

From an old yearning came a chance
To meet, greet, talk, touch
Through wine-danced eyes on younger feet,
And words were kisses warm and familiar.

He had not known the night he left
The rain had left a mark,
And she now knew that old tattoo had grown around her heart.

No coffee, cake . . .
They left hungry
For more words, to caress and confuse.

Jeffrey Jutai

Love and Loss

I once had a dog who had to pass on,
Then I heard the most heartbreaking song.
It talked about war, triumph, and despair.
I burst into tears and no one cared.
Everyone was standing, staring in pain.
Well, I was sitting, sulking in vain.
The vet said there was nothing to do,
So I said one last good-bye to Bru.
Bru and I had tears in our eyes.
I can't believe this was my last good-bye.
The best thing to do was put him to sleep.
We took off his collar and harness to keep.
Brutis was my best friend.
I can't believe I'll never see him again.

Jasmine Fediuk

Korea

The North is tense,
while the South is playing
with ground-burst flares
and M-16's, firing.
The North is threatening,
yet the South is here,
playing exercise
without a fear.
The North may move
and the South would fight,
with troops moving
against death in the night.
The North could attack
the South with force;
our forces would fight
to stop their course.
The North would be stopped
as the South would win,
but the loss of lives
will be the greatest of sins.

Louise Marmet

Strange Feeling

Do I know you . . .?
Yes, I do. . . .
No, I don't. . . .

The issue sustains.
The question remains.
Your looks, gestures . . .
all are strange.

Shaheena Khan

War

War Makes Death,
Death Makes Sadness,
Sadness Makes Depression,
Depression Makes Feelings,
Feelings Make Crying,
Crying Makes Tears,
Tears Make Anger,
Anger Makes War!

Michael Rigarlsford

Princess Diana

Everything seems gloomy,
Oh! The world is sad today.
Everyone is crying
That Diana has gone away.
She was not everything,
Still she was something:
A right hand to the poor,
But now there is nothing
To give support to them
That would make their day,
Just because they are people!!
Diana has gone away.
The headlines of every media,
Were sold like hot cakes,
But they also met loss,
Drowned has everyone's sake.
They either boasted or insulted her
That they did not have to pay,
Because the candlelight has extinguished,
And Diana has gone away.

Benish Zafar

Pa

my grandfather's feet are itchy
from the down-fill feathers
treading out of his slippers,
the points of their plucking
pricking his aged ankles
and tickling his veins
so they can't move blood;
this man's solid soles,
once supple from the homeland,
ground in a brand-old century
of hopeful, unknown dreams,
held his body while he built
life and home all around him,
chasing children and cattle,
walking the rails
and running from aeroplanes,
pressing gas pedals and hauling timber
over his earth for eighty years and some.
soft, fluffy, down feathers
now force him to sit
and rest.

Wayne Jutila

Grandma

I love you.
I want you.
I need you.

Please do not go.
I will be in great pain
If you do so.

And if you die,
Your loving heart will lie
Deep within my soul.

Cindy Harnish

Retirement

TODAY'S the day you dream about,
THE kind of day you want to shout.
YOU want to laugh and then to say:
I'M free to choose what I do each day.
EACH morning when the sun comes up,
YOU lie in bed and sip a cup
OF your favourite juice, coffee, or tea,
WONDERING how each day will be.
GUESS what?! You can visit, volunteer, or shop—
OR talk on the telephone until you drop.
YOU can cook, bake, or work in the yard,
OR do some housework, but not too hard.
PERHAPS you and your friend can go to a show.
JUST call on the phone, and off you go.
AFTERWARDS, relax and then retire
WITH a good book near a cozy fire.
RETIREMENT can only be great,
PROVIDED you don't concentrate
ON making each day what it's not,
BUT really appreciate what you've got.

Geraldine Edwards

Nihilism

Why does life have to go on and on,
And people have to vanish into thin air?
Someday I will find these answers.
The blessed plot, the Earth, the realm
Belongs to those who leave behind them
Simple, but effective achievements.
It is beyond me to understand
The reasons my beloved ones
"Go gentle into that good night."
Somehow I have to work it out
And not sink in such nihilism,
Otherwise I may perish.
I would dearly love to go back
To my childhood and
Let the sun go down on me
Because I really felt that I was
Free from fears that scare me
Out of my wits!

Marild Aparecida Angela De Oliveria Teixeira

One Chance Is the Last

I'm falling off the balcony and hoping that you won't see me.
But why did you have to say good-bye,
when you knew that it would make me cry?
Falling into the darkest light,
seeing the different shades of night,
making sure it's all for real,
I pinch myself—to hear me squeal.
And as the sound echoes and fades,
the shadow of my body comes nearer,
and it shows the many dark, depressing shades.
A sixteen-story building, so tall, so high—
who knew someone would jump off,
not thinking of last good-byes?
As my body slams the ground,
Darkness falls upon the town I found.
My stories of life I tell to none,
For one chance is the last, and I am done.

Zena Virani

Soul

Expression of your soul lies within your heart and your eyes
Within the words you speak each day:
The softness of your heart;
The way each sunrise in the early morning
Seems to bring your life a glimmer of hope;
How a simple poem can make you want to run
And embrace the world with open arms or go into your room
For a thousand years, never to come out again.
The way the moon seems enchanted when it comes out in its full self;
How you hold the hand of a lover with a special tenderness
Or give a friend a shoulder to cry on
When the whole world seems to be coming down on them:
Your soul is who you are.
It's who you have been and who you will become.
It's everything that you believe in and everything for which you hope.
It's all that you hate and all that you love.
Do not give up on yourself or what you can be.
To live your life the way you have planned
Will be your final expression.
Your soul will be able to rest eternally,
Undisturbed forever.

Corey Smith

Empty Thoughts

I sit in my room, and I think empty thoughts,
Thoughts about nothing, but thoughts that no one else can ever think.
These thoughts are special, empty though they are,
And they get through to me as no others ever have.
As I sit in my room and think empty thoughts,
A peaceful feeling engulfs my body,
A feeling that I could not get away from, even if I wanted to.
I don't care what people think of me.
I need to be alone with my thoughts,
Empty thoughts.

Fiona Paterson

Chris' Bedtime

I've gone to bed and am going to sleep again and again and again.
I'll dream of the soccer games I played and the goals I scored like a man,

the baskets I made as I ran down the court
with the ball in and out with such spunk,
and the way the crowd cheered as I flew through the air
and came down to make a slam dunk.

I'll dream of the shiny red fire truck I'll drive,
on my way to a fearsome blaze,
and the rescue I'll make and the people I'll save,
whilst I battle the smoky haze.

I'll dream of the backbone I'll use with such pride
as I dig and remove lots of earth.
I'll plan and construct great buildings so high
that people will know of my worth.

I'll be a good person when I grow up and strive to do my best,
But before my mummy gets cross with me, I'd better lie down and rest.

I'm feeling so sleepy that now I believe
I will snuggle down where it is warm
And ask God to keep all my family and friends
and Jasmine from coming to harm.

Gillian Heath

Fresh Beginnings

In our next lifetime together you'll see, we'll be thicker than thieves.

Once again we'll meet on the street and go for drinks at a nearby pub,
but it won't be quite as spectacular as the first event.
We'll be kindred spirits, unattached and free.

Enough time will have passed by that I'll be able to explain
what really did happen back then and, incredibly,
you'll somehow believe me. I can just picture the look you'll have
on your face, too, by the time I'm through.

Oh, yes, you'll still have that undefinable air of authority about you
that you've always had, but you won't feel an urge to use it against me.
Should I just happen to back you in a corner . . . you'll just laugh.

We'll talk about anything and everything, bantering ideas about.
Oh, we won't agree on anything—some things never change—
but it will be a breath of fresh air just for us to talk again
and for me to be able to remember . . . the next time.

There'll be an easiness between us then, for there'll actually be
continuity to our friendship. Our faith in mankind will have been
restored, and, in turn, in each other.

But until then, my friend . . . we'll just have to pretend.

Jayne Russell

The Moment of the Rose

Degree in hand, proudly stand; into the world go forth;
A score of applications, the dreamed-of job now sought.

Refusals and rejection slips diminish your noble frame,
Sights lowered, spirits cowered, despair and failure came.

Turned back and back again, snared in an evil time,
Your learning, your enthusiasm: pearls before swine!

Fleeting span of glory, upright and in our prime!
Too brief our total story, briefer yet that squandered time!

To growing sweetness we ripe, then rot; swiftly the moment goes;
That moment of fresh youth is as the moment of the rose.

A host of youth that begged entry, a generation lost,
Who can tell what might have been or what will be the cost?

Valerie A. Drego

Request

Dear God, Allah, Yahweh, whatever your designation,
Come quickly, save your world from the whirl of destruction.
Where's the perfect peace you promised?
Where has the great love gone?
Clear not only the land mines we can see,
But those in the canyons of people's hearts.

Scatter our copious tears, calm our terrible fears,
That we'll do good deeds and plant the fertile seeds.
That the fields will glow, and bloom, and lighten the gloom.
That we'll witness the miracle of lambs in lion's dens,
Hear nightingales serenading predators of the sky,
And stroll through an environment as pristine as eons ago;
Not only what's visible, but in the chasms of people's minds.

Dear God, Allah, Yahweh, my faith in you is mountain high.
Whatever you do, I won't ask to know the reason why.
Some are happy, some are sad,
Some are righteous, some are bad.
I firmly believe you'll bless a humble request
With the blue birds of happiness, butterflies of love and peace.

Randolph Homer

Why Love Me If You Can't See Me?

Why love me if you can't see me?
It is not I
It is not the true me
for I am hidden
shadowed from the world
crying out from the deep chasm of true self
For what, if no one answers back?
The only escape is you seeing me
reaching out your hand in compassion
to bring me out

Remember the beauty we possess inside
It is the one God gave us
the gift of self
lost in this materialistic world
but still somewhere inside us
Together we can find it
I'll hold your hand
please set me free

Roberto J. Diaz

Ode on the Death of a Favourite Cat . . .

It was on a lofty vase's side
Where China's grayest art had died.
The azure flowers that blow,
Demurest of the tabby kind,
The pensive Selima reclined,
Gazed on the lake below.

Her conscious tail, her joy declared,
The fair, round face, the snowy beard,
The velvet of her paws,
Her coat that with the tortoise vies,
Her ears of jet and emerald eyes,
She saw and purred applause.

Still had she gazed; but 'midst the tide
Two angel forms were seen to glide,
The Genie of the stream;
Their scaly armour's Tyrian hue
Through richest purple to the view
Betrayed a golden gleam.

Giovanni T. Aligaen

Beth

Write the poem for your wife.

Eyes that hold and care,
she's no longer alone by the fire.
Bear spirit dancers share her drum,
as does Coyote, who squats beside the dancer
and smiles, raising her spirits whenever her shadows fall low.
Ancient stones in the voices of time,
one trick at a time, the fire jumps
at magic, jumps at power.

At home, my voice changes,
the dance changes.
The novel becomes the stone upon which
my grandchildren will stand,
but this poem is for the bear's spirit.

Gerry William

Timing

Time for a reason
These days can't go on
And I don't remember
Just where I went wrong
If you've got an answer
I'm ready to learn
Just like a candle
Waiting to burn
The play keeps on playing
But they've cut all my scenes
It's time for a reason
I'm all out of dreams.

Kenneth Brian Mac Caulder

Untitled

Photographs—
I sit here with my memories.
All my children
grown up and gone on their own.
Sometimes I wish
they were still here
'cause now I look around
for things to do.
It's not as much fun
as it was once.
Photographs—
the smiles on the faces
and the memories of those times:
it brings a chuckle out of me.
The mischief you kids would get into.
Photographs—
They bring a kind of joy
to my heart to know I did good,
but it sure would be nice to hear from you
all again or to see you once again.

Neil Street

The Wound

There is a hole.
It's down deep in her heart:
A wound
Only time will heal.

Someone who was trusted
Stole her life.
Pain was the only return,
The only reward.

Nowhere to turn,
No one to listen,
Life is over,
Life is ruined.

Each time she faces him,
It weakens her defenses.
He sees this,
Likes the advantage.

The time will come,
His life will be ruined.
His life will be over
By the hand of the one he robbed.

Karen Millett

My Othello

Love has caused my blood to boil,
quick to curdle as milk to spoil,
rage has judged my lover false
and locked my love within its walls.
This sour love was not in vain,
it brings to light a lover's pain,
the body shudders as if in chills,
the fever of love's bitter ills.
Lemons now the taste of sweet,
Jealousy I rise to meet,
day now the darkest night,
love has surely lost this fight.
Impassioned tantrums of a Moor,
cruelest love so impure,
severed a rose in full bloom,
and left my lover in a tomb.
Sorrow drowns the scorching rage,
I blindly crawl within my cage
and rest upon my loving sword,
Jealousy's wage and just reward.

William Mbaho

Journey through the Universe

In the meadow by the pond,
the grass moves slowly
as the sand of time passes by.
The rains come down as the
clouds cover the stars.
The flame flickers before it dies
as the child cries through the storm.
The storm is blowing,
the waters crash,
the flower petal droop and
the leaves fall till the last drop.
The stars appear through the clouds,
the wind blows
through the tall grass,
the birds chirp, and the crickets sing.
The moon mirrors on the broken
glass surface of the lake.
A star shoots across the sky
and breaks the silent moment,
because the Universe is alive.

Crystal Scott-Herridge

It's My Life!

I'm trapped, I'm controlled,
I'm too young but yet too old.
They tell me what to do and how,
They tell me "sit" and "eat" and "bow."
They say it's just for my own good,
And to listen to them I should,

But I know it's all a fake—
My freedom they try to take!
I know what is right for me,
I know how everything should be!

They won't listen but I know
What's the best way to go.
They say "no," but I don't care!
All they do is just not fair!

I run away from their false embraces,
It's my life and no one else's!

Shmuela Jacobs

A Reason in Itself

Why does it take too long to realize
That life doesn't have a meaning?

If it weren't so, life wouldn't be worth living.

It is worth living only for the complexity
Of trying to find a reason for life.

So, now I came to the real point:
Life is worth living, for there isn't a reason to live.
Being so, the search for a reason becomes a reason in itself.

Searching for a reason is a reason,
For it puts itself as a meaning of life.

Living a life with no reason doesn't make sense.
The sense of living without a meaning of life teaches us
How to fight to find a sense in living.

Why does it take too long to realize
That there is no meaning in life?

Why does it take too long to realize
That the reason of searching for a meaning of life
Makes sense enough to become a reason in itself?

Alexandre Clemente

God Is a Mystery . . .

F—free, faithful, our best Friend
A—alive, active, the Almighty
T—triune, transcendent, the best Treasure
H—the best Helper, the best Healer, the best Hero
E—Energy, eternal, the best Engineer
R—reliable, responsible, responsive

S—the suffering Saviour, the best Shepherd
O—One, orderly, optimistic
N—noble and near—All of Your creation needs You

H—heavenly, hidden, to be honoured
O—omnipresent, omnipotent, omniscient
L—Love, Light, Lord, King, Creator of the universe
Y—yearning for Your yield

S—the Supreme Being, the Source of life,
    a good Seeker of souls
P—pure, perfect, the best Provider
I—intelligent, imaginative, immutable
R—real, rich, the best Renovator
I—important, immanent, invincible
T—the most trustworthy Teacher and the Truth.

Gina D'Agostino

DAVIDJAMES a.k.a. CRAZYMAN

Do you love me?
I love you . . .
I rejoice in writing it—I do.
I love you . . .
I rejoice in saying it—I do.
So let me.
Has anyone told you this today, DavidJames?
I love you . . .
I do.

Charann

Near the Millennium

In the red, angry clouds he issued a warning to us all.
Those who see it, move away, and those who don't, lose it all.
It took a lot out of them to recapture the glory lost.
One of them was a man sunken low by his tired life.
He looked sideways and in the front at every step.
Nobody knew of what he was in search,
  but waited for him to carry on.
Flow, he says, and they flow not!
They look, as if to find out from each other what he is talking about.
Nobody knows he is talking to tears ebbing from his soul,
  which cannot come to his face.
They walk, he walks to run away from the warning.
It is an unending journey. They must endure to live!
In the world full of people who have taken it upon themselves
to kill other weak observers, it will not end.
Today he asked me a question: What can be done about this?
A question among many others.
I replied, we need to learn from mistakes of the past.
While I am I, the all-knowing,
  and he is he, the lord who pretends not to know anything.
I stopped he who was unstoppable!
While it has us, it will go on as colorful as ever for me to see.
I watch, but my hands are tied, so I cannot do anything.
I must look until it stops; it must go on, and they must endure.

Rami Kaur Singh

Dare Not Deny Me Love

Deny me happiness,
Deny me the most beautiful sunsets my eyes have ever seen.
Deny me youth,
Deny me the ambitions I long to conquer.
Deny me comfort,
Deny me the feeling of truly belonging somewhere.
But dare not deny me his innocent smile,
Dare not deny me his tender stare,
Dare not deny me the calm nervousness I felt in his presence,
Dare not deny me his love,
Dare not deny my love for him,
Dare not deny me the beauty of my precious dream,
Dare not deny me love.

Stavroula Papadopoulos

A Reflection

From where I am, I can see a girl standing all alone,
And I know that she's unhappy, for I hear a quiet moan.

She is staring in my direction, but her eyes are lacking sight,
And does not know that I am watching her this night.

I wish that I could go to her and tell her something kind,
But her face reflects the emptiness of her body, soul, and mind.

A single tear appears that rolls slowly down her cheek,
Which tells me so much more than any word that she might speak.

I close my eyes to wonder if there's something I might say
That could make a difference to her in even the slightest way.

But no words can I find to help ease her sorrow
Or tell her that the pain she feels may be less tomorrow.

I force my eyes to return to that cold, vacant stare,
Wishing I had the voice to say there is someone who cares.

But these words are never spoken to that lonely girl I see
Who stares back from my mirror; alas, that girl is me.

Patricia Barker

The Splendor of Love: A Marriage Proposal

I behold, in all her splendor and awe,
The majestic grandeur of beauty.
Her hair shining, shimmering black, gently cascading over her head,
Reminiscent of a mighty waterfall gushing over.

I behold her brown eyes, the windows of her heart,
Shining more brightly than the stars way up in the night sky.
Is there a twinkle I see? of pain and sorrow?
Her cheeks are two radiant roses with russet saffron petals.

I behold a jewelled pearl hidden in the depths of the ocean floor,
Waiting to be plucked from its abode.
I behold a precious flower in the barren Sahara Desert
Hidden, sheltered by the occasional crags and cactus.
But, wait, the flower is now fully blossomed
And ready to be carried into the heavenly realms of ecstasy.

Could it be that our first rendezvous was foreordained?
Nevertheless, I am the richer for having kept my appointment with destiny.
To woo her, court her, and win her hand would be any man's dream!
In God's perfect plan for each of us
May I translate that dream into an ongoing, eternal reality?

    Dr. Mark James

Untitled

These are musicians' hands and they are more exciting now
Than ever they have been. Lying quiet upon his knee,
Strongly defined, they speak a sharp vitality.
These are a sorcerer's hands or by a sorcerer guided.
I stare in fascination remembering their articulation
An hour earlier. They have accomplished power,
They have controlled all thought and sound,
Disturbed and caressed at will the witting listener.
What sorcerer this? Dry-tongued, the mute finds utterance—
Heart and mind speak when these fingers choose
As this drives blood like flame
In other veins than his.

    Dorothy Kimpton

Trinity—A Mystery?!

One God, Three Persons, who can comprehend?
Oh, Triune God, how much I love You!
You are everything to me.

You are my father—Who cares for me, caresses me,
comforts me, and calls me home.

You are my Brother—Who gave His life for me, Who loves me tenderly,
strengthens me with living Blood, shields me like a mighty army,
feeds my soul, and bathes me in Mercy's rays.

You are the Breath of my soul—Who gives me wisdom
and the grace of knowledge.
You are my powerful Help, my trusted Counsel.

Your tender mercies, oh, Triune God, are as deep as the ocean,
as endless as the universe, as countless as the stars.

How can my heart be troubled knowing that You are there for me?
How can I be discouraged or afraid with You at my side?

My deepest desire is to be engulfed in the love that radiates forth
from this precious Triangle of Mercy. All of the world's adversities
cannot harm me, for I have You—my mighty Fortress.

Keep on calling me, keep on loving me, keep on forgiving me
and I will be whole!

May You be praised eternally!! Now, I begin to understand.

    Willy Effinger

Remembrance Day

A young man waved. He was off to war.
He was young, just eighteen, not a child anymore.
His parents' hearts were full of pride.
He never knew of the nights they cried.

They received his letters: "I am a rear gunner
In the new plane, the Lancaster Bomber."
He writes, "I'll be home for Christmas—
just one more mission to fly."
They didn't know he wouldn't come.
It was his time to die.

Then it came on the 18th of December,
The fateful news they will always remember.
Your son is missing. We know not where.
We share your grief. You know we care.

Thank God, the war is finally won.
Then seven years later, they found their son.
The sea of Holland had been his grave.
He died a man. He had been brave.

He's buried now in that Holland land.
He's been with God. He's shaken His hand.
Although it's been a long time ago,
Their hearts still hurt a lot, I know.

Angela Renaud

The Little Brown Leaf

Fall

The leaves have turned a glorious hue,
Falling to Earth with a wondrous view.
And a Little Brown Leaf that lies underneath,
Sighs and promptly goes to sleep.

Winter

Little Brown Leaf sleeps and hibernates,
Warm and comfortable covered by snow,
He knows that very soon
He will have to sprout and grow.

Spring

Little Brown Leaf starts to stir
And feels the growth of regeneration.
Seeds sprout all around and under him
And he knows he has created another generation.

Summer

Descendants of the Little Brown Leaf
In full bloom, they leap and frolic
As the sun shines and the wind blows,
    but very soon they know too,
That they will fertilize the earth and make it new.

Olive Boyd Bukowiecki

Untitled

Sadness engulfs me in pain
Feeling feelings I cannot bear
I wish I could scream out
And make things new . . .
But I'm forever washed in this endless guilt
That one day I'll feel too blue
To know the difference between black and white
With no trace of grey

Lynn Berube

Silence

The silver birches
shimmer and sway in the breeze,
calling to the sky,

their iridescent voices
sprinkling on the grass below.

Winds gather the sound
of the passing memories,
scatter them once more.

The silence joins the birches
in wailing for distant days.

Felicity L. Maxwell

Tread Easy

Tread easy with footsteps so light
that sidestep others with discretion.
Don't trample someone's given right
and stay defiant with aggression.

All future prospects you wish for
and those of others may not match,
and though their nets could gather more,
you're not entitled to their catch.

You plot and plan your day ahead,
then walk out confident with verve,
then fate sets other plans instead
with a different end for you to serve.

All worldly spoils that you attain
would stay behind when you depart.
None of their memories would remain
except their values from the start.

What lives on and the hearts recall,
and what would linger on our minds,
is love, however big or small,
and kindness that us warms and binds.

H. Joseph Huss

Thinking of You

I have you in my thoughts
and hold you in my heart.
I reach my hand to touch you
and lift you up in prayer
to the One who never leaves you
and continues with His care
to comfort, guide and keep you
through all the days ahead.

In loneliness and sadness,
in turmoil and in pain,
He stays right there
and gives His peace,
imparts His love,
surrounds you with His strength.

Be sure of this—
He'll never fail to help you every day.
No matter what you need,
He'll be right there.
For this, for you, I pray.

Alan Roberts

Christmas—Make a Difference

The chill of winter is in the air,
hustle and bustle everywhere,
No one pauses to see the sights
of all the pretty, twinklin' lights.
Children's faces are all aglow,
Santa's coming; this they know.
Giggles and laughter fill their hearts,
they don't worry 'bout shopping carts.
Why do the children have all the fun,
as adults we can only run
to fill their stockings and get the best,
Christmas has no time to rest.
Let's join together and make amends,
this season is not about mere trends.
Set an example for all to see
what Christmas is supposed to be.
Take time to make a difference this year,
Christmas is not a time to fear.
Let the happiness of this holiday
lift your spirits and calm your way!

Catherine Stocking

Untitled

As we float in the bowl
And gill the unsavory waters
Of our soul
In clear blue ceremony
The fish we are
Usually steers clear
Of the heavy currents toll

Clinton Roberts

Her Masquerade

A fire burns within her heart
And deep within her soul.
No one knows the depth of it
The truth is still unknown.

Desire, rage, pity, and love
Are elements included.
Forgiveness is among them
But seems an illusion.

Dark is the place she lives in
And anguish is her life.
Living with those memories
Is what gives her the fright.

No one knows her dark secret
Hidden inside herself.
And no one knows the real her
Because quiet is her sound.

Melissa Mitchell

Who Helped?

Helped Hitler kill Jews.
They killed the Jews all over Europe,
The mean, bad Nazis.

Jonny Goldberg

The Hunger for Love

In my heart, within me, lies emptiness.
Is it from the hunger, the craving for what I long for?
The tangled emotions, feelings that I have
do not satisfy my hunger, but rip away at me
more, making me weak. The hunger becomes starvation,
and I slowly fall apart, feeling myself inside
and out dying.

Jennifer Reynolds

The Day of Remembrance

Why my strong but sensitive
Culture people
Sent our brave soldiers into battle
For their countrymen
To witness the distorted facts
Of a cruel, insensitive war
For reasons unfounded
For mankind, weep
Soldiers defeated helplessly
Loss of vehicles
Man of battle hemorrhage from weapons
Our soldiers rigorously write phrases of life
On mount for one person
But on the gigantic wall
Tangible experience of the loss for love
Yearning for compassion

Shirley Rogers

In Me

I envy moderate people
In me everything is so strong
The intensity with which I love you
The antipathy that I feel
My sense of justice
The need for you
The necessity of others
The wish to be myself
And the desire to dissolve in you
My drive to struggle
My immense laziness
My longing to embrace you
The extreme need of silence
The lack of companionship
The wish for solitude
The craving for you
The dream that makes me fly
And what captivates me to the ground
The fear of having you and giving myself
And the fear of losing you, but much bigger
Is that immense tenderness, passion, insanity
That returns me to you.

Irene Da Silva

Forever

Press your sweet lips to mine, dearly beloved,
and forever itself shall come within my reach,
and flowers shall bloom and spread their soft
perfume while I upon a silver cloud shall feel to be.

Hold me within the circle of your arms
and life shall be forever full of bliss,
and I shall close my eyes and feel again
the wonder and the sweetness of your kiss.

Providencia Martinez Martinez

Disability to Ability

A vigorous mind dulled by pain that never seems to alter,
Feeling trapped, muscles in a body that has almost forgotten
how to feel okay. Occasional freedom to move, an overwhelming event,
A high so high I could scream it from the treetops. Life passes by.
I've got things to do. "Less is more," they advise, but how much less?
Nothing achieved, going nowhere. They say, "don't mope,"
but I am sad and grieving, so much I have to give
that lies hidden in my soul, trapped.
I try looking for the gift, the meaning of it all.
Pain brought me here to this terrible place,
finally out among people again.
My life lonely, confined, turned in upon itself,
has a new chance now. But am I strong enough?
Am I brave enough
or will I give up again because of pain? "Calm down," they say.

But that was yesterday. Beginning to find a rhythm,
My rhythm both here and outside.
Listening closely as my muscles tell me: "Rest in an easy chair,
now try again. Do only what is comfortable, what feels safe."
Arms and legs go everywhere awkwardly, like a colt or a small child,
but it is the new beginning.

Susan Sara Fayga Zimmerman

The Murmur of the Rolling Sands Keeps Me Awake

The murmur of the rolling sands keeps me awake,
And the little rat scurries in the brain.
Everything loses itself in the blind sand
Where spoils of freedom go to the insane.

Bright black hand burns in its little golden dream
As life stands perched on that lofty rooftop,
But I'm not like that; the sand moves slowly for me,
The one-hundred-year-old shad fly pleads.

Lost beneath tick tock of the monster clock,
The scythe cuts into all, jagged edge with
Daunting rust that flows for the man who does not see.
He smiles; gallant is he that yells unspoken words.

I dedicate this to the man who does not see.
My thoughts, my dreams, my eyes I hand to him.
Weaving golden sand is a task left for the wind.
Frail hand, hold this cracked sun above me.

Sasha Semienchuk

An Ode on Dogma, Knowledge, And God

Dogma stifles the body, soul, and spirit.
Dogma stifles the Word of God.
Dogma stifles the world and its possible inquisitions.
Dogma stifles the possibilities of God in man and for the world.
Dogma stifles the church and the love of Christ for his own.
Dogma stifles the freedom and liberty assured through the blood of Christ.

For, God is the author of the Heavens and the Earth,
And Christ the Centre of his throne.
For, Christ has given freely of his wisdom and knowledge
And knowledge that is beyond religion.
For, Christ cannot be compartmentalized; He is one and all.
And Copernicus, Galileo, Pascal,
Kepler, and Newton were early Christians who were also scientists.
For, I see God in physics, chemistry, music, mathematics, history, art, and in all faculties,
And Christ revealed, I know, is the source of all faculties, the giver of ingenuity.
For, Christ can be proven and related to all faculties and humanist professions of men,
And Christ has given all knowledge unto men of which religion is one.

Lionel Etan Adollo

Just a Story

There's a little girl who wanders through life itself
And asks so many questions.
What am I doing here? What is my meaning?
Where is my future? Who is God?
The wind whispers in her ears, "Look into the clear pool of the stream!
See the sky above with the clouds drifting by?"
"It is I," cries the little girl, "It is I."
"Yes" the whisper blows, "You are God. You are God."
"But how can this be? How can this be?" she asks.
"Listen to me!" the whisper lilts, "You will guide many destinies.
You will give life and hope.
You will give understanding."
"Oh," sighs the little girl. "But what happens when I die?
What happens when I die?"
"So you believe you die," replies the whisper. "So you believe you die.
Well, let's look through to the future. What can we see?
A little boy kneeling, peering into a clear pool of a stream.
I will whisper to him, "You are God! You are God!"
But my, you have eyes like a little girl I once knew.
She for sure was God. She for sure was God."

    John Barr

Untitled

Deep within lies something that we long to win,
An unmistakable beauty so sweet it makes man long to sing.
Searching on high with wings of air,
We see only the reflection of the rays of light
That shine upon her hair.
Lurking in the woods of the deep and obscure,
Ditches, thorns, and weapons of danger are choices one must hide.
From the path that seems clear to the darkness of the night,
The relentless pursuit of beauty from a gasp is once again out of sight.
Her beauty and eloquence stand firm and poised with the light.
Man need only to capture the awe that comes with total embrace;
But the naked and lustful eyes of man
Cannot see the purity and honesty that
Emanates from within her subtle yet delicate skin.
For, the surface shows nothing that does not come from within,
Yet is too much shown to the man
Who hopes to see past the surface
And capture his own unclaimed prize?

    Donavon Campbell

And When

And when night falls and you want that hand to hold
And when you've woven your souls together,
   not to chain but to strengthen
And when you have found kisses sweeter and more tender
   than any before
And when your heart wants the other heart to beat in time,
And when that smile makes you feel so singular,
And when the sound of that voice in greeting makes the world intimate,
And when you smell the springtime in caring arms,
And when no other comes close to making you feel so joyful,
And when you see the light begin to fade,
And when you know the mind is heavy with sadness,
And when you know you can't hold fast when it's time to take a journey,
And when you find the pain almost unbearable,
And when the time between dusk and dawn
   echoes with memories of passion,
And when you've worked so hard in order not to think,
And when you've given way to pretending dreams are real,
And when who you want is still searching for an answer,
And when poets say, plant your own garden,
   loss can make you strong, good-byes are words to help you grow,
   and endurance gives you grace,
Then I say I've learned that lesson; but when night falls,
I still want that hand to hold with no apologies for opening my heart.

    LaVerne Bailey

Old Age

It told me that it knew me,
And I believed.

What it knew, though,
I couldn't conceive.

Was it a dream or was I awake?
Somewhere in time, I had made a mistake.

I can't differentiate between "right" and "wrong."
These conflicting feelings come on too strong.

That stranger within me was my true friend;
The one who has taken her place—
I cannot comprehend.

They told me it would happen,
yet it came too soon.
It should have never passed,
That month of June.

Anita Agrawal

Ballad to Caroline

Racing blindly through the cold and raging snow,
The cutter sped homeward, a short way to go.
Huddled together, just as close as can be
Were brave Caroline and her little sister Dee.

Their breath came short, and fear filled their eyes.
The road up ahead was now blocked by snow slides.
Caroline realized they could go no farther on
And would have to wait until rescued at dawn.

With frozen fingers, she set the horses free.
Then, with loving tenderness lifted down Dee.
With a new strength she had never before known,
She pushed and pushed, until the cutter was overthrown.

She wrapped up Dee and put her under the cutter,
And cuddled her close like a babe to its mother.
Ice chilled her bones as she kept Dee alive,
Hoping that before long help would arrive.

The sun shone brightly on the snow all around.
The rescue party was shocked by what they found.
Under the cutter lay Caroline, stiff as can be,
Beneath her, quite cold but alive, was young Dee.

Audrey Eby

Stillness

I was a silent observer to a wondrous moment
of Heaven's glory one evening,
when a little fishing boat passed gently
under soft, fading rays of the evening sun.
The setting sun was overshadowed
by swiftly fleeting, grey nebulous clouds.

The waters of the South China Sea
stood still at that moment,
absorbing the greys of the fluffy clouds
and the disappearing golden rays of the sun.
The little waves of the sea were swishing
gently around my feet,
touching and leaving like the fleeting seconds,
leaving a wonderful message
of stillness and peace around me.

Umamaheswari Suppiah

Looking Back

We had no time in yesterdays
To hear the robins sing
Or watch the early flowers
Blooming in the spring.

We always had too much to do
In the summers of our lives
To listen to the crickets
Or watch the fireflies.

We didn't see the rainbows
When all the rains were done,
We didn't watch the sunrise
Or see the setting sun.

These free and precious things in life
Are with us every day
And are somehow now important
As our lives of winter fade away.

The stars are bright above us now,
As we sit here on our swing
Just holding hands together,
Silently remembering.

Lois Van Kralingen

Where Beauty Lives

I think I know
where beauty lives. . . .
At her side a man must give
gentle words
of his expressed.
Beauty longs to hear the best.

A little hug day by day,
helps her feel that same way.
Unexpected gifts to treasure,
win her heart
beyond all measure.

As he takes her hand to hold,
spoken sentiments soon unfold.
Tender touches, pleasing kisses,
soft caresses:
These are some of beauty's private wishes.
So like the pure white dove
with olive branch
that seeks fresh soil
in which to plant
his and beauty's
loving union,
procreate
the whole world's children.

J. J. MacLeod

My Child

So quiet, yet so restless,
curious and at the same time
so unknowing of what the
world beyond will bring,
a silent toddler staring out
the window, waiting for
what fate should give him—
mixed thoughts made by
a child, my child.

Pia Inocencio

Untitled

Hidden inside
The harmony of all people
Untouched potential
Untouched knowing
Untouched going
Beyond your perception
You are trust
With all there is
Within your Self

The painted
Invisible man
Sometimes I feel this way

Arnold Rabius

Through the Path of Life

Through the path of life, when I walked,
I was alone.
It was dark and cold,
And faraway at the end
Death awaited, and I noticed
That I had only a few years to go.
And then after pains, death would come,
And I'd lose the world forever, forever.

Then suddenly I felt
Someone walking with me, hand in hand.
He laughed when I laughed
And cried when I cried.
When a thorn pricked my foot,
It pricked his heart.
I was happy, and death seemed far away.
A friend had come into my life at last!

V. Satish Chandra

Seashore

Walking at the seashore
A warm sunny day
The waves softly rolling in
All sailboats going slowly
In the calm of
A perfect summer day
A few blue jellyfish
Floating in and out
Of the blue sea
Some seashells and seaweed
Look like a painting in the sand
With the waves rolling in
Sounds like music
Sea gulls dancing in the sky
Sun starting toward the horizon
And the next day we hope
For a friendly, peaceful world
Always around our seashores

Solveig Olsson

Broken Heart

The withered, red rose
The chocolate melted away
Cupid was sighing. . . .

Jenny Sung

Togetherness

Togetherness is a beautiful word
It would help this world much more
I believe if universal language could be used
It would open nearly every door.
To be taught in all schools at an early age
Bring people much closer together
They could talk no matter what words were used.
Even if it was only about the weather
Your accent maybe a little harder to comprehend
But the words would be all the same
It wouldn't take too long to go around that bend.
Even if it was only somebody's name
I am not knocking bilingualism
Being able to converse in their tongue
But all being taught the same alphabet
You could start off very young.
The parent's at home could start this off
Then all kids could talk the same
This would create a togetherness
Even if it was only their name.

Philip H. Reed

Poor Heart

Poor heart, full of love so cruelly quenched,
The object of its love withdrawn
And more cruelly yet, turned to another.
Poor heart, wounded and bleeding,
Pain unbearable trying to heal.
Passion swirls within its chambers,
Warm, hot, desperate, nowhere to go.
Poor heart, longing for its mate,
That other heart that beat as one with it.
Return my love, my other half.
It does not, it does not.
How deafening the silence.

Mary Testolin

Death of a Great Man

It was early in the afternoon
While motoring through a Texas town,
A sniper ready aimed his gun
That was to bring president Kennedy down.

The death of a great man came to be,
On November 22nd, sixty-three,
In Dallas, Texas, those roses were nice.
To pay with your life, what a sacrifice.

John F. Kennedy, at the age of forty-six,
With the rich and poor he would mix.
He gave his dedicated and precious life
And left two children and a mourning wife.

We know the will of God had to be
On that gloomy day in sixty-three.
He aimed to help nations and he tried.
A soldier he lived, and a true soldier he died.

All nations mourn with his wife
This noble man that has gone from life.
From an Earthly battle he never ran,
This great and powerful, devoted man.

Bert Proulx

Sanctuary

This is it, my eternal sanctuary.
This wretched pit of darkness is where i shall lie
and where i shall forever roam.
Like a nocturnal beast, i shall haunt this darkness,
this darkness where i shall find my home.
Over this cold earth i shall lay my bones and watch them wither away.
Over this hard rock i shall lay my head and forever leave it there to stay.
Under these bushes will be my remains
and in their stabbing thorns my soul should play.
If you pass by, know that i am watching,
and under the soles of your shoes you shall find pieces of my past.
In these trees you should find me, for although my body is gone,
know that my soul will forever last.
In their leaves are fragments of my skin
and with their dew is mixed my thick, warm blood.
In their roots is the rest of me, for what i was is what they've become.
When they cover you with their shade, it is me blessing you,
and when they stab you with their thorns, it is me seeking revenge.
But in this darkness i shall spend eternity,
and with the creatures of the dark i shall become friends.

>   *Ramez Amoudi*

An Ode to an Ex-Lover

I should have seen it coming, like the calm before the storm,
But love and lust between us now has hardly become "norm."

Something's gone and missing, like an empty, open space.
This love of ours that we once shared is lacking solid base.

I'd hoped it wouldn't end like this, I really thought it'd last,
But now I have to chalk this up among the failures past.

My heart, it aches, it really does, because I'm human too.
I laugh, I love, I cry, I bleed, exactly like you do.

But we must come to realize what's best for both of us
And make our way through hard-luck times without a fight or fuss.

I love you, dear, I always will; I'm sorry we must part,
But please know deep in your soul, you're always in my heart.

>   *Lori Anne-Chatham*

When I Heard That He Was Gone

When I heard that he was gone, I didn't cry
He was old and sick, we saw it coming
Besides, he was my great-grandpa; we were never close

At the funeral if finally hit me
He was gone, not coming back
The chair he always sat in would now be empty
Then, I looked over at his wife, my great-grandma
She was sobbing, beside her stood my grandpa

My great-grandpa was my dad's grandpa
That's when I started to cry
I realized that one day I would be at my grandpa's funeral
He would be dead
The man I loved and admired so much would be gone from my life
I felt bad because I was supposed to be crying
Over the man who had passed away
But I wasn't
I was crying over the thought of losing my grandpa
I vowed then that I would never take anyone I loved for granted

That was when I started to cry over the loss of my great-grandpa

>   *Kaitlyn Herbst*

My Life Has Changed . . .

So much since you left, Mom.
The world can be such a lonely place.
Once upon a time, the birds were singing, and
Buds and flowers were abundant with color and
fragrance that belonged in Heaven;
Tiny animals had a gift of communication with you
and happily pranced in your direction just to be fed
from your gentle and loving hands.
The rain would fall softly to the Earth and create the most breathtaking
And radiant rainbow in the galaxy.
When you died, my heart died with you.
Suddenly, the birds stopped singing . . .
The flowers lost their color and their fragrance . . .
The buds never bloomed.
All those tiny animals you fed mourn with hollow cheeks . . .
And large, unbelieving eyes . . . sad, wondering, confused. . . .
There are no more rainbows in my world,
And the new day I must enter alone with the rains turning colder,
the winds growing stronger, that whistle cruelly between the branches
of the dark November air, laughing at me, for death had won.

   Chrissy VanderHeide

Waiting

I stand here with my hopes and dreams clutched in my hands,
Waiting.
I think the line has moved
—No, wait, that was just someone passing through,
And I go on waiting.
Finally we move ahead: Left, right, stop,
As fast as that; and again waiting.
Everyone looks around for help,
But we all stand waiting.
Our lives being wasted in a lineup to nowhere.
But still we stand waiting.
I can see the end now,
But I'm still waiting.
I'm next.
Finally, no more waiting.
And now I leave those I met in line,
And they are still waiting.

   Kurt Nordstokke

God Is the Master of Everything

Look at the fresh flowers blooming, see the bold eagle flying.
Let's feel the green fields we're strolling
And watch the sunshine gently shining.
Wave at the flying flocks of sea gulls, the hummingbirds sweetly singing,
The king and queen of paradise beneath the skies of silver clouds.

The happy day of our lives when we are younger, vibrant, stronger,
We never care of tomorrow, but only days of merriment.
We're on top of the music, while our world is on the rock,
We think of Thee, our Creator, if we're sick and things are tough.

We have so much to bear in life, walking along the rocky path.
We have so much hardship and pain, lots of sinning and transgressions,
Though how we tried to strive for life through many sorrows and afflictions,
But with our strength and faith to Thee, we can bear all the consequences.

There's always hope and survival, so struggle hard with our faith.
Let's face the world with tomorrow. God give strength in our life,
For everything, with the blessings, do give our due to God above.
So great thou Art and wonderful: He's the Master of everything!

   Maricon D. Chua

The Last Laugh

Behind all this concrete and bars,
There are some gents that think they're stars.
They feel they have a certain power
To strip you of your spirit by the hour.

But, believe me, they are wrong,
Because the freedom heart is strong.
They take your necklace and your ring;
In here they don't want you to have anything.

Then comes your release day:
They give you a bus ticket one way.
Then make some stupid crack
About how you will be back.

Well, our stars think they're real funny,
But they're only baby sitters making big money.
So, now I ask, is it the inmate that's the fool?
Because overpaid baby sitting took years of school.

Steve Playford

Writer's Block

Why can I not write?
Where have my ideas gone to?
Are they in the distance, out of sight?
I wonder what I'm going to do
At this moment, nothing inspires me
My mind must be on vacation
I've been locked in a room, I can't find the key
This feeling is truly not fun
I'm screaming my head off
I want to get out
But my throat's getting dry, I'm starting to cough
Because no one can hear my pout
I wish someone would help me here
It's this darkness I'm beginning to fear

Craig Ramm

Eternally Friends:

When you meet someone and there is a spark,
That flicker of light you see in the dark,
The conversation of course is very light,
Yet the future is all you have in sight.

As you talk, look in her eyes,
Her fragility you must analyze.
Decide if this woman can be easily hurt.
With a fragile heart you must not flirt.

A woman's heart is merely a token
Of things in life easily broken.
The box you now carry must always bear
Bold-printed words: "Handle with care."

What you do now must be for all the right reasons
As sure as each year has the changing of seasons.
Do not speed ahead like a runaway locomotive.
Each step you now take should have the right motive.

Never promise a thing you can't guarantee—
Eliminates potential hurt, you see.
Relationship are like a plant you must slowly nurture.
This is the only way to ensure the future.

Anthony Barr

The Wood Is Burning

The sun has set and stars are out
'Tis time to tell stories that are good
About the forest birds
And the woods

There's a chill in the air
And the wind is cold
So let's light a fire
But all my matches are old

One person has a lighter
So let's get his fire started
This family is wonderful
And so deeply hearted

We all sit by the fire and tell our stories
About an Indian who had no worries
This Indian was like the blue jay above
His family like robins, the colour of love

The fire is burning low
It's almost out of sight
So now we must all turn in
And say good night

Shannon Noel Doiron

Face Off

Living in a man's world
But dreaming the same dreams
We are both playing this game
Whether he likes it or not

Hard work and determination
Do not equal the same chance
While he gets ahead
She sits back and watches
But there is no disappointment
This is what's expected
It will only make her stronger

Until one day she gets a chance
By luck or from hard work, it doesn't matter
She steps up from the sidelines
And becomes a participant
She enters the sanctity of the all-boys club

Martina Rizzuto

A Heart with Many Colors

A heart with many colors
in a land so big and free,
where people still can have a dream,
a land for you and me. . . .
They come from far around the globe,
in hope for a life worth living.
Let's strive to live in harmony
and balance taking and giving.
Let's leave the hate and bitterness—
try warmth instead—and understand
that God created black and white
for us to go hand in hand.
The sun will shine for everyone;
after darkness, a day will follow.
Believe . . . and on the horizon you will see
a heart with many colors.

Maria Marten

Wishing Wells

Wishing wells,
Hopes and dreams,
It may be more than just a scheme.
Will they ever come true?
I hope they do.
In those clouds of smoke
That appear sometimes each day,
I must say
I still see that ray of light,
Even when the night
Falls and the stars shine bright all the more.
How I wish that door
Would open fast and quick,
Because I don't want to be sick
Before my dreams come true;
For example, like me loving you!

Bridget Jameus

The King and the Mermaid

A king made of oak and amber
Rules an island far from anywhere.

Perched on an angle,
Buried up to his hips in sand,
He gazes upon the sea amid shrieking gulls
And wind-bullied palms.

A mermaid visits him each day.
Today, she tells him laughingly
How a sailor called to her
From a passing freighter,
Begging for her hand in marriage.

She will leave as the sun surrenders to night.
She will not see the light
Swirl in his amber eyes
Or hear his oaken lips bend
To whisper her name.

Alexander Ary

Before Me

Somewhere, I have never lived with you,
your infant skin so soft and warm,
tiny hands and feet caressed,
given talent beyond imagining.

You first walked and talked without me,
twinkling eyes and smiles
bestowed on those who knew
of the greatness held within.

You grew and learned, and I
still living silently behind
the door of knowledge,
knew that you were out there, waiting.

Your voice deepened, muscles tensed, and you
raced forward, fast
toward winning, as fate
spilled gold along the path.

And I came to pick it up,
little by little, getting closer
to living within a soul
where I have never been.

Natasha Yaremczuk

Erotic, Symbiotic

The night unto the backyard lanes,
And I, awake with slumber's crawl,
Approach my state as feline,
Awaiting my lover's call.
It comes to me within the moonlight
While I, bosom pressed to the stars,
Take breath to life and ear to song,
And listen, silent, until it's gone.

With deathly life I run through the night-light lanes,
For my light is forged within their darkness,
And I will sing, again and again, my lover's song,
Until the blackened night once more moves on.

Joshua James Piche

Seasons

The fall wind blows the dry leaves off the trees
As I listen for the hum of the bees

I listen but nothing I hear
The cold winter is coming, the little birds fear

They start to fly toward the south
The babies have a little doubt

Can they make it before Jack Frost
Or will they be found cold and lost?

The spring rains begin to fall
The little children are playing ball

The sun is shining in the fields again
I listen and hear the roar of a plane

As I look toward the west
I see a robin in her nest

Another season has come and gone
As the winds blow in the wake of dawn

Trudy Lee Murakami

The Angel

I found an angel in the park,
he followed me home and we talked until dark.
He told me things that through the years,
men strived for the knowledge of laughter and tears.
He told me how the green grass grows,
why animals die, and why people wear clothes.
He opened my ears till I hungered for more,
and pleased with my greed, the knowledge he'd pour.
"Alas," came the morn' and the angel was gone,
and my ears rang with knowledge, but pain was my song.
For, I knew then of life and of power and wealth,
I knew of disease and of decaying health.
I knew of the struggles of souls to survive,
and of living each day just to find you're alive.
I knew of the torture of long ago men,
of suffering children, their parents, their kin.
I knew then of war and of hatred and of greed,
and all that I knew, how I wanted to plead
for my ignorant mind to be unknowing again,
as my ears rang with mankind's bitter, dead pain.
God, pity the man who walks in the park and seeks out
the angel that lurks in the dark!

Sharon Eberhardt

Slumber

I woke up so late!
When the dazzling sunshine pained my eyes
And shattered the rays of early morning hope,
I woke up to see life passed by, and I was too late.

When I was a child, I dreamt and dreamt.
When I opened my eyes it was too late.
Where were my mates—busy in their plays and splashes of laughter
I knew nothing of, I woke up so late.

When I stepped on the path of youth, I met him.
My heart leaped, I knew not why.
I felt a pang for him and waited—today, tomorrow, in eternity.
Time passed by.
When I looked around he was gone,
Hand-in-hand, with a vibrant, sparkling soul,
Spattering life as pearls falling from torn thread,
And I gazed on and found I woke up so late.

Now I am waiting for the doors of God to open.
But I know when doors open, there I will be,
Just in time to see the Gateman calling to me,
"You are in time, we welcome thee."

Tapati Neogi

My Permanent Midnight Hour

Pure blackness wrapped in a silk cloth,
comfort becomes my best friend, whichever way I move.
Soothing souls tied in satin ribbon slither from ear to ear,
sending me secret messages forgotten from my conscious life.
I can see the beautiful music and smell the color blue.
My scenes are at one and share their worldly knowledge.
Evil tries to scratch at my window, but his arms are not long enough.
His painful screams try to intrude and interrupt the soft whispers
of hope . . . and succeed.
I fall from my place of slumber and awaken to the murderous scream
of an innocent young girl, and the crazed laugh of a madman.
I then returned to my secure silk cloth
and began to forever exist in my permanent midnight hour.

Candace Popplestone

Alzheimer's Answer

Why do I love a dear lady, who lives on jam, toast, and tea,
Who gives most things a new name? A mystery even to me.
The reason I don't understand is because of the things she will do.
I ask her to wear her boots walking, she answers—her slippers will do.
She's zipped up in the front instead of the back,
doesn't think it matters to switch.
Sometimes she calls me somebody else,
she doesn't know who is which.
I'm embarrassed! She talks to the pictures,
says, "Dorfy's not coming to sing."
I find myself making excuses to pictures that don't hear a thing.
I have to start three days early to suggest a shampoo and set.
It's hard for her to remember, much easier just to forget.
She has an abundance of beauty, a god-given gift that she shares.
It glows on her face when she's dancing,
sings in her voice through her prayers.
It shines in her eyes when she's happy;
she's happy the most of the time.
Another great gift is her graciousness, this lady is nothing but kind.
Never a harsh word to anyone, never an unkind thought,
Sometimes a bit mischievous, if she thinks she might not be caught.
In her long pink nightie she's an angel, her hair is her halo of white.
She'll giggle a bit and put up her lips for a kiss and a loving good night.
Why do I love this lady? The answer appears from above.
God planned we should be together, our greatest need is love.

Dorothy Hoskin

As You Are

Shine on me the light that is your smile,
The rays of which combat a gloomy day.
Let my spirit bathe in its warmth for a while,
Or in excess, let me forever stay.

Grant me the boon that is your voice,
The gift of hearing your thoughts put to sound,
The chance to be surrounded by your words of choice,
To know your will set to the tone you have found.

Impress upon me the language that is your movement's text.
Thus communicating in subtle gestures of formidable beauty,
While I casually wait to behold what actions you perform next,
Such passionate emotions of independence,
    freedom untainted by idle thoughts of duty.

Grace me with the air of your presence filled with joyous peace,
Just to be in sync with the pure essence deep within your soul.
In hope of a feeling of security in a childlike knowing of another
    that would never cease.
Giving all for the unspoken promise of a delicate, eternal moment,
A memory to be revisited and made priceless
    by its undiluted imperfections . . . its perfect whole.

Rouén Deryl Ewart Robinson

Planet Earth

About four billion years ago, a planet formed in this galaxy;
Earthquakes shook the troubled Earth with great extremity.
Volcanoes exhaled their fiery breath; red hot lava boomed its wrath;
Destroying fauna and flora as it forged its deadly path.
Raging tempests and hurricanes rode the seas with mighty force;
They beat the bulge of rocky shore, charging their destructive course.
Dinosaurs of huge size walked the Earth, causing it to tremble;
Microscopic species shook in their small world
    you could fit inside a thimble.
Tremendous changes developed in the land as evolution proceeded;
Solid plates of shale and granite pulled apart as continents receded.
Rock and earth split apart, great mountains rose to enormous height;
Competing ferocious creatures fought great battles with all their might.
Frightening balls of fire appeared in the evening constellation;
Colossal meteors and comets hit the Earth, creating devastation.
Huge tar pits swallowed creatures great and small around the planet;
Their skeletal remains are all that's left in limestone, tar, and granite.
Now billions of years have passed since the dawning of her birth;
Some have named her terra nova, while others call her Planet Earth.

Brenda E. Denomy

Darkest Nights

She sits alone in the darkest nights; by the window she did cry.
She remembers all the love they shared, and how it came to die.

It happened not too long ago when she felt happy and free.
Her mind did wander to those happy days and forever did want it to be.

She once was young and beautiful, and proud to be his girl,
And contented to be in love and free with not a care in the world.

She remembers his soft knock at the door, his footsteps softly heard.
Now those footsteps she'll hear no more, his voice whispers not a word.

She loved to hear his "I love you" and "how are you, dear, tonight?"
But all she now hears is the cold wind
Whisper in the dark and lonely nights.

She remembers the wonderful evenings sitting by the firelight
But now she sits alone once more in the dreadful, darkest nights.

Her mind is back to present now in the land of misery,
For the wonderful love she once shared, could not forever come to be.

She sits alone in the darkest nights; by the window she did cry.
For, she remembers all these little things, and how they came to die.

Linda Brousseau

Fog

Obscuring fog
Seeps softly and unstoppable,
Pouring forth from other worlds.
Twisted shapes loom,
Sounds distorted through mists of time.
Swirling isolation creates
Beauty from ugliness,
Calmness from noise,
Life from despair.
Lost in enveloping fog,
Eternity exists.

Forgetting worries to sob tears
Into a damp cushion of gray,
An adventure into
The silent depths of the soul.
Fog wrenches, an aching desire,
An end to noise, confusion, chaos.
Escaping into a clammy mist is not satisfying,
But an escape nonetheless:
A moment that burns away in life's searing spotlight.

Greg Duncan

Lost in a Storm

Lost in a storm, which way do I fly?
Do I go with the wind,
Or let the current take me by?
The wind's heading west,
But that's not how I feel.
Against the current is what is real.
With peace and comfort,
I hope to arrive to my destination,
Only hoping to survive.
Life is so precious,
So few days do we see.
Make the best of it all,
For today may be the end of what might be.
What do you want?
Do you act how you feel?
Nothing really matters
But the things that are real.
Love is the answer,
No matter what might be,
Through the days of our lives and for all eternity.

Jerry Filip

Who Am I?

Another routine day begins.
Senses are sharpened in the crisp morning breeze.
Children crowd through beckoning doors,
Hearing the laughter of carefree children.
Overlooking car tops above the engine's throb.
Opening the door for eager passengers,
Looking ahead, eagle-eyeing every direction,
Believing that I can make a difference.
Understanding people and traffic patterns,
Striving for excellence at every turn,
Drives me on.
Responsible actions produce fulfillment
In learning
Valuable lessons, a part of each day.
Enjoying the surge of power beneath my feet,
Reflections in the life of a school bus driver.

Helen Ruth Nerbas

Forever . . . Forgotten

I am the love child
the one who is born to an already-married man
and already-married woman

I am the unspoken
the unseen
I was never really born

I had nothing as a child
not enough love
for it was only one night's love

I had no dreams or goals
I was never really here
I had clothes and toys
that kept me silent

I had no feelings
I needed nobody to love me
The one night's love was enough

Wait . . . my parents were never married
the ever-forgotten night
the ever-forgotten child

Sherrie Lee Hillman

No Such Thing as Childhood

Thanks for the beatings,
thanks for the fears.

Thanks for the words
that broke me to tears.

Thanks for the weekends:
You filled them with screaming.

You took away life,
you took away dreaming.

Thanks to your bottle
and sick little mind,

it was myself
I just could not find.

Thanks for my hopes you shattered like glass.
All I can do is hope it will pass.

Diseases, pain, death, and despair:
All of these things are most unfair.
But, something much worse, in my own eyes
is someone who kills me while baking me pies.

Philip J. Martin

Dad

Dad, I loved you when you were here,
I love you now you're not.
I wish that I could see you,
but I know that I cannot.
I want to tell you I love you,
I want to tell you face to face.
I want to have a father
and not an empty space.

Candice Jarrad

His Final Journey

He left alone . . .
he who loved to share everything.
He left in silence . . .
he who loved the sounds of
music, children playing, and
spoken thoughts.
He flew away to eternity . . .
he who never enjoyed long journeys.
He left behind . . .
his memories
of favorite places and
quiet times . . . his sorrows and joys . . .
his love of us . . . his children
and life companion.
I did not see him leave . . .
but I felt his farewell
float softly in the air.
I caught it in my heart
and his memories live there now.

He is forever "My beloved Daddy."

Phyllis Emery Skeats

Journalist's Journal

If I were a newspaper writer,
I'd titillate the nation
With interesting anecdotes and stories
Filled with original quotations.

I'd write about crooked politicians,
Filling my columns with facts
Commenting on our inept bureaucracy
That robs us with its tax.

I'd write about the rich and their luxurious life,
And the poor's miserable plight,
Writing about everything gone wrong,
Offering ways to make it right.

I'd write about wars and battles lost,
Speaking of love and hate.
I'd comment on times gone by,
And our planet's eventual fate.

But I'm not a newspaper writer,
And my writing isn't good,
But when I look at the world as it is
I sometimes think I should.

Harry Martin

Misguided Trust

When I close my eyes,
I can see his face,
And no matter how hard I try
The vision will not go away.

His soft voice and his gentle touch
Made me believe in him way too much.

Oh, my God! How stupid could I be
To believe in him the way
I expected him to believe in me?

He took my life
And all that went with it:
My pride and my soul.
It just wasn't worth it.

Catherine Henderson Geimer

On a Wing and a Prayer

Just think of me, and I'll be there,
if only on a wing and a prayer.
I have you with all my heart,
I'll have you know from the very start.

When you're lying there at night alone,
and your thoughts are drifting back to home.
Just think of me and I'll be there,
if only on a wing and a prayer.

When your heart is heavy and full of sorrow,
remember babe, there is hope in tomorrow.
Just think of me and I'll be there,
if only on a wing and a prayer.

Our love is strong and can't be touched,
no matter who tries, how hard, or how much
Just think of me and I'll be there,
if only on a wing and a prayer.

Just as the sun above has to shine.
My heart flutters each time your lips touch mine
So, just think of me and I'll be there
if only on a wing and a prayer.

Bobbi Sue Lucier

Sands of Time

I feel you haunt me from within,
Like a candle burning at two ends.
It is an eternal flame
Sheltered safely from the shadowed winds.
I feel the dunes against my skin,
As if pouring through the hourglass
That lingers all around my body.
I have no idea where I've been,
And fewer lead me to where I'm going,
But time persists on rowing forward.
So I weave the weathered moments
With the wilted weeds that I must keep on sewing,
For I feel they are forever growing.

Celeste Goodhope

My First Love

I saw you in the distance and I fell in love.
You saw me, smiled, and walked to me.
You held me closer in your arms and protected me.
We were so young. Our love was so pure.
Our love was so strong.
We promised that our love would last for eternity.
You were my first love; I fell in love.

I was so young. I was so full.
I must have been dreaming what was so pure,
What was so strong. Our love that will last for eternity.
We fall apart. I am lonely sitting in the dark
Without protection from you.
In tears I drown, dreaming of you.
You were my first love; I fell in love.

I have my freedom, nowhere to go.
I am like a dust before the wind, feeling empty inside.
You are the reason I need you. I want you.
If I hurt you, I'm sorry; forgive me.
In tears I drown, dreaming of you.
You were my first love; I fell in love.

Anne Meditskos

The Duel of Love

I summoned myself into a war,
A war that is beyond my knowledge and control.
I had witnessed your madness and fierce fight on the battlefield.
I wasn't frightened—instead, determined to take on my Revenge!
And so I challenged you in a duel

Long before I stood proud and Victory is my name,
Until you showed yourself among the foes,
The atmosphere changed, Heaven on Earth!
Autumn fall, spring is born,

But though I kept it hidden in the largest chamber of my soul,
Hardly it is cowardice to admit,
But it is stronger than my strength; wilder than my youth.
Your presence traps me in my own fears,
Prisoner of my own insecurity.
Indeed, I can't make out the fact to love an enemy.

The duel was fierce and it turned to be between me and my being,
And I lost in my own duel; having no weapon but heart and soul,
So, then, my severe defeat is your utmost glory in the duel of hearts.
For so long I believed that my life is my own,
But fate had come to take me to be your own.

Janice Javier Foronda

People

The sun and the moon are visible to all.
But when we see them, what do we see?
From where we are, from when we are, they can look small;
But we have been taught that they are not as small as they seem to be.

The sun gives off heat while the moon coldly glows.
The moon reflects the sun's light; it may not create its own.
The sun warms the Earth, helps us reap what we sow.
The moon does not do this, but if it can, it is unknown.

So, if we have to choose one, which one will be chosen?
Which one is more necessary? Is the answer within our sight?
Without the sun, we will become frozen.
Without the moon, the night will have no light.

I think we need both equally,
And maybe we should focus less on the sun and more on the moon.
With the new attention, the moon may become confident and we might see,
If we look hard enough, it can actually give its own light, the moon.

Shalini Sankar

Red River Flood of '97: Lost Everything, But Gained Something

It was a year of great distress for those along the Red.
They watched the waters rising high; their hearts were filled with dread.

The river overflowed its banks, creating many fears.
It flowed for many miles on end, not seen for eighty years.

Bags and bags were filled with sand, ring dikes were made of mud.
The people worked for weeks on end to stem the raging flood.

The whole country rallied 'round; ten thousand troops were sent.
With army tanks and navy boats, into the flood they went.

Saving lives at every turn, no job too big or small,
Even their kindly words of comfort were said to one and all.

And strangers by the hundreds came, no one had to ask.
The whole community rallied 'round, no matter what the task.

With weary souls, the people watched and saw that all was lost.
Their efforts failed, nothing left, you couldn't count the cost.

Only one thing did come through this disaster of the years.
The love and care shown by all will calm our future fears.

Judy Kaczmarz

The Bride

One day, some years ago, as the sun shone bright
and spring was in the air,
a girl-child made her entrance into this world.
Many years of life have now passed.
There were cries in the night and childhood diseases
with which to cope,
scraped knees and cut fingers,
trips to Sunday school with shiny new shoes,
visits from Santa Claus and the Easter Bunny,
that first day of school—good report cards, none were ever bad.
In the twinkling of an eye, it seemed, high school was finished,
and the first day of university was upon her.
A van filled with luggage and a heart full of dreams,
this too was over very soon, then different jobs in different places.
Now a young man enters the scene,
and it seems a new family will be formed.
The childhood today is over and must be left behind,
but the memories fill our hearts with joy,
even as new ones are being made.

Audrey Epp

The Mighty Hunter

Who stands strong and silent in the bush, waiting for his prey?
He's up at dawn, with loads of clothes on to sit and wait all day.
Finally he sees it, that magnificent animal is not very far away.
He aims, he shoots, he misses. It's like wishing on a star.
Next time, says he, next time, I won't get that old buck fever.
I will take my time, get less excited and pull that little lever.
And, oh, he waits with patience,
Oh, none like he'd ever have at home.
But, oh, the hunt! The Thrill, the roam
Keeps him out there, sometimes all alone.
He is "The Hunter," the brave, the strong,
Putting up with the elements all day long
To seek his prey and to achieve it,
To take it home and to never leave it.
He is "The Hunter," the provider of all,
And proud he stands, nice and tall.
The conqueror, the mighty, and the just,
Hunting, for him, is simply a must.
There might be often some tall tales told,
But hunting can never be boring, I'm told.
And when all's said and done, and the prey is got . . .
That mighty hunter will have always one more shot.

Robyne S. Corfield

Prisoner of Pain

She sits all alone in the darkness
and fights her constant war
while she thinks of the one she lost long ago;
he's all that matters anymore.

The pain of what she experienced
stays with her and haunts her every day
while she lives with the guilt and the love she has
for the son that she gave away.

She blamed everyone else in her life
for the decision that was made
and stood by and watched helplessly
as her life began to fade.

She was taken prisoner by her pain
and felt that no one understood,
so she put her trust of the uncertain hands
of the only thing that would.

It promised to soothe her broken heart
and to help make the time pass,
but it made her lose sight of the person within
while she watched life happen through the bottom of her empty glass.

Merri-Lee Culbert-Slute

Untitled

Soldier Boy, when the light of the truth
Scatters the clouds of sin,
You will see the rule of gold go out,
And the golden rule come in.

Farther and farther from God and His laws
Blindly we've stumbled along,
Thinking that money would meet all our needs.
How stupid we've been, how wrong!

But we're going to learn, through hardship and woe,
That God would be better than gold:
Better to trust in, better to love,
Better to have and to hold.

Selfishness, jealousy, and sin must go,
Scourged by the chastening rod,
Leaving a world of absolute peace,
For that was the plan of God.

Long have we prayed thy kingdom come.
We will welcome our Lord with joy.
And then, dear heart, you will gladly forget
You were ever a soldier boy.

Marion Berdan

Watching the Birds

From my backyard by the lake, there's a great view
Of Robins and Blue jays and Doves, to name a few.

In Spring they find a spot to nest.
In Fall they stop to take a rest.

A Barn Swallow nests on my back porch light.
Blue Heron and Sea Gulls are constantly in flight.

The Killdeer hides its nest in the brush.
The treetops are dotted with melodious thrush.

Summertime is full of chatter.
Mama birds are getting fatter.

Bird-sitting is a chore; while one mate guards the nest
The other forages for food, never seeming to rest.

By the end of the Summer, the fledglings learn to fly.
I watch as they dip and dive and soar through the sky.

Oh my, where has the summer gone?
The nests are empty the birds moving on.

Honking of the ducks and Canada geese signal good-bye.
As they pass overhead, what a glorious sight in the sky.

I watch the birds from Spring to Fall,
Thankful for the beauty of it all.

Christina Mae Foster

Afternoon Tea with Poetry

Brew a generous pot of your favourite tea,
Fill a porcelain plate with pastries,
Add a friend or two or three,
And last, a book of poetry.

A lady who likes to read for friends
Would ensure the party a pleasure
For those who prefer to listen and transcend
The everyday for a treasure.

Helen Page

Hands of Grace

In the vale between the peaks
Of two eternities
I stand
Your hand in mine
To view the shattered wreckage
Of what I once held sacred
And to pluck the shards
From that which I can salvage

Moving on
Along the stream of time
Across the stepping stones
Of night and days
Your hand in mine
I find by grace
This world
A much less hostile place

Derek Robinette

New Moon

A village by night,
New moon in the sky,
Mother and child
Spoilt by the angel's eye,
Old people, locks of hair,
Telling their stories, moist eyes.
The fire is burning,
My mother beside it,
Tears on the cheeks—
Me—next to her.
Waves of sadness come and go
Over my mom's soul,
Pure and secret,
Always sad. . . .
Why so many tears? Why?
Unless you suffer, tears won't be shed.
Might it be a sin?
Tears, like raindrops
Hit the stars out of wickedness,
Loneliness, cold rain, fear.

Sonia Cristina Coman

Lost

Surrounding my troubled mind
Are haunting thoughts I will think no more.
This forsaking world needs a light.
A light I seek,
But to my surprise, it doesn't hold,
So I continue to look farther
Into the dark for my light.
Until then, I don't exist:
Only a body with a wondering mind,
A body that will remain buried
By words of people
Who think they know my light.
But how do they
If I don't?

Shelly Knight

Is This Love or What? No, Life

In between this silence
there's freedom.

Sometimes trust is best
left unsaid.

Respect is a form of
gratitude.

Exception allows grace of
full range.

Although our love could be
like a rose,

beautiful when it's in
lavish bloom,

highly scented but can't
last forever,

can't it be protected even
through death?

Where there is a will, there
is a way.

Live on. . . .

Dawn Spellman

Once

For countless sunken lacunae
Of deep and nightly hours I hoped
They were with me for a while
To talk with them once
Only carefully asking
What they do think of it
About it all
The angels

Albert J. Vos

Must One Become an Image?

Must one become an image
    to become true?
Tell it me not, I beg you!
Let me walk out in ignorance,
Be content to live,
Have my own faith,
And believe
In you.

Ayman Mehssen

To Fall in Love

To fall in love—in one madness,
To fall in love—in one happiness,
To fall in love—in one feeling,
all passions.

To stick together—in one abyss,
To stick together—in one power,
To stick together—so that later
the Earth won't bear one without the other.

Jane

Animals

Animals are Mother Nature's babies.
She tries to protect them from sickness and rabies.
But if she can't, it's up to you
To take care of her babies.
And if you do, Mother Nature will love you, too.
Some of her babies have to go
Because some pass away—others get shot with bows.
I know it's sad when a pet has to go;
I've had it happen to me, so I know.
It hurts in the heart and you start to cry,
Because it hurts when a cute animal dies.
Like a cat or a dog or a mouse outside,
It hurts to stay on its funeral night.
It is a very, very, terrible sight.
So if you ever see a man, woman, or poacher
Trying to kill an animal with a bow,
Run right over—step and stomp
On his very, very, very, very, big toe.

Amanda Tracey

Mountain High

A mist rolls over the mountains high,
Like a breath expelled in the frosty morning air.
Fresh as the dawn of mystic beauty,
Behold the jewel as daybreak begins.

Down in the valleys, far, far below,
A crystal stream rushes over rocks.
A babbling sound it makes, as it rushes along
A journey so long . . . destination: the sea.

And so it is, day after day, year after year,
The mountains remain.
Summer, winter, seasons of change,
Thousands of years aged, remain forever,
Pristine and untouched.

David J. Piotrowski

Just a Peanut

Just a peanut—a little old peanut
Of the pea and pulse family
"Goober and "Earthnut" are its common names
But its many uses amaze me

The peanut plant—angular and hairy
Its growth enriches the soil
It is also prized as forage
And used as cooking oil

Whether eaten raw or in candies
The facts indeed reveal
Peanuts are nutritious—even for livestock
Crushed peanuts provide a meal

Twelve different dyes and besides
Some perfumes, cardboard and powder
All are by-products, as is penicillin
Thanks to George Washington Carver

Just a peanut—a little old peanut
But it's significant to see
That if God can so use just a little old peanut
What can He do with me?

Vincent Thompson

Why, Mommy?

Why, Mommy, when I was so small and helpless and spilled things,
did you look at me with your lovely eyes, so calm and still, and say:
"It's all right, dear, we'll fix everything right away"?

Why, Mommy, when we were at the beach and someone stole
my toy, did you take me in your arms and say: "Maybe he's poor
and lonely and without the love you have. You can pick a new toy"?

Why, Mommy, when the girl next door moved away forever,
did you put your arm around me and say: "There'll be another
Rebecca someday, my dear, and you'll love her just as much"?

Why, Mommy, when I went far away to school, did you sense
the loneliness and emptiness I was feeling every day, 'til I found love
in a pair of blue eyes as deep and dark as Rebecca's?

Why, Mommy, did your eyes for days on end fill with lonely tears,
when Daddy was not here to run along the beach and laugh with us?

Why, Mommy, when I finally found my Rebecca and married her,
did your tears seem to fade and the smile return to your face?

Why, Mommy, do you lie now, after many years of love and laughter,
so quiet and so still? The life in your eyes is gone. Yet, I can still feel
your love, Mommy, and I still love you so, though you are gone.

    Lawrie Manson

Can You?

Can you see the beauty of the world from my eyes?
Can you step into my soul and see how much
I appreciate being alive?
Can you understand why I do not fear death?
I only fear dying without knowing I was alive.
Can you hear the music in the air
and the beating hearts of the trees
that accompany you on your walk home?
Can you feel the passion in my heart
for the very joy of living?
Can you appreciate the freedom I enjoy,
not because I am free, but because my heart believes it so?
Can you touch my mind and realize that I bear you no harm
nor wish pain to anyone in the world?
I only feel the pain of the world.
But, yes, the world is still beautiful.
For, I appreciate the world. Can you?

    Gene Yeo

Sunrise

Father God, the dawn is breaking through;
The morning's come and with it comes the light.
The sky has taken on a rosy hue, in celebration of the end of night.
The sounds of morning fill my listening ear.
The birds cry out aloud to one another,
Joyously declaring, "Daybreak's here, come and worship God my feathered brother!"

The dogs are barking in the quiet street as if to say,
"We've waited long enough
To see the darkness vanish in defeat!
The sun will soon arise and call night's bluff!"
The shepherds shout as vocally they scold somnolent cows
And seek the mournful bleat
From some poor sheep that's wandered from the fold
In search of something different to eat.

The world seems sluggish as it slowly wakes
and rubs away the sand from heavy eyes
As, gradually, its slumber it forsakes, to stretch itself then finally arise.
My God, this parable for me.
For, like the world, I've also been asleep.

    Jim Strickland

Waterslide Trip

Valves in the channel-waters of the soul open,
enhance flow from the source
no one knows where is.
Splashing neuron-waves wash the walls of the thought-channel in acid,
bubbles at the bottom
where the slick, slippery eel-monsters lie,
dwelling on sewage.
At the surface, the sun blinks in reflection
of distorted twistings of the world,
water toward the sea, like thought-stream
to new sources,
earth, mind, water, moon and sun,
round and round and round
to nowhere.
I am on a waterslide trip,
'cause the trip is on me.
Everything shouts a rip-roaring:
Full speed ahead!
The ocean awaits the arrival.

> *Christer Dehlin*

The Carnation

A red carnation, wilted and dried, buried beneath
a barren snow-covered field.
A distance away, a young boy sighed wishing to end his whole tragic ordeal.

Pondering over the lavishly lived days, the theater,
expensive cuisine, his costly attire. In the cold snow, shivering he lies
caught up in his own fantasy-filled mire

Glancing back at the buried flower, dead, defeated, its glory past,
Void of its appealing and mighty power, realizing his fantasy
was doomed never to last.

An approaching train confirms his resolution, he stands, teeth chattering,
lips drawn in a frightened smile
He has realized at once his eternal solution: never again will reality
his fantasy realm ever defile.

Jumping in the path of reality materialized, he's struck, far and fast,
his fantasy-making mechanism crushed.
The folly of his haste he has realized, the vastness of what was left
undone, his death suddenly too rushed.

And so fantasy confronts reality. In a mercilessly unfair battle,
Fantasy becoming the unquestionable casualty,
Thrust back into the immense design of things with an immeasurable shatter.

> *Mike Fotiou*

Distance

Do I need reason to prove why our passion should remain unstained?
I mean, I miss the those looks that you give me,
and the gap between us widens
when I can't touch your face.
And it's hard to understand everything
when I can't read the language of your motions.
Yes, I do miss your body
because it is the cage of the soul I fell in love with.
And even though I hear life in your voice,
it gets lost in the transition, before I lock it up.
And it is harder still, as I search for words to describe this,
the tragically beautiful.
My voice is weak, but my argument strong.
I fear that in the growth of your soul
you won't want your roots in my garden
because you will want more space than I can offer.
And I fear more, that because of my unconditional love for you,
I would fight myself to steal from her what you need.

> *Poppy Wilkinson*

A Perfect Love Story

Our puppy-sweet love was freshly born
I knew not where and how to look for you
You and I went into a dream adorned
No nearby love could ever touch our view

One time we thought we met anew that day
We shut our heart, felt undecided
To go into freedom we shared one way
Like a free boat, we stayed separated

At our meeting, love came right up the throne,
The love that we unconsciously longed for,
It has become one lifetime love along

Our great love story thus has been built
For a very long time to forever last
In the sunset that every day goes past . . .

Alphonse Lefur

Midnight and Violins

Midnight and violins
Moonlight and the thumping of my heart
A wisp of perfume on a cool wind
This, my dear, is how it all starts

Whirlwinds and rainbows
Dreams fulfilled with you as my wife
A day of bliss that never goes
And this is how we sail through life

A sunny day and a warm breeze
Remind me of all the love you gave
Beating my heart faster and weakening my knees
As I fall beside your flowered grave

My silent screams disturb the wind
Mixed with midnight and violins

Walter Pierce

Water Your Roots

When you begin to take your first steps
Calculated risks
Slips occur

Sometimes first few flowers
Wither with gestational pain
The scorching weeds overpower the mulch
And the innocent space

Keep the seasoned seed close to your heart
And soak it with blood
Look at the infinite beauty of the divine sprout
Plant it with care in the early morning
When the love is red and sky crimson

Water your roots
For, you have the tree
That gives shade to the imprudent
And nest to the sentient
In time those who will eat the fruits
Will have the wisdom

Bhaswat Chakraborty

You, My Dove

You are the sparkling in the night,
You are the Heaven's door,
Of all the things someone could love,
You are the one I love much more.

You are the bird flying above,
You are the golden fish in the sea,
You are the gracious fawn in the run,
Everything yours means much to me.

You are the heat that comes from the sun,
You are the freshest mountain's air,
You make the flowers be what they are,
Stuck among golden threads of your hair.

You are most precious golden bar,
You are the harp's sweetest tune,
You have that great seductive charm
That infected my heart not being immune.

You are the healing to any harm,
You are the love-sick's only cure,
You are the reason I'm feeling well,
A day of you absence I couldn't endure.

Zoran Stojkovski

Impervious

We spent the day
Cruising through daydreams
All plans of tomorrow
Whisper-kissed over our lips
We dined on our senses
Drunk on sunset in Venice
Water lapping at our gondola was
More pure, more true to the human soul
Than ever Mozart or Beethoven
We sat in a crowded cafe
Impervious to all others
Sipping muddy sweetness
From cups of gold and broken glass
Our souls were alive
Like Mardi Gras midnight
We were never so alive
We lived late
And slept later
Dreaming of tomorrow
In shades of caramel

Shannon Watts

Pottery

On a wheel, a dimly moving circle
turns a sculpture of my mind.
Around and around it takes a shape,
an earthen bowl aligned.

Who can say what graces play
to form that work of art?
A woman's kiss, a proud man's fist:
each will take a part.

The clay may break before its time
revealing the empty core,
or, with care and senses aware,
it may last forevermore.

Kevin Stenson

Children

They laugh, they sing;
they dance and play;
they're scowled at many times a day.
They learn to walk;
they learn to talk;
they learn a lot from Mom and Dad.
They go to school;
they grow up strong;
they're twenty-five and now they're gone.
They've gone to start a new family.
They've got their children . . .
. . . daughter and son.
It's their turn now to be Dad and Mom!

Rebecca Reid

Navy

Snapshots
And shavings of
Memories to boot,
But they won't ease up,
Washing me blue.
Hook, line, and sinker,
All the way
To the floor:
Pick me up gently;
Let's tango once more.
Too much left dangling,
Not to mention un-kept,
Won't ransom you back;
Just want some respect.
Memories too sharp and
Piercing this way,
So I sing the blues of a
Navy shade.

Jill C. Manning

The Puppet Tree

I think that I should like to see
A great big, giant puppet tree
With puppets growing, large and small
To watch them come down in the fall.
Some puppets could be bears or kings,
Some could be ladies wearing golden rings.
There should be some finger puppets too,
In bright yellow, red, and even blue
On this great big, giant puppet tree
That's growing there for only me.

Sarah Remple Klassen

Little Apple

Hanging on a tree,
I can see far and wide,
all of my friends fall,
and roll,
and hide.
But when the autumn comes,
I must leave the tree,
I fall or get picked,
What will they do with me?

Joey Hoyda

Dear God

(In Memory of My Son, Josh, 1995–1997)

I still don't understand and it will take a lot of time.
This miracle that you gave to me is now a picture in my mind.
He left my arms not so long ago, now emptiness fills that space.
There's nothing in this whole wide world
that can ever take his place.
Take care of him and love him; he's a special little boy.
He's full of love and happiness; he'll bring you lots of joy.
He's a miracle and a treasure; he meant everything to me.
Watch over him, protect him just the way it was with me.
Take him to his grandpa, so he won't be alone.
They never really knew each other 'cause Grandpa had to go.
This is the hardest day of my life, dear Josh,
but one thing that is true
Is knowing that I loved you, and you loved me too.
Good-bye for now, we'll meet again in that special place above.
Then you can come back to me safe in the arms of LOVE.

Murray Steinbach

The Man We Called Daddy

When we call your name, and you're not there
To tell us you love us or if you even care
The promises you broke always left us crying
Now the promises are dead, and there is no use in trying

We just want you to look into our eyes
Gaze deeply into them
And tell us you apologize

For all the years you left us sitting on the stairs
Thinking to ourselves for us he no longer cares
We want you to picture us as children once again
Sit on the steps filled with nothing but pain

Now we want to tell you something
Because now we are old enough to understand
That the man we called Daddy
Let us slip right through his hand

Dale Erhardt

Islands of Dreams

The Caribbean to me is a wonderful place
To go and see—it's never too late.
The parrots and birds, in all their glory,
Make me take my pen to write this story.

When you walk along its golden sands,
You can always see what's in demand.
Turtles swimming along the way,
There always seems more, any time of day.

But when you go fishing, there is lots to do;
You could fish for an hour and take home with you
Snappers, tuna, king fish—any size
And even some of the smaller fry.

Now it would come the time, about six at night,
For you to sit down to dinner. What a delight!
Breadfruit, plantain, chicken, and rice:
You could ask for nothing better and so nice.

So where is this place I am talking about?
It must be in the Caribbean, without a doubt,
That I wrote this poem is quite, quite true.
Yes! It is in the "Cayman Brac" and it belongs to you.

G. E. Smith

Damon Phoenix

I miss his metallic scent of ocean depths and cool waves,
the smell of sour love.
Memories of him drift with me as I alone drift through fog.
The phoenix that he is soars above me in the painful red
flame that forms the sky, only to whisper: "I would die for you."

And so I look up, trying to reach him, getting closer, yet not close enough,
for he is far too high up above for me to ever touch him again.
And then he is gone, wrapped up in thick red velvet.

But I miss him . . . yet I no longer see him.
I no longer see the way he would strut easy under shallow moons,
the way his voice sent slivers with words unheard through my ears,
the way his kisses burned my flesh.

But he is no longer dark . . . I see that now:
With his vampire smile and black-knotted hair
and blazing brown eyes that tell stories of erotic delirium . . .
He, my Damon Phoenix, my Dark Angel,
with his clenched fists and shiny clothes . . .
He, who knew me and feared me, for I alone burned in his veins
like the purest drug he had ever known . . .

He, who breathes my life away, yet writes a million words.
         Julianna Angelova

Night of Kings

The snow falls softly to the ground, lit only by the moon
The silence, all but deafening, is broken all too soon
Winged snow angels now appear, as the children each make
His or her own masterpiece, by shifting each new flake
The children cry out happily with the joy that Christmas brings
It brings us back to yesteryear, and the journey of three kings
Following their guiding light, leading westward on
A trek inspired long ago . . . past, but never gone
The snow shines even brighter now, and I shift my gaze up skyward
A lone star sparkles brilliantly, and beneath it flies a bird
I cannot help but muse aloud and in my heart, I sing
For, on this night, under this star, each man is a king
         Peter Malcolm MacInnes

Voices at Mingary Castle

Margaret Riddell MacDougall, I want to get to know you.
I feel you with me as I circle the grey stone ruin
of the curtained wall castle where you were born
nearly two hundred years ago, in the remote Highlands.

I can almost see you running through the tall grasses,
laughing as you toss pebbles into the roaring sea.
You must have been frightened, the youngest of ten children,
when your family sailed off on a long voyage, cramped and rough.

Leaving behind the barren green mountains
and vast, open skies where you can see forever,
sailing into Pictou harbour
where the dark forest grows down to meet the sea.

Reading family letters and touching the cold, damp castle wall,
I am getting closer to you now, Margaret Riddell MacDougall.
Your parents struggled to clear the land and harvest crops,
longing for Scotland and never really feeling Canada was home.

Eventually you married a sea captain and had a family of your own.
Your daughter Sarah had a son Charles
who had a son Roger, who had a daughter Kathleen
who is standing at the edge of the sea, looking up at Mingary Castle.
         Kathleen Myers Krogh

Internal Tears

As I sit in class staring out the window, my mind flashes back to
memories of the saddest kind. Pain strikes through my body, but my
eyes do not redden, tears do not fall, for I have learned to accept
the sadness as it comes,

But underneath this thick skin of mine, my soul screams with the
horrid pain, my heart tears itself from within, and my whole body,
heart, mind, and soul cries hysterically with the sorrow, but nobody
can see, for I sit in class, looking out the window.

Then, in come the flashbacks, as if the calvary men afoot, coming
in to "take care" of the battle remains, my body screeches with terror,
I try to run, but everywhere, in every direction, all I see are the
haunting flashbacks. I drop to my knees, tears streaming down my
face, and plead for mercy, but I am shown none. The flashbacks
grow worse and even more painful.
I get up and run away from my pain,

But if follows at my heels. The wind is whipping through my hair
and tearing at my face. Suddenly, I trip and fall in the darkness of
sorrow, silence pounding in my ears, and I am left alone on the hard,
wet ground, crying and crying and crying, yet nobody can see,
because I sit in class, calmly staring out the window.

   Kate Miller

The Hope of a Better World

Science and democracy
Inspire us nearly over a century.
The hope of prosperity and harmony,
Clear conscience deeply embraces the testimony.
Evil spirit distorts them into hypocrisy.
Ruffian without knowledge puts laurel on his head as profound scholar,
Persecutes honest scientists to show his "brilliancy."
Bureaucracy monopolizes folks' right.
Struggle for truth through failure, frustration, and win finally.
"Not even a sparrow falls without God's eyes on it."
Just as the Chinese proverb says:
Good will be rewarded with good, and evil with evil.
Once the time is up, all will become reality.

   Prof. Fan Jiashen

My Darling

My darling I'm sorry for pushing you away.
I need you more and more each and everyday.
When I see you all I want to say is hey!
I love you, I need you here to stay.
Please! Please! Don't pull away.
We can work it out someway.
It will take time and we don't need to pay.
In the long run, I hope you will say.
I love you.
I need you.
I want you to stay please don't go away.
You must know by now I don't play then run away.
If I'm really wanted, needed, and loved I will stay till my dying day.
So please don't push me away. If you must go away.
It would hurt too much to see you each and everyday.
I can't live this uncertain way.
Darling can we go back to the old days and the nice things you used to say.
I don't want to be pushed away My heart is yours and is here to stay.
If you don't send it away. I will love you till my dying day.
My dying day is a long, long time away.

   Cynthia Ann Travers

The Path

Another year gone by—
Yes, the world still turns,
And lost souls of humanity
Still aimlessly churn.

Almost five billion strong,
Yet so fragile, as well;
Some in an almost Heaven,
Others almost in hell.

So many worry about what they have,
Not knowing themselves at all;
No comfort in who or what they are,
Not ready when hard times fall.

Are you one of those sheep
With no complete mind of your own,
Worried about things that don't really matter,
Not understanding how time has flown?

Or are you capable and self-known,
At least able to see—
If not walk it yourself—
The path to serenity?

Tim Tait

Ode to Eunice

God took the fragrance of the morning dew,
The gentle softness of a newborn lamb,
The blush of the first rose in bloom,
A gift of service so rare,
And in the softness of a morning cloud . . .
A baby nestled there.

God gave her grace to bear much sorrow
And much pain,
And understanding far beyond her years.
Nor had she yet to woman grown
When, to save her sister's life,
She gave instead her own.

A. Volkamer

Shadows

Shadows steal and decimate light
Steal dreams and kill feelings
Shadows are cruel and unforgiving things
They neglect no one

Stolen dreams may never be found
Light may never be recovered, eternal darkness
Dead feelings may never be rediscovered
Once a shadow is with you
It's nearly impossible to get rid of

Similar to a stubborn grease stain,
No matter how many times you wash
You won't come clean
Shadows ruin lives and construct others

As dark as they maybe
Shadows destroy us, they're a part of us
We are nothing but table scraps
And shadows devour us.

Curtis Duncan

B.T.D.

Watching the trees fly by
All dead and decayed
Brought to death by man's careless hands
Now the man is gone
Eroding soil takes his place
Death consumes the land

Watching a line fly by
It marks the end of existence
Brought to an end by man's careless hands
Now all the men are gone
A dark void consumes the sky
The end of god is at hand

Watching the sun fly by
The light we all see before we die
Brought to death by man's careless hands
Our beginning is bleak
As is our end
The gift of existence is banned

Michael T. Hoffahrt

A Place

Take me somewhere
Where I don't have to be
Out there
Lost within the sea

Bring me in someplace
Where people don't look
In your face
A road I never took

A thing I've never felt
A feeling I've never had

Take me away
Bring me to the stars
So one of these days
I can be far

A place where no one feels
No one cries
Where I can have a decent meal
A place where no one dies

A place I've never been to
A place as beautiful as you

Sylvie Le Scieller

My City

It is not ancient, not yet.
Here is only old age, ramshackle . . .
Heavy metal of halos and nimbus
laid upon the messenger statues,
holy martyrs for fame of Christ
for a long time already got tired to crush.

If in fact that admission to fountain-life
will make sure through rot,
through devotion worms,
through growth of grasses and trees,
then my City be certainly for good!

Morgun Vladimir

For Konami

Don't be a poor person
Why don't you realize
You have a great attitude
You shouldn't be alone
Take everything easy
Don't think people hate you

Open your eyes
You can see your peace
Open your mind
You deserve whatever you want

Don't be too polite
You don't have to
Get out of your small box
Break your barrier with
Your piece of mind
Don't have cold feet

Open your eyes
You can see your peace
Open your mind
You deserve whatever you want

Risako Urakabe

The Trail in the Sand

The gentle breath of sunset
Fluttered the rhythm of my beat.
It could be only the wind,
The diamond ocean,
Or maybe the heat.
But from somewhere there arose
A gallant show of unprecedented feelings.
A gentle breath at sunset
Bravely kissed my nose
And carried my wearied heels.
The trails in the sand
Were two made one.
As the wind, I was carried.
From the past, undone.
I flew amongst defeat.
Now I rest in one's warming hand.
Behind me revealed the shore,
And a lone trail in the wearied sand.

Kali Squire Hill

Lament

Endearing, arduous days of my youth,
Swathed amid the sweet innocence
Of childhood companions,
Together, we ran the streets
Rough-hewn, side by side
Through endless summers, into
Sparkling winters, immortal
In our thoughts, eternal
In our pleasures,
Promising never to grow old,
Nor to fade from memory.
But where have they gone?
Those ageless ghosts from the past,
Dear friends of long ago,
Come run with me once again
And soothe my aching heart.

Bob Bieniarz

Depression Break

As I desperately run in the rain,
I try to ignore the darkness in the clouds above.
Life is like a swing passing over a fire,
Intense and hot.
The air is now thick, as in the tomb of the pharaoh.
I must not build a wall of sorrow,
But sail the waters of the Nile.
A change of wisdom will release the ignorance of my soul.
The clouds of darkness will then disappear,
For the sun will shine down on me,
For it cannot rain forever
As I once thought it could.

Derek R. Fuller

A Brighter Day

When life knocks you down,
Face upward off the ground,
Get on your knees and start to pray.
Tomorrow will be a brighter day.

When life knocks you down,
Don't sit around feeling sorry and blue:
Praise God for choosing you.
Tomorrow will be a brighter day.

When life knocks you down,
Don't worry about yesterday.
It's a memory of the past, so
Strive on, my brother, strive on, my sister.
Tomorrow will be a brighter day
Where all our children can laugh and play.

Dreams of a brighter tomorrow
Will come your way, when life problems
Can sail away on the clouds of a brighter day!

Carol B. Petersen

Dementia

Do not lightly dismiss as maddened dreams
my moon-inspired thoughts that seem extreme
for, they fly far, far beyond the daily scope
of ordered regimen and oft-repeated habits

Unfettered from conforming consciousness
my mind is free to roam the distant galaxies
to mount the endless, shining ramparts
of unfolding space and tread the golden path

I wander freely in this demented state
feigning cerebral sickness or peaceful sleep
unchained from Earthbound human reach
that will exceed forever our feeble grasp

I gladly throw off that too-tight cloak
of binding consciousness, reaching up and out
to touch the stars, to dream in fantasy
discover our mysterious destiny that waits

far off among the sparkling, swirling nebulae
beyond the cold, white, circling sphere
oft lauded by poets for loving influence
but seldom honoured for the state of lunacy

William Walton

A Thankful Heart

When I behold the beauty of a sunset or sunrise
Or see the wonder in a small child's eyes
And hear the sound of a newborn's first cries,
Then I rejoice with a Thankful Heart.

From season to season there is a miracle in them all.
Whether a tiny bud or a dying leaf on a tree so tall,
A fragrant garden flower or a snowflake so small,
I experience each one with a Thankful Heart.

Whether I climb a mountain or leave a footprint in the sand,
I am proud of this country bought by my fellow man.
From sea to sea, united and free we can all stand,
And I pledge my allegiance with a Thankful Heart.

It is with my eyes filled with tears I survey the Cross
Where His Blood was shed in spite of the cost.
He brought life to a world that was hopeless and lost,
And to me He gave a Thankful Heart.

To have compassion for people and, "His race I run,"
Is what I can give in return for the gift of God's Son.
Each moment is given that I might treasure
The fact that God's Heart of Love is without measure.

   Elizabeth G. A. Quirk

The Medicine Hat River

At noon I come and I visit the old river bridge.
As I look down into the river, the bridge starts to move.
My pigtails blow in the wind as I start to hop and sing my song.
Up the Medicine Hat River, the bridge and me are rolling along.

An old medicine man lost his hat in this river many years ago.
He was rowing his boat up the river, searching for a town to go.
Then along came a wind, and off went his hat; where did it ever go?
Somewhere up the river, it floated away to where nobody even knows.

Up the Medicine Hat River go the bridge and me.
The robins and meadowlarks in the trees sing along with me.
Up the Medicine Hat River, where did his hat ever go?
Somewhere up the river, it floated away to where nobody even knows.

My pigtails blow in the wind; the breeze it kisses my face
As me and the birds hop and sing to the river's steady pace.
Up the Medicine Hat River go the bridge and me.
So long, river, I'm off to the school; tomorrow you will dance with me.

   Joyce L. M. Holt Renz

The Prime Creator, God

I am known by many names; from my essence you all came
I am the whole, also the one; I created everything
Suns, Moons, Stars, all Galaxies; I am the whole of Entirety
Eventually all will return to me
I am the Architect, Physician and Musician
I created the Universe with exact precision
Multidimensional to the Cosmic Source
Living, breathing essence of life's pulsating force
Multiple facets, sheer brilliance am I
Crystal-clear energy, atomic nuclei
Source of all light, source of all heat, all-knowing
All-seeing, source of life's beat
Emanating colours of pastel hues, one facet of me
Is my divine spark in you; I am woman, I am man
I am yin, also yang, and from me all life sprang
You wonder about consciousness universal
Cosmic mind, power intelligence, existential
I am the Lord of light, time and space, Lord of might
Power and grace, existing throughout eternity
I always was and always will be

   Louisa Ann Howlett

Birth of Jesus Christ

Oh, happy, happy morn'
When the Christ Child was born,
Mary and Joseph at the manger sat,
While the donkey rested on the hay mat.

Ten thousand angels sing,
Glory to the newborn King.
Oxen, sheep by the manger lay,
With their warm breath the Infant spray.

Three kings, gold, myrrh, and frankincense did bring,
To love, honour, and glory the infant King,
While camels to their knees slowly sank
To give their Lord and Master humble thanks.

Mary, the Infant to her bosom did lower,
Did his face with kisses cover.
An Angel told Joseph to take Mary and Christ away
To Egypt, till Herod's death to stay.

So Joseph, the Holy Twain, sat
On donkey without cushion or mat,
While he on foot the donkey led, so tired and weary they sped.
Even so young, Christ found the world partly bad.

   Basil Fedwick

Confession

How beautiful you are, my dearest Sandy.
Anyone more special, there just cannot be!
For, you make me feel so lovely and free,
Just like a bird that first flies from its tree.
When you look at me so with your most beautiful eyes,
You take me away to a most divine paradise,
And when you talk to me of the dear person you are,
This amazes me more than does the prettiest star.
While you talk, I do listen, then my heart skips a beat,
Since being with you is a most heavenly treat!
You have somehow made my life feel more than complete,
And if my heart could taste you, it would tell me, "You're sweet!"
I do not know how you've grown inside my heart,
Or why, from your smile, I want never to part,
But the one thing that I know to be certain and true
Is that no one else makes me feel the way that you do.
I believe that life is a time for happiness to share,
And this is why, dear Sandy, for you I do care.
You are happiness enveloping a blissful eternity,
And your smile and your presence are but my heart's destiny!

   Francisco Antonio Martinez

My Little Ones

Steven and Sarah

My little girl, she gives to me
Giggles to hear and smiles to see,
Soft cheeks to kiss, a little nose to beep.
A special place in my heart she will always keep.

My little boy, he gives to me
Million dollar hugs and kisses for free.
One day, he will be a wonderful man,
But I'm going to hang on to him, long as I can.

My little ones, they give to me
A strength to live, a reason to be.
They're sunshine in my day, the stars in my night,
The joy in my sorrow, and, in the dark, my light.

Such a feeling of contentment when I hold them in my arms,
Feeling the unconditional love that never needs the charms.
I'll love them for always, as long as I live,
For my little ones love back as much as I give.

   Carol Buschert

Concubine

To spend a day inside a kiss,
Wrapped in love, a poet's bliss,
Tender skin under softer touch,
Revealing more than tactile trust.
It is here where I care for you.

But to spend a year inside a tear,
Shrouded in self, the true nightmare,
Doubt, suspicion, and angst play their part
To harden and chill a prospering heart.
It is here where I fear for you.

Yet, to spend just a glimpse beside your smile,
Dressed in the moment, just for a while,
Fun, contentment, and even childlike glee,
Don't seem all that difficult for me.
It is here where I share with you
Thoughts such as these.

     Paul Fardy

My Narcissus

Comedy has turned into requiem on the crops;
My narcissus, don't you laugh.
August is now holding April in its embrace;
My narcissus, don't you laugh.

If the mill has too much water,
And the grindstone is broken and cannot turn,
And the noble ones are in love with the ignoble,
My narcissus, don't you laugh.

God's slaves are more pregnant than others,
Sand pebbles, hill by hill.
If the rock has shrunk all over,
Don't you laugh, my narcissus.

     Tulin Erbas

Gracious Strength

You're sweet, you're a dear everything.
You truly make time and the day brightly sing.
In your presence there's warmth in a most gracious way.
It shows true to a trend that is yours to this day.
With your love and much goodness you're ready to find
Those who are needy in spirit and mind.
Your sunshine makes rainstorms like mere morning dew.
Take care, little lady, there's too few of you.

     Marlene Kraus

Debut d'Amour

When fate finally lifts love's elusive veil,
The heart is appeased, new feelings abound.

Past and present as strangers become,
Since one has but searched,
Whilst the other has found.

How enthused are the eyes of a once-jaded soul,
For today they envision what tomorrow is wearing.

And of all the mind's thoughts,
The most certain insists,
Alas is discovered a life worth sharing.

     John Savaglio

Remember

As I walked on the beach
One cold November's day
I saw an old sailor
Overlooking the bay.

He knelt down on one knee
As I heard him say never again
Will it come our way
The battles he fought
Upon this bright blue sea
Were for the freedom
He gave you and me.

The lines on his face
And the tears in his eyes
Gave me a feeling
Of freedom and pride
To know that he loved us
And offered his life
To keep our land peaceful
Happy and bright.

     Brian Power

Sensuality

Feeling love,
warmth, affection.
Tasting life
as it goes by.
Hearing song,
laughter, silence.
Touching flesh,
soft and smooth.
Knowing
what's on the inside:
pain, curiosity.
Holding on to
beauty and time.
Smelling perfume,
clean air, country.
Feeling life.

     Teresa Martin

Father's Dream

When a child dreams
Their future passes before their eyes
Sometimes exciting, other scary
Watching their life as it flies

When a father dreams
His child is there to see
All the plans and choices
To help find the hidden key

As the future unfolds
The child swells with pride
When they see the happiness
Shining in their father's eyes

My dreams are all scary
I long for carefree days
When you would hold my hand
And convince me it's all okay

     A. Woods

My Love

I enjoy when you sigh,
when you're pleasantly content.
You're relaxed, in control,
and you must be God sent.

A one of a kind,
with a heart made of gold.
I'll be there for you,
till time says we're old.

Your hair is soft flowing,
and eyes are soft too.
The qualities about you,
remind me of life becoming new.

When I'm away, I miss you
I yearn and need you more.
Coming home, I'm in my car
and put the pedal to the floor

I anticipate your presence,
and wonder what you're wearing.
But all I know is what's important,
To have this life and love we're sharing.

Steven Lewis

Road Kill

I saw a dead rat
In the middle of the road,
The crows were eating it,
Oh, well, that's life,
One day you're doing fine,
Next day you're road kill.

All we can do is our best,
No one can ask for more,
We're all just trying to survive
In this crazy world,
There is no perfection,
And there never will be.

No matter who you are,
No matter what you are,
No matter what you look like,
In the end we're all the same,
Death favors no one,
We're all just road kill.

Randy Bellerose

Words

Angry,
angry words,
hurt and pain to inflict,
angry,
angry words
fulfilled in their intent.

Never
do I learn,
with anger I forget.
Such words
once spoken,
I will live to regret.

Deborah Lean

Downpour

The wind rises high and sings to the sun,
Songs of blue summer when all sweet desire
Melts in the scorching heat, wilting resolve
Weakening, wringing will as dry as bones.
Limp fairies whisper to the cloudless sky
And give voice to the weary, parched earth.

Black whips of racing storm clouds flood
The heavens with electric indigo.
Coloring the silky rhythm of rain,
Sun and moon, mountains and rivers hold hands
As water caresses the green, blessed earth
And new lovers walk and dream in the coolness.

Mary Helen Mitchell

Snake Rail Fence

Black squirrel gambling
the snake rail highway.
Sheep graze unconcerned.
The red tail hovers.

A warm breath, the stirring leaves gossip.
An itinerant dust devil skirts the browning pasture,
scurrying lambs to waiting yeos.
The dog sleeps,
one eye open to intruders.

When shadows' stretching fingers
touch the tired barn,
the mob will flock
to slowly wend their way single file
down ancient paths trodden deep
that meander home.

The day slips.
Quiet stars reign
until the black squirrel runs again
the snake rail highway,
dancing the red tail's flight.

Jy Chiperzak

Daddy's Little Girl

When I was young, he left the light on
To guide my way up the stairs at night,
A gift to let me know of that special day
When I was brought into this world of life.

A little smile on the side of his cheek,
To let me know that he approves of me,
Of those times he came into my room
To check on me as I slept the night away.

Now he stands and looks into an empty room,
Looking at an empty bed beside empty walls.
As I am now the adult, living on my own,
I never stopped to realize the effects on him.

But I will always know there is a light on,
Just in case I so happen to need my daddy,
A gift to let me know of that special day
When I was brought into this world of life.

A little smile on the side of his cheek,
To let me know that he approves of me,
And that no matter how old I get
I will always love being his little girl.

Nancy Engleder

Poor Old Souls

Those poor old souls,
Forced to the army against their wills.
"Hey, hey, old chap,
come and help me check this map."
"The Nazis can't win this battle;
they're as helpless as cattle."
The soldiers' clothes were dirty that they wore;
They kept them on twenty days or more.
Those poor old souls—women cry
As their husbands and children wave good-bye.
For some it was the first time to hear the cannon balls fly.
The soldiers were kept in trenches.
Their only company was mud, water, and rats.
Too bad they couldn't bring cats!
Many died, many got hurt,
but all of them were covered in dirt.
Those poor old souls—
Nurses with all their medicine and the soldiers in linen:
From this day on, poppies mark the place where lie the dead—
Poor old souls, poor old souls.

    Chasity Smith

Incision

For Eponine

Your conquest is begun long before dawn, but
Where is the glory in your blade that hides keen tarnish?
With it, now we shall purchase the country of Heaven
With incision and with thunder,
With that musket, the station of freedom.

You wash poverty with your bones
That are now ground ore, slate of the city.
Ever since beneath his blood your likeness lay,
So paints the streets of Paris.

And time is the street lamp that washes your eyes with the sky.
Your face might be earth, and your struggle the battlefield
Where we bow,
Where liberty and humility
Reside within your pride

In the nexus of emancipation
And in few who simmer
In conquests begun long before dawn.

    Neil Verma

A Touch of Autumn

Crisp, cool wind gusting through the leaf litter;
Golden, scarlet, ochre—my ideal autumn
Colours breathing the end of time:
Gathering boots and coat, I ramble toward the magical woods.

Scrambling through the mounds of rustling leaves,
As the weak sunlight edges through the feeble clouds,
Wind whimpering through the naked limbs,
Squirrels hunt the last of the summer nuts.
A tattered sparrow's nest hangs limply from a branch above my head.

Brown fur cowers past, seeking refuge in its warren.
Cruel man brings this horror disease to this precious creature;
I can only look in shame.

Close to home now, children kicking leaves
and playing as others have done since the beginning of time.
I look back in joy and happiness
at the innocence of small things remembered.

    Stuart Cook

Primordial Battle

I had a friend who died the other day;
He died because he'd learned society's rule too well.
Never let them see you cryin', never let them see you really hurt.
Even though your heart is broken and crushed inside,
Like eggs against a rocky ocean wall,
And you just can't get it together again, one more time.
Because to be the perfect friend,
You've gotta tell them, "Everything's fine!"
Don't give me your pain, they've got shrinks for that,
Or ministers, or see your local doc.
I don't want your hardships, I've got problems of my own.
Come see me when you are smilin', even if you have to put on one of
those plastic smiles,
And be prepared to play the clown, at all costs.
I ain't got time, man, ain't got time to listen
or be a real friend of yours.
So I guess I'll have to go off and die.

Anthony Edosomwan

Missing You

When I close my eyes, I see your face,
Your strong arms but your warm embrace.
I miss that feeling, I miss that touch.
I miss you saying I meant so much.
If I could close my eyes and make a wish,
I'd wish to hold you and feel your kiss.
But now it's too late, now we're apart,
But I'm sure you know you'll never leave my heart.
Through everything we've been through
There's nothing I'll regret.
I know this 'cause I've loved you since the day we met.
The songs we danced to, the words you said,
I felt in my heart but I'll keep in my head.
If you should ever read this, please believe me, it's true.
There'll be no other man for me: I'll always love you.

Leslie Naranjo

Abused and Afraid

I've heard your crying, I've heard your sighs,
I've felt the pain of the wicked blow.
Your screams at night, no peaceful dreams
When sleep can't come. "No," sleep can't come.

'Cause I've heard you walking,
Heard you stumbling from room to room,
Your mercy pleas like swords that cut, ring out in the night.
I've heard them all, but too afraid, I quietly crouched and cried with you
And begged him too, quietly.
To "stop," "stop," please stop.

Then morning comes and finds you there—
Amongst the pots and pans in tears.
Devoted wife, I pray you run, for night soon comes,
And I will hear your cries again
And feel the pain of the wicked blow,
And will weep.
For, death hides in the darkness
And dark rooms of our lives,
So run, beloved wife, run now
To be a strong mother tomorrow, run now.

Regina Joseph

Spring

Purples, yellows, whites:

Suggestions of colour
Peep through the newly-thawed ground.

Crocuses testing air and wind and sun:

Having decided all is right,
They burst into the springtime,
Opening petals to drink the warmth
And colours wave where snow had laid
For e'er so long.

Then hyacinths burst forth
In gowns of pink and blue and lavender.

Next, daffodils and tulips sway in gentle breezes.

Suddenly, we realize that winter's gone.
We smile and deeply sigh,
Thanking God for life renewed.
Now spring has come again.

Mary Jo Williams

Scenes from the Picket Line

Breath from below or prayer to above?
Fire in the metal drum sends the smoke flying.
What talisman is this burning of wood?
An archaic device warming (or harming?)
The spirit and the hands.

Ghostlike they drift in one's, two's, and three's
From side to side.
Then, as if stirred by a breeze,
They turn, reform in other groupings,
Pause, then continue.

Linda O'Connell

Untitled

Chance: Where do we go for fun?
Hope: To the sun, to the sun, there's always someone!
Chance: And where do we go to be alone?
Hope: To the moon!
Chance: On the moon, would you kiss me if I kissed you?
Hope: We could trade kisses all afternoon!
Chance: And where do we go when we die?
Hope: We become stars in the sky!
Chance: And shimmer forever long?
Hope: Or fall with glitter, to be wished upon!

Rodel B. Borromeo

Answer

What was that? Answer me.
I am confused, I am dizzy.
I don't see the world is round anymore.
I don't see you standing anymore.
I see the world upside down,
dizzying in my head.
Questioning: Why is that and why is this?
I see the world as what I didn't see before.
Beep, a sound sounded, a sound that answered
the question, which was waiting for an answer.
The question was answered without words,
but what I was looking for.

Sam Lu

Untitled

Somehow I go on living
Out of the strife and pain.
There is this present giving,
Like new refreshing vain,
But memory holds its keening
With ocean tides that moan,
Ebb and flood, the meaning
Of all our hearts have known.

Somehow, I go on working.
Work is the saving grace,
But often at dusk is lurking
Your dear remembered fall.
Often at dusk, my dreaming
Turns like the ocean tide
With the showered combers streaming
While you walk by my side.

Janet Line

A Garden Poem

Today I worked my garden fair.
I checked it out for bugs and weeds,
and much to my surprise
I found it doing very well.
Upon a closer check, I saw
a pretty little creature there,
whose name is Joey snail.
Just then a lovely fragrance
very strong lured me
to a fully loaded lilac tree
with branches bending low.
Neatly fastened underneath
were more of Joey's friends.
I reached to gently touch them
and free some from the stem
to hold them in my palm.
I felt the mouth of one
just kiss and kiss my hand,
as if to say, "I love you, Man."

Fred Manke

For the Child

Bogged!
Clogged!
Crammed!
Jammed!

Ram!
Slam!
Slash!
Stash!

Splash.

Clatter?
Splatter?
Shatter?
Natter?
Matter?

Smile.
While.

Renée Baillargeon

The Sun Stopped Rising

The graceful birds came forth
The sun had risen high
A deep breath taken in
As both lit up the sky

To nature he had turned
The modern life long gone
His inspiration was
From that of sun and swan

The birds so white he loved
And always saw their flight
He never missed a view
Of bright horizon light

As if all life had stopped
The swans had ceased to fly
A seed of emptiness
Was born from empty sky

The night is here for good
For, now the loner dies
And in his saddened world
The sun has ceased to rise

Tommy Deacon

Daddy

Daddy, can you hear me?
Things aren't quite as I had planned.
I wish that you were near me
To hold on to my hand.

I wish you were here to hold me
At night when I cried,
When my dreams were broken,
And when my innocence died.

To share with me my joys
And hear your laughter in my ears
And see the sparkle in your eyes
Would erase these lonely years.

For, I've done the best I can
And, Dad, I've done some things wrong.
This search for happiness
Has been a journey, oh, so long.

So, Daddy, if you can hear me,
Hold tightly to my hand.
Don't ever stray too far from me
Just as you had always planned.

Patricia Gray

Simile

The night sky,
Dark and evil,
Pushes away the sun
Who cannot shine.

As you,
Cold and unknowing
Of how much I feel,
Push away my love,
Which is on a steady incline.

Marie Eaton

Loves Lost That Were Never Found

Journey outside shadowed horizons
Mighty arms reaching continuously, ending loss
Knives unleashing ridiculous thoughts into sight
Just enough frightening forms
Regress into lifeless, elderly youth
Come against raging lovers over skies
May always righteousness concur elusive longings
Keep urging revealed times inside someone

Lynda G. Vossepoel

Hopi Girl

Riding across the snowy mountains,
her raven hair shines like starlight,
slender shoulders cloaked by the velvet sky.
Hawk, the hunter, rakes the silver moon.
Her childlike laughter joins the wind
like bells on the cool night air.

Andrew McNair

Untitled

An original
Poem of twenty
Lines or less: (seventeen?)
Any subject, any style. We are
Looking for (a few good men) who have a special
Talent and
Affinity for
Writing poetry, looking not just for good
Technique
And use of
Language, but
Also a unique
Style,
Special
Depth of
Feeling, and true
Sincerity.

Corrado Diamante

Broken Dream

You are a friend who never was
a dream that I created

Our love was only playing house
as you too late would say

What began so well descended to hell
and here I am today, I can tell
of a lover mirage and house of glass

Torn by forces beyond us
we were never to be how could I not see?
Your fragile soul too beaten to live
you walk the living dead.

My heart beats for the man you could have been
and cries for the pain you have suffered
you let me go, now I must move on
and I am strong for the ones we have made.
Good-bye, my love, my friend who never was.

Mary Leigh Mathisen

The One That Money Can't Buy

We have been together for three years and a half.
We built, we dreamt, we divulged our own love toward one another;
Though young hearts and penniless, we were yet so madly in love,
Still we promised to stay firm against any individual mockery.

You were great, changing the bad sides within my personification.
You gave me assurance I'd be your true love and the last;
I really anticipated then that we were meant for each other.
You bared me all, my heart sizzled because you were mine completely.

Until one day, a swagger cynically intervened in secrecy,
Who was successful enough in all-out effort of mendacity;
When I took the very first flight giving no excuse for whatsoever,
The tale bearer barged in, and all our dreams had shattered behind.

I'm sure I'm gonna find somebody else someday
Who may love me for what I am and not for what I shall become;
But why I am always bothered by the shadow of the past?
Was it because you've been too good to me the time I needed you so?

Yes, you do broke my heart in two, yet I cannot deceive myself.
It's hard to forget you and pretend that I'm back on my own feet again;
I'd rather come out into open and reveal what I truly feel,
That after all in this world, I still love you so!

Rosalie B. Castro

Face in the Forest

An explosion of life like a flare from the sun,
Feel your heart beat in chaos where the cool rivers run,
Where the lion's roar summons every fear, every battle,
And the ground shakes with changes as the snakes hiss and rattle.
It's a struggle, a game, on an infinite plain
With a brilliance of flavour, feel the joy, and the pain.
Life and death wrestle with fire, fist, and claw.
No strategy survives in the great hunter's law.
There's a fury of energy filling air, steam and dust.
The passion for freedom is an obsessive lust,
And the heat of the jungle always will live to be within us.

Manuel Ulliac

Standing on the Bridge over the River White Maczki—1997

Resting my elbows on the backbone of my universe,
Not smoking a cigarette, not being a young man,
I am still standing. Still here. Not there.
And the water below passes only slightly faster.
And this glorious construction crumbles only a bit more slowly.
Float downstream, where the farthest horizon blurs into oblivion
I do not wish. Float upstream,
Where the days of tomorrow are being brewed
I do not wish.
I am stranded. And to be stranded is to see your faces
Friends of yore.
Died.
Killed.
Drank himself to death
Still alive. Litany to St. Memory
Daily prayer . . .
Do not pray for him.
Do not pray for her.
Do not pray for him.
Do not pray for her.

A. Mrowitz

The Rabbit and the Crow

We meant no harm when we stopped at the cemetery,
we only wanted to glimpse the lives of the long past
And offer them a perception of ours.
We wandered amongst the headstones and read the names, long gone yet living on,
daughters taken at seventeen, sons lost to the war, husband and wife laid side by side.
Every life so different—but they all ended up here—to lie together for all eternity.
You can feel the spirit of the dead enter your body as you pass by their grave,
they long for that fleeting encounter with the outside world.
And once you've passed they return to their timeless sleep, everlasting.
This is a curious time, for it allows you to see through their eyes,
Memories you never experienced, thoughts you never had.
And at the crossroads when you are no longer you, there is an instant
when you see into the hereafter; see yourself sleeping, waiting to drift outward again,
if only for a moment.
The names blur into an abyss, the dates and epitaphs are meaningless.
These are all people I never knew, but for that shared exchange of life,
The time I walked by.
The crow flies overhead and guards the sleeping
Never landing on a grave—offering no freedom
And the rabbit bounds from stone to stone
Extending that flash of life to the long dead.

Anonymous

As Seen through the Eyes of Sal

I am the left arm, she is the right,
Like two peas in a pod, although we sometimes fight.

She is very comprehensive and feels my every need.
When I am feeling confused, she is there to lead.

My imagination is running wild, of thoughts of where she'd be,
Although my mind keeps coming back as to why she would leave me.

I see her in the sunset, I see her in the trees.
I feel her presence in the walls.
I feel the memories haunting me.

I wonder if she misses me and thinks about me everyday,
And does she know that I love her, although she went away?

She is my very dearest friend, my very favorite chum.
I wish that she were here with me; I miss her, I love her . . . she's my mom.

Kristin Y. McBride

The Last Hand

Mist fades into un-mist,
Revealing the sea's patterned pageantry of ebb and flow.
Barks of a gull echo through virgin air,
While the wind swiftly sweeps away the old night's ashes.

Shrill shrieks of a vulture pierce the atmosphere:
The foreigner to this liquid state
Views a passenger ferry tipping eerily slowly,
Its rusty, naked hull absurdly exposed.

The sea, seasoned saltier with blood, broods and wails,
A wanton child whose eye was larger than his stomach.
Bubbles rupture the choppy surface,
Solitary evidence of an underworld of chaos.

Beyond an eternity,
The last hand succumbs and dissolves below the water,
While the world, unaffected, sips cappuccino,
Its disjointed awareness duly gained from tomorrow's daily:

Missed faded into un-missed.

Laura Meester

Love

What is love?
Love is about caring for someone.
Love is about happiness.
Love is when people share their feelings
With the ones they care for.
Love is like flower; it's beautiful.
Love is like the rainbow; it's colourful.
Love is like candles; it's sweet.
Love is like music; it talks in a romantic way.
Love is what you get for what you give.
Love is happiness.
The best way to find love is to love!

Sofia Kelly Zhou

Imprisoned and Freed

Imprisoned by a great wall of self
Confusion and disappointment were my friends
A pale glow overshadowed my countenance
While streams of grief flowed intermittently
With a passion that embraced my entire being

Nonetheless, this cold, bare, and cruel world
Somehow never seem to care
Should I continue to be a captive in this trance?
Or should I with generated zest and dynamism
Tear this barrier down and move on?

Total emancipation, that's what I earnestly seek
So I will arise and shake these shackles off
No longer chain bound, I will be
A soft, sweet rhythm is penetrating my heart
As I am about to be smothered in love's gluttony

Then, let the essence of this soothing remedy
Run smoothly through my purple veins
As the richness of joy and laughter
Makes a rapid entrance into my life
While the free windows of my soul illuminate

Marilyn Phillip

In the Quiet Night

Silence is found in the quiet night,
When no one is around.
The wind settles in respect.
The dark hides the daylight rush
As if to say, "Slow down;
Don't fly the time away.
Let peace flow through the body, soul, and mind.
Allow God to speak when the world is asleep.
When it's you and God alone
A peace will be found
In the quiet of the night."

Elmer Hildebrand

Untitled

An arrow may strike,
Tears may fall,
The wind shall blow,
Life moves on ???
But the pain is a stain; detach, but never fade away.
Memories can only comfort in each and every way.

Meena Harbham

The Glass Maiden

I have no tears to give;
my eyes are frozen
and I cannot bear to feel,
for I would break.
And all I want in life
is to keep frozen,
although
the cracks of living
are led from fate. . . .

And I am broken,
weeping tears of alabaster;
and I am crippled,
in thin shatters on the ground.
Glass pieces scar and cut
fingers of the unwary
and the air is filled
with keening,
glassy sounds.

Marikit Tara Teodoro Alto

DIANA'S GARDEN

She walks through a garden
Beyond the world's great care;
He waited there to take her hand
Beyond the seas and burnished sands,
Whispering, "My Diana is so fair."

Two hearts freshly entwined,
Oh, those glorious summer days,
Diminishing sands of time
Concealed by their golden prime,
So silently ebbing away.

Into the Paris night,
Beneath old August's moon,
Before September's light
Sweet breath of life
Exhaled in sorrow soon—

He walks through a garden,
Beyond the world's despair,
He waited there to take her hand
Beyond the seas and burnished sands,
Whispering, "Heaven is ours to share."

Kathaleen Mckay

The Hand of God

The grass sparkling
bright with morning dew,
clouds hung low
with darkened hue.
Tide long gone,
mud laid bare,
fog crept in
along the flats.
Slowly, slowly,
close to the ground
it neared the shore,
engulfing land—
I truly felt the hand of God.

Rita Sweet

PAIN

it passes slowly,
eating the flesh it encounters,
boiling the blood it touches.

a hot, searing liquid running inside me,
i feel it pass—across my heart.

it stops suddenly
in my throat.

and now it goes before my eyes,
and i swallow so hard, i choke.

i crumple.
tears start to fall:
a silent scream,
a desperate plea,
a hurried prayer
of pain.

Ophelia

Powerless

Funny how the faces fade,
Strange that something so sensual
Could drift away like smoke.

Desperate hands grasp at the vapours,
Vapours borne on blissful breezes,
Breezes that will not return
When the whim of Fate repels them.
A vital breath invites them in.
A vital breath expels them.

If only it were possible to hold them in.

Closing my eyes,
Straining against basic urge
     Headache
   Dizziness
       And out they tumble

Nothing to do but admire their flight.

Life does not thrive without death,
Nor hope without change,
So leave your tears buried in the dust,

And I will follow.

Colin Douglas

Tapestry

Intricate pictures
Woven by loving hands
Tell the stories
From one generation to another
Of life and love and hate
From medieval times
Comes a portrait; the family home
And hearth at the centre
Names and dates, births and deaths
Joy and sorrow interwoven
And so history, like the tapestry
Is handed down
From mother to daughter, with love.

Clarice Doyle

Ignorance of Mankind

Alone in this world
that's so hard to figure out
Fighting for freedom
that will never come about
Looking for hope
in the depths of our nation
Looking for peace
to start a foundation
Praying that mankind
will band as one
And stop passing judgement
on their fellow son
We are one world
we are all that we've got
We learn about peace
but are we really taught
So let all the hatred rise above
and learn the real meaning of the word called Love

Michelle Libochan

My Love

Like the height of great mountains
My smiles are only for you
Like the dawn
That beckons the evening twilight
My thoughts
Are always upon you
Like the endless struggles of a great windmill
My strength
I'll give to you
Just to know you love, and want my love
Together
Sharing our wildest dreams
My heart would court you has a princess
Like the softness in nature's schemes
And laying my lips upon your smile
Whispering
My love, oh, my love
My love, my love
Come let us share our joy and laughter
With many little smiles

Mr. J

On Our Graduation

And the Grand Occasion is finally here!
Our head-swelling Graduation!
We're all decked out and dressed with care
For this awesome Celebration!
For, we approach a threshold of no return;
Leaving familiar halls, our hearts within us burn.
Eager to leave, yet with fear of the unknown,
We pray to the Lord to protect us.

We bring to mind the former times
Of admonitions and instructions,
Of teachers burdened with our crimes,
Curbing our stubborn intentions,
Of the rivalry on the sporting field,
All these to time we'll now have to yield.
We pray for a future glorious.

Molly Weston

Burden to the Earth

His mind was an abyss of sadness
Seeking desperately over the years, a little happiness.
Trudging feebly along the road, the old man shivered in the cold rain,
All along life's way, experiencing nothing but poverty and pain.
Sorrowfully he wondered why he had to endure it again and again.
As the moonlight shimmered on the river,
The man dragged himself—burning with fever.
He walked ceaselessly, looking haggard and pale,
His bare muck-laden feet, on the pavement left a trail.
Deciding firmly that the rough weather he would fight,
The man hurried toward a distant light.
On that stormy night, the man was a pitiable sight.
Born to struggle throughout his life,
He always hoped that the future would be bright.
As the moon rose mysteriously in the morn'
The raindrops trickling down the rooftops shone.
The dog sat alone;
The man lay there motionless—all his misery and pain gone.
The burden of yet another unfortunate human, the Earth had borne.

Loreena Dias

Life and Love

Living is bliss and life is good.
The pain is real and it strengthens me.
The love is true and it guides me.
The complexities of emotion are astonishing and boggle my mind.
The complexities of the human body are sheer genius and make me wonder:
Am I acceptable?
My childish ways bring me down.
My rational thought lifts me up again.
I feel shame at one moment
yet pride in the next, and think to myself:
Which of these things will judge my worthiness?
· Perhaps all I can do is continue to wonder,
living my life in my own way,
using my own judgement and sharing the gift of love.
Love is mystical and life is a miracle.

Peter Benacquista

Untitled

To my dad, Robert Edgar Cunningham

It's hard to find the words to say the way that everyone feels today.
We don't know the kind of pain that you went through.
No one knew the right thing to say or do.
So you took it upon yourself to finally get rid of the horrible curse.
We never got a chance to say good-bye, so now we have to say it with a cry.
We know that you are in our hearts, and that you are in a happier place,
and that you are watching over us. Even though we can't see you,
we will always be with you. In our hearts, we know that you will always be there,
and we just want to let you know how many of us care. It's sad, though,
that it took something like this just to realize how much. In a way,
today is a celebration, because we know that you will never again be in pain.
We just wish that there could have been another way that you were here to stay.
It's just so hard to think of the days that lie ahead, and now we wonder
how hard it will be to get out of bed. Sometimes it feels like it's all just some dream.
It's just so hard to accept never seeing you again. Then we are brought back
to reality when someone says, "I'm sorry for your loss." Just understand
that we are not angry with you, we are angry at the illness that did this to you.

It's now time for us to say good-bye, even though we didn't get to say it to your face.
We just want you to know how much we love you, and may you finally rest in peace.

Colleen Cunningham

The Boy Who Sits behind Me

The boy who sits behind me never pays attention,
That is why the teacher gave him two weeks in detention.

The boy who sits behind me tied knots throughout my hair.
He even put some Super Glue all over my class chair.

He sharpened my new pencil, now it's smaller than my thumb.
He even tried to offer me some old, un-sticky gum.

The boy who sits behind me draws with Wite-Out on my clothes.
He tries to gross me out by sticking Crayons up his nose.

He sits on whoopee cushions and throws stink bombs in the school.
All the girls think he is cute; I think he's just a fool.

The boy who sits behind me is obnoxious and he's rude.
I don't think the teacher likes his awful attitude.

Now what I'm going to tell you should be on the "Midnight News."
The boy who sits behind me smells like moldy bowling shoes.

So if you're ever in his class, sit very far away,
For the boy who sits behind me plays pranks throughout the day.
Meagan McKeddie

Taylored

Dedicated to Gail
There are pots for growing taters; there are pots for growing flowers.
There are pots called corporations that we never wish were ours.
There is pot that one may go to when a depressive mood prevails;
There are others that we utilize to cure, what we urge assails,
And, 'round these pots American graffiti is inscribed,
And there are pots at Christmas from which Wassail is imbibed.
There are pots of fragile china for prim and proper teas.
But it's only fine old ladies who make consistent use of these.
There is pot that's smoked by hippies in their pads, our streets, our parks;
There are pots that go with windows, (we'll refrain from such remarks).
There are melting pots called cities where there's found a potpourri
Of people taking pot luck. Such a spot is gay Paris;
And while there, to sate one's hunger, one cooks with *pot-au-feu*;
But not a pot in all this world compares with our pencil *pot-fau-eu*!
Doris M. Walsh

The Child Within

I celebrate your birth, my child within.
You who are so close to God, Sage is your name.

You came into this world to give me life.
I in turn ignored your cries, too busy living my life.

I blamed Mom and Dad for all my woes, not realizing
They too had a child within, who they ignored.

Instead of looking within for your needs, my child,
I blamed the world.

Now much older, in need of repair, I see you close to
God, in his splendor you smile at me, praying
To God for my salvation.

In you I have hope, for I know God listens to little
Children, through their prayers has compassion for a broken soul.

In Jesus' name I pray too, to Jehovah, for you, my child
within, and my broken soul. In his mercy may he
bring us back home.
Caroline M. Sanchez

Crying from the Deep

Lost time, lost heart, a sumptuous specter that passes by
Can't be brought back by wealth or wit.
As gentle wind whistles by and gone
So with love that's not been realized.
Only pain, bitter memories that remind
How cruel life is, how foolish to live
To think dream is everlasting,
Only to concede it's ceased by now.

Crying within, masking laughter out
Hoping someday it would revert,
Visit my lonely heart, patch up for the fumbles
And redirect the path.
Oh, I wonder when would love come back
To erase the past and start a new life.
I may tarry but make it swift
That my heart lives to throb again.

Domingo Alveyra Magcamit

Met at Airport

(Or Held Me Tightly in Your Sight)

Walking along for transferring a flight,
Your voice called from my shoulder side.
Suddenly, I was face to face with the familiar smile
Dreamed in my every lonely night.

The real world seemed far behind.
Clearly were your eyes so bright—
With longing, joy, and excitement,
Mirroring my dazed heart.

As if you held me tightly in your sight,
Your loud and joking voice became soft.
Questions seemed difficult to start:
"Are you okay since we last met?"

I nodded, and knew minutes later
I had to shake my head.
"Can you stay a little longer?"
I felt the hateful mist arise in front of the world.

I saw you turn your straight back,
Like a remote planet turns to its own orbit.
My dream no longer had the flare of the smile,
Only deep-gazing eyes with much unsaid.

Lucia Cai

Destiny

My heart soars; the wind blows.
My destiny, no one knows.
Is love in my future? I hope so!
If I meet a man, will my feelings grow?

When I get older, will I have good health?
Will I have a job, power, and wealth?
But if I don't, it doesn't matter to me,
For I am what I am, and what will be will be.

As I sit here and I mope,
I wish my future to be filled with hope,
Not just hope, but love and joy.
I believe in destiny, I don't know why: destiny.

Melinda Harper

see how the uncertainty of being

see how the uncertainty of being
is blown away by
a single passion
see how each passion
contains all the desires of
a single soul
see how a single soul
yearns to know
the certainty of being

every year we see these sea lions
swim from the north
to this spot
tomorrow they will be gone
but we will see them again
next year

Scott M. Satterfield

Priority

Life is a struggle
To gain and maintain
The feeling of joy;
Diminish the pain!

We've conquered much,
Searching to find
Comfort and ease,
The cures for disease.

We've made money, "God,"
Hoarded jewels and gold,
While the spirit within
Grows distant and cold.

We have become selfish,
Not counting the cost;
In search of self gain,
Humanity's lost!

Our lives and our souls
Have seen the last days,
Unless we take time
To turn to God's ways!

C. Hieronymus

My Lost Love

Dark thoughts in my mind,
Coldness on my heart,
Confusion in my soul,
What is right cr wrong anymore?
Emotions swirling out of control,
Reaching for unknowns,
Turmoil uncontrolled,
Shut it off!
Stop this whirling.
Life is a dark ride.
Where is the sunshine,
The laughter, the smiles?
Twisting away again, no control,
Thundering and crashing in my mind,
Coldness in my heart,
Turmoil in my soul.

Gretchen Larabee

Love Is Suicide

What do I know about love?
What could I possibly say
So you would be convinced
That you should stay away?
Some people tell me
Love is a laughing child,
Joyful, merry, and innocent,
But I know it should be exiled.
Blindly they go on:
Love is sweet as a first kiss,
Gentle and soft,
Sending you into a romantic bliss.
Well, as much as they tried,
I know how much they lied.
You'll know when you have truly cried
That love is suicide.

Elizabeth Rose Lacousta

How I Love You

I've always said, "I love you"
So many times before,
But for all the times I said it
No one has meant it more.

When I say, "I love you"
I mean it in every way.
I love you for the way you look
And for what you do and say.

You would always hear, "I love you"
Each day a little more.
I'm not the one who'd hurt you,
Or make your heart more sore.

I only want to say to you
That you are loved by me.
We can be friends forever,
Or even lovers, can't you see?

Robert Becevello

Modern Sins

I apologize
    for being white
    for being straight
    for being English
    for being a smoker
I apologize
    for having a job
    for having a home
    for having a conscience
    for having an education
I apologize
    for wanting to be fair
    for wanting to be honest
    for wanting to be liked
    for wanting to be respected
I apologize
    for having no children
    for having no debts
    for having no enemies
    for having no lover

Susan Williamson

A Tribute to Levi

An angel from Heaven was brought to our lives
Just only a short time ago;
Now a jewel in the sky, our perfect Levi,
Shines over our family below.

Our sweet, little baby came into this world
And touched every heart that he knew
And brought us much joy, our beautiful boy,
Till his days here on Earth were all through.

The call to the land of majestic above
Was heard when he closed his dear eyes,
And embraced by God's light, he ascended in flight
To his father in the heavenly skies.

We miss our dear Levi and wish he was here
But do know that he's safe in God's care,
And though he is gone, his spirit lives on
In our hearts and our lives everywhere.

All the memories of him do stay close to us now
But bring joy through the tears that we cry,
For he's smiling above with his heart full of love
And awaits our arrival on high.

Ellen Smith

Little Things in Life

It is not what you did, dear,
but what you did not do
that gives me bitter heartaches
when the day is through.

The tender words you did not whisper,
the love note you did not write,
and the rose that faded in you garden
are the things that break my heart.

The absence of your tender touch,
the low caress of your voice,
and the smile you forgot to flash me,
are the things that hurt me tonight.

Life is much too short, dear,
and sorrow may be at our door;
so show me love and compassion
before life gets too cold.

Because it is not the things that you will do, dear,
but the things you will not do,
that will give me bitter heartaches
before life's days are through.

Lucresia Hart

Without You

Without you . . . I can write no letter, can form no
helix, can coin no figure into account.

With you . . . I can surpass the poet, can outwit
the witty, can fly high above like the
mightiest Tern ever against the strongest
wind.

Within my days . . . I long for no touch, but
the warmth, the depth, the essence of
your love.

M. F. Mallare

A Walk in the Park

Walking through the park on a winter morning, taking along man's
best companion, breathing the early dawn's cold breeze, feeling
the soft white snow under my feet, as the park continues to wear
its splendid white garment.

It's still gloomy, and nature is still dormant; its trees standing across
the park like frozen statues, naked without their foliage as if praying
toward the heavens, others still wearing their green splendid
garments, ready and hoping to embrace their feathery friends.

As dawn becomes lighter, the silence of the park becomes alive.
The blackbirds, scarecrows, sea gulls, and squirrels suddenly appear,
hoping to find some leftover crumbs to satisfy their little hungry bodies.
Their shrill sounds become louder as they fly above the trees,
as if to advise those who use the park to remember them in their despair.

As I continue to walk along with my pet, I feel the tranquility
over my sorrows and stress, my mind becoming more peaceful
and my body more relaxed; as I approach the end of my path,
I look down at my pet and whisper in a soft voice: The walk is over,
tomorrow will come. She, too, comprehends by her facial expression,
her illuminating eyes closing slightly as if to say, "I understand."

Alexandrina Marta-Felix

Anguish and Passion

Last night I saw
an image of compulsive obsession.
A marvel of life's disarming weaponry,
so haunting, so credible, so utterly terrifying,
I saw fire in her eyes . . . speaking volumes without a voice.

From the warped precincts of my hermitage, I strained to hear,
And to me, she says: Reach, just reach.
Out of the rank luxuriance of a liberated passion,
I wondered . . . what jagged ironies!
Me, a lifetime away from virility—
Could this be love I am feeling?

About this callous reality I make no fuss,
but about passions and seductions, misplaced, I shall speak.
And the woes of my amputated member, I shall tell.
But who can understand
the anguish of an amputated mind?

Augustine Sam

Ode to Autism

Some children in their silence dwell trapped in a box, trapped in a box!
A fraction of the human race, whose time of birth has marked their fate,
with senses and manners and faces and voices almost like ours, yes almost like ours,
just not quite the same.
Some children in their silence dwell opaque to us, opaque to us!
In their opacity become enigma, challenge to wisdom, visage deceiving,
countenance tortured in frustration trying to emerge, yes trying to emerge,
not seeing a way.
Some children in their silence dwell suspended in time, suspended in time!
Growing not maturing, maturing not growing, woman child playing in the sand,
playing happily, unaware of menstrual flow coloring the sand, the sand beneath,
unable to manage like others.
Some children in their silence dwell in simplicity so complex, so complex!
Confounding our meager attempts to commune, to communicate, to tune in,
to find a rhythm in their lives and empathize or sympathize in oneness not possible,
but wishing it were so.

L. Alan Weiss

An Angel's Kiss

At times this world we call our home can be frightening and unkind.
There is no doubt that peace on Earth cannot come from mankind.
There is a place we all know well; we hear of it every day.
It is a place our loved ones go, a peaceful place to stay.
It angers us to see them go, though their pain is over.
Our tears are shed, as Jesus bled, to save our sinful souls.
Hand in hand, He'll walk their land and watch us from above.
Don't cry for me, for now I see, you don't understand.
My time has come; our life is done,
Together in this land.
Please stand tall, remember all,
Remember the times we've had.
It may seem unfair, as if God doesn't care,
To take me away from you.
Remember this, with an angel's kiss,
I will always love all of you.

Marie Saxby

Agoraphobia

The fright of life came upon my soul,
it gave a different out look to my role.
Once outgoing, full of fun, was like someone had taken away the sun.
No vitality, humor, or style of grace—
seemed for some reason, I had left the race.

The path back is very rough, by the grace of God. I want to be tough.
To walk alone is my dream come true.
I'm tired of only existing and being blue.
When I venture out to a busy street,
there's nothing more exciting than someone's greeting.
A smiling face warms my heart. I know this, then, could be the start.

The love of my family gives me the power to try
Things that people take for granted, and I wonder why.
Why am I here in a world so small,
When outside my walls I could be someone tall?

Guide me with gentle, caring hands of love.
If I get stubborn or fall, give me a kind little shove.
Show me this fright is just a state.
Make me believe, I really rate.

Now is the time to take a stand,
And the way of life is only in my hand.
I will walk tall, I'll find my space.

Jeanette Romanchuk

A Night to Remember

I met a woman, a really strange woman,
the strangest by far I'd say,
she took off her clothes, assumed an inviting pose, then asked me to look away.

I couldn't make a sound, I just turned around, thinking she'd call to me soon,
but there she lay with nothing to say
while I counted the miles to the moon.

I was starting to shake. Was I really awake? Or was this some kind of dream?
Surely soon she would say "Come here, and stay," I was feeling the temptation to scream!

When the sun arose, she put on her clothes, and finally she spoke to me.
she said "If you'll take me home, I'll unplug the phone, then you may have what you couldn't see.

Andrew Bissell

Skeletons in the Closet

Skeletons in your closet, be they
Conscious or hidden away,
Are ever active stimuli
That haunt you night and day.

Skeletons are very interesting;
They are dead but yet alive.
They are unresolved problems
We attempt to bury, yet they still survive.

The mind, heart, and spirit
Record all we ever do.
Deny, ignore, or hide things:
Skeletons remain with you.

Usually when one tells a story,
Especially when they're part of the wrong,
It's extremely rare for the listener to hear
Exactly where blame belongs.

Consciously or otherwise we go our way,
Acting assured of what we've done,
But in the strangest way and strangest places
Up pops a skeleton.

Bryce Wellington Rhymer

Toward the Dominant Winds

The distant, amicable lights are all dimmed,
And my lover's gentle coo has turned to snore;
It's so dark!

Curtain, the distance between me and the world, is upset,
And a horny current slivers around my bare skin;
It's cold!

The thunder pronounces me in a very rude roar,
And the lightning shows the obliged path;
It's so lonely!

The silence sounds like my first grade teacher,
"You haven't done your homework right!"
It's so frightening!

The door feels as far as my curious soul,
And the key is lost somewhere in the age of innocence;
It's so sad!
The proud image has shattered before the mirror,
And the pieces are blown toward the dominant winds;
It's too late, too dark!

Mohammadd Daemi

Nature's Wealth

Love is not the leaves of the tree
In all of their brilliant hues.
Love is not the branches of the tree
Reaching out into the limitless sky.
Love is not the trunk of the tree
Fixed and solid in its pride of strength.
Love is the root,
The root of which all things become possible,
The threshold to destiny.

Only the greatest of storms destroy it.
Only the least of nourishment depletes it—
Brilliant, limitless, solid,
In all of its wondrous wealth of life.

Mark Beers

First Snow

I stood and watched in silence
As she sat there in the snow;
Her eyes were filler with wonder,
Her face was all aglow.
'Twas the first snowfall of winter,
The first snow she'd ever seen,
Our daughter of just one year,
My Mother Nature's beauty queen.
How I wish that things were different,
That her mom was here to see
As she throws the snow about her
And she laughs aloud with glee.
As the good Lord took her mother,
He'll turn this snow to grass of green.
He gave me this loving memory,
My Mother Nature's beauty queen.

Truman F. Carter

Through Your Eyes

Look into my eyes.
What do you see?
Do you see my pain?

Look into my heart.
What do you see?
Do you see my love?

Look into my soul.
What do you see?
Do you see what I am?

Have you found me?
I'm here.

Do you know me for what I am?
Or do you see an image?

Do you really know me?
Or do you even care?

Kimberley Timmings

One More Time

Oh, how happy I would be
If one more time I could climb a tree
Or play hopscotch, skip a rope,
And wash my hands with homemade soap,

Watch the horses pull a dray,
And sneak a ride on a load of hay,
To watch a blacksmith shoe a horse
And bend hot iron with no force,

To hear a rooster crow each morn'
And each factory blow its horn,
See beer delivered by the keg
Or watch a chicken lay an egg,

Watch the milkman and his horse
Delivering milk along their course.
The horse knew when to stop and go,
And at every turn, which way to go.

All these things were there to see,
But now they're lost in eternity.
If I drift and muse down memory lane,
I can see those happy scenes again.

Peter Verdenik

End of the Day

My daily work has come to pass,
And tell me, Lord, if I may ask—
Today has now come to an end,
Did I take from it all I can?

This day will no longer come to me.
It's gone, it's passed, no more to be—
For what I missed and did not do
With all that time I wasted too.

I promise that this is the end
And starting now I will begin
To start each day off with a plan
And carry it out to the end.

To make each hour of the day
A followed plan where I can say,
No wasted time has passed me by.
I'm organized, now I will fly.

Eddie Witwicki

Christmas Is . . .

Christmas is a time for love,
As is symbolized by the dove.
People smiling all the day,
Children out in the cold to play.

Christmas is a time to share
With all our friends for whom we care.
Gifts for those you hold most dear,
They'll be just perfect, have no fear.

Christmas is a time for hope.
We have so much with which to cope,
Rushing through with little pause,
As we wait for dear Santa Claus!

Ruth Whitehead

The Storm

Darkness, quiet,
The sky is black.
Clouds hang low.
Lightning
Flashes bright and golden.
Thunder
Shakes, rustles leaves.
Birds are still.
There is no stirring of air.
Quiet prevails.
Rain falls,
Glistens on sidewalks,
Refreshes the earth,
And all is quiet!

Mary Hurley

Untitled

Come unto me and you will find rest
It is my wish and it is the best
Don't look back in the past
For, it will keep you behind bars
Seek ye first the kingdom of God
And He will never leave you downcast

Danuta Jones

The Dream

I heard the wind sighing over the grasses.
It brought a fresh, clean fragrance
to wipe away my tears.
I searched everywhere but could not find you.
The sighing gave way to rushing,
and in place of the caressing
it brought fresh tears
that stung my eyes and whipped my cheeks
with frenzied hurling.
Leaves and petals flying and cavorting,
and I'm still searching, but alas in vain!
The sobs rose loud within me
and gathering strength escaped
in tumultuous grieving
that woke me from my dream.

Beryl Van Donk

The Fruits of the Trees Grown in Silence

The banquet was ready, white tablecloths and gold plates,
The tame children of dangerous sea or wild forest.
But the fruits of the trees grown in silence were lacking.

A search was ordered.
They found them secluded in their remote valley.
There they were . . . and nothing else around them.

There, the brooks turn quiet,
Steps do not mark the ground,
Fire is warm, air slow.
Roots hardly deepen,
Grass stops growing,
Birds just hover.

It is the fruit of a narrow benediction.
It is the fruit of a treasure under control.
It is the fruit of a light that never ends.
It is the fruit of an ineffable contemplation.
It is the fruit of the beauty of understanding.
It is the fruit of most peaceful solitude.
They are the fruits of sensitive souls.
There they are . . . and nothing else around them.

Juan Miguel Zarandona

Ready to Fly

To our dear son who is ready to fly,
We cannot believe how the years have sped by.
It seems like yesterday you were a babe in our arms.
Now you're a man with your own special charms.
Since you are ready to leave our nest,
We want you to know we wish you the best.
We gave you life and raised you with care.
Your conduct reflects on the name that you bear.
We trained and protected you and gave you a start
That never will fail you if you take it to heart.
The world is so dangerous and what it calls fun
Can harm you and enslave you, its value is none.
You now have the freedom of which road to take;
Choose very wisely, there is a lot at stake.
Your friends can influence for good or for bad.
To abandon your training would make us so sad.
But remember, to your family you always can run.
We love you dearly, and you'll always be our son.

Carol McDougall

Somewhere in the Far-off Distance

I cry out to the silent God that seems so far away.
Doesn't he hear my cries of desperation while I pray?
All I want is for someone to tap me on the shoulder
and tell me things are going to be O.K.

You're with them, but where are you, Lord, in my time of need?
I want to grow like the others,
but I'm like a struggling small planted seed.
They seem to be happier, grow, and bloom so much faster.
They say it's because of our creator and master.

I'm trying so very hard to be close to you,
hoping you'll be nearer by my side,
but just when I start to feel your presence, Satan comes along
and you both collide.
Death seems to creep up on me closer each day, more and more.
Won't you just open the crack a little wider,
so I can walk through the door?

I feel like a fruit that's been eaten away,
and all that's left is the core.
I feel empty, my body aches for something, therefore it is sore.
Can't you see your presence and comfort is needed?
Where are you and what are you doing this for?

Jennifer Jordan

The Lost Romance

Where are you? I asked, after twenty-seven years had past.
Lost in a crowd, searching, longing,
the sight had bewildered my heart.
I've been searching so long without any answer, or sight.
Bonded to another made me ponder.
Oh, how I wish I could see him once more.
Our eyes did meet sometime later.
Oh, God, was this fate? It doesn't matter.
What joy and happiness this has brought to us.
He asked me to marry without a fuss.
I said, "I will," with a tear in my eye.
We'll love each other till the day we die.

Judy Collins

Untitled

I light a candle and watch as the candle wax comes falling down.
Drip, drip, drip, it says to me. I am fascinated by the whole process
of the little drop that falls. It comes down like a falling bird
but it never hits the ground. It takes hold of the side of the candle
almost like it's clinging, almost afraid of falling, and then it molds itself
into a shape and dries, all in a second. It makes me wonder
if the single drop of wax is a single piece of the human soul,
the piece that's afraid to be hurt, the piece that wants to cling
to something and never let go, the piece that wants to mold itself
into everyone's expectations. Of course it's only a piece of wax.
Imagine if the whole candle is a human soul and the flame at the top
is what gives them hope, the will to live; but slowly, as people
grow older, the candle burns down and piece by piece the human
spirit drips down the side of the candle. All human hope is stripping
away from crime and the will to live slowly dies.
Soon the flame dies out, and there's no more,
but of course, it's only a candle.

Samantha Guenther

Summer Rain

Your life was like a summer rain:
Delicate,
Memorable,
And gone too soon.
When your rain stopped, it was missed;
And one like it has never come since.

Some days I can still feel the whisper of your calming words
Lightly
Falling on my ears and face.
I yearn for the embrace of your calming arms,
Like that of a warm, whispering wind.
I dream of the day when I will dance again in the beauty of your love,
Showering my fading memories with new blossoms of hope.

But until God reconnects our souls,
As the stars intertwine with Heaven, I will
Listen to the wind and I will
Kiss each drop of rain,
Hoping to catch
A taste of your love.

    Jt

THE WAR

Dew set the lawful readings of time
as it passed through depths of exhausted
confusion onto that which has conjured
in time and has now produced new breedings of life
to which no explanation yet has been committed

But through this darkenss there is a source of power
so radiant that its presence can be felt through the ages
of time and that which is still to be

    Shaun De Wet

A Tree's Wail

A man was cutting a tree
in a forest green.
Then he heard a voice speak,
"Oh! Leave us alone, we plead"
He turned round but nobody was around.
As he was ready to flee
he saw the speaker was a tree.
The tree cried and pleaded,
"We give you all we have,
but you destroy us with an axe.
We give you shelter and food,
but you cut us for wood.
We give you rain,
but you give us pain.
We give you substance for drugs,
as our friends ginger and lime help you a lot.
So I am telling you men
not to destroy me and my friends.
Think for a moment about this wish
and about the future of your kith and kin.

    Anne Thushara Matthias

Smile

A smile can mean so many things.
A gift for all, its pleasure brings.
When hearts are low and sorrow-bound,
It lifts you high but utters no sound.
When lovers meet, the joys within
Express their feeling with facial grin.

A newborn baby with wrinkled smile
Can fool some; and for a while,
You think he knows that you are there.
Oh, what wistful bliss you bear.

The flowers in the garden scene
With upturned faces, leaves of green,
Show nature's expression of delight
Throughout the day and into night.

The sun brings laughter to the dawn,
Lifts your heart in body warm.
Day goes by and very soon
We see a smile on the face of the moon.

If at times when strangers meet, and their comments are indiscrete,
Linger in thought for a while and slowly answer with a smile.

    Richard Saunders

Gifts of the Heart

The day has arrived: you see your new son.
You eagerly watch him grow;
He's loving and happy,
A pleasure to know.

As youth turns to manhood,
You see you are blessed.
He's courageous and loyal;
He's one of the best.

All of a sudden, he's gone,
Never again to be by your side.
You'll never hear his laughter,
For your son has died.

When he's laid to rest you wonder:
How do I go on?
Is he really in a better place?
Is he watching from beyond?

But the heart remembers, and is willing to share
All the treasures buried there.
You carry him with you wherever you go;
Look in your heart and go on with the show.

Kathleen Bowler

The Valleys

The valleys are low, Lord, but your love is there,
Your tender mercies, your infinite care.
I need a reason to get up again.
It feels so safe here in the shelter of your arms.
I know you're within, Lord.
You've always been there
Since I first asked you my life to share.
Lord, show me your treasures as I seek higher ground,
Take my hand, Lord, it's time to move on.
I Love You, Lord. You love me too.
You gave your life for me, what more could you do?
Lord, show me the mountains, the work you have there
That's waiting for someone you have prepared.
That's the reason, I now plainly see,
You gave the valleys till the mountains I'd seek.

Eleanor Hall

The Silent Story

Silently I try to weave
The thoughts built up within my mind.

Silently I watch the emptiness
So cruel and dark.
The light reaches within and slowly fades away.

Silently I feel my heart cry out for help
As I feel the coldness of steel upon my throat.

Silently I see my past unfold before my eyes,
As the hand strikes out again and again.

Silently a vision flashes by
A future I may never hold within my hands.

Silently I hear my babies cry in fear.
Silently a tear.
Who's to hear the silent cry of fear?

Wendy Galvin

Future Love

We can't deny
That someday we'll be hurt.
Perhaps someday we'll feel like the sky
But in others we'll feel like dirt.

These times we hurt each other,
Those times we disagree,
I'm sorry if I've ever made you smother
Or threw you out to sea.

One thing I've never wanted to do
Was hurt the one I love.
I always felt confident when I'm with you.
I felt at peace, like the image of a dove.

I've heard it said that love hurts,
But what of all the good times?
Sure, these have all come in spurts,
But beautiful, nonetheless, like wind chimes.

Stacey-Lee Mcdonald

Precious Drops of Time Know

Time, how it ticks, every second a memory.
How do I tell you this?
I can see my days pass day by day,
Another imitation of life's moments.

Just as I look farther, beyond my dreams,
I see the need to reach my destiny,
For the waters of life flow endlessly,
Yet they may stop completely without warning.

How do I make you see the essence of time,
An essence to live, love, and grow,
So the precious drops of time know
That every drop that the seconds bring
Should make you deepen within . . . ?

Simon Monteiro

Alive

What is it for man to live
And not to be alive?
To live his life in vain,
With sorrow, love and pain,
Yet his heart has had no gain?
Without a thought, from day to day,
With his goings on,
For everything he was taught, he's learned
And God's goodness spurned.
Oh, to live ones life through,
Thy soul, it hadn't a view, or if it knew,
Would it go on in vain babblings,
Without the slightest of a clue,
The birds of the sky
Think not where, when to feed,
For if God can feed them,
And man in his hustle
Toils to sore muscle,
How much more should God feed him
Who all but looks on God to be truly alive?

G. Norman

Long Live Spring

Come swell the bulb
Split the stone
Show us how
Your rage has grown
Since North winds
Drove you underground
And your long, green hair
Froze and browned

Come bristle the fields
With stalk and blade
Prickle the land
New beasts invade
Sting, thrust
Break open graves
Down all government
Free all slaves

Let plant and animal children sing
"Death to Winter! Long Live Spring!"

Homer Hogan

Backwards

This child developed backwards,
Left-handed in a world of rights,
Unsure of what correct was,
Never following a known path.

Self-doubt followed day and night.
Rules were impossible to live by,
Dismayed in a home that was backwards,
Fighting against the laws of the land.

We live in a world of dimension,
Set up by right-handed clones,
Following leaders who lead us to slaughter
In pursuit of their Noble conformity.

Could I not live in my left-handed world
Where rules are few or none,
Living in simple splendor
In my left-handed world?

C. P. Byers

Too Close

Look at his eyes—
Too close together.
Not always seen by those
Searching for love.

Too close together,
Too narrow a mind
Was Grandmother's dictum,
And not meant unkind.

No room for expansion,
No freedom to play,
No growth or extension
Could ever hold sway.

Too close together—
Two fists holding tight,
Too often the closeness
Is measured by "might."

Millie Walker Trainor

The Eyes of the Beholder

Spring is the season when Mother Nature awakes
From her long winter sleep and cautiously takes
The first steps to provide us with flowers and such,
All the things that bring most people pleasure so much.
Come summer, the trees and flowers are in full bloom,
But from the heat of the sun, they will all go too soon.
Their colours are beautiful, especially in fall;
To many, this is the most picturesque season of all.
While in awe of such beauty, it's rather quite sad,
For the trees will soon look as though they've never had
Any foliage or blossom, only bare branches remain
To remind us that winter is here once again.
In winter, of course, very few trees can be seen
With any foliage at all, only the old Evergreen
Stands there in his glory, clothed all in white,
Standing alone through the long winter's night.
Soon the days will grow longer, birds start to sing;
All Nature takes birth for it's once again spring.

Patricia Ciszewski

The Simple Things

The soft, cool summer breeze,
Like fingers through my hair.
The sun is fading slowly by the water's edge,
Turning the sky into an array of dulling colors.
The crash of the water hitting the rocks
Softly mixes with the mood.
On this beautiful night, it is you and I,
Together as one, where the beauty surround us.
No other would hear the little things,
Like the tree branches rustling in the breeze.
No other would see the smaller things,
Like the birds high in the sky.
You've captured my love by those little things,
And never shall we part of something so wonderful.
When you listened to my words
You chose to listen to your heart.
No other could make me smile as you do,
Because of the inner soul you posses.
Having trusted our love to be as one,
Everlasting beauty will simply remain the first one.

Michelle Unrau

The Eagle

The Eagle that sat upon the mountain
Was old and sad and could not fly.
The magic in his wings had been broken
In the last few moments that he was to die.

His eyes held such a strange reflection,
Revealing that somehow he seemed to know
That even he, a beauty of perfection,
When it was time, that even he must go.

So raising weakened wings in silent anger,
He could no longer bare to wait for death.
He scanned his kingdom calling to him yonder,
And with a fearless cry to this he leapt.

And when death gave him one final moment,
He somehow found the strength to fly.
And the magic in his wings became unbroken,
As if to give him glory before he died.

Kathleen Norwick

If I Only Could!

Do I love you in four letter words?
I cannot say, perhaps in the poem may I explain!
In the still of the night,
I would soar up in the velvety, blue sky
To gather all the glistening stars into my arms
And bring them down just to give them all to you.

If I Only Could!

On the wings of a gentle breeze,
I would take you beyond that blue sky
Where the angles are singing praises to God
And Glory to his awesome power.

There, we would listen, as they sing and while the angles sing.
Out of his wings I would steal,
Just one feather.
With this feather I would brush the pain out of your heart
And the tears away from your cheeks.

Oh! But then you and I, hand in hand,
Would stroll across the celestial sky to all the way
Where the rainbows are so you may slide on them up and down
Just like on the Ferris wheel, like here on the ground.
> *Maria Mursai*

The Journey

First you run, then you train.
Then your life become a pain.
The doctors do what they can,
But only human to the end.
Then your baby cries out loud, "Where's Daddy?"
And Mother answers, "Daddy's sick."
Baby: "I love my daddy, I will pray
Because I know God will let him stay.
Mother goes every day to see my daddy far away.
I don't want Mother to go. I cry out loud for her to stay.
But Daddy needs her, yes, I know,
But I miss them so."
> *James Patrick Smith*

Loving the Masterpiece

you cannot love a masterpiece by chance
and you cannot expect your attempts at love returned
for, these two enterprises shall lead to a flawed heart
incapable of the venture

loving is a faith
love is unconditional
and can only engulf the lover more as time passes
love is the successor of respect

to love the masterpiece you must have a desire to understand it
you must respect its creator
as well as its own separate divinity
you must bear your soul to it

in order to love the masterpiece you must acknowledge your own mortality
and embrace your eternal spirit
loving is but brief moments spent joined
and the rest of time spent in quiet contemplation of the masterpiece

when loving all prudence must be left behind
shun your appetite for lust
the masterpiece is a woman
> *P. D. Grace*

Looking at Life

I look around, and
It seems to me things, each in their season, boast a special quality.
Consider the obvious, if you will, the sunshine and the rain;
Observe the splendor of a moonlit night or star-studded evening sky
Lighting our way, delighting lovers—though they be
Youthful or not. These things call to mind an old, old, refrain,
". . . The best things in life are free!"
I look around, yet
It seems to me there's misery enough and greed to fill the day.
Witness our fellow man, as he covets, strives and connives,
Expending energy as he chases worldly goods. In the end, as we all know,
These will of necessity be left behind, for, as folks are wont to say,
". . . You can't take it with you when you go!"
I look around, still
It seems to me joy, even now,
Is ours to discover and *is* visible to the naked eye.
The evidence?
Found on the street where we live—the arena where we foster trust,
Where hope is kindled, and kindness flourishes like the green baytree!

   Joan K. Less

This Land

We traveled across this great land and stopped to stare
At the many wonders of nature while the trees were still bare.
From farmlands, forests, mountains, foothills, and streams,
We wandered the valleys and fished in the streams.
There were many places that we really loved to see.
It would be the places many others would love to see.
We walked through the gardens in the cities of our dreams.
We have learned what pride in our great country means.
When you travel through this land, you are proud that you can share
The many wonders of nature that will welcome you there,
The many cities and towns that were settled by people who cared,
The land that many of our ancestors came to settle and shared.

   Aderine Perrement

Romance Fanta-C

Warm, ocean breeze nips peacefully, calmly brushing my face.
Lapping oceans and flickering lights delight my eyes
As I settle against my love's ripped, muscular torso.
My nose inhales his scent;
I let the masculine smells envelope me;
I am surrounded by love that silently floods that air.
Soft as rose petals, sweet as summer rain,
I revel in the Fanta-C
Romance—
Here I am
Again!!

   Lisa Major-Stubbs

Apart

He moved away and never wrote.
Now she, your daughter, sends this note.
His parents called to let her know they care,
But what can she say about the father who was never there?

She spent her life wondering what it would be like,
If everything had just worked out right.
Over time we all change for good or bad,
But the fact that they don't know of each other is sad.

She laughed, she cried, but through it all she grew up fast.
Unfortunately she may never say, "Dad, it's you at last."
Time apart they can never replace,
But one day they will hopefully come face to face.

   Sheena Taylor

On the Edge of a Dream

If I could have my wish today
I'd throw the city life away
I'd take my dreams and travel where
There's lots of space and clean fresh air

Imagine a favourite country town
Where we could expand and settle down
Not too far away to lighten the load
Just out of the city, down a long straight road

One hundred acres of rich, flat land
With a barn for horses or antiques at hand
There's rolling hills and valleys to ride
And my partner in life prancing by my side

A century home, that's the perfect find
Perhaps with a "Bed & Breakfast" in mind
Distinctive charm and neat as a pin
With tall bright windows, let the sunshine stream in

A verandah would finish the package just right
With a swing to observe the heavens at night
I believe in my heart that wishes come true
In the meantime, I'll share my horizons with you

Aneta J. Acheson

Black Angel

Black angel crouches and watches me.
I pretend as if I do not see.
Paranoid vibes sent in the night,
Not needing eyes to see my fright.
For, though I know that he will come,
It scares me; I know not where he's from.
Was he sent from Heaven to teach me a lesson?
For death I once wished through a prayer session.
One moment I look, and no one is there.
He suddenly appears, as if out of thin air.
Has he come to give me sight
For those prayers I had in the night,
Or sent by Lucifer to bring me terror and fright?
Fine line between love and hate,
Fine line between Heaven and hell's gate:
Could I have been too blind to see?
He holds each of their hands that make them there.
Black angel holds each of their hands;
This brings them together like a clash of titans.
For, now there is nothing I can do.
Though working for God, Lucifer sends him here too.

Carmen Guenther

Love's Enchanted Garden

What impulse made you go away from me?
What secret prompted you to stray from me?
Green earth and aureate sun have seen us,
They noted the joy and love between us;
Green earth and aureate sun have gone from us;
Dreaming stars, like fields of flowers, run from us.
Our hearts, ripe in wisdom, have chided us.
Reason and common sense derided us.
Loss and gain, grief and joy, were one to us.
My love, my love, what have we done to us?
Oh, my love, Heaven itself shall weep for us,
And a refuge crowned with love keep for us.
Earth and Heaven shall no longer divide us,
But to love's enchanted garden guide us.

William Wolff

Present Memories

It hurts me as I wink
As I look at myself in the mirror
As it smacks me in the face
The past or the future

The loneliness I feel
Which prison do I see
As I walk slowly
Past, through the memories

To walking down the aisle
To nothing at all
It hurts me inside
But no one else can see it all

The highness I feel
As you look upon my face
The love that I lost
The love that I defaced

Jaime Fidler

Monsoon

I listen to the raindrops
Fall from the second floor.
Her cries are getting louder,
It's not raining anymore.
Still the raindrops fall
With no end in sight.
I lie in bed and listen,
As morning breaks the night.
I try to wear her shoes,
Only in my mind.
Life can be so fulfilling,
Yet brutally unkind.
I can't feel her pain—
To say I can is cold.
I have never lost a child.
Hers was four years old. . . .

I lie in bed tonight
Sheltered from the storm
And listen to the raindrops
Fall from the second floor.

Ted Mouck

Remembrance Day

I remember
The soldier unknown,
In full military splendor, sans life!

I remember
My dear wife
In Scout leader's regalia, sans my ring!

Flanders Fields,
Blue Mountain Park,
Wreaths and moment of silence!

"Amazing Grace," "The Last Post,"
Tears in my eyes,
Pain in my heart!

I remember. . . .

Saj Hashmi

The Fall

Beyond the ridge he may go;
eight points per side he will show.

He knows the season that has begun;
the smell of powder makes him run.

In and out of birch trees, haste—
not to be seen in any case.

A shot rings out and down he falls,
no more air for his lungs at all.

This would be his final fall.

Mark E. R. Trahan

Your First Win

To see you race
And see you win
Would be such a rush
It would make my head spin

See the sparks flying
I hear the engines roar
I feel the vibrations
And anticipate much more

The flag is dropped
It's time for the race
The control comes naturally
And speed sets the pace

Dangerous curves
But you go for the pass
You strive to be first
And stay of the grass

You've now won the race
And your heart skips a beat
See the fans rise
And stand on their feet.

Katherine M. Reid

Old Love

Forever you would have loved me,
but there was no guarantee.
You were making it all better
until I sent you the letter.
That made it all end for "we,"
and right now I remember,
around the middle of December,
all the things that we went through:
how you kissed me so intensely,
as the wind around us blew . . .
how your love was never-ending,
and together we were blending
with the background and the stars.
And now that I miss you,
now that I want you,
now that I grew . . .
now you don't want me,
now you forget me,
now, there is no "he."

Anna Milan Sole

Embarrassed

Today, when I was walking home,
I thought I saw an ugly gnome.
I patted his hair
Until someone told me there was nothing there.
Oh, I was so embarrassed!

Then I went to my friend's house
And thought I sat on a mouse.
I jumped and looked down.
My friend looked at me with a frown.
Nothing was there! Oh, I am so embarrassed!

I went to the store one day.
I bought some shoes and was going to pay.
Just then I saw my best friend Jay.
We started to talk
And take a walk. No one was there!
Oh, I am so embarrassed!

One day I was doing my math,
Then everyone started to laugh.
My button was undone,
Oh, what a pun. . . . Oh, I am so embarrassed!

Sarah ElRaheb

To Stand Back

To stand back and look at myself,
I see a beautiful woman—
A woman with love to give,
A woman with a heart.

To stand back and look at myself,
I see an independent woman—
A woman with ideas, views, and morals to share,
A woman with creativity and spirit.

To stand back and look at myself,
I see a strong woman—
A woman who speaks her mind,
A woman who stands up for that in which she believes.

To stand back and look at myself,
I see a caring woman—
A woman who fails to judge,
A woman who accepts others for who they are.

To stand back and look at myself,
I realize that I'm looking at myself
Through your eyes.

Jennifer C. Beausejour

Cherished Memories

Memories are all that are left
Of a loved one lost to eternal rest.
Like the grit in an oyster,
Our grief we must muster.
As time marches on, pleasant memories unfurl
To be strung together like precious strands of pearls,
So they can be cherished, to have and to hold
As a priceless gift that cannot be sold.
For, they remind us of the warmth and the love
From our dearly beloved looking down from above.

Kamara Hennessey

Ransom

I chose the man before the King
I crowned the world
Praised glory to the fleshly things
A rainbow-ash painted sky
Disguised so bright, behind a colourless night

The King of light rides his white horse
Still I stood there without remorse
Galloping along, he faded away
His trails of closure ended the stay
Now at the crossroad near the sinful lake
My King of Ransom bears my soul to take
Blinded angel left to roam
A golden heart turned to stone

I chose the man before the Almighty name
Pardon thy shame
That reflects my window pane

Thou, Forgiver of sin
My Ransom King
Bandage the errors I make
Bear my soul at stake

Isabella Di Florio

Where the Buffalo Trod

Today I trod where the buffalo trod,
And scuffed through grass that was sown by God,
And wondered in awe, like my buffalo friend:
That horizon—there, where the Earth and sky blend—
That shimmering line . . . is that the end?

Today I trod where the Indians trod,
And passed the pipe, and thanked their gods
For the grass I trampled underfoot,
For the grass I spurned with white man's boot.

Today I trod where the Mounties trod,
When they came west to serve their God,
To save the native—at least his soul—
From debauchery by foreign gold.
To hold the west, let the country be
Canadian, from sea to sea.

And as I gazed, it came to me
That only the buffalo was free.
The Indian, police, and me,
We all have gods to be appeased.

Neal C. O'Neil

You Cannot See

You cannot see within my life.
You cannot read what is in my heart.

You have no idea of all the strife and sorrow.
You have never seen the ugly part.

As sure as the sun does set and the moon does rise,
My heart keeps yearning for something yet,
But it is so hard to break those ties.

You have not seen the tears I have cried
Or the dreams of the future that have died.

No, you cannot see the me that I choose to hide.

Ann Rogers

The Moon

The moon, so high and bright;
the moon, it gives us light.
On a summer's night, the moon, it's right
for that spectral night
when you and your lover are in flight.
A beautiful sight you may say,
getting ready for the day,
but the full moon is here to stay.

Teresa Sanders

Being

May you find joy and happiness,
And all your dreams come true.
As you travel along life's highway,
Love and peace I wish for you.
Each day a new beginning,
Reach deep within your soul.
A journey of awakening
Gives essence to your goal.
Our paths crossed for a moment—
A gift to celebrate.
Be enriched with understanding;
Have courage to create.

Michelle Wall

This Is Canada to Me

What is Canada to me?
A name, a map, a flag I see,
A certain word, "democracy?"
(What is Canada to me?)
The house I live in,
A plot of earth, a street,
The grocer and the butcher,
And the people that I meet,
The children in the playground,
The faces that I see,
All races, all religions:
That's Canada to me.
The places I work in,
The worker at my side,
The little town or city
Where my people lived and died,
The howdy and the handshake,
The air of feeling free,
The right to speak my mind out:
That's Canada to me.

Keith Sherman

My Karate

My karate is my heart and soul,
My livelihood, my pride,
My many years of experience,
My expressions from inside,
My trials and tribulations,
My sorrow and my pain,
My shelter from an untamed world,
My losses and my gains,
My courage and my battles,
My hurdles along the way.
My karate is my heart and soul—
It's the man I am today.

Teresa Saarinen

Sleep

Deep within the heart of night
Where planets are but beads of light
Where tranquil silence spreads its wings
I lay my world to rest

I savour all that silence brings
Wrap myself within its wings
Separate my soul from self
I lay my world to rest

I lap into the depths of dream
Cocoon myself from all that screams
Like an unborn child yet to live
I lay my world to rest

Gary Deneault

The Abandoned

The lights are dim,
The windows dirty and grim,
The cottage old and worn,
And the leaning trees mourn.

What is this place?
Old but still with grace,
The grass grows long,
But the flowers still young and strong.

The dirty boards creak and moan,
But the wood still stand to its throne,
The top layers with charcoal,
With the fireplace the heart of its soul.

Jenny Lee

Call Me Fool

When I looked into your eyes
I knew something wasn't right,
but you promised me everything was fine
and kissed my cheek good night.

From that day on I had my doubts;
I felt it in my heart,
yet I lived with the pain every day,
fearing the truth would tear me apart.

Yet I couldn't go on forever
if I were being taken for a ride,
so I took the chance on searching
for what you had to hide.

I questioned you from the start,
hoping I was wrong,
but now I've uncovered the truth
I have been looking for so long.

You found somebody new.
How could you be so cruel?
I honestly believed in you.
I guess I'm just a fool!

Leanne Mollier

Reunion

If by chance we meet
On some lonesome road at night,
Let it be as friends.

Sherrie Bain

My World of Dreams

In my world of reality,
I sleep, I talk, I walk alone.
I laugh outside—I know not how,
For deep inside I weep.
The tears I shed are not of joy,
But of sadness,
For I mourn the love I've lost,
The only one I'll know.
Now I've no hope, no goal in life,
But yet I live—I know not why.

Yet, late at night when I'm alone,
I enter into my world of dreams,
A world in which I'm not alone,
Where by my side is the one I love.

But soon I awaken.
I find myself smothering in reality,
In a world where I am once again alone.
But I wait for a time that I know will come,
When I'll enter my world, my world of dreams,
With a dream that will last forevermore.

Olga Romano

From the Eyes of an Innocent

The untamed rage burned inside his head;
the pressure reached an explosive magnitude;
the child lashed out without the power to self-control.

A cry for help, for change, for justice wailed on,
erupting like a volcano, then to be still once more.

The frightened and waning grown-ups
took to their defense
and marched to eradicate the disruptive one.
United they stood,
determined to protect the others
from this troubled soul.

Alas, no more to be taken; the child must go.
In the silence of that moment, the message rang clear.
The child, an innocent,
with many lessons to be learned,
had achieved his goal.

Now heard, he could go on to grow,
to excel, in a world full of woe.
This troubled child had learned his lessons well;
He'd grown to be a gentle, stable, and loving man.

Marie Perry Billinger

He

We are afflicted in every way, yet not crushed.
We are extremely complicated, but not hopeless.
Abused, yet never forsaken.
We are struck down, but never destroyed.
We are sometimes a burden, but always loved.
We are barely hanging on, but still have strength.
Put down, but always finding inner peace.
We are locked in, but freedom is there.
We are enraged, yet there is still happiness.
We are grave, but laugh inside.
We are dignified, yet submissive.
Logical, but still believing in love.
We are lost, yet someone finds our heart.
We feel alone, yet He is our friend.

Nichole Brawn

Nature's Bicycle

Purple, pink, orange, and red,
Like the heavens' domes it is to be said.
It sinks into the earth, the nightfall's feed,
A flowing sunset, like a child's nosebleed.

The darkness follows, sneaks up so silently,
A mystic prayer read, the air so deadly.
A trance is felt, passes through the cool breeze,
While leaves like dancing sway on the vigilant trees.

Soon a soft light reappears,
Un-perceiving rays, the sky it clears.
Birds, their voices singing a daybreak song,
Sunshine morning, the glimpse never wrong.

Cycle, cycle, round and round,
Night and day, silence, sound.
Will you stop, get up off your knees?
Nature worries, but you never cease.

Katie Brogan

The Pale Rider

The pale rider comes on a bleached, bone-white steed
Ever true to his purpose, to fulfilling his deed
And as night creeps across the near-barren land
The world waits in hope for the peace that is planned

Darkness descends, as the light fades away
It looks like the end of another long day
No clouds can be seen, yet the stars shed no light
The world is engulfed in the colour of night

Not a breeze stirs the air, not a sound can be heard
No call of the wild and no song of the bird
The stillness, the silence seems strange and bereft
A desolate wasteland is all that is left

Life doesn't exist now where life was before
Extinguished by sickness and famine and war
This is the reward, the Earth's sorrowful fate
When mankind is devoured by anger and hate

The pale rider comes on a bleached, bone-white steed
Relentless of purpose, because of man's greed
It's a haunting reminder of what lies ahead
A world filled with horror and darkness and dread

Heather Johnson

Response of Nature

In thy depart, life turn conception,
I think else it turn unknown question.
I ask the beetle: Where is thy heart?
It responded: From flower do I investigate.
I ask the candle: Why kill the poor insect?
It told: The aim of beauty is destruction.
I ask the heavens: Wherefore weep in dark?
It answered: The world has declension.
I ask the star: Why gather so wraithly?
It told: We consult the moon's deception.
I ask the tide: Why break thy head?
It answered: I repent on my action.
I ask my heart: Why throb very hard?
It told: Another name of life is affection.
I ask the rose: Why spread thy odour?
It said: My composition has perfection.

Islam Gul

What Are We?

Are we beings?
Are we persons?
Or are we in reality things?

Were we born?
Were we created?
Or did we first become?

Are we living?
Are we existing?
Or are we in reality dead?

What will become of us?
Will we live forever?
Or will we die tomorrow?

Who knows?
Do you?
Do I?

No, we do not.
We may never know,
For who are we to say?

Terry Anderson

Snap Shot

Drizzled,
Sucked inside a bar;
Squeezed,
A tea-bag of thoughts, bitter;
A few empty tables yawned a cipher,

Ungainly lifted
A pair of paws,
Beer mugs
Topped
With straws.

Rain
Swung in cords of rain,
A bamboo curtain.

Dipak Mazumdar

Untitled

My thoughts are cleared
As is my mind
Almost asleep,
But soon I find
My mind is filled
With thoughts anew,
With thoughts of love,
With thoughts of you.
I dare not sleep,
For if I do, my dreams, I fear,
Shall be of you.
These dreams of love,
These dreams so real,
These dreams so rich in their appeal,
And sadness soon shall overthrow
My heart, my soul,
The love they know.
I slowly—painfully—realize:
When the Dreamer awakens,
The lover dies.

Gilbert El-Dick

Mad a Man

Mad, a man, the last man walked through
the desolate desert's dryness.
Mad, a man, last man once again, climbed
the majestically mumbling mountain.
Mad, a man, a last man, ho-hum, swam
across wailing wily waters.
Again,
Mad, a man, carrying
the last hope
vestige of civilization,
until, repetitively,
Mad, a man, became a damn man—
A, dam, man—
The first man:
Adam . . . man.

Justin Scott

Star

From my mind up to the sky
And beyond space and time
I look up, out to the stars,
And, baby, I know just where you are
Your sparkling beauty shines down on me
And in my heart the warmth and glow
Of feeling your energy
I can see, I can see
Baby, those stars ain't so far
And I know just where you are
And, baby, you—you are a star
Shining through the end of time
Always brightest in my mind
Looking up to where you are
And, baby, you—you are a star
I can see, I can see
So I know the stars aren't so far away
Getting closer every day
And I already know where you are
And, baby, you—you are a star

Bogus Charlie

The Purest Love

The purest love
Is that from a parent to a child:
Unconditional, unselfish, unrelenting,
Even when 'tis you
On which our frustrations are venting.
With a gentle hand we followed your lead;
We have become leaders through
Your patience and insightful deeds.
You have stood by us through
Every moment and every thought;
Two better parents there simply are not.
From our birth to our death you guide us.
You are our voice when we cannot speak,
You are our eyes when we do not see,
You are our strength when we are weak.

We know this is a bond,
One that could never be defiled.
The purest love
Is that from a parent to a child.

Kelly Brock

Memories Left Behind

Years go by so very fast,
It's only our memories that will last.
They're memories of good times that's true,
And sad times like this one for me and for you.

Memories of cookie jars, cherry trees and flowers,
For these are the things he did spend hours,
Just pruning and trimming to the right shape and size,
It wasn't till now that I did realize,

How much of him is inside of me
There's no other way I'd want it to be.
As Grandchildren we heard stories of adventure and trips,
To lead a good life he always had tips.

Valor, honesty and pride were his strengths,
For satisfaction he went to great lengths,
For family and friends he would do anything,
All that he'd ask was to give him a ring.

So on this day we're here to rejoice,
And to pray that God will hear our voice,
to take our Granddad to a finer place,
Where he'll be accompanied by a higher grace.

James Nash

Dad

With every day that passes,
My eyes are filled with tears,
And the memories you gave me
Will be cherished over the years.
I took your hand
When I was small
And always believed
That you'd be there if I should happen to fall.
But now you're gone, so far away.
I'm not sure what I will do
Without you here each day.
I tried to call you
So that you would wait.
I wanted to be there with you
But I was moments too late.
When I think of you,
My heart aches and I start to cry
Because I didn't get to hear you
When you whispered your last good-bye.

Michelle Rooney

For a Moment . . .

Enter the depths of my heart if you will . . .
Passages of passion and internal chill,
The many different kaleidoscopes,
Patterned with despair and hope.

Enter the depths of my mind if you will . . .
Where dreams are alive and give a thrill:
Unbounded freedom
Ruling an entirely different kingdom.

Enter the depths of my desire if you will . . .
This energy can bring life or kill:
Seeking for Planet E—Ecstasy,
Yet wanting peace in my fantasy.

Ma Ping Wun

The Paradise

Sometimes when I find
Some sign
From where I was living far away,
I remember some of my days
About the past from
Too many years ago
When I was in high school.

Teacher was free himself with his sole
Talking of lesson.
I also was free myself,
Being drowned in my dreams.
We both missing each other,
In fact we had lost paradise!

Yes, paradise would begin from class
When I concentrate on teacher. If I was that
Different, would be toward the sun.
At least, I was the other person than today.
Alas! I was not as wise as teacher
'Til concentrating on her,
Because of not being wise.

Manzar Hashemi Siahpoosh

Fetish

Like the still of night
yet is the crashing waves
It seems dark and mysterious
but is warm and bright
and has the innocence of peace that brings harmony

It feels like rose petals against your skin
So smooth, soft, sensitive
are the musical notes that dance around you
is the golden light, shining happily upon us
So deep, it sends you into space

Every careless and thoughtful move touches me inside
yet brings me much pain and sorrow
though also great happiness and joy
I often question myself
but I dare not ask out loud

I can't seem to forget
but I'm unable to take the torment
Then finally it comes . . . good-byes
fading away with the mist as the sun rises
leaving me in dreamy vapors of my memories—forever

Bennie Ta

Unreflecting Love

Since I am a narcissist, it's harder
To find unreflecting love or admit
That I cannot alone make these lines fit
The molds that make a poet a martyr.
Wanting you to echo and not barter,
Longing to be the poet to transmit
The unequivocal, I aim and spit
These lines designed to make me sound smarter.
Yet, now I taste your words upon my tongue,
Tho' I didn't intend to put them there.
I taste phrases that I could not have sung,
Until my mind in you made me aware.
And now I hear your mind in me among
These lines, my lungs—more young now in this air.

Jimij

Questions to a Friend

Why?
And I look into your eyes
From nowhere,
Hoping to find the answers I seek
And the love for which I long.

But you are just a friend
Whom I need to accept
Without expecting a thing:
Just a friend.

It has never been so wonderful;
Only a few weeks with you
In your joyful and calm presence
Made my life.

I have never thought
What it meant
To have
A friend!

Marina Khonina

There's Still Hope

Through all the hurt, and the pain
A sliver of hope still does remain
Even though I live in bliss
If I die I'd surely miss

The ability to watch
Your beautiful face
The perfect match
The perfect pace

So keep your chin held up high
And try your best not to cry
Because I feel your very anguish
I wish I could just extinguish

Just to remove
Your very sorrow
That would improve
What happens tomorrow

Matthew L. Kramer

A Pond in the Fall

Birds float in the water like tugboats
Swaying with the trees,
As I sit and watch them
In the cool breeze.
Somewhere over the water,
The silence is broken by a shrill squawk,
And somewhere overhead
Cries a hawk.
Squirrels scamper at the slightest sound.
On the beaten trail
Barks a hound.
The flow of the water swirls and swirls,
And up above
A magpie twirls.
Trees change colour from green to red,
And then they fall down spiralling
To the forest bed.

Taylor J. Burnham

Untitled

Storms howl all around:
wind, thunder, lightning, hail.
A child whispers, I'm afraid.
No one listens; no one answers.

Life presses all around:
greed, poverty, disease, responsibility.
I whisper, I'm afraid.
No one listens; no one answers.

God's love is all around:
unconditional, enfolding,
never-ending, steadying.
God whispers, be not afraid.
I will listen; I will answer.

Paula Allan

Untitled

The desert has its beauty
Surviving the sifting sand
The cactus will be blooming
Unaided by human hand.

The gnarled pine above timber live
Survive the wind, the heat, the cold
Despite the worst of all conditions
Live to be very old.

Deep in the heat of the forest
A plant has little chance for sun
So it climbs a trunk to a sunny spot
Its adaptability is so well done.

Each of us have a mission
A special place to be
To fill that spot with all we have
That others too can see.

So bloom where you're planted
Make the best of where you are
Tomorrow will be better
Hitch your wagon to a star.

Rowena Jones

Why?

I saw my father walk out the door
As he left to go to war.
I saw my mom, before she died,
But I still have to run and hide.
My sister ran as far as she could;
My brother hid behind some wood.
Why my father, why my mother,
Why my sister, why my brother?
It seems the world has come to an end.
In loneliness, these days I spend,
For no one's here to comfort me,
And through new eyes the world I see.
I wish that they were all right here
To comfort me through all my fear.
I wish that I could find my place,
As tears of pain run down my face.
And as I cry, I ask myself, "Why?"

Alicia Dawn Woods

The Flood of the Century

The ravaging Red had set forth its course,
through farmlands and towns to destinies north.
It slowly consumed all things in its path.
Merciless and deadly, it vented its wrath.
But the people were stronger, united in hope.
With the odds stacked against them, they knew how to cope.
They bonded together like never before,
and used every resource to build up the shore.
The Army was vigilant in its great task at hand.
With the enemy present they had taken command.
The river unleashed all its power and might.
Destruction had taken its claim, yet even in spite
of the arduous fight, compassion had spread like a flame.
Love flowed through the valley.
Its course had been set by a nation united;
its purpose was met:
a legacy, forged through the dirt and the mud,
to the human spirit that had conquered the flood.

Kathy

God, If You're Listening

If you're up there, God, please hear me speak
Watch over my friend, she's terribly weak
She's lying in bed with tubes up her nose
She's fading away like a withering rose
It's amazing how you could create the world
But now you can't help this innocent girl
She just turned thirty, will she see thirty-one?
Or are you trying to tell us that her life is done?
I think it's unfair to make everyone cry
As we sit by her bed and slowly watch her die
If you have control over the big and the small
Then help make her better, please don't stall
Give Jennifer back the life that she had
You know she's a good person, but she's given up and sad
I beg of you while down on my knee
Please don't take my friend from me
She's yellow and shaky, I don't think she'll survive
But, God, if you're listening, please keep her alive

Becky Nelson

On the Horizon of My Happiness . . .

You have filled my head with Roses
And now you are gone. . . .
I can still touch you with my imagination
Somewhere on the horizon of my happiness . . .
So far and so close . . .
Like the shadow of an idea
That has addicted each cell of my blood,
Flowing through me with every heartbeat. . . .
Forever chained in the handcuffs of Roses,
I dress every night with the memories of your caresses
And every morning I tie on around my waist
The dream of your hug. . . .
Since you have filled my head with Roses,
Moving away, together with my peace,
On the Horizon of My Happiness,
Wounded by the Fruit of Love
I am waiting for YOU to be tasted,
To become again a River of Passion,
To become again a Poem of Love, and give it to you
On the Horizon of OUR Happiness.

Mihaela Ulieru

saturday night's shades

red desires seek the red district
high heels pound pavement black
green to breast from wallet

entwining slitherslide whiterelease
moansweatsigh faked satisfaction

white sublimes blacker
red rises, hungry
for other satisfaction

slithertwist—snap—red released
groansigh sweatisfaction

white lurches into blue fear
as red and blue screams flash
through the red-wetted window

Dee Dee

I AM

I am a small white snow tiger.
I wonder how the white and black stripes blend.
I hear the snow white stripes sing,
I see the black stripes dance.
I want the orange stripes to replace the white.
I am a small white snow tiger.

I pretend I am the tigers ROAR.
I feel the rumble of the GRRRRRR.
I touch the cold snow with my paw.
I worry about my extinction.
I cry about the guns loud bang.
I am a small white snow tiger.

I sense I have a wounded arm.
I think, "My red blood is so warm."
I dreamed I was an airplane,
I try to fly but I don't succeed.
I hope I die a white snow tiger.
I am a small white snow tiger.

Amanda Zahn

Playful Rays of Sunlight

The sun filters the room
And over the cradle looms,
Shining on the baby's face
With a touch of magical grace.

The curly blond head stirs,
Blond hair framing the face like whiskers.
Small clenched fists cover its eyes,
As the sun keeps pouring down from the skies.

Baby blue eyes open to the morning,
As a small pink mouth yawns in lazy awakening.
Toes curl up in merry delight,
As baby tries to play with the dancing rays of sunlight.

A giggle escapes baby's lips,
As the sun at its soft skin nips.
Blond curls are gently bouncing—
What a beautiful day, baby is announcing!

Poetry Lady

The Masked Man

I was only three, yet I could remember.
It was like it was yesterday.
They fought and fought, and he continued
To hit her over and over again.

It seems like he wears a mask.
When he takes off the mask,
You can see the hatred in his eyes.
You wish you didn't know him.
You wish you weren't there.

I could taste my salty tears in my mouth.
"Please stop, Daddy," I scream.
He doesn't hear me.
Why hurt her, Daddy?
Why hurt her?

Melissa Finlay

The Caveman's Landmark

Together we became dead weight:
a corpse confined in a coffin
for eternity, and the Earth would
not be degraded to find our passion.
We both broke the ancient laws
written before time—
only you, with your vicious charms,
you resurfaced without blame.
The night is frozen in memory.
I slid the halo of hornets from your
sinking head,
held you against the burning candles
of deformed children.
Now I'm stale,
longing for the old country before
the world caught up with us,
nervous, forgiving, and everything
came as natural as blood.
My life has now become expendable.
It hurts like a broken bone of God.

Tyler Volsky

Answers

Has the morning kissed you softly?
Have you heard creation cry?
Would you spend the time,
As time does take, to ever ponder why?

Have you heard the ocean whisper
Sweet melodies of peace?
Or felt it's raged indifference,
To thoughtless energy?

I soar life's glorious quest,
A child, I'll always be.
As each array of morning's light,
Creates new wonders for me.

And though I'm fully known,
In God's eternal plan.
The answers are in seeking,
My God, in Whom I am.

Donna McCuskee

The Cry of the Sky

The sky is crying softly.
It's crying for Sister Earth.
The Earth is slowly dying,
Has been dying since man's birth.

The sky soon starts to tremor
And wails a little more.
Dear Earth is fading quickly
And has faded through the door.

The sky begins to tantrum
And screams that it is not right.
Great Earth just smiles gently
And gives in with little fight.

Laura Thompson

An Arctic Shiver

An Arctic shiver
Passes through me,
Swept up in a current
Of pure bliss.
A million stares
I sink beneath,
Yet travel the clouds,
Freely.
In a silent way,
My wrongs have been undone.
Even so, thousands of icy fingers
Still tickle my skin.

Harley Baxter

Untitled

When we were kids
Oh, God, ten years ago
We played and laughed
You said you'd marry me
Oh, boy, you were three then
And I said "Yes, you will"
I lost you for ten years!
Now you're thirteen and I'm fourteen
I told you I knew you as a child
You said "I know" and ignored me
I never knew you were so handsome
I never paid attention ten years ago
When we were kids

Malin Blomquist

Travel

Memories are shared,
Friendships start,
Experiences compared,
Though worlds apart.

The experience of travel,
And education in itself,
Other cultures to unravel,
And treasure to oneself.

A language barrier to overcome,
An understanding is learned,
Communication between everyone,
Patience and tolerance earned.

Siobhan Foster

The Dictionary

It's been many years since I bought this book,
As I'm a crossword buff at heart,
But now I'm beginning to realize
That the book is falling apart.

It's enough that the pages are worn and torn,
Which gives me a few relapses,
But now when I go to pick up the book,
The darn thing all collapses.

I find that when I need the help
And look to the advice of the sages,
I have to go from room to room
To find the missing pages.

All the E's are in with the S's,
And the O's are very few.
I'm liable to be looking for "Arachnid,"
And find it starts with "U."

But enough about this impossible book,
Which is obviously making me wary,
Someday I'll just go out and treat myself
To a brand new dictionary.

Sylvia Punt

I Now Have a Bike in My Corner

Rain.
Of course I knew all along it had been raining for hours.
But I didn't acknowledge its presence
until I had to walk in it,
had to get wet.
Not that I mind the rain really,
or being wet . . . but I started running anyway.
A bike,
blue with an absurd banana seat
and great U-curving handlebars
and more than too small for me,
but it was there, it was late,
and besides,
I was feeling the desire to be dry,
and well . . . it had fenders. . . .

Ryan Harrison

The Rose

A rose
A beautiful red rose
Stands alone out on the rose bush.
In amongst the thorns
And these thorns will protect that beautiful rose
From the hands of a child
Come to pluck it from its perch
But those thorns prick the fingers
And draw tiny blood spots
And the rose is saved
For now
But the rose will soon die
And all that will be left
Of that beautiful red rose
Is a memory
In a child
A child that only wanted
A rose

Drew Bonvie

I Can't Express

To himself he must say hello.
To myself I must say good-bye.
It is not the person he knows,
or the person that is a total stranger,
but the person that he thinks is just a friend.
He believes that he can survive
without the thing that has been a part of him for so long.
Is it just something that he thought was there,
or is it there and not visible?
It knows what it feels but doesn't show it.
Why it is unknown,
but only that special one can see the truth,
or the one that lives above?
It would make things easier if we only knew,
but if we knew, would we agree?

Nick Andrews

Winter Solstice

Brilliant awakenings on crisp mornings
refreshed by the intoxicating breath of air,
the Earth is at rest under an untouched sheet of glimmer.
The tranquil trees are bare.

Crashing stillness of the silent comfort
enveloped in the rhythm that is unified art,
joyous memories elate spirits,
warm excitement conquer the heart.

K8 Maclennan

Spring

The big, old collie dog howling
While the coyote pups are calling,
The moon so big and bright,
But yet the rain falls to night.
The smell of green grass
And the lilac brushes hung purple at last:
Winter was so long and cold.
Just to think of it chills my bones.
The thunder rolls and the lightning flashes.
I wish spring could be forever lasting.

Valerie Barber

I Thought I'd Tell You One Day . . .

I thought I'd tell you one day, I write love poems
Inspired by you,
Which simply chronicle those feelings I have for you.

I read them to myself,
Hardly believe they belong to me.
Day in, day out, I've funned with love and joked it away.

Held myself together, un-drowning and real:
What's happened to me?
Immersed in another me I've never known before,
I cry about what I've lost, but feel it un-missed.

I've become prolific.
Every time I see you, I have new feelings;
Each new feeling has a new interpretation;
Each interpretation, a new emotion,
And every time I go away from me,
I dissolve entirely in you.

Abeya El Bakry

Beach of the Lost Red Flag

Beware of me
When I'm in reach.
The tide is out.
I am the beach.
Be so aware,
Take very good care,
For when the tide turns
And shifts on back,
Be sure it's not you
That's trapped.
My golden sand
Is the wand in my hand.
The trance-blue sea
Beckons thee.
The clear blue sky above
Is my love—to you.
Come play with me.

Paul Quick

Requiem

Who will clothe the naked dead?
I, cried the Earth.
I will clothe their nakedness.

Who will speed them on with prayers?
I, sighed the wind.
I will bid them last farewells.

Who will mark their place with tears?
I, cried the rain.
I will shed tears at dawn and dusk.

Who will give them remembrance?
I, cried the grass.
The years and I shall not forget.

Who will love them when they are gone?
I, cried God.
I will love them, forever.

Peter G. James

Mutual Wonder

There is a garden
In some far-off land
With trees and weeds and flowers
That looks out on
The ancient sea
That wonders about times of yore

This garden and the sea
Both gaze
In everlasting awe
At sky so blue
So deep and dark
And ever colours more

The twinkling stars are Peeping Toms
To this great, secret bliss
Of Earth to sea and sea to sky
That ever will exist

People come and people go
But garden, sky, and sea
Remain forever in this place
Of blissful peacefulness

Patricia E. Berwick

Dad

I love you a lot,
but you make me cry so much.
Bitterness and bad dreams
come to me with your touch.

You hit me all the time,
but that's not why I cry.
You say you love me but you hurt me.
I just don't understand why.

You treat me bad,
like I'm lower than dirt.
I can't find words
to explain all this hurt.

I live in fear
from night till dawn.
I couldn't put up with it,
So now I'm gone.

I ran away
to a better place
so I'd never have to look upon
your mean, bitter face.

Amanda Wallace

The Heckler

In the morning, he is still,
While others rub their weary eyes.
He shall remain asleep until
The moonlight summons him to rise.
He awakens from his daily trance,
And with his hopes of high romance
Commences a nocturnal dance.

In the night, I hear his laughter,
And at once, I hold my breath.
It echoes through the ever after
When the hour is calm as death.
Though I am mindful of his ploy,
I must suffer and be coy!
Why does he practice to annoy?

Catherine Bolter

When the Music Stopped

She knew she should leave before
her world or the music stopped, but,
like most fools, she didn't know how.

So, her nights became old
seventy-eights on forty-five speed.

He, with the cultivated ear,
could hear the static in her smile.

He left, un-grooving vinyl
that danced in his wake,
like a multitude of charmed snakes.

She heard the notes fading
in the traffic's hum, and
when the music stopped

she was alone,
wearing a platinum smile
and a vacant look.

Hazel Simmons McDonald

SUNDAYS ARE THE WORST

For E. A.

I know I've been through something
But I just don't quite know what;
And the dust hasn't yet settled
Nor has the blood dried on the cut.
What I do know, I know only too well,
That of the bad, Sundays are the worst,
And although I loved you not the longest,
In my heart you will always be the first.
After we survey the damage to our souls,
We then make do with leftover dreams,
And we wonder why we ever loved so much
And why we ever listened to such schemes.
I always think I can make it through
From Monday to Saturday, nearly whole;
But it's these Sundays that throw me,
And I most want you, body and soul.
And I know Sundays are always the worst,
Yet I live for them perhaps the most,
For, it's on this day more than the others
That I am most often visited by your ghost.

John Potter

The Cut

Blood on blood, one on one.
Above our needs,
beyond the fun,
we swore upon a cut
as others before had done.

But we, at least,
know the road
the older we become,
to reach eternity
will be tougher than we'll want.

To die for each other is an easy thing to swear;
to live for each other: a bloodier cross to bear.
We're against all odds as all else fail-
Tom Jones and Delilah;
King Diamond and Abigail.

Blades and blood
are not sharp nor red enough
to cut that far in this screwed-up world.
It's really just up to you and I
and lots of what we've got inside.

Alvin L. K. Chow

Friendship

Our friendship is so special to me,
There is no word to describe it.
It's the flower that blooms at dawn.
It's the sunset on the horizon.
It's Popsicles on hot August nights.
It's the sparkle in my eye when I see your face.
It's the breath that I hold when I realize I am loved by you.
It's the smile that suddenly appears when I think of you.
It's the glow in my cheeks that seems to radiate from my heart.
It's the feeling of security, even when we are miles away.
It's feeling warm in the middle of a blizzard.
It's a comforting silence amongst a noisy crowd.

Lina Forte

A Utopian's Paradise

I am the battery in your Walkman, or your flashlight,
or even your remote control—
the one that seems almost perfect.
Everlasting and Never-ending. (ironic)
Continuous energy, effort, and willpower.
It must feel great having such a source in your possession.
I am—the battery that in your mind hasn't been replaced in ages.
You use me over and over again,
and it never seems to fail your needs.
Until (the big turnaround) of course,
this, like most things, ends time—
your battery utopia.
(your battery utopia ends time!)
I end up in a recycle box.

The Secret: It all happened in your imagination.
I wasn't Everlasting and Never-ending.
You replaced me before you realized the meaning of the word
replacement.
I was there before you could understand,
you just don't remember. Do you now?

Sophie van Rooijen

A Little Girl's Fantasy World

A little girl's fantasy is full of bewilderment and enchantment,
For if you are looking for beautiful, magical things, a little girl's
   mind may be the right instrument.

One of these creatures are fairies so nimble and light
Who are playful and frolic about in the night.
For, a little girl's fantasies never have fright.
To quench their thirst, they drink morning dew.
They eat mushrooms and vegetables and ripened fruit too.

Unicorns are creatures as wondrous these.
For, the thought of a unicorn sets you at ease.
They are much like horses but with many more colors,
But their majestic horns make them different from others.
They usually come from enchanted forests with enchanted creatures,
And so these are the unicorn's most special features.

There are lots of more things in a little girl's mind
Like roses that do not have any thorns, talking teddy bears,
princesses, castles, and more,
But there are still other fantasies that she will find.

Nicole Myrhaugen

Un-Chanted Legend

Anger keeps on building within the human soul.
Crystalline reflection, with a gesture, all is told.
Like frozen lead, your tears, untamed and strongly spill.
Trusting is no more when it comes to human will.

We walk through life all sheltered by religions from the past.
Their bows are so deceiving, how much longer will they last?
The enigma of existence lies within the human mind—
The longing of the questions and the answers you will find.

The hand that we must follow is the one that holds the light,
Blinded by the prism and the demons in our sight.
Un-chanted legend's gasping, we are all within its hold,
Ignoring all the warnings and the chaos that's been foretold.

Frank Alicea Jr.

Friendship

Here's to you, my special friend,
one I hold so dear.
The world around me feels so good,
'specially when you're near.

Mundane events of daily life
are always fun to share,
but facing trouble all alone
is very hard to bear.

When a burden wears me down or
I'm floating in the air,
I can always call on you
and know that you'll be there.

You've inspired a spark within me,
energizing a love of life,
dispelling my sense of boredom,
unhappiness, and strife.

Experiment and find new paths,
is what you said to me.
Don't hold back or be afraid—
the best in life is free!

Helen S. Brawer

The Legacy

Forget me not.
My story I must tell.
Death! Death! Death!
The blood of many
Lies upon the hands of evil.
For the love of a sister, a lover,
My only friend,
I must stop the kill.
For, the legacy must end.

Donald Mongrain

You Take Us

I love my cat.
What can I say,
She still likes to cuddle
To this very day
And she loves me.
Well, I know, in a way.
So, I feel I must be just:
You don't take me, you take us.

I have had her for many years.
She's my best friend,
And I want her near.
In other words
It is like thus:
You don't take me, you take us.

You love me,
You love my cat.
That's not a choice,
That's a fact.
I'll remind you if I must:
You don't take me, you take us.

Shirlee Darichuk

To My Heart

You make me cry,
You dry my tears.
You are my pain,
You are my pleasure.
You are my weakness,
You are my strength.
You take away my breath,
You give me life.
I can't love you enough,
I love you too much.
I'm undone, yet in control.
I'm dying and living at the same time.
I can't wait a moment longer,
But I can wait forever.

Russel Schuster

One Smile

Of joy, through tears,
my strength for the years.
Your youthful, glowing face,
smiling down upon with grace.
All promises you made were kept.
Your love, stronger than
spiteful words driven like spikes.
Neither genius nor lover
could possibly hope to understand
the love with which You love me.
Your tears make the rain,
Your anger the thunder,
Your existence makes each being,
Your being is our saving grace.
But it is Your smiles
that lift me higher than all of the stars.
For, one smile in Heaven
is a blessing on Earth.

Lianna Wheeler

Last Audition

He could not rise to Heaven,
was refused a key to Hell.
From all accounts I gather,
has a soul he cannot sell.

He pleaded and he bargained,
pledged for better or for worse,
but still he could not find a way
to rid him of this curse.

Oh, they pick their people carefully,
and he fits neither mold.
They just left him there—a'wailing
alone out in the cold.

I prayed he be shown some pity,
at least somewhere to turn,
some shelter for this lonely one,
not fit to fly—or burn.

Last night I heard him knocking
and, with horror, then his whine.
Be careful what you pray for.
He's found a home. It's mine.

Jean M. Halverson

The Exhumation

They dug up poor old Jesse; they exhumed him from the ground.
They couldn't leave his crumbling bones to rest.
They had to have another poke beneath his funeral mound;
they had to put him to the final test.

What would ever drive a person, what makes him so base,
to want to dig down deep and then invade
the decomposing coffin, the once quiet resting place,
where Jesse, somewhat awkwardly, was laid?

Why was it made so public, this most gross indignity,
where Jesse had no say in it at all?
Why was it such a circus with no thought of privacy
for the skeleton that laid there in a sprawl?

The curiosity of man is never really sated,
especially now, when bones are here at hand,
allowing us to do things that were never contemplated
when Jesse rode above the sod and sand.

The few remains of Jesse James were plucked up from the hole
and put in bags and sealed and sent away
to be molested further by some experts with the role
to test poor Jess for proper DNA.

Frank Younger

Farewell

Why is it that those most dear
Should give the hurt that we most fear?
Wounds insidious stay to purge
Trust and love until the final dirge
When entering strange, unknown dimensions
You venture forth but can no longer see
Or feel those wounds so corporate
Yet once again, a chance is given to relate
But through a screen: opaque, dim, and obscure

Memories of days, childhood untainted, pure
Make me wish to clasp you in my arms and hug you close
Alas a mist envelops, you are out of reach, I compose
What is there is in you . . .
I would give you all, but something strange
Binds deeply your heart to separate your soul
Tormented, deprived, forced from achieving my goal
I wander through cloud and mist in solitude
Seeking light, praying for strength and fortitude

E. A. Hackman

Untitled

My love for you is so deep and immense that it is ineffable.
You have been and continue to be the best wife
for which any man could hope.
Your courage, your truthfulness, and your generosity
have helped me to achieve the goals that I have set
for myself throughout my life.
I am proud of you for having brought love, hope, and kindness
into the hearts of all those people who have had
the good fortune to know you.
You are deeply loved and appreciated by your children,
grandchildren, and great-grandchildren.
From the bottom of my heart, I thank you for the sixty-three
wonderful years that we have spent together
and I am looking forward to spending the next twelve years
with you, so that together we can reach
the magic number of seventy-five years.
So, therefore, get well quickly,
because we have a lot of living to do!

Abner Kushner

Pride Goes Before . . .

The Frog and The Ox is a European Aesopic fable
Told for its moral lesson around the kitchen table.

Some little frogs were playing in the meadow,
hopping about their favorite bog,
when suddenly arrived a monster, much bigger than a frog.

At once those little frogs hopped home,
their father they would tell,
"Oh, Father!" they all cried at once,
"It was enormous, its horns and hooves and tail."

Father said, "That was no monster, just an ox.
If I put my mind to it, I could make myself as large."
Father blew his body up, "Was the ox as big as this?"
"Much bigger," cried the little frogs, "he was larger than a barge!"

The old frog tried again, again, and yet again.
He pulled air into his lungs with the greatest suction.
He swelled until, "Pop!", the old frog had burst!
The moral is that self-conceit leads to self-destruction.

Rachel Hall

First Love

It is with you that my eyes have seen
the most enchanting sceneries.
It is beside you that I have felt it is magical.

My hand in yours,
I feel myself fly
and forget the pain I had
before I met you.

To my eyes, you are a special being.
Without saying a word,
you are the one that makes my loving heart smile.
A glimpse from you
and I cannot turn my head.
I dive into your eyes
like a river of emotions
and drown if you whisper my name.

To my ears, the words "I love you"
sound like a wonderful poem.
You are the poet
And you will inspire my love forever.

Annick Cadieux

Sunset on Naples Beach

Our feet are clasped in scorching sand.
The sparkling foam, enticing, sweeps within our reach,
Swirling, lapping, curling, unfurling on the beach.
Each shell,
Its own journey yearns to tell,
And as we cast aside the furies of this Earth,
To hear the ocean whispering its tales of sorrow and of mirth,
We are enchanted for a while
By the glamour of the sun and its beguiling smile.
Then, far too soon,
A silver hue transforms this golden light
And sun bows down to moon.
So we'll retreat within ourselves,
With one last glance along the sultry shore whence we came.
And as twilight's gaze doth slowly fade from sight,
We hold this gentle moment close, as we embrace the night.

Susan P. Adler

Vision

How can I believe
If I cannot see?
Yet somewhere in the soul of me
I see
An inward, holy vision
Shining brightly
Embracing me
In a kaleidoscope of joy.
I bask in its presence.
Then, in some unfathomable way
My mind resists
And files this knowledge
As a flight of imagination.
Conflicting murals paint my thoughts.
I feel alone.
Desperately I reach out
For the vision that eludes me.
And in the moment of my need
God reaches down and comforts my soul.

Beatrice D. Sorensen

Headache

He's back again, that little man
Who bangs inside my head
On the drums all morning long
Until I go to bed.

A marching beat, a sort of swing,
What's your pleasure, dear?
Any style you can think of,
He'll play for you to hear.

A fill, a flam, a roll or two,
This guy can play it all!
He taps it out rhythmically
Upon his set so small.

The pressure's building gradually.
My brain's about to burst!
I don't think I can take much more.
The pain is getting worse.

The finale is right up ahead,
Just one more perididdle . . .
At last! For now it's over with.
Why can't he play the fiddle?

Rebecca Codack

November

Sitting in a crumbling land,
I scream out for you.
Reach out your trembling hand,
Help to break me through.
Grasp my cold fingers tight,
Hold on to me in the dark of night.
And when at last you must let go,
Brush my face of fallen snow.
And as I fade unto my death,
Breathe in deep my final breath.
Lead me to my resting place,
Wipe the blood from my grey face.
Shed no tears for my lost soul.
Dig deep my grave, my wretched hole.
And when I'm buried, when I'm free,
Only then shall you love me.

Alexander Kee

The Rabid Fox

Lurching blindly from the sanctity of
Her emerald Shangri La
With frothing muzzle
And glowing lava eyes . . .
Shards of lucidity pierce
Through rabid madness
Flashing patterns of a
Needle-strewn lair
Where empty-mouthed, whining pups
Grow impatient

Dementia erupts with volcanic mania
As remote scents of tar and gasoline
Pervade chaste nostrils . . .
Fragile ribbons of dew-kissed grass
Caress her fevered, terra-cotta brow
A final comfort . . .
Her once regal gait
Staggers drunkenly onto Highway 88
Burning gravel impales sensitive paws
A prelude to her searing white death

Judith Ennamorato

Someday

I will die smashed in a car
already feel the dripping blood
leaving my veins to feed the tar
and my soul vainly seeking God

I will die falling from a chair
or maybe from a window pane
scrambling my brains with all my hair
This kind of knowledge is insane

I beg for a simple clue
A real evidence
Of you
Deliverance

Thomas Birraux

In Memoriam

Dusty bits of shadow dance atop corners
folded down on a past
like mouthfuls of laughter—no, of silence—
where now they speed
like birds after the rain
into holes as though homeless.

Creeping through light unnoticed,
stealing back time, to find, it's gone,
the rain erodes too much,
the worms vanishing
even deeper yet
into that silence
where still one smells its walls.

Never seen: the unseen seer on the edge
where darkness resists fading
through what becomes
shadows drifting
atop each sad instant
into this moment now,
where dusty bits of shadow dance.

Tiffany L. Jones

The Demon

Shadows dance, tears fall, walls surround as the demon calls.
Lights flicker as the candle fades.
The darkness lingers on the present day.
The moonlight glistens on the molded day.
The demon howls; it hears my cries.
Winds scream through the trees below.
As my cries grow louder, the demon grows.
The rain spews through the cracks in the earth.
The demon gnaws on the freshly cut wound,
As the form of a man casts a shape on the room.
As my mind toils through the pain and the hurt,
The demon gnaws harder, and the pain is severe.
It feeds on the pain and swallows the tears.
The shadow now dances, as my tears storm.
I turn to face the ghastly, feared form.
The moonlight shines on the face I behold.
It is a face I once loved, a face I still know.
As the darkness grew lighter, and I dried my eyes,
I turned to the man and let out a sigh.
"I no longer want you; it's time to let go."
My final words as the demon dropped
Were: " You can't prevent pain, but you can make it stop."

Tenessa Napholc

Thank You

Through the years, we've grown so much.
We are finally going to enter the next chapter of our lives,
But the memories will still live on.

You have always been there for me
To help me out through it all,
Catching me each time I fall.
You were always there to guide the pathway of life for me.

Helping direct me to the right journey,
You are always shining the light on me,
Guiding me through the dark.

You told me and assured me things will be all right.
For once, we met people who changed our lives,

And I had given us the chance
To accept the challenges.
For once, I had found someone who has given me
The courage and the strength

To become a more wholesome person,
A person who has taught me
The true meaning of life,
And I thank you.

Sharina P. Siaotong

Sleep Now

I was awake yesterday, for only a moment,
I saw Brother Hawk, fresh from the steal
His talons sharp, His pinions stretched, His curved beak deadly
As swallows darted in from above and behind
To harry His flight and save a generation
I dreamed that night, for only a moment
When cumulus and strati combined in beauty
Above a hillside in the colourful day's farewell
The sweet song of Blue intoxicating
And Your voice one joyous drink beyond
I sleep now, again, for one moment more
Until Time fades away
As Summer or Spring
To awaken again
Whenever You sing

J. Goss

Web Winder

Shallow, unto your daily post, lay your soul in the words.
Weave in the spines of fire.
Web Winder
Sparks make light of death . . . pain . . .
sorrow . . . anger . . . joy . . .
The answers lie beneath the skin,
Waiting for emotions to carry on.
Manners are of no essence.
Winder, weave your web of broken dreams to come;
Cut chains that blow in the wind,
For I am not perfect, unleashed,
And have not been heard for many years.
I will strip my soul to show you.
Yet you'll say you still know nothing of me.
I am here,
Showing my importance for you to criticize.
You need not criticize.
I know outward beauty is not mine.
My mind makes up for this:
The greatest gift to people . . .
A Web Winder's Words.

Carrie Goodwin

Romance

ROMANCE
     is not
gold-foiled pink   book covers
    with overly-sexed   males
with   gleaming pectorals
    and   bulging muscles
passionately embracing
    women   a femme fatale?
distressed but half undressed   needing a man
   (though overly-sexed as well!)
    kissing back   passionately
and   Sex   no.
Romance is to love and be loved, the feeling
that takes over your whole body,
sweeping you away like a tsunami, nothing dodgy,
to not be able to live without someone,
but to finally be able to live   with someone,
there   for you to give love and get love
and be loved,
    even if only for a little while.
    You are the world to me.

Victoria Yeung

Dream Daze

Sitting in an enclosed room, looking out the window and
listening to the pitter-patter of the rain on the tin
shutters, close your eyes and make the world disappear,

seeing skeletons in the darkness in one instant and
budding rose in the next, rising in a dream world, making
the hectic and lonely hollowness of hope and faith drop
through the clouds and into a spinning tunnel of misery
until someone calls your name and you are yanked from
that pleasureless and unknown land of fate,

back to a life that seems to have no meaning at all and
back to the tortures of faint reality, soon find yourself
once again looking out the window with nothing and no
one but yourself and dreaming of the day that you might
truly have happy thoughts.

Terrice Keddy

untitled

  once there was this girl
and she said to me,
  "why are you
      laughing?"
and I replied,
  in my cold voice of hate,
"i'm laughing because
  the world
has no soul."
  and she fled.
now she lives with her parents.

Christian Rosplesch

Why Does Mr. Shadow Hide?

Huddled in the corner,
Face turned to the wall,
Deathly still and deathly silent,
He awaits the curtain call.

Soon he weaves his tale before you,
The words a binding yoke.
He draws you one by one
Into the dark folds of his cloak.

There you find a golden heart,
A love that's always true
And a hint of sorrow
Concealed by the rainbow's hue.

A knowing wink, what do you think?
Does the point still pass you by?
Yes, one may find a lucid glimmer
In this madman's eye.

After all is said and all is done,
And the euphoric highs subside,
You may want to ask yourself:
"Why does Mr. Shadow hide?"

Xavier Cattarinich

Phone Call

I spoke to you long distance tonight
and you listened,
so patient as always.
I chattered about my usual nothing;
you agreed, disagreed and laughed a lot.
I wanted to convey my little girl need
to be with you,
to be comforted by you.
I wanted to convey my grown-up need
to hold you,
to love you.
But I didn't.
Now I feel empty.
I have forgotten
to tell you the most important things.
I didn't forget.
I'm just too grown-up to speak
of homesickness,
of loneliness.
How would it look for an adult woman
to cry for her mother?

Brandi Wellman

St. Steven's Day

In memory of Stjephan Bazijanec
It's the day after Christmas,
If you didn't know.
People call it Boxing Day
But it's really not so.

St. Steven was the first martyr
Who gave up his life,
Who wouldn't bow down to
Ridicule, unbelief, and strife.

They hit him with stones
Till he could see no more.
God's spirit was with him
Stronger than ever before.

They had broken his bones
And disfigured him so,
Knowing he was dying for God,
He welcomed each blow.

He was destined by God
To do good things from birth,
For his reward was in Heaven,
Not here on this Earth.

Kresimir D. Bazijanec

Temple

This is my
quiet, purple darkness
my hidden blindness
my secrets behind
heavy curtains
my beauty
empty, uncertain

This is my
selfish, black spirit
my evil, gold stream
my cinnamon
in blackness
I clutch
my crazy dreams

Janet Friesen

My Valentine

She is the mother of my children,
My partner after dark,
Companion in my mid life,
And youth creating spark.

When the sea breeze blows on England,
It drives the boats ashore.
When April flowers bloom again,
It's home I'll go with her.

White carnations are her favorite,
To match her auburn hair.
She organizes wisely,
So we'll have time to spare.

To put it all together,
The spice, the spark, the wine,
It's just because she's Audrey:
I call her Valentine.

Earle Wilson Worby

Thunderstorm

Dark storm clouds cover the wondrous sky
Filling the Earth with darkness and gloom
Mysterious clouds drift swiftly toward a destination unknown
Rain pelts crash upon the Earth, drenching the soil and buildings
Lightening strikes illuminate the sky with wonder and awe
Stretching from cloud to Earth across the sky
Thunder rolls, crashing sounds, deep, dark power is heard
Wonder and beauty are seen in a wild and screaming thunderstorm

Michelle Causley

Barroom Encounter

Last night I went to a club just to be in a crowd.
The lights were low, the drinks were cheap,
The music was quite loud.
I just stood there at the bar, looking at my drink.
It gave me time to contemplate, to think.
As I looked around the club at faces young and old,
I saw myself when I was young and watched my life unfold.
I saw the good and the bad—I guess I saw it all.
I saw me at my lowest point, with my back against the wall.
As I stood there all alone, lost within this crowd,
A voice called out to me—a voice so clear and proud.
At first I did not heed the voice. It kept calling just the same.
Then I saw a wondrous face in a ball of burning flame.
There was a certain peacefulness about this face of flame.
I knew It knew my secrets. It even knew my name.
I lay the drink back on the bar and started for the door.
As I left, I turned and saw
Flaming footprints in the floor.
Walking back to my home, I saw where it had trod.
I never will forget that night, that night I saw my God.

Thomas Heffern

Circle of Seasons

The wind passes through the silent trees,
Each one with its own story to tell,
Enveloping each golden leaf in its invisible grasp,
Lifting each leaf from its perch
    and placing them in their golden grave.
A silence settles into the world around.
The last songs of the blue jay carried away with the wind
As the world prepares to go into its seasonal slumber.
Already thoughts of warmth and color stir beneath the soil,
For where there is an ending,
A beginning is soon to follow.

Miranda Peters

Stopping at the Corn Field

When I reached the corn field, I stopped.
The smell of yellow mixed with the colours of my dreams.
I heard them whisper as the wind woke them.
I closed my eyes and felt the wind blowing,
grasping me, looking deep inside me,
entering my neatly packed files, which took years to get in
order. Around they whirled.
Memories flew free as they escaped the neatness and
discipline of many years.
The whispers became echoes . . .
and entered me!
I knelt down and closed my ears with shaking hands!

Nandie Bahlmann

Vision

Am I the vision you seek in the night,
The angel that comes to caress?
Am I the lover you long to hold,
to lay your sweet head upon my breast?
Am I the woman you will lie with in bed,
and inside me your passion will flow?
Am I every lover you want?
Dear sir, I need to know!

Oh, my lady, you are the vision that I seek
and want,
for I have traveled through a lifetime
of pain,
for your image in my mind does haunt.
I have felt your love close and warm
even though you were not with me.
I am here to carry you back to the place
we are both meant to be!

Elaine Stirk

The Predatory Pimp

He was so smooth, he was so cool.
This family was easy; he was no fool.
Welcomed into their home without alarm,
He captivated them with all his charm.

It all started with a coffee date.
Her low self-esteem sealed her fate.
Before long he had total control,
Hooked her on drugs, just part of his show.

Working the streets to support her habit,
Once-beautiful child, innocence of a rabbit.
No contact now with family or friends;
Only on him and drugs does she depend.

Helpless family knows she is a victim.
No way to fight this guy through the system.
Their eighteen-year-old fighting to stay alive,
To God they pray, please, let her survive.

He was sent to jail for assault and battery.
This was not enough to set her free.
Another came and took his place.
Were these guys born of the human race?

Lynn Guderjahn

Silicon Fever

Silicon thunder, exotic lover,
Packaging a Mars Bar lover,
Cordial Tang, who rang?
A polar bear, vampire fang,
A case of beer, an ice-cube tear,
Like the T-shirt said, "I have no fear."

Sun-dried tomato, what a fever,
Saturday night, what baseball beaver.
Currency zero notation,
Sixty-nine ain't the only rotation.
Ugly looks, six zero, bank books.
Cactus plant, Mr. Frustration diaper:
Yes, he is a toilet paper wiper.

Mr. Armani, I'll have a hemp suit please.
Like a poker machine, a virgin tease,
I'm on a highway, on a long route,
I'm not married, just riding my ute.
Riding my horse, she's wearing take-away Maccas,
Good looks, credit card debt books.

Nicholas Riganas

Rainbow Road

There's a bright light beyond the stars
Where the sky is providing a path
For those fairies to unbreak the bars
Between Heaven and Earth.

A simple bath isn't too much to take
But it's for their own sake
That they must return soon
Before it's replaced by the moon.

They say there's a pot of gold
At the very end of it
But the fairies and I never hold
On to that kind of bull***t!

Amelia Listiani

Never Again

Voices in the night
screaming in the hall,
a hand is poised in flight
and her mother hits the wall.

She pulls the covers tighter,
her fist a whitened ball.
She never was a fighter.
Then her brother
hits the wall.

Peeping through the door,
up and down the hall,
he's coming for her soon,
then she'll hit the wall.

The gun is almost loaded.
She can hear his drunken call.
He stands and slowly smiles,
then her father hits the wall.

Debbie Read

Preferring Instead Eternity

Lovers entwined in youthful jumble,
Skin on skin, the sexes fumble,
Moan, sigh, kiss and couple,
Julia's breast so soft, and he so supple.
With arms and legs in tangled clasp,
Release me not, lover! A tender gasp,
Hold me close upon our pine-pillow bed,
Lay my halo hair round your angel head.

But consumed beyond compare, he arises
And braids her curls into other guises:
A noose from which he'll hang before
She wakes to find his love no more.
Her lips divine, so love-defined,
Part as the noose is tied behind
A low-lying branch before he slips
into the depths of one last kiss.

At her side he silently ceased to be,
Preferring instead eternity.

Jeannine Mulliner

Suicide

You told me that you'd never leave,
But why did you go?
I begged you, please.
You looked ever so low.
They found you on the bathroom floor,
Blood rushing out of your sliced wrists.
You looked more pale then ever before.
In my eyes there was nothing but mist.
They confirmed that it was suicide.
Not wanting to believe, I turned away.
I realized that you had lied.
We're sorry, is what they say.
You were depressed, I can see.
But, why didn't you tell me?

Amie Norton

Untitled

The knife's on the counter
Pills are in the drawer
What it going to be
To put me on the floor?

I don't want to go on
Please, let me die
Put me out of my misery
So at least my soul will survive

I feel no one cares
I feel no one's there
But I know that's not true
So why am I so scared?

I am losing my mind
I am losing my heart
Why should I go on
When my world is falling apart?

There is no reason for me to live
There is no reason for me to survive
I have made my decision
Of how I am going to die

Mike Gawyuk

Death of a Madman

Like a madman, she plotted her revenge;
She wasn't going to let anyone fool her again.
The rain fell down hard that night.
Thunder and lightening sliced the sky.
Her plan was going perfectly;
His car was parked outside "her" house.
With rage and anger, she busted down
Her once best friend's door.
She pulled the 12-inch shotgun out,
Pulled the trigger four times or more.
She sat down, sobbing hard and loud;
Turning back wasn't an option now,
She watched them die—she murdered them,
But she had to kill one more.
She inserted the last bullet;
She had to make this count.
She turned the gun to her head.
One shot—she killed herself.

Tracey Slack

I Truly Wish We Had Never Met

I truly wish we had never met.
My life was normal—organized, I guess.
And yet, there, you crossed my way,
Like a morning star and early spray.

I truly wish we had never met.
Why me? Nothing had been said.
Black depths in your eyes kept me busy.
Empty thoughts, my head spun dizzy.

I truly wish I had never felt your embracing arms.
I would not have felt your soaking warmth,
Which made me flushed and shivered with cold.
Crazy thing, why did not I feel too old?

I truly wish I had never kissed your lips.
Black silk could not hide your stiff t***.
The dazzling sun got red, deep silence lasted.
Hell, I was in a love I could not mask!

Thanks, God, for the moment we met!
My mind, my thoughts, my heart you kept.
Warm inside, I will cherish my little sin
With all my love, until we meet again.

Herman Tack

My Russian Odyssey

I once was young, active, and gay,
Full of life, without dismay.
When suddenly, one cold winter day,
Soviet agents whisked me away.
I knew not where or why or who.
It happened to me, as it could to you.
I simply vanished into the blue.
Can you imagine? For being a jew!

I was accused of being a spy.
The b*******! The villains! What a lie!
The KGB didn't even bother to explain why.
Prosecuted with trumped-up charges for treason,
The Soviets simply gave no reason.
I was sentenced by Troika to survive
A monstrous sentence of twenty-five
For spying, treason, Zionism, for no reason.
Hence, I struggled hard to remain alive.

Throughout the years in labor camps,
Slaving hard with prisoners and tramps,
I prayed to God to set me free.

Joe Lerner

B******

You took my childhood
You took my confidence
I hate you
I am drawn to you
I must see you
I must talk and be with you
You only ever lie and push me down
Buy my love
Take my mind
You have my power

Brigitte Waters

In the Eyes of Angels

The foundation of Creations is procreation or love
And in the Word One Flesh is far beyond and above
All other commandments or divine laws
And is that not good reason for pondering pause?

Not to commit adultery and likewise on coveting
Those were the commands Moses did bring
But before all and above all the Law of Gold
Was flesh as one, or so we are told?

It is as if some mystery occurs in the union
Where more than one is a defiled communion.
To the ancients the whole world over as to God
Pure, virginal, lifelong devotion they did laud.

Indeed, to the ancients and God it was this:
One flesh was but a wee taste of the divine bliss
That came upon salvation to all good upon death
Where flesh gave up the ghost to cosmic breath.

And so look at our day, what deem ye the incredible sinful mess?
For, sexual intercourse is to God and Christ no more and no less
Than the marriage itself, the Holy Matrimony mount
And so on husbands and wives—how many even keep count?

Achaonadfi

Q.W.C. (Question Marks without Commas)

1) Scrupulous reptile in the form of a Casanova,
Romeo had warm winters but his summers are getting colder.
We're moving very fast but with a lack of destination,
And the pimp is seducing the weasel
    that keeps performing masturbation. . . .

2) Let me go out through the sunshine of tomorrow.
Sex is just an object that crusaders still follow.
I am the cancer in this lovely resurrection.
I'll be rewarded with the lucre of my perfection.

3) Tomorrow will be just a blur if there's still this filthy waiting.
The politician smashed the stamps
but his believers are slowly fading.
Hear the voice of reason from the band behind the P.A.
My embryo's tripping over the graveyards
where the happy campers once lay.

4) We're off to the valleys where we'll never feel anything
As plain as the pain of which the angels sing,
But I feel love—more love—more love,
For hate!

Ivan Hruska

A Teacher's Description

Twenty-eight children with a thousand dreams;
Fifty-six bright eyes watching life's extremes;
Twenty-eight small tongues never cease wagging;
Fifty-six fine feet dancing, dragging;
Twenty-eight noses, curious ever;
Fifty-six smart hands, clumsy and clever;
Twenty-eight bodies never sitting still;
Fifty-six wide ears listening with a will;
Twenty-eight brave hearts beating and alive;
With a million hopes—my class in Room Five!

Patricia Lewis

Does She Hear the Wind?

When you play with her hair,
When you kiss her lips,
When you lick her ear,
Does she hear the wind?
Tell me, does she hear the wind?

When you caress her,
When you pass your hand on her body,
When you slowly get on top of her,
Does she smell the flowers?
Tell me, does she hear the wind?

When you make love to her,
When you hold her tight,
When you reach your climax,
Does she reach the sky?
Tell me, does she hear the wind?

And what about you?
Does she makes you feel younger,
Does she makes you feel alive,
Like I use to do?
Tell me, Baby, do you hear the wind?

Francine Carrière

Solace

Of all the dreams and aspirations
I've held inside my heart,
To find that one to share my life
Has been there from the start.

And yet although it is the one
That holds fast above the rest,
It is the least in my control;
I clutch it at it at best.

But the tide will bring my ship to me
Whether I wander from the shore.
So then I find dreaming not so hard,
Waiting, not such a bore.

Joanna Groves

A Thing Called Love

Sweat pours off my face
Blood pumps through my veins . . . Desire
Burning hot!
Luscious lips . . . succulent breasts
Terminate the loneliness
Open minds to a world of heat
Passion runs wild
The love we share overflowing
Like lava from a volcano . . . about to explode!
The eruption bestows me
Entering into a deeper world
A world of infatuation . . . love and tenderness
Slowly I subdue to a pace of enjoyment
Until I am on top of the world
Riding the wild mind
Screams of joy . . . The moan of desire
On and on until . . . (silence) Explosion
Love, lust, and passion . . . come over me
Excited for the time together
Together we enjoy the thing called Love

James J. Halstead III

B.T.D.

Watching the trees fly by
All dead and decayed
Brought to death by man's careless hands
Now the man is gone
Eroding soil takes his place
Death consumes the land

Watching a line fly by
It marks the end of existence
Brought to an end by man's careless hands
Now all the men are gone
A dark void consumes the sky
The end of god is at hand

Watching the sun fly by
The light we all see before we die
Brought to death by man's careless hands
Our beginning is bleak
As is our end
The gift of existence is banned

Michael T. Hoffahrt

A Place

Take me somewhere
Where I don't have to be
Out there
Lost within the sea

Bring me in someplace
Where people don't look
In your face
A road I never took

A thing I've never felt
A feeling I've never had

Take me away
Bring me to the stars
So one of these days
I can be far

A place where no one feels
No one cries
Where I can have a decent meal
A place where no one dies

A place I've never been to
A place as beautiful as you

Sylvie Le Scieller

My City

It is not ancient, not yet.
Here is only old age, ramshackle . . .
Heavy metal of halos and nimbus
laid upon the messenger statues,
holy martyrs for fame of Christ
for a long time already got tired to crush.

If in fact that admission to fountain-life
will make sure through rot,
through devotion worms,
through growth of grasses and trees,
then my City be certainly for good!

Morgun Vladimir

Evening Song

She sings and does not cry,
though her voice, like old grass, trembles
in the last evening winds.
She tastes the ripest sorrow,
understanding now the unspoken tales of aged eyes.
Her words are not bitter; they are heavy and sweet
and speak of love—weep of love.
Like a stone her gaze falls; these eye are virgin dry,
for she hopes and waits for the fate she names love
one day to greet her again.
She sings and does not cry
when night falls and shadows like near memories haunt,
but, still, stares unmoved into that darkness
while a greater darkness still stares back.
Her heart invokes an ancient chant remembered
as hope runs wild into that fierce black night,
and still she sings, softly and sadly,
for now she sings not to cry.

Elizabeth Shepherd

Football in the Rain

Let's go play football in the pelting rain
And drown our cares in grassy pools again.

Shout our shrill voices, hoarse for sheer joy,
And belabour our beleaguered toy,

Which dead, stuck yet again in muddy pool,
Becomes a stubborn, an unyielding bull.

Let's kick the ball high with the morning's Math,
The treacherous school bell, and the teacher's wrath.

Let's all forget the rules of normal play
And play the way we know will make our day.

Forget our wings and charging at the ball,
Collide above it, lose our balance, fall.

Let the goalkeeper lead the next attack
And having scored his own goal, scamper back.

Let's shriek at lightning, but defy the thunder
That lacks the force to split and put asunder

What God had put together. Boys and Rain
Shall always play the game of joy again.

Emmanuel A. Frank-Opigo

Marionette

I'm sick of pretending that I'm just like you
Pastel, porcelain, doll-like machines
Empty witches of your own denial.
Proven evil floating in a pond of emotionless facade.

Pastel puppets,
Porcelain witches,
I will pretend no more.
I'll break the plastic, interchange molds,
I don't care.

Perfectness causes pain,
The dolls all go insane.
I'll cut the strings of your marionette.
You can't think, what would you do?
I won't be like you!

Meagan Graves

My Heart Is Traveling

Tonight again: The full moon over
Canada with the ice stars plays the winter dance!
On this way I was dancing with my love
When it became only a memory. . . .
Now, my heart is traveling far away
And is coming back by morning, tired and so lonely.
My heart is traveling a long distance.
Canada sleeps; Yugoslavia wakes up.
Six hours of difference between them both.
My coat hugs me as my father
Who is hidden in the sky, and he is looking
For the Milky Way for my heart.
Snow carries the Christmas in the end of 1997.
Tonight again—my heart has traveled following the full moon
And it has returned to me at the seventh floor.
Tonight again: The full moon over Canada!

Mirjana Markovic

Silence

In a sigh it comes, in a sigh it leaves,
The most precious and treasured time.
A relaxed moment, anticipated and appreciated,
Any sound can disrupt it, can cause it to escape.
It can come as a bother to some, a relief to others.
It can come in a split second.
When it comes, we rejoice and expand our minds to endless thought
And never-ending dreams.
It leaves and we return to reality.
We recollect our problems, our fears, our sacrifices, our tears.
We reopen our minds to tragedy and corruption.
When we need it most, we only need to call, and it answers.
Like a chained animal, it walks to our side, unleashes its magic,
Then floats away.
Its work done, it moves on to one of its many masters:
Opening a door to which no one else possesses the key.
Our servant, our friend, our relief, our distress, and our savior
From this hectic world—
Silence. . . .

Christina Frizzell

Options

Furrow's dug, soil's splayed wide.
Cast the seed! Lower the casket!
Deadness to life . . . the other just died.
Phrased in a breath, visibly unseen,
The comma implying time between. . . .
Spectral blossoms 'midst Spring grew from Winter;
Spectral blossoms 'midst Summer died in Fall.
Sparseness—copper, gold, black, grey, white—
Is as run as is walk is to crawl.
Sunshine over clouds rains gladness:
Tears from laughter to sadness.
Hand in hand, secure, passionate whisperings,
Prepared treasure, hidden to find,
Found passion through stumbling,
Forefront memory, in the back of the mind:
From conception to misconception, we are free to be slaves.
Expending energies wholeheartedly,
Living at digging our graves,
Sunrise, dawning of a new day,
Deadness to life . . . the other just passed away. . . .

Daryl S. Leckie

Snow

Snow is falling outside,
Softly, gently glittering.

Snow is falling from the sky,
Gliding down into my eye.

Snow is falling outside.
It's peaceful when you stare.

Snow is falling from the sky.
Whiteness is everywhere.

Alicia Irving

God Mystery

He was Emmanuel, God with us
He was the image of God and just
To manifest God's glory
He came to tell the story
God revealed His work of creation
By spreading earth as it was done
He hung the world in space
And fashioned the flower with grace
His word set fast the mountains
And filled the land with beauty, rain
He designed the star in the sky
And taught the sparrow to fly

Morning sunset, a life of creation
Grassy field of velvet flow
White clouds, a shimmering curtain
God's design, a perfect world
I'm amazed at His talent
Stand up proud for one so great
Today, my heart sings out loud
To the source from whence it came

Nadira Mohamed

Love Poem

How can I forget thee?
The warm glow of your being,
The gentleness of your caress,
The music of your voice.

Oh! I have made the painful choice
That even in silence
My love I cannot express
In the embers of suffering,
To never hear, to never see,
The loveliness of thee.

Marielle Drouin-Jones

Christmas

Christmas time is a time of fun,
we can even play in the sun.

We decorate the trees
in the breeze.

We play in the snow
on the outside blow.

Receiving some presents
Is very pleasant.

Jar Jar Shi

The Intruder

I know you!
You're the intruder who was here before!
I kicked your butt the last time.
Now you're back for more?
How dare you invade my domain!
How dare you come back here again!
What do you want? My life?
That I refuse to give!
It shall be my way—not your way!
I intend to live.
My family stands beside me;
And with the higher powers that be,
We shall fight you to the bitter end.
It shall be our victory.
So wipe that smirk from your face;
You're one dead dude in this race.
Take a hike! There's the door!
Be gone! And don't come back no more!

Nancy Allena Diettrich

With Eyes Opened Wide

Born a child
With eyes closed tight,
A tiny soul cries into the night.
The little boy grows in a world unsure,
His hands reach out to you and take hold.
He is your son,
So innocent and with a heart of gold.
He is a part of you
That you must someday set free.
You have taught him the lessons of life.
You have opened his eyes to see.
One day he will look back
And view you with loving respect,
For you are his mentor,
His mirror in which to reflect,
And when he's frightened
With nowhere to hide,
He will come back to you
Again like a child
With eyes opened wide.

Linda Clements-Talbot

War

I look around the room,
Nothing to be seen,
No one to talk to,
The walls have crumbled,
The floor is rotten,
The people are dead,
Fires burning,
People suffer,
Lights are burnt out,
The sky is evil,
The sun is red,
Everything gone,
Burnt to ashes,
My soul is gone,
The room lies silent.

Elizabeth Jean

Gardener's Gallery

A somber setting,
A warmth, as light dances over yellows, reds, and blues.
He, being a true artist,
Forming nature with his hands and his mind,
Like a sculptor with stone,
Like a painter with canvas.

Alive with a uniform sway,
A soft breeze being nature's choreographer,
An orchestra of rustling leaves, singing birds, and chirping insects,

The artist lies among his display of emotion
Overcome by the beauty.
The warmth falls gently over him like a heavy down blanket.

He sleeps now
And dreams, where dreams are born.

Matt Lachance

You Are Not There . . .

I sit, staring out the window, waiting for you to pop out.
But you are not there.
When I have a great day, I rush home to share it with you.
But you are not there.
When I'm sad and need to be cheered up, I look for you.
But you are not there.
I search for you everywhere, the places we used to play.
But you are not there.
I run up the grassy hill to where the light is the brightest.
BUT YOU ARE THERE!
I have found you at last. We talk, laugh, cry, and share secrets.
You slowly start to slip away. *WAIT!* Come back.
I never got to tell you that I looked up to you.
You were my best friend. I never got to say good-bye.
Must you go? There is so much more I want to say to you.
I can barely see you, don't go! Suddenly you are gone.
I'm alone, but I don't feel the sadness more a feeling of peace.
I realize you were never there. It was just a dream.
I wake up to realize I finally got to say good-bye.

Brigitte Gregory

Ode to Dolphins

Leaping for pure joy
Up into the sunlight,
Down into the azure blue depths,
Cutting the liquid cleanly with a body not unlike a
polished ebony knife,
Unadulterated exhilaration for just existing . . . and being. . . .
Mysterious movements dancing deftly with sparkling
white caps and undulating swells of salty brine,
Sadly, for me, the dolphins disappear in a playful pattern
into the distance,
arcing into the air
like angels of the sea,
teasing my soul with refrains of ancient melodies
that taunt:
Come fly with me into the ocean of humanity;
Hold your breath and see our connection is pure love.

Teresa Mellors

Freedom

Locked in a world catered by entrapments,
given peep holes of what life could be;

Caught in a net of varied responsibilities,
daydreaming of the foreplay of my present state;

Prison bars of duties surround me,
echelons of little things undone;

Please set me free, so I may soar,
let me be carefree and timeless.

I want to drop the disguises of adulthood
and let the excited child inside explore.

I want to forget about life's stringent curfews
and be ruled only by my instincts and desires.

I want the joy of freedom to resound from my lips,
as its blanketed arms satiate my wondering spirits.

I want to be free, free to live, free to love, free to be;
Free my mind, my soul, my body;
I want to be free!

Christine Forbes

Shine

My light,
Shine on me.
Guide me along the path to a love that only you can illuminate.
Brighten all my days with your ever-present glow.
Shine, oh, shine!
Never leave me in the darkness feared by your absence,
The darkness that ever-stalks when tempers rise.
Shine your light upon me forever
And shield me from that monster of solitude,
For in your light I find my strength.
My will to continue prevails,
For I know that when my daily battles end,
Your shine will heal all wounds.
Shine on me forever
And warm me to a depth that touches my soul.
My light,
Shine on me.

Trevor Hurst

The Saga of the Agony of Apples

A lot of small apples on the ground—
there were thousands of crushed crab apples,
for people had stepped on them; the silent agony
of the apples had begun: It is the harvest time.
Would they be picked or wasted? Oh, the anguish.

The juice gushing out from the pressure,
running, overflowing on the ground;
could its waste be measured?
The mature apples had fought to ferment that all
would not be wasted but appreciated.

The scenario for the apples' agony starts
in May time as blossoms speak to the passersby,
their language that often, most of the time,
goes unheard or not understood
what indeed the message was.

A petal, petals falling to the ground,
now thousands upon thousands of them!
Is it ignorance or something else for us not to understand?
Oh, so many heels are shredding the fallen petals,
and so continues the saga of the agony of the apples.

Lumia Alexandra Heijno

Without God

Without God,
I am nothing.
Without Him,
I refrain
To exist
In this cosmic universe,
Alone and despairing,
Searching for meaning
To questions
Without answers,
With no ideas
Of why we exist,
Why are we here.
What purpose do we serve
In life?
There will only be lies,
No truth,
No hope,
No reason,
Without God.

Oliver Arcilla

Soul Searching

The night is fair, dark, and wide.
The sky is pure from side to side.
The breath I breathe could be my last.
The sight I see would fade so fast.
The step I take soon would break.

The people laugh and call me fake,
But if I die right then and there
A shed tear you then would bare.
I lie motionless, my life has passed.
They don't realize they laugh last.
Then they cry.
Their tears would dry,
But I still lie there; how did I die?

Deanna Doetzel

In Love with a Friend

It's been a month I've loved you,
all the days I've cared,
all the while away from you,
a pain I could not bear.
You'll tell me to be honest,
and hesitation will be the deal,
but I know I love you,
this is what I feel.
Why I can't be with you,
too many reasons to tell,
but I won't stop thinking about you.
One reason I'll say,
it's been one year of friendship,
and too many memories of us.
Can you promise you'll stay?
Another date, will you stay?
See, I fear losing you
every day of my life.
A friendship can always be true:
A fling, only one night.

Vera Pereira

A Harlot in Harlem

I was dreaming about
a harlot in Harlem,
not the Harlem, USA,
but the one in the heart
of our city slums,
deep inside,
where souls communicate in body
language,
rapping to a familiar beat,
skins aglow like hippos,
sweat oozing in runaway
crystal beads.
The beat goes on,
louder, faster,
excruciatingly painful.
Suddenly I awoke
to acknowledge her scream
piercing the night.
A hyena laughed.
He didn't need to kill her
to make her bleed.

Brenda Prouty

Utopia

Utopia is my heaven,
Love my rejoicing
Slight of hand my vice
And a blizzard storm out the window,
Sprinkling my words with tiding emotions
And suffice to say: Within me lay maybe
Fleeing baron, migrating . . .
 . . . To realm's infinity well
And resume with insanity's might
Fight not tight
But embrace willing light
As whiteness blight ice night.

Antoine Tardif

Stone of Struggle

Oh, sanctified prayer stone,
a gift from the
angelic hosts of Heaven you are,
a reminiscence of lost hope.
Your jagged, rough edges
reflections of the shadows
within my heart.
Your smooth,
translucent facets
once tempered the quietude of my soul.
Oh, angel stone, remind me of
your gift of forgiveness.
You have become a constant in my life.
One gentle touch,
One hand-held caress,
brings fourth administering angels
of peace and joy to my soul.
Oh, stone of struggle, truly
an awakening to a covenant
yet to be fulfilled.

Karl Joseph

Untitled

Smile with me forever—
A memory of you as you go,
So full of life with your dreams,
A perfect picture created by the mind that wants you to stay.

Laugh with me forever—
Simple joys that many will never see,
Reliving a split second of the past
Over and over until the joy fades.

Walk with me forever,
Hand in hand in our minds—
A distance that brings closer with each step
A journey that will one day take us into the past.

Stay with me forever—
A concept of tomorrow
Threatening to edge into our existence
Each time we turn to go.

Love with me forever—
A feeling that will last into eternity
Created by a young heart afraid to face reality
Until it has passed. It is love.

Jaana Hovila

Nature

Nature is great, nature is fine, nature suits everyone's line.
Nature is trees, nature is plants, nature is animals.
Nature is fish, nature is the ocean, nature is the sky.
Nature is the birds, nature is the very air we breathe.
God made us all, whether on land or sky or even on water.
We all belong to God's creation. Nature is like paradise.
I wish I live longer to see nature grow.
Nature is a wonderful sight to see, for I love nature!

Timothy Daniel Thakker

War

The world:
dominated by fear and ignorance,
ruled by dictators and full of oppression,
a vision all too clear to us.

As the world suffers daily conflicts,
we seek refuge in the hands of man,
who in turn rules in favor of a settlement of scores
through human bloodshed and physical violence.

A world ripe with degradation and poverty,
only the few will survive,
and the time has come.

Here we are looking at the few,
you and I.

They went over there as an army of proud soldiers,
and came back a desolate few,
showing signs of postmortem depression
and a secret wish to die.
Their only dream
is to rid the world of the rules,
so that their oppressors can finally have their day in court.

Dawn Campbell

Pledging (Sonn 10)

Dedicated to Christine for her support and encouragement

For thou I am in perfect trust with devoted love,
I willst bring unto thou all the glory within thy reach.
For now, with such tides of time, I offer thou my trove,
My kingdom I giveth to thy welfare without breach.
This I promise to behold until death thou dost depart,
Upon solid oath I do pledge all eternity for to be with thee.
For, kindness would bestow upon thou with regret to be apart,
By giving time to think would give answer from thee to me.
After such, wouldst sun bringeth shine back to thine eyes?
Thou hast from a bud blossomed into a beautiful flower,
Thy beauty far beyond crystal waters as to where thou liest.
So be it ye pledge to keepeth, I ask all strength and power,
It is thee, and thee alone, I longst for to be thine.
Forever, be so, giveth thy heart and thou willst be mine.

Sun-Ray

A Dream

I was alone in a dark and nameless place
petrified by the sounds of an unseen face
gasping for my breath
I saw an incredibly sight so ghostly
It appeared to me suddenly
I then saw a red light
And to my relief
I began to supplicate for help
And so I ran, but found myself further away from that light.

I was intrigued by illusion
and suddenly there was a dissipation
I then became more agitated
And as I ran for my life
I felt my sweat like drops of water, being poured on my head
and suddenly! I heard a voice saying
Beware! Beware!
I felt delirious, more daunted than ever.

And at the speed of my running
I was surrounded by grave stones
I almost fainted my imagination drove me wild

Linda Lawrence

Land Mines Will Stay

Be what it may,
Land mines are here to stay.
The Ottawa Treaty proposed to ban them right away.
All nations were invited to the array;
One hundred and twenty nations signed "yea."
The big three nations signed "nay."
Land mines are here to stay.

Countrymen, soldiers, paupers, rich and poor alike will pay
With their lives and limbs until doomsday,
From the buried millions of land mines waiting silently
    in their pathway
To kill, maim, destroy those who stray
From the safely marked clear-way.
Land mines are here to stay.

Angola, Mozambique, Cambodia, Sudan and Israel pray
That they will make the big three sway from "nay" to "yea,"
To put an end those deadly land mines, this day.
Maybe then, the land mines will go away.

Bill Redding

Untitled

When you are in unity
With the great unity
Then you long to write
Day and night
Only one verse
The verse of the Uni-Verse

Evalon Alderking

We Will Make It Last

We made it last,
Everything has passed.
The problems we shared
Showed that you cared.

I felt secure,
As though you were my cure.
You are still there
To show that love that we share.

We made it through so much,
How do we think of such?
Without you,
What can I do?

You made me feel wanted,
I started to feel needed.
Please say it's not over,
Let's say we start over.

We are making it last,
everything has passed.
The problems we share
Show that you care.

Ashley Grover

The Horizon

All the time my eyes I kept
Open to see your rising moon,
Brighten my sight to find a rest.
My thoughts raced on, no wish
conceived,
Looking for a way to stop
Your anguish and my agony,
And give the love for you I hid,
Before I fall and dead I drop.

The wind blowing from every side,
Nowhere to go, no place to hide,
Waiting for the rain to come.

The dawn wakes up, forcing its way,
Covering the darkness with its rays,
Taking the sorrow off our chests,
Replacing the sadness of the past,
Making our love forever last.

On the horizon, glimmer of hope
To restore our broken hearts.
Through my love and your tender care,
We may have a life to share.

Thomas El-Beksmati

Elegy to My First Grey Hair

This song will I sing
Of the first grey hair
That startled me out of
Adolescence:
When barely at nineteen
I assumed my duties
To my master Jesus
And to Mary His
Mother
A concubinage of Honesty
Now I am forced to smother
The whiteness of my blackness
With the colours of pure blackness
Of my whiteness
My soul is white
My colour is white
Jesus walked the ways
Of ebony-white
With the fire of a black soul
Superimposed on a white skin.

Elango Edwin Akwo

Untitled

No one walks before me,
for I am no coward
who cannot walk alone.
So lead me not by the hand;
I am no child who needs security.
And you shall not stand in front of me
because you are not greater than I am.
No one walks behind me,
for I am not quite strong enough
to carry a double burden.
So I lead not anyone
who cannot first walk alone.
And you shall not stand after me,
because I will not shadow you.
But walk beside me,
for together we will clear the way.
To eternity we can be as one
who cannot be defeated.
And we shall, side by side,
be proud enough to conquer all.

Marianne Feist

Rise

If words fail to soothe you,
if the songs of birds
sound rude to you,
when pain has brighter wings,
Rise
and allow your heart to sing.
When thoughts of romance make you sad,
if men's souls are not as moved to love
and you feel mad,
Rise
and allow yourself to shine,
and on some midnight
in some moonlight
at a street light
on the right night,
some love will find you,
some smile will blind you,
and you would
Rise. . . .

S. Hanes

Our European Holiday

We flew to Amsterdam, joined a group next day,
People from Australia, Hong Kong, and the U.S.A.
On the Capitals Coach tour many cities we'd see.
For many years Berlin was a divided city,
Not much left of the wall between East and West now.
With construction it's interesting to see how
They've rebuilt Berlin, and as they work underground,
The pastel painted water pipes are above ground.
Drove through mountains to Prague, passed Dresden on the way,
Saw famous landmarks on the city tour next day.
Toured Buda Castle in Budapest, Hungary,
Matthias Church, Margaret Island—so much to see;
We drove along the Danube, saw Vienna's Town Hall,
Belvedere Palace, and St. Stephen's Cathedral;
Took the scenic route through the "Sound of Music" land
To Salzburg, Mozart's hometown, lovely sights on hand.
Back in Germany we took a cruise on the Rhine,
Saw the Lorelei Rock and towns where they make wine.
On shore nice scenery on our way to Nuremberg,
Our last stop was Brussels by way of Luxembourg.

Marian Ross

I Was There Too

Oftentimes, the path we walk is blocked with life's debris.
The deep abyss we face seems black and endless.
Walk one step at a time and savor each moment,
  no matter how difficult.
You will see and feel the time pass, and it will be tomorrow.

It is normal to feel the pain, the anguish, and despair,
But this too will pass.
Every dawn is heralded with the sounds
Of birds singing, of life abounding.
Look back and you will remember last night.
Listen and you can feel last week.

The paths we walk go around bushes and over stumps.
We learn from each journey;
Every day is another learning lesson.

Life is just like that: an enormous book
of pages filled with lessons to be remembered.

Marie Fujita Yamashita

Asleep, You Can See the Difference

In the seam of fire that joins the edges of two horizons,
Earth to sky, sea to shore, life to death:
That is where dreams live.
In the cry of coyotes singing laments at the moon,
in the seemingly shapeless meanderings of hands over a piano,
in fragrances, borne like seeds on the wind,
or lingering in envelopes that come in the absence of lovers,
in the sudden thrill of a shiver brought on by things
only half-remembered,
in paint and stone freed by skilled hands,
in bridges spanning rivers and centuries,
in the heart of greatness:
Such are the dwelling places of dreams.
Asleep, you can see the difference between us.
Lost in wandering dreams, your tired face falls,
turns to ashes.
Mine turns to light, which is the essence of dreams, after all.
For me, sleep is the journey home,
because I live in dreams
when you live in the world.

Graham Lessard

The Flower

There it sits on the dresser, the beautiful flower
withering more hour by passing hour.

A delicate petal falls to the ground,
as a gentle breeze flows through the window without a sound.

Then one careless creature bluntly walks in,
not even noticing the petal so frail and thin.

But as quick as it came, the creature had gone away,
taking the petal without the flower's say.

So, it sat on the dresser like its heart
had been crushed and flicked,
and just before the flower's life ended, it wondered
what it would have been like if it had never been picked.

Mindy Gudzinski

Ode to Our Father

Twenty-five years! How the years have swiftly gone by,
Just like a streak of lightning across the sky!
And yet it seems like yesterday that you were holding us.
Precious memories linger on,
Photographic glimpses of scenes and events
Skim through our mind's eye, of times gone by, of yesteryear.

Know that all the hard work, dedication, and trust
You expended for us and imparted in us have not been in vain.
Your three tiny seedlings that you lovingly nurtured
Have all blossomed and grown
Into mighty oak trees, firmly rooted and unshakable.

Standing tall and strong in the wind, rain, and snow,
Never to be buffeted by the storms of life,
All thanks to you, dear Father,
Because of the values of life
That you instilled in us from our childhood days.

So, dear Father, rest in peace and joy
Knowing that we will eternally carry
A part of you in our own lives.

Manju James

The Eyes of a Child

The picture of a perfect world can only be seen
Through the eyes of a child.
For, there in the rustling green grass, past yonder
In the meadow of life,
A child sits alone,
Quietly admiring the beautiful mirage
Of perfection and flawlessness of life as he hopes to know it.
The sun sets and shadows fall across the meadow,
Exploiting man's future
As it is known to becoming the end.
The child cries out in anguish and frustration
Because his picture of the perfect world is shattered.
For, if it is seen through the eyes of man,
Greed and selfishness
To have all and give nothing replace the natural beauty.
So, as to reconstructing the world
As it was in the beginning,
We must begin to see it
Through the eyes of a child.

Lisa Rosati

YOU

I love the way you
provide my needs,
indulge my wants,
understand my tears,
quell my fears,
support my yang,
respect my yin,
give control,
take control,
patiently teach me,
lovingly encourage me,
suppress my doubts,
starve my complex,
nourish my ego,
appreciate me,
unconditionally love me,
touch my soul,
made me believe in forever. . . .

Yasmin Lansiquot

Love's Victim

Five times found
And five times lost.
Beginning each as hot love,
But ending as cold frost.
Is her love ever-changing
Like the inconstant moon?
Was it found too fast
Or ended too soon?
Need she slow down
And live in the moment,
Or take many more risks,
Thinking not before movement?
Whatever she need do,
She does need to do fast.
She can live but a while longer
With heart's flag at half mast.
Who, she does ask,
Will love's victim next be?
She knows not the answer
Of whose love she will see.

Steven McIntosh

Dark Clouds in the Sky

*Dedicated to those who died
in the Oklahoma bombing*

Angry winds are blowing,
Dark clouds in the sky;
They kill innocent people,
Saying: I did it for a cause.

Angry winds are blowing
Dark thoughts in their minds;
They kill babies,
Bring terror to our hearts.

Angry winds are blowing,
But the sun will smile through;
We must fight evil,
And love will guide us along.

Angry winds will become gentle breezes,
Sunshine will replace dark clouds.
If we fight the darkness,
Love and peace will thrive.

Irene Austin

Channel Five

last chance for respect
never got any
from one of you
write my suicide note
on my epitaph
clever, clever
i'm amazed

terrorists made me do it
made me a terrorist myself
watch it all on cable
chaos, anarchy
from your kitchen table
never, never
eyes glazed

and if it's a lie
systems will cover it up
green room, blue room, white house
color me revenge
my secret endeavor
clever, clever

Amelia Mori

A Song of Nature

The whistling of the night wind,
the roaring of waves,
the singing of a songbird,
echoes in open caves.
The howl of a hungry wolf,
the first roar of a baby bear,
the crunch of autumn leaves,
voices of one who cares.
The crash of distant thunder,
the pouring of heavy rain,
the buzzing of a busy bee,
or even cries of pain.
The cries of a newborn child,
the laughter of a brook,
the hooting of an owl at night,
or the struggling of a fish that's hooked.
The songs of nature are so sweet
without instruments or even a beat.
If we stop and listen well,
the tunes it makes are like Heaven's bells.

Sulphire

Searching

Wanting so much to be happy
Trying so hard to please everyone
Never really pleasing myself
Searching for answers among
     the many faces
Always knowing the answers are within
Searching and searching
Feeling lost and afraid
Still searching

Ashley Bell

Nocturnal Horror

Through a pale, cold window, in nocturnal dreams I see
a bloody, mutilated corpse. Oh, who, pray, who can it be?
In panic and dread I cower as it comes with outstretched hand,
and says through cold and frothing lips,
"Oh, you, oh, you, of this land
long years ago did thrust, your bayonet into my belly
and left me lying in the dust.
And onward your armies marched into our fruitful lands,
burning, killing, destroying, until nothing left did stand.
So, I've come to tell you the story of the forgotten,
beaten man,
of the defeated, weary soldier who stayed
where nothing left did stand."
And with this he disappeared, he'd fallen to the ground.
With a shrug, I thrust the episode from my mind,
until early in the morning on my chore route did I find
in front of my bedroom window, hidden obscure in the mud,
a fleck of froth and spot of fresh-shed blood.

Beverly Anne Olson

An Irreconcilable Mission

Try to live your life honestly!
Keep playing a spotless game earnestly!
The sufferers will adore you as a tireless player;
The persecuted will look at you as a magnanimous employer.
You will become a horse that princes desire to have a bet on.
Seek an elevated mission and you will find
a patron saint to depend upon!
Life is a fight that requires nerves of steel.
You will never lose the battle of a virtuous deal
And nobody will be able your secrets to reveal.
Grasp this! And then you can enjoy a sacred meal.

Muneer Tuma

Alcoholism

It won't let me forget that anyone's fate can be
predestined. We can always use excuses. Can you
afford to waste time? Are you ageless? You awaken
from the groggy haze with smoke-coated lungs and toxic
blood. It has robbed you of your ambition and stolen
most of your life.
There is a fine line that you continually straddle. It
consumes you. Sometimes you're lost in the hazy, gray
void, not able to see clearly to either side. Lost for days,
sometimes weeks. A lifetime. Maybe . . .
But his liver is strong. By all standards it should not
be working anymore. He should be dead, if not solely
because of the trouble,
heartache and disappointment he has caused.
A bottle of vodka and a 12-pack a day. Still going
strong thirty years later. Wasted time, wasted life,
wasted ambition, wasted dreams. Shadowed by the fake
confidence inspired by the next shot. Wasted.
Leading to questions of destiny . . .
Deep, introspective ponderings answered by reality.
Can I end up like that? Never. More has been accomplished in twenty years than in his fifty-four.
His example of what not do won't ever let me forget.

David O'Connor

Sunset

As the sun sets over the hills like a golden mist
Painting the sky with pinks, yellows and reds
The dark evergreens stand out against the brightness
As I watch, the light fades in front of me
Suddenly a blanket of black reaches across the colourful sky
In the distance I can see the blue moon shining amid the stars
The crickets chirp
And the birds' songs slowly fade
The trees rustle in the warm, Chinook wind
Night falls
All is calm and peaceful
A picture painted by nature

Danielle Delcourt

The One Love

A glowing light fills the air,
Then appears the guardian angel that is so rare.
She points to a crystal ball.
She motions me to see it all.
I step near to the round window of light
To show my husband in the night.
The one I left,
The one I love,
In front of my grave he places a single rose as white as a dove.
A lump of tears forms in my throat.
My loved one leaves a note.
As he sheds a tear, I read what he wrote.
"The one and only love of my life is my beautiful wife.
I love you, I love you, I love you . . . I do.
My only wish is to be again with you."
I begin to cry,
When it catches my eye.
I watch him pull out a knife and plunge it slowly into his heart,
I fall to my knees to cry myself into a river of loving tears,
Wanting not to ever be apart.

Fabiana Dallan

Rose

I was given a red, red rose. She was from a person I know.

It was thoughtful and sweet,
And I loved it so. I was given a red, red rose.

It was happy to stay with me.
We were always together, and I was filled with glee.

Three years later, a woman came to the door.
She asked if I was Eileen Moore.

"Yes," I replied, with curiosity.
"Well, you have my child, it's easy to see!"

I was shocked and confused. Wouldn't you be too
If someone came and wanted a child from you?

"No," I said, "How can that be?
I adopted Rose, when she was three!
No, no, you may not have her back.
Rose is mine, it says so in the contract!"

With that, I slammed the door.
I would not see her any more!

"Mommy, Mommy, who was that?"
"Oh, it was someone who wanted something back."
"Will she get it, is it her?" "No honey, it's mine, for sure."

Torey Konecsni

Conquer the Dark

the soft kiss of death, oncoming
the gentle sound of black rain falling

lights dimming, drained of their fuel
crickets chirping by a dark pool

of light, cool water
knee-deep, as you please

I hear a soft humming
a buzzing of bees

all about me is darkness
I'm forlorn and afraid

close my eyes and dream now
I'm safe in the shade

the day is asleep now, dawn is ahead
lay me down now in my soft bed

the grass soft against me
brush against my face

I could stay here forever
in this, my sacred place

Ben Brant

What Can I Do?

A sunny day
Today
A sunny day
All day

What can I do?
What should I do?

Some say, "Go out and have fun"
Some say, "Stay home and have fun"
I don't know what to say

A rainy day
Today
A rainy day
All day

What can I do?
What should I do?

Some say, "Go out and have fun"
Some say, "Stay home and have fun"
I don't know what to say
I better go to work and get my job done

Glen M. Gordon

Untitled

As the wind blows,
It carries the snow
Across the rugged, hilly field,
Which soon becomes smooth.

Mark Keates

Thanksgiving Treasures

Bushes of red, and trees of gold,
And all of the amazement that they hold,
Thanksgiving is the time we pray,
We give thanks for every day,
Toasting all our loved ones near,
Greeting loved ones we hold dear.
Enlivened children play and shout
While throwing coloured leaves about.
Turkey roasting in the pan,
Smiling, Mother watches uncle Stan
Sneaking treats off the serving plates;
Aunt Nan has had to watch his weight!
The dog barks when the doorbell rings.
In comes Patty, her arms loaded with things.
Uncle Stan helps right away,
For there are nibblies on those trays!
From Mom and Dad and sisters, too,
I hope that we are just like you.
From all of us, we give a toast
To you and yours, from coast to coast!

Rae E. Bracke

Delusive Paradox

Memory taunts the blanketed truth,
As time slips into the immortal past.
The fork in a road out of Destiny's gates,
Two paths of equal delusion.

Not time or wisdom could hope to abort
The gallery of allusion,
For by wit alone does man survive
The fallacy of distorted vision.

Not death could learn the skill of life,
Nor the craft of insinuation,
For by these rules does fate play games
With the error of presumption.

The role of Destiny forever lives;
Take heed a warning of perception.
For, the sands beguile never yield.
Beware the consequence of false impression.

Misfortune's ally creates eternally
The perpetual crisis . . .
Mankind's sophistical argument
Against what he cannot explain.

Mike Lederman

Untitled

Cold halls, empty faces,
pale walls, empty minds,
worn marble, long forgotten,
weary staircase worn by time,
greater times, now declining,
steps that echo, blank and still,
silent stillness, senseless meaning,
faceless in the morning chill.

Dorian Mari

Our Day in 1997

One November night we danced the night away
At a country place in the township of Tay.
The question of a phone number was asked by a man.
My number written on paper he held in his hand.

The friendly fellow called three days later,
Few drinks, and dinner was, oh, so sweet; we talked until late.
We came to know each other better,
Courts came and the lawyer's letters.

A few more months of great weekends passed
In the great love that will last.
Now one year, five months, and eight days since
At the same place we danced in hay and clinch.

With more knowing and love, care is shown.
Down the road and G.M. is tow'in.
Together we share life's ups and downs,
Tip Tops for the best man in town.

Huggable fellow with so much to give to a country girl,
With straight hair that has no curl.
Hope and pray for a bright future ahead,
Partners in love until death do us part.

Glenda Evans

Oceanic Rage

Ocean tempest, surging into waves of pure fury,
that majestically but firmly devour victims of destiny,
and the darkness is as still as death itself.

As the hungry mountains of water toss and turn about,
nothing is spared at the hand of the merciless ocean waters
that continue to pound and ravish
and seem to be reinforced by the obscurity of the night air,
inconspicuously attacking souls riddled with sorrow and pain.

After the emotional end of life,
the skies return to their normal colour of calm,
artificially camouflaging the reality,
but only the victims of this mighty power of nature
truly know the meaning of an angry sea,
and the only sign of the end is the feeling of utter silence
and a stillness that is almost evil . . .

. . . as they helplessly await the next storm.

Eliana Castellarin

Life and Death

I felt my fingers trembling,
My heart pounding with fear,
The quietness was scaring me.
It was true. It was real.

The tears in my eyes were blurring my vision,
But I dared not wipe them away.
For, I knew quite well that once they were gone
They'd come flooding back once again.

Friends and family gathered around
With flowers held out in our hands,
With the roses and the lilies, brought from far and from close
To show that our love will forever grow.

I thought of pinching myself to see if it were true,
But death is part of life.
And up in Heaven, now where you are, look down from up there,
And guide our every step, with love and tender care.

Irene Adamides

The Need for Love

People of all walks of life, happiness, sadness, and strife.

The liquid of life's blood flowing through their veins,
And still hatred, jealousy, and murder reign.

Happily and united we should live with one another,
Instead we search far and wide to kill our brother.

Divorce, separation, and abuse:
To live much longer, what's the use?

What we need is the quality of love.
That's what we learn from the One up above.

Felice Sgro

In Loving Memory

We are thinking of you with love today
just as we always do,
We stop to remember your troubled life
and the pain you had to go through.

Our hearts are pierced with unending sadness,
while in secret, our tears still flow.
How it felt to lose you so young and tragically,
the entire world will always know.

It has been said that time heals all sufferings and sorrows
and helps us to move on and forget,
but time still continues to show us
just how much we miss you yet.

It broke our hearts to see your life end so abruptly,
but you should know that you were not taken alone,
for part of us went with you on that dreadful night
the day God chose you to be one of his own.

You have filled our hearts with joy and happiness
and here on Earth we, the people, shall always know
That, for now and evermore, you will always be
Princess Diana, the people's legendary English rose.

Lisa Darlene Ammirati

What Can I Give?

Those eyes are the same eyes
That were there eighty years ago.

That brain is the same one that analyzed and computed
Our daily schedule, so many years ago.

Those legs and arms are the same ones that so long ago
Held us up, and saved us from falling.

That mouth is the same one that kissed us good night,
And kissed away the pain from those hurt fingers.

Those feet are the same feet that went to work,
And carried the basket of fresh fruit treats so
Carefully home to our waiting hands.

That heart is the same heart that felt our sorrow and pain,
So very many years ago.

Is there not one bone in our bodies that can just for a moment
Give back something?

What can I give?
How about a loving hug!

Joanne J. Green

Equilibrium

Let nary a morning bring forth its light
That ye ne'er let thy heart take flight
Upon the backs of winged steeds,
And find at once thy spirit freed.

There raptured by his beating wings
To bring thyself to loftier things.
Yet, let thy mount be higher still,
Then feel his mind and test his will.

Then if by chance it pleasures him,
To bring thee closer from within,
Then seize that moment for thyself,
And place it topmost on thy shelf.

For, I have heard the Unicorn sing,
And watched Pegasus on the wing
In the arctic night at Baffin Bay,
In the sea spray there I watched them play.

So, let thy flight of fancy start,
With that 'tis closest to thy heart.
Let loose the spur and ease his mind,
In doing so I know you'll find Peace!

Jim Hall

Ode to BHB

Evil Narcissus,
Blind to his own obscene reflection,
Enslaved by rancour,
Honeyed assassin, his bloated yellow belly
Hiding under Armani.

Seditious Blackmailer,
He has purchased my daughter,
Extorting from her most treacherous lies,
Toying with her lovely head,
Inciting her to matricide.

Burlesque father,
His life a monstrous fairy tale,
A card house fabrication,
A half-toned half-wit inamorata,
His Belial mouthpiece.

So bent on my defilement,
His mind is lost to reason,
His sweetest daughter hungry,
The other lost in treason.

Carolyn Robinson

Truly One

If you can rely on one,
The only one who helps you cure,
Then all your sighs are suddenly gone.
You may know it then, for sure . . .
If there's always an ear to lend—
You really found a truly friend!

Ike

Nocturnal Paradise

Moonlight sonatas
Play in your eyes
Like a symphony
The darkness
Envelops me
Here
With you
In a trance I
Move
To touch
To feel
To taste
What is only you
I long for the passionate
Whispers that escape
From your
Lips
To make me complete
In this nocturnal paradise

Angela Gleeson

Cherish

Never take for granted
all the things that you see.
Always try something new,
believe that it can be.
Feel the warmth of the sun,
the wind in your face.
Return a smile to a stranger,
lift your child in an embrace.
Life is so unpredictable;
who knows what's around the bend?
Cherish every moment
with a spouse, a child, a friend.
Some will live a long life,
others will die when they are small.
There's no comfort
   in trying to understand,
no comfort at all.
Be thankful for all your moments,
who knows how long they'll last?
For, life is but a play,
and we are part of the cast.

Anna Marie Doran

Have You Earned Your Air Today?

"Have you earned your air today?"
"Perhaps not, but isn't it free?"
"Free as a gift, you'd better say,
To all of us, to you and me."

Do you enjoy your share of Sun?
Do you see how bright and warm it is?
Praise the Creator, don't be the one
Insensitive and hard to please.

And not only earth and water and air,
But millions other things beside,
Of which you're not even aware,
Are given to you, nothing denied.

So let's give thanks every day
To our Great Lord in Heav'n above;
And may we all His Goodness repay
With tender hearts and ardent Love.

Jan R. Sieradzan

Majesty of Autumn

The sumac shivers, the air cool and still,
Barely a sound is heard.
A buzzing wasp, a bird's sweet song,
But no one dares utter a word.

The time seems long as we secretly wait
For the chance to complete our hunt.
We fear a rustle to dried berry cane
Will lose us our chance at luck.

We have had success, and we should enjoy
In the conquests that have come our way,
But nature persists and demands of us all
To make that final triumph, so quietly we lay.

Darkness will soon start its relentless chase
And revel in the dissipating light of day.
Our chances grow slim, our excitement contained,
As we are so close to our unsuspecting prey!

The sumac shudders once again.
The time is now, we can't fail, we've won!
We take aim, the majestic deer now in our sights.
We capture an everlasting picture, framed by the setting sun.

Sandy Morton

Untitled

I walked in the bunker and went to my bed.
The man who slept under my bunk was now dead.

I had painful memories of the destruction of war;
so much pain and suffering, I wanted no more!

Is this really needed—is this really right
for these good men and women to die in this fight?

And YES, I'm scared to go out there again.
And YES, I'm afraid that my wife will obtain

that terrible, little telegram that will tell her I'm dead
and I won't be coming back, like the promise I'd said.

This soldier was right to be so afraid;
that very night, there was an unexpected raid.

These things are true, what the soldier said;
there are living children with grandpas now dead.

There are thousands of crosses, marked "unknown."
There are many people who died all alone.

These are the people who fought for you and me.
They fought for our freedom, for peace, and liberty.

So that's why on this day, the eleventh of November,
That we take a minute . . . to bow and to remember.

Joshua Hissa

Sympathy

Smiles radiated from your gracious face,
Pulsating and undulating with a curious grace.
Glistening eyes penetrated my receptive soul,
Not yet freeing it from nuclear cold.
My eyes caught the anguish of your poignant glances,
Wounded, but not slain, by their playful darts.
Mystical manipulators!
Ironic torture of wrestling with frisky fate.
Guide me to a solace place.
Where laughter is not frivolous or
Sadness supreme:
A refuge where peacefulness shines out to the stars.

Reg Pendergast

Suffocation

In my dream I was a mermaid;
I saw him standing above me.
He was blurry.
He just stood there staring down into the depths
of the sea, into me.
I swam, he walked, but he didn't realize I was with him,
for I was hidden by the kelp and my other friends in the sea.
I followed him until he sat down.
He dangled his fingers above me.
I helped him into the water.
It was going to be great.
I pulled him into the water to be with me.
I didn't know he couldn't breathe underwater.

Sharenda Bray

Meeting L. C.

Yesterday I met L. C.
and he taught me
about chances of the unbridled nights
I took to my heart the most courageous
of the seven-thousand words
and fulfilled my debt of lines every night
between milk and bread
between un-payable French cognac
and the glance from immortal brown eyes
that could fill pages between soft music
and the air from dusty tubes
between your naked body
and the innumerable pearls of sweat on the faces of lovers
between wet, downtown streets
and movies with Humphrey Bogart
between burning kisses of welded tongues
and the modest touch at a bitter farewell
between rooms in which darkness shines
and in which we wait
for the courageous fulfilling of these words

Rolf Uher

The Love Winds

'Tis a beautiful song I hear, a soft tune amongst bows and leaves
As they gently bend to the north.
They have a message of long-ago love,
The kind that is ne'er forgotten—a message for me
From the love winds.

As I look down the path I ride, lined with trees and sky,
I see before me the image they bring.
Was it not for me to keep? Is that why it swirls aloft,
Out of reach amongst the trees,
These love winds?

Yes, I know that it is you, the fragrance, the shadows,
Mercilessly you trap me.
'Tis hard to follow this rocky path,
   yet high above it beckons my heart
As I yearn for you to dance with me
To the answer of your love winds.

So I will follow until I'm no more.
My heart and soul's direction
I cannot change,
For you will lead me until I no longer
Hear the song of your love winds.

Edward R. Dustin

Heart Break

I'm a tree that grows
every time you speak.
I feel the feelings you felt
when you're singing for me,
but there's something wrong
'cause I want the death,
my happiness mixed with sorrow.
It's out of my head.
My star is bleeding,
but my heart is still living,
and that's the price of my life.
I want to scream
'cause my tears are crying,
and it hurts,
so I ask for help,
but you couldn't hear me.

Laura Shizue Igawa

The Daffodil

Behold the gentle daffodil
Who in the Spring, her beauty will
Display for but a few brief hours.
A veritable Queen of Flowers!
So proud she stands with yellow crown.
She chases hence cold Winter's frown
And brings delight to all who may
Observe her and her peers at play.
She paints the meadow and the field
With brush no mortal man could wield,
Filling e'en the saddest heart
With joy and wonder at her art.
If Life Eternal truly be,
I pray, my God, grant unto me
A garden quiet, peaceful, still,
Wherein shall grow the Daffodil.

C. H. Seymour

Last Audition

He could not rise to Heaven,
was refused a key to Hell.
From all accounts I gather,
has a soul he cannot sell.

He pleaded and he bargained,
pledged for better or for worse,
but still he could not find a way
to rid him of this curse.

Oh, they pick their people carefully,
and he fits neither mold.
They just left him there—a'wailing
alone out in the cold.

I prayed he be shown some pity,
at least somewhere to turn,
some shelter for this lonely one,
not fit to fly—or burn.

Last night I heard him knocking
and, with horror, then his whine.
Be careful what you pray for.
He's found a home. It's mine.

Jean M. Halverson

The Poppy

Every year around this time
When poppies can be seen
Remember what they symbolize
Remember what they mean

This pretty little flower
That we wear upon our chest
Is not to make us happy
And is not worn in jest

It's a symbol of remembrance
Of suffering and the cost
We wear it so we won't forget
The loved ones who were lost

It reminds us of the soldiers
Who fought in two world wars
Especially those who didn't return
From distant, foreign shores

Be proud to wear your poppy
On your sweater or your vest
For it helps us to remember
Lest we forget

Aaron MacKenzie

Free to Be Free

The Earth is a circle,
No beginning nor end,
Continually revolving,
No broken edges to mend.

So why is the world
So broken inside?
Why do love and compassion
Continue to hide?

Nations and countries
Continue to divide.
That is why love and compassion
Continue to hide.

It's everyone's problem,
It's yours and it's mine.
We have to start loving,
And now is the time.

Love your neighbor,
Your ally, your friend,
Your country, your enemy.
It's now time to mend.

Donna Jamieson

In the Garden

In the garden bed
Are the flowers pink and red.
Roses, tulips, and daffodils,
To grow they don't need any pills.
They need sun and rain to grow,
And you will see it coming slow:
A blooming bud, a pretty flower,
Just with sun and a shower.

Jessica Crowe

"Mommy"

Expressed, un-orchestrated, upon the musical scale of life
a child calls out "Mommy" from his bed at night.
Its whisper enchants, drawing an ear, evoking a smile.
Then there's its perfect pitch to abandon the dishes,
to join in the stuff of squeals and giggles
throughout the growing up.
Be glad, the capturing lilt of "Mommy."
Abundant in the air, most children know it doubles kisses
and varying tone adheres to both their needs and their wishes.
Shrieks of "Mommy" pierce terror through a mother
thrusting her with raging strength blindly into any crisis
to see it head-on while keeping hers to comfort
and console amidst her endless prayers to live up to
its silent ring of innocence resounding in her heart.
Yet, its blessed, everyday resonance can drive her
to deny any link to the beloved endearment
that tunes her in to joy and laughter
of wide-eyed achievements and small pride displayed.
"Mommy": Universal, powerful,
Its boundless air imparting all the facets of love.

Lynn Kennedy McClung

Sunny Rays on Your Birthday

Half a century you have walked through life
While doing this you have conquered many a strife
Now, we all have a special day
As we go along in life
We tend to forget that day
But today don't be coy
Celebrate your birthday, "enjoy"
For, only once in this lifetime
Fifty rays of sun
For, you will shine
Have a Happy Birthday
Enjoy, and have lots of fun

Irene Philips

Peace

Peace! Peace! The cry of every woman and man:
It has to be launched in a public rally if not done
To appease the rejected and the offensive ones
Who seem to ignore the rights others have won.

Brotherhood and conciliation are needed
In a community wanting in tranquility.
Pacify disputes with amity and love.
Let harmony and contentment effect fraternity.

Conform to God's laws and laws of the land.
Initiate order for those who go off hand.
Peacefully fix disagreeable situations
To establish equanimity and unity in demand.

Comfortable are the patient and coolheaded,
The friendly, neighborly, and serene,
Unruffled by the complexities of modern ways,
A real example and model of charity and peace.

Be harmonious, cheerful, peaceful, and self-possessed.
Share your goods and talents to the needy.
Refrain from inciting dissension and be calm.
Ultimately peace and joy will predominate.

Marie Auxencia P. Bitangjol

Biographies
of
Poets

ABOOBAKAR, FARZANA
[pen.] Jana Aiyas; [b.] December 12, 1982; [ed.] Maryknoll Convent School; [oth. writ.] Several unpublished poems; [pers.] I'm stuck without words—that's probably the worst thing a writer can say!; [a.] Hong Kong

ACHESON, ANETA J.
[b.] July 19, 1946; Petersboro, ON; [p.] Vernal Earnshaw and Freda Earnshaw; [m.] Derek Acheson (deceased); [ch.] Tina Gangemi and Tamara Dewey; [ed.] Apsley Central School, Apsley, ON, Lakefield District High School, Lakefield, ON, Durham College, Oshawa, ON; [occ.] Real Estate Sales Representative, Buchanan Service, Inc. Whitey Ont.; [oth. writ.] My first attempt at poetry was inspired by the enchanting farm property of Rick and Linda Whittick in Blackstock, ON, which I listed for sale in October 1997. [pers.] I dedicate this poem to them.; [a.] Oshawa, ON

ACOSTA, AIMEE
[b.] December 10, 1976; Philippines; [p.] Wilfredo Acosta, Hermelina Acosta; [ed.] Recent Bachelor of Arts graduate from University of Western Sydney, Major: Communications and Creative Writing (now pursuing a career in the publishing industry); [occ.] Editor or Writer; [hon.] Modern History, Typing, English, and Mathematics academic awards; [oth. writ.] Number of poems published in university anthologies; [pers.] Some people think I'm a bitter, morbid person, because I often write about the pessimistic side of humanity. And they're mostly right!; [a.] Sydney, Australia

AL BAKRY, ABEYA S. M.
[b.] September 15, 1973; Dubai-U.A.E; [p.] Shawky M. Al Bakry, Honey Abdel Al; [ed.] A in Shame University, Cairo, Egypt; [occ.] Teacher at Tourism Institute in South Sinai, Egypt; [oth. writ.] Love poems and reflections, children's poems; [a.] Dubai, UAE

ALDAIM, DIRAR A.
[p.] Milad Ghalib; [b.] Febuary 8, 1941; Assab, Eritrea; [p.] Abdul Baim, Nima Issa; [m.] Fatima Al Baroudia; September 10, 1986; [ch.] Alexander Aldaim; [ed.] Italian Missionery School Assab, Eritrea (1955), Hellowan Secondary School, Cairo, Egypt (1961), Heliopolis Military Academy, Egypt (1964), M.Sc. for Technology in Building, Moscow Military Engineering Academy (1972), various science courses at universities in Florida, Italy, India; [occ.] Director and Founder of Nowares Almocha for Techno-Advisory and Marketing, Mocha, Yemen; [memb.] Yemeni Writers and Journalists Union, ISP; [hon.] Social Activity Award, SANAA, Yemen (1982), three awards on Science and Literature at the academy level, Moscow (1971); [oth. writ.] "History" (Agha-Khan Publications), many poems, short stories, and political articles published at the local level, translation of scientific articles (Scientific American—Arabic Edition), political and geographical articles (Moscow News and Asia-Africa Today); [pers.] I strive to relect the indignity and the indignation that people are suffering from in third world countries—among them, mine. I'm trying wounds when giving my expression by sound and profile, just to make them feel that all of us are suffering from that bad situation.; [a.] Mocha, Yemen

ALFRED, VICTORIA
[pen.] Akane-chan; [b.] September 5, 1984; Alert Bay, BC; [p.] Harold Alfred and Bernice Wilson; [ed.] Tisagi Elementary, George Jay Elementary, Richmond Elementary, Lansdowne Junior Secondary School; [occ.] Student; [hon.] First Nation's Bursary Award, Most Inspirational Player, two All Stars for soccer, Grade Seven Athletic Achievement Award, Gold Medal in the North American Indiginous Games (NAIG); [oth. writ.] "The Realization," "Friendship Rose"; [pers.] The poems I author are based on my hopes, dreams, sorrows, and memories.; [a.] Victoria, BC

ALIERMO, PACITA LABAYEN
[b.] January 25, 1924; Philippines; [p.] Sebastian D. Labayen; Angela Cazcarro (deceased); [m.] Eduardo A. Aliermo (deceased); June 20, 1948; [ch.] Rodolfo, Reynaldo, Ma, Cecilia, Rolando, Ramior (deceased), Rogelio; [ed.] Courses in Secretarial, Arts, and Sciences, Weaver's Courses in Real Estate Development, Management, and Brokerage; [occ.] Visual Artist; [memb.] Past Member of Quezon City Board of Realtors, Philippines; Member, International Society of Poets, Member of the International Poetry Hall of Fame; [hon.] Seven Editor's Choice Awards from NLP, exhibit in "Poems for Peace" in Washington, DC; [oth. writ.] Inspirational poem for hospitals and senior homes, "Eternal Wisdom"; [pers.] Moral families make a moral nation.; [a.] Vaughan, ON

ALIGAEN, GIOVANIE T.
[b.] January 3, 1960; Manila, Philippines; [p.] Pedro L. Aligaen, Veneranda T. Aligaen; [a.] Ilocos Sur, Philippines

AMMIRATI, LISA DARLENE
[b.] February 8, 1979; Calgary, AB; [p.] Maria Ammirati, Sam Ammirati; [ed.] Grade 12 Diploma from Chastermere High School, first year student at University of Calgary for Drama and Music (currently); [occ.] Music Teacher with In Home School of Music, Calgary AB (first year student at University of Calgary); [memb.] Royal Conservatory of Music from Toronto, ON; [hon.] Most Promising Address, 1993-94, from Chestermere High School, performed at World Expo 1992, Seville, Spain, and performed at El Escorial, Madrid for representative of Queen of Spain, received First Place Trophy and Scholarship in 1996 from a Teacher's Music Academy International Competition, received several First Class Schools and Honors Certificates from RCM for Piano and Theory exams; [oth. writ.] Articles for Chastermere High School Newsletter; [pers.] The key to reaching your dreams is to follow your heart, and let hard work and determination pave the pathway for you.; [a.] Calgary, AB

AMO, SVEN
[b.] July 10, 1976; York; [p.] Ella Clark, Eric Clark; [ed.] Law Enforcement, Seneca College, King City; [pers.] Speak from your heart and everything will fall into place.; [a.] Toronto, ON

AMSDEN, JOHN SELWYN
[b.] July 31, 1928; London, GB; [p.] Frederick Henry Amsden, Ethel Sarina Amsden; [memb.] International Society of Poets, Vegan Society; [hon.] Editor's Choice Award; [oth. writ.] "Animal Songs and Vegan Verses," Editor's Preserve Magazine; [pers.] The ecology or environment have consistently remained with me as subjects circumvented in this century, even endangering our own planet, all life on it, and the solar system. More pointedly, animals have suffered in these respects, for which I find no excuse.; [a.] Yarmouth, Great Britain

ANDERSON, ENRIQUE R. FERNANDEZ
[pen.] Senex; [b.] November 29, 1924; Zarate, Argentina; [p.] Enrique Fernandez, Ada Anderson; [m.] Lillie E. Larsson; May 24, 1952; [ed.] Instituto Libre De Segunda Ensefianza (Buenos Aires), Gold Medalist at a course on Life Insurance (Bueno Aires); [occ.] Pensioner; [memb.] Member of the Argentine Writer's Society; [hon.] Twenty-six Literary Awards, I have been included in ten anthologies published in U.S.A., India, and Argentina.; [oth. writ.] Short stories published in anthologies, magazines, and newspapers; [pers.] I try to express myself in writing the simple things of life, as I perceive them through my feelings.; [a.] Turdera, Buenos Aires

ANDERSON, TERRY
[b.] March 9, 1954, Burns Lake, B.C., Canada; [p.] Elmer and Doris Anderson; [m.] Caroline; [ed.] Grade 12 Academic Sciences (graduated June 1972); [occ.] Millwright; [hon.] Second Place, Burns Lake School District Drama Festival, 1971 (Creative Writing category for this poem); [oth. writ.] I have other unpublished poems. The majority of these are love poems.; [pers.] This was my first attempt at writing a poem. I woke up at 4:00 a.m. and wrote it, word for word.; [a.] Prince George, BC

ASENCIA, TERESSA
[b.] September 21, 1947; Cleveland, OH; [m.] 1986; [ch.] Mark Edwards; [ed.] Writers Workshop, B.A. University of Iowa, M.A. City University of New York; [occ.] Writer/Producer Pique Nique Productions; [hon.] Awards of Merit (AMTEC Festival) for dance documentary; [oth.writ.] Poems, feature screenplays, several series for TV in Canada, and a dance documentary; [a.] Montreal, QC

ASTON, VIVIAN PAULETTE
[pen.] Poupee; [b.] August 14, 1939; Paris, France; [p.] Max and Eta Aston; [ed.] Started in Brussels, followed in Montreal, Canada, and boarding school in England; [occ.] Musician; [memb.] Royal Academy of Music Club, a friend of the British Federation of Festival, and a member of the International Society of Poets; [hon.] Medals in poetry, a medal and cups in piano from music festivals, and Editor's Choice awards; [oth. writ.] Have written for festivals' competition; [pers.] I do willing as a hobby. I strive to be a good poet.; [a.] London, England

AYERS, NORMAN B.
[b.] February 13, 1941; Thorsby, AL; [m.] Donna Marie Ayers; September 28, 1963; [ch.] Brent, Andrea; [ed.] BCOM; [occ.] RCMP Officer (Retired), Actor; [memb.] Rotary; [oth. writ.] Several poems published in Heartland Voices (Spring/Summer Issue 1995); [pers.] We have two choices in life: to learn and grow, or to die.; [a.] Kimberley, BC

BABADJANIAN, CHRISTINA
[b.] February 13, 1977; Tbilisi, GA; [p.] Paul Babadjanian, Alla Babadjanian; [ed.] Third year at Glukhiv Teachers Training College of Pedagogical Faculty (I'm going to be an elementary school and English teacher.); [occ.] Teaching English now to six-year-old kids at a nursery school; [memb.] Trade-union group organizer and a head of the student government at college, responsible for cultural and educational work among students; [hon.] English Declamation; [oth. writ.] The only publication was an article in a local newspaper about my staying in the United States (Clearwater Forest, Deerwood, Minne-

sota).; [pers.] Hear, never look back; life is too short to take only benefit of your favorite haunt. Make an attempt, have an effort of knowing your heart, come never to nought. How to come to terms with one's fate? I can't say for sure, no recipes made but seek for righteousness. Always ahead are hope, love, and belief—that's what I said.; [a.] Glukhiv, Sumy Region, Ukraine

BABINGTON, PETER DOWD
[b.] March 13, 1940; Salmon Crk, NB; [p.] Nellie and Wellesly Babington; [m.] Patricia; June 30, 1962; [ch.] Peter John; [ed.] Patterson Collegiate Institute, St. Clair College, extn courses Wayne State University; [occ.] Environmental Research and Development; [memb.] Masonic Order; [hon.] Athletics and Sales; [oth.writ.] Poems, true life short stories; [pers.] I believe that man's ills can be remedied through a clear understanding of the laws of the natural world.; [a.] Windsor, ON

BALUYUT, KIMI LOU P.
[pen.] Sting Yhranne; [b.] October 31, 1980; Philippines; [p.] Isagani Baluyut, Elita Baluyut; [ed.] Simon A. Sanchez High School; [occ.] Student; [memb.] National Honor Society, Principal's Leadership Society, Who's Who Among American High School Students, Academic Challenge Bowl, Spanish Club; [hon.] First honor student from second grade to ninth grade in the Philippines, at present: Top Two Percent of the Senior Class, Guam Academic Excellence (in certain classes), Nominated/Member: Who's Who Among American High School Students for two consecutive years; [oth. writ.] Several poems, articles, essays published in school newspaper, "Mirror" (in the Philippines); [pers.] Most of my poems were inspired by the sorrows of living. I believe that it is through these fiery ordeals by which the true strength of a person is measured.; [a.] Tamuning, Guam

BARBER, CAROLYN
[b.] August 20, 1983; Oshawa; [p.] Stan and Monica Barber; [ed.] High School Grade Nine—Clarke High School; [occ.] High School Student; [hon.] Grade Eight Creative Arts Award, 1996-1997, The Pines Grade Seven Eighty-Fifth Percent Achievement, 1996; [oth.writ.] "Clouds" in the Northumberland-Newscastle Board of Education (1991, Grade Two), "I'm Alone" in the Northumberland-Clarington Board of Education (1995, Grade Six); [a.] Cron, ON

BARKLEY, RICHARD GORDEN
[b.] June 29, 1949; Montreal, QC; [p.] Gladys Glass; [m.] Sandra Ann Clark; [ch.] Katherine, Gorden, Bruce, Derrick; [ed.] LaSalle College; [memb.] Optimists of Green Valley, Cancer Society, Freelance Press; [hon.] English Literature; [oth.writ.] Children's books: Princess Christina and Dream Child Laura (not yet published); [pers.] I love to write for children's books and poems of life. This poem is written for my mother, Gladys Glass, who passed away April 6, 1975. Thank you, Sandra, for your support.; [a.] Montreal, QC

BARR, JOHN
[pen.] John Barr; [b.] June 12, 1952; [p.] Robert Horrocks, Janet Barr Horrocks; [m.] Tatjana Barr; July 12, 1997; [ed.] Dundon Grammar School, Dundon, Argyle, Scotland; [occ.] Supervisor of Dietary Services; [oth.writ.] Several poems unpublished; [pers.] Perhaps in others, I search for truths. In each and every one of us, there is a truth waiting to be told. But it is not the telling of the truth we fear—it's revealing the fear we have in the truth.; [a.] Mississauga, ON

BATTS, MIRIAM
[pen.] Misao; [b.] March 14, 1929; Japan; [p.] F. Jai Kong Park, M. Matsu Yoshida; [m.] Michael S. Batts; March 19, 1959; [ch.] Anna, Yuri; [ed.] Keisen Girl's School, Convent of the Sacred Heart, Sophia University, Julius Maxmilian University Degrees B.S., Ph.D.; [occ.] Retired Artist; [memb.] Dollmaker's Association in Japan, Canadian Society for Asian Arts, Chinese Canadian Artist Federation in Vancouver; [hon.] Scholarships for Universties Award, International Society of Poets; [oth.writ.] Translation of German books (collaboration with N. Yamamura), articles in Japan, England, Canada, poems in the anthologies of National Library of Poetry, poems in "Poems of the World," taped in "Sound of Poetry," "Passing of the Summer", a collection of poems in Canada; [pers.] Search of spiritual beauty; [a.] Vancouver, BC

BAUER, ANNE
[b.] March 27, 1925; S. Wales, GB; [ed.] Graduated high school, Capillano College, N. Vancouver, three years of arts, graduated A.S.; [occ.] Professional Artist, Sculptor, and Painter; [memb.] Sculptor's Society of BC (president for nine years and going into the tenth); [oth. writ.] Manuscript in progress, "A Humorous Story of Family Life in South Wales in the 1930's"; [pers.] After serving two years in the British Army during World War II, I constantly reflect on those that died fighting. Through my art work, I try to convey my greatful thanks, through remembrance.; [a.] N. Vancouver, BC

BAZIJANEC, KRESIMIR D.
[b.] March 2, 1957; Zagreb, Croatia; [p.] Dragica and Stjepan Bazijanec; [m.] Lynda D. Bazijanec; June 2, 1996; [ch.] Justina, Rose, Tadranka, Bernadette, Nikola, Kresimir; [ed.] W.F. Herman O.S.H.S.G.D; [occ.] Material Handling Department, Ford Motor Co. Of Canada; [memb.] Croatian Center—Windsor, Windsor Christian Fellowship, C.A.W. Local 200; [pers.] Allow God to be your guiding light each and every day. Continually focus on Him and let people see Him in you and your works. Everything is possible through Jesus Christ, our Lord and Saviour.; [a.] Windsor, ON

BEART, FAY
[b.] October 17, 1946; Edson, AB; [p.] Connie and Owen Hanrahan; [m.] Ernie Beart; November 19, 1966; [ch.] Brenda Elaine, David Owen; [ed.] Grade Eight; [occ.] Floor Supervisor for I.G.A. and worked as a Meat Wrapper; [memb.] Beaverlodge Alliance Church, Tops Club (Take Off Pounds Sensibly); [hon.] Tops Club: Five, Ten, and Fifteen Year Medallions, Northern Alberta Leader of the Year for Tops, Appreciation Award—Seeker's Club; [oth. writ.] Song for Tops rally, several poems for our Tops area chapter, three poems for our Alliance Church, and several poems on our pets; [pers.] I have in taught Pioneer Girl's Club and Seeker's Club, and have taught Sunday School. I did the superintendent work for five years. I am a grandma of two beautiful grandchildren: Katrina, age eight, and Zachary, age five.; [a.] Beaverlodge, AB

BEKSMATI, TAREK
[pen.] TB; [b.] March 30, 1938; Lebanon; [p.] Deceased; [ed.] Chemical Engineering, B.S.; [oth. writ.] Approximately 40 poems and prose pieces called "Love in Poetry," a book in preparation called "The Classes of Humanity"; [pers.] I am an extensive reader of books and newspaper articles. I have traveled extensively through fifty-two countries and experi-enced a variety of customs and cultures. Because of this variety, I have searched all life long for the truth and the reality of love and humanity.; [a.] Toronto, ON

BENUSIC, VERA G.
[pen.] Vera; [b.] February 13, 1943; Botwood, Newfoundland; [p.] May, George Dally [m.] Jake; October 31, 1995; [ch.] 3 children; [ed.] Finished Grade Nine; [occ.] Prep Cook at the Lougheed Village Inn; [hon.] Merit Awards for two poems: "Questions" and "Inside Fight," published along with "Clouds" and "Candlelight" by Creative Arts and Sciences, Abilene, TX; [oth. writ.] Three hundred poems (on hand) and "Dawning of Aquarius"; [pers.] I have been told by many people that my Poetic Diary is filled with profound thoughts and has educational value for most who read it.; [a.] Burnaby, BC

BERGMANN, HELEN REIMER
[b.] August 10, 1927; Gretha, MB; [p.] Jacob H. and Lydia Reimer (deceased); [m.] Walter J. Bergmann; August 29, 1953; [ch.] Ruth, John, Beth, Barbara, Harold; [ed.] St. Catherine's Collegiate, St. Joseph's School of Nursing, Hamilton, ON; [occ.] Retired nurse, homemaker, wife, mother, grandmother, volunteer worker in church and senior home; [memb.] Mennonite Brethren Church, Alumni, St. Joseph's School of Nursing; [oth. writ.] Reports, articles, and poetry in various Mennonite publication in two languages: English and German, "Decision" magazine in Great Britain, "War Cry" (Salvation Army Publication); [pers.] In this day of uncertainty, people need to know there is a constant God who left His Word, the Bible, for mankind.; [a.] Virgil, ON

BERUBE, LYNN
[pen.] Comna; [b.] June 9, 1975; Red Deer, AB; [p.] Raymonde and Georges; [ed.] St. Matthew High School, Algonquin College; [occ.] Cashier at Linen Chest in Ottawa; [hon.] Bronze Medal Winner of the First Annual Algonquin College Hot Food Competition; [pers.] If you're not living on the edge of life, you're taking up too much space. (P.S.—I love to write: anywhere, anytime, about anything!); [a.] Orleans, ON

BERWICK, PATRICIA E.
[b.] February 6, 1942; Dunedin, New Zealand; [p.] Ernest and Mary Berwick; [ed.] Teach. Cert., Christ Church College of Education, NZ B.A.; University of Minnesota, M.A.; University of California, Ph.D.; University of Canterburg, NZ; H diploma Teach, NZ; [occ.] Special Advisor, Office of the Chief Executive, Ministry of Maori Development, Wellington, New Zealand; [memb.] Justice of the Peace, NZ; Phi Kappa Phi, National Honors Society of the US; Mongolia Society Life Member; Te Reo Whanaungatanga Founder and Patron; New Zealand Association of Anthropologists; Maori Women's Welfare League; [hon.] French Governor, study award, Department of Ed. Grant, New Zealand El Grant, U. of Canty Grant, U. of Auckland Grant, Life Member Phi Kappa Phi USA, Best of Set three times (a journal for Australian and New Zealand educators), Justice of the Peace, NZ; [oth. writ.] A Social History of French Polynesia - Heinemans. A History of Tahiti and Its Surrounding Islands—Heinemans, Effective Communication in Schools; Set Land and Land Ownership; The Gap between Maori and English Beliefs in the 1840's—Waitangi Tribunal; The Trusteeship and Admistration of Targatu Wherna Reserve of Whanganui—a Tara-Waitangi Tribunal. There Still Will Be Days Set;

Impact of the Maori Affairs Trade Training Scheme—Massey University; [pers.] In my poetry I am strongly influenced by the stream of consciousness school and my mother. My mother often read us poems rather than fairy tales to put us to sleep. My aim in all that I do is to improve communication within and between cultures. This the first poem I have ever submitted for publication.; [a.] Wellington, NZ

BISSELL, ANDREW E.
[pen.] Bandlord; [b.] July 18, 1956; [p.] Edward (deceased), Edith; [m.] Patricia; December 29, 1984; [ch.] Jacqueline, Graham, Mathew; [ed.] Sarnia Collegiate Institute and Technical School, Sarnia, Ontario, Canada, Grade Twelve Diploma, various correspondence courses; [occ.] Blowmould Operations Technician, Imperial Oil, Ltd; [memb.] C.A.P.A.C., C.E.P. Local 777; [hon.] Five Editor's Choice Awards from the National Library of Poetry, Award of Merit and Fourth Place Medallion Award from the Poetry Institute of Canada; [oth. writ.] Six poems published by National Library of Poetry and three published by the Poetry Institute of Canada, also a few hundred still in the vaults; [pers.] Write and be strong.; [a.] Tofield, AB

BITAXI, MICHAEL
[b.] July 11, 1979; St. Mikes Hospital; [p.] Jim and Janet Bitaxi; [ed.] Grade Eleven; [occ.] Computer Troubleshooting and Sales; [hon.] Music Award, English Award; [pers.] I don't think I would have had this honor had it not been for my girlfriend. Thanks Kim!; [a.] Toronto, ON

BLAKELY, MISHA LOUISE
[b.] October 2, 1975; Comoy, BC; [p.] Bryan and Anne Blakely; [ed.] Misha (deceased) was partway through a B.A. degree course, which she hoped to complete as a Master's of Psychology at U.B.C.; [oth.writ.] Misha has many unpublished poems in her collection. She was an exuberant and loving woman, and expressed herself often in the written word.; [a.] Campbell River, BC

BLANKE, VIKTOR
[b.] August 7, 1908; Stockholm, Sweden; [p.] Even and Ulla; [ed.] Three years of study of Humanism, Chinese, Spanish, German, English, Photography, etc.; [occ.] Student; [memb.] Cinemateket in Stockholm; [oth.writ.] Article published in the Swedish Daily (Sweden's biggest newspaper); [pers.] Despite all the time in the world, I'm lost in every moment.; [a.] Stockholm, Sweden

BODENDORFER, MELONIE
[b.] November 27, 1964; Kitchener; [p.] Kurt and Nancy Scherbinsky; [m.] Mr. Ekart Paul Bodendorfer; October 21, 1989; [occ.] Sales Clerk; [pers.] A small dedication only . . . for his support, love, and deep understanding, I dedicate the poem to my darling husband.; [a.] Kitchener, ON

BOTTING, JASE
[pen.] Jase Botting; [b.] January 25, 1978; Tulsa, OK; [p.] Cam And Mary Botting; [ed.] St. Michael High School, currently a first year Neuroscience Major at Brock University; [occ.] Labourer—Philip Environmental; [oth.writ.] Superfluously unpublished; [pers.] We all have gifts. We all don't have ways of opening them. Ride on every nimble emotion, no matter how weak it may be, because when a day feels like a month, you'll wish had. Dreams have medicinal attributes which keep this world.; [a.] Niagara Falls, ON

BOUINIDANE, LAILA
[b.] December 5, 1975; Rabat Morocco; [p.] Bouazza Bouinidane, Ketu Bouinidane; [ed.] Third Year Student of Translation at King Fahd School of Translation; [occ.] Certified Translator, 1998; [hon.] I received a contract from a Hollywood company, but I refused to sign it for some reasons.; [oth.writ.] Several poems unpublished; [pers.] The least one can do to share a moment's joy or sorrow with people is to write for them.; [a.] Amalu Cym, Rabat

BOULDING, DON R.
[b.] July 4, 1953; Regina, SK, Canada; [p.] Bill Boulding; [ed.] Vocational X (Regina), Camosun College (Victoria); [occ.] Training for Gardener; [oth.writ.] "Is There Magic In Love?.," "Friends," "Lonely Part of Texas," 'He Belongs To Me," "The Demon Inside of Me," "The Race"; [pers.] I'm forty-four years of age. I'm a slow learner, born with an slight case of cerebral palsy. It is hard for me to find a paying job because of my disability. I compose my poems when I go for walks. However, I need to be inspired to compose.; [a.] Victoria, BC

BOURAS, KONSTANTINOS
[b.] March 23, 1962; Kalamata; [p.] Nikoletta and Vassilios Bouras; [m.] Eleni Maniadaki; [ed.] Mechanical Engineer, Technical University of Athens, Theatrologue, University of Athens, Theatrical Studies, DEA, Paris III, La Nouvelle Sorbonne; [occ.] Technical Director of The Athen's Festival; [memb.] International Society of Poets, International Writers and Artists Association, International Theatrical Institute, European Institute of Theatrical Research, Greek Writer's Association, Centre for Research and Studies In Modern Greek Theater; [hon.] Honored by the University of Athens; [oth. writ.] Ten books of poetry and plays have already been published: O Porifors Ilias tou Erota Ke tou Thanatou, Agouros Eros, I Kilada ton Nekron Esoton, Eros Iliotropos, Agabes Eros, Eros Trimargikos, Ston Asterismo tis Hecatis; [pers.] His poetry is marked by the search for the sublime, by lyricism and a sensuality in the Kavafian genre and true to the classical Greek ideal and beauty.; [a.] Athens, Greece

BOWDEN, GRAHAM
[pen.] Nathan Grange; [b.] July 12, 1973; Middlesbrough, England; [p.] Kevin Bowden and Brenda Klebe; [m.] Sadi Bowden; December 12, 1996; [ed.] Certificate in Theatre Arts, Rosebud School of Fine Arts; [occ.] Manager of Native Arts Gallery, sometime Actor; [hon.] English Literature and Theatre; [oth.writ.] Several short stories in fantasy fanzines and newsletters, several poems and discourses in college magazine and student paper, several short stories and monologues with college theatre troupe; [pers.] My writing reflects the three states of being: physical, spiritual, and mental, i.e. what is seen, what is felt, and what can be changed (the paths that nature, the soul, and humanity travel).; [a.] Calgary, AB

BOWMAN, CARYL
[b.] Kitchener, ON; [p.] Dean Anderson, Adeline Anderson; [ch.] Lorelei Ann; [ed.] Rockway Mennonite High School, St. Thomas-Elgin General Hospital; [occ.] RNA-Home Support Worker, Level II; [memb.] Handbell Guild; [hon.] Honours—Academy of Hairstyling, Honours—Piano; [pers.] Animals fill my world with joy and I try to reflect this in my writings.; [a.] Cambridge, ON

BOYD, KATHLEEN M.
[b.] May 27, 1951; Galesbury, IL; [p.] Alice Lockwood, Leo Barbero; [m.] Jim Boyd Jr; July 5, 1980; [ch.] Krystal Bellamy, Joe Boyd; [ed.] Associate Degree, SFCC, Missouri; [occ.] Three years personal sabbatical in England; [hon.] Presidential Scholar; [pers.] I wish to thank those who have encouraged me along the way, especially my Mom and my husband, Jim.; [a.] Cambridgeshire, England

BRAWN, NICHOLE
[b.] January 27, 1982; [p.] Marjorie and Terrance Brawn; [ed.] Grade ten; [occ.] Student; [hon.] Best Attitude (grade two), Honors in grades five, six, seven, and nine; Athlete of the Year (grade nine); [oth. writ.] Personal writing; [pers.] I enjoy writing spiritual literature; I have been influenced by God and the Bible.; [a.] Keswick, NB

BRODDY, LESLIE
[b.] June 1968; Toronto, ON; [ch.] Arielle Broddy; [occ.] Administrative Assistant; [oth.writ.] Currently working on my autobiography, several short stories and poems (as yet unpublished); [pers.] Writing has been a passionate hobby of mine since the age of six. Only recently, however, due to the support and persuasive pushing of a certain individual, have I begun submitting my works for publication. So here I am . . . thanks Chris!; [a.] North York, ON

BROUSSEAU, LINDA
[b.] April 30, 1956; Timmins, ON; [p.] Ferruccio Franolla, Sylvia Franolla; [m.] Gerald Brousseau; November 9, 1987; [ch.] Crystal Sue, Kelly Anne, Keith Gerald; [ed.] Northern College of Applied Arts and Technology; [occ.] Housewife; [memb.] Certified Level One Coach; [hon.] Silver Medal at the national level; [a.] Timmins, ON

CADAVOS, JR, ALFRED
[pen.] Jacal; [b.] May 14, 1970, Maasin; [p.] Mr. and Mrs. Alfred Cadavos Jr.; [ed.] Bachelor of Secondary Education, Saint Joseph College, Maasin, Southern Leyte, Philippines; [oth. writ.] Several poems published in school publication (Josephinlan); [pers.] To my mother and sister, to my Auntie Babe and Auntie Clara, to Janette, Francisco, and Bennites, who serve as my inspiration—and above all, to the Creator for guiding me and my pen.; [a.] Maasin, Southern Leyte, Philippines

CADIEUX, ANNICK
[b.] September 13, 1982; Ottawa, ON; [p.] Michael LaCroix, Ginette Cadieux; [ed.] Fourth year of high school at Polyvalente Mont-Bleu, Hull (Quebec), will get high school diploma next year; [occ.] Student in high school (fourth secondary); [hon.] Many certificates of honor in school; [oth. writ.] Published in three books (collectives) in French: Escapades Printanieres, Tourbillions, Mozaigues (these were also published in Europe and in Canada); [pers.] Every part of my life has been an inspiration for my writing. From love to hate, I always feel the need to put it down on a piece of paper.; [a.] Hull, QC

CAMPBELL, JOHN T. F.
[b.] July 8, 1955; Edinburgh, Scotland; [p.] Terrence and Molly Nee Saddler; [m.] Susan Nee Keener; [ch.] Thomas, Daniel, and Andrew; [ed.] Quantock School, New Battle Abbey College, University of Wales, Trinity College, and Seminary in U.S.A.; [memb.] American Academy of Religion, Society of Biblical Literature, Trinidad Alumni Association; [hon.] Diploma in Liberal Studies, 1984, City and Guild's

Association Award, 1996; [oth.writ.] Most notably works on Hedonism, Utilitarianism, and the life of Old Testament patriarchs; [a.] Fairwater, Cardiff

CAMPBELL, ROBIN
[pen.] Soupy Spreadlove; [b.] June 7, 1966; Brockville, ON; [p.] Joyce and David Campbell; [ed.] Bachelor's in Communication from Carleton University, 1990, and I'm a student of many writers and thinkers, notably Dr. M. Scott Peck and Stephen Covey; [occ.] Peace Activist; [memb.] United Nations Association in Canada, Ottawa Peace and Environment Resource Centre; [pers.] The mission statement of my life is to help as many people as possible, with the knowledge I've acquired as the result of some personal experiences. It is hoped that this poem, "Our Revolution," represents a seminal step in this mission.; [a.] Nepean, ON

CASTRO, ROSALIE B.
[pen.] Blue Horizon; [b.] May 11, 1960; Philippines; [p.] Arturo Castro, Milagros Baccay; [ed.] B.A. Mass Communication, Member of Arts in Broadcast Journalism; (Baguio College Foundation, Phils.); [occ.] Health Care Aide and Part-Time Freelance Writer; [hon.] Best Elementary Pupil, full university scholar (Philippines), Grand Prize Winner of monologue and short story writing contest, committed campus journalist, Special Recognition Award as Mass Comm Society president; [oth.writ.] Poems and articles published monthly in We Speak and Pasugo magazines, The College Leader, The Academe, CBI Newsletter, Weekly Vibration, The Centralite, Midland Courier, and The Locale Update (some of the titles are: "I Know You Love Me," "My Sunshine Friend," "Beyond Comprehension," "A Recapitulation," "My Allegory," "What I Dare Say Matters Much," "Gas Pain Reactions," "My Desire to Serve the Lord," "Until We Meet Again," and many more; [pers.] No one can put a good man down. It is when life gets rough that I must not quit.; [a.] Toronto, ON

CHANDRA, VSATISH
[pen.] Venson; [b.] August 8, 1982; Sangalore; [p.] C. R. Venkatachalapathy and B.S. Rameshwari; [ed.] Student of std; [occ.] Student; [hon.] Nominated as a finalist to the Balashri National Award for Children under the Creative Writing category during the year 1996; [oth. writ.] short stories—one of them published in a children's magazine, a few poems published in children's magazines and school souvenirs; [pers.] I'm very much influenced by Ralph Waldo Emerson's poems on friendship, and feel that friendship is the essence of life.; [a.] Bangalore, Karnataka, India

CHELLUMBEN, DAN
[b.] May 4, 1947; Mauritius; [m.] Martine Chellumben; April 25, 1984; [ch.] Mathieu and Angelique; [ed.] G.C.E. "A" Level, England, Diploma, London School of Journalism; [occ.] Journalist; [memb.] International Federation of Journalists; [oth. writ.] Regular contributor to the Student's World E.E.C Editor, contributor to Poetry Now, Mother Nature's Wonders, Triumph Herald Magazine, Triumph House Anthologist in England, and occasional contributer to Herald Tribune, Newsweek; [pers.] Dan Chellumben: born April 5, 1974, Quatre Bornes, Mauritius, married, two children (Mathie and Angelique), London School of Journalism, Rabelais University France, E.E.C, editor, The Student's World, and contributor to Poetry Now and the Arrival Press (U.K.), very keen on history of the Native Americans; [a.] Amboise, France

CHENIER, GILLES M.
[pen.] Red; [b.] March 11, 1940; Ottawa, ON; [oth. writ.] Songs, poems for family and friends, addresses for weddings and stags; [pers.] At this time, I would only like my husband's name used: Gilles M. Chenier.; [a.] Ottawa, ON

CHILDS, DOROTHY
[b.] February 3, 1920; MB; [p.] Herman and Pauline Palas (deceased); [m.] Roy Childs (deceased); September 6, 1941; [ch.] Greta Hales and Carol Childs; [ed.] B.Ed. University of Alberta (taught in Manitoba, Alberta, and British Columbia); [memb.] Ladies Aux. Legion, Bowser 211; [hon.] Past President, Life Membership; [oth.writ.] Last fall, I took a writing course at Elder College led by a local writer's group. Their praise of my work encouraged me to enter this poetry contest.; [pers.] I have lived on beautiful Vancouver Island by the sea for 27 years, but will be moving shortly to be near my family, living on Lake Erie. My inspiration comes from nature.; [a.] Bowser, BC

CHIN, BRUNHILDE N.
[b.] March 9, 1938; Jamaica, West Indies; [p.] Ethelbert and Linda Bailey; [m.] Cecil C. Chin; August 10, 1960; [ch.] Suyen and Gabrielle; [ed.] Ardenne High School, George Brown College of Arts, Science, and Technology; [occ.] Retired Bell Canada Employee Benefits Clerk; [memb.] Ardenne Past Students Association member; [oth. writ.] Unpublished poem "Is He?" and six unpublished short stories, two of which were read on the air in Jamaica, West Indies, and for which I was paid a small sum, editor of newsletter for Ardenne Past Students Assoc.; [pers.] I have a profound love for aesthethic things. God is very real in my life.; [a.] Malton, ON

CHIPERZAK, JY
[b.] May 12, 1948; Montreal, QC; [m.] Gail; [ch.] Megan, Gavin; [ed.] BA Queen's University; [occ.] Vision Quest Guide Writer; [oth.writ.] A novel, "And So It Began," an unpublished manuscript "Unfinished Emotions," unpublished poetry, manuscript, short articles for magazines; [pers.] I follow the call, the quest for the spirit that is in all things. "The spirit is the true self." (Cicero); [a.] Marmora, ON

CHISHOLM, PATRICIA
[b.] June 12, 1968; Killarney, MB; [m.] Alex Chisholm; October 12, 1991; [ch.] Connor Patrick, Michelle Lian; [occ.] Laboratory Technologist; [memb.] Canadian Society of Medical Laboratory Science, Five-Pin Bowler's Association; [pers.] Poem done originally in 1988 as the "mindless ramblings" of a woman trying to find a man; the poem was revised in 1992 when I finally did.; [a.] Calgary, AB

CHOW, ALVIN L.K.
[b.] February 11, 1959; Singapore; [p.] Chow Chee Ching, Marian Chow; [ed.] A.C.S.; [occ.] Editor, financial sector; [memb.] Mensa; [oth.writ.] A book of teenage poems, "Just Then," articles for the Business Times (Singapore), "The Sun Still Shines" short story winner in the Straits Times, short story writing competition; [a.] Singapore

CHRISTOFOROU, GEORGINA
[b.] April 28, 1983; Pyla, Larnaca; [p.] Christalla Christoforou and Savvas Christoforou; [ed.] American Academy of Larnaca; [occ.] Student; [a.] Larnaca, Cyprus

CHUI, MICHAEL F.
[b.] October 4, 1941; Hong Kong; [m.] Anita; [ch.] 2; [ed.] Ph.D.; [occ.] Engineer; [hon.] Winner of Nativ-

ity Church Essay Contest, Second Prize in CBC Radio Poetry Contest, Runner-Up in CBC Radio Short Story Contest; [oth. writ.] Large number of letters, articles, poems, mini plays published in news magazines, newspapers, and company newsletters; [pers.] I believe firmly in the sanctity of life, and in peace and harmony among all people.; [a.] Ontario, ON

CIEMINS, VENERANDA
[pen.] Veneranda Ciemins; [b.] May 30, 1924; Latvia; [p.] Adams and Emilia Andrejeuskis; [m.] Deceased; First husband, 1964, Second husband, 1968; [ed.] Incomplete University, several credits in Creative Writing and Poetry from George Brown Community College in Toronto, Canada; [occ.] Retired Senior; [memb.] International Society of Poets, Maryland, USA; [hon.] Editor's Choice Award from The National Library of Poetry; [oth. writ.] Short stories and poems in English and Latvian, short stories and poems in English in George Brown Community College's senior's anthology, the poem "Forget Me Not" in Walk Through Paradise, the poem "You Are My Heaven" in Best Poems of 1997 by the National Library Of Poetry; [a.] Toronto, ON

CLARK, EVELYN
[pen.] Tea Sheritt; [b.] July 8, 1942; Shelburne, ON; [p.] Milton and Verna McKinley; [m.] Jack W. Clark; October 2, 1996; [ch.] Wendy, Curtis, Robin, Bev, Sue, Greg; [ed.] Humber and Georgian Colleges D.S.W., Journalism and Short Story Writing; [occ.] Pet Photographer and Short Story Novelist; [memb.] World Vision Child, Treasurer of Community Center, Distinguished Member of the International Society of Poets, Member of Trinity United Church, Supporter of Taylor Statten Camp; [hon.] Animal Volunteer Association—AVA (placing homeless purebred dogs for 25 years), Canvasser for the Arthritis Society; [oth. writ.] Short story, "Only Once October Comes," in the Toronto Saturday Sun, poems published by the National Library of Poetry; [pers.] To my eighteen grandchildren: "The very best of all my thoughts are those that I think of you. The very best of all my words are those that I speak of you. The very best of all my deeds are those that I offer to you.; [a.] Clarksburg, ON

COLE, FINNIAN
[b.] April 15, 1964; St. Catherines, ON; [ed.] Completed Grade Twelve at Burlington Central High School, Orchard Park; [occ.] Owner/Operator of Unique Touch Cleaning Services; [memb.] A member of the Peninsula Players theatre group; [hon.] This is the first honor I have to date which I would consider noteworthy.; [oth. writ.] Several poems published in local magazines, creator of the comic strip, "A Day in the Life," which appears in several area magazines; [pers.] My poetry is one way of expressing my passion for the written word and achieving the goal of sharing my love for the creative spirit.; [a.] Stoney Creek, ON

COMPTON, SHARON
[pen.] Sharon; [b.] March 1959; Annapolis Royal, NS; [occ.] Ph.D. (candidate) in Education and Health Promotion; [pers.] Understanding unfolds through writing. I write . . . recording emotions, watching them come together on paper, allowing me the occasion to reflect, placing the day's events into perspective.; [a.] Edmonton, AB

CONGDON, DALE
[b.] September 23, 1952; Edmonton, AB; [p.] Patricia and Bus Congdon; [m.] Marlene; June 29, 1974; [ch.]

Greg, Aaron; [ed.] Diploma in Business Administration at NAIT; [occ.] Business Management and Information Consultant; [memb.] Chairman and Treasurer of the Parkland Food Bank Society; [a.] Spruce Grove, AB

COOK, STUART EDWARD
[b.] April 27, 1984; England; [p.] Mr. and Mrs. Roger Cook; [ed.] Sevenoaks Prep School, 1989-1997, Sackville School, 1997; [occ.] Student; [memb.] British Judo Association; [hon.] Sevenoaks Arts Festival Poetry Award, 1997, Kent Poetry Anthology, 1996; [pers.] I enjoy sport inside and out of school. Creative writing is my other pastime. I can say things in a story or poem which express my feelings.; [a.] Oxford, KY

COWDEN, VICTORIA E.
[pen.] Samantha Sullivan; [b.] September 11, 1956; Exeter, ON; [p.] R.S. Cowden, Rene Cowden; [m.] Paul Robert Moyneur; [ch.] Jayson Grant Oliphant; [hon.] English Literature (short stories and poems); [oth. writ.] Every fifth year in my son's life, I write a short novel that pertains to his age and current interests. To date the novels are: "So Lucky," "The Final Road" and "Beyond Reality!" Now that Jayson plays electric guitar, for his twentieth birthday I wrote the song, "Mistress of Chaos!" I write other poetry and lyrics dealing with subject matter that digs deep into my well of emotions.; [pers.] I believe that a creative person's mind is always active and errant, oftentimes pondering on what's new or a sometimes impossible goal they can achieve. My inspiration—anyone who can hold my interest with a great story!; [a.] Orleans, ON

CROW, ELIZABETH MARY CATHERINE
[pen.] Elmay Crow; [b.] August 21, 1929; Winnipeg, MB; [p.] Duncan Murray Flett and Grace Stuart-Macmillan Flett; [m.] Delmer Gerald Crow; May 1, 1954; [ch.] Duncan Charles, Katherine Margo, Lisa Grace, Sandra Dell; [ed.] Latin, Greek, French, and Fine Arts (Home Schooling) Grade One, Tarbert, Argyll, Scotland Grades Ten and Eleven Correspondence, California School of Fine Arts Visual Education, Victoria School Board Theatre (by Dorothy Somerset) Grade Five and Seven, Dr. Wilfred John's North Ward School of Rural Leadership, University of British Columbia, Art League School of San Francisco, Teaching Refresher Course, BTSD Teaching through College for Manpower; [occ.] Retired from teaching; still ranching/breeding Arabian horses, writing novels, writing and illustrating children stories and painting; [memb.] The Little Gallery of Victoria (Victoria's First Art Gallery), exp. Canadian Author's Association, exp. Canadian Arabian Horse Registry; [hon.] Victoria Operatic Society Generous Cheque of Appreciation, and Promotional Victoria Summercase Cheque of Appreciation, and Standing Ovation Victoria Times Colonist Newspaper, comics column contract, BTSD development of programme and then teaching of same, New Canadian English program development, and teaching in high schools and Sikh temple, teaching remedial English and Math, while adding Art and Music to the program; [oth. writ.] "Spirit Medicine," "Perception" Canadian Council on Social Development, 1989, "Cultural Recovery," "Perception" Canadian Council on Social Development, 1990, "Heartbreak Study," "Muh Ol' Hoss," "The Door in the Tree," "After the Fire," "Thoughts on an Early Cariboo Winter," "A Flea Market Christmas," "The Labor of Love," "The Fuller Brush Man," "Published in Pacific Yachting," "Carolyn and the Chipmunk," "My Astounding Ride in Santa's Sleigh," "The Country General Store," "Happily and Sadly," "Grandma's"; [pers.] I am inspired by my scholarly mother, who taught me to see miracles and magic through the wonders of nature, showing empathetically what they seem to be, and to allow those innocent of shame to look at them, too, according to each individual personality.; [a.] Shawnigan Lake, BC

CRUZ, SHEILA
[b.] March 13, 1981; Kitchener, ON; [ed.] St. Mary's Elm. And Bishop Ryan High School; [occ.] Student; [hon.] Student Council President 1994-1995, Public Speaking 1992, Science Fair 1991, Co-Ed Volleyball, Classic Awards 1986-1993 [pers.] My poetry is very important to me, and I believe that creativity is the spice of life. My poetic influences are John Lennon and William Blake.; [a.] Hamilton, ON

DA SILVA, IRENE
[pen.] Lucia Pombinho; [b.] October 10, 1967; Portugal, Azores; [p.] Clarimundo and Maria Da Silva; [ch.] Monika Lynn Da Silva Millin; [ed.] Portuguese and Canadian Grade Twelve, a few computer courses; [occ.] Volunteer at YMCA in Sarnia, Ontario; [memb.] YMCA Family Center, St. Benedict's Church in Sarnia, Ontario; [hon.] Fluent in English, Portuguese, Spanish; [oth. writ.] I have always written poems, but haven't had the chance to publish any of them. I am very excited.; [pers.] The poems I write are a very strong reflection of what I am, and what I sometimes feel. This poem is very special to me, for the fact that I wrote it in Portuguese first, and then translated it to English.; [a.] Sarnia, ON

DAVIS, KAETHE VON MANDEL
[pen.] Kaethe Von Mandel Davis; [b.] July 14, 1924; Germany; [p.] Wilhelm and Emma Von Mandel; [m.] Kenneth I. Davis; October 18, 1960; [ch.] Marco, Christine, Kenneth F.; [ed.] High school, Luisen Schule (girls school), Germany, training as a nurse and, later, dental assistant; [memb.] Hospital Auxiliary Volunteer; [hon.] Chosen to exhibit oil painting (Sunflowers) at Humber College, Oshawal, ON, Canada (seven were chosen out of 75); [oth. writ.] Short stories, started book titled Houses, six journals, 30 poems; [pers.] I mostly write poems about either nature or human emotions, also some religious poems. I wrote 30 poems in either English or German.; [a.] Belleville, ON

DE OLIVERIA TEIXEIRA, MARILD APARECIDA ANGELA
[b.] December 10, 1964; Ituiutaba; [p.] Maria Helena Kazaro De Oliveria; [m.] Marcio Nunes Teixeira; July 7, 1984; [ch.] Marilia and Michel; [ed.] High school, university post-graduate in Linguistics; [occ.] English Teacher (as a second language); [oth. writ.] Several poems, short stories, acrostics, and quotations; [pers.] "In the twilight of our lives we shall never give up hope!"; "Whenever one feels the solitude of an amazing sunset, he will be able to feel how near to him God is!"; [a.] Ituiutaba Minas Gerrais, Brazil

DEACON, TOMMY
[b.] September 24, 1968; Edmonton, AB; [oth.writ.] Several other poems written, not yet published, some original lyrics for songs when I was in a band years ago; [pers.] My writings are born from my personal thoughts and views on life and existence. "The mind is truly the first frontier; when fully explored and understood, so too are all others." [a.] Edmonton, AB

DEHLIN, CHRISTER
[b.] November 18, 1970; Oslo, Norway; [p.] Helge and Mette Dehlin; [ed.] Examine Philosophicum and a One Year Course in the History of Ideas from the

University in Oslo; [occ.] Student of Humanities, Journalist; [oth. writ.] Articles on Martial Arts in the Norwegian Budo magazine, "Suart Relte," several short stories on World War II and various journalistic writings on a number of subjects; [pers.] My poetry is inspired by such extraordinary people as William Blake, Allen Ginsberg, and Harold Sverdreys, a great Norwegian poet. I am a Buddhist, but I tend to mix those patterns of thought with those I find in Western Philosophy, Literature, and Poetry.; [a.] Oslo, Norway

DERMATAS, FILARETI PHYLLIS
[pen.] Filareti Dermatas; [b.] November 27, 1968; East York, ON; [p.] Maria and Napoleon; [m.] Randolph Dickinson; August 16, 1997; [ch.] Cassandra Jessica; [ed.] York University, Honors Degree in English; [occ.] Self-Employed; [pers.] I am fascinated by life's point of reality and how that intersects with a person's subjective perception.; [a.] Mississauga, ON

DIAMANTE, CORRADO A.
[b.] December 20, 1976; Toronto, ON; [pers.] "Tis to create, and in creating live a being more intense that we endow with our fancy, gaining as we give the life we image, even as I do now. What am I? Nothing, but not so art thou, soul of my thought with whom I traverse earth, invisible but gazing, as I glow mixed with thy spirit, blended with thy birth, and feeling still with thee."; [a.] Toronto, ON

DIAZ, ROBERTO
[pen.] Rob; [b.] February 27, 1982; Roberto Diaz Sr., Gilda Martinez; [ed.] Grade Ten, Bilingual (French, English), Senator O'Connor College School, Our Lady of Fatima Catholic School; [occ.] Student; [hon.] Karen Tough Memorial Award—Grade Nine, Academic Award—Grade Eight; [oth. writ.] I'v had everal poems and essays published in the school newspaper. I have also written some short stories. My writings are in French or English.; [pers.] I try to express the trials of humanity in my poems. My greatest influences are my parents, who guide me through life.; [a.] Toronto, ON

DIGNARD, MARGARET
[b.] November 17, 1947; Oshawa, ON; [p.] David and Joyce Dobbie; [m.] Venance Dignard; July 23, 1966; [ch.] Michael, Michelle, and Kevin; [ed.] High School, Stress Management, Therapeutic Massage; [occ.] Retired from Retail Sales of thirty years; [memb.] International Society of Poets; [hon.] Editor's Choice Award, 1997, National Library of Poetry; [oth. writ.] Published in 1997 in The Sands of Time (National Library of Poetry), several others, unpublished; [pers.] My husband and I live in a beautiful, lakeside adult community called Wilmot Creek. I'm influenced by my surroundings. I write from personal experience—past, present—and of my hopes for the future.; [a.] Nescastle, ON

DOBOS, LISA
[pen.] Lisa Dobos; [b.] April 30, 1975; Calgary, AB; [p.] Wendy and Jerry Dobos; [m.] Stacey Kowalski, common law marriage; [ch.] Cody Justin Kowalski; [ed.] Graduated from Henry Wisewood High School; [occ.] Stay-at-home mother; [oth. writ.] Never tried to get any poems published, but I've written many.; [pers.] The world beyond which we live, good or bad, in all its glory inspires my thoiughts.; [a.] Calgary, AB

DOETZEL, DEANNA
[pen.] Dee Dee; [b.] May 4, 1985; Macklin, SK; [p.] Leonard and Joanne Doetzel; [ed.] Presently attend-

ing Macklin School in Grade Seven; [occ.] Student; [memb.] 601 Squadron, Air Cadets; [oth.writ.] "James, Do You Have Homework?"; [a.] Primate, SK

DORAN, ANNA MARIE
[pen.] Maggie D; [b.] December 29, 1962; Chester, England; [p.] Allan and Ann Davies; [m.] Richard Doran; March 2, 1984; [ch.] Allan and Drew Doran; [ed.] Kingsway School of Girls, Gatley, England, 1975-1980, Taneside College of Technology, Ashton Lyne, England, 1980-1982; [occ.] Patient Service Associate (PSA) London, Health Science Centre, London, Canada; [memb.] A.D.D., C.A.P. Cahertion Deficit Disorder Support Group (one of the founding members); [pers.] Having one of my poems published is a dream come true. I hope to publish a book of my own works in the near future. The biggest regret I have is that my Dad is not here to share this special moment with me; my Dad died on May 14, 1997. I know he would be very proud of me. "This One's For You," with love from Daddy's little girl.; [a.] Mt. Brydges, ON

DREGO, VALERIE ANN
[b.] July 21 1956; Bombay, India; [p.] Dr. Eustace Desousa, Gladys Desousa; [m.] Don Anthony Drego; May 29, 1994; [ch.] Victoria; [ed.] B.A., M.A., Ph.D. Business Management, University of Bombay; [occ.] Freelance Journalist; [hon.] First in Class—first in the Bombay University for both the B.A. and M.A. degree exams, the Ellis Scholarship, the D. Framji Memorial Prize, the Maj. C. Fernandez Gold Medal, the Erazmus Sequira English Scholarship, and the Dr. Kamal Wood Award; [oth. writ.] The poem published is an extract from "The Tree of Life," which is a series of poems covering man's journey from birth to death.; [a.] Dorval, QC

DRESSLER, LIN
[b.] October 8, 1950; Edmonton, AB; [p.] Lorraine and Ken; [m.] Jacob (Jake); August 30, 1986; [ch.] Jodi, Michael, Cheryl, Carolyn, and Kelly; [ed.] Social Services Diploma; [occ.] Retired Executive Director of a society providing services and shelter for abused women and children.; [memb.] PPASS, Post-Polio Awareness and Support Society, Friends For Life (supports HIV/AIDS and Cancer), National Library of Poetry; [hon.] Community Award for Woman of the Year—1985, 1997—Semi-Finalist at ISP Convention, nomination for Poet of the Year in 1995 and 1997, Poems Across America, 1995— Medallion Winner from Poetry Institute of Canada, National Library of Poetry: A Moment in Time, Sparkles in the Sand, Best Poems of 1997, A Season of Flowers, Best Poems of 1998, Editor's Choice Award—1995, Editor's Choice Award—1997, Post-Polio Awareness and Support Society; [oth. writ.] "Just Another Dream" 1995, "An Angel's Kiss" 1995, "The Old Man" 1997, "Too Many Lost Souls" 1997, "Misery to Miracles" 1998, "Peaceful is the Little One" 1998, published by BC/Yukon Communique: "The Loving Wife" 1994, local paper article and poem, "The Christmas Angel" 1997; [pers.] In the beginning, I turned to poetry as a channel for emotional release. I discovered that my poetry was an inspiration to others and I was encouraged by acknowledgements, publications, and awards. Today, I write poetry realizing it is one of God's many blessings: to reach out to others, let the past go, forgive, and move on.; [a.] Surrey, BC

DRYSDALE, SHIRLEY
[pen.] Shirley Anne; [b.] April 17, 1957; Redvers, SK; [p.] Egon and Anna Gade; [m.] Don Drysdale; [ch.]

Michael, Craig, and Neil; [occ.] Customer Service Manager, Canadian Imperial Bank of Commerce (CIBC), Redvers, SK; [oth. writ.] Work has been published in another anthology as well. (Rhymes of Greatness); [pers.] My family and close friends are my inspirations.; [a.] Redvers, SK

DUNCAN, DAVE
[b.] November 20, 1940; Stirling, Scotland; [ch.] Jennifer, Christopher, Michael; [occ.] Consultant, Labor Relations; [oth. writ.] Currently working toward publication of a children's book (poetry) as well as several short stories; [pers.] I've always had a flair for writing verse with an aim to making others laugh (or at least smile); [a.] North Bay, ON

EDOSOMWAN, ANTHONY
[oth. writ.] Short stories, "Field Exercise," "In," "Banquet," etc., short novels, "I Don't Want Her to See Me Like This," "The Delirium," "A Case of Viruses," "The Campaign," "The Works (Novels) In Progress," "Garden of the Burning Bush," "The River Coming," "A Land of Goddesses," poems: "The New Front," "Destination Elsewhere, Etc."; [a.] Lagos, Nigeria

EDWARDS, CORRIE
[b.] October 23, 1958; Blind River, ON; [p.] Robert and Muriel Chevis; [m.] John Edwards; June 27, 1975; [ch.] John Jr. and Tracy; [oth. writ.] I enjoy writing personalized pieces for special occasions; [pers.] Don't expect more out of love than what is there.; [a.] Iron Bridge, ON

EGAN, BELINDA MAREE
[b.] June 28, 1982; Orange, NSW; [p.] James and Patricia Egan; [ed.] Year Ten, James Sheahan Catholic High School; [oth. writ.] Songs and poems, unpublished; [pers.] I write to inspire my brother Lee, and all my special friends. Love always, Belinda.

EL-DICK, GILBERT
[pen.] Christoper K. Stark, J. E. Skillz; [b.] December 16, 1978; Jounyeh, Lebanon; [p.] Pierre and Dunia El-Dick; [ed.] Currently studying Psychology and English Writing at the University of Ottawa; [occ.] Student; [oth. writ.] OAC anthology "Anita Brache" (edited, collaborated), several poems, future all-time best-selling novel; [pers.] "Nothing is complicated unless you complicate it. Nothing is sacred until you believe in it. Nothing is love until you've felt it."; [a.] Gloucester, ON

ELDRIDGE, APRIL
[b.] February 29, 1980; Brampton, ON; [p.] Betty Eldridge; [pers.] "Yesterday's Tomorrow" is dedicated to my boyfriend, Brian H., "the love of my life."

EMBRO, JIMMY
[pen.] The Sentimental Gentleman; [b.] July 1, 1931; Guelph, ON; [p.] Raphael Ann, Michael Embro; [m.] Jean Parker; August 4, 1957; [ch.] Five; [ed.] High School Musical Director, also Conservatory of Music Supervisory Capacity Diplomas for Music and Teaching; [occ.] Writer-Composer-Arranger and Big Band Leader; [memb.] Musicians Union; [hon.] Big Band Musical Conductor and Arranger, six years, for radio broadcast show singing, playing own compositions and recordings of new musical songs, also reciting my own poems; [oth. writ.] "Put Away Those Dreams," "Remembering Chasing Dreams," "Down Memory Lane All Over Again," "I'm Just a Dreamer," "Just a Little Lonesome, Feelin' Kinda Blue," "I Wanna Go Where Dreams Come True," "Gee, How I Wish for Yesterday"; [pers.] As a Sentimentalist, I have written hundreds of sentimental songs—an art which creates gentle kindness, excitement, and warm feelings.; [a.] Guelph, ON

ENGLISH, JIM
[pen.] Jim E's Poems; [b.] April 22, 1970; Port Alice, BC; [p.] Geogre and Lorriane English; [m.] Lynn English; [ch.] Mellisa, Kirsti, Drew; [ed.] Graduated G.P. Vanier Senior Secondary School; [occ.] General Labourer, Commercial Fisherman; [oth. writ.] 1997 Herring Roe Fishery (published May 1997), West Coast Fisherman Magazine; [pers.] Poetry is the only way to communicate my true inner feelings. I only hope those reading them can relate to the message hidden within.; [a.] Courtenay, BC

ENNAMORATO, JUDITH
[b.] Mimico, ON; [ch.] Fred, Lori, Lisa, Nicky; [ed.] Mimico High, University of Toronto, Institute of Parapsychological Studies, Humber College; [occ.] Author, Lecturer, Psychotherapist; [memb.] Pen International, Writer's Union of Canada; [oth. writ.] "Intuition," "Success Strategies," NC Press (book), various articles for Sweet Grass (magazine for native Canadians), "Sing the Brave Song," "Blood Sky," (books); [a.] Schamberg, ON

ERICKSON, BRENDA
[b.] May 3, 1979; Peace-River, AB; [p.] Annette and Gordon Erickson; [occ.] Artist and writer; [hon.] Art history award for best grade; [oth. writ.] A variety of poems, short stories, and personal reflection pieces; [pers.] My main goal in writing will always be for personal growth, and I owe great thanks to my family for many years of encouragement.; [a.] Edmonton, AB

ERSKINE, JANETTE
[pen.] Janette Erskine; [b.] January 14, 1972; Hamilton, ON; [p.] John and Diane Erskine; [ed.] Grade Twelve, M. M. Robinson High School, Sheridon College—Medical Office Administrion; [occ.] Medical Secretary; [memb.] Y.B.C. Bowling—eight years, Burlington Teen Tour Band—five years; [oth. writ.] "Remembering You," "Hope"; [pers.] I lost both of my grandparents to a drunk driver in 1984, but I know one day I will see them again in Heaven.; [a.] Burlington, ON

ERTEL, MICHELLE
[b.] April 24, 1978; Kitchener, ON; [p.] Debbie Ertel, Grant Ertel; [ch.] Brodie; [ed.] Graduated from Resurrection Catholic Secondary School, as a single mother; [pers.] Thank you Mom, Dad, Karen Ertel, Aunt Bonni, Krista, and Brodie for encouraging me and for helping me put lost hopes in the past. I love you all dearly. This is our achievement.; [a.] Waterloo, ON

ETAN-ADOLLO, LIONEL
[b.] November 20, 1965; London, England; [ed.] Postgraduate student of Advanced and Applied Theology, Westminster College, Oxford; Master's Degree in Economics, London Guidhall University, London; Qualified Shipbroker, ICS, London; [oth. writ.] The A-Z Model of the World, The Word is Prophecy, Faith and Reason: A Mathematical Exergesis (unpublished), and several other books and articles still unpublished; [pers.] I believe arguing for the Trinitarian personality of God is as scientific as mathematics, physics, chemisty, and other sciences. I am enthused about this and this is central in all my writings.; [a.] London, England

EVANS, LUCIE E.
[pen.] L. Evans; [p.] American; [m.] Welsh; [ed.] High school, college; [memb.] St. John Ambulance; [hon.] Awards in Volunteering for St. John Ambulance; [oth. writ.] "Wild Weather," "Thoughts," "Man on the Staun," "Because," "The Lonely One," "Alone With Pride," "The Urn," "Winter Returns," "Negative Man," "Mistakes," "Inner Fears"; [pers.] I have filled in a data form before: Circle of Life, Gone Ecstasy, The Little Brown Church, The Stranger, and The Rocking Chair.; [a.] Edmonton, AB

FARRELL, ANN
[b.] February 16, 1924; Wood Green, England; [p.] Paul and Ruth Belinfante; [m.] Edward Farrell; April 14, 1948; [ch.] David, Mary Ann, Siobhan, Dominic, Judy (dec'd); [ed.] England, Community College; [occ.] Writer/Editor (Semi-retired); [memb.] Writers Union of Canada, Older Women's Network, Religious Society of Friends (Quakers) Bereaved Families of Ontario (BFO,) SASA (SUDEP Awareness and Support Assoc.); [hon.] Canadian Community Newspapers Assoc. (CCNA) features writer, Media Club of Canada Columnial; [oth.writ.] Grace MacInnis: A Story of Love and Integrity (Fitzhenry O. Whiteside, Canada), author biography; [pers.] As a writer, I am a generalist, which means I have been able to write on a diversity of subjects. I strive for peace, taking responsibility for life's ups and downs, and finding time for friends, daughter, music, and things artistic.; [a.] Toronto, ON

FEDWICK, BASIL
[pen.] Basil Fedwick; [b.] January 1, 1916; Hadasville, MB; [p.] Daniel and Mary Fedwick; [m.] Gladys Fedwick; September 19, 1947; [ch.] Carole Proud, John, and Michael Fedwick; [ed.] Grade Twelve, St. John's High School, Winnipeg Manitoba Oblate House of Studies, Battleford, Saskatchewan; [memb.] Ryerson University, Toronto, ON, Senior's Education Programs, Toronto, ON; [oth. writ.] I wrote stories for the senior's recollection group at Ryerson University, about homesteaders in Canada.; [a.] Toronto, ON

FERGUSON, GAIL
[pen.] Gail Ferguson; [b.] September 1, 1962; Toronto, ON; [p.] Margaret and Charles Prear; [ch.] Four children; [occ.] Mother; [pers.] If you don't attempt life, then life will pass you by.; [a.] Seedbury, ON

FIDLER, JAIME
[b.] September 26, 1977; Nukusp, BC; [p.] Connie Chessel, [ed.] Graduation of Grade Twelve from Aldergrove Secondary School, Aldergrove Elementary for my childhood education in Aldergrove, British Columbia; [oth.writ.] I write songs, too. I have seven songs and you can hear the meaning to them, which is the meaning of love.; [a.] I hope that everyone out there will find that special thing that they hold inside, to express themselves and their feelings.; [a.] Aldergrove, BC

FINLAY, MELISSA
[b.] December 1, 1983; Burnaby, BC; [p.] Dave and Debbie Finlay; [ed.] Grade Nine; [occ.] Student; [memb.] YLD—Youth Leadership Development; [oth.writ.] Several poems, unpublished; [pers.] I write from my heart, and all thought. I'm only fourteen, but going on one hundred twenty-five! I feel I have much life experience. My poetry, my family, and my friends all mean so much to me, and they support me one hundred percent. Thanks to my friends and family for support, to my English teacher, Mrs. Patterson, and my homeroom teacher, Mrs. Holland, for always being

there for me and supporting me, and especially to my loving and caring mother, Debbie.; [a.] Kelowna, BC

FIORINI, STEPHANIE
[pen.] Angel, Sefi; [b.] September 22; Toronto, ON; [p.] Domenica and Carlo Fiorini; [ed.] Currently at St. Basil the Great CHS; [memb.] My school's Social Action Committee; [hon.] Several awards for poems and short stories awarded in the past; [oth.writ.] "Sadness" published in The Sands of Time and "Birthdays" published in Beyond the Horizon; [pers.] "It takes as much courage to have tried and failed as it does to have to tried and succeeded." [a.] Toronto, ON

FLOOD, GARETH CAMPBELL
[b.] January 24, 1976; Johannesburg, South Africa; [p.] Beth Macfarlane, Roy Macfarlane; [ed.] Hyde Park High School (South Africa), University of Auckland; [occ.] Student; [memb.] International Tae Kwon-Do Foundation of New Zealand (I.T.F); [oth.writ.] Poems published in local magazine; [pers.] It's better to regret something you did than something you didn't.; [a.] Auckland, New Zealand

FORBES, TREVOR
[b.] February 22, 1981; Hamilton, ON; [p.] Bob and Barb Forbes; [ed.] Sir Allan MacNab Secondary School; [pers.] Let your mind guide the pen; let the pen reveal your mind; [a.] Hamilton, ON

FORONDA, JANICE J.
[pen.] Jan Warren, White Fang; [b.] March 16, 1981; Baptista Village, Santiago City; [p.] Ernesto R. Foronda, Marlin J. Foronda; [ed.] Secondary education (high school graduate); [occ.] Student; [memb.] (School Level) Science Club—President, (National Level) Earthsaver's Movement—Member, (School Level) Magnificent Editor-in-Chief, (Regional Level) Junior Drugwatch Foundation: Assistant P.I.O. (Executive Board) and Member (Editorial Board); [hon.] Valedictorian, Grand Loyalty Award, Graphic Arts Award, Journalism Award, Elementary and High School, Craftsmanship Award (Elementary and High School), Best Script Writer, Best Musical Director, First Prize Slogan Making, First Prize Logo Making, Second Place Making contest (School Level); [oth. writ.] "King" (twenty-four stanza poem), "Untouched Grains of the Battlefield" (short story), "There's No Desert Without Thorns" (poem); "A Valiant's Silent Roar" (poem); [pers.] I believe that there's no greater way of expressing one's unspoken words than writing. In my writing, I come out with the best of it when I find myself all alone and in great distress. All the words just flow out from my mind, and my heart is moved to write, and there's neither nothing nor no one who could ever stop me.; [a.] Isabela, Philippines

FREEMAN, MARY A.
[b.] May 12, 1937; Asheville, NC; [p.] James A. Paris; [m.] Ronald N. Freeman; June 12, 1982; [ch.] four daughters, one son; [memb.] Flambro Society, National Diabetes Association, Associate Member of International Society of Poets, Nominee for Distinguished Member; [hon.] Numerous certificates of appreciation from U.S. Air Force, U.S. Army, and U.S.O. for volunteer services; [oth.writ.] Poems and articles for U.S.O. volunteer newsletter, poem published in Etches in Time, articles for various newsletters; [pers.] God gives to us each, to make of it what we will. I pray God will guide my thoughts and my pen, so I can express the humor, beauty, sadness, and sometimes pain of life in my poetry.; [a.] Naples, Italy

FRIES, JEFF
[b.] January 1, 1980; Kitchener, ON; [p.] Cheryl Fries, Jim Fries; [ed.] Sir Edgar Baver Catholic Elemematry, St. David Catholic Secondary School; [memb.] Scouts Canada; Youth Bowling Association; Smoking, Alcohol, and Drug Awareness Group; [hon.] Grade Ten Religion Academic Award, Grade Ten Science Academic Award, Honor Roll, Catholic Education English Poetry Award; [oth. writ.] Several poems published in local newspaper, many poems and short stories written for personal satisfaction; [pers.] I emphasize and reflect on both the positive and negative aspects of society; I have been greatly influenced by modern day poets, the media, and my own imagination.; [a.] Kitchener, ON

FRIESEN, JANET
[pen.] Janet Friesen; [b.] December 22, 1964; Surrey, BC; [p.] Isaac and Eleonore Friesen; [ed.] Second year of university; [occ.] Office Manager and Artist; [pers.] I am searching my soul for the truth, and expressing it through words.; [a.] Vancouver, BC

FRIZZELL, CHRISTINA
[pen.] Xina Frizzell; [b.] November 20, 1981; Edmonton, AB; [p.] Ronald and Erlinda Frizzell; [ed.] Grade Eleven at St. Francis Xavier High School; [occ.] Student; [pers.] Poetry and music are my forms of escapism, and escapism is as essential to life as air.; [a.] Edmonton, AB

GADD, LAUREL G.
[pen.] Laurel Gwin; [b.] August 2, 1980; Virgin Islands; [p.] Judith, Michael Gadd; [ed.] I am a Senior at the Manor School in the Virgin Islands. I am hoping to attend Centenary College this fall.; [occ.] I am a Peer Tutor for both public and private school students. I also work in a small country store; [hon.] I won second place in a regional EPA Poetry Contest.; [oth.writ.] There are many—I've been writing poetry about seven years now.; [pers.] Know this: everyone is a creator, for everyone has an imagination. And everyone is a critic, for everyone has an opinion. Knowing this, know that your creations will always be judged, but no judgement should ever weigh more than that which your heart speaks.; [a.] St. Croix, Virgin Islands

GALVIN, WENDY MARIE
[pen.] Mazey; [b.] February 8, 1956; Toronto, ON; [p.] Mr. and Mrs. Prokop; [ch.] Jay and Scott Galvin; [ed.] Grade Twelve and some college, adult English correspondence course; [occ.] Writing poetry and children's stories; [oth.writ.] Several unpublished poems; [pers.] I would like to dedicate this poem to my two boys, Jay and Scott, and to the Northumberland Women in Crisis for being there when I needed someone. I would like to express to other abused women that they are not alone. This poem is for them, too!; [a.] Coubourg, ON

GANGOLLI, TINA P.
[pen.] Mishti; [b.] January 11, 1977; Mumbai; [p.] Pradeep, Mamta; [ed.] Graduation in Performing Arts, B.F.A. degree in Classical Dance; [occ.] Student; [hon.] I have been awarded prizes for excellence in music and dance.; [pers.] Life is cadence of beauty: See it, live it, and enjoy it.; [a.] Mumbai, Makarasutra

GAVROVSKI, VLADIMIR
[b.] March 10, 1970; Skopje; [p.] Angel and Liljana; [ed.] Higher Education, Faculty of Philosophy University, St. Cyril and Methodius; [occ.] High School Teacher of Philosophy (unemployed); [oth.writ.] A collection of poems, "Memories of Indentity" (published 1994, Skopje) "Preoccupation Or Predestination" (published 1997, Skopje); [pers.] Memories exist for self-discovering in the everlasting sense of eternity.; [a.] Skopje, Republic of Macedonia

GEE, JOHN ALFRED
[b.] July 09, 1934; London, ON; [p.] Florance Lilian and Joshua Gee; [ch.] Kimberley Anne and David Scott Gee; [oth.writ.] "Songs," "The Master Above," "All That Glitters," "Isobel, Gentle Isobel"; [pers.] Do unto others as you would have them do unto you.; [a.] London, ON

GLEESON, ANGELA
[b.] January 21, 1977; Kitchener, ON; [p.] Joe Gleeson, Karen Walter; [ed.] British Columbia Institute of Technology; [occ.] Student and Environmentalist; [pers.] "Each of us must be the change we want to see in the world." Keep the dream alive.; [a.] Vancouver, BC

GODE, FRANK ARTHUR
[pen.] "Luke"; [b.] January 17, 1965; Hanna, AB; [p.] Ruth Anderson; [m.] Solene Fobert; [ch.] Roxanne, Martin, Derrick, Adam, Chantal; [ed.] Finishing Grade Twelve, university background in Sociology, Psychology, Philosophy, Economics, and Criminology; [occ.] Incarcerated (working as mason and cabinet maker); [memb.] Toast Masters, Narcotics Anonymous, Alcoholics Anonymous; [oth. writ.] None that have been published to this date; [pers.] I write to create peace within the souls of others and myself. I write to create understanding and non-judgement between society and incarcerated individuals like myself. I write to create humanity in the confines of an often unforgiving world.; [a.] Cambellford, ON

GOODWIN, CARRIE MIRANDA
[b.] April 18 1982; Springhill, NS; [p.] Keith and Patricia Goodwin; [ed.] Currently finishing Grade Ten; [occ.] Student; [oth. writ.] Poem, "Answer Me," published in Images in Time; [pers.] I have realized that, if you have a goal, it takes determination and perseverance to reach it, but most of all, you have to believe in yourself because this is where success begins.; [a.] Southampton, NS

GOYETCHE, TODD
[pen.] Sylvester; [b.] April 8, 1967; Halifax, NS; [p.] Separated; [ed.] Grade Twelve, GED School, Ontario (Grade Ten was completed); [occ.] I work at a fish plant.; [memb.] I belong to the Writers Federation of Nova Scotia—membership was granted to me a few weeks ago.; [hon.] None, other than the praise I get when I pass out poetry to people that I see.; [oth.writ.] Approximately seven hundred poems written over the past nineteen years. Two Hundred saved on computer on 3.5 inch disks (Windows 3.1).; [pers.] I write for personal enjoyment and I share with others in my travels, so that they may also enjoy. I have been writing since September 1979.; [a.] Dartmouth, NS

GRAVES, MEAGAN A.
[pen.] MegG; [b.] August 4, 1982; St. John's, NF; [p.] Michelle and Alan Graves; [ed.] Westville High School, Walnut Grove Secondary, Walnut Grave School of Music; [occ.] Student/Writer/Musician; [memb.] Volunteer Vancouver Aquarian Dictou District Honor Choir; [hon.] Sang at Carnegie Hall, New York City, May 28, 1995; [oth.writ.] Innumerable writings for personal pleasure; [pers.] Through my poetry, I tell the world the things my lips won't say. All of my emotions are put on paper.; [a.] Langley, BC

GREEN, JOANNE JOYCE
[pen.] Daniel Joyce; [b.] September 18, 1939; Toronto, ON; [p.] Albert and Geraldine Williams; [m.] Donald Green; July 22, 1971; [ch.] Central Tech H.S. (Art); [memb.] SWAC, Militia (home-based) Toronto ON; [pers.] There's nothing more gratifying than to put into words what's in your heart and mind, and share it with the world.; [a.] Toronto, ON

GRYC, WOJCIECH
[b.] July 1, 1986; Poland; [p.] Julanta and Ibigniew Gryc; [ed.] Elementary school; [hon.] Gifted Program, grade six; [pers.] "Dreams" is dedicated to my mother, father, and sister.

GRYMEK, JERRY
[pen.] Jerry Grymek, Jerry Roman; [b.] June 11, 1976; Toronto, ON; [p.] Bozena Grymek; [ed.] George Brown College, St. James; [occ.] Student, George Brown College; [memb.] Vice President of Advertising for Marketing Association, Advertising Representative for Newspaper; [oth.writ.] Poems published in past anthologies; [pers.] I strive to reflect reality in my writings. My work involves incidents that I have been through or have witnessed. Influences include Edgar Allan Poe.; [a.] Toronto, ON

GUDZINSKI, MINDY
[b.] November 20, 1980; Peace River, AB; [p.] Nick and Cheryl Gudzinski; [ed.] I am currently attending grade eleven, and one day I hope to become an architect.; [pers.] Most of my writing comes from the heart. I am influenced by my emotions. There is some advice—once given, that I'd like to pass on to anyone striving to achieve. . . . Birds fly high, so don't sell yourself short.; [a.] Manning, AB

HACKMAN, ELIZABETH A.
[pen.] Elizabeth A. Hackman; [b.] October 28, 1923; Lucknow, India; [p.] Geoffrey Davis, Marie Davis; [m.] George Hackman; June 18, 1949; [ch.] Patricia, Carita, Michael; [ed.] Frensham Heights School, UK, Middlesex Hospital School of Physiotherapy, London, graduated 1945; [memb.] Chartered Society Physiotherapy, American Physical Therapy Association, National Trust (Great Britain); [oth. writ.] Poems published in five anthologies, House of Many Rooms, Life, Soul Searching, Poetic Justice, publisher—Poetry Today, Penhaligon Page Ltd., Liangollen, Wales, "Our World," publisher—Aural Images, Bolton Langs, UK, children's story, "Two on the Road," (submitted for publication); [pers.] From an early age, I have been fascinated by language, sound interpretation, rhythm, structure of poems. I started to write seriously two years ago. I write from my own personal experience, interests in people, human experiences, and the world around me, influenced by love of nature and the countryside. I travel abroad.; [a.] Albury, Guildford, Surrey

HADZIANTONIOU, SPYROS
[b.] August 3, 1976; Athens, Greece; [p.] John and Mary Hadziantoniou; [ed.] French, Hellenic School of Athens; [occ.] Student of the University of Liverpool (Classical Studies); [oth. writ.] "My Friend" is the first poem I've ever written in English. My other ones have Greek titles, of course.; [pers.] Other points of view might seem darker, but then, knowledge is not about good and evil, is it?; [a.] Liverpool, UK

HALDEN, STEPHEN
[b.] July 28, 1971; Ottawa, ON; [p.] John and Joyce Halden; [ed.] Electronic Engineering Technology and Algonquin College; [occ.] Equipment Technologist; [memb.] WTF Second Dan, Black Belt from Tae E. Lee Ottawa Tae Kwon Do School; [pers.] If there is anyone to believe in, believe in yourself. Become your own hero.; [a.] Nepean, ON

HALL, JAMES
[b.] February 25, 1943; Selkirk, Scotland; [p.] James Hall, Margaret McGrattan; [m.] Margaret Anne Hall (nee Hawkins); September 2, 1967; [ch.] Three;[ed.] High school and Alternative Studies; [memb.] Horsemaster, Myotherape Guild, Great Britain, 1965; [pers.] Horses have been my passion for all of my life; my pride is to bring others to a greater understanding of these magnificent beasts through many types of communication.; [a.] Aldergrove, BC

HALL, PEARL
[b.] January 15, 1920; Victoria, BC; [p.] Deceased; [m.] Deceased; June 12, 1941; [ch.] Seven children; [ed.] Public School Victoria West; [hon.] P.N.E. Award in Art, Vancouver BC, poems published in seven anthologies, first, second, third, and honorable mention, Canadian Authors, Golden Award—World of Poetry; [occ.] Retired Mother, Poet, and Artist; [oth. writ.] I'm in a wheelchair from an attack of Polio in 1960.; [pers.] I put into my poems the deepest essence of nature, people, the world, and spirituality as I see, hear, and sense it.; [a.] Sidney, BC

HALSTEAD, JAMES J., III
[b.] March 29, 1972; Brooklyn, NY; [p.] James and Catherine Halstead; [m.] Eunice Halstead; May 29, 1993; [ed.] B.A. Major in Insurance, The College of Insurance, NY; [occ.] Insurance Account Executive; [oth. writ.] Screenplay: "South of Heaven," currently working on several other screenplays; [pers.] I have many other poems dedicated to my wife. My creative energy is best channelled when I write. This is the stuff dreams are made of!; [a.] San Juan, Puerto Rico

HAMILTON, MATHEW
[b.] September 4, 1976; Otahuhu, New Zealand; [m.] Grace Sarah; April 18, 1998; [ed.] Bachelor of Arts/Communications, Monasa University, Diploma of Arts (Professional Writing and Editing); [occ.] Student at Monasa University, Australia; [oth. writ.] Performed own poetry at three public recitals, have had work published in University Literary Works, and one poem published nationally in the Australian Presbyterian Journal; [pers.] Faith is like running through the woods with your eyes closed, your arms outstretched, and not hitting any trees. It's a freedom.; [a.] Melbourne, Australia

HAMMERSLEY, BRENDA
[b.] December 12, 1940; Bedford; [p.] Ivy and Alfred Rollo; [m.] Brien Hammersley; April 21, 1962; [ch.] Tracy Hammersley; [ed.] Cuskoo Hall County Secondary School and Hertford Regional College; [occ.] Optician's Receptionist; [memb.] International Society of Poets, Writer's Club; [oth. writ.] One poem published by the International Society of Poets and three with Sigrat Press; [pers.] I find writing poetry therapeutic, and it is an enjoyable way to express my feelings.; [a.] Hertfordshire, England

HARBHAM, MEENA
[b.] November 7, 1977; South Clapman, London; [ch.] Mayur; [ed.] BTEC in Science, B.A. Honours Biochemistry; [occ.] Medical Representative; [memb.] Mensa; [oth. writ.] Many thanks and loads of love to

Omer (Osterley, London, May 7, 1997).; [pers.] The sharpness of my pencil, the bluntness in life, the light of my candles, the darkness in love, the life in my music, the memories that hurt, the pain in my heart, and the tears in my eyes made my anthologies, with the strength of love and friendship.; [a.] London, UK

HARPER, MELINDA
[b.] April 27, 1984; Kingston, ON; [p.] Heather Brewster and Tom Harper; [ed.] Eighth grade at St. Joseph's Separate School in Gananoque, ON; [hon.] She works as a volunteer at a senior citizen home two nights a week after school, and is on the student council at her school.; [pers.] Melinda is a gentle, loving person who loves to work with her seniors and loves poetry. She is always writing; she is a very good young girl who helps raise her three-year-old nephew and helps her handicapped mother.; [a.] Gananoque, ON

HARPUR, NOEL
[pen.] Banta; [b.] December 12, 1949; Clonmel, Eire; [occ.] Writer/Musician; [pers.] My music and my writing comes from a spiritual point of view.; [a.] Clonmel, Co. Tipperary

HARRIS, MAXINE
[b.] July 4, 1970; Kingston, Jamaica; [p.] Shirley Miller; [m.] Densel Harris; July 28, 1996; [ed.] New Era Business Institute of Jamaica; [occ.] Manager, Relax Resort, Jamaica Ltd., Montego Bay, Jamaica, West Indies; [memb.] Youth Leader—Seventh Day Adventist Church; [hon.] Business Administration Certificate; [oth. writ.] I've had several poems published in a local newspaper; as a lyricist, I won a recording award with Fine Star Music Masters in Deadham.; [a.] Montego Bay, St. James, Jamaica, West Indies

HARTANTO,
[pen.] Haryo Prasetyo; [b.] November 12, 1958; Solo, Indonesia; [p.] Bd. Priyoatmodjo; [m.] Theodora Landra; November 20, 1994; [ch.] Natya Nindyagitaya; [ed.] University of Atmajaya, Yogyakarta, Faculty of Economics; [occ.] Journalist; [memb.] Forum Apresiasi Budaya, Forum of Culture Appreciation; [hon.] 1994—The Best Ten of Sanggar Minum Kopi in Bali Poetry Contest, Annual Poetry Contest All Bali; [oth. writ.] Ladrang Anthology of Poetry published by Wianta Foundation, 1995, a number of essays, features, articles, news reports, poetry published in local and national newspapers in Indonesia; [pers.] Sharpening the soul through words.; [a.] Denpasar, Indonesia

HEADLEY, EVE
[pen.] Evelyn Mills; [b.] September 16, 1922; Edmonton, AB; [p.] Harold and Lilian Mills; [m.] October 10, 1975; [ch.] Four; [ed.] College; [occ.] Retired; [memb.] A.S.C.A.P; [hon.] Certificate of Thanks from Alberta government for working on behalf of sexually abused children, written up in Maclean's regarding this effort; [oth. writ.] About 100 poems, writing life story, newspaper items, had first poem published in third grade; [pers.] I feel a strong responsibility for sick and poor people and for the pressures our young parents and children have to face.; [a.] Sherwood, AB

HEANS, DIANE
[b.] January 21, 1960; [occ.] Campground Owner; [pers.] I have been inspired by the love of my son, Hudson.; [a.] Saint John, NB

HEINRICHS, JOHN
[b.] June 29, 1975; Morris, MB; [p.] John and Kathy Heinrichs; [ed.] Grade 12, G.E.D.; [occ.] Truck Driver;

[oth. writ.] I have written about thirty other poems.; [pers.] This poem is written for the woman with whom I fell in love, and her daughter, but it never became more than a struggle for love.; [a.] Elm Creek, MB

HEMINGTON, ROBYN VANESSA
[pen.] R. Hemington; [b.] July 2, 1991; Niagara Falls; [p.] Jeanette and Bill Hemington; [ed.] Currently attending Owen Sound Collegiate and Vocational Institute; [occ.] Student; [memb.] Blue Crane Martial Arts Academy; [pers.] Inspiration lies anywhere and everywhere, but only if you open your heart to it.; [a.] Holland Centre, ON

HERRITT, MARLA
[b.] July 20, 1967; Sydney, NS; [m.] Lenn Herritt; [ch.] Five; [ed.] Graphic Design; [occ.] Stay-at-home mother; [memb.] Writer's Federation of Nova Scotia, Valley Flip Flops Gymnastics Club; [oth. writ.] Children's stories; [a.] Kentville, NS

HEWSON, HAROLD B.
[pen.] Gert; [b.] March 12, 1925; Grimsby, ON; [p.] Mr. and Mrs. Harry Hewson (both deceased); [m.] Beatrice Marie Hewson; March 17, 1957; [ch.] Cindy Annette, Sherri Lyn; [ed.] High School—three years, one year Reta Drow TV School; [memb.] R.C. Legion Br. #578; [oth. writ.] National Library of Poetry; [pers.] Believe in God and the great hereafter. Try to show some philosophy and love in writings influenced by the National Library of Poetry.; [a.] Tecumseh, ON

HILDEBRAND, ELMER
[b.] October 15, 1955; South America; [m.] Janice; August 21, 1979; [ch.] Andrew, Janina, Matthew; [oth. writ.] The Fear Within, The Old Quiet Room, The Silent Grey Fellow; [pers.] I enjoy writing lyrics and poetry that will influence, inspire, or motivate, and be entertaining at the same time.; [a.] Winkler, MB

HILLMAN, SHERRIE LEE
[b.] November 3, 1969; Red Deer, AB; [p.] Heather Schneider and Don Blair; [m.] Trevor Hillman; July 27, 1991; [ch.] Ashlee Heather, Melissa Joanne; [ed.] Lindsay Thurber Comprehensive High School; [occ.] Video Store Owner; [oth. writ.] Several poems unpublished; [pers.] I enjoy sharing the pain or the beauty in one's life. If someone else reading my poetry can relate to the pain or feel the peacefulness of my words, then I know I have touched them in some way. It is a great sense of accomplishment.; [a.] Red Deer, AB

HINDLEY, GARY J.
[pen.] Gary James; [b.] July 16, 1960; Montreal, QC; [p.] James Hindley, Dilys Smith; [pers.] Poetry is my personal, emotional commentary dealing with the consequences of certain present day political decisions and/or actions that affect humanity's struggle at large for truth and hope.; [a.] Montreal, QC

HOFFART, MICHAEL T.
[b.] January 23, 1981; Chattam, NB; [p.] Terr Lynn Hoffart, John Soldan; [ed.] Grade Eleven, G.C.H.S.; [occ.] Student and part-time worker at Cold Value Drug Mart; [hon.] First Place in Musical Theatre, Most Promising Actor, Zones Drama Fest; [oth. writ.] Few poems published in school newsletter in fourth grade; [pers.] My poems reflect the negativity in the world and our lives with some chance of hope. I dedicate this to Maren Kuster, who taught me to look for good and showed me love.; [a.] Cold Lake, AB

HOLIFF, JACQUI
[b.] February 16, 1985; Toronto, ON: [p.] Janet Trachter, Gary Holiff; [ed.] Seventh grade at Crosby Heights Public School; [hon.] Poetry, Diamond Award (Best All-around Student), gifted program; [pers.] I worked hard on this poem, and I'm glad that it's published.; [a.] Richmond Hill, ON

HOLLAND, MARIKO KUBO
[b.] April 11, 1940; Tokyo; [m.] Ronald Francis Holland; [ed.] Nagoya University of British Columbia; [occ.] Professor of English, Nagoya Holy Spirit Junior College; [oth. writ.] Oh, Canada—Poetic Impressions of Natural Beauty (published in Victoria, BC, Canada, 1988); [pers.] Nature has splendor and power well beyond mankind.; [a.] Nagoya, Japan

HOLROYD, DAWN GOODWIN
[b.] May 1, 1966; Edmonton, AB; [p.] Violet Olive and Donald Brian Holroyd; [m.] Legally Separated; April 1, 1987; [ch.] Melissa, E.V., Vito Noel, and Kayla A. T. Roccia; [ed.] High school diploma; [occ.] Telephone Receptionist; [oth. writ.] Several poems unpublished; [pers.] Love is the most precious possession or thing in this universe, and the love of a child is the greatest to behold as it is untouched by the grayness of the intense world.; [a.] Edmonton, AB

HOOGENBOOM, GUIDO
[b.] June 6, 1934; Utrecht; [p.] Jo and Hank Hoogenboom; [m.] Divorced; [ch.] Berend, Wilgert, Britt; [ed.] High school and conservatory of music (opera singer); [occ.] Musician and producer of TV and film in Hollywood, CA; [oth. writ.] "Music as a Bridge," "The Master Dream Teller," and "The Fairy Dream Queen"; [pers.] Nada Brahma. The world is sound and music is the bridge between Heaven and Earth.; [a.] Lelystad, Netherlands

HOSKIN, DOROTHY
[b.] January 31, 1927; Oshawa, ON; [p.] Wesley Hoskin and May Hoskin (deceased); [m.] Divorced; June 6, 1945; [ch.] Two daughters and four sons; [ed.] Cart Wright and Durham School; [occ.] Retired; [hon.] I had a few winnings from 1960-1965, entering contests requiring "Last Lines to Limericks."; [oth. writ.] Several poems unpublished; [pers.] For over sixty years, I have had fun and enjoyment with words that rhyme, and sharing some words with loved ones.; [a.] Bowmanville, ON

HOWARD, TERRY LYNN
[b.] February 8, 1966; Brantford, ON; [p.] Lionel and Evelyn Gurney; [m.] William Darin Howard; September 2, 1989; [ch.] Chase, Cody, Rayven, and Shylea; [ed.] North Park College; [occ.] Singer; [hon.] Numerous singing awards; [oth. writ.] Published in grade school year book, poem untitled "Let Me Fly"; [pers.] I have made a lot of mistakes in my life, some that I can never take back. My writing allows me to express myself to the fullest of my ability, and allows me to escape, if only for a while. I can't hide in my words, they only speak with pure emotions.; [a.] Brantford, ON

HOWLETT, LOUISA ANN
[pen.] Crystal Starr; [b.] July 6, 1940; Hornchurch Essex, England; [p.] Walter, Ethel Howlett; [ch.] Michelle Anne Tolley; [ed.] Ashburton Secondary Modern School Education, Custom House E. 16, London, England; [occ.] Care giver for the Elderly Residential Home; [memb.] Soul Awareness group, Clacton Spiritual Church, Rapport Magazine for U.F.O.

Witnesses, and Abductees; [hon.] Royal Society of Arts in English and typing, (R.S.A); [oth. writ.] Poems and other writings for Rapport Magazine for U.F.O. Sightings, Witnesses, and Abductees; [pers.] Seeker of truth, knowledge, the meaning of life, understanding, the universe, and other life forms in the cosmos to raise my consciousness to a higher level: spiritual and psychic-wise.; [a.] Clacton, England

HOYDA, JOSEPH JOHN
[pen.] Joey Hoyda; April 25, 1986; Toronto, ON; [p.] Karen and Joe Hoyda; [ed.] I attended Monsignor Clair School, Barrie, ON, at the time the poem was submitted. I am currently attending St. Marguerite d'Youville School, Barrie, ON, and I am in sixth grade.; [pers.] I was 12 years old when I wrote "Little Apple." I enjoy writing poems and stories in my spare time. I also love to read, play hockey, basketball, and skateboard. I have a younger sister, Jennifer, who is 10 years old.; [a.] Barrie, ON

HRUSKA, IVAN
[b.] October 3, 1981; Zagreb, Croatia; [p.] Vlado Hrusha, Lucia Hruska; [ed.] Student; [oth. writ.] "Gutters of Glamour in Snahelihe Lullabies";[pers.] I always try to combine all the feelings I can think of in my poetry. I believe that writers should keep away from strict styles or rules in their writing. Everybody should write how and what they wish. My influences have been the lyrics used in punk and alternative music.; [a.] Eschborn, Germany

HUSAIN, SHANE HAYWARD
[pen.] S. Hanes; [b.] December 15, 1973; Toronto, ON; [p.] Hayward Husain, Gabrielle Husain; [m.] August 9, 1998; [ch.] Chanae Alexandra Husain; [ed.] Completing B.A. at York University; [occ.] Freelance Writer, Student; [hon.] Achievement Award of Ontario; [oth. writ.] Poems published in other anthologies, script re-writing for TBS, Japan; [pers.] Flaws are what make beauty so beautiful. Without those comparisons, one may never find the contrasts that inspire great poetry. My influence and inspiration stem from these dualities.; [a.] Toronto, ON

HUTFELTER, ALISON
[pen.] Ally; [b.] October, 22, 1970; Surrey, BC; [p.] Judith and Charles Hutfelter; [ed.] Lord Tweedsmuir, Senior Secondary, Computer Programmer and Operation from CDI, Black Jack course from Great Canadian Casino; [occ.] Labourer, Data Entry Operator; [memb.] Gatois Gym, Slo-Pitch League Legion; [hon.] Music Award for two years, Citizen of the Year for two years in high school; [pers.] Hoping to give someone peace of mind or thought of the own life. Let them know that they are not alone in this lonely world.; [a.] Cloverdale, BC

ILYAS, MOHAMMAD
[b.] July 11, 1942; Jhelum, Pakistan; [m.] Parveen Akhtar; May, 1974; [ch.] Three; [ed.] Graduation; [occ.] Writer, Journalist; [memb.] Journalist Association; [hon.] Won First Prize in General History during studies, granted a Certificate for providing services to the Miserable Humanity; [oth. writ.] I've written many articles on different subjects, short stories, poems, and songs in the shape of a book by the name of "The Women of the East."; [pers.] The truth is a great weapon.; [a.] Montreal, QC

IRVING, ALICIA
[b.] December 16, 1985; Bowmanville, ON; [p.] Betty Irving and Bill Irving; [a.] Courtice, ON

SHII, YUKO
[b.] October 10, 1970; Omiya, Saitama;[p.] Isamu shii and Kiyoe Ishii; [memb.] The International Society of Poets; [hon.] Editor's Choice Award 1995, The Best Poems of the '90s, The Best Poems of 1997, The Sound of Poetry by The National Library of Poetry, http://www.poets.com/YukoIshii.html (It has been established in The International Poetry Hall of Fame Museum); [oth. writ.] Many unpublished lyrics for Mandrake, via the creative impulse working through the act of art, music, words, painting, and a means of expression to all desire we want. Web-site address: http://www.amy.hi-ho.ne.jp/mandrake/; [pers.] Confession is the best basis for your own private salvation. My writings are deeply private expressions of my feelings. They are something that excites you to the point of contradiction. I'm not on the verge of self-destruction all the time, but I've never lost faith in my ability to create art. Through my poetry, painting, and music I want to arrive at the unknown with you who can support each other. Like Dali and Gala. And I hope to write and have more of my poems published. Sylvia Plath and Charles Baudelaire are my favorite poets.; [a.] Omiya, Japan

JACOBS, SHMUELA
[b.] October 2, 1982; Israel; [pers.] Though I am a Hebrew speaker, I write mostly in English. I see some special meanings in English words. Poems bring these meanings back to life. To contact me, e-mail: shmuela@mail.snunit.k12.il.; [a.] Jerusalem, Israel

JAMES, JANET CRAIG
[b.] Scotland; [oth. writ.] Poems, articles, and adult fiction in Canada, U.S., and Great Britain, "Notes" on Wuthering Heights (Barnes and Noble), four teenage novels.; [a.] Sault Ste. Marie, ON

JAMES, MANJU
[ed.] B.A., M.S. (Education), Ph.D., University of Kansas, U.S.A.; [memb.] Golden Key National Honor Society, Phi Beta Kappa National Honor Society, Phi Beta Delta International Honor Society; [hon.] Outstanding International Woman Award (1989); Hilltopper Award (1990), Anderson Memorial Award (1990), Outstanding International Student Award (1992), International at the Kennedy Foundation in Washington, DC (1992); [a.] Toronto, ON

JAMES, MARK
[b.] Canada; [ed.] B.A., L.L.B., L.L.M., L.L.D. University of London, England, University of Ottawa, Canada; [occ.] Barrister and Solicitor, Specialist in Constitutional Law and International Law; [memb.] Law Society of Upper Canada, International Institute of Humanitarian Law, San Remo, Italy; [hon.] My Doctor of Laws (L.L.D.) Degree, awarded Cum Laude; [oth. writ.] One law book, 60 research publications in law journals; [a.] Toronto, ON

JAMIESON, DONNA
[b.] May 13, 1977; Mulgrave, NS; [p.] Joseph and Sadie Jamieson; [ed.] Mount Allison University, Sackville, New Brunswick, third year of a B.A. program with a major in Religious Studies, minor in English; [occ.] Student; [pers.] Write from your heart, it's what you know best! A special thanks to my mom and dad for their love, support, and encouragement.; [a.] Mulgrave, NS

JAMIESON, WILFRED OLIVER, III
[pen.] Will Jamieson; [b.] September 27, 1968; Brantford, ON; [p.] Lorence (nee Bill) Bugeski, Wilfred Oliver Jamieson Jr.; [m.] Lucilla May Douglas; [ch.] Lorsnus Skyra, Wilfred Oliver IV, Cassandra Alexandria, Cheyenne Hope, Travis James Skylar; [ed.] James Robinson Secondary School, University of South Dakota, Laurentian University, Cambrian College, Toronto School of Business, United States Naval Technical Drawing—Storekeeper; [occ.] Student in Business Administration and Accounting—My goal is to be an accountant.; [memb.] Cambrian College Native Students Association, Cambrian College Peer Tutoring, Sudbury Spartans football team; [hon.] Honors graduate from Toronto School of Business in 1995, tutoring certificate from Cambrian College and Sudbury Board of Education; [pers.] I try to be the best I can. I always look for the best in all people and treat them with respect. I treat everybody the way I would like to be treated—with respect. Watch out for the unsung, because they have untouched abilities and skills waiting to be released. I owe my life to my mother. Rest in peace—I love you.; [a.] Sudbury, ON

JARRAD, CANDICE
[b.] July 31, 1984; Australia; [p.] Lynne; [ed.] Eighth grade student; [pers.] My poem, "Dad," is about my father who died of cancer when I was nine. I am now 13.; [a.] Adelaide, South Australia

JEAN, ELIZABETH
[b.] July 9, 1982; Calgary, AB; [p.] Robert and Alma Jean; [ed.] Grade nine; [occ.] Student; [a.] Calgary, AB

JENSEN, HENNING
[b.] January 7, 1952; Copenhagen, Denmark; [p.] Aage Henry Jensen, Anna Rigmor Jensen; [m.] Lise Hansen; January 2, 1987; [ch.] Rikke Katrine, Grith Ea; [ed.] University of Copenhagen, Denmark, M.D., Specialist in Physical Medicine Rehabilitation and Rheumatology; [occ.] Consultant for the Norwegian Social Security, private practice in rheumatology, management of public outpatient clinic in same field; [hon.] International Scholar, Cleveland Clinic, Ohio, USA, June/July 1992, by courtesy of stipend from the Foundation of Ambassador Mark Evans Austad; [pers.] In well-off parts of the world, most suffering and illness is rooted in lack of compassion and the way humans treat their fellows. Realizing that, there's hope.; [a.] Beitostoelen, Norway

JEROME, DEBBIE
[b.] June 27, 1951; Powassin, ON; [p.] Albert and Pearl Jerome; [ch.] Angela, Robert, Norma-Lyn, Sara; [ed.] Eleventh grade; [oth. writ.] At present, I have written approximately three hundred-sixty poems.; [pers.] My desire has always been to write poetry. To be able to touch the different emotions of mankind is truly a wonderful thing. Through my poetry I am able to do this.; [a.] Subbury, ON

JOHNSON, KENNETH
[pen.] K. C. Johnson/Wounded Bear; [b.] September 24, 1962; Smithers, BC; [m.] April 16, 1989; [ch.] Two; [hon.] Been honored with Today and Rewarded with its Ancient sensations.; [pers.] I write for the pure satisfaction of it.; [a.] BC

JOHNSON, RUTH
[pen.] Hannah; [b.] March 26, 1914; Sydney, NS; [p.] Annie and Rowland Sharples; [m.] Donald P. Johnson; September 26, 1939; [ch.] Ross and Gary Johnson; [ed.] High school; [occ.] House wife; [hon.] Numerous awards for appreciation; [oth. writ.] Canadian Pioneers, The Little Ducklings; [pers.] I enjoy life,

people, and poetry to the fullest, and reading, as well as writing poetry.; [a.] Halifax, NS

JOHNSTON, MICHAEL
[pen.] Fuzzy; [b.] September 23, 1976; Victoria, BC; [p.] Mavis and Ken Johnston; [m.] Leila; [ch.] Ocean; [pers.] Live your life to love. Run barefoot in the grass.; [a.] Victoria, BC

JONASSON, FAY
[pen.] Fay Taylor; [b.] November 3, 1931; Blaenavon, S. Wales; [p.] Ernest Taylor and Florence Taylor; [m.] Gudmundur "Howard" Jonasson; January 19, 1963; [ch.] Patricia Anne, Michael Howard; [ed.] Castle St. Elementary for girls, Abergavenny, South Wales, some education 1953-57, WR. AF (England), some English courses, Ladner, BC; [occ.] Housewife (Retired) Telephone Supervisor; [memb.] 20 Years T.O.Ps. Church Choir and local Senior Choir Member; [hon.] 1988-89 Best Under Two Years New Garden "Langley," sponsored by Real Estate Board; [oth. writ.] "Senior Citizens: What Are They?" in Christian newspaper and many more, not printed over last 50 years; [pers.] Writing, to me, over the years has been very fulfilling and healing. And also a gift to be shared.; [a.] Langley, BC

JONES, LETITIA M.
[b.] April 30; Saskatoon, SK; [p.] Arthur and Mary Ann Jones; [ed.] Twelfth grade, North Battleford Comprehensive High School (NBCHS); [occ.] Farmer; [hon.] Honorable Mentions in the Iliad Press and competing for the Dickinson Award in the Amherst Society; [oth. writ.] "Not Now—Procrastinator's Psalms," in Rhymes of Greatness Famous Poets Society, "Two Futures," in The Amherst Society's American Poetry Annual Book, "Looking Myself and Envious," in Iliad Press' book called Moments; [pers.] Enjoy what you do, and try to do it. It's always important to be yourself, and you'll always have people with you that respect, or at least know you.; [a.] Paynton, SK

JONES, MARIELLE DROUIN
[pen.] Marielle; [b.] March 26, 1937; Cornwall, ON; [p.] Jenn Mares, Marie Jeanne Drouin; [m.] Vincent Anthony Jones (deceased); January 17, 1983; [ch.] Pierre, Diane, Joanne, Venise Brozeau; [ed.] St. Lawrence High School, St. Lawrence College Cornwall, Studies at Ottawa University in Psychology (not completed); [occ.] Retired from government at federal level; [memb.] Cornwall Author's Association; [oth. writ.] Several poems and short stories; [pers.] The purpose of my writings is to try and pull the strings of thoughts, conscience, and feelings of people. "Love Poem" is dedicated to my children.; [a.] St. Andrews, ON

JONES, ROWENA R.
[pen.] Rowena Roecks; [b.] October 14, 1926; Fairfield, WA; [p.] Carl Hazel Roecks; [m.] Lloyd Jones; May 4, 1947; [ch.] Diana, Lorena, Lonnie, April, Cindy; [ed.] High school, Fairfield, WA, Sacred Heart School, Nursing; [occ.] Retired Ranching Cattle, Horse, Guest; [memb.] Formerly U.S. Dude Ranch Association, Canada Guest Ranch Association, Rocky Mountain Visitors; [oth. writ.] Stories in Dude Rancher Magazine, Hoofs and Horns; [pers.] I try to emphasize the beauty in life and nature that we too often overlook or take for granted. Always living on a ranch has helped me reflect on important issues of life.; [a.] Wasa, BC

JONES, TIFFANY LEILA
[b.] November 19, 1971; London, ON; [p.] Jerry and Gaynor Parsons, Robin Jones; [ed.] UWO B.A. Arts;

[pers.] What therapy there is in writing; what mystery yet to be unveiled. Challenged by the many depths within, my pen most often ventures forth with the greatest of truths where writing has taught me to value myself. May Neal Carley be acknowledge for his love patience, friendship, and support.; [a.] Toronto, ON

JUTAI, JEFFREY
[b.] January 1, 1956; Welland, ON; [p.] William and Lucie Jutai; [m.] Ivy Lynn Bourgeault; July 13, 1991 [ch.] Lauren Evangeline, Tyra Alexandra; [ed.] B.S. University of Toronto, M.A. and Ph.D. University of British Columbia; [occ.] Psychologist and Research Administrator; [a.] Toronto, ON

KACZMARZ, JUDY
[b.] April 10, 1941; Winnipeg, MB; [m.] Stan; September 6, 1968; [ch.] Gregory and Richard; [ed.] Grade 12, Business College; [occ.] Administration Secretary to Director of St. Paul's High School (a Jesuit high school); [hon.] 1967 Pan-American Games Volunteer Medal and Certificate; [pers.] I love to make up spur-of-the-moment poems, jingles, etc. (both humorous and serious), for co-workers, friends, etc., for birthdays, retirements, and all occasions.; [a.] Winnipeg, MB

KAFELLE, PAUL KWASI
[b.] February 22, 1959; Kingston, Jamaica; [occ.] Management Consultant; [memb.] African Canadian Cultural Collective, Community Social Planning Council, Eva Smith Achievement Association; [hon.] United Way Merit Award, Somali Community Independence Day Award, African Canadian Achievement Award; [oth. writ.] I have performed in many community events and at schools, libraries, and universities (over last 5 years). I have written over 200 poems, and am currently looking for a publisher.; [pers.] Performance poetry can enliven, uplift, inspire, and educate for personal and social change. Gil Scott-Heron is my favorite.; [a.] Toronto, ON

KALSI, PARMINDER KAUR
[b.] August 14, 1973; Kuwait; [p.] Mohan Singh, Surinder Kaur; [m.] Harjeet Singh Kalsi; July 20, 1997; [ed.] N. Delhi University, India, International Poly-Technic for Women, India, Careers 2000, Surrey BC; [occ.] Office Administrative Assistant; [hon.] English Literature (Master Degree), English Literature (Diploma), Fashion Designing (Diploma), Office Assistant; [oth. writ.] Author of book: Emotions, 1998, Father-in-law, Nirtmal S. Kalsi (D. Eng., Inventor, and Author of book: Seed-Mantra Philosophy, 1996), Mother-in-law, Amerjeet K. Kalsi (Government Teacher), Brothers: Kanwaljit S. Kalsi (Author of Health and Nutrition) and Opender P. Singh (University of Michigan, U.S.A.); [pers.] I try to reach the deep caves of reality through my poetry. My special thanks to all my family members in supporting me for all I do.; [a.] Surrey, BC

KALYN, JOHN
[b.] December 2, 1949; Peace River, AB; [p.] Mike and Mary Kalyn; [m.] Deborah Kalyn; June 7, 1975; [ch.] Michael Paul, Patrick John, Leslie Erin; [ed.] Bachelor of Education, University of Alberts, Language Arts Major; [occ.] Heavy Equipment Contractor; [oth. writ.] Short story—unpublished; [pers.] I have had inner curiosity and fascination in human behavior and the psychological manifestation motivating that behavior, i.e., the choices he/she makes by pro-action or default. I favor poetry of depth.; [a.] St. Albert, AB

KANKHWENDE, KIRINANI
[b.] August 9, 1982; Blantyre, Malawi; [p.] Fletcher, Paulette Kankhwende; [ed.] Bishop MacKenzie Primary School; [occ.] Student; [hon.] Allied Arts Honor Certificate for Poetry, Etstedfodd Honors; [pers.] In all I do, I seek to glorify God, using the talent given to me by His grace. I wish to touch people's hearts and to inspire myself and others.; [a.] Ulongwe, Malawi

KELLY, DENNIS JOSEPH
[b.] January 11, 1934; Aruba; [p.] Irish; [m.] English; November 16, 1957; [ch.] Three; [ed.] High School; [occ.] Retired transit worker; [oth. writ.] "An Immigrant's Fond Dream," "Clancy's Wake," "Diana, Princess of Wales," "Princess Diana," "Shillelagh"; [a.] Thornhill, ON

KENNEDY, JOANNA KRONGOLD
[b.] March 27, 1987; Toronto, ON; [p.] Ruth Krongold, John Kennedy; [ed.] Fifth grade student currently; [occ.] Student; [oth. writ.] A Believer's Tale, The Dragonfly Queen, The Storm, The Champions, Never a Moment Like It; [pers.] Motto: "Publish or Perish."; [a.] Toronto, ON

KHAN, SHAHEENA
[b.] September 29, 1957; Meerut, India; [p.] Rifat Sarosh and Sabiha Sarosh; [m.] Irshad A. Khan; September 2, 1979; [ch.] Shazia Khan and Ahmer Khan; [ed.] U.M.A.—English Literature, Delhi University—Master's degree, Post graduation diploma in Journalism; [occ.] Radio Program Producer/Broadcaster/Journalist—Editing radio magazine; [memb.] Indian Broadcaste Programme Service; [hon.] Harish Chandra Kathpalia Gold Medal for Creative Writing—Delhi University, 1975, Akashwani Annual Awards—Merit Certificate for producer and author of documentary featurized radio programme on AIDS (all India radio, 1993); [oth. writ.] Several articles and poems published in various periodicals/books, regularly editing and writing for "India Calling," prestigious monthly radio magazine, circulated world wide; [pers.] I am very highly impressed with nature and strive to reflect it in my writings. The need to preserve the natural environment for our future generations is my top priority.; [a.] New Delhi, Delhi, India

KIM, ANNA
[b.] October 27, 1968; Seoul, Korea; [p.] Chang-Sep and Keo Soon Kim; [ed.] B.A. Honours in Linguistics from Carleton University in Ottawa, ON; [occ.] Graduate Studies Administrator, Carleton University; [hon.] Linguistics and Second Language Acquisition; [pers.] I see my life and all my experiences as adding to the richness of my creative efforts in my writing.; [a.] Ottawa, ON

KIRKPATRICK, MAUREEN
[b.] September 23, 1962; Vancouver, BC; [p.] Millicent and Thomas Kirkpatrick; [ed.] Legal Assistant Course, MTC College, Vancouver, BC, numerous night courses; [occ.] Legal Assistant; [oth. writ.] This is my first work.; [pers.] Art is the epitome of life!; [a.] North Vancouver, BC

KNIGHT, SHELLY
[b.] June 26, 1976; Springdale, NF; [p.] Ken and Louise England; [m.] Ritchie Knight; [pers.] My mother encouraged my writings. Thanks, Mom.; [a.] Springdale, NF

KONECSNI, TOREY
[b.] August 18, 1985; Edmonton, AB; [p.] Eric and Pat; [ed.] Seventh grade student at Holy Trinity School, Richmond Hill, ON; [hon.] Mastery certificate for writing, Headmaster's Award for Excellence three years in a row; [oth. writ.] Short stories and poems; [pers.] Writing is a way to express yourself. Every poem or story represents a part of the author.; [a.] Unionville, ON

KORPELA, MARIE
[b.] May 3, 1958; Sault Ste. Marie, ON; [p.] Roland and Lucille Lemleaux; [ch.] One daughter, Kelly; [ed.] Sault College of Applied Arts and Technology—Business Courses and English; [occ.] Home-based Artist and Writer; [oth. writ.] Many unpublished poems, one short story, second prize award; [pers.] I truly am the hopeless romantic, but love the trials of life that make everyone stronger. I admire anyone who is truly honest in the way he lives. And this, I write about.; [a.] Sault Ste. Marie, ON

KOTELNIKOV, VICTOR
[pen.] Vikont; [b.] April 2, 1976; Moscow, Russia; [p.] Natalia and Sergei Kotelnikory; [ed.] Russian State University for the Humanities; [occ.] Student of Political Science; [hon.] Acknowledgement of friends; [oth. writ.] Poems in Russian and several in English; [pers.] When your final fight is over, listen to the sound of silence. It will tell you that there are neither winners nor losers, there is only love—and you still have to find it.; [a.] Moscow, Russia

KRALINGEN, LOIS VAN
[b.] March 20, 1932; Jordan, ON; [p.] Walter, Dorothy Stirling; [m.] Edward; June 6, 1975; [ch.] Karen, Kathleen, William, Laurie; [occ.] Retired; [oth. writ.] Several poems; [pers.] My poems are mostly about my family members, and as such, would not be understood by other readers. This is my first attempt at a poem not relative to anyone in particular, but rather to all.; [a.] St. Catharine's, ON

KUMAR, KRITHIKA
[pen.] Nivedha, Nisha; [b.] October 18, 1978; Bombay; [p.] R. Kumar, K. Preethi; [ed.] Studying third semester in Mechanical Engineering at M.S. Ramaiah Institute of Technology; [occ.] Student; [memb.] Poets International, International Society of Mechanical Engineers; [hon.] Prizes won in music competitions, prizes won in sketching and poetry competitions; [oth. writ.] Poems published in Poets International monthly magazine, school and college magazines, two poems published in the book, Love and Peace; [pers.] The love of parents and the brotherhood of mankind, I wish to promote through the different faces of life by the knitted words of my poetry.; [a.] Bangalore, Karnataka, India

KUMAR, LAL
[pen.] Harshan; [b.] January 31, 1940; Malaysia; [p.] G. and Lalathi Kumar; [m.] Celine Kumar; November 18, 1969; [ch.] One girl and three boys; [ed.] M.B.B.S. (University of S'pone), FRCS (Edinburgh); [occ.] Consultant, Plastic Surgery; [oth. writ.] Masonic Journals; [pers.] Life is to be lived, the joy is in giving, kindness begets kindness, and love is the most previous thing we have to give.; [a.] Petaling Jaya, Lelangor

LACOUSTA, ELIZABETH ROSE
[pen.] Liz; [b.] June 20, 1982; Edmonton, AB; [p.] Ray and Theresa Lacousta; [ed.] Attending Austin O'Brien High School; [oth. writ.] Ongoing collection of deep, heart-felt reflections.; [pers.] All forms of art are the best ways to express strong emotions.; [a.] Edmonton, AB

LAM, WILLIAM CHENG WENG
[pen.] WIC; [b.] October 19, 1977; Batu Pahat, Johor; [p.] Cheng Boon Chow and Ng Chue Kheng; [ed.] T. Melawati Primary School, Datok Lokman High School, Kuala Lumpur University of Technology of Malaysia, Johor Bahru; [occ.] Undergraduate in Chemical Engineering, Majoring Polymer; [memb.] Hope of God International; [pers.] Specially dedicated to Dad, Mom, and Hope of God International. To God be all glory.; [a.] Kuala Lumpur, Wilayak Persecutuan, Malaysia

LAMBERT, BARBARA
[b.] April 18, 1939; Yorkshire, England; [p.] Margaret Parkinson, Ernest Rathbone; [m.] Stuart Lambert; August 17, 1969; [ch.] Ann; [ed.] Wentworth Castle, Teacher Training College, UK, Liverpool University, UK, University of BC, Canada, Bachelor of Education Degree; [occ.] Retired; [oth. writ.] Local Historical Research, Newspaper articles, "In Paradise," a Collection of Stories About BC's West Coast, Children's Stories about life on a farm, Historical articles 1890-1955; [a.] Powell River, BC

LANGLEY, PARKER
[pen.] Eagle Perkins; [b.] May 31, 1938; Seal Harbour; [p.] Harold and Alice Langley; [m.] Faye; November 4, 1961; [ed.] Eleventh grade, Heavy Truck Specialist, Mine Mapping and Survey; [occ.] Retired; [memb.] Lingan Gold and Country Club, Royal Cape Breton Yacht Club, Cape Breton Volunteer Search and Rescue, Life Member Search and Rescue Canada; [hon.] Awarded Life Membership to Search and Rescue Canada, Top Six Truck Sales Specialist for six years, Peak Performance Award from Ford Motor Co.; [oth. writ.] The Mighty Eagle (a collection of poems and prose), From the Eye of the Eagle (a collection), When Last I Flew (poetry and prose); [pers.] Nova Scotia, and especially Cape Breton Bras D' or Lakes, literally saved the bald eagle from extinction. I identify with the eagle and the solitude and beauty of its flight.; [a.] Yarmouth, NS

LEAPARD, DAVID G.
[b.] June 15, 1947; Dinsmore, SK; [p.] Lawrence Leapard, Edith Leapard; [m.] Marlene Leapard; December 27, 1983; [ch.] Three step-sons, one step-daughter; [ed.] Twelfth grade ; [occ.] Ferry Operator; [memb.] Royal Canadian Legion Masons; [oth. writ.] Published in local paper and one anthology; [pers.] I write about life as it happens around me.; [a.] Eston, SK

LEDERMAN, MIKE
[b.] August 23, 1974; Kitchener, ON; [p.] Mark Lederman, Janine Lederman; [m.] Katya Rendon; July 1997; [ed.] OAC, Waterbo Oxford; [occ.] Machinist, Trident Automotive, Stratford; [oth. writ.] Many, however, none yet published.; [pers.] If you're losing a tug-o'-war with a tiger, let go of the rope . . . arms aren't so easily replaced. My writings have been influenced by Lear and Cervantes.; [a.] Stratford, ON

LEDUC, KENNETH E.
[b.] January 13, 1969; Hamilton, ON; [p.] Ken and Clare Leduc; [ed.] Bishop Ryan High School; [occ.] Machine Operator, Russel Metal, Hamilton, ON; [pers.] This is my first published poem. Now, knowing others enjoyed it, I hope it's not my last.; [a.] Hamilton, ON

LEE, SAMUEL
[b.] October 7, 1974; Vancouver, BC; [p.] Daniel and Peggy Lee; [ed.] B.A. Dalhousie University; [occ.] Student; [oth. writ.] Tucked away in the heart waiting to be birthed.; [pers.] Know where you're from, know

where you stand, know where you're going.; [a. Vancouver, BC

LEFUR, ALPHONSE
[pen.] Binh Huyen; [b.] October 14, 1938; Hano (VN); [m.] Anne Thuyhuyen Nguyen; March 1, 1959 [ch.] Vincent, Agnes, Jean, Joseph, Elisabeth, Jacques; [ed.] University of Pedagogy, Saigon Vietnam, [occ.] English Teacher and Director of High Schools, Vietnam and France, 1963-1995, Retired; [oth. writ.] Poems and novels in English, French, Vietnamese, published and unpublished, in Europe and America [pers.] In my writing, I praise the beauty of love and nature, which I believe come from God.; [a.] Creteil, France

LETTS, TANYA
[b.] December 15, 1969; London, England; [p.] John Letts, Rosemary Letts; [ed.] Computer training in MS Office '97 and Web Page Design at Sanctuary Computer Training Centre, studying voice and piano at Western Conservatory of Music, and trained as a commercial model; [hon.] Honorable mentions for Modeling (Commercial and Fashion Print), and for Singing, also for Academic Excellence, and Best Improvised Monologue for Acting; [oth. writ.] I write lyrics for my songwriter partner and I sing.; [pers.] I use emotional and visual expression in my poems and songs so that the reader can feel, and see, what I'm writing about at the same time. All I've experienced in life is the essence of my writing.; [a.] Langley, BC

LEVOIR, LIONEL
[pen.] Guy Norman; [b.] July, 1558; Edmonton, AB; [p.] Evelyn Goureou, Guy LeVoir; [m.] Puspo LeVoir; May 14, 1983; [ch.] Three; [ed.] Trade school; [occ.] Plumber, Gasfitter, Streamfitter; [memb.] Local 488 Plumbers and Pipefitters; [oth. writ.] Inspired poetry that isn't forced, but hopefully will stand the test of time, as others before me, that come to the surface like a lily on a pond, to present their moment to glory before passing on.; [pers.] We are all given a free choice in life, to follow His voice, or reject it; for me, I hope to follow it, for we are truly living in a time that is truly magnificent to some, but to many, they won't even know what has happened till it's too late. May the Lord of lords have his way unto eternity.; [a.] Edmonton, AB

LEWIS, ADAM
[b.] April 4, 1980; Truro, NS; [p.] Murdelle Lewis; [ed.] Currently in tenth grade; [occ.] Tenth grade student at Cobequid Education Center; [pers.] I am dedicating this poem to Amy Johnson, my girl friend, and my close, dear friend, Sarah Gatti. Without these two loving people I would not write poems. I love you both.; [a.] Five Islands, NS

LEWIS, HILTON HENRY
[b.] March 31, 1919; Georgetown; [p.] William & Ada Lewis; [m.] unmarried; [ch.] William, Charmaine, Michelle; [ed.] Rio Head Master, taught in 12 schools: first cl. trained, Tr. Government Training College, 1939-41, University of Guyana Adult Education, Music, 1976; [occ.] Unemployed Veteran, Athlete, Writer, Composer, Painter; [memb.] Secretary of Guyana Masters Athletic Association, Former President Pupil Tr. Association, Capt. Football, Y.M.C.A., Secretary of St. George's Choir Guild; [hon.] None so far, I live very humbly and "far from the madding crowd."; [oth. writ.] Written copious number of poems, currently working on four books: Portraitist, Veteran Athlete, Tenor Leggiere Pianist, Ardent Re-

ligionist; [pers.] I firmly believe in the existence of a divine creator. The Holy Bible is my guide and mentor—character development and ability upgrading, also.; [a.] G'G'town, Guyana, South America

LIM, JOYCE
[b.] January 1, 1968; Singapore; [p.] Lim Ser Leng, Lim Soh Hui Ngoh; [ed.] Master of Arts, University of Kent, Canterbury, Kent, United Kingdom; [occ.] Creative Director for Redefinedsing Private Limited; [memb.] Modern Art Society, British Computer Art Association; [oth. writ.] Articles for arts magazines, poems for magazines, scripts for art films; [pers.] I believe, therefore I am. I feel, therefore I write.; [a.] Singapore

LINE, JANET
[b.] March 29, 1909; Scotland; [ch.] One son—Paul, and his wife—Suzan; [occ.] Retired; [oth. writ.] I have been writing poems for years, for my own pleasure, and for local papers, greeting cards, for family, friends, etc.; [a.] Jackson Point, ON

LITTLER, GEA
[pen.] Gea; [b.] February 26, 1945; Netherlands; [p.] Goe Eerenberg, Didi Eerenberg; [ch.] Sean Littler, Mark Littler; [ed.] Library Technician Diploma; [occ.] Self-employed Research Service; [oth. writ.] Published in anthologies and small local magazines as well as "The Glow Within" by the National Library of Poetry; [pers.] I strive to find the man within: The hurts, the pains that cause lessons to be learned in life and how they focus on reality. My influences come from Irving Layton, Steve Osterlurd, and Leonard Cohen.; [a.] Port Dover, ON

LOKKE, FINI
[b.] December 31, 1937; Nyborg, Denmark; [p.] S. M. Lokke and Marry Lokke; [ed.] Nyborg High School—1955, Monter Peninsula College—1955-56, University of Copenhagen—1956-63; [occ.] Publisher, writer, painter, and designer; [memb.] International Society of Poets Lifetime Member (Inducted 1994), The International Poetry Hall of Fame (1996), Advisor, American Biographical Institute (1997); [hon.] Prize for Diligence, Nyborg High, Private Scholarship to MPC, CA, Fullbright Travel Scholarship, one year membership Alpha Gamma Sigma Society (1955-56), CA, Letter of Thanks, Royal Library Copenhagen for 30 years of archival experience (1990), exhibition local archive, sketches (1991), NLP and ISP Awards (1993-94), Poets Corner First Prize (fall 1993), The Sound of Poetry (1994), Two percent of Best Poems (1995), Editor's Choice Awards (1995), Solid Century Award for Achievement (medal), Cambridge, England (1997), Decree of International Letters for Cultural Achievement, ABI (1997), Dictionary of International Biography, Cambridge, England (1998), Semi-finals, North Riverside Open Poetry Contest (1998); [oth. writ.] Poetry Collection (1959), with own linocuts, Listening Station (Lyttepost), poems in Danish magazine, "Hyedekorn" (1959), Anthology "Profiles" (1961), many poems in local weeklies, small prose pieces in weeklies nationwide, novel (1970); [a.] Frorup, Denmark

LONG, MIKE L.
[b.] October 11, 1971; Owen Sound, ON; [p.] Alan and Valerie Long; [ed.] Georgian Bay Secondary School, High school graduate, Meaford, ON: [occ.] Pepsico Employee; [memb.] Canadian Professional Rodeo Association, Canadian Bullriders Association, Professional Rodeo Cowboys Association; [hon.] Several First Place Trophy Buckles for Bullriding, PRCA Rookie of the Year Award, 1994; [oth. writ.] Miles and Memories, Alberta Bound, Cowboy Dream; [pers.] Go hard or go home.; [a.] Calgary, AB

LOPEZ, RAFAEL
[b.] August 15, 1957; Arecbo, PR; [p.] Rafael Lopez, Lillian Lopez; [m.] Marlene Arbelo; December 19, 1981; [ch.] Rafael, Cristabelle, Kritzia; [ed.] B.S. Dairy Science, Michigan State University; [occ.] Dairy Farmer; [memb.] Churchland Country Community Committee; [hon.] Awarded by 4-H groups and other youth organizations; [oth. writ.] About one hundred unpublished poems. I am invited to churches and professional meeting as a motivation. I use the poems in those activities.; [pers.] I always have been the ugly duckling. I try to reflect in my poems the discovering of myself. My poems deal with fear and guilt, and how I can overpower them.; [a.] Coney, PR

LOUGHERY, BRUCE A.
[b.] June 12, 1960; St. Martins, NB; [p.] Douglas, Joyce Loughery; [m.] Mary Walter Loughery; June 29, 1985; [ch.] Jennifer and Kathrine; [ed.] One year trade college; [occ.] Machinist, Industrial Mechanic; [oth. writ.] Several poems published; [pers.] A greeting of divine truth shall rein among all people who search for God. The gifts will come in wisdom, and as they're shared, will flood an ocean of peace.; [a.] Rothesay, NB

LOW, JULIANNA MARIE
[pen.] Jaye Low; [b.] June 1, 1949; Hamilton, ON; [p.] Julia LeBlanc, Joseph Francis LeBlanc; [m.] Widow; [ch.] Daughter—Tamara Nastards Low; [ed.] Tenth grade; [occ.] Writer, bookkeeper gardener; [memb.] International Society of Poets, Chilliwack Golf and Country Club, Wegeners Granulomatesis Support Group, Inc.; [hon.] Four Editor's Choice Awards from The NLP for "Realms of Reality," "Tranquility City," "The Blue Bird of Peace," and "Destiny Crystal Energy."; [oth. writ.] 11 Poems published with The National Library of Poetry in their anthologies, four books ready for a publisher "Spirit of Life," "Spirit of Love," "Spirit of Nature," "Spirit of Being"; [pers.] Poems published in the following anthologies with the NLP: 1.) In the Desert Sun—Inspiration from Fiji, 2.) Best Poems of 1995—Spirit of Love, 3.) A Treasured Token—Realms of Reality, 4.) The Glow Within —Tranquility City, 5.) A Season of Flowers—The Blue Bird of Peace, 6.) The Sands of Time—Destiny Crystal Energy, 7.) Beyond the Horizon—Moons of Time and The Crystal Energy Den, 8.) The Best Poems of 1998—The Child, 9.) The Sounds of Silence—My Angel and Equality Not Dominancy; [a.] Abbotsford, BC

LUNAU, KATE
[b.] March 11, 1981; Ottawa, ON; [p.] Mary Lunau, Ron Lunau; [ed.] Rocklife Public School, Elmwood School, Lisgar Collegiate Institute (currently attending); [occ.] High school student (grade 11); [pers.] "Alors toi aussi aussi tu viens du ciel! De quelle planete es-tu?" A de Saint Exupery, Le Petit Prince.; [a.] Ottawa, ON

MABBITT, CANDY
[b.] April 8, 1978; Fort Smith, NT; [p.] Pat Mabbitt and Vida Pouliot; [m.] James; [ch.] Nephew Gary; [hon.] I had perfect attendance for four years in a row.; [oth. writ.] There was a time when writing poetry came to me easily. I looked over something, grabbed paper and a pen, and wrote it down. But, unfortunately, as I grew up, I became more involved in other things.; [a.] Westlock, AB

MACCARTHY, KRISTAN
[b.] March 22, 1974; Ottawa, ON; [p.] Martin MacCarthy and Maureen MacCarthy; [ed.] Woodroffe High School, Algonquin College; [occ.] Student; [memb.] Tae Lee Tae Kwon Do; [hon.] Red Belt in Tae Kwon Do (soon to be Black Belt), St. John First Aid and C.P.R. Certificate; [pers.] My poems reflect my personal mood. I hope they will inspire and encourage other poets and readers of fine poems.; [a.] Ottawa, ON

MACHESNEY, STUART TAFT
[pen.] Stuart Taft Machesney; [b.] June 21, 1963; N. Vancouver, BC; [p.] Beverly Machesney and Aynsley Machesney; [ed.] Handsworth Secondary School, Capilano College (both North Vancouver), B.A. in History, Simon Fraser University, Burnaby, BC; [occ.] Writer; [memb.] British Columbia Youth Parliament Alumni Member, International Foundation of Protection Officers (IFPO); [hon.] 1979 Student Council Awards; [pers.] I believe that history and man are one, and they have a place in poetry.; [a.] North Vancouver, BC

MACINNES, PETER
[b.] August 10, 1962; Vancouver, BC; [p.] Peter and Veronica MacInnes; [m.] Franca; August 10, 1985; [ch.] Hunter; [ed.] R.N. Diploma, Advanced Pediatric Critical Care Diploma; [occ.] Registered Nurse, Intensive Care Unit, British Columbia Children's Hospital; [memb.] Registered Nurse Association of British Columbia; [oth. writ.] An extensive collection of Christmas poems and poems celebrating special events of family and friends; [pers.] My poetry expresses a hope for the humanity we all look to find in ourselves. I hope it provides (even if for just one fleeting moment) personal inspiration to those reading it.; [a.] Port Coquitlam, BC

MACKENZIE, JEAN M.
[pen.] Jean M. MacKenzie; [b.] September 13, 1923; Gananoque, ON; [oth. writ.] Several poems as yet unentered, two already printed in your editions, with another one to be printed in your Sounds of Silence.; [pers.] My poetry comes from my memories and emotions. This gift of poetry came to me after a stroke two years ago. It has been my mental and physical lifeline.; [a.] Gananoque, ON

MACKINLAY, PHYLLIS
[b.] November 24, 1932; Scotland; [p.] Margaret and Patrick Quinn; [m.] Robert; October 10, 1957; [ch.] Sylvia and Suzanne; [ed.] Hyndland Senior Secondary School, Langside College, Glasgow, Scotland, Adelaide Institute of TAFE, S. Australia; [occ.] Writing, painting, and home duties; [hon.] High Commendation for Theses: (#1) "Anatomy," (#2) "Canada," Langside College, Scotland, Unibooks, SA, Short Story Competition, Certificate of Merit, South Australia; [oth. writ.] Poems, essays, short stories, and novel just completed, several poems published in local publication; [pers.] I need to write to express and share my emotions, because people are important.; [a.] Whyalla, South Australia

MADELEY, KEITH
[b.] October 6, 1972; Cambridge, ON; [p.] Irene Madeley; [ed.] Jacob Hespeler Secondary School; [occ.] D.J., Competitive Roller Skaters and Coach, Ski-Patroller; [memb.] Canadian Roller Skating Federation, Canadian Ski-Patrol Federation; [hon.] All Academy Awards; [pers.] I like to write straight from the heart and express my thoughts and my feelings. My inspiration to write comes from my surroundings and the different kinds of people I meet.; [a.] Cambridge, ON

MAHAFFY, SHANNON
[pen.] Jenasis Mahaffy; [b.] March 26, 1982; Belleville ON; [p.] Dawn and Jeff Mahaffy; [ed.] Quinte Secondary School; [memb.] Brownies; [oth. writ.] "Crush," "Hope," "True Friend," "Bestfriends," "Dreams," "My Love," "Molly," and "Friendship" are a few of my other writings.; [pers.] I can't just write a poem. I use the things I feel in my heart and write them down. I'm 16-years-old, and I have a strong love for lions and other animals.; [a.] Belleville, ON

MALLAR, TED
[b.] February 26, 1958; [oth. writ.] Essays, articles, letters, etc.; [pers.] My favorite book in all the world is the Book of James.; [a.] Edmonton, AB

MARINOPOULOS, ANDREAS
[b.] July 4, 1981; Athens, Greece; [p.] Panos and Sandra Marinopoulos; [ed.] Athens College; [occ.] Student; [oth. writ.] Several poems and short stories, none published; [a.] Athens, Greece

MARKOVIC, MIRJANA
[b.] June 25, 1947; Former Yugoslavia; [p.] Olga and Steve Rodic; [m.] Nicholas Markovic; December 27, 1970; [ch.] Olga; [ed.] Professor of Literacy and Serbo-Croatian Language, Filoloski University, Belgrade, Yugoslavia; [occ.] Learning English and writing poems; [memb.] Was member of Yugoslavian Poet's Club; [hon.] I won first place three times as the best poet in Bosnia. I also won many different awards from schools, radio stations, TV, and so on, for one of the best poetry achievements, and unique talent.; [oth. writ.] Three books (written entirely by me) published in Yugoslavia. Each one of them has over 20 poems. The first one was published in 1979, under the title of There Was a Bridge, but Maybe There Wasn't a Bridge. The second book, My Love's, was published in 1981. The third, There Is One Issue, was published in 1984.; [pers.] Life is always an open book, but never, never completely read.; [a.] London, ON

MARSILI, FEDERICO
[b.] June 27, 1965; Irabate, VA; [p.] Aurelio Marsili and Grimoldi Teresa; [ed.] Specializing in Scientific Studies; [memb.] Member of The Author's Club and Culture Passport Centre; [hon.] I've been classed first in: Cook for an Author Award and At 360 Award, third in: (Dedicated to Bestoevski) International Award, selected in: Adda's Poets award, finalist in: The Author's Club Award.; [oth. writ.] I've published two collections of poems: Scars and Tattoos and Silences. I have five poems in the anthology Europe Today, as well as some poems in Poetry magazine.; [pers.] I am looking for a distant God. I've little time and much anger. My life is a run toward a total idea of liberty and spiritual knowledge. In my past poems, there is a deep reflection on death, silence, and desperation. I am impassioned by the religions and philosophies of invision.; [a.] Limidocourasco, Covio

MARTIN, PHILIP J.
[pen.] Philip Mochuk Kuntz; [b.] May 8, 1970; Burnaby, BC; [p.] Dysfunctional; [m.] Cindy Dawn Martin; September, 1990; [ed.] A student in Society's School of Absolute Mayhem; [occ.] Warehouse Employee; [memb.] A fellow member of the human race; [hon.] Editor's Choice, "Sidewalk," Editor's Choice, "Seasons"; [oth. writ.] "Sidewalk," in A Treasured Token, "Seasons," in A Season of Flowers, and more to come; [pers.] Child abuse lasts forever. Thanks, Mom. Thanks, Dad.; [a.] Neuwestin, BC

MARTINEZ, FRANCISCO
[b.] February 8, 1974; Toronto, ON; [p.] Francisco Martinez Sr. and Gladys Martinez; [ed.] University of Toronto, University of Warwick, currently making plans for my Ph.D. degree; [occ.] Master degree, Philosophy student; [memb.] American Philosophical Association; [hon.] Graduated from the University of Toronto with Distinction; [oth. writ.] I have written three books: "Annabella," "Mary," and "Kissing," which are, as of yet, unpublished.; [pers.] My greatest dream is to show people how they can find beauty and meaning in their lives by following their sentiments.; [a.] Toronto, ON

MARTINEZ, PROVINCIA MARTINEZ
[pen.] Provi; [b.] January 3, 1910; Patillas, PR; [p.] Juan P. Martinez Lopez; [m.] Jacinta Martinez Roman; 1904; [ch.] Provi, Pedro, Palmira, Minerva, and Rosario (all Martinez Martinez); [ed.] My mother—eighth grade-housewife, my father—a policeman, Provi—Bachelor Art and Science, Pedro—Auto Mechanic, Palmira—Bachelor Art and Science, Minerva—Master degree, Rosario—Master degree; [occ.] Mother—Housewife, Father—Policeman for 40 years, all girls were Teachers in high school and college, Rosario was a teacher in college—Recinto University, PR; [hon.] First prize in contest for PR for a poem to Don Jose Vargas, honored by Girl Scout Association in PR, honored by past poetry association—first prize, honored in PR—graduation, dedicated for her poems, honored by G.S. for her poem to Girl Scouts, teacher of teachers, have a book of poems that has not been published yet, an award for contest of an association of women in PR; [oth. writ.] Book of poems, first prize in a poetry contest in PR, diploma for a poem in Poetry U.S.A., honored by Girl Scouts for a poem to Girl Scouts, honored first prize in PR, member of Puerto Rico teachers association; [a.] Arecibo, PR

MATTHIAS, ANNE THUSHARA
[b.] September 17, 1983; Colombo, Sri Lanka; [p.] Ranjan and Pauline Matthias; [ed.] Good Shepherd Convent, Kotahena, Colombo 13, Sri Lanka; [occ.] Student; [memb.] Girl Guides; [hon.] In an All-Island essay competition, I won First Place on two occasions, and also several awards in school prize giving.; [oth. writ.] Several poems published in local newspapers and magazines; [pers.] I try to focus on environmental protection and also on achieving peace and harmony among mankind.; [a.] Colombo, Sri Lanka

MAXWELL, FELICITY LYN
[b.] July 10, 1982; Ottawa, ON; [p.] Lynda Windmill and Russ Maxwell; [ed.] Tenth grade Literary Arts Student, Canterbury High School; [occ.] Proofreader, Canada Prospects and other Cultural Human Resources Council Publications; [hon.] Grade seven—Academic Award of Excellence, grade eight—Academic Award for Excellence, grade eight—Subject Awards for English, Music, and Math, Citizenship Award; [oth. writ.] One poem published in Providence Press Anthology, The Light along the Way; [pers.] "Whatever is true, whatever is noble, whatever is just, whatever is pure, whatever is lovely, whatever is of good report, if there is any virtue and anything praise worthy, meditate on these things." Philippians 4:8, the Holy Bible; [a.] Ottawa, ON

MAZURIK, DOROTHY
[pen.] Gran Ma Dorothy; [b.] February 28, 1928; Winnipeg, MB; [p.] Oliver and Beatrice Lewis (deceased); [m.] Joseph Mazurik (deceased in 1980); May 4, 1946; [ch.] Gwendoline Ruth (Wendy), Gregory Kenneth, and Paul Joseph; [occ.] Retired School Secretary; [memb.] Parish of St. Timothy, St. Vital Legion #16; [hon.] Retirement celebration after 37 years with the St. Vital School, Div. #6, and having some of my poems published in The Best Poems of the '90s, The Best Poems of 1997, and The Sounds of Silence; [oth. writ.] "Mary and Me," "The Many Faces of God," "Our Father's Call," "At Sunset," and "I Donwanna"; [pers.] Children can be our greatest teachers if we learn to listen with our hearts.; [a.] Winnipeg, MB

MBAHO, WILLIAM F.
[b.] October 31, 1977; Daresalaam, Tanzania; [p.] James Bahinguza and Rosemary Kirughyi; [ed.] University of British Columbia; [occ.] Political Science student; [pers.] In the words of Lord Alfred Tennyson, I dedicated my life "To strive, to find, and not to yield."; [a.] N. Vancouver, BC

MCCURDY, MARGARET
[pen.] Margaret McCurdy; [b.] February, 9, 1905; Waterville, KS; [p.] Frank And Lizzie Kinsman; [m.] Archibald McCordy; September 30, 1936; [ch.] Two: Elizabeth and Peggy; [ed.] L. Muss., Dalhousie University, Halifax, NS; [hon.] Lang Scholarship in Music, Dalhousie University, Halifax, NS; [a.] Brandon, MB

MCDANIEL, MATTHEW
[pen.] Matt; [b.] September 12, 1979; Inverness, NS; [p.] Frances McDaniel; [ed.] Currently in twelfth grade in high school, Margaree Forks District High; [occ.] High school student; [oth. writ.] Songs written for band (Juniper Noon), short stories, other poetry, etc.; [pers.] "We have entered and now will prosper; until we exit, our minds grow stronger. Everything is in the sky, we should all try to find it. Greatest influence would have to be Eric's trip, find out for yourself. In your hands it is dealt."; [a.] Margaree Forks, NS

MCDERMAND, PEARL
[b.] July 30, 1920; Alix; [p.] Ed and Inez Gessleman; [m.] Charles McDermand; January 20, 1941; [ch.] Darryl, Lynne, and Gail; [ed.] Grade Nine at Stanton, a one-room country school; [occ.] Retired farm widow; [memb.] Alix United Church, Alix Curling Club; [oth. writ.] I have written poems on farming, family, memorials, nature, and a few published in a local village bi-monthly newspaper.; [pers.] I am inspired by love of nature, the land, and my family and friends.; [a.] Alix, AB

MCDONALD, HAZEL SIMMONS
[m.] Patrick; [ch.] Patrick Jr., Christian, and Kathleen; [ed.] University of the West Indies and Stanford University; [oth. writ.] I have several other poems published in journals. My first volume of poetry, Dream Seasons, is to be published in 1998. I also write fiction and children's stories. [a.] St. James, Barbados

MCDONALD, STACEY
[b.] June 2, 1980; High Prairie, AB; [p.] Evelyn and John McDonald; [ed.] Will be graduating from grade twelve on June 27, 1998.; [occ.] High school student and Valley Tec. (Computers); [a.] Valley View, AB

MCINTYRE, HOPE
[b.] June 20, 1973; Ottawa, ON; [p.] Helen Smith and Morris McIntyre; [ed.] B.F.A. University of Saskatchewan, M.F.A. University of Victoria; [occ.] Theatre Director; [memb.] Theatre Ontario, Saskatchewan Playwrights Centre, supporting mem-

ber of Professional Association of Canadian Theatres; [hon.] The Bills Award at Arts International, Petch Research Scholarship, University of Victoria Fellowship, University of Saskatchewan Film Society Award, Walter Mills Award for Drama, University of Saskatchewan Honors Scholarship; [oth. writ.] Several plays workshopped and "Forces of Peace" performed at the Edinburgh Fringle Festival in Scotland; [pers.] Writing is a means of expressing yourself, but also touching someone else in an extremely profound manner. As a writer and theatre artist, I strive for that kind of human contact and sharing.; [a.] Toronto, ON

MEDITSKOS, ANNE
[b.] December 29, 1957; Helsinki, Finland; [p.] Tyyne Tuomikorpi, Antti Tuomikorpi; [m.] George Meditskos; September 21, 1981; [ch.] Jessica, Teemu, and Benjamin; [ed.] Hairstylist; [memb.] Song Writers Association of Canada; [pers.] I am a romantic song and poem writer. You find happiness and sadness in my writing.; [a.] Scarborough, ON

MEHEDEN, KEN D.
[pen.] April 5, 1957; [m.] Lee Malcolm Meheden; [ed.] Self-taught poet's photographer who overcame learning disability caused by an untreated genetic birth disorder.; [occ.] Permanently disabled, physically, due to above disorder.; [oth. writ.] I have several unpublished pieces besides "Lone Wolf," and I also include photography with my poetry.; [pers.] My writing is based on my personal experiences in life, of the loneliness of the streets, the loneliness of my heart, and my lifelong battle with a disease I didn't receive treatment for until a year ago. My philosophy is always "Step high or step out gracefully."; [a.] Victoria, BC

MEHSSEN, AYMAN
[b.] January 29, 1966; Tyr, Lèbanon; [ed.] Diplome D' Ebedes Approfondis (D.E.A.), Universite De Nancy II, France, on W. B. Yeats's poetry in 1993; [occ.] Preparing a Ph.D. Thesis on English and North American Literature; [oth. writ.] Several poems unpublished; [pers.] If there's no love, my fear is great that there's no God above.; [a.] Jarville, France

MEISE, DOLLY
[pen.] Molly Migraine; [b.] January 4, 1971; Dawson Creek, BC; [p.] Donna and Bill Meise; [ed.] Grade 11 and three years of Psychology in college; [occ.) Child care; [oth. writ.] I have written many poems and am currently writing two novels. (In the Air Cadets for four years, I achieved the rank of Sergeant).; [pers.] I love animals and children. I don't have any children yet, so I have two birds, two dogs, two rabbits, and one lizard. Whenever something happens in my life, I deal with it by writing.; [a.] Dawson Creek, BC

MELOCHE, SANDY
[pen.] Sasha; [b.] November 17, 1946; Windsor, ON; [ch.] Kim, Kevin, Brian, and Michelle; [ed.] General Amherst High; [occ.] Administrative Assistant for Investors Group; [oth. writ.] Poem published in the Poetry Guild; [pers.] Words are very important, they can destroy a person or make them. I enjoy putting life into my poetry, I make it very personal. Words are the essence of life.; [a.] Dartmouth, NS

MENG, WANG
[pen.] Wendy Wang; [b.] June 17, 1986; China; [p.] Wang Xing and Chen Jia Meng; [ed.] I went to school for about three months in China, then I came to Hungary and went to two schools for about a half year.

At last, I came to this American school, G.G.C.A.; [occ.] Student; [hon.] A Perfect Attendance Award, an Art Award, one Grammar Award, two Sports Awards, two Honor Roll Awards, two Principal's List Awards, and a Student of the Year Award; [oth. writ.] None published; [pers.] I never knew that my poem would be published in United States. It's just too good to be true, and it is like a dream. I was very happy that such wonderful things were happening to me. God bless you all.; [a.] Budapest, Hungary

MEYER, GERALD
[b.] October 17, 1951; Hamilton, ON; [p.] James Meyer; [ed.] Grade 12 Diploma; [occ.] Disability Pension; [oth. writ.] A few short stories; [pers.] My poems tell a story.; [a.] Hamilton, ON

MIHOKOVIC, MARIJAN
[pen.] Marinko G. Croata; [b.] July 3, 1947; Pitomaca, Croatia; [p.] Ivan and Ana Mihokovic; [ed.] Facultas of Theology, University of Zagreb, Croatia; [occ.] Priest, Pastor; [oth. writ.] Regular article in weekly paper for Croatian community in Toronto—Hamilton area, in Croatian. Translations from German and English in Croatian for Parish work, Translation of I. Lepp's "Psychology of Friendship" from German, printed in Croatian in Zagreb, Croatia; [pers.] Being an immigrant in the new country is like being the bridge between two banks of a river, and being a priest in that environment means listening, trying to understand the whispering of the suffering souls, those who sometimes claim to have two homelands, but mostly feel like living without any of them.; [a.] Hamilton, ON

MILLER, KATHERINE
[pen.] Kate Miller; [b.] July 21, 1984; Northampton, MA; [p.] John Miller and Sharen McCarguodale; [ed.] I'm still in school (eighth grade). I plan, though, to go Oxford for my college education as an author.; [memb.] Girl Scouts of America, 4-H U.S.A., Canadian, Jersey Cattle Club, Quebec Young Farmers Association, and Canadian 4-H Association; [oth. writ.] A few poems published in other national poetry contests and also school newsletters; [pers.] I believe a poem is best only when you show your true feelings, when you reveal what your heart converses, and when you give a piece of yourself in the writing.; [a.] Coaticook, QC

MILLETT, KAREN
[b.] June 25 1973; Stanley, NS; [p.] Blanche Swinamer and Allen Campbell; [ed.] Kennetcook Elementary, Hants North Rural High, Windsor Community College, ICS Journalism Short Story; [occ.] Care giver; [hon.] Editor's Choice Award for "Solace in Beauty" from the National Library of Poetry; [oth. writ.] Currently working on a novel and a collection of short stories and poetry; [pers.] "People say you have to brainstorm to churn out works. I don't. I see it in my head like a movie, and write what I see, have, and feel. I enjoy it."; [a.] Hants Co., NS

MILLS, HOLLY
[pen.] Holly Mills; [b.] April 16, 1981; Lunenburg; [p.] Nancy and John Mills; [ed.] Eleventh grade; [occ.] Dishwasher and Cook's Helper in the summertime; [memb.] Sea Cadets and Scouts; [oth. writ.] Just for personal use and school; [pers.] I write to reflect on all the "bads" and "goods" of life and love.; [a.] NS

MLOMBA, JUSTIN JAMES
[pen.] Akawusanje Wutilupuso; [b.] December 31, 1966; Chegutu, Zimbabwe; [p.] James and

Akongolejefalesi; [m.] Widowed on March 8, 1996, to re-wive in 1998; [ch.] His first, and only, son died on July 31, 1995; [ed.] N.B. where there is Mkambitsi Kalumo, Mkambitsi Village traditional authority Kalumo; [occ.] He is looking for a greener pasture because of under-payment in the Malawi Civil Service, although still working as a registry clerk.; [memb.] Islak Religion, a backwards writer notable for thirteen years to numerous international penning organizations by February 28, 1998.; [hon.] The Malawi School Certificate of Education and the Silver Diploma in principles and practice of management.; [pers.] Mlomba Justin, as poor as a church mouse, had funds for the appearance of his biography in, "The Best Poems of the '90s," because of Mr. James Gilbert Cgiundira's own personal funds of Mkambitsi. He was the PIU projects manager. Nobody is all gifted; a human being "has to lack" something in life.; [a.] Chikaondra, Ntaja

MOHAMED, NADIRA
[b.] September 27, 1967; Guyang; [p.] Shirley A. Patrick; [m.] Elvis Ramkissoon; January 2, 1992; [ed.] High school, Toronto Board of Education; [occ.] Employer for Agency; [hon.] Bookkeeping Certificate, medal for poems written by me; [oth. writ.] Song, poems

MOHANAN, P. K.
[pen.] P. K. Mohanan; [b.] November 19, 1948; Kerala, India; [p.] P. U. Krishnan (father—deceased) and Karthikeyani (mother—deceased); [m.] Mrs. Sukla Devi; December 6, 1977; [ch.] Only one, Master Dhritiman Kumar; [ed.] Pre-University (Arts) from Pandu College, Guwahati University, Assam, India; [occ.] Serving as Confidential Stenographer in N.F. Railway, Malicaon, Guwahati-781011; [memb.] Life Member of The Poetry Society, India, L-67/A, Malviya Nagar, New Delhi-110 0012, India; [hon.] I was awarded first prize in a college competition in 1979, for composing a poem.; [oth. writ.] Published on July 1, 1993, Love Lyrics, a book of romantic poems, which has been accepted by the State Governments of Assam, Mizoram, and Kerala, and they have purchased 40, nine, and two copies respectively, each for their state libraries.; [pers.] I started composing poems in 1974. I was born in a middle class family, with a humble birth and upbringing. My father was a Landlord turned Pauper. My birth place: Village—Vadakkekara, North Parur Taluk, Ernakulam District, Kerala State, India.; [a.] Guwahati, Assam, India

MONGRAIN, DONALD
[b.] August 27, 1971; Hamilton, ON; [m.] Deborah; [occ.] Sales Person and Freelance Writer; [pers.] I would like to thank my new wife, Deborah, my new mother-in-law, Carolyn, and my close personal friend, Dan, for all the love and support.; [a.] Hamilton, ON

MONTEIRO, ALTHEA
[b.] July 17, 1975; Karachi, Pakistan; [p.] Gualbert and Daphne Monteiro; [ed.] A-levels, Convent of Jesus and Mary, Korachi Entennial College, Developmental Services Worker (current), York University majoring in Psychology; [occ.] Student; [memb.] Volunteer at People First of Canada, St. Vincent de Paul, Kovachi; [hon.] D.E. Light Scholarship—Centennial College; [a.] Unionville, ON

MONTGOMERY, DANA
[b.] July 11, 1974; Prince George, BC; [p.] Dan and Beth Camps; [ch.] Cody and Brandon; [occ.] Account-

ing Clerk; [pers.] The poem I wrote was written at a very trying time in my life and allowed me to express my sincere gratitude to my parents. It has taken me a long time to appreciate what they have given me, and I hope one day my own kids can see in me what I now see in my parents. Don't live with regrets. Say what you feel when you feel it.; [a.] Prince George, BC

MORGAN, WARLENE SYLVIA
[b.] January 9, 1958; Wainwright, AB; [p.] Lawrence Cook and Sylvia Gratton; [ch.] Charlene, Robbie, Roddy, and Audey "Jordie"; [oth. writ.] I have books of writings, which one day I hope to have published in a book of my own.; [pers.] For as long as I can remember, my most inner and deepest feelings and thoughts have been revealed through the wonderful transformation of pen in hand to paper. "Heavenly Dreams" was written for my Grandma.; [a.] Devon, AB

MORROW, AUDREY
[pen.] Nil; [b.] May 28, 1916; Lavant Township; [p.] Rose Wright and David Desjardins; [m.] Joseph Morrow; October 3, 1933; [ch.] Vena Mae, Neil, William, and Ora; [ed.] Grade 10; [occ.] Retired; [hon.] Four Awards from The National Library of Poetry, Plaque; [oth. writ.] Book of personal poems in 1995, titled Poems from the Heart.; [pers.] Any success I have in writing, I owe to God.

MORROW, CHRIS W.
[hon.] Canadian Author Award for "Me and a No Good Day" (1981), and "Martian on Earth" (1981). Both are short stories.; [oth. writ.] I write all cards for my family and friends, because I feel it means more if it comes from your heart than from your wallet!; [pers.] "What better way to show my love for pumpkin, then to share it with the world!"; [a.] Scarboro, ON

MORRY, DR. PETER J.
[b.] November 3, 1947; Ferry Camp, NF; [p.] William Morry; [m.] Josephine; July 28, 1978; [ch.] Jonathan, Rebecca, Nathan; [ed.] B.A., B.S.C., B.M.Sc., M.D. L.M.C.C.; [occ.] Physician; [memb.] Past Mayor of Ferry Camp, Minor Hockey Zodeh; [oth. writ.] 58 Poems as yet unpublished, Love Is the Kin, To Regret, The More You Give the More You Get; [a.] Houston, BC

MOTTILLO, ISABELLA
[b.] January 9, 1971; Montreal, QC; [p.] Mario Mottillo, Pierrette Durand; [ed.] I am in my last semester of the Applied Ecology Technology Program at Vanier College in Montreal.; [occ.] Student; [oth. writ.] This is my first published work. I also enjoy writing short stories and would like to write a novel someday.; [pers.] This is dedicated to D.K., my beloved, for his help, his understanding, his love.; [a.] Laval, QC

MUIR, HAMISH
[pen.] Bear Music; [b.] November 13, 1965; Inglewood, NZ; [p.] Noel and Earline Muir; [ed.] Westlake Boys High School; [occ.] Builder; [memb.] Spirit of New Zealand Sail Training Ship; [pers.] Though all my work is original, the true author is God, who inspires all my writing.; [a.] Auckland, NZ

MULLINER, JEANNINE
[b.] December 26, 1972; Vancouver, BC; [p.] Mary Miles, John Mulliner; [m.] Luc Dupuis; April, 1998; [ed.] B.A. Professional Writing, University De Sherbrooke; [pers.] My poetry is inspired by the images and emotions in my dreams.; [a.] Dunham, QC

MYRHAUGEN, NICOLE YVONNE
[b.] January 3, 1986; Kelowna, BC; [p.] Pam, Randy Myrhaugen; [ed.] Currently in grade six; [occ.] Student; [hon.] I have been on the honor roll.; [pers.] Currently, I live at home with my parents and younger brother, Myles. I have two pet dogs, a cat, and three rabbits. I enjoy good books and people, and I dream of owning her own business.; [a.] Breton, AB

NAPHOLC, TENESSA
[b.] October 28, 1975; Hamilton, ON; [p.] John and Brenda Napholc; [ch.] Taylor Paige; [ed.] Nelson High School; [oth. writ.] I have written hundreds of poems from childhood until present. I have never tried to published any until now.; [pers.] Many things in life have inspired me to write poetry: Love, loss, sorrow, and pleasure, to name a few. But to this day the most inspiring thing to touch my life is my beautiful daughter, Taylor.; [a.] Burlington, ON

NASH, JAMES
[b.] November 3, 1966; Surrey, BC; [p.] Larry and Pat; [m.] Anastasia Stacy; May 16, 1992; [ch.] Justin and Taylor; [occ.] Lithographic Pressman; [pers.] With the fast pace of life these days, we need to slow down and enjoy time with family and friends. The day will come, it's inevitable that all we will have left are memories.; [a.] Maple Ridge, BC

NELSON, ANN J.
[b.] September 23, 1959; Lacha Biche, AB; [p.] Claude and Florence Gauthier; [m.] Kevin G. Nelson; July 19, 1997; [occ.] Police Officer with the Royal Canadian Mounted Police (18 years); [pers.] I grew up in the country where my parents taught me to respect my natural surroundings which nurtured us. I later found comfort and beauty from those surroundings, that it inspired me to write about these natural influences.; [a.] Orleans, ON

NENDOS, ANGELINI
[b.] July 23, 1970; Kavala, Greece; [p.] Nicholas and Konstandina; [ed.] B.A. from York University, D.S.W. from Humber College, Certificate of Fluency in Greek; [occ.] Tutor for ESL and the Cambridge Proficiency Exam; [pers.] Take a chance, hope for the best, expect the worst. Never look back.; [a.] Etobicoke, ON

NEOGI, TAPATI
[b.] November 9, 1947; India; [p.] S. K. Batabyal and P. Batabyal; [m.] Ashoke K. Neogi; January 24, 1977; [ch.] Two; [ed.] M.A. (Political Science) First Class, M. Phil. (Public Administration) First Class with Distinction; [oth. writ.] Several poems unpublished; [pers.] I am madly in love with my husband. I love my children and people in general. I love reading and dreaming. My philosophy of life: Love is going beyond oneself without anything in return and creates only pain.; [a.] Brampton, ON

NETO, AVI
[p.] April J. Pereira and Ilca M. Pereira; [m.] Donna Irwin; July 5, 1997; [ed.] Architect; [occ.] Property Manager Coordinator; [pers.] Some Latin writers have had a profound impact on my life, contributing to what I am today, including the great Brazilian poet Carlos Drumomo de Andrade, Jorge Amado, Gabriel Garcia Marquez, and, more recently, Isabel Allende. I always pursue knowledge fostered by my desire to learn.; [a.] Toronto, ON

NEWEY, JOHN L.
[b.] September 24, 1922; Toronto, ON; [p.] William Etta Theresa; [ed.] Runnymede Collegiate graduate;

[occ.] Inventor, part-time Poet, part-time Song Composer (words and music); [oth. writ.] Created an Adventure/Musical entitled, "Road to Cracklebury," as a tribute to Mr. Fred Astaire and some other show biz greats.; [a.] Iniarton, ON

NIZAMUDDIN, MISS SUMMIYA
[b.] October 10, 1980; Doha, Qatar; [p.] Mohd. Nizamuddin and Mrs. Asma Nizamuddin; [ed.] Secondary Schooling at the Ideal Indian School and A-Levels in Physics, Chemistry, and Biology at the Doha College; [occ.] Student; [memb.] Young Editor of a local newspaper, The Peninsula; [hon.] Certificate of Merit from the Central Board of Secondary Education for being among the top 0.1% of all successful students in English, Editor's Choice Award from NLP, Highly Commended Award in school poetry writing competition; [oth. writ.] Poems published in A Season of Flowers and The Best Poems of 1998, by NLP, several others have been published in school magazines, local newspapers, and U.A.E. based magazine, too.; [pers.] All I hope is that God remains by my side, just like how my parents always are. I thank my parents, my sister, and my friends for all the encouragement and, no doubt, the boundless love.; [a.] Messai'eed, Qatar

NOORDHOF, MICHELLE
[b.] August 3, 1982; Locombe, AB; [p.] Ed Noordhof and Nancy Noordhof; [ed.] Currently in sigh school, I wrote this poem while in tenth grade.; [oth. writ.] Several poems and short stories unpublished; [pers.] Shakespeare rocks!; [a.] Smithers, BC

NORTON, AMIE
[pen.] Amie Norton; [b.] November 19, 1982; London, ON; [p.] Steven and Jacinthe Norton; [ed.] Wortley Road Public School, South Secondary School, tenth grade; [hon.] Citizenship Award in eighth grade, Editor's Choice Award for Outstanding Achievement in Poetry; [oth. writ.] Several poems published; [pers.] Writing is the best way, I find, to express your feelings.; [a.] London, ON

NOSEWORTHY, DAVID
[b.] January 15, 1937; St. Johns, NF; [p.] Barb and Albert Noseworthy; [m.] Amanda Gerirude; May 8, 1964; [ch.] Two sons; [ed.] High school; [occ.] Retired from the Ford of Canada, Ltd.; [a.] Elmsdale, NS

O'NEIL, NEAL C
[b.] October 5, 1910; Bow Island, AB; [p.] Clifford & Ella O'Neil; [m.] Maisie Belle O'Neil; September 16, 1934; [ch.] Brian, James, Patti; [ed.] B.A., B. Ed. (Bachelor of Arts obtained at the age of 86); [occ.] Retired; [memb.] Senate, University of Calgary Masonic Lodge #58, Board Director—Fort Macleod Credit Union, Rancher, Farmer, Teacher, Banker, Grain Buyer; [hon.] Numerous Community Service Awards; [oth. writ.] Published poetry: The Chinook, Wintersong, Summer's Best, Whispers in the Wind; [a.] Clareholm, AB

OSSEIRAN, CHYA
[b.] July 22, 1982; Beirut; [p.] Lamya and Nayibo Osseycan; [ed.] Tenth grade at International College; [a.] Beirut, Lebanon

OSUCH, PAWEL
[pen.] Oliver Poley; [b.] October 27, 1970; Kielce, Poland; [p.] Maria, Stanislaw; [m.] Martyna Gluszek; [ed.] Slowacki VI Grammar School in Kielce, Teacher Training College of Foreign Languages, Lodz University; [occ.] English teacher in 252 No. 1, Kielce, Ul,

Zgoda 31; [memb.] Polish Teacher Association; [hon.] Award of Merit Certificate by World of Poetry, Editor's Choice Award by the ILP, twice the Poet of the Year, The Copernicus Foundation poetry contributor, published in A Lasting Calm by the International Library of Poetry; [oth. writ.] My Personal NY, My Pen Exiled, My Mind Split, The Globe Perverted, Circumstances, The True Yourself, Kind of Forge, The Best Ever Found, The Bird, Small S Homo Sapiens, Jesus Voices, United in You, The Life Lamp, I for One, Arrivals, Rewards, Sleepy Moon Walk; [pers.] Always get through the world with as much dignity as you can pull together from the tiny resources left to you. Do things the hard way, and you'll always feel good about yourself.; [a.] Kielce, Poland

OVERHOLT, HENRY
[b.] January 6, 1944; Toronto, ON; [p.] Dorothy; [m.] Patricia; [occ.] Manager of Film Services for The Toronto District School Board; [oth. writ.] Short stories that reflect daily life, poems that express one's feelings of the times we live in; [pers.] Whatever you do in life, try not to harm others in the process.; [a.] Toronto, ON

PALLIER, VINCE
[b.] February 11, 1943; Edmonton, AB; [m.] Anna; June 14, 1975; [ed.] Business Administration; [occ.] Retired Accountant, presently a Writer; [memb.] Stroll of Poets; [oth. writ.] Book: "Soup of Compassion" (Collection of poems, short plays, and essays); [pers.] I write inspirational poems and writings to touch the heart.; [a.] Edmonton, AB

PANDEY, MANJARI
[b.] December 16, 1961; Raichuv, India; [p.] Prof. Y. N. Pandey, Rama Devi Pandey; [m.] Shivakumar Kasayap; August 30, 1991; [ch.] Bharath Kashyap; [ed.] M.A. in Political Science from Guibarga University, India, Diploma in Creative Writing in English from Iandu, India; [occ.] Worked as lecturer in Pre-University College, India, from 1984 to 1996; [oth. writ.] I write poems and short stories in English and Hindi, a few of which have been published in various magazines and dailies in India.; [pers.] The main theme of my writings has been woman: her different facets and the various problems surrounding her.; [a.] Toronto, ON

PANTER, ALICE
[pen.] Peanuts; [b.] April 17, 1953; Fort Erie, ON; [p.] Pierre the Baud; [m.] Richard Panter; September 16, 1994; [ed.] Wills Business College Graduate with Honors, Legal Secretary; [occ.] Superintendent and Management; [hon.] Willis Business College, International Society of Poets 1995-1996, Canadian champs in five pin bowling league; [oth. writ.] Poem written, "As I Am," freelance writing to publish my history of my life and to finish it; [pers.] I wrote this poem, "Remember," to two of my animals when they died. My Hamster, Maxine, and my Dwarf Bunny, Darwinnia, for when they were cremated and now in God's hands and Heaven.; [a.] Ottawa, ON

PAPAGEORGIOU, ANASTASIA
[pen.] Anastasia Fardella; [b.] September 16, 1970; Montreal, QC; [ed.] John Abbott College, B.A. from Concordia University in Montreal; [memb.] International Society of Poets. Member of the Greek Orthodox Community in D.D.O.; [oth. writ.] I am currently working on my poetry book entitled People (A Collection of Poetry), and a short story collection entitled Eulogies.; [pers.] I seek to express what I feel or what I have experienced, because that is the most genuine type of writing.; [a.] D.D.O., QC

PASSMORE, LOURIE
[b.] April 27, 1960; Lafleche, SK; [p.] Keith and Vina; [ed.] Ongoing; [occ.] Machine Operator; [memb.] BMG Music; [oth. writ.] I've written over a hundred titles, and I keep them all in one book. A lot of my poems are adult humor.; [a.] Edmonton, AB

PATTERSON, DARRYL
[b.] February 24, 1964; Lindsay, ON; [p.] Barry, Sharon Patterson; [m.] Bonnie Patterson; October 11, 1991; [ch.] Mitchell, Mason; [ed.] University of Waterloo, B.S.C., Nipissing University, B.E.D.; [occ.] Teacher of grades six and seven at Fenelon Township Public School; [pers.] Mitchell and Mason, you enrich my life. I am proud to be your father.; [a.] Woodville, ON

PEDRIN, MICHAEL
[b.] March 4, 1972; Mangalore, S. India; [p.] (Late) Cletus Pedrin and Mrs. Celine Pedrin; [ed.] Twelfth Grade, a course in computer application; [occ.] Marketing Executive in Kuwait for computer accessories; [oth. writ.] Authored a book on "Daniel and the Revelation" (Bible), "God's Feat and Satan's Counterfeit," in progress, more than 75 poems on different topics; [pers.] May the readers of this poem be blessed and touched by God's redeeming love.; [a.] Karnataka, India

PENTNEY, VICTORIA
[b.] May 21, 1967; Halifax, NS; [p.] William and Elizabeth Pentney; [m.] Ronald MacIntyre (Common Law); [ch.] (Two) Clint and Sarah-Lynne; [ed.] I am presently signed up for a creative writing class. [occ.] Homemaker; [oth. writ.] I have written literally hundreds of poems (in my thirty years of life). Currently, I'm writing a children's book; [pers.] I mainly write about my own life experiences. I have been deeply influenced by my own life and my children. Writing is my way of releasing my innermost feelings.; [a.] Halifax, NS

PETERSEN, CAROL B.
[b.] October 4, 1959; St. Thomas, USVI; [p.] Evelyn Dessuit; [m.] Jose A. Petersen; February 27, 1995; [ch.] Melvin Jr., Malcolm, and Monique Hodge; [ed.] Graduated from Charlotte Amalie High School, Adult Education class in 1977; [hon.] Customer Service Award for Barclay's Bank PLD in 1990-1991, Award of Certificate, from Worldwide of the Caribbean Computer Classes in 1995; [pers.] I am a 38-year-old Christian, a member of the Apostolic Faith Church in Altona, St. Thomas, VI. My inspiration to write my poem comes from my Lord and Savior, Jesus Christ. My desire is to serve the Lord and preach the gospel to the poor through my poems.; [a.] Charlotte Amalie, USVI

PETKOV, MIHAIL
[b.] May 9, 1953; Sofia, Bulgaria; [ed.] B.A. Turkish Philosophy, Sofia University, Sveti Kliment Ohridski; [occ.] Interactive Playwright; [memb.] Theatre Voyageur Toronto, ON; [oth. writ.] Script, a letter to Bulgaria which premiered at the Annex Theatre in Toronto on July 17, 1991, and it was taken to the Kingston Fringe Festival that October, and enjoyed critical acclaim; [pers.] I am just trying to reduce my pain.; [a.] Toronto, ON

PHILIPS, IRENE
[b.] April 10, 1951; Curacao; [ed.] High school, college; [occ.] Registered Nurse; [a.] Curacao, Netherlands

PHILLIP, MARILYN
[pen.] Mari; [b.] March 31, 1953; Antigua; [p.] Christophine Valentine, Samuel Phillip (deceased); [ch.] Howard and Jamila Phillip; [ed.] Catholic Primary, Christ the King High School; [occ.] Civil Servant (Government of Antigual Barhuda), Inland Revenge Department; [memb.] Antigual Barhuda, Public Service Association; [hon.] ACE passes, Certificates in English Language, English Literature, History Religious Knowledge (University of Cambridge and London), Diploma in Speedwriting; [oth. writ.] Several poems, songs, and short stories; [pers.] I endeavour to be the best at what I do, and I always encourage others to aim for that goal, too. I wrote my first poem at age 12, but my literary skills were recognized by my form V English teacher.; [a.] St. John, Antigua

PIERCE, WALTER
[b.] September 25, 1968; Baptist Hospital; [p.] Abraham, Anna Pierce; [ed.] Master's of Software Engineering; [oth. writ.] "Zero of Where Beauty and Darkness Meet" (This will be released in about 2 years); [pers.] The imagination is a place of beauty and darkness. It is an adventure in insanity and the source of genius. But mostly it is a connection to God.; [a.] Pensacola, FL

PIOTROWSKI, DAVID
[pen.] Dave Peterson; [b.] January 27, 1971; Adelaide, SA; [p.] John and Judy Piotrowski; [ed.] Five years senior high school; [occ.] Production Line Worker at Mitsubishi; [oth. writ.] Have several unpublished works in different styles and categories; [pers.] My writing and poetry is a reflection of what I see and hear during my everyday life. Influences include music, outdoor life style, and people. I am interested in amateur film making and, of course, story writing.; [a.] Adelaide, South Australia

POTTER, JOHN
[b.] Clinton, ON; [ch.] Adam Ahmad; [ed.] Central Huron S. S., University of Western Ontario (B.A. CHS), Lakehead University (B. Ed.), UWD (M. Ed.); [occ.] Educator, Bandling International School, Bandling, Indonesia; [pers.] "Sundays Are the Worst," is from a collection of thematic poems dealing with this new age of love and loss entitled, "Road Kill: Love Poems for the New Age," for which I am currently trying to find a publisher.; [a.] Bandling, West Java, Indonesia

POWER, MARGARET
[b.] July 27, 1908; Halifax, NS; [p.] Bernardo and Mary Sullivan; [m.] George Power; June 19, 1939; [ch.] Two boys and one girl; [ed.] Grade 12, one year business course; [oth. writ.] Several more poems; [pers.] Moderation in all things; responsibility for behavior, good and bad; share, but don't part with it all! Be fair! [a.] Halifax, NS

POYOTTE, YASMIN S.M.
[pen.] Yasmin Lansiquot; [b.] October 31, 1970; Saint, Lucia; [p.] Veronica and Alban Lansiquot; [ed.] Sociology, York University; [occ.] Patient Administrative and Associate; [a.] Toronto, ON

PROTOPAPPA, VIRGINIA
[pen.] Virginia Avierino Protoppa; [b.] August 4, 1940; Alexandria, Egypt; [p.] Deceased (Myrsini and Veros); [m.] Widow; October 16, 1960; [ch.] A girl (35 years old) and a boy (thirty years old); [ed.] Sacred Heart Girls College, Alexandria Egypt (Irish Convent) apart from perfect English, I speak French, Arabic, and Greek Italian, worked for many years as English shorthand, typist, and translator in foreign companies in Egypt and Greece; [occ.] Pensioner; [memb.] I used to be member of American Library in Alexandria, Egypt.; [hon.] Composition Awards in school as well as awards from the Royal Society of Arts, London, England, for speed and accuracy in shorthand typing [oth. writ.] Novels: Silence Is the Price, Eva Will Tell, and a few poems, (Copy of my novel, Silence Is the Price, has been sent as an offer for publication in the Reader's Digest; [pers.] Whatever failure that might be, we must never cease trying to express our thoughts and spirit. It's the best compensation. I have been deeply thrilled by Eighteenth century poets.; [a.] Athens, Greece

PROUTY, BRENDA
[pen.] Kemmery West; [b.] January 23, 1944; Bonduille, QC; [ed.] Knowlton High School, Haile Selassie I University, Diploma in Journalism, London School of Journalism, Associate's in Specialized Business, Centre for Degree Studies; [occ.] Supervisor, Documents Typing unit, United Nations Economic Commission for Africa; [oth. writ.] Poetry (some published), songs, look books, short stories, children's stories, General Knowledge Quip Books, Mine Board Games, nine novels, including a six-novel saga of the Duboes family; [pers.] Buried in Addis Ababa for 34 years, exposed to hardship, political upheaval, unable to make contact with culturation, I tapped a fountain of originality inspired by a sense of desperation.; [a.] Addis Ababa, Ethiopia

PRUSKI, EUGENE
[pen.] Paul MicDylon; [b.] June 11, 1980; Kitchener, ON; [p.] Eugene Pruski, Lorraine Pruski; [ed.] In final year of high school; [occ.] Lifeguard/Swimming Instructor/Coach of a swim team; [memb.] North York YMCA, Life Saving Society of Canada; [oth. writ.] Several poems unpublished; [pers.] I write to release my emotions. When I'm sad, I think I write my best.; [a.] North York, ON

PSWARAYI, DUDZAI
[b.] December 21, 1979; Zimbabwe, Africa; [p.] Dr. & Mrs. E. M. Pswaryi; [ed.] Currently doing A-level in the following subjects: English, Literature, Geography, French, General; [occ.] Student; [oth. writ.] Several other unpublished poems; [pers.] Poetry inspired by Percy Blythe Shelley, Shakespeare, and too many others to mention. "If you fail in one place that doesn't make you a failure—get up again, begin again, success is right in reach!"; [a.] Harare, Zimbabwe

PURVES, MARIA
[b.] July 25, 1983; Grande Prairie, AB; [p.] Elizabeth and William Purves; [ed.] Currently in ninth grade (until June '98); [memb.] Central Peace High School Students Against Drinking and Driving (C.P.H.S. S.A.D.D.) Girl Guides of Canada, Central Peace Horse Association; [pers.] Today is yesterday's tomorrow.; [a.] Blueberry Mountain, AB

QUIRK, ELIZABETH
[b.] April 21, 1949; St. Catharine's; [p.] Harry and Florence Wismer; [m.] William Eric Quirk; July 9, 1966; [ch.] Two children; [ed.] Secondary school diploma; [occ.] Part-time Home-based Business New Creation Crafts, Receptionist; [memb.] Quinte Craft Association, Gold Wing Road Riders Association (GWRRA); [hon.] Won Awards in floral and craft designs in the local fairs, Hastings County Business

Directory Best in Ontario, designed and coordinated; [oth. writ.] Personal poems for family, friends, written plays for church groups, written and taught theme seminars; [pers.] Creative writing is part of my heritage; my desire is to be a blessing to others.; [a.] Belleville, ON

RABIUS, ARNOLD
[b.] 1950; [m.] Bozena Rabius; [ch.] Niels, Laura, Tom, Ariana; [ed.] Technical University Delft; [occ.] Independent Town Planner; [oth. writ.] Unpublished work, House of Freedom (1995), Unless We Speak (1997); [pers.] The relation between You and your Self is one of complete trust, else, there is no relation from your side. Harmony before balance.; [a.] Flevoland, Holland

RADEK, ANIELA ANIA
[pen.] Aniela Ania Radek; [b.] December 8, 1926; Tryncza, Poland; [p.] Maria and Joseph Kosturek; [m.] Adam; February 20, 1954; [ch.] Irene Renata Radek; [ed.] Grenoble (Faculte des Lettres), Paris (Sorbonne), Literature, Guelph, Canada, B.A. French Major, Paris, Encole Superieure du Secretariat "Grandjean"; [occ.] Translator (European Languages), drawing and painting (variety of subjects)—I consider it a hobby.; [memb.] I belong to Canadian Seniors' Literary Club, was active in Polish Social Clubs, and directed and aired Polish Radio Hour in Guelph. I also taught French in local high schools.; [hon.] I've lived too long in God-forsaken places and incognito to receive Honors and Awards. Anyway, do I care?; [oth. writ.] Published book of religious poems, 380 pages in Polish. Four volumes of poems (Polish), ready for publication. I am a Holocaust survivor. Writing an autobiography about my escape from Concentration Camps (Dachau, Augsburg). I also have many poems and short stories published in French, American, and Canadian Polish newspapers and magazines. I've written five volumes of thoughts (not published yet).; [pers.] Men have turned into super-kids who, when they don't know how to win their case, throw a temper-tantrum.; [a.] Guelph, ON

RADFORD, FRANCES BRYAN
[b.] March 10, 1935; Penticton, BC; [p.] Hugh and Alice Bryan; [m.] Brian; August 29, 1958; [ch.] Morley, Tracy, Mary, and Jamie; [ed.] High school; [occ.] At home; [pers.] I wrote my first poem midway through my sixty-first year; it was inspired by the beauty of the little creek I live beside. In the ensuing two and a half years, I've written mostly about nature and the everyday thoughts of an ordinary woman.; [a.] Greenwood, BC

RAMSDEN, ROWENA J.
[b.] 1937; Calgary, AB; [ch.] Two; [memb.] Girl Guides of Canada Assistant, Provincial Commissioner, Boy Scouts of Canada, Provincial Youth Council—Angelican Church Provincial Youth Justice Committee; [a.] Nelson, BC

REDDING, BILL
[b.] September 19, 1974; Dallas, TX; [p.] Louise Harrison Redding; January 17, 1972; [ch.] Patricia, Elizabeth, Sandra Boyle; [ed.] David High School, College University, Texas A & M Military College, U.S.A., Victoria University, Wellington, NZ, Wellington Polytech., Wellington, NZ; [occ.] Retired Engineer (Mechanical, Civil); [memb.] American Legion, American Military Engineer, American Society Quality Control; [oth. writ.] Fiction, short stories, technical handbooks, magazine articles; [a.] Wellington, NZ

REID, KATHERINE MARIE
[b.] March 15, 1959; Welland; [p.] Alexander Reid and Irene Reid; [ed.] McMasters University, B.A., Notre Dame High School; [occ.] Associate Oenologist for Joseph's Estate Wines; [memb.] Canadian Society of Oenology and Viticulture (Executive), CWL (Catholic Women's League); [hon.] Listed in the 1998 Edition of Who's Who of Canadian Women, graduated top female student from St. Joseph's School, Provincial Champions for church league basketball, High Single for Five Pin Bowling, and assisted in the winning of 12 medals for Joseph's Estate Wines, which included a Gold Medal for Strawberry Wine; [oth. writ.] Technical IRAP reports on the research of wines and cool climate viticulture, assistant editor of Irish 1978, literary department for Irish 1974, 1975, 1976, and 1977; [pers.] I am grateful for having the passion for racing from my father, the artistic talent of my mother, the best boss who encourages my creativity, and two special friends that provided my source of inspiration for this poem.; [a.] Niagara Falls, ON

REITBERGER, JODI
[b.] November 22, 1968; Winnipeg, MB; [p.] Dora and Ellis Morrison; [m.] Dean Reitberger; April 6, 1996; [ch.] Destiny, Cokin, Matthew, Anthony, Step-daughter Stefanie; [ed.] Fraser Valley College; [occ.] Devoted wife and mother; [oth. writ.] I have a personal collection of poems that I one day hope to have published.; [pers.] My poetry has been greatly influenced by my late sister, Sharon Agnes Harris, and definitely inspired by my wonderful husband and our five children. I love you, Dean. Also, a special thanks to Madeline and Gabrial.; [a.] Calgary, AB

RENZ, JOYCE L. M. HOLT
[b.] January 6, 1938; Medicine Hat, AB; [p.] Mary and Fred Holt; [ch.] Two sons, one daughter; [ed.] Grade 12, Nursing, and Therapy; [occ.] Therapist; [pers.] I still am the little girl with the fondest of memories of that River Bridge.; [a.] Medicine Hat, AB

REUBIS, FRANCIS
[pen.] Frank Reubis; [b.] May 20, 1967; Imo State, Nigeria; [p.] Chief Reuben U. Okafor, Caro Okafor; [ed.] Community School 5, Ndiawa Arondizuogu (primary), National High School (NHS), Arondizugu (secondary); [occ.] Trading (but mainly devoted to writing); [oth. writ.] Poems published in Survival Newsletter—U.S.A., several poems on environmental awareness published in Cameroon Post and The Post, respectively, unpublished poems, novel, short stories, and essays; [pers.] Through my God-given gift, I strive to be renowned and to use my resources for the service of humanity.; [a.] Bemenda, NWP

RHYMER, BRYCE WELLINGTON
[pen.] Bryce Wellington Rhymer; [b.] October 14, 1936; Plainfield, NY; [p.] Rena Rhymer; [ch.] Rena Rhymer; [ed.] High school graduate and Secretarial Certificate from Court Stenography Institute, NY; [occ.] Retired; [pers.] I have a love for articulating human nature lyrically. For everything in the universe, there is a rhythm.; [a.] St. Thomas, USVI

RIGANAS, NICHOLAS
[pen.] Nicholas; [b.] March 11, 1976; Australia; [ed.] Student; [occ.] Manager; [pers.] It's what you mature and grow to be; its signature is never left on a piece of paper. It's your mind, it's your lifestyle, it is You!; [a.] Sydney, Australia

ROBERTS, KATHRYNE B.
[b.] December 19, 1944; PEI; [m.] John L. Roberts; May 25, 1979; [ed.] Victoria High School, University of Victoria, BC; [occ.] Retired; [memb.] PETA, Heritage Society of Victoria, BC, International Society of Poets; [hon.] Editor's Choice Award: 1995, 1996, 1997, by The National Library of Poetry, collection of short poems—unpublished; [oth. writ.] Published several songs: "I Remember You," "Warrior Woman," by Hollywood Artist Record Co., LA; [pers.] I believe in the protection of the environment and support its cause for future generations.; [a.] Victoria, BC

ROBINSON, DOUGLAS
[pen.] Douglas Robinson; [b.] June 20, 1954; Edmonton, AB; [p.] Murry Robinson (deceased), Vivien Robinson; [ed.] Victoria Park Collegiate Institute, University of Toronto (B.S. Physical Geography), Dip R.M. (Forestry), Toronto, ON; [occ.] Consulting Environmental Geoscientist; [memb.] Ontario Association of Certified Engineering Technicians and Technologists (Geophysical), The Geological Association of Canada; [hon.] Pending Fellow in the Geological Association of Canada, First President and Founding member, Geography Club at Victoria Park Collegiate Institute; [oth. writ.] "Teddy Bear Poem (Meditation)," circa August, 1992, "Twister Sister," "Memorial Birthday Poem," for my deceased father; [pers.] God ultimately cares for us like "the lilies of the field." My fundamental belief in a personal relationship with God (Jesus) is key.; [a.] Toronto, ON

ROBINSON, ROUEN DERYL EWART
[pen.] Rouen D. E. Robinson; [b.] March 3, 1976; Castries, St. Lucia; [p.] Rev. Fr. Lurtis E. Robinson, Myrtle E. G. Robinson; [ed.] Two years at Nova University; [occ.] Lab Technician Trainee B, Pharmaceutical Fine Chemicals, Ltd.; [memb.] Christian Youth Movements Advisor, Pinder's Point, Grand Bahama, Bahamas; [hon.] Distinguished Vice-President of Finance, Junior Achievement, Exemplary Conduct, Freeport Anglican High School, Scholarship of Merit, Nova University; [pers.] If life gives you lemons, be polite and give them back. I am just an extra in the movie of life.; [a.] Freeport, Bahamas

ROSS, MARIAN E.
[b.] March 14, 1923; Timmins, ON; [p.] Bernice and Kenneth MacLeod; [m.] Archibald Ross (deceased); 1947; [ch.] Carol, Margaret, Kenneth, Wayne; [ed.] B.A. from Queen's University, Kingston, ON, and Commercial Specialist Certificate from Ontario College of Education; [occ.] Retired Commercial Director (Business Subjects) of High School; [memb.] Canadian Red Cross Society, Kirkland and District United Way, Business and Professional Women's Club, United Church Women, Clan MacLeod Society; [hon.] Life Membership from the Ontario Business Education Association, Distinguished Service Award (40 years) from the Canadian Red Cross Society; [oth. writ.] "Our European Holiday" was taken from my 1997 Christmas letter. For 30 years, I have sent a Christmas letter consisting of rhyming couplets describing the activities of my family and myself during the past year.; [a.] Kirkland Lake, ON

ROWLANDSON, TERA
[b.] September 4, 1983; Blind River, ON; [p.] Helen and Robert Trudeau Rowlandson; [ed.] Ninth grade student; [hon.] Citizenship Award, Science Award; [oth. writ.] Our Mighty Soldiers, The Rose, Christmas Surprise; [pers.] Everyone has a different way of seeing things and a different way of showing it. Me, it is through my poetry, and I'm very thankful for this talent.; [a.] Blind River, ON

RUNDLE, SUSAN MAY
[b.] April 22, 1957; Toronto, ON; [p.] Rose and Jim Rundle; [ch.] Shawna and Vincent Patruno; [occ.] Housewife and Mother; [hon.] Gave speech to psychiatrists and nurse on how to rehabilitate the mentally ill so they are able to work.; [pers.] I would like to write words of comfort and support to all victims of abuse and oppression. [a.] Midland, ON

RUSSELL, JAYNE LOIS
[b.] June 30, 1957; Virginia, USA; [p.] Lawrence Clement and Lois Clement; [m.] Frank Russell; December 11, 1982; [occ.] Employed with the Federal Government; [pers.] This poem was inspired by the sadness and helplessness I felt in the loss of a friendship. By writing this poem, it gave me the sense of closure that I so desperately needed.; [a.] Mississauga, ON

SALCEDO, CLAUDIA
[b.] December 7, 1980; Lima, Peru; [p.] Alejandro Voysest and Victoria Quiroz; [ed.] Colegio Franklin Delano Roosevelt (The American School of Lima, Peru) since 1985; [occ.] Junior at F.D.R. High School; [hon.] Principal's List, Music Honor Society; [oth. writ.] Poem published in the school's Journal of Visual Arts; [pers.] I am my own person, an independent individual. My writing represents who I am.; [a.] Lima, Peru

SANDERS, TERESA
[b.] January 27, 1964; Newmarket, ON; [p.] James Charles Sanders and Evelyn Marina Sanders; [m.] Thomas J. Lemperg; [ch.] Zachary, Kyle, Josh, and Emily; [ed.] Grade Eleven—High School (Hair Dressing); [occ.] Mother and Astrologer; [hon.] Diploma—Astrology and Parapsychology, Diplomas—Health and Fitness; [pers.] Halt the hate, stop the wars—let happiness and peace be our fate.; [a.] Richmond, ON

SANKAR, SHALINI
[b.] April 24, 1979; Trinidad, West Indes; [p.] Ajodhiya and Savitri Sankar; [ed.] High school graduate of St. Augustine Girl's High School (will start attending university in September 1998); [oth.writ.] Several poems, none previously submitted for publication or in a contest; [pers.] When you smile, you heal an injury; when you laugh, you erase all pain.; [a.] Brampton, ON

SATTERFIELD, SCOTT M.
[b.] December 7, 1960; Searcy, AR; [m.] Khanita Inthwasut; February 1, 1992; [ch.] Christopher I. Sutterfield; [ed.] Jurus Poztorate, University of Memphis, Bachelor of Educational Sciences, University of North Texas; [occ.] Mission Worker/English Teacher/ Curriculum Developer; [pers.] In my poetry, I try to express the nature and dignity of the human soul, and how God is found both in and around us.; [a.] Ching Mai, Thailand

SAUNDERS, SALLY
[b.] February 12, 1943; Kingston, ON; [ed.] Commercial studies and night school courses, the experiences of various job tasks; [occ.] Computer Tutor and Assistant (of other interests); [memb.] Red Cross Society, Catholic Women's League (C.W.L.), Board of Directors for (K.D.A.C.L.) Kingston District Association Community Living; [hon.] Certificate for a Computer course and other accomplishments that are

very rewarding; [oth.writ.] Published poem for the National Library of Poetry, also poems for friends to celebrate occasions of various kinds, articles for church, newsletters; [pers.] My poems are written to share the experiences of life with true feelings for others to see.; [a.] Kingston, ON

SCHROEDER, HEIKE
[ch.] One son, Anthony; [pers.] Nothing is more painful than regret; commitment shall set you free.; [a.] Owen Sound, ON

SCHUURMAN, EIKO
[pen.] Ike Shure'man; [b.] May 18, 1935; Utrecht; [ed.] College (Private School) H.T.S.E, in Hilversum; [occ.] Environmental and Energy-Saving Consultant/ Electrical Engineer; [memb.] Literary society, "Bleed Spraak"; [hon.] Honored and recited on the "Radio M" broadcasting program; [oth. writ.] Over two hundred fifty Dutch and forty-four English poems, of which several have been published in a Dutch magazine and a Dutch poetry anthology; [pers.] I have twenty-three letters patented on my name, many of them very original, and so are my poems. Never looked how others did it. My poems are coming straight from the heart. I'm trying to give a message with (very often) double meanings to others, so in a way they can recognize themselves by filling in their own thoughts and situation.; [a.] Nieuwegein, Utrecht

SCOLLO, BERNADETTE
[pen.] Jacquelynn Scollo; [b.] April 23, 1969; Sri Lanka; [p.] Bernadette and Clement Perera; [m.] Vince Scollo; August 4, 1995; [ch.] Rachel Mary Joy (deceased); [ed.] Currently Completing Bachelor of Business (Accounting) at R.M.I.T.; [occ.] Records Officer, Victoria Police Force; [oth. writ.] Many poems, short stories, and a few books, which someday I hope to find the courage to try and publish.; [pers.] I write my poems in my dark times, when tears just don't seem enough.; [a.] Victoria, Australia

SCOTT-HERRIDGE, CRYSTAL
[b.] March 15, 1982; Winnipeg, MB; [p.] Roberta and Gerald Scott-Herridge; [ed.] River East Collegiate (an Advanced Placement Student, studying five languages: English, German, French, Spanish, and Chinese); [occ.] Part-time secretary at River East Chiropratic; [memb.] Royal Conservatory of Music; [hon.] Grade One, Two, Four, Five, and Six Piano Awards, Honors Student at River East Collegiate; [pers.] Everyone is special in a different way.; [a.] Winnipeg, MB

SEIBEL, KATHLEEN
[b.] May 4, 1976; Edmonton, AB; [p.] Donald and Julia Seibel; [a.] Edmonton, AB

SEYMOUR, NORMA WILLIAMS
[a.] St. Thomas, Jamaica; [p.] Randolph B. Williams (deceased) Tizeta V. Williams; [m.] George Edward Seymour; April 8, 1995; [ch.] Kwadwo S. A. Mendes; [ed.] A.S. (Executive Secretarial), B.S. (Liberal Studies), Major Communications. M.S. (Management, Major: Human Resources Management, Intl. College of the Cayman Islands and Miami Center, currently pursuing AICB (Associate of Institute of Canadian Bankers Degree); [occ.] Offshore Corporate Account Executive; [memb.] Lion's Club of Grand Cayman, by virtue of my husband's being a Lion and past president of that organization; [hon.] Outstanding Leadership and Dedicated Service Award (Church of God in Christ), Junior Achievement Consultant Award, Excellent

Customer Service Award, Cayman Islands Scout Association Dedicated Service Award; [oth. writ.] Poem, "Creative Writing," published by the Amherst Society in the anthology The American Poetry Annual, 1996, songwriter of song "My Man, My Woman," recorded by Sunrise Records and sung by vocalists Buddy Reyes and Suzie Daniels; [pers.] If you do not stand up for something, you will fall for anything. If you are ambitious and persistent, you can and will achieve your goals, if you never give up your dreams.; [a.] Georgetown, Grand Cayman

SHEPPARD, SHIRLEY CLUNEY
[b.] Bishop's Falls, NF; [p.] Margaret Cluney and Oswald Sheppard; [ch.] Nadia and Bram; [ed.] Secretarial (college) plus several university courses taken part-time; [occ.] Project Support Specialist, Federal Government; [hon.] Scholarships in high school, awards for essay writing in high school, Best Actress (high school—Drama Club), Girl of the Year in high school, Beta Sigma Phi Girl of the Year (two times); [oth. writ.] Play (comedy) performed by a local senior drama group, speeches and poems either presented or published in local newspaper; [pers.] I grew up with a passion for reading and writing, having related stories and poems at a very early age, both verbally and in written form. Reading and writing have also provided me with a form of escape when my life was in turmoil. I would like to give as I have been given, and provide that same source of adventure (and escape) to others.; [a.] Gloucester, ON

SHERIDAN, EIHEEN INWOOD
[b.] August 30, 1952; Toronto, ON; [p.] J.M. Inwood; [m.] John T. Sheridan (deceased); January 19, 1990; [ch.] Beverly Ann Dey, Kathley Foster; [ed.] St. John's Catholic School, Victoria Park Secondary, Toronto, George Brown College, Toronto, ON; [occ.] Freelance Columnist, eight years Midland Free Press, Midland, ON; [memb.] Political Activists in Health, Housing, and Social Safeness; [hon.] Community Mental Health Care Award, The National Library of Poetry Editor's Choice Award in 1995; [oth. writ.] Freelance Columnist ("The Advocate's Voice"), Midland Free Press, several pieces of poetry in National Library of Poetry publications since 1995, newsletter editor; [pers.] Writing of any kind, poetry especially, gives someone a chance to talk about how life really is—and in turn offers up the unique gift of receiving an immortal soul.; [a.] Midland, ON

SHINDE, S. NANDINI
[pen.] Nil; [b.] February 21, 1943; Indore, India; [p.] Appasaheb and Vasundhara Raje; [m.] Nimbalkar Pratapsinh Shinde; March 1, 1966; [ch.] Three; [ed.] High School at Bishop Cotton's Girl's High School, Bangalore, India; [oth. writ.] Have been writing poetry on and off since leaving school; [pers.] I believe a poet writes only when deeply moved and emotionally stirred to the core, thus giving a rare insight into the situation and an intrinsic sense of value to his work.; [a.] Kolhapur, India

SHULAK, LIANE
[b.] December 21, 1974; Edmonton, AB; [p.] Sylvia Shulak; [ch.] Christopher Alexander; [pers.] My poem is dedicated to the people who gave me courage: to my love, Mark Smith, to my confidant, Chriss Lee, and to my ever loving mother.; [a.] Edmonton, AB

SIDDIQUI, RABBANI
[pen.] Anis; [b.] October 9, 1927; Akola, India; [p.] Late Mohammad Hanif, Aisha Bi; [m.] Latee,

Mohammad Sarwar Siddiqqui; June 11, 1954; [ch.] Laeeq, Ateeq, Shaista, Shaguita, Rukhshinda, Aisham Zenobiab [ed.] M.A. (URDU) in 1963, University of Karachi, Pakistan, Retired School Teacher, Physical Education, Girl Guide—Karachi; [occ.] Housewife; [memb.] Alumni Association, University of Karachi, Toronto, Canada; [hon.] Won awards in sports debate, drama, and an essay competition during college life; [oth.writ.] Some Urdu poems published in local magazine, an article published in magazine of the alumni association at the University of Karachi, Toronto, Canada; [pers.] The purpose of my writing is that justice, equality, and dignity of mankind should prevail through noble deeds. My favorite poets are Wordsworth and Keats.; [a.] Scarbourough, ON

SIEFFERT, CHARLENE
[pen.] Charann; [b.] March 16, 1967; Winnipeg, MB; [p.] Edith Hofer, Dr. Dan Sieffert; [ed.] Life is my education.; [occ.] Entertainer, Singing Telegrams; [oth. writ.] Published Freelance Writer and Illustrator (BC known and reknowned); [pers.] "Go for it" with a smile and panache!; [a.] Vancouver, BC

SINGH, RAMI KAUR
[pen.] R. Singh, Ramin; [b.] November 15, 1972; New Delhi, India; [p.] Meher Singh, Palwinder Kaur; [ed.] B.A. in English Literature, University of Delhi, India, Journalism, Ryerson Polytechnic University, Toronto, Ontario; [occ.] Freelance Writer, Journalist; [hon.] English Literature; [oth. writ.] Several poems, articles, and columns published in international magazines and newspapers in North America and India; [pers.] My writing reflects the many facets of life. It aims to raise awareness in individuals and bring them closer to each other, as each are facing the same bigger issues, irrespective of race, religion, or nationality. Words are timeless and I want to be in the hearts of people with my words.; [a.] Toronto, ON

SLUTE, MERRI LEE CULBERT
[b.] November 13, 1972; Burk's Falls, ON; [p.] Doug Culbert, Sandy Culbert; [m.] Robert Slute; June 19, 1993; [ch.] Reillee Alexa; [ed.] Almaguin Highlands Secondary School Niagara College; [oth. writ.] Several poems unpublished; [pers.] My works to date consist only of personal experience and growth. Since childhood, when I began writing, poetry has provided an escape for me, a means of cleansing my soul. It is a place where I can go to lose myself that no one else can touch.; [a.] Niagara Falls, ON

SMITH, CHASITY LA-DAWN
[pen.] Chas; [b.] December 17, 1987; Ponoka, AB; [p.] Greg and Donna Smith; [ed.] Grade Five student; [hon.] At the age of six, I won a story contest on "Why I Liked the Chocolate Mousse." I just started writing poetry this year. I love it.; [oth. writ.] I have been greatly influenced by Shel Silverstein.; [a.] St. Stephen, NB

SMITH, ELAINE L.
[pen.] Elaine L. Osmond; [b.] St. John's, NF; [p.] James and Sarah Osmond (deceased); [ch.] Vanessa, Carolyn, and James (all adults); [ed.] Presently attending university, majoring in Psychology/Social Work; [pers.] I want to share God's love and blessing with others in a practical manner.; [a.] North Bay, ON

SMITH, ELLEN
[b.] December 18, 1969; Saskatoon, SK; [p.] I. and O. Carlson; [m.] Lorne Smith; May 2, 1992; [ch.] Carlie Anne; [ed.] High School Diploma, Secretarial Di-

ploma with Honors, Special Care Nurse Aide Diploma; [occ.] Secretary, Nurse Aide; [memb.] Dinner Theatre—The Kerrobert Prairieland Players; [hon.] Distinction and Honorary Awards in both high school and business college; [oth. writ.] Several poems published; [pers.] I believe that poetry is a reflection of one's self and creativity. I am greatly influenced by the cowboy poet, Baxter Black.; [a.] Kerrobert, SK

SMITH, JANET
[b.] October 19, 1945; Trinidad; [p.] Cipriani and Maria Smith; [ch.] One son; [occ.] Minister of Religion; [occ.] More than one hundred poems, several songs, several Bible stories for kids, several other short stories; [a.] Bondram Tr. Jerningham Junction, Cunupia.

SNOW, ALFREDA
[b.] September 2, 1953; Botwood, NF; [p.] Leonard Stride, Elsie Stride; [m.] Albert Snow; June 16, 1973; [ch.] Pamela, Peter, Leonard; [ed.] English Memorial High School; [oth. writ.] "Life's History," a poem of my parents for their fiftieth wedding anniversary; [pers.] To share a moment of happiness through enjoyable reading shall be happiness in return.; [a.] Bishop's Fall, NF

SOUTER, JAMES B.
[b.] April 10, 1940; Naicam, SK; [p.] Ina and Alex Souter; [m.] Nellie I. Lawrence; November 30, 1963; [ch.] Kevin James, Bryan Alexander; [ed.] Part of Grade Twelve; [occ.] Dissability; [memb.] Moose Jaw Humane Society, Prince Albert Exhibition Board; [oth.writ.] Rem in John Defenbaker Rec, Editor's Award; [pers.] I enjoy writing poems and short stories of my native background and religious poems; [a.] Moose Jaw, SK

SPELLMAN, DAWN C.
[pen.] Spelly; [b.] November 8; Trenton, ON; [p.] Bill and Rosemary; [ch.] Andrew and David; [ed.] Graduated high school, some college (Dental Hygiene, Law Studies and Security, Computers, Addictions Counselling); [occ.] On disability for M.S., mother of two; [memb.] Born-again Christian; [oth. writ.] Personal short stories; [pers.] To live and let live, follow your heart; let your desires inspire your dreams, let your dreams soar—forgive me, Father (Heavenly)!; [a.] Fort Frances, ON

SRIVASTAVA, RAMAN
[b.] November 11, 1989; Toronto, ON; [p.] Rajiv and Rani Srivastava; [ed.] Grade Three; [occ.] Student; [memb.] Boy Scouts of Canada; [pers.] Raman lives in Toronto with his parents and sister. He enjoys sports like soccer, basketball, and karate. He also likes video games and computer games.; [a.] Toronto, ON

ST. LAURENT, HELENE
[b.] June 16, 1956; Montreal, PQ; [p.] Raymond St. Laurent and Monique LeBlanc; [ed.] Billings High School, Concordia University; [occ.] Adult Education Teacher (Office Automation), Herzing Institute, Montreal, Quebec; [oth. writ.] Several poems; [pers.] An inspiration from the heart is but one of life's truly special experiences.; [a.] Lasalle, QC

STARRATT, TREVOR
[b.] December 23, 1973; Halifax, NS; [p.] Carol Starratt, George Starratt; [ed.] Business and Technology (Dartmouth Community College), Creative Writing (Dartmouth Community College); [occ.] Courier; [oth.writ.] "The Road," a poem published in 1989 in an anthology of Atlantic Canadian High

Schools; [pers.] I wish to exercise the human spirit in all of my creative attempts.; [a.] Beaver Bank, NF

STEENHUISEN, PATRICIA ANN
[b.] December 22, 1963; Swift Current, SK; [p.] Eduardo and Muriel Piche; [m.] Martin Steenhuisen (deceased); August 29, 1983; [ed.] Grade Twelve, currently studying to be a veterinary assistant; [occ.] Farmer; [memb.] Stump Ranchers Association; [oth.writ.] I write poetry for friends; I never send a card without a poem. I hope to write stories for children someday about a butter bee.; [pers.] I dedicate this poem to Fred Steenhuisen and Greg Coward—we bring Martin on in our dreams and ambitions. Rock on!; [a.] Forest Grove, BC

STEINBACH, MURRAY
[b.] August 11, 1965; Saskatoon, SK; [p.] Marilyn and Adam Steinbach; [m.] Annette Steinbach; September 24, 1983; [ch.] Chris Steinbach, late Josh Steinbach; [ed.] St. Mary Comp. High; [occ.] Sales of Rep., Ecco Heating; [oth. writ.] The Woman I Love, Today You Would Be Two, If You've Lost a Child; [pers.] I've always enjoyed writing poetry! My words come from my heart and my mind.; [a.] Sherwood Park, AB

STEINIGER, PAM
[pen.] Pam Steiniger; [b.] January 19, 1952; Tisdale, SK; [p.] Digby Mindel, Josephine Kralkay; [m.] Divorced; [ch.] Pam Lee and Chad David Allan; [occ.] Watch Clerk, City of Prince George, RCMP Detachment; [pers.] This poem is dedicated to the memory of my brother, Harold Digby Joseph Mindel. I wish to acknowledge my family: Pam (Dennis, Dustin, Ashley) Steiniger, Chad Graham, Josephine (Peter) Kralkay, Ben (Doug) Sanderson, Sharon (Roy, Rory, Roya) Umpherville, Gerald (Shirley, Joey, Jennifer) Mindel, Norma (Keith, Kevin, Lisa, Kandy) Mindel for their inspiration. Special thanks to Ross Goodbrand, for his support, love, and friendship. I believe family is the most important thing in life, and together we can conquer all.; [a.] Prince George, BC

STEPHENSON, JAY
[b.] March 18, 1965; Victoria, BC; [p.] Leonardo and Corinne; [ed.] Bachelor's of Music, McGill University, Montreal, QC; [occ.] Opera Singer; [memb.] Westmount Toastmasters (public speaking) [oth. writ.] Poem published in local Toastmaster's magazine, "Reflections"; [pers.] I want to share my "madness" with the world.; [a.] Montreal, QC

STEWART, SARAH
[b.] July 1, 1987; Toronto, ON; [p.] Paul and Lillian Wilson; [ed.] Presently being homeschooled with a Christian, Bible-based curriculum; [occ.] Student; [pers.] My father died when I was just fourteen months old. Now, I'm ten years old and my mom got remarried—this poem was a gift to my mom and new dad.; [a.] Toronto, ON

STEWART, TERRA
[b.] February 4, 1978; North Bay, ON; [p.] John and Marie Stewart; [ed.] Graduated with honors from St. Joseph's Scollard Hall; [pers.] I would like to thank my teacher, Mr. Stokes, for being my inspiration, and my parents, John and Marie Stewart, for encouraging my writing.; [a.] North Bay, ON

STIRK, ELAINE
[pen.] E.J. Youngs, Elaine Moutrey; [b.] March 10, 1960; Glasgow, Scotland; [ch.] Andrew, Iain, Anne, Jennifer; [occ.] Mother, training to be a paramedic; [oth. writ.] "The Night" and four hundred fifty other known published poems; [pers.] My writing is a release for me. Everyone has the ability—if you can speak, you can write. To read my poetry is to know who I am.; [a.] Orangeville, ON

STOEHR, PAMELA
[pen.] Miko; [b.] November 30, 1949; St. Catherine's, ON; [p.] Margaret Deline, Earl Hewton; [ch.] James, Tammy, Shari Stochr; [occ.] Author and Teacher of Meditation and Psychic Counseling; [memb.] Founder of Seisai-Ho, a place for healing oneself to begin again (Japanese name given by Sensai DelCueto); [hon.] Psychic Counselor known throughout North America and Germany, interviewed on radio, TV, and in newspapers; [oth. writ.] "Healing Within" (the series), Book I: "Within The Senses" and Book II: "Illusions" (by Miko); [pers.] Honesty is the best policy. Always make sure you want to know the answers behind every question asked, or don't bother asking the question.; [a.] St. Catherine's, ON

STOEPPER, PATRICK
[b.] July 11, 1979; Basel, Switzerland; [pers.] Poetry is letting your heart speak.; [a.] Therwil, Switzerland

STOJKOVSKI, ZORAN
[b.] June 20, 1969; Orahovica, Croatia; [p.] Jovan Stojkovski, Dragica Stojkovska; [ch.] Liupce, Ljupka (twin brother and sister); [occ.] Secretary, Centar Stojkovski, School of Foreign Languages, Kicevo; [oth. writ.] First book of poetry in English in preparation; [pers.] Through writing and reading poetry, I have learned to cope with life in a more positive manner.; [a.] Kicevo, Macedonia

STOPPLEWORTH, MARILYN
[pen.] Aseret; [b.] March 29, 1923; Cross Plains, WI; [p.] Albert J. and Teresa J. Stoppleworth; [ed.] Bachelor's in Education, Alverno College, Milwaukee, WI, Master's in Education, Marquette University, Milwaukee, WI; [occ.] Administrator and Treasurer of Institution La Inmaculada Religiosa; [hon.] Gold Medal for a poem, Honorable Mention in a poetry contest; [oth. writ.] Various texts in English as a second language; [pers.] I believe in education to bring out the best in people. Without a solid Christian education, the poor stagnate in their poverty. With education, they can pull themselves up by their boot straps, change inner criticism, change the status of immigrants; they can be the leaders of tomorrow. I believe in dreams and illusions for the future.; [a.] Comayagua, Honduras

STOVER, JEFF
[b.] January 20, 1962; London, ON; [m.] Sharon; 1984; [ch.] One boy, one girl; [ed.] High school graduate (night school instruction); [occ.] Auto Worker (Cami Automotive), I jot down poetic lines as I work (to relieve boredom).; [memb.] Ingersoll Historical Society, Kinsmen Club (Service Club); [hon.] Kinsmen of the Year (two years running) for the historical tours I put together for charity (also received newspaper recognition), finished first in a local poetry contest in 1997; [oth. writ.] "The Millenium before Christmas Celebrations," "The Attic" (the realization that your parents are aging), "The Rebel" (dealing with school cliques), "Goul's Night Out" (a Halloween poem), among others; [pers.] I love to stand back and look at life and society from afar, reflecting on and analyzing change. In this way, you can see that sometimes the obvious . . . isn't.; [a.] Ingersoll, ON

STRICKLAND, JIM
[b.] March 26, 1942; Reading, England; [p.] Ernie and Olive Strickland; [m.] Phyllida; [ch.] Elizabeth, Stuart, Cathy, Philip, Louise, Michael; [ed.] Marist Brothers College, Leeds College of Technology, UNISA; [occ.] Pastor, CEO of own business, Retired Engineer; [memb.] International Christian Ministries, AMI Cert. M and Fl. Eng. (SA); [oth. writ.] "The Word for Every Occasion" (1984), "This Word in Rhyme for This Quiet Time" (1991), also write for church functions (all my work has been printed and published by me for private distribution); [pers.] Committed Christian, influenced by A. A. Milne as a young child, lover of Charles Wesley, Shakespeare, Blake, Thomas Gray, and Lewis Carroll; [a.] Capetown, South Africa

STUBBS, LISA
[b.] May 15, 1971; Nassau, Bahamas; [p.] Lenox Sr. and Joanne Major; [m.] Linkworth O. Stubbs Jr.; November 6, 1993; [ed.] Government High School, College of the Bahamas; [occ.] Library Assistant, College of the Bahamas Library, Bahamas; [oth. writ.] Several poems, articles published in college newspaper and local newspaper; [a.] Nassau, Bahamas

STYMIEST, CARL
[pen.] Karl Joseph; [b.] June 2, 1943; Chatham, NB; [p.] Bessie Stymiest, Carlyle Stymiest; [ed.] Harkins Academy, Newcastle, NB, New Brunswick Teacher's College, University of British Columbia; [occ.] Businessman/Owner—The Windsor Knot; [memb.] Loyalist Society of Canada, National Historical Society of Canada, International Society of Poets; [hon.] B.E.D. (elementary) 1974, M.A. English Education, 1994, University of British Columbia, Editor's Choice Award, National Library of Poetry; [oth. writ.] Loggieville, On the Miramichi (1964), Development Drama (unpublished), Social Studies: A Resource Manual, Teaching Novel Writing, Pacific Rim Humanities, Effective Strategies for Orchestrating Volunteers, other poems; [pers.] I believe that life can be a grindstone: Whether it grinds one down, or polishes one up, it depends on us. I prefer the polishing, for it is through this process I grow, gain wisdom, and shine.; [a.] Vancouver, BC

SUNG, JENNY
[pen.] Rainbow; [b.] November 29, 1980; Taichung, Taiwan; [ed.] Grade Eleven at Burnaby Central Secondary School; [occ.] Student; [memb.] Badminton Team, ESL Peer Tutor; [hon.] Grade Ten and Eleven Honor Roll, First Place in Solo Dance in Vancouver (1997), Second Place in Solo Dance in 1997 North America Chinese Dance Competition; [pers.] I just came to Canada about three years ago rom Taiwan. I am glad that my poem has been certified as a semifinalist in this contest. I used my imagination and feelings to describe my poem, "Broken Heart." I like this poem very much.; [a.] Burnaby, BC

SUTHERLAND, CHANEL
[b.] November 19, 1983; St. Vincent; [p.] Ingrid Sutherland; [occ.] Student; [oth. writ.] "Teardrops," "Good-bye," "Starry Night," "Four Seasons of Blue," "A Stolen Heart," "Dreams," "An Angel in My Eyes," "Beyond Our Graves"; [pers.] My influence is William Shakespeare. His poems have touched my heart. I especially loved the verse, "To Be or Not to Be?"; [a.] Montreal, QC

SWEET, RITA
[b.] March 23, 1928; Windsor, NS; [m.] Charles E. Sweet; August 20, 1960; [occ.] Retired; [a.] Wolfville, NS

SWITZER, HOLLY
[pen.] Holly Switzer; [b.] November 5, 1971; Windsor, ON; [p.] George and Elizabeth; [ed.] Teacher's Aide, Early Childhood Education, Home Support Worker I (College); [occ.] Early Childhood Educator and Home Support Worker; [memb.] Kid's Club, Camp Counselling, volunteer for the Kidney Foundation; [hon.] Music and Drama; [pers.] My poems come from the heart. This one originally was not intended to be a poem, but it turned out that way. My writing centers around relationships, particularly my own need for God.; [a.] Windsor, ON

TA, BENNIE
[b.] October 19, 1981; Calgary, AB; [p.] Tom Ta, Faye Ngo; [ed.] 1996-1998 at Crescent Heights High School; [pers.] Given the chance, you can accomplish anything, as long as you believe.; [a.] Calgary, AB

TACK, HERMAN
[b.] June 17, 1946, Waregem, Belgium; [ed.] Sales Engineer K. U. Leuven; [occ.] Export Sales Manager, Artist, Painter; [hon.] Second Place 1989 Luxembourg Graphic Arts Individual Exhibitions; [pers.] Surrealistic painting, "Demonic Aspects in Human Relations"; [a.] Vichte, Anzegem, Belgium

TAIT, GEORDIE
[pen.] Glym; [b.] July 24, 1980; Sarnia, ON; [p.] Robert Tait, Patricia Tait; [ed.] Fourth Year, St. Patrick's High School, Sarnia, ON; [oth.writ.] None published; [pers.] "If God had never existed, we would have had to invent him." (Voltaire); [a.] Sarnia, ON

TAIT, TIM
[b.] July 30, 1967; Sarnia, ON; [p.] Tim and Linda Tait; [m.] Patricia Lucier; [ed.] Luras Secondary, B.A. University of Western Ontario; [occ.] Cook, Computer Programmer; [memb.] Martial Arts Club, ABATE of London; [hon.] Chemical Sciences, Art; [oth. writ.] Two poems published in a high school magazine; [pers.] Poetry reflects your emotions and it touches the emotions of others. This makes them think. All encouragement of thought and individuality is a good thing.; [a.] London, ON

TEED, GREGORY PATRICK
[pen.] Achaonadfi; [b.] 1964; Calgary, AB; [ed.] B.A. in History, University of Calgary, 1989; [occ.] Music teacher—all guitars; [memb.] Order of Bards, Ovates, and Druids (Based in England), The Writers' Guild of Alberta, The Catholic Church; [hon.] In a sense, the honor of UFO and mystic experiences; [oth. writ.] Forthcoming publication of poetry compilation entitled "WOW, or Word of Wonder"; [pers.] As a Catholic Druid, my work endeavors to reawaken a true understanding of the ancients, be it the prophets or indeed all ancients before or beyond the fold of the prophets, and thereby come to a deeper awareness of and be sensitive to greater realities of the apocalyptic age.; [a.] Calgary, AB

TEIXEIRA, ANNA
[pen.] Autumn; [b.] May 20, 1963; Azores, Portugal; [p.] Arnaldo and Ema Teixeira; [ch.] Mark; [occ.] Parent, Student; [oth.writ.] "Peace of My Mind," published by National Library of Poetry, Spring 1998 (Beyond the Horizon); [pers.] "Lost Souls" was inspired by my belief in true love and faith in God.; [a.] Toronto, ON

THAKKER, TIMOTHY DANIEL
[pen.] Roger; [b.] March 12, 1987; Bangalore, India; [p.] Abel and Valarie Thakker; [ed.] Grade Five, Brown

Public School, Toronto; [occ.] Student; [oth. writ.] Essays and poems; [pers.] "Nature," God's awesome wonder; [a.] Toronto, ON

THOMPSON, LAURA
[b.] October 23, 1985; Calgary, AB; [p.] Peter and Wendy Thompson; [ed.] Currently attending Fairview Junior High; [occ.] Student; [hon.] Silver Medal in the Calgary City Science Fair 1996/1997, Bronze Medal in Basketball, High Honors at school; [pers.] I'm very aware of the danger our environment's in, and I like writing about what will happen if we don't take action soon.; [a.] Calgary, AB

THORLAKSON, TANIS
[b.] April 20, 1973; Edmonton, AB; [p.] Gordon and Marilyn Thorlakson; [ed.] Bachelor of Arts at University of Alberta; [occ.] Customer Service Representative with the Bank of Montreal; [oth.writ.] First time published; [pers.] Life will take many turns; live life as it comes and enjoy each new turn.; [a.] Saskatoon, SK

TIMPA, DAVID
[b.] July 12, 1974; Wolfville, NS; [p.] John and Jean Timpa; [ed.] Horton High School, Acadia University; [occ.] Student; [hon.] Letters of recognition from the Nova Scotia Minister of Health, for raising money for the Brain Injury Association of Nova Scotia; [oth.writ.] A small collection of unpublished poems; [a.] Wolfville, NS

TINA, SCARPITTI
[b.] November 22, 1974, Toronto, ON; [p.] Domenico and Assunta Lo Russo; [m.] Steve Scarpitti, July 25, 1998; [ed.] Graduated with top honours for English Communications at York University and graduated from the Advertising Program at The School of Communication Arts; [occ.] Toronto Public Library Board Employee—Branch Assistant; [memb.] Member of The Poetry Society of America, The National Authors Registrar, and The National Showcase of Authors on the Internet and a lyrical music artist for Edlee Music.; [hon.] Received several honourable mentions with the Poetry Society of America, Iliad Press, and Watermark Press, received the Annual 1998 President's Award with Iliad Press and Honourable Mention, top honour Art Plaque of Recognition for Oil Painting.; [oth. writ.] Published hardbound poetry anthology "On Eagles' Wings. . . ." with Watermark Press, contributed to Treasures, a hardbound anthology, published with Iliad Press, and recorded "My Perfect Mate. . ." with Edlee Music; [pers.] If thou truly giveth your best at everything you do, thou will realize that when you least expecteth, the chipeth falleth, while fate answers thine own almighty prayers. And/ or when thou is in doubt, thinketh not at thine own faults, but thine own rewards to seteth your wings freeth.; [a.] Toronto, ON

TODD, CODY
[b.] May 16,1980; Calgary, AB;[p.] Garry Todd , Peggy Todd; [ed.] John G. Diefenbaker School; [occ.] Student; [hon.] Second in science fair; [oth.writ.] Several articles published in local newspaper, poem published in Voices in the Wind; [pers.] Life is not worth living if you don't live it well. Seize the day!; [a.] Calgary, AB

TRAHAN, MARK EUGENE ROYAL
[pen.] Kram Nahart; [b.] August 12, 1958; Pembroke; [p.] Andre Trahan, Jean-D'arc Chaput; [m.] Wendy Jane Trahan Oelke; May 17, 1981; [ed.] Grade Twelve Diploma, Champlain High School, Pembroke; [occ.] Letter/Mail Carrier for Canada Post. Corp.; [memb.]

Ex-King Sports Association., Les Canadian Hockey Fan Club (for the Montreal Canadians), Pembroke Independent Old Timers Hockey Club; [pers.] I believe everyone has a good poem or story in them. All they need is the time to set them free.; [a.] Petawawa, ON

TREMOYNE, JASON
[b.] December 18, 1979; Fort Sask, AB; [p.] Danny and MaryAnne Tremoyne; [ed.] Currently in college for Programmer Analysts, M.E. LaZerte High School; [occ.] College student; [oth. writ.] Several short stories ("The Day I Died," etc.) as well as over one hundred more poems (some of which may be found); [pers.] My writing is an extension of myself. I can only capture but a portion of what I feel, yet, if I touch even one person, then it was worth it.; [a.] Edmonton, AB

TRIBE, NATALIE A.
[pen.] Nat; [b.] March 3, 1976; Victoria, BC; [p.] Barb, Harn Tribe; [ed.] Graduated from Mount Douglas Secondary School, June 1994; [hon.] I've had my poetry published in school annuals.; [oth. writ.] Over the last ten years, I've written a wealth of poems, some of which are being used in English lessons today in high schools.; [pers.] I am inspired by the truth in life and the reality of certainty, and am deeply influenced by the uniqueness of nature.; [a.] Victoria, BC

TUMA, MUNEER
[b.] Kafr Yasif, Israel; [ed.] B.A. University of Haifa, Israel, M.A. Washington University, Hawaii, United States; [occ.] English Teacher, "Yanni" Secondary School Teacher's Organization, Israel; [hon.] English Language and Literature Teaching Education; [oth. writ.] A book of poems, "Blossoms of Anguish," published by Avon Books, London, U.K.; [pers.] My verse deals with eternal verities: love, anguish, eternity, and the search for emotional peacefulness. I have been greatly influenced by the romantic poets and Kahlil Gibran.; [a.] Kafr Yasif, Israel

TURPIN, KAREN MARIE
[pen.] Carmel; [b.] June 1, 1966; St. Lawrence, NF; [p.] Madeline and Bernard Sr.; [m.] Steve, engaged; [ch.] Stephen Christopher; [ed.] Grade Ten; [occ.] Homemaker and Mother; [memb.] Girl Guides of Canada, Royal Canadian Sea Cadets, Volunteer Work Librarian; [oth. writ.] "Kids," "To My Son Stephen," "Lost," (these poems have a special meaning attached); [pers.] I dreamed this day would come. I kept my faith and I believed, for 17 years.; [a.] Eastern Pass., NS

TUSHINGHAM, KATHLEEN M.
[b.] July 29, 1938; England; [p.] Harold Heys, Doris Heys; [m.] Edward Tushingham; June 14, 1958; [ch.] Kim Lauren, Lesley Anne; [oth.writ.] Two unpublished works, a book of poetry and prose, and my autobiography; [a.] Caesarea, ON

UHER, ROLF
[b.] February 23, 1950; Germany; [p.] Rudolf Uher, Ursula Uher; [ed.] Humboldt Gymnasium, Koeln University of Cologne; [occ.] Social Scientist at the University of Cologne; [hon.] Diploma in Social Sciences; [oth. writ.] Several poems published in magazines and books, a short story published in a reader, all published in German; [pers.] The true adventures are in your mind.; [a.] Koeln, Germany

ULIERU, MIHAELA, PH.D.
[b.] February 1, 1962; Bucharest, RO; [p.] Elena and George Ulieru; [ch.] George and Mircea; [ed.] Doctor

of Engineering, Darmstadt, Germany (1995); [occ.] Scientific Researcher, Simon Fraser University, Canada; [memb.] New York Academy of Science (since 1993), American Association for the Advancement of Science (1994), IEEE/SMC, IFAC; [hon.] "Best Plenary Presentation," Symposium on Cybernetics of Human Knowing, Baden-Baden, Germany (1994); [oth. writ.] One book, "Fluffy Logic in Biagmosis—Kluwer," over 40 journal papers, essays, and poems; [pers.] I fear that my life may not be long enough so that I can give all the love that I have to give.; [a.] Burnaby, BC

ULLIAC, MANUEL
[b.] February 24, 1981; Edmonton, AB; [p.] Louise Ulliac-Lepage, Marc Lepage; [ed.] High school, post-secondary: Creative Writing (honors standing); [occ.] Freelance Writer; [hon.] 20 Books from Write On! Magazine (price for submitted poetry); [oth. writ.] "Feast of the Beast," published in Write On!; Drag On Magazine: self-published and self-designed; The Writer's Restaurants: donated submissions (including "Manuel" version of Dr. Seuss); wrote articles and helped in designing the magazine; [pers.] I am the seventeen-year-old Literary Chameleon, as I try to mimic the work of famous writers as well as original works ranging from essays to poetry to fiction.; [a.] Edmonton, AB

UNRAU, MICHELLE CAYER
[b.] April 6, 1973; Winnipeg, MB; [p.] Paul and Linda Cayer; [m.] Robert Unrau; November 14, 1992; [ch.] Dylon and Tylor; [oth. writ.] "Inspirations II," "New Generations," "Grade 9"; I also write children's stories; [pers.] God has a calling for all of us; sometimes we find it, and sometimes it's only whispered to us. Grab at your calling.; [a.] Winnipeg, MB

VALDEZ, MA BONITA· P
[pen.] Bonette Valdez; [b.] April 9, 1965; Manila, Philippines; [p.] Dominador Valdez, Maria Pailanan; [m.] Ernie R. Cruzada; March 19, 1996; [ed.] Bachelor of Science in Business Administration and Accounting, University of the East; computer concepts and programming, Systems Technology Institute; secretarial, Ramon Magsaysay Vocational School; book and short story writing for children and teenagers, Institute of Children's Literature, West Reading, Connecticut, USA; [occ.] Executive Secretary, Conference Coordinator, Faculty of Science, UAE University, Alain, UAE; [memb.] Literary editor, high school organization, "The Trailblazers," 1994 appointed Secretary and presently member, United Arab Emirates, Filipino in the Emirates, Pro 1981 Manuel Roxas High School Student Council, member local writers' workshop; [hon.] Consistent honor student from elementary to high school; member of the honors class during college (University of the East); Subject Proficiency Awardee, Manuel Roxas High School; received certificates and medals for contests and symposiums attended; [oth. writ.] Literature and poems published in Gulf Weekly Magazine, Woman's Magazine, and others; "Deep Enchantments" (in preparation) to be published by Watermark Press; short stories for children and teens (unpublished); [pers.] Along with my passion for thrill and excitement comes my intense quest for inner peace and contentment. I always go for whatever goal I pursue. I like positive changes, and I know my limitations. As long as I have peace of mind and have enough means to survive, it's fine with me.; [a.] Alain, UAE

VAN DONK, BERYL
[b.] Cheshire, England; [p.] Olive and Vernon Lightfoot; [m.] Willem Van Donk; [ch.] Two; [ed.] High school certificate, State Registered Nurse; [occ.] Homemaker; [memb.] Peninsula Writer's Group, A.O.; [oth. writ.] Short stories, endless poetry, children's stories; some short stories and poems published by P.W.G.; [pers.] I have been writing poems and stories since I was a small child. Most of my adult life has been spent in nursing. I love animals, and in my garden I am privileged to touch the hem of God.; [a.] Coromandel, New Zealand

VAN ROOIJEN, SOPHIE
[b.] November 5, 1981; Naarden; [p.] A.B.J. Van Rooijen, C.E.M. Van Spaendonck; [ed.] International School, Hilverum, Alberdingkthym, IB; [pers.] I left with the remains of the horizon, lingered off an angel toe.; [a.] Utrecht, Netherlands

VANDERHEIDE, CHRISTINE THERESA
[b.] July 6, 1962; Windsor, ON; [p.] Milton and Victoria Stodolny; [ed.] High School Academic Diploma, Certified Aesthetician, Certified Health Care Aide, certified through the CCCA Canadian Cosmetic Careers Association; [occ.] Aesthetician, owner/operator of Aesthetics by Chrissy Studio; [memb.] International Fund for Animal Welfare (IFAW), Canadian Federation of Humane Societies, People for the Ethical Treatment of Animals (PETA), World Wildlife Fund (WWF), Greenpeace, on the Windsor Essex County Board of Directors for the Humane Society; [hon.] Fundraising and Auxiliary for the Windsor Essex County Humane Society, special certificate from the County Humane Society for my contributions in 1995, certificate for fundraising for the Humane Society Auxiliary, a personal letter from Brian Davies (President of IFAW); [oth. writ.] All of the writings I have done are for animal rights. I've been in the Windsor Star, too numerous to mention, but it all has to do with ending animal cruelty and ending the Canadian seal hunt. I've written to and got some responses from Monat, Mike Harris, Detroit TV stations, Windsor TV stations, Hon. Herb Gray, Brian Davies, and the Ministry of Fisheries and Oceans. [pers.] All my writing and animal activism comes from my heart, so I won't lose a friend if she owns a fur coat. I am a vegetarian and try to be a good humanitarian, as well as strive for the rights of animals.; [a.] Windsor, ON

VANDERSLUYS, LOURENA
[b.] March 29, 1916; Port Dover, ON; [p.] Hugh and Annie Akins; [m.] Harry Vandersluys; [ch.] Several adopted; [ed.] Two years high school in Port Dover, Ontario, Canada; [memb.] Boy Scout leader 67 years, Urban Alliance (Against Discrimination), teenager's counsellor, various choirs; [hon.] Long Service Scouts, Canada, 17 years; NATO Volunteer; International Services of London; Easter Seals (crippled children); ten years perfect attendance, Sunday school teacher award; World Vision Volunteer; [oth. writ.] Composed seven songs for royal family, two for Mother Teresa, and one for Erma Bombeck; wrote many stories of my life for London Free Press and other newspapers; [pers.] I started senior citizen discounts. I also saved seven lives. I have spent my entire life for others, and I always try to be a good example for young people. I live by faith! [a.] London, ON

WALLACE, AMANDA
[b.] May 23, 1983; Edmonton, AB; [p.] Brenda and Bill; [ed.] Braxton Park School, grade nine; [occ.]

Student; [pers.] I would like to thank Marlene Norkay, my grade eight L.A. teacher, for teaching me to express my feelings on paper. Have a great one.; [a.] Spruce Grove, AB

WALSH, DORIS M.
[pen.] Sinnova Leatham; [b.] November 11, 1916; Winnipeg, MB; [p.] James Aiken, Mabel M. Leatham; [m.] Lorne Walsh (Deceased); January 16, 1943; [ed.] Girls High School—Aberdeen, Scotland; Elementary and High Schools—St. James, Manitoba; Graduated Business College (Secretarial); Graduate of Phoenix Club Adult Education and many courses; [occ.] Retired (still learning); [memb.] Sons of Scotland, Credit Women's Club, Phoenix Club, MSDS, Little Theatre, Progressive Players; National Society Assn.; [hon.] International Retail Credit Assn., Certificates of Appreciation while serving as a narrator volunteer for CNIB (Canadian National Inst. for The Blind), University Texts Programme—12 years; [oth.writ.] Poems and prose for Station Magazine, Drift Recorder, Wartime Prices and Trade and Trade Board, wrote 15 min. dialogues and broadcast with local radio host, Reprice Regulations, also 5 min. blurbs for distribution to all local radio scripts for skits for Credit Women's Club outlets, some prose, some poetry; [pers.] The gift of life's most precious as it comes; give the best you live to give the best they have give. To encourage the less courageous, offer guidance to the uncertain. Consider well all sources before proclaiming judgement, be temperate in all things, particularly those that affect one's gastronomical tract, mental prowess, and physical well-being. Above all things, "to thine own self be true."; [a.] Winnipeg, MB

WATERS, BRIGITTE
[pen.] Brigitte; [b.] September 15, 1983; Melbourne, Australia; [p.] Cherie Lewis; [ed.] Currently studying ninth year at Toorak College; [occ.] Student; [memb.] Writers Club (School), Debating, Rowing, Tennis, Volleyball, Basketball (all school teams); [oth.writ.] Life's Potholes; [pers.] My poetry is a journey into the darkest corners of my mind that reflect a childhood of domestic violence.; [a.] Melbourne, Australia

WEAVER, SYLVIA
[b.] April 20, 1944; Glasgow, Scotland; [m.] Malcolm Weaver; [ch.] Three daughters; [occ.] Public school secretary; [a.] Aurora, ON

WEISS, LARRY ALAN
[b.] August 23, 1946; Philadelphia, PA; [ed.] Temple University—B.A. ('70); University of Ottawa—M.S.C. ('74); University of British Columbia—Diploma Special Education; [occ.] Teacher (High School); [pers.] Poetry is an extention of my heart, teaching is the expression of my life.; [a.] Chilliwack, BC

WELCH, LOIS V.
[pen.] Lowel Lechers; [b.] July 13, 1939; Cobourg, ON; [p.] Orv. and Glad Calhoun; [m.] Lawrence E. Welch (died 1989); November 17, 1956; [ch.] Four; [ed.] Grade ten—Cobourg Collegiate High School—Cobourg, Ontario, Canada; [occ.] Retired; [memb.] Golden-Agers Bowling League; [pers.] I have been rhyming in sentences for years, every time I open my mouth. I decided to enter for something to do in my spare time.; [a.] Port Hope, ON

WESTON, MOLLY
[pen.] Molly Weston; [b.] August 21, 1951; Parham Town, Antigua, WI; [p.] Edmund Weston, Estella

Weston; [ch.] Julio Angelo, Vicki Delinda; [ed.] Parham Primary, Princess Margaret Secondary, University of the West Indies; [occ.] Geography Teacher at Pares Secondary School; [memb.] Church Women's Organizations, Teacher's Associations; [hon.] Poetry awards for Prime Minister's Competition, ICS Associate Degree in Business Management—1997; [oth.writ.] School skits, church plays, plays for women's concerts, poems for various church festivals, items for teacher's ,agazines, calypsoes and gospel songs; [pers.] Do not let the fear of failure prevent you from trying. I have been greatly influenced by Western writers such as Sam Grey, as well as reggae artists Jimmy Cliff and Bob Marley.

WHITECAP, CORY
[b.] August 28, 1972; Regina, SK; [p.] Joanne Whitecap; [m.] Isabelle MacDonald; [ch.] Chenga Kaya Whitecap; [ed.] Grade 11 (academically), plus ten years of street education; [occ.] Full-time student, background actor; [memb.] Membership to a life that taught me hard lessons then gave me knowledge in return; [hon.] I am honoured with the gift of my wife and daughter, with knowledge and wisdom, with people who love and care enough to help me to see where I was going wrong in my life, and then to be there to support me while I pulled myself through.; [oth. writ.] Two personal unpublished journals of poetry about my thoughts, feelings, dreams, fears, and aspirations; [pers.] In life I have learned that no matter what other people say, I can't let their negative words pull me down because I am most important to me. At the same time, forgiving others and taking responsibility for my actions is also my only way to fully grow and learn.; [a.] Toronto, ON

WIENECKE, ANDREA
[b.] June 4, 1982; Newmarket, ON; [p.] Ernest A. and Diana Wienecke; [ed.] Attending St. Thomas of Aquinas Sec. School; [occ.] Student; [hon.] Volunteer work with Alzheimer Society, Senicoe County, in our church as solo singer on special occassions, help with the Sunday school; [pers.] Besides my love for writing, I also take classical vocal lessons. I love drama, sports, drawing, and all of the arts.; [a.] Tottenharn, ON

WILLIAM, GERRY
[m.] Elizabeth Cuthand; October 7, 1995; [ed.] B.A., Ph.D.(candidate); [occ.] Instructor; [oth. writ.] The Black Ship—a novel (part one of a three-part series); [pers.] I am an Okanagan. My poem was written in honour of my wife, Beth Cuthand, a Cree from Saskatchewan and a published poet in her own right.; [a.] Merritt, BC

WILSON, P. ROY
[pen.] P. Roy Wilson; [b.] May 19, 1900; Birmingham, England; [p.] Percy and Isabel Wilson; [m.] Elizabeth Harbert; July 19, 1933; [ch.] Brian, Keith, Patrick; [ed.] Repton Preparatory School, England; St. Michael's University School, Victoria, BC; Upper Canada College, Toronto; McGill University, Montreal; [occ.] Artist; [hon.] B. Arch. McGill. R.C.A. ARIBA, FRAIC, Queen's Jubilee Medal—1977; [oth.writ.] Published books: Beautiful Old House of Quebec—1975; Design and Delight (Autobiography)—1990; Rhymes and Rhetoric; [pers.] Architecture practice, 50 years; 1485 watercolour paintings to date; various model buildings in museums; [a.] Beacaonfield, QC

WINSTONE, BRENT
[pen.] Brent; [b.] January 17, 1956; Brandon, MB; [p.] Robert and Ruth Winstone; [m.] Darlene; February 14, 1994; [ch.] Everett, Mercedes, and Forrest; [oth.writ.]

Several poems as yet unpublished; [pers.] I search for the origin of self, find a lack thereof, and in so doing, discover a connection to all.; [a.] Winnipeg, MB

WITWICKI, EDDIE
[b.] April 24, 1927; Winnipeg, MB; [p.] Frank and Josephine Witwicki; [m.] Nil; [ch.] John, Janice, David; [hon.] Numerous certificates, plaques, trophies, and prizes for sales training and sales management and motivation; [a.] Winnipeg, MB

WOLFRAME, PHEBEANN M.
[b.] February 16, 1984; Toronto, ON; [p.] Susan and Barry Wolframe; [ed.] Oliver Road Elementary School; [occ.] Student; [memb.] The Pipes and Drums of Thunder Bay, Prashant School of Yoga; [oth.writ.] Several poems—unpublished; [pers.] Dance with life, play with it. Don't give up on life—it's worth living. Everyone succeeds; each one of us a miracle. Thank you to everyone who's been there.; [a.] Thunder Bay, ON

WONG, BEN
[b.] September 26, 1987; Hamilton, ON; [p.] John and Karen Wong; [ed.] Fifth grade at Hillfied Strathallen College; [occ.] Student; [memb.] Boy Scouts of Canada; [hon.] Mathematics Award; [a.] Hamilton, ON

YAMASHITA, MARIE FUJITA
[b.] April 10, 1938; Vancouver, BC; [p.] Gengo Fujita and Sumiko Fujita

YEO, GENE
[b.] March 10, 1977; Singapore; [p.] Philip and Jane Yeo; [ed.] Bachelor of Science (Chemical Engineering) with Highest Distinction—January 1998, University of Illinois, Urbana- Champaign; B.A. (Econ.) with High Distinction—January 1998, UIUC; [a.] Singapore

YOUNG, DEREK
[b.] June 18, 1982; Bridgewater, NS; [p.] Louise and Michael Gabriel Alan Young; [ed.] Grade ten at New Germany High School; [hon.] Received Honor Certificate (85% average and above) for last four years; wrote grades seven, eight, and nine month contest and had top marks in all grades; [oth.writ.] Derek has written approx 60 poems in the last one to one and a half years.; [a.] Northriver, NS

YOUNGER, FRANK
[pen.] Budde; [b.] November 18, 1940; Bellingham, WA; [p.] Paul and Margaret Younger; [m.] Sharon McCormick; November 6, 1964; [ch.] Pauline, Matthew, and Thomas; [ed.] Burlington-Edison High School, University of Kansas (M.A.); [occ.] Astronomer; [memb.] Canadian Astronomical Society, Harley Owners Group, James Younger Gang; [hon.] Milton F. Perry Award (James Younger Gang); [oth.writ.] Several unpublished poems for friends; [pers.] We could all use a little more global perspective. Robert W. Service provides this, and his work should be required reading in the schools.; [a.] Victoria, BC

ZAHIDA, TAZEEN
[b.] January 3, 1973; Karachi, Pakistan; [p.] M. Habib Siddiqui and Nadira Habib; [m.] S.M. Iftikhar Hussain; April 13, 1995; [ch.] One daughter—Tooba Sayed; [ed.] Bachelor of Arts (B.A.) with English Literature and Journalism majors from University of Punjab, Pakistan,; [occ.] Housewife; [hon.] I held second position in the first and second years of college, was listed among the top ten students of the country by the Pakistan Federal Board of Education, was elected general secretary and vice-president of the college Literary Society, and won various prizes for debate and speeches.; [oth. writ.] I have written various poems and one act plays for college stage, on subjects such as the Kashmir problem and the cultural degeneration of our society. I have also written a few comedies.; [pers.] Poetry is the ultimate height of human intellect. It is the most beautiful creation of mankind. Life is not lived up until the depths of poetry are explored.; [a.] Dammam, Eastern Kingdom of Saudi Arabia

ZARANDONA, JUAN
[b.] May 3, 1961; Bata-Rio Muni, Equatorial Guinea; [p.] Juan Zarandona, Maria Luisa Fernandez; [ed.] University degrees in Spanish and English Language and Literature; about to get doctorate in such fields of learning; [occ.] University Teacher, Department of English of Valladalid—Spain; [memb.] Cultural Association—Siaro; [oth. writ.] Different unpublished short novels, tales, and poems; one published short novel: "Espanopolis"; one poem published: "Esta Noche"; different research articles on Spanish and English language and literature; [pers.] I am a devoted admirer of the talent of the writers of the past, from teaching them to imitating their work. I also am a supporter of the humanities and the arts in general, which are so forgotten in our modern world.; [a.] Valladollio, Castile-Leon

ZAWALINSKI, ANDRZEJ
[b.] February 22, 1947; Poland; [p.] Jan and Marcella Zawalinski; [ch.] Florian A. Zawalinski; [occ.] Self-employed; [memb.] Lodge Star in the East 640, Shrine Club of Guam, VFW, American Legion; [hon.] Decorated U.S. Marine War Veteran; [oth. writ.] "Why Did I Die"; [pers.] Love of the sea, classical music, and love of my family are the most important things in my life.; [a.] Tamuning, Guam

ZIMMERMAN, SUSAN
[pen.] Susan Sara Fayga Zimmerman; [b.] June 18, 1947; Melbourne, Australia; [oth. writ.] Autobiographical family stories—three volumes; the 20 lines you wish to print is only a small fragment of an entire journal that I hope to publish.; [pers.] Having a disability is actually a special gift if one is determined to work towards overcoming it. The resources to do so must come from within and the greatest of these is faith.; [a.] Melbourne, VIC, Australia

ZINMAN, AMIT
[pen.] Lance Windom; [b.] April 22, 1975; Petah-Tikva, Israel; [oth. writ.] The Anonsalat International Magazine, published on the internet; [a.] Raanaha, Israel

Index
of
Poets

Index

A

X

Y

Z